D0495224

Excel 2000 VBA Programmer's Reference

John Green

Stephen Bullen

Felipe Martins

wrox

Programmer to Programmer

Excel 2000 VBA Programmer's Reference

Published by
Wiley Publishing, Inc.
10475 Crosspoint Boulevard
Indianapolis, IN 46256
www.wiley.com

Copyright © 2003 by Wiley Publishing, Inc., Indianapolis, Indiana

Published simultaneously in Canada

Library of Congress Card Number: 2003107075

ISBN: 0-7645-4401-2

Manufactured in the United States of America

10 9 8 7 6 5 4 3 2 1

1B/RT/QW/QT/IN

No part of this publication may be reproduced, stored in a retrieval system or transmitted in any form or by any means, electronic, mechanical, photocopying, recording, scanning or otherwise, except as permitted under Sections 107 or 108 of the 1976 United States Copyright Act, without either the prior written permission of the Publisher, or authorization through payment of the appropriate per-copy fee to the Copyright Clearance Center, 222 Rosewood Drive, Danvers, MA 01923, (978) 750-8400, fax (978) 646-8700. Requests to the Publisher for permission should be addressed to the Legal Department, Wiley Publishing, Inc., 10475 Crosspoint Blvd., Indianapolis, IN 46256, (317) 572-3447, fax (317) 572-4447, E-Mail: permcoordinator@wiley.com.

LIMIT OF LIABILITY/DISCLAIMER OF WARRANTY: WHILE THE PUBLISHER AND AUTHOR HAVE USED THEIR BEST EFFORTS IN PREPARING THIS BOOK, THEY MAKE NO REPRESENTATIONS OR WARRANTIES WITH RESPECT TO THE ACCURACY OR COMPLETENESS OF THE CONTENTS OF THIS BOOK AND SPECIF-ICALLY DISCLAIM ANY IMPLIED WARRANTIES OF MERCHANTABILITY OR FIT-NESS FOR A PARTICULAR PURPOSE. NO WARRANTY MAY BE CREATED OR EXTENDED BY SALES REPRESENTATIVES OR WRITTEN SALES MATERIALS. THE ADVICE AND STRATEGIES CONTAINED HEREIN MAY NOT BE SUITABLE FOR YOUR SITUATION. YOU SHOULD CONSULT WITH A PROFESSIONAL WHERE APPROPRIATE. NEITHER THE PUBLISHER NOR AUTHOR SHALL BE LIABLE FOR ANY LOSS OF PROFIT OR ANY OTHER COMMERCIAL DAMAGES, INCLUDING BUT NOT LIMITED TO SPECIAL, INCIDENTAL, CONSEQUENTIAL, OR OTHER DAMAGES.

For general information on our other products and services or to obtain technical support, please contact our Customer Care Department within the U.S. at (800) 762-2974, outside the U.S. at (317) 572-3993 or fax (317) 572-4002.

Wiley also publishes its books in a variety of electronic formats. Some content that appears in print may not be available in electronic books.

Trademarks: Wiley, the Wiley Publishing logo, Wrox, the Wrox logo, the Wrox Programmer to Programmer logo and related trade dress are trademarks or registered trademarks of Wiley in the United States and other countries, and may not be used without written permission. All other trademarks are the property of their respective owners. Wiley Publishing, Inc., is not associated with any product or vendor mentioned in this book.

Trademark Acknowledgements

Wrox has endeavored to provide trademark information about all the companies and products mentioned in this book by the appropriate use of capitals. However, Wrox cannot guarantee the accuracy of this information.

Credits

Authors
John Green
Stephen Bullen
Felipe Martins

Development Editors
Dominic Shakeshaft
Dominic Lowe

Editors
Peter Morgan
Adrian Young

Technical Reviewers
Stephen Bullen
Steve Danielson
Ron Landers
Duncan Mackenzie
Bill Manville
Tom Ogilvy
David Rowlands
Joe Sutphin

Cover
Andrew Guillaume
Image by Rita Ruban

Design/Layout
Mark Burdett
John McNulty

Index
Catherine Alexander

About the Authors

John Green

John Green lives and works in Sydney, Australia as an independent computer consultant, specializing in Excel and Access. With 30 years of computing experience, a Chemical Engineering degree and an MBA — he draws from a diverse background. He wrote his first programs in FORTRAN, took a part in the evolution of specialized planning languages on mainframes and, in the early 80's, became interested in spreadsheet systems including 1-2-3 and Excel.

John established his company, Execuplan Consulting, in 1980, specializing in developing computer based planning applications and in training. He has led training courses extensively for software applications and operating systems both in Australia and overseas.

John has had regular columns in a number of Australian magazines and has contributed chapters to a number of books including "Excel Expert Solutions" and "Using Visual Basic for Applications 5", published by Que.

Since 1995 he has been accorded the status of MVP (Most Valuable Professional) by Microsoft for his contributions to the CompuServe Excel forum and MS Internet newsgroups.

Email: jgreen@enternet.com.au

Stephen Bullen

Stephen Bullen lives in Milton Keynes, England with his wife and two dogs and is soon to become a father of twins. After graduating from Oxford University in 1992 with an MA in Engineering, Economics and Management, Stephen joined Price Waterhouse Management Consultants where he spent five years developing Excel applications for a wide range of multinational corporations.

In 1997, Stephen started his own company, Business Modelling Solutions Ltd, specializing in Excel and Access development and consulting. The BMS web site, www.BMSLtd.co.uk, contains a large number of examples of his work, including tools and utilities to extend Excel's functionality and many examples of Excel development techniques. The entire site was recently awarded the accolade of 'VBA Power Tool of the Month' by Microsoft.

Stephen enjoys helping other Excel users and devotes a lot of his spare time to answering questions in the CompuServe Excel forum and Microsoft's Internet newsgroups. In recognition of his contributions and knowledge, Microsoft has given him a 'Most Valuable Professional' award every year since 1996.

Stephen can be contacted by email to Stephen@BMSLtd.co.uk, though any Excel support questions should be asked in the newsgroups.

Felipe Martins

Felipe Martins is an MCSD and MCT who has been programming with Office products and VB for many years, building applications in the manufacturing, healthcare, and aerospace industries. He currently works for ImagiNET Resources Corp. as a Senior Solutions Developer. ImagiNET Resources Corp supplies clients with leading edge business solutions by employing highly skilled and experienced people who are experts at using Microsoft technologies.

Currently Felipe can be found somewhere in a Starbucks in Winnipeg, Canada.

Felipe Martins can be reached at fmartins@imaginets.com

Acknowledgements

I want to thank a number of people who have helped me gain some knowledge of Excel VBA. I was off to a jump-start when I discovered books by Reed Jacobson and John Walkenbach, but my real education began in the Excel forum on CompuServe, back in 1994, when the forum was sponsored by Microsoft. It was heady stuff, to have access to the best brains and expertise in the world in my chosen line of work. In particular, I was influenced by Jim Rech and Bill Manville and, a little later, by Rob Bovey and Stephen Bullen. They, and quite a number of others, will recognize some of their ideas in this book and Stephen has been gracious enough to write three of the book's advanced chapters.

All of us were awarded the status of MVP (Most Valuable Professional) by Microsoft for our part in answering the daily flood of questions posted to the forum, but it is we who have benefited the most from the exchange of ideas that has occurred and continues to occur. Since Microsoft moved its support platform to the Internet news groups, the emphasis has gradually shifted away from CompuServe, but the same spirit lives on. Indeed, I must thank Alan Beban who has made a comprehensive study of ways to generate range object references and shared his findings in the newsgroups.

I would also like to thank the two Dominics — Lowe and Shakeshaft — at Wrox Press. Without their constant sympathy and encouragement, I would never have made it. Adrian Young and Peter Morgan merit special thanks for their invaluable help in editing the material into an acceptable state, along with the, it seems to me, countless reviewers who made many useful contributions. Finally, I must thank Felipe Martins and Stephen Bullen who worked together to ensure that the reference section was complete, accurate and useful. *John Green*

I would like to thank John Green for asking for my assistance in the writing of this book. I was a little daunted by the task at first, but hope that my first attempt at technical authoring is well received. I would also like to thank my wife Yvonne for her support and understanding. Without her encouragement I may not have risen to the challenge. A big 'woof' goes to my trusted friend Max who kept my feet warm during some very late nights while I worked on these chapters. Lastly, I'd like to thank the people at Wrox Press and the book's technical editors (you know who you are) for helping to make this the excellent book that I hope you'll agree it is. *Stephen Bullen*

To my beautiful wife, Angie, and to my daughter, Marissa. *Felipe Martins*

Dedication

To Peg, Rob and Vic, none of whom will ever read this book, but without whom this book would *never* have been read. *John Green*

Table of Contents

Table of Contents

Table of Contents

Table of Contents

Table of Contents

Table of Contents

Table of Contents

Table of Contents

Table of Contents

Table of Contents

Introduction

A Brief History of Spreadsheets

Excel made its debut on the Macintosh in 1985 and has never lost its position as the most popular spreadsheet application in the Mac environment. In 1987, Excel was ported to the PC, running under Windows. It took many years for Excel to overtake Lotus 1-2-3, which was one of the most successful software systems in the history of computing at that time.

There were a number of spreadsheet applications that enjoyed success prior to the release of the IBM PC in 1981. Among these were VisiCalc and Multiplan. VisiCalc started it all, but fell by the wayside early on. Multiplan was Microsoft's predecessor to Excel, using the R1C1 cell addressing which is still available as an option in Excel. But it was 1-2-3 that shot to stardom very soon after its release in 1982 and came to dominate the PC spreadsheet market.

Early Spreadsheet Macros

1-2-3 was the first spreadsheet application to offer spreadsheet, charting and database capabilities in the one package. However, the main reason for its run-away success was its macro capability. Legend has it that the 1-2-3 developers set up macros as a debugging and testing mechanism for the product. It is said that they only realised the potential of macros at the last minute, and included them into the final release pretty much as an afterthought. Whatever their origins, macros gave non-programmers a simple way to become programmers and automate their spreadsheets. They grabbed the opportunity and ran. At last they had a measure of independence from the computer department.

The original 1-2-3 macros performed a task by executing the same keystrokes that a user would use to carry out the same task. It was, therefore, very simple to create a macro as there was virtually nothing new to learn to progress from normal spreadsheet manipulation to programmed manipulation. All you had to do was remember what keys to press and write them down. The only concessions to traditional programming were eight extra commands, the /x commands, which provided some primitive decision making and branching capabilities, a way to get input from a user and a way to construct menus.

One major problem with 1-2-3 macros was their vulnerability. The multi-sheet workbook had not yet been invented and macros had to be written directly into the cells of the spreadsheet they supported, along with input data and calculations. Macros were at the mercy of the user. For example, they could be inadvertently disrupted when a user inserted or deleted rows or columns. Macros were also at the mercy of the programmer. A badly designed macro could destroy itself quite easily while trying to edit spreadsheet data.

Despite the problems, users revelled in their newfound programming ability and millions of lines of code were written in this cryptic language, using arcane techniques to get around its many limitations. The world came to rely on code that was often badly designed, nearly always poorly documented and at all times highly vulnerable, often supporting enterprise critical control systems.

The XLM Macro Language

The original Excel macro language required you to write your macros in a macro sheet that was saved in a file with an .xlm extension. In this way, macros were kept separate from the worksheet that was saved in a file with an .xls extension. These macros are now often referred to as XLM macros, or Excel 4 macros, to distinguish them from the VBA macro language introduced in Excel Version 5. The macro language consisted of function calls, arranged in columns in the macro sheet. There were many hundreds of functions necessary to provide all the features of Excel and allow programmatic control. The XLM language was far more sophisticated and powerful than the 1-2-3 macro language, even allowing for the enhancements made in 1-2-3 Releases 2 and 3. However, the code produced was not much more intelligible.

The sophistication of Excel's macro language was a two edged sword. It appealed to those with high programming aptitude, who could tap the language's power, but was a barrier to most users. There was no simple relationship between the way you would manually operate Excel and the way you programmed it. There was a very steep learning curve involved in mastering the XLM language.

Another barrier to Excel's acceptance on the PC was that it required Windows. The early versions of Windows were restricted by limited access to memory and Windows required much more horsepower to operate than DOS. The Graphical User Interface was appealing, but the trade-offs in hardware cost and operating speed were perceived as problems.

Lotus made the mistake of assuming that Windows was a flash in the pan, soon to be replaced by OS/2, and did not bother to plan a Windows version of 1-2-3. Lotus put its energy into 1-2-3/G, a very nice GUI version of 1-2-3 that only operated under OS/2. This one horse bet was to prove the undoing of 1-2-3.

By the time it became clear that Windows was here to stay, Lotus was in real trouble as it watched users flocking to Excel. The first attempt at a Windows version of 1-2-3, released in 1991, was really 1-2-3 Release 3 for DOS in a thin GUI shell. Succeeding releases have closed the gap between 1-2-3 and Excel, but have been too late to stop the almost universal adoption of Microsoft Office by the market.

Excel 5

Microsoft took a brave decision to unify the programming code behind its Office applications by introducing VBA as the common macro language in Office. Excel 5, released in 1993, was the first application to include VBA. It has been gradually introduced into the other Office applications in subsequent versions of Office. Excel, Word, Access, PowerPoint and Outlook all use VBA as their macro language in Office 2000.

Since the release of Excel 5, Excel has supported both the XLM and the VBA macro languages and the support for XLM should continue into the foreseeable future, but will decrease in significance as users switch to VBA.

> *VBA (**Visual Basic For Applications**) is an object oriented programming language that is identical to the Visual Basic programming language in the way it is structured and in the way it handles objects. If you learn to use VBA in Excel, you know how to use it in the other Office applications.*

> *The Office applications differ in the objects they expose to VBA. To program an application, you need to be familiar with its **Object Model**. The Object Model is a hierarchy of all the objects that you find in the application. For example, part of the Excel Object Model tells us that there is an* Application *object that contains a* Workbook *object that contains a* Worksheet *object that contains a* Range *object.*

> *VBA is somewhat easier to learn than the XLM macro language, is more powerful, is generally more efficient and allows you to write well-structured code. You can also write badly structured code, but by following a few principles, you should be able to produce code that is readily understood by others and is reasonably easy to maintain.*

In Excel 5, you wrote your VBA code in modules, which were sheets in a workbook. Worksheets, chart sheets and dialog sheets were other types of sheets that could be contained in an Excel 5 workbook.

> *A module is really just a word processing document with some special characteristics that help you write and test code.*

Excel 97

In Excel 97, Microsoft introduced some dramatic changes in the VBA interface and some changes in the Excel Object Model. From Excel 97 onwards, modules are not visible in the Excel application window and are no longer objects contained by the workbook object. Modules are contained in the VBA project associated with the workbook and can only be viewed and edited in the Visual Basic Editor (VBE) window.

In addition to the standard modules, class modules were introduced, which allow you to create your own objects and access application events. Command bars were introduced to replace menus and toolbars. User forms replaced dialog sheets. Like modules, user forms can only be edited in the VBE window. As usual, the replaced objects are still supported in Excel, but are considered to be hidden objects and are not documented in the Help screens.

Excel 97 also greatly increased the number of events that VBA code can respond to and formalised the way in which this is done by providing event procedures for the workbook, worksheet and chart sheet objects. For example, workbooks now have 20 events they can respond to, such as `BeforeSave`, `BeforePrint` and `BeforeClose`. Excel 97 also introduced ActiveX controls that can be embedded in worksheets and user forms. ActiveX controls can respond to a wide range of events such as `GotFocus`, `MouseMove` and `DblClick`. In previous versions of Excel, objects such as buttons embedded in worksheets could only respond to a single event, usually the `Click` event.

The VBE provides users with much more help than was previously available. For example, as you write code, popups appear with lists of appropriate methods and properties for objects, and arguments and parameter values for functions and methods. The **Object Browser** is much better than previous versions, allowing you to search for entries, for example, and providing comprehensive information on intrinsic constants.

Microsoft has provided an Extensibility library that makes it possible to write VBA code that manipulates the VBE environment and VBA projects. This makes it possible to write code that can directly access code modules and user forms. It is possible to set up applications that indent module code or export code from modules to text files, for example.

Excel 97 has been ported to the Macintosh in the form of Excel 98. Unfortunately, many of the VBE help features that make life easy for programmers have not been included. The VBE Extensibility features have not made it to the Mac either.

Excel 2000

Excel 2000 has not introduced dramatic changes from a VBA programming perspective. If you are an Excel 97 user, you will find that 99% of what we have to say in this book applies to you and most of it applies to Excel 98.

There are a large number of improvements in the Office 2000 and Excel 2000 user interfaces and improvements in some Excel features such as PivotTables. A new PivotChart feature has been added. Web users will benefit the most from Excel 2000, especially through the ability to save workbooks as web pages. There are also improvements for users who need to share information, through new online collaboration features. The new Office clipboard, which can store up to 12 objects, will help many users.

One long awaited improvement for VBA users has been in user forms. It is possible to create a modeless dialog box in Excel 2000 for the first time. Previously, Excel only supported modal dialog boxes, which take the focus when they are on screen so that no other activity can take place until they are closed. Modeless dialog boxes allow the user to continue with other work while the dialog box floats above the worksheet. Modeless dialog boxes can be used to show a "splash" screen when an application written in Excel is loaded and to display a progress indicator while a lengthy macro runs.

Excel 2000 VBA Programmers Reference

This book is aimed squarely at Excel users who want to harness the power of the VBA language in their Excel applications. At all times, the VBA language is presented in the context of Excel, not just as a general application programming language.

The pages that follow have been divided into three sections:

❑ Primer Excel VBA

❑ Working with Specific Objects

❑ Excel 2000 Object Model and VBE Object Model Reference

The Primer has been written for those who are new to VBA programming and the Excel Object Model. It introduces the VBA language and the features of the language that are common to all VBA applications. It explains the relationship between collections, objects, properties, methods and events and shows how to relate these concepts to Excel through its Object Model. It also shows how to use the Visual Basic Editor and its multitude of tools, including how to obtain help.

The middle section of the book takes the key objects in Excel and shows, through many practical examples, how to go about working with those objects. The techniques presented have been developed through the exchange of ideas of many talented Excel VBA programmers over many years and show the best way to gain access to workbooks, worksheets, charts, ranges, etc. The emphasis is on efficiency, i.e. how to write code that is readable and easy to maintain and that runs at maximum speed. The final three chapters of this section, written by Stephen Bullen, address the following advanced issues: writing code for international compatibility, programming the Visual Basic Editor and how to use the functions in the Win32 API (Windows 32 bit Application Programming Interface).

The final section of the book is a comprehensive reference to the Excel 2000 Object Model. All the objects in the model are presented together with all their properties, methods and events. I trust that this book will become a well-thumbed resource that you can dig into, as needed, to reveal that elusive bit of code that you must have right now.

Primer in Excel VBA

Introduction

This chapter is intended for those who are not familiar with Excel and the Excel macro recorder, or who are inexperienced with programming using the Visual Basic language. If you are already comfortable with navigating around the features provided by Excel, have used the macro recorder, and have a working knowledge of Visual Basic and the Visual Basic Editor, you might want to skip straight to Chapter 3. If this is not the case, this section has been designed to provide you with the information you need to be able to move on comfortably to the more advanced features presented in the following chapters. We will be covering the following topics:

❑ The Excel macro recorder

❑ User defined functions

❑ The Excel object model

❑ VBA programming concepts

Excel VBA is a programming application that allows you to use Visual Basic code to run the many features of the Excel package, thereby allowing you to customize your Excel applications. Units of VBA code are ofter referred to as macros. We will be covering more formal terminology in this chapter, but we will continue to use the term macros as a general way to refer to any VBA code.

In your day to day use of Excel, if you carry out the same sequence of commands repetitively, you can save a lot of time and effort by automating those steps using macros. If you are setting up an application for other users, who don't know much about Excel, you can use macros to create buttons and dialog boxes to guide them through your application as well as automate the processes involved.

If you are able to perform an operation manually, you can use the **macro recorder** to capture that operation. This is a very quick and easy process and requires no prior knowledge of the VBA language. Many Excel users record and run macros and feel no need to learn about VBA. However, the recorded results might not be very flexible, in that the macro can only be used to carry out one particular task on one particular range of cells. In addition, the recorded macro is likely to run much more slowly than code written by a user with the knowledge that you will find in this book. To set up interactive macros that can adapt to change and also run quickly, and to take advantage of more advanced features of Excel such as customized dialog boxes, you need to learn about VBA.

> Don't get the impression that we are dismissing the macro recorder. The macro recorder is one of the most valuable tools available to VBA programmers. It is the fastest way to generate working VBA code. But you must be prepared to apply your own knowledge of VBA to edit the recorded macro to obtain flexible and efficient code. A recurring theme in this book is to record an Excel procedure and then show how to adapt the recorded code.

In this section you will learn how to use the macro recorder and you will see all the ways Excel provides to run your macros. You will see how to use the **Visual Basic Editor** to examine and change your macros, going beyond the recorder and tapping into the power of the VBA language and the **Excel object model**.

You can also use VBA to create your own worksheet functions. Excel comes with hundreds of built-in functions, such as SUM and IF, which you can use in cell formulas. However, if you have a complex calculation that you use frequently and that is not included in the set of standard Excel functions — such as a tax calculation or a specialized scientific formula — you can write your own **user-defined function**.

Section 1: Using the Macro Recorder

Excel's macro recorder operates very much like the recorder that stores your greeting on your telephone answering machine. To record a greeting, you first prepare yourself by rehearsing the greeting, to ensure that it says what you want. Then you switch on the recorder and deliver the greeting. When you have finished, you switch off the recorder. You now have a recording that automatically plays when you leave a call unanswered. Recording an Excel operation is very similar. You first rehearse the steps involved and decide at what points you want to start and stop the recording process. You prepare your spreadsheet, switch on the Excel recorder, carry out your Excel operations and switch off the recorder. You now have an automated procedure that you and others can reproduce at the press of a button.

Recording Macros

Say you want a macro that types six month names as three letter abbreviations, "Jan" to "Jun", across the top of your worksheet, starting in cell B1. I know this is rather a silly macro as you could do this easily with an AutoFill operation, but this example will serve to show us some important general concepts:

❑ First think about how you are going to carry out this operation. In this case, it is easy — you will just type the data across the worksheet. (However, a more complex macro might need more rehearsals before you are ready to record it.)

❑ Next, think about when you want to start recording. In this case, you should include the selection of cell B1 in the recording, as you want to always have "Jan" in B1. If you don't select B1 at the start, you will record typing "Jan" into the active cell, which could be anywhere when you play back the macro.

❑ Next, think about when you want to stop recording. You might first want to include some formatting such as making the cells bold and italic, so you should include that in the recording. Where do you want the active cell to be after the macro runs? Do you want it to be in the same cell as "Jun", or would you rather have the active cell in column A or column B, ready for your next input? Let's assume that you want the active cell to be A2, at the completion of the macro, so we will select A2 before turning off the recorder.

❑ Now you can set up your screen, ready to record.

In this case, start with an empty worksheet with call A1 selected. If you like to work with toolbars, use View | Toolbars to select and display the Visual Basic toolbar as shown below on the top right of the screen. Press the Record Macro button, with the dark blue dot, to start the recorder. If you prefer, start the recorder with Tools | Macro | Record New Macro… from the Worksheet menu bar.

In the Macro name: box, replace the default entry, such as Macro1, with the name you want for your macro. The name should start with a letter and contain only letters, numbers and the underscore character with a maximum length of 255 characters. The macro name must not contain special characters such as ! or ? or blank spaces. *It is also best to use a short but descriptive name that you will recognize later.* You can use the underscore character to separate words, but it is easy to just use capitalization to distinguish words. Call the macro MonthNames1, because we will create another version later.

In the Shortcut key: box, you can type in a single letter. This key can be pressed later, while holding down the *Ctrl* key, to run the macro. We will use a lower case *m*. Alternatively, you can use an upper case *M*. In this case, when you later want to run the macro, you need to hold down the *Ctrl* key and the *Shift* key while you press *M*. It is not mandatory to provide a short cut key. You can run a macro in a number of other ways, as we will see.

In the Description: box, you can accept the default comments provided by the recorder, or type in your own comments. These lines will appear at the top of your macro code. They have no significance to VBA but provide you and others with information about the macro. You can edit these comments later, so there is no need to change them now. All Excel macros are stored in workbooks. You are given a choice regarding where the recorded macro will be stored. The Store macro in: combo box lists three possibilities. If you choose New Workbook, the recorder will open a new empty workbook for the macro. Personal Macro Workbook refers to a special hidden workbook that we discuss below. We will choose This Workbook to store the macro in the currently active workbook.

> *If you choose to store your recorded macro in the Personal Macro Workbook,*
> *the macro is added to a special file called* Personal.xls, *which is a hidden*
> *file that is saved in your Excel start up directory when you close Excel. This*
> *means that* Personal.xls *is automatically loaded when you launch Excel*
> *and, therefore, its macros are always available for any other workbook to use. If*
> Personal.xls *does not already exist, the recorder will create it for you.*
> *You can use* Window | Unhide *to see this workbook in the Excel window, but*
> *it is seldom necessary or desirable to do this as you can examine and modify*
> *the* Personal.xls *macros in the Visual Basic Editor window. An*
> *exception, where you might want to make* Personal.xls *visible, is if you*
> *need to store data in its worksheets. You can hide it again, after adding the*
> *data, with* Window | Hide. *If you are creating a general purpose utility*
> *macro, which you want to be able to use with any workbook, store it in*
> Personal.xls. *If the macro relates to just the application in the current*
> *workbook, store the macro with the application.*

When you have filled in the Record Macro dialog box, click the OK button. You will see the word Recording on the left side of the Status Bar at the bottom of the screen and the Stop Recording toolbar should appear on the screen. Note that the Stop Recording toolbar will not appear if it has been previously closed during a recording session. If it is missing, refer to the instructions below under the heading "Absolute and Relative Recording" to see how to re-instate it. However, you don't really need it for the moment because we can stop the recording from the Visual Basic toolbar or the Tools menu.

> *If you have the Stop Recording toolbar visible, make sure*
> *that the second button, the Relative Reference button, is not*
> *pressed in. It should appear flat on the toolbar surface, not*
> *indented as it appears in this screenshot. By default the*
> *macro recorder uses absolute cell references when it records.*

You should now click on cell B1 and type in Jan and fill in the rest of the cells as shown below. Then select B1:G1 and press the Bold and Italic buttons on the Formatting toolbar. Click the A2 cell and then stop the recorder. You can stop the recorder by pressing the Stop Recording button on the Stop Recording toolbar, by pressing the square Stop Recording button on the Visual Basic toolbar — the round Start Recording button changes to the Stop Recording button while you are recording — or you can use Tools | Macro | Stop Recording from the Worksheet menu bar. Save the workbook as Recorder.xls.

```
Microsoft Excel - Book1                                    _ □ X
File  Edit  View  Insert  Format  Tools  Data  Window  Custom  Help   _ ё X
D ё ∎ ё ᴅ ᵷ ∽ ⋅ ᵷ Σ ʄᵥ ᴢ₊ 🎲 ❔    »  10 ▼  B  I  U  ≡ 🎛 $ ⁺₀ ⁺₀₀  »
      A2        ▼        =
        A      B      C      D      E      F      G      H      I      J
 1            Jan    Feb    Mar    Apr    May    Jun
 2
 3                          ▼ Stop R X
 4                          ∎  🔳
 5
 6
 7
┃◀ ◀ ▶ ▶┃ \Sheet1 /              │◀│
Ready    Recording
```

It is important to remember to stop the Recorder. If you leave the recorder on, and try to run the recorded macro, you can go into a loop where the macro runs itself over and over again. If this does happen to you, or any other error occurs while testing your macros, hold down the *Ctrl* key and press the *Break* key to interrupt the macro. You can then End the macro or go into Debug mode to trace errors. You can also interrupt a macro with the *Esc* key, but it is not as effective as *Ctrl+Break* for a macro that is pausing for input.

Running Macros

To run the macro, either insert a new worksheet in the Recorder.xls workbook, or open a new empty workbook, leaving Recorder.xls open in memory. You can only run macros that are in open workbooks, but they can be run from within any other open workbook. You can run the macro by holding down the *Ctrl* key and pressing *m*, the shortcut that you assigned at the start of the recording process. You can also run the macro by clicking Tools | Macro | Macros... on the Worksheet menu bar and double-clicking the macro name, or by selecting the macro name and clicking Run.

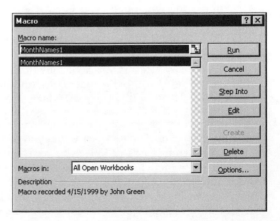

The same dialog box can be opened by pressing the Run Macro button on the Visual Basic toolbar.

Notice here that I have provided you with a number of different methods to do the same task. This is the way I do it in my training courses. I find different people have different habits and don't like being forced into a different mode. So I'll leave it up to you to home in on the alternative you prefer and ignore the others.

Short Cut Keys

You can change the shortcut key assigned to a macro by first bringing up the Macro dialog box shown above, using Tools | Macro | Macros or the Run Macro button on the Visual Basic toolbar. Select the macro name and press Options. This opens the following dialog box:

It is possible to assign the same shortcut key to more than one macro in the same workbook using this dialog box (although the dialog box that appears when you start the macro recorder will not let you assign a shortcut that is already in use).

> It is also quite likely that two different workbooks could contain macros with the same shortcut. If this happens, which macro runs when you use the shortcut? The answer is, the one that appears closest to the top in the Macro dialog box. As the macros are presented in a list that is sorted by the macro names, it is always the macro that comes first alphabetically that runs.

Shortcuts are appropriate for macros that you use very frequently, especially if you prefer to keep your hands on the keyboard. It is worth memorizing the shortcuts and you won't forget them if you use them regularly. Shortcuts are *not* appropriate for macros that are run infrequently or are intended to make life easier for less experienced users of your application. It is better to assign meaningful names to those macros and run them from the Macro dialog box. Or you can run them from buttons that you add to the worksheet or place on the toolbars. You will learn how to do this shortly.

Absolute and Relative Recording

When you run `MonthNames1`, the macro returns to the same cells you selected while typing in the month names. It doesn't matter which cell is active when you start, if the macro contains the command to select cell B1, then that is what it selects . The macro selects B1 because you recorded in **absolute** record mode. The alternative, **relative** record mode, remembers the position of the active cell relative to its previous position. If you have cell A10 selected, and then turn on the recorder and you go on to select B10, the recorder notes that you moved one cell to the right, rather than noting that you selected cell B10.

We will record a second macro called `MonthNames2`. There will be three differences between this macro compared with the previous one:

❑ We will use the Relative Reference button on the Stop Recording toolbar as our first action after turning on the recorder.

❑ We will not select the "Jan" cell before typing. We want our recorded macro to type "Jan" into the active cell when we run the macro.

❑ We will finish by selecting the cell under "Jan", rather than A2, just before turning off the recorder.

Start with an empty worksheet and select the B1 cell. Turn on the macro recorder and specify the macro name as `MonthNames2`. Enter the short cut as upper case *M* — the recorder won't let you use lower case *m* again. Click the OK button and depress the Relative Reference button on the Stop Recording toolbar. The button should now appear to have a shadow around it, rather than look flush with the toolbar surface.

> **If the Stop Recording toolbar does not automatically appear when you start recording, click on** View | Toolbars **from the** Worksheet **menu and select** Stop Recording. **The** Stop Recording **toolbar will now appear. However, you will need to immediately click the** Stop Recording **button on the** Stop Recording **toolbar and start the recording process again. Otherwise, the recorded macro will display the** Stop Recording **toolbar every time it is run! The** Stop Recording **toolbar will now synchronize with the recorder, as long as you never close it while recording.**

If you needed to re-synchronize the Stop Recording toolbar using the instructions above, upper case M will already be assigned. If you have difficulties assigning the upper case M short cut to `MonthNames2` *on the second recording, use another key such as upper case N, and change it back to M after finishing the recording. Use* Tools | Macro | Macros... *and, in the* Macro *dialog box, select the macro name and press the* Options *button, as explained in the Short Cut Keys section above.*

Type "Jan" and the other month names, as you did when recording `MonthNames1`. Select cells B1:G1 and press the Bold and Italic buttons on the Formatting toolbar.

> **Make sure you select** B1:G1 **from left to right, so that** B1 **is the active cell. There is a small kink in the recording process that can cause errors in the recorded macro if you select cells from right to left or from bottom to top. Always select from the top left hand corner when recording relatively. This has been a problem with all versions of Excel VBA.**

Finally, select B2, the cell under Jan, and turn off the recorder.

Before you run `MonthNames2`, select a starting cell, such as **A10**. You will find that the macro now types the month names across row 10, starting in column **A** and finally selects the cell under the starting cell.

Before you record a macro that selects cells, you need to think about whether to use absolute or relative recording. If you are selecting input cells for data entry, or for a print area, you will probably want to record with absolute references. If you want to be able to run your macro in different areas of your worksheet, you will probably want to record with relative references.

If you are trying to reproduce the effect of the *Ctrl+Arrow* keys to select the last cell in a column or row of data, you should record with relative references. You can even switch between relative and absolute recording in the middle of a macro, if you want. You might want to select the top of a column with an absolute reference, switch to relative references and use *Ctrl+Down Arrow* to get to the bottom of the column and an extra *Down Arrow* to go to the first empty cell.

> *Excel 2000 is the first version of Excel to let you successfully record selecting a block of cells of variable height and width using the* Ctrl *key. If you start at the top left hand corner of a block of data, you can hold down the* Shift+Ctrl *keys and press* Down Arrow *and then* Right Arrow *to select the whole block (as long as there are no gaps in the data). If you record these operations with Relative referencing, you can use the macro to select a block of different dimensions. Previous versions of Excel recorded an absolute selection of the original block size, regardless of recording mode.*

The Visual Basic Editor

It is now time to see what has been going on behind the scenes. If you want to understand macros, be able to modify your macros and tap into the full power of VBA, you need to know how to use the Visual Basic Editor. The VB Editor runs in its own window, separate to the Excel window. You can activate it in many ways.

First, you can activate it by pressing the Visual Basic Editor button on the Visual Basic toolbar. You can also activate it by holding down the *Alt* key and pressing the *F11* key. *Alt+F11* acts as a toggle, taking you between the Excel Window and the VB Editor window. If you want to edit a specific macro, you can use Tools | Macro | Macros… to open the Macro dialog box, select the macro and press the Edit button. The VB Editor window will look something like this:

It is quite possible that you will see nothing but the menu bar when you switch to the VB Editor window. If you can't see the toolbar, use View | Toolbars *and click on the* Standard *toolbar. Use* View | Project Explorer *and* View | Properties Window *to show the windows on the left. If you can't see the code module on the right, double-click the icon for* Module1 *in the Project Explorer window.*

Code Modules

Your macros all reside in **code modules** like the one on the right of the VB Editor window above. There are two types of code modules — **standard modules** and **class modules**. The one you see on the right is a standard module. You can use class modules to create your own objects. You won't need to know much about class modules until you are working at a very advanced level. See Chapter 13 for more details on how to use class modules.

Some class modules have already been set up for you. They are associated with each worksheet in your workbook and there is one for the entire workbook. You can see them in the Project Explorer window, in the folder called "Microsoft Excel Objects". You will find out more about them later in this chapter.

You can add as many code modules to your workbook, as you like. The macro recorder has inserted the one above, named Module1. Each module can contain many macros. For a small application, you would probably keep all your macros in one module. For larger projects, you can organize your code better by filing related macros in separate modules. Modules behave like word processing documents. You can edit the code using standard Windows techniques and there is a multilevel Undo facility.

Procedures

In VBA, macros are referred to as **procedures**. There are two types of procedures — sub procedures and function procedures. You will find out about function procedures in the next section. The macro recorder can only produce sub procedures. You can see the MonthNames1 sub procedure set up by the recorder in your code module in the above screenshot.

Sub procedures start with the keyword Sub followed by the name of the procedure and opening and closing parentheses. The end of a sub procedure is marked by the keywords End Sub. Although it is not mandatory, the code within the sub is normally indented, to make it stand out from the start and end of the procedure, so that the whole procedure is easier to read. Further indenting is normally used to distinguish sections of code such as If tests and looping structures. Any lines starting with a single quote are comment lines, which are ignored by VBA. They are added to provide documentation, which is a very important component of good programming practice. You can also add comments to the right of lines of code. For example:

```
    Range("B1").Select    'Select the B1 cell
```

At this stage, the code will not make perfect sense, but you should be able to make out roughly what is going on. If you look at the code in MonthNames1, you will see that cells are being selected and then the month names are assigned to the active cell formula. You can see that you could edit some parts of the code. If you had spelt a month name wrongly, you could fix it, for example. Or you could identify and remove the line that sets the font to bold. Or you can select and delete an entire macro. You can also see the differences between MonthNames1 and MonthNames2. MonthNames1 selects definite cells such as B1 and C1. MonthNames2 uses Offset to select a cell that is zero rows down and one column to the right from the active cell. Already, you are starting to get a feel for the VBA language.

The Project Explorer

The Project Explorer is an essential navigation tool. In VBA, each workbook contains a project. The Project explorer displays all the open projects and the component parts of those projects, as you can see here:

You can use the Project Explorer to locate and activate the code modules in your project. You can double click a module icon to open and activate that module. You can also insert and remove code modules in the Project Explorer. Right-click anywhere in the Project Explorer window and click Insert to add a new standard module, class module or UserForm. You can right-click Module1 and choose Remove Module1… to delete it. (Note that, you can't do this with the modules associated with workbook or worksheet objects.) You can also export the code in a module to a separate text file, or import code from a text file.

The Properties Window

The Properties window shows you the properties that can be changed at design time for the currently active object in the Project Explorer window. For example, if you click on Sheet1 in the Project Explorer, the following properties are displayed in the Properties window. The ScrollArea property has been set to A1:D10, to restrict users to that area of the worksheet.

You can get to the help screen associated with any property very easily. Just select the property, such as the ScrollArea property, which is selected above, and press *F1*.

Other Ways to Run Macros

You have seen how to run macros with short cuts and how to run them from the Tools menu. Neither method is particularly friendly. You need to be very familiar with your macros to be comfortable with these techniques. You can make your macros much more accessible by attaching them to buttons. If the macro is worksheet specific, and will only be used in a particular part of the worksheet, then it is suitable to use a button that has been embedded in the worksheet at the appropriate location. If you want to be able to use a macro in any worksheet or workbook and in any location in a worksheet, it is appropriate to attach the macro to a button on a toolbar. There are many other objects that you can attach macros to, including combo boxes, list boxes, scrollbars, check boxes and option buttons. These are all referred to as **controls**. See Chapter 10 — Adding Controls for more information on controls. You can also attach macros to graphic objects in the worksheet, such as shapes created with the Drawing toolbar.

Worksheet Buttons

Excel 2000 has two different sets of controls that can be embedded in worksheets. One set is on the Forms toolbar and the other is on the Control Toolbox toolbar. The Forms toolbar has been inherited from Excel 5 and 95. The Forms controls are also used with Excel 5 and 95 dialog sheets to create dialog boxes. Excel 97 introduced the newer ActiveX controls that are selected from the Control Toolbox toolbar. You can also use these on UserForms, in the VB Editor, to create dialog boxes.
For compatibility with the older versions of Excel, both sets of controls and techniques for creating dialog boxes are supported in Excel 2000. If you have no need to maintain backward compatibility with Excel 5 and 95, you can use just the ActiveX controls, except when you want to embed controls in a chart. At the moment, charts only support the Forms controls.

Forms Toolbar

Another reason for using the Forms controls is that they are simpler to use than the ActiveX controls. They do not have all the features of ActiveX controls. For example, Forms controls can only respond to a single, predefined event, which is usually the mouse click event. ActiveX controls can respond to many events, such as a mouse click, a double-click or pressing a key on the keyboard. If you have no need of such features, you might prefer the simplicity of Forms controls. To create a Forms button in a worksheet, click the fourth button from the left in the Forms toolbar shown below:

You can now draw the button in your worksheet by clicking where you want a corner of the button to appear and dragging to where you want the diagonally opposite corner to appear. The following dialog box will show, and you can select the macro to attach to the button:

Click **OK** to complete the assignment. You can then edit the text on the button to give a more meaningful indication of its function. After you click on a worksheet cell, you can left-click the button to run the attached macro. If you need to edit the button, you can right-click on it. This selects the control and you get a short cut menu. If you don't want the short cut menu, hold down *Ctrl* and left-click the button to select it. (Don't drag the mouse while you hold down *Ctrl*, or you will create a copy of the button.)

If you want to align the button with the worksheet gridlines, hold down *Alt* as you draw it with the mouse. If you have already drawn the button, select it and hold down *Alt* as you drag any of the white boxes that appear on the corners and edges of the button. The edge or corner you drag will jump to the nearest gridline.

Control Toolbox Toolbar

To create an ActiveX command button control, click the sixth button on the Control Toolbox toolbar shown below:

When you draw your button in the worksheet, design mode is automatically turned on and the Exit Design Mode toolbar appears with a button that you can use to turn off design mode. This little toolbar is situated on the lower right side of the worksheet on the screenshot below. Don't worry if it does not appear. You can use the identical button on the Control Toolbox toolbar.

When you are in design mode, you can select a control with a left-click and edit it. You must turn off design mode if you want the control to respond to events.

```
 Microsoft Excel - Recorder                                        _ □ ×
  File   Edit   View   Insert   Format   Tools   Data   Window   Custom   Help        _ ₧ ×
  [toolbar icons]                                              B   I   ≡ ▤   »
 CommandBut... ▼        =    =EMBED("Forms.CommandButton.1","")
        A        B        C        D        E        F        G
  1              Jan      Feb      Mar      Apr      May      Jun
  2     ┌─────────────────────────────────────────┐
  3     │ ▼  Control Toolbox                     ×  │
  4     │ [control toolbox icons]                  │
  5
  6
  7      □        □        □                    ┌────┐
  8      □  CommandButton1  □                   │ ▼ ×│
  9      □                  □                   │ ✎  │
 10      □        □        □                    └────┘
 11
 12
 ◄ ◄ ► ►  Sheet2 / Sheet1 /              ◄
  Ready
```

You are not prompted to assign a macro to the ActiveX command button, but you do need to write a click event procedure for the button. An **event procedure** is a sub that is executed when, for example, you click on a button. To do this, make sure you are still in design mode and double-click the command button. This will open the VB Editor window and display the code module behind the worksheet. The Sub and End Sub statement lines for your code will have been inserted in the module and you can add in the code necessary to run the MonthName2 macro, as shown:

```
 Microsoft Visual Basic - Recorder.xls [design] - [Sheet2 (Code)]         _ □ ×
  File   Edit   View   Insert   Format   Debug   Run   Tools   Add-Ins   Window   Help   _ ₧ ×
  [toolbar icons]                                                         »
 Project - VBAProject        ×     CommandButton1      ▼     Click           ▼
  [icons]                              Private Sub CommandButton1_Click()
 ⊟ VBAProject (Recorder.xls)               Call MonthNames2
   ⊟ Microsoft Excel Objects          End Sub
     Sheet1 (Sheet1)
     Sheet2 (Sheet2)
     ThisWorkbook
   ⊟ Modules
     Module1
```

To run this code, switch back to the worksheet, turn off design mode and click the command button.

If you want to make changes to the command button, you need to return to design mode by pressing the Design Mode button on the Control Toolbox toolbar. You can then select the command button and change its size and position on the worksheet. You can also display its properties by right-clicking on it and choosing Properties to display the dialog box opposite:

Properties - CommandButton1	
CommandButton1 CommandButton	
Alphabetic	Categorized
(Name)	CommandButton1
Accelerator	
AltHTML	
AutoLoad	False
AutoSize	False
BackColor	&H8000000F&
BackStyle	1 - fmBackStyleOpaque
Caption	Type Month Names
Enabled	True
Font	Arial
ForeColor	&H80000012&
Height	39.75
Left	21.75
Locked	True
MouseIcon	(None)
MousePointer	0 - fmMousePointerDefault
Picture	(None)
PicturePosition	7 - fmPicturePositionAboveCenter
Placement	2
PrintObject	True
Shadow	False
TakeFocusOnClick	True
Top	82.5
Visible	True
Width	89.25
WordWrap	False

To change the text on the command button, change the Caption property. You can also set the font for the caption and the foreground and background colors. It is also a good idea to change the TakeFocusOnClick property from its default value of True to False, if you want compatibility with Excel 97. If the button takes the focus when you click on it, Excel 97 does not allow you to assign values to some properties such as the NumberFormat property of the Range object.

Toolbars

If you want to attach a macro to a toolbar button, you can modify one of the built in toolbars or create your own toolbar. To create your own toolbar, use View | Toolbars | Customize... to bring up the Customize dialog box, click New... and enter a name for the new toolbar:

Customize	? X
Toolbars	Commands	Options
Toolbars:	
☑ Standard	New...
☑ For	**New Toolbar** ? X
☐ 3-D	Toolbar name:
☐ Au	MonthTools
☐ Ch	
☐ Ch	
☐ Circ	
☐ Clip	
☐ Con	OK Cancel
☐ Dra	
☐ Exi	
☐ Ext	
☐ Forms	
☐ Full Screen	
☐ Picture	
	Close

Staying in the Customize dialog box, click on the Commands tab and select the Macros category. Drag the smiley icon to your new toolbar, or an existing toolbar. Next, either click the Modify Selection button or right-click the new toolbar button to get the following short cut menu.

Click on **Assign Macro…** and select the name of the macro, MonthNames2 in this case, to be assigned to the button. You can also change the button image by clicking on Change Button Image and choosing from a library of images, or you can open the icon editor with Edit Button Image. Note that the Customize dialog box must stay open while you make these changes. It is a good idea to enter some descriptive text into the Name box, which will appear as the tooltip for the button. You can now close the Customize dialog box.

To run the macro, select a starting cell for your month names and click the new toolbar button. If you want to distribute the new toolbar to others, along with the workbook, you can attach the toolbar to the workbook. It will then pop up automatically on the new users PC as soon as they open the workbook, as long as they do not already have a toolbar with the same name.

There is a potential problem when you attach a toolbar to a workbook. As Excel will not replace an existing toolbar, you can have a toolbar that is attached to an older version of the workbook than the one you are trying to use. A solution to this problem is provided in the next section on Event Procedures.

To attach a toolbar to the active workbook, use View | Toolbars | Customize… to bring up the Customize dialog box, click the Toolbars tab, if necessary and click Attach… to open the Attach Toolbars dialog box as follows: Select the toolbar name in the left list box and press the middle button, which has the caption Copy>>.

If an older copy of the toolbar is already attached to the workbook, select it in the right hand list box and press Delete to remove it. Then select the toolbar name in the left list box and press the middle button again, which will now have the caption Copy >>. Click OK to complete the attachment and then close the Customize dialog box.

Event Procedures

Event procedures are special macro procedures that respond to the events that occur in Excel. Events include user actions, such as clicking the mouse on a button, and system actions, such as the recalculation of a worksheet. Excel 2000 exposes a wide range of events for which you can write code . You have already seen an event procedure. It was the click event procedure for the ActiveX command button that ran the MonthNames2 macro. You entered the code for this event procedure in the code module behind the worksheet containing the command button. All event procedures are contained in the class modules behind the workbook, worksheets, charts and UserForms. You can see the events that are available by activating a module, such as the ThisWorkbook module, choosing an object, such as Workbook, from the left drop down at the top of the module and then activating the right drop down, as shown:

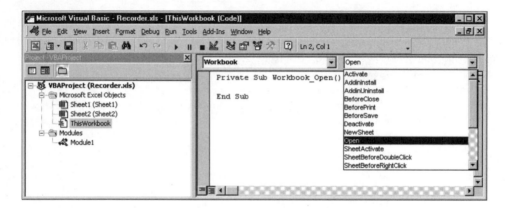

The Workbook_Open() event can be used to initialize the workbook when it is opened. The code could be as simple as activating a particular worksheet and selecting a range for data input. The code could be more sophisticated and construct a new menu bar for the workbook.

> For compatibility with Excel 5 and 95, you can still create a Sub Auto_Open(), in a standard module, that runs when the workbook is opened. If you also have a Workbook_Open() event procedure, the event procedure runs first.

As you can see, there are many events to choose from. Some events, such as the BeforeSave and BeforeClose events, allow canceling the event. The following event procedure stops the workbook being closed until cell A1 in Sheet1 contains the value True.

```
Private Sub Workbook_BeforeClose(Cancel As Boolean)
    If ThisWorkbook.Sheets("Sheet1").Range("A1").Value <> True Then
    Cancel = True
End Sub
```

This code even prevents the closure of the Excel window.

Removing an Attached Toolbar

As mentioned previously in this chapter, if you have attached a custom toolbar to a workbook, there can be a problem if you send a new version of the toolbar attached to a workbook, or the user saves the workbook under a different name. The old toolbar is not replaced when you open the new workbook and the macros that the old toolbar runs are still in the old workbook. One approach that makes it much less likely that problems will occur, is to delete the custom toolbar when the workbook is closed. Place the following code in the workbook's ThisWorkbook module:

```
Private Sub Workbook_BeforeClose(Cancel As Boolean)
    On Error Resume Next
    Application.CommandBars("MonthsTools").Delete
End Sub
```

The On Error statement covers the situation where the user might delete the toolbar manually before closing the workbook. Without the On Error statement, this would cause a run time error when the event procedure attempts to delete the missing toolbar. On Error Resume Next is an instruction to ignore any run time error and continue with the next line of code.

Summary – Recording and Running Macros

In this section, you have seen how to use the macro recorder to turn a manual operation into a macro. Although we used some very simple examples, you can record the most complex manual operations in the same way. You have seen the difference between absolute and relative recording, and many different ways to run your macros. You have been shown the Visual Basic Editor, the Project Explorer and the Properties windows. You have also seen how to utilize event procedures to tap into the wide range of events that Excel exposes. Although we have covered a lot of ground, there is lots more to come.

Section 2: User Defined Functions

Excel has hundreds of built in worksheet functions that you can use in cell formulas. You can select an empty worksheet cell and click the Paste Function button on the Standard toolbar to see a list of those functions. Among the most frequently used functions are SUM, IF and VLOOKUP. If the function you need is not already in Excel, you can write your own user defined function (or UDF) using VBA. UDFs can reduce the complexity of your worksheet. It is possible to reduce a calculation that requires many cells of intermediate results down to a single function call in one cell. UDFs can also increase productivity when many users have to repeatedly use the same calculation procedures. You can set up a library of functions tailored to your organization.

Creating a UDF

Unlike manual operations, UDFs cannot be recorded. You have to write them from scratch using a standard module in the VB Editor. If necessary, you can insert a standard module by right-clicking in the Project Explorer window and choosing Insert | Module. A simple example of a UDF is shown here:

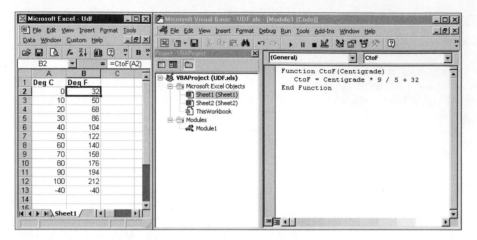

We have created a function called CtoF() that converts degrees Centigrade to degrees Fahrenheit. The function is visible in the VB Editor to the right. In the worksheet on the left, column A contains degrees Centigrade. In column B, we have used the CtoF() function to calculate the corresponding temperature in degrees Fahrenheit. You can see the formula in cell B2 by looking at the formula bar:

```
=CtoF(A2)
```

The formula has been copied into cells B3:B13. You can see the code for the function in the VB Editor:

```
Function CtoF(Centigrade)
    CtoF = Centigrade * 9 / 5 + 32
End Function
```

The key difference between a sub procedure and a function procedure is that a **function procedure** returns a value. CtoF() calculates a numeric value, which is returned to the worksheet cell where CtoF() is used. A function procedure indicates the value to be returned by setting its own name equal to the return value. Function procedures normally have one or more input parameters. CtoF() has one input parameter called Centigrade, which is used to calculate the return value. When you enter the formula, =CtoF(A2), the value in cell A2 is passed to CtoF() through Centigrade. In this case the value of Centigrade is zero. CtoF() sets its own name equal to the calculated result, which is 32 in this case, as shown above. The result is passed back to cell B2. The same process occurs in each cell where you enter a reference to CtoF().

A different example that shows how you can reduce the complexity of spreadsheet formulas for users is shown opposite:

The lookup table in cells **A1:D5** gives the price of each product, the discount sales volume — above which a discount will be applied, and the percent discount for units above the discount volume. Using normal spreadsheet formulas, users would have to set up three lookup formulas together with some logical tests to calculate the invoice amount. Instead, we create the following function:

```
Function InvoiceAmount(Prod, Vol, Table)
    Price = WorksheetFunction.VLookup(Prod, Table, 2)
    DiscountVol = WorksheetFunction.VLookup(Prod, Table, 3)
    If Vol > DiscountVol Then
        DiscountPct = WorksheetFunction.VLookup(Prod, Table, 4)
        InvoiceAmount = Price * DiscountVol + Price * _
                        (1 - DiscountPct) * (Vol - DiscountVol)
    Else
        InvoiceAmount = Price * Vol
    End If
End Function
```

The `InvoiceAmount()` function has three input parameters: `Prod` is the name of the product; `Vol` is the number of units sold and `Table` is the lookup table. The formula in cell **C8** defines the ranges to be used for each input parameter:

```
=InvoiceAmount(A8,B8,$A$2:$D$5)
```

The range for the table is absolute so that the copies of the formula below cell **C8** refer to the same range. The first calculation in the function uses the `VLookup` function to find the product in the lookup table and return the corresponding value from the second column of the lookup table, which it assigns to the variable `Price`.

> *If you want to use an Excel worksheet function in a VBA procedure, you need to tell VBA where to find it by preceding the function name with* `WorksheetFunction` *and a period. For compatibility with Excel 5 and 95, you can use* `Application` *instead of* `WorksheetFunction`. *Not all worksheet functions are available this way. In these cases, VBA has equivalent functions, or mathematical operators, to carry out the same calculations.*

In the next line of the function, the discount volume is found in the lookup table and assigned to the variable `DiscountVol`. The `If` test on the next line compares the sales volume in `Vol` with `DiscountVol`. If `Vol` is greater than `DiscountVol`, the calculations following, down to the `Else` statement, are carried out. Otherwise, the calculation after the `Else` are carried out.

If `Vol` is greater than `DiscountVol`, the percent discount rate is found in the lookup table and assigned to the variable `DiscountPct`. The invoice amount is then calculated by applying the full price to the units up to `DiscountVol` plus the discounted price for units above `DiscountVol`. The result is assigned to the name of the function, `InvoiceAmount`, so that the value will be returned to the worksheet cell. If `Vol` is not greater than `DiscountVol`, the invoice amount is calculated by applying the price to the units sold and the result is assigned to the name of the function.

Direct Reference to Ranges

When you define a UDF, it is possible to directly refer to worksheet ranges rather than through the input parameters of the UDF. This is illustrated in the following version of the `InvoiceAmount()` function.

```
Function InvoiceAmount2(Prod, Vol)
    Set Table = ThisWorkbook.Worksheets("Sheet2").Range("A2:D5")
    Price = WorksheetFunction.VLookup(Prod, Table, 2)
    DiscountVol = WorksheetFunction.VLookup(Prod, Table, 3)
    If Vol > DiscountVol Then
        DiscountPct = WorksheetFunction.VLookup(Prod, Table, 4)
        InvoiceAmount2 = Price * DiscountVol + Price * _
                        (1 - DiscountPct) * (Vol - DiscountVol)
    Else
        InvoiceAmount2 = Price * Vol
    End If
End Function
```

Note that `Table` is no longer an input parameter. Instead, the `Set` statement defines `Table` with a direct reference to the worksheet range. While this method still works, the return value of the function will not be recalculated if you change a value in the lookup table. Excel does not realize that it needs to recalculate the function when a lookup table value changes, as it does not see that the table is used by the function. Excel only recalculates a UDF when it sees its input parameters change. If you want to remove the lookup table from the function parameters, and still have the UDF recalculate automatically, you can declare the function to be volatile on the first line of the function as shown:

```
Function InvoiceAmount2(Prod, Vol)
    Application.Volatile
    Set Table = ThisWorkbook.Worksheets("Sheet2").Range("A2:D5")
    ...
```

However, you should be aware that this feature comes at a price. If a UDF is declared volatile, the UDF is recalculated every time any value changes in the worksheet. This can add a significant recalculation burden to the worksheet if the UDF is used in many cells.

What UDFs Cannot Do

A common mistake made by users is to attempt to create a worksheet function that changes the structure of the worksheet by, for example, copying a range of cells. **Such attempts will fail**. No error messages are produced, Excel simply ignores the offending code lines, so the reason for the failure is not obvious.

> **UDFs, used in worksheet cells, are not permitted to change the structure of the worksheet. This means that a UDF cannot return a value to any other cell than the one it is used in and it cannot change a physical characteristic of a cell, such as the font color or background pattern. In addition, UDFs cannot carry out actions such as copying or moving spreadsheet cells. They cannot even carry out some actions that imply a change of cursor location, such as an Edit | Find. A UDF can call another function procedure, or even a sub procedure, but that procedure will be under the same restrictions as the UDF. It will still not be permitted to change the structure of the worksheet.**

A distinction is made (in Excel VBA) between UDFs that are used in worksheet cells, and function procedures that are not connected with worksheet cells. As long as the original calling procedure was not a UDF in a worksheet cell, a function procedure can carry out any Excel action, just like a sub procedure.

It should also be noted that UDFs are not as efficient as the built in Excel worksheet functions. If UDFs are used extensively in a workbook, recalculation time will be greater compared with a similar workbook using the same number of built in functions.

Summary – User Defined Functions

In this section, you have seen how to create your own functions (UDFs) to simplify your worksheet calculations. A UDF can allow a worksheet user to perform complex calculations very easily. UDFs do impose calculation overheads, but the trade off is that they are easy to use and reduce the likelihood of errors. To maximize calculation efficiency, UDFs should only access data via their input parameters. UDFs can't carry out any actions that would change the structure of the worksheet. They can only return values to the cells in which they are used.

Section 3: The Excel Object Model

The Visual Basic for Applications programming language is common across the Office 2000 applications. In addition to Excel, you can use VBA in Word, Access, PowerPoint and Outlook. Once you learn it, you can apply it to any of these. However, to work with an application, you need to learn about the **objects** it contains. In Word, you deal with documents, paragraphs and words. In Access, you deal with databases, recordsets and fields. In Excel you deal with workbooks, worksheets and ranges. Unlike many programming languages, you don't have to create your own objects in Office 2000 VBA. Each application has a clearly defined set of objects that are arranged according to the relationships between them. This structure is referred to as the application's **Object Model**. This chapter is an introduction to the Excel object model, which is fully documented in the reference section.

Objects

First, let's cover a few basics about Object Oriented Programming (OOP). This not a complete formal treatise on the subject, but it covers what you need to know to work with the objects in Excel. OOP has a very basic premise that we can describe everything known to us as objects. You and I are objects, the world is an object and the universe is an object. In Excel, a workbook is an object, a worksheet is an object and a range is an object. These objects are only a small sample of around two hundred object types available to us in Excel. Let us look at some examples of how we can refer to Range objects in VBA code. One simple way to refer to cells B2:C4 is as follows:

```
Range("B2:C4")
```

If you give the name Data to a range of cells, you can use that name in a similar way:

```
Range("Data")
```

There are also ways to refer to the currently active cell and selection using short cuts:

In the screenshot opposite, `ActiveCell` refers to the B2 cell, and `Selection` refers to the range B2:E6. For more information on ActiveCell and Selection, see Chapter 3 — the Application Object.

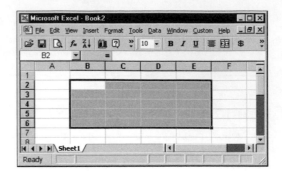

Collections

Many objects belong to **collections**. A city block is a collection of high-rise buildings. A high-rise building has a collection of floor objects. A floor is a collection of room objects. Collections are objects themselves — objects that contain other objects that are closely related. Collections and objects are often related in a hierarchical or tree structure.

Excel is an object itself, called the `Application` object. In the Excel `Application` object, there is a `Workbooks` collection that contains all the currently open `Workbook` objects. Each `Workbook` object has a `Worksheets` collection that contains the `Worksheet` objects in that workbook.

> Note that you need to make a clear distinction between the plural `Worksheets` object, which is a collection, and the singular `Worksheet` object. They are quite different objects.

If you want to refer to a member of a collection, you can refer to it by its position in the collection, as an index number starting with 1, or by its name, as quoted text. If you have opened just one workbook called `Data.xls`, you can refer to it by either of the following:

```
Workbooks(1)
Workbooks("Data.xls")
```

If you have three worksheets in the active workbook that have the names `North`, `East` and `South`, in that order, you can refer to the second worksheet by either of the following:

```
Worksheets(2)
Worksheets("East")
```

If you want to refer to a worksheet called `DataInput` in a workbook called `Sales.xls`, and `Sales.xls` is not the active workbook, you must qualify the worksheet reference with the workbook reference, separating them with a period, as follows:

```
Workbooks("Sales.xls").Worksheets("DataInput")
```

When you refer to the B2 cell in `DataInput` while another workbook is active, you use:

```
Workbooks("Sales.xls").Worksheets("DataInput").Range("B2")
```

Let us now look at objects more closely and see how we can manipulate them in our VBA code. There are two key characteristics of objects that you need to be aware of to do this. They are the **properties** and **methods** associated with an object.

Properties

Properties are the physical characteristics of objects. Properties can be measured or quantified. You and I have a height property, an age property, a bank balance property, and a name property. Some of our properties can be changed fairly easily, such as our bank balance. Other properties are more difficult or impossible to change, such as our name and age.

A worksheet Range object has a RowHeight property and a ColumnWidth property. A Workbook object has a Name property, which contains its file name. Some properties can be changed easily, such as the Range object's ColumnWidth property, by assigning the property a new value. Other properties, such as the Workbook object's Name property, are read only. You can't change the Name property by simply assigning a new value to it. You refer to the property of an object by referring to the object then the property, separated by a period. For example, to change the width of the column containing the active cell to 20 points, you would assign the value to the ColumnWidth property of the ActiveCell using:

```
ActiveCell.ColumnWidth = 20
```

To enter the name Florence into cell C10, you assign the name to the Value property of the Range object:

```
Range("C10").Value = "Florence"
```

If the Range object is not in the active worksheet in the active workbook, you need to be more specific:

```
Workbooks("Sales.xls").Worksheets("DataInput").Range("C10").Value = 10
```

> VBA can do what is impossible for us to do manually. It can enter data into worksheets that are not visible on the screen. It can copy and move data without having to make the sheets involved active. It is therefore very seldom necessary to activate a specific workbook, worksheet or range to manipulate data using VBA. The more you can avoid activating objects, the faster your code will run. Unfortunately, the macro recorder can only record what we do and uses activation extensively. Recording is a very useful way to get a starting point for a macro, but the code will usually be very inefficient.

In the examples above, we have seen how we can assign values to the properties of objects. We can also assign the property values of objects to variables or to other objects' properties. You can directly assign the column width of one cell to another cell on the active sheet using:

```
Range("C1").ColumnWidth = Range("A1").ColumnWidth
```

You can assign the value in C1 in the active sheet to D10 in the sheet named Sales, in the active workbook, using:

```
Worksheets("Sales").Range("D10").Value = Range("C1").Value
```

You can assign the value of a property to a variable so that it can be used in later code. This example stores the current value of cell **M100**, sets **M100** to a new value, prints the auto recalculated results and sets **M100** back to its original value:

```
OpeningStock = Range("M100").Value
Range("M100").Value = 100
ActiveSheet.PrintOut
Range("M100").Value = OpeningStock
```

Some properties are read only, which means that you can't assign a value to them directly. Sometimes there is an indirect way. One example is the `Text` property of a `Range` object. You can assign a value to a cell using its `Value` property and you can give the cell a number format using its `NumberFormat` property. The `Text` property of the cell gives you the formatted appearance of the cell. The following example displays $12,345.60 in a dialog box:

```
Range("B10").Value = 12345.6
Range("B10").NumberFormat = "$#,##0.00"
MsgBox Range("B10").Text
```

This is the only means by which you can set the value of the `Text` property.

Methods

While properties are the quantifiable characteristics of objects, methods are the actions that can be performed by objects or on objects. If you have a linguistic bent, you might like to think of objects as nouns, properties as adjectives and methods as verbs. Methods often change the properties of objects. I have a walking method that takes me from A to B, changing my location property. I have a spending method that reduces my bank balance property and a working method that increases my bank balance property. My dieting method reduces my weight property, temporarily.

A simple example of an Excel method is the `Select` method of the `Range` object. To refer to a method, as with properties, you put the object first, add a period and then the method. The following selects cell **G4**:

```
Range("G4").Select
```

Another example of an Excel method is the `Copy` method of the `Range` object. The following copies the contents of range **A1:B3** to the clipboard:

```
Range("A1:B3").Copy
```

Methods often have parameters that you can use to modify the way the method works. You can use the `Paste` method of the `Worksheet` object to paste the contents of the clipboard into a worksheet. If you do not specify where the data is to be pasted, it is inserted with its top left hand corner in the active cell. You can override this with the `Destination` parameter (parameters are discussed later in this section):

```
ActiveSheet.Paste Destination:=Range("G4")
```

Note that the value of a parameter is specified using `:=`, not just `=`.

Often, Excel methods provide short cuts. The previous examples of `Copy` and `Paste` can be carried out entirely by the `Copy` method:

```
Range("A1:B3").Copy Destination:=Range("G4")
```

This is far more efficient than the code produced by the macro recorder!

```
Range("A1:B3").Select
Selection.Copy
Range("G4").Select
ActiveSheet.Paste
```

Events

Another important concept in VBA is that objects can respond to events. A mouse click on a command button, a double click on a cell, a recalculation of a worksheet and the opening and closing of a workbook are examples of events. All of the ActiveX controls from the **Control Toolbox** toolbar can respond to events. These controls can be embedded in worksheets and in UserForms to enhance the functionality of those objects. Worksheets and Workbooks can also respond to a wide range of events. If you want an object to respond to an event, you enter VBA code into the appropriate event procedure for that object. The event procedure resides in the code module behind the `Workbook`, `Worksheet` or `UserForm` object concerned.

For example, you might want to detect that a user has selected a new cell and highlight the complete row the cell is in and the complete column that the cell is in. You can do this by entering code in the `Worksheet_SelectionChange()` event procedure. You first activate the VB Editor window and double click the worksheet in the Project Explorer. From the drop downs at the top of the worksheet code module, choose `Worksheet` and `SelectionChange` as shown below, and enter in the code shown:

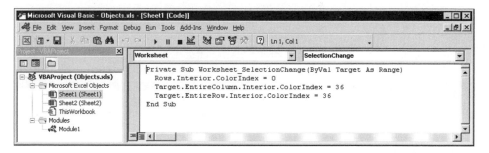

This event procedure runs every time the user selects a new cell, or block of cells. The parameter, `Target`, refers to the selected range as a `Range` object. The first statement sets the `ColorIndex` property of all the worksheets cells to no color, to remove any existing background color. The second and third statements set the entire columns and entire rows that intersect with the selected cells to a background color of pale yellow. (This color can be different, depending on the color palette set up in your workbook.)

The use of properties in this example is more complex than we have seen before. Let's analyze the component parts. If we assume that `Target` is a `Range` object referring to cell **B10**, then the following code uses the `EntireColumn` property of the **B10** `Range` object to refer to the entire B column, which is the range **B1:B65536**, or **B:B** for short:

```
Target.EntireColumn.Interior.ColorIndex = 36
```

Similarly the next line of code changes the color of row 10, which is the range A10:IV10, or 10:10 for short:

```
Target.EntireRow.Interior.ColorIndex = 36
```

The Interior property of a Range object refers to an Interior object, which is the background of a range. Finally, we set the ColorIndex property of the Interior object equal to the index number for the required color.

This code might appear to many to be far from intuitive. So how do you go about figuring out how to carry out a task involving an Excel object?

Getting Help

The easiest way to discover the required code to perform an operation is to use the macro recorder. The recorded code is likely to be inefficient, but it will indicate the objects required and the properties and methods involved. If you turn on the recorder to find out how to color the background of a cell, you will get something like the following:

```
With Selection.Interior
    .ColorIndex = 36
    .Pattern = xlSolid
End With
```

This With...End With construction is discussed in more detail later in this chapter. It is equivalent to:

```
Selection.Interior.ColorIndex = 36
Selection.Interior.Pattern = xlSolid
```

The second line is unnecessary, as a solid pattern is the default. The macro recorder is not sophisticated enough to know what the user does or doesn't want so it includes everything. The first line gives us some of the clues we need to complete our code. We only need to figure out how to change the Range object, Selection, into a complete row or complete column. If this can be done, it will be accomplished by using a property or method of the Range object.

The Object Browser

The Object Browser is a valuable tool for discovering the properties, methods and events applicable to Excel objects. To display the Object Browser, you need to be in the VB Editor window. You can use View | Object Browser, press *F2* or click the Object Browser button on the Standard toolbar to see the following window:

The objects are listed in the window with the title Classes. You can click in this window and type an *r* to get quickly to the Range object.

Alternatively, you can click in the box, second from the top with the binoculars to its right, and type in range. When you press *Enter* or click the binoculars, you will see a list of items containing this text. When you click on Range, under the Class heading in the Search Results window, Range will be highlighted in the Classes window below. This technique is handy when you are searching for information on a specific property, method or event.

You now have a list of all the properties, methods and events (if applicable) for this object, sorted alphabetically. If you right-click this list, you can choose Group Members, to separate the properties, methods and events, which makes it easier to read. If you scan through this list, you will see the EntireColumn and EntireRow properties, which look likely candidates for our requirements. To confirm this, select EntireColumn and click the ? icon at the top of the Object Browser window to go to the following screen:

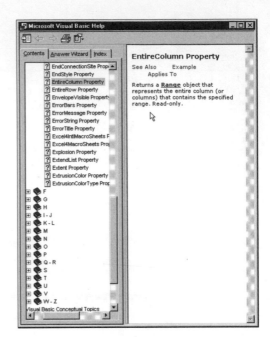

You can click on Example in
the Help screen to see samples
of code using this property.
See Also can often lead to
further information as well. It
only remains now to connect
the properties we have found
and apply them to the right
object.

Experimenting in the Immediate Window

If you want to experiment with code, you can use the VB Editor's Immediate window

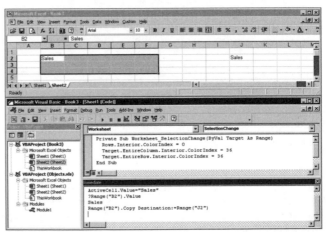

Use View | Immediate
Window, press *Ctrl+G* or
press the Immediate
Window button on the
Debug toolbar to make
the Immediate window
visible. You can tile the
Excel window and the
VBE window so that
you can type
commands into the
Immediate window and
see the effects in the
Excel window as
shown:

You type in the commands and press *Enter*. The command is immediately executed. To
execute the same command again, click anywhere in the line with the command and
press *Enter* again.

Here, the Add method of the Workbooks collection has opened a new empty
workbook. The Add method of the Worksheets collection has added a new worksheet
to the workbook. The Select method of the Range object, has selected the range
B2:F4. The Value property of the ActiveCell object has been assigned the text
"Sales". If you want to display a value, you precede the code with a question mark,
which is a short cut for Print.

```
?Range("B2").Value
```

This code has printed "Sales" on the next line of the Immediate window. The last command has copied the value in B2 to J2.

Summary – The Excel Object Model

In this section you have been introduced to the concept of the Excel object model. You have seen how you can use properties and methods to manipulate objects and how to write code to respond to events. You have seen that the macro recorder is a valuable tool for disclosing the appropriate objects, methods and properties to carry out a task. You have also seen that the recorder is often not sufficient — it produces inefficient code that is not always flexible enough for your needs. In order to go beyond the recorder, you need to be familiar with using the Object Browser and the Help screens. You have also seen how you can use the Immediate window to test lines of code.

Section 4: The VBA Language

In this chapter you will see the elements of the VBA language that are common to all versions of Visual Basic and the Microsoft Office applications. We will use examples that employ the Excel Object Model, but our aim is to examine the common structures of the language. Many of these structures and concepts are common to other programming languages, although the syntax and keywords can vary. We will look at:

- ❏ Storing information in variables and arrays
- ❏ Decision making in code
- ❏ Using loops
- ❏ Basic error handling

Basic Input and Output

First, let's look at some simple communication techniques that we can use to make our macros more flexible and useful. If you want to display a message, you can use the MsgBox function. This can be useful if you want to display a warning message or ask a simple question. In our first example, we want to make sure that the printer is switched on before a print operation. The following code generates the dialog box below, giving the user a chance to check the printer. The macro pauses until the OK button is pressed:

```
MsgBox "Please make sure that the printer is switched on"
```

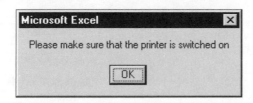

MsgBox has many options that control the type of buttons and icons that appear in the dialog box. If you want to get help on this, or any VBA word, just click somewhere in the word and press the *F1* key. The Help screen for the word will immediately appear. Amongst other details, you will see the input parameters accepted by the function:

```
MsgBox(prompt[, buttons] [, title] [, helpfile, context])
```

Parameters in square brackets are optional, so only the prompt message is required. If you want to have a title at the top of the dialog box, you can specify the third parameter. There are two ways to specify parameter values, by position and by name.

Parameters Specified by Position

If you specify a parameter by position, you need to make sure that the parameters are entered in the correct order. You also need to include extra commas for missing parameters. The following code provides a title for the dialog box, specifying the title by position:

```
MsgBox "Is the printer on?", , "Caution!"
```

Parameters Specified by Name

There are some advantages in using the alternative method of specifying parameters. If you specify parameters by name, you can enter them in any order and you do not need to include dummy commas. You do need to use : = rather than just = between the parameter name and the value, as we have already pointed out. The following code generates the same dialog box as the last one:

```
MsgBox Title:="Caution!", Prompt:="Is the printer on?"
```

Another advantage of specifying parameters by name is that the code is better documented. Anyone reading the code is more likely to understand it.

If you want more information on buttons, you will find a table of options in the help screen as follows:

Constant	Value	Description
vbOKOnly	0	Display OK button only.
vbOKCancel	1	Display OK and Cancel buttons.
vbAbortRetryIgnore	2	Display Abort, Retry, and Ignore buttons.

Constant	Value	Description
vbYesNoCancel	3	Display Yes, No, and Cancel buttons.
vbYesNo	4	Display Yes and No buttons.
vbRetryCancel	5	Display Retry and Cancel buttons.
vbCritical	16	Display Critical Message icon.
vbQuestion	32	Display Warning Query icon.
vbExclamation	48	Display Warning Message icon.
vbInformation	64	Display Information Message icon.
vbDefaultButton1	0	First button is default.
vbDefaultButton2	256	Second button is default.
vbDefaultButton3	512	Third button is default.
vbDefaultButton4	768	Fourth button is default.
vbApplicationModal	0	Application modal; the user must respond to the message box before continuing work in the current application.
vbSystemModal	4096	System modal; all applications are suspended until the user responds to the message box.
vbMsgBoxHelpButton	16384	Adds Help button to the message box
vbMsgBoxSetForeground	65536	Specifies the message box window as the foreground window
vbMsgBoxRight	524288	Text is right aligned
vbMsgBoxRtlReading	1048576	Specifies text should appear as right-to-left reading on Hebrew and Arabic systems

Values zero to five control the buttons that appear. A value of 4 gives Yes and No buttons:

```
MsgBox Prompt:="Delete this record?", Buttons:=4
```

Values 16 to 64 control the icons that appear. 32 gives a question mark icon. If you want both value 4 and value 32, you add them:

```
MsgBox Prompt:="Delete this record?", Buttons:=36
```

Constants

Specifying a `Buttons` value of 36 ensures that your code is indecipherable to all but the most battle hardened programmer. This is why VBA provides the **constants** shown to the left of the button values in the help screen. Rather than specifying `Buttons` by numeric value, you can use the constants, which provide a better indication of the choice behind the value. The following code generates the same dialog box as the last one:

```
MsgBox Prompt:="Delete this record?", Buttons:=vbYesNo + vbQuestion
```

> The VB Editor helps you as you type by providing a pop up list of the appropriate constants after you type `Buttons:=`. Point to the first constant and press + and you will be prompted for the second constant. Choose the second and press the *Spacebar* or *Tab* to finish the line. If there is another parameter to be specified, enter a "," rather than *Spacebar* or *Tab*.

Constants are a special type of variable. They are variables that do not change, if that makes sense. They are used to hold key data and, as we have seen, provide a way to write more understandable code. VBA has many built-in constants that are referred to as **intrinsic constants**. You can also define your own constants, as you will see later in this chapter:

Return Values

There is something missing from our last examples of `MsgBox`. We are asking a question, but failing to capture the user's response to the question. That is because we have been treating `MsgBox` as a statement, rather than a function. This is perfectly legal, but we need to know some rules if we are to avoid syntax errors. You can capture the return value of the `MsgBox` function by assigning it to a variable.

However, if you try the following, you will get a syntax error:

```
Answer = MsgBox Prompt:="Delete this record?", Buttons:=vbYesNo + vbQuestion
```

The error message, "Expected: End of Statement", is not really very helpful. You can press the Help button on the error message, to get a more detailed description of the error, but even then you might not understand the explanation!

Parentheses

The problem with the above line of code is that there are no parentheses around the function arguments. It should read as follows:

```
Answer = MsgBox(Prompt:="Delete this record?", Buttons:=vbYesNo + vbQuestion)
```

The general rule is that if you want to capture the return value of a function, you need to put any arguments in parentheses. If you don't want to use the return value, you should not use parentheses, as with our original examples of using MsgBox.

> *The parentheses rule also applies to methods used with objects. Many methods have return values that you can ignore or capture. See the section on Object Variables later in this section for an example.*

Now that you have captured the return value of MsgBox, how do you interpret it? Once again, the help screen provides the required information in the form of the following table of return values:

Constant	Value	Description
vbOK	1	OK
vbCancel	2	Cancel
vbAbort	3	Abort
vbRetry	4	Retry
vbIgnore	5	Ignore
vbYes	6	Yes
vbNo	7	No

If the Yes button is pressed, MsgBox returns a value of six. You can use the constant vbYes, instead of the numeric value, in an If test.

```
Answer = MsgBox(Prompt:="Delete selected Row?", _
                Buttons:=vbYesNo + vbQuestion)
If Answer = vbYes Then ActiveCell.EntireRow.Delete
...
```

InputBox

Another useful VBA function is InputBox, which allows you to get input data from a user in the form of text. The following code generates the dialog box shown:

```
UserName = InputBox(Prompt:="Please enter your name")
```

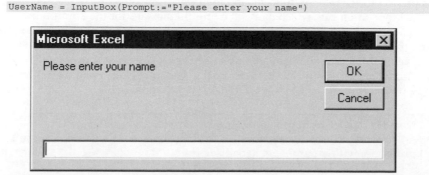

InputBox returns a text (or string) result. Even if a numeric value is entered, the result is returned as text. If you press Cancel or OK without typing anything into the text box, InputBox returns a zero length string. It is a good idea to test the result before proceeding so that this situation can be handled. In the following example, the sub does nothing if Cancel is pressed. The Exit Sub statement stops the procedure at that point. Otherwise, it places the entered data into cell B2.

```
Sub GetData()
    Sales = InputBox(Prompt:="Enter Target Sales")
    If Sales = "" Then Exit Sub
    Range("B2").Value = Sales
End Sub
```

In the code above, the If test compares Sales with a zero length string. There is nothing between the two double quote characters. Don't be tempted to put a blank space between the quotes.

Calling Function and Sub Procedures

When you develop an application, you should not attempt to place all your code in one large procedure. You should write small procedures that carry out specific tasks. You should test each procedure independently. You can then write a master procedure that runs your task procedures. This approach makes the testing and debugging of the application much simpler and also makes it easier to modify the application later. The following code illustrates this approach, although, in a practical application your procedures would have many more lines of code:

```
Sub Master()
    SalesData = GetInput("Enter Sales Data")
    If SalesData = False Then Exit Sub
    PostInput SalesData, "B3"
End Sub

Function GetInput(Message)
    Data = InputBox(Message)
    If Data = "" Then GetInput = False Else GetInput = Data
End Function

Sub PostInput(InputData, Target)
    Range(Target).Value = InputData
End Sub
```

Master uses the GetInput function and the PostInput sub procedure. GetInput has one input parameter, which passes the prompt message for the InputBox function. GetInput tests for a zero length string in the response and returns a value of False if this is found. Otherwise GetInput returns the response. Master tests the return value from GetInput and exits if it is False. Otherwise, Master calls PostInput, passing two values that define the data to be posted and the cell the data is to be posted to.

Note that sub procedures can accept input parameters, just like function procedures, if they are called from another procedure. You can't run a sub procedure with input parameters directly.

*Also note that, when calling PostInput and passing two parameters to it,
Master uses the general rule that says not to put parentheses around
parameters only whenusing a return value from the procedure.*

When calling your own functions and subs, you can specify parameters by name, just
as you can with built-in procedures. The following version of Master uses this
technique:

```
Sub Master()
    SalesData = GetInput(Message:="Enter Sales Data")
    If SalesData = False Then Exit Sub
    PostInput Target:="B3", InputData:=SalesData
End Sub
```

The Call Statement

When running a sub procedure from another procedure, you can use the Call
statement. There is no particular benefit in doing this, it is just an alternative to the
method used above. Master can be modified as follows:

```
Sub Master()
    SalesData = GetInput("Enter Sales Data")
    If SalesData = False Then Exit Sub
    Call PostInput(SalesData, "B3")
End Sub
```

Note that, if you use Call, you must put parentheses around the parameters you pass
to the called procedure, regardless of the fact that there is no return value from the
procedure. You can also use Call with a function, but only if the return value is not
used.

Variable Declaration

You have seen many examples of the use of variables for storing information. Now we
will discuss the rules for creating variable names, look at different types of variables
and talked about the best way to define variables.

> Variable names can be constructed from letters and numbers and the
> underscore character. The name must start with a letter and can be up to
> 255 characters in length. It is a good idea to avoid using any special
> characters in variable names. To be on the safe side, you should only use
> the letters of the alphabet (upper and lower case) plus the numbers 0-9
> plus the underscore (_). Also, variable names can't be the same as VBA
> words, such as Sub and End, or VBA function names.

So far we have been creating variables simply by using them. This is referred to as
implicit variable declaration. Most computer languages require you to employ
explicit variable declaration. This means that you must define the names of all the
variables you are going to use, before you use them in your code. VBA allows both
types of declaration. If you want to declare a variable explicitly, you do so using a Dim
statement or one of its variations, which we will see shortly. The following Dim
statement declares a variable called SalesData:

```
Sub GetData()
   Dim SalesData
   SalesData = InputBox(Prompt:="Enter Target Sales")
   ...
```

Most users find implicit declaration easier than explicit declaration, but there are advantages in being explicit. One advantage is capitalization.

> You might have noticed that, if you enter VBA words in lower case, such as inputbox, they are automatically converted to VBA's standard capitalization, InputBox in this case, when you move to the next line. This is a valuable form of feedback that tells you the word has been recognized as valid VBA code. It is a good idea to always type VBA words in lower case and look for the change.

If you do not explicitly declare a variable name, you can get odd effects regarding its capitalization. Say you write the following code:

```
Sub GetData()
   SalesData = InputBox(Prompt:="Enter Target Sales")
   If salesdata = "" Then Exit Sub
   ...
```

You will find that, as you press *Enter* at the end of the line 3, the original occurrence of SalesData loses its capitalization and the procedure reads as follows:

```
Sub GetData()
   salesdata = InputBox(Prompt:="Enter Target Sales")
   If salesdata = "" Then Exit Sub
   ...
```

In fact, any time you edit the procedure and alter the capitalization of salesdata, the new version will be applied throughout the procedure. If you declare SalesData in a Dim statement, the capitalization you use on that line will prevail throughout the procedure. You can now type the variable name in lower case in the body of the code and obtain confirmation that it has been correctly spelled as you move to a new line.

Option Explicit

There is a way to force explicit declaration in VBA. You place the statement Option Explicit in the Declarations section of your module, which is at the very top of your module, before any procedures, as follows:

```
(General)                              GetData

   Option Explicit

   Sub GetData()
      Dim SalesData
      SalesData = InputBox(Prompt:="Enter Target Sales")
      If SalesData = "" Then Exit Sub
      Range("B2").Value = SalesData
   End Sub
```

> Option Explicit only applies to the module it appears in. Each module requiring explicit declaration of variables must repeat the statement in its declaration section.

When you try to compile your module or run a procedure, using explicit variable declaration, VBA will check for variables that have not been declared and highlight them and show an error message. This has an enormous benefit. It picks up spelling mistakes, which are amongst the most common errors in programming. Consider the following version of GetData, where there is no Option Explicit at the top of the module and, therefore, implicit declaration is used:

```
Sub GetData()
    SalesData = InputBox(Prompt:="Enter Target Sales")
    If SaleData = "" Then Exit Sub
    Range("B2").Value = SalesData
End Sub
```

This code will never enter your data into cell B2! VBA happily accepts the misspelled SaleData in the If test as a new variable that is empty and that it considers being a zero length string for the purposes of the test. Consequently, the Exit Sub is always executed and the final line is never executed. This type of error, especially when embedded in a longer section of code, can be very difficult to see and has even been known to drive people crazy.

If you include Option Explicit in your declarations section, and Dim SalesData at the beginning of GetData, you will get an error message, "Variable not defined", immediately you attempt to run GetData. The undefined variable will be highlighted so that you can see exactly where the error is.

> You can have Option Explicit **automatically added to any new modules you create. In the VB Editor, use** Tools | Options… **and click the** Editor tab. **Check the box against** Require Variable Declaration. **This is a highly recommended option. Note that setting this option will not affect any existing modules, where you will need to insert** Option Explicit **manually.**

Scope and Lifetime of Variables

There are two important concepts associated with variables, **scope** and **lifetime**. The scope of a variable defines which procedures can use that variable. The lifetime of a variable defines how long that variable retains the values assigned to it. The following procedure illustrates the lifetime of a variable:

```
Sub LifeTime()
    Dim Sales
    Sales = Sales + 1
    MsgBox Sales
End Sub
```

Every time you run LifeTime, it displays a value of one. This is because the variable Sales is only retained in memory until the end of the procedure. The memory Sales uses is released when the End Sub is reached. Next time LifeTime is run, Sales is recreated and treated as having a zero value. The lifetime of Sales is the time taken to run the procedure. You can increase the lifetime of Sales by declaring it in a Static statement:

```
Sub LifeTime()
    Static Sales
    Sales = Sales + 1
    MsgBox Sales
End Sub
```

The lifetime of Sales is now extended to the time that the workbook is open. The more times you run LifeTime, the higher the value of Sales will become.

The following two procedures illustrate the scope of a variable:

```
Sub Scope1()
    Static Sales
    Sales = Sales + 1
    MsgBox Sales
End Sub

Sub Scope2()
    Static Sales
    Sales = Sales + 10
    MsgBox Sales
End Sub
```

The variable Sales in Scope1 is not the same variable as the Sales in Scope2. Each time you execute Scope1, the value of its Sales will increase by one, independently of the value of Sales in Scope2. Similarly, the Sales in Scope2 will increase by 10 with each execution of Scope2, independently of the value of Sales in Scope1. Any variable declared within a procedure has a scope that is confined to that procedure. It is only visible to that procedure. A variable that is declared within a procedure is referred to as a **procedure-level** variable.

Variables can also be declared in the declarations section at the top of a module as shown in the following version of our code:

```
Option Explicit
Dim Sales

Sub Scope1()
    Sales = Sales + 1
    MsgBox Sales
End Sub

Sub Scope2()
    Sales = Sales + 10
    MsgBox Sales
End Sub
```

Now you will find that Scope1 and Scope2 are processing the same variable Sales. A variable declared in the declarations section of a module is referred to as a **module-level** variable and its scope is now the whole module. It is visible to all the procedures in the module. Its lifetime is now the time that the workbook is open.

While you are editing and debugging a module, it is quite likely that static and module-level variables will lose their values due to the changes and the need to recompile the module.

If a procedure in the module declares a variable with the same name as a module-level variable, the module-level variable will no longer be visible to it. It will process its own procedure-level variable.

Module-level variables, declared in the declarations section of the module with a `Dim` statement, are not visible to other modules. If you want to share a variable between modules, you need to declare it as `Public` in the declarations section:

```
Public Sales
```

`Public` variables can also be made visible to other workbooks, or VBA projects. To accomplish this, you create a **reference** in the other workbook to the workbook containing the `Public` variable. You do this in the VB Editor using Tools, References....

Variable Type

Computers store different types of data in different ways. The way a number is stored is quite different to the way text, or a character string, is stored. Different categories of numbers are also stored in different ways. An integer, a whole number with no decimals, is store differently to a number with decimals. Most computer languages require that you declare the type of data to be stored in a variable. VBA does not require this, but your code will be more efficient if you do declare variable types. It is also more likely that you will discover any problems that arise when data is converted from one type to another, if you have declared your variable types. The following table has been taken directly from the VBA Help files. It defines the various data types available in VBA and their memory requirements. It also shows you the range of values that each type can handle:

Data type	Storage size	Range
Byte	1 byte	0 to 255
Boolean	2 bytes	True or False
Integer	2 bytes	-32,768 to 32,767
Long (long integer)	4 bytes	-2,147,483,648 to 2,147,483,647
Single (single-precision floating-point)	4 bytes	-3.402823E38 to -1.401298E-45 for negative values; 1.401298E-45 to 3.402823E38 for positive values
Double (double-precision floating-point)	8 bytes	-1.79769313486231E308 to -4.94065645841247E-324 for negative values; 4.94065645841247E-324 to 1.79769313486232E308 for positive values

Table Continued on Following Page

Data type	Storage size	Range
Currency (scaled integer)	8 bytes	-922,337,203,685,477.5808 to 922,337,203,685,477.5807
Decimal	14 bytes	+/-79,228,162,514,264,337,593,543,950,335 with no decimal point; +/-7.9228162514264337593543950335 with 28 places to the right of the decimal, i.e. the smallest non-zero number is +/-0.0000000000000000000000000001
Date	8 bytes	January 1, 100 to December 31, 9999
Object	4 bytes	Any Object reference
String (variable-length)	10 bytes + string length	0 to approximately 2 billion characters
String (fixed-length)	Length of string	1 to approximately 65,400 characters
Variant (with numbers)	16 bytes	Any numeric value up to the range of a Double
Variant (with characters)	22 bytes + string length	Same range as for variable-length String
User-defined (using Type)	Number required by elements	The range of each element is the same as the range of its data type.

If you do not declare a variable's type, it defaults to the Variant type. Variants take up more memory than any other type because each has to carry information with it that tells VBA what type of data it is currently storing, as well as store the data itself. Variants use more computer overhead when they are processed. VBA has to figure out what types it is dealing with and whether it needs to convert between types in order to process it. If maximum processing speed is required for your application, you should declare your variable types, taking advantage of those types that use less memory when you can. For example, if you know your numbers will be whole numbers in the range of -32000 to +32000, you would use an Integer type.

Declaring Variable Type

You can declare a variable's type on a Dim statement, or related declaration statements such as Public. The following declares Sales to be a double precision floating point number:

```
Dim Sales As Double
```

You can declare more than one variable on a `Dim`:

```
Dim SalesData As Double, Index As Integer, StartDate As Date
```

The following can be a trap:

```
Dim Col, Row, Sheet As Integer
```

Many users assume that this declares each variable to be `Integer`. This is not true. `Col` and `Row` are `Variants` because they have not been given a type. To declare all three as `Integer`, the line should be as follows:

```
Dim Col As Integer, Row As Integer, Sheet As Integer
```

Declaring Function and Parameter Types

If you have input parameters for sub procedures or function procedures, you can define each parameter type in the first line of the procedure as follows:

```
Function IsHoliday(WhichDay As Date)

Sub Marine(CrewSize As Integer, FuelCapacity As Double)
```

You can also declare the return value type for a function. The following example is for a function that returns a value of `True` or `False`:

```
Function IsHoliday(WhichDay As Date) As Boolean
```

Constants

You have seen that there are many intrinsic constants built into VBA, such as `vbYes` and `vbNo` discussed earlier. You can also define your own constants. Constants are handy for holding numbers or text that do not change while your code is running, but that you want to use repeatedly in calculations and messages. Constants are declared using the `Const` keyword, as follows:

```
Const Pi = 3.14159265358979
```

You can include the constant's type in the declaration:

```
Const Version As String = "Release 3.9a"
```

Constants follow the same rules regarding scope as variables. If you declare a constant within a procedure, it will be local to that procedure. If you declare it in the declarations section of a module, it will be available to all procedures in the module. If you want to make it available to all modules, you can declare it to be `Public` as follows:

```
Public Const Error666 As String = "You can't do that"
```

Variable Naming Conventions

You can call your variables and user-defined functions anything you want, except where there is a clash with VBA keywords and function names. However, many programmers adopt a system whereby the variable or object type is included, in abbreviated form, in the variable name, usually as a prefix, so instead of declaring:

```
Dim SalesData As Double
```

you can use:

```
Dim dSalesData As Double
```

Wherever dSalesData appears in your code, you will be reminded that the variable is of type Double. Alternatively, you could use this line of code:

```
Dim dblSalesData As Double
```

For the sake of simplicity this approach has not been used in this Primer chapter, but from Chapter 3 onwards, one or two letter prefixes are added to *most* variable names. This is the convention used in this book:

One letter prefixes for the common data types:

```
Dim iColumn As Integer
Dim lRow As Long
Dim dProduct As Double
Dim bChoice As Boolean
```

Two letter prefixes for Strings, Variants and most object types:

```
Dim stName As String        ' Some code in later chapters uses just s-
Dim vaValue As Variant      ' Some code in later chapters uses just v-
Dim rgSelect As Range
```

No prefix for loop counters and general (rather than specific) object names:

```
Dim i As Integer
Dim Rng As Range
Dim Wkb As Workbook
```

Object Variables

The variables we have seen so far have held data such as numbers and text. You can also create **object variables** to refer to objects such as worksheets and ranges. You use the Set statement to assign an object to an object variable. Object variables should also be declared and assigned a type as with normal variables. If you don't know the type, you can use the generic term Object as the type.

```
Dim MyWorkbook As Object
Set MyWorkbook = ThisWorkbook
MsgBox MyWorkbook.Name
```

It is more efficient to use the specific object type if you can. The following code creates an object variable Rng referring to cell B10 in Sheet1 in the same workbook as the code. It then assigns values to the object and the cell above:

```
Sub ObjectVariable()
    Dim Rng As Range
    Set Rng = ThisWorkbook.Worksheets("Sheet1").Range("C10")
    Rng.Value = InputBox("Enter Sales for January")
    Rng.Offset(-1, 0).Value = "January Sales"
End Sub
```

If you are going to refer to the same object more than once, it is more efficient to create an object variable than to keep repeating a lengthy specification of the object. It is also easier to write the code and the code is easier to read. Object variables can also be very useful for capturing the return values of some methods, particularly when you are creating new instances of an object. For example, with either the Workbooks object or the Worksheets object, the Add method returns a reference to the new object. This reference can be assigned to an object variable so that you can easily refer to the new object in later code:

```
Sub NewWorkbook()
    Dim Wkb As Workbook, Wks As Worksheet

    Set Wkb = Workbooks.Add
    Set Wks = Wkb.Worksheets.Add(After:=Wkb.Sheets(Wkb.Sheets.Count))
    Wks.Name = "January"
    Wks.Range("A1").Value = "Sales Data"
    Wkb.SaveAs Filename:="JanSales.xls"
End Sub
```

This example creates a new empty workbook and assigns a reference to it to the object variable Wkb. It then adds a new worksheet to the workbook, after any existing sheets, and assigns a reference to the new worksheet to the object variable Wks. It changes the name on the tab at the bottom of the worksheet to "January" and places the heading "Sales Data" in cell **A1**. Finally, it saves the new workbook as JanSales.xls.

Note that the parameter after the Worksheets.Add is in parentheses. Because we are assigning the return value of the Add method to the object variable, any parameters must be in parentheses. If the return value of the Add method were ignored, the statement would be without parentheses as follows:

```
Wkb.Worksheets.Add After:=Wkb.Sheets(Wkb.Sheets.Count)
```

With...End With

Object variables provide a useful way to refer to objects in short hand and are also more efficiently processed by VBA. Another way to reduce the amount of code you write, and also increase processing efficiency, is to use a With...End With structure. The last example above could be re-written as follows:

```
With Wkb
    .Worksheets.Add After:=.Sheets(.Sheets.Count)
End With
```

VBA knows that anything starting with a period is a property or a method of the object following the With. You can re-write the entire NewWorkbook procedure to eliminate the Wkb object variable, as follows:

```
Sub NewWorkbook()
    Dim Wks As Worksheet
    With Workbooks.Add
        Set Wks = .Worksheets.Add(After:=.Sheets(.Sheets.Count))
        Wks.Name = "January"
        Wks.Range("A1").Value = "Sales Data"
        .SaveAs Filename:="JanSales.xls"
    End With
End Sub
```

You can take this a step further and eliminate the Wks object variable:

```
Sub NewWorkbook()
    With Workbooks.Add
        With .Worksheets.Add(After:=.Sheets(.Sheets.Count))
            .Name = "January"
            .Range("A1").Value = "Sales Data"
        End With
        .SaveAs Filename:="JanSales.xls"
    End With
End Sub
```

If you find this confusing, you can compromise with a combination of object variables and With...End With:

```
Sub NewWorkbook4()
    Dim Wkb As Workbook, Wks As Worksheet

    Set Wkb = Workbooks.Add
    With Wkb
       Set Wks = .Worksheets.Add(After:=.Sheets(.Sheets.Count))
       With Wks
          .Name = "January"
          .Range("A1").Value = "Sales Data"
       End With
       .SaveAs Filename:="JanSales.xls"
    End With
End Sub
```

With...End With is useful when references to an object are repeated in a small section of your code.

Making Decisions

VBA provides two main structures for making decisions and carrying out alternative processing, represented by the If and the Select Case statements. If is the more flexible, but Select Case is better when you are testing a single variable.

If Statements

If comes in three forms: the IIf function, the one line If statement and the block If structure. The following Tax function uses the IIf (Immediate If) function:

```
Function Tax(ProfitBeforeTax As Double) As Double
    Tax = IIf(ProfitBeforeTax > 0, 0.3 * ProfitBeforeTax, 0)
End Function
```

IIf is similar to the Excel worksheet IF function. It has three input arguments. The first is a logical test, the second is an expression that is evaluated if the test is True and the third is an expression that is evaluated if the test is False. In this example, the IIf function tests that the ProfitBeforeTax value is greater than zero. If the test is true, IIf calculates 30% of ProfitBeforeTax. If the test is false, IIf calculates zero. The calculated IIf value is then assigned to the return value of the Tax function. The Tax function can be re-written using the single line If statement as follows:

```
Function Tax(ProfitBeforeTax As Double) As Double
    If ProfitBeforeTax > 0 Then Tax = 0.3 * ProfitBeforeTax Else Tax = 0
End Function
```

One difference between IIf and the single line If is that the Else section of the single line If is optional. The third parameter of the IIf function must be defined. In VBA, it is often useful to omit the Else:

```
If ProfitBeforeTax < 0 Then MsgBox "A Loss has occured", , "Warning"
```

Another difference is that, while IIf can only return a value to a single variable, the single line If can assign values to different variables:

```
If JohnsScore > MarysScore Then John = John + 1 Else Mary = Mary + 1
```

Block If

If you want to carry out more than one action when a test is true, you can use a **block If** structure, as follows:

```
If JohnsScore > MarysScore Then
    John = John + 1
    Mary = Mary - 1
End If
```

Using a block `If`, you must not include any code after the `Then`, on the same line. You can have as many lines after the test as required. You must terminate the scope of the block `If` with an `End If` statement. A block `If` can also have an `Else` section, as follows:

```
If JohnsScore > MarysScore Then
    John = John + 1
    Mary = Mary - 1
Else
    John = John - 1
    Mary = Mary + 1
End If
```

A block `If` can also have as many `ElseIf` sections as required:

```
If JohnsScore > MarysScore Then
    John = John + 1
    Mary = Mary - 1
ElseIf JohnsScore < MarysScore Then
    John = John - 1
    Mary = Mary + 1
Else
    John = John + 1
    Mary = Mary + 1
End If
```

When you have a block `If` followed by one or more `ElseIf`s, VBA keeps testing until it finds a true section. It executes the code for that section and then proceeds directly to the statement following the `End If`. If no test is true, the `Else` section is executed. A block `If` does nothing when all tests are false and the `Else` section is missing. Block `If`s can be nested, one inside the other. You should make use of indenting to show the scope of each block. This is vital — you can get into an awful muddle with the nesting of `If` blocks within other `If` blocks and `If` blocks within `Else` blocks etc. If code is unindented, it isn't easy, in a long series of nested `If` tests, to match each `End If` with each `If`:

```
If Not ThisWorkbook.Saved Then
    Answer = MsgBox("Do you want to save your changes", _
                    vbQuestion + vbYesNo)
    If Answer = vbYes Then
        ThisWorkbook.Save
        MsgBox ThisWorkbook.Name & " has been saved"
    End If
End If
```

This code uses the `Saved` property of the `Workbook` object containing the code to see if the workbook has been saved since changes were last made to it. If changes have not been saved, the user is asked if they want to save changes. If the answer is yes, the inner block `If` saves the workbook and informs the user.

Select Case

The following block If is testing the same variable value in each section:

```
Function Price(Product As String) As Variant
    If Product = "Apples" Then
        Price = 12.5
    ElseIf Product = "Oranges" Then
        Price = 15
    ElseIf Product = "Pears" Then
        Price = 18
    ElseIf Product = "Mangoes" Then
        Price = 25
    Else
        Price = CVErr(xlErrNA)
    End If
End Function
```

If Product is not found, the Price function returns an Excel error value of #NA. Note that Price is declared as a Variant so that it can handle the error value as well as numeric values. For a situation like this, Select Case is a more elegant construction. It looks like this:

```
Function Price(Product As String) As Variant
    Select Case Product
        Case "Apples"
            Price = 12.5
        Case "Oranges"
            Price = 15
        Case "Pears"
            Price = 18
        Case "Mangoes"
            Price = 25
        Case Else
            Price = CVErr(xlErrNA)
    End Select
End Function
```

If you have only one statement per case, the following format works quite well. You can place multiple statements on a single line by placing a colon between statements:

```
Function Price(Product As String) As Variant
    Select Case Product
        Case "Apples":   Price = 12.5
        Case "Oranges":  Price = 15
        Case "Pears":    Price = 18
        Case "Mangoes":  Price = 25
        Case Else:       Price = CVErr(xlErrNA)
    End Select
End Function
```

Select Case can also handle ranges of numbers or text, as well as comparisons using the keyword Is. The following example calculates a fare of zero for infants up to 3 and anyone older than 65, with two ranges between. Negative ages generate an error:

```
Function Fare(Age As Integer) As Variant
    Select Case Age
        Case 0 To 3, Is > 65
            Fare = 0
        Case 4 To 15
            Fare = 10
        Case 16 To 65
            Fare = 20
        Case Else
            Fare = CVErr(xlErrNA)
    End Select
End Function
```

Looping

All computer languages provide a mechanism for repeating the same, or similar, operations in an efficient way. VBA has two main structures that allow you to loop through the same code over and over again. They are the Do...Loop and the For...Next loop. The Do...Loop is for those situations where the loop will be terminated when a logical condition applies, such as reaching the end of your data. The For...Next loop is for situations where you can predict in advance how many times you want to loop, such as when you want to enter expenses for the 10 people in your department. VBA also has an interesting variation on the For...Next loop that is used to process all the objects in a collection — the For Each...Next loop. You can use it to process all the cells in a range or all the sheets in a workbook, for example.

Do...Loop

To illustrate the use of a Do...Loop, we will construct a sub procedure to shade every second line of a worksheet, as shown below, to make it more readable. We want to apply the macro to different report sheets with different numbers of products, so the macro will need to test each cell in the A column until it gets to an empty cell to determine when to stop.

Our first macro will select every other row and apply the formatting:

```
Sub ShadeEverySecondRow()
    Range("A2").EntireRow.Select
    Do While ActiveCell.Value <> ""
        Selection.Interior.ColorIndex = 15
        ActiveCell.Offset(2, 0).EntireRow.Select
    Loop
End Sub
```

ShadeEverySecondRow begins by selecting row 2 in its entirety. When you select an entire row, the left-most cell (i.e. in column A) becomes the active cell. The code between the Do and the Loop statements is then repeated While the value property of the active cell is not a zero length string, i.e. the active cell is not empty. In the loop, the macro sets the interior color index of the selected cells to 15, which is gray. Then the macro selects the entire row, two rows under the active cell. When a row is selected that has an empty cell in column A, the While condition is no longer true and the loop terminates.

You can make ShadeEverySecondRow run faster by avoiding selecting. It is seldom necessary to select cells in VBA, but you are led into this way of doing things because that's the way you do it manually and that's what you get from the macro recorder. The following version of ShadeEverySecondRow does not select and it runs about six times faster. It sets up an index i, which indicates the row of the worksheet and is initially assigned a value of two. The Cells property of the worksheet allows you to refer to cells by row number and column number, so when the loop starts, Cells(i,1) refers to cell A2. Each time around the loop, i is increased by two. We can, therefore, change any reference to the active cell to a Cells(i,1) reference and apply the EntireRow property to Cells(i,1) to refer to the complete row:

```
Sub ShadeEverySecondRow()
    Dim i As Integer
    i = 2
    Do Until IsEmpty(Cells(i, 1))
        Cells(I, 1).EntireRow.Interior.ColorIndex = 15
        i = i + 2
    Loop
End Sub
```

To illustrate some alternatives, two more changes have been made on the Do statement line. You can use either While or Until after the Do, so we have changed the test to an Until and we have used the VBA IsEmpty function to test for an empty cell.

> The IsEmpty function is the best way to test that a cell is empty. If you use If Cells(i,1) = "", the test will be true for a formula that calculates a zero length string.

It is also possible to exit a loop using a test within the loop and the Exit Do statement, as shown below:

```
Sub ShadeEverySecondRow()
    i = 0
    Do
        i = i + 2
        If IsEmpty(Cells(i, 1)) Then Exit Do
        Cells(i, 1).EntireRow.Interior.ColorIndex = 15
    Loop
End Sub
```

Yet another alternative is to place the While or Until on the Loop statement line. This ensures that the code in the loop is executed at least once. When the test is on the Do line, it is possible that the test will be false to start with, and the loop will be skipped.

Sometimes, your code makes more sense if the test is on the last line of the loop. In the following example, it seems more sensible to test PassWord after getting input from the user, although the code would still work if the Until statement were placed on the Do line.

```
Sub GetPassword()
   Dim PassWord As String, i As Integer
   i = 0
   Do
      i = i + 1
      If i > 3 Then
         MsgBox "Sorry, Only three tries"
         Exit Sub
      End If
      PassWord = InputBox("Enter Password")
   Loop Until PassWord = "XXX"
   MsgBox "Welcome"
End Sub
```

GetPassword loops until the password XXX is supplied, or the number of times around the loop exceeds three.

For...Next Loop

The For...Next loop differs from the Do...Loop in two ways. It has a built-in counter that is automatically incremented each time the loop is executed and it is designed to execute until the counter exceeds a pre-defined value, rather than depending on a user specified logical test. The following example places the full file path and name of the workbook into the center footer for each worksheet in the active workbook:

```
Sub FilePathInFooter()
   Dim i As Integer, FilePath As String

   FilePath = ActiveWorkbook.FullName
   For i = 1 To Worksheets.Count Step 1
      Worksheets(i).PageSetup.CenterFooter = FilePath
   Next i
End Sub
```

Excel does not have an option to automatically include the full file path in a custom header or footer, so this macro inserts the information as text. It begins by assigning the FullName property of the active workbook to the variable FilePath. The loop starts with the For statement and loops on the Next statement. i is used as a counter, starting at one and finishing when i exceeds Worksheets.Count, which uses the Count property of the Worksheets collection to determine how many worksheets there are in the active workbook. The Step option defines the amount that i will be increased, each time around the loop. Step 1 could be left out of this example, as a step of one is the default value. In the loop, i is used as an index to the Worksheets collection to specify each individual Worksheet object. The PageSetup property of the Workbook object refers to the PageSetup object in that workbook so that the CenterFooter property of the PageSetup object can be assigned the FilePath text.

The following example shows how you can step backwards. It takes a complete file path and strips out the file name, excluding the file extension. The example uses the FullName property of the active workbook as input, but the same code could be used with any file type. It starts at the last character in the file path and steps backwards until it finds the period between the file name and its extension and then the backslash character before the file name. It then extracts the characters between the two:

```
Sub GetFileName()
   Dim BackSlash As Integer, Point As Integer
   Dim FilePath As String, FileName As String
   Dim i As Integer

   FilePath = ActiveWorkbook.FullName
   For i = Len(FilePath) To 1 Step -1
      If Mid$(FilePath, i, 1) = "." Then
         Point = i
         Exit For
      End If
   Next i   If Point = 0 Then Point = Len(FilePath) + 1
   For i = Point - 1 To 1 Step -1
      If Mid$(FilePath, i, 1) = "\" Then
         BackSlash =i
         Exit For
      End If
   Next i
   FileName = Mid$(FilePath, BackSlash + 1, Point - BackSlash - 1)
   MsgBox FileName
End Sub
```

The first For...Next loop uses the Len function to determine how many characters are in the FilePath variable and i is set up to step backwards, counting from the last character position, working towards the first character position. The Mid$ function extracts the character from FilePath at the position defined by i and tests it to see if it is a period. When a period is found, the position is recorded in Point and the first For...Next loop is exited. If the file name has no extension, no period is found and Point will have its default value of zero. In this case, the If test records an imaginary period position in Point that is one character beyond the end of the file name. The same technique is used in the second For...Next loop as the first, starting one character before the period, to find the position of the backslash character, and storing the position in BackSlash. The Mid$ function is then used to extract the characters between the backslash and the period.

For Each...Next Loop

When you want to process every member of a collection, you can use the For Each...Next loop. The following example is a re-work of the FilePathInFooter procedure:

```
Sub FilePathInFooter()
   Dim FilePath As String, Wks As Worksheet

   FilePath = ActiveWorkbook.FullName
   For Each Wks In Worksheets
      Wks.PageSetup.CenterFooter = FilePath
   Next Wks
End Sub
```

The loop steps through all the members of the collection. During each pass a reference to the next member of the collection is assigned to the object variable Wks.

The following example lists all the files in the root directory of the C drive. It uses the Microsoft Scripting run time library to create a Files object containing references to the required files. The example uses a For Each...Next loop to display the names of all the files:

```
Sub FileList()
   Dim FileSystem As Object, MyFolder As Object
   Dim MyFiles As Object, MyFile As Object
```

```
    Set FileSystem = CreateObject("Scripting.FileSystemObject")
    Set MyFolder = FileSystem.GetFolder("C:\")
    Set MyFiles = MyFolder.Files
    For Each MyFile In MyFiles
        MsgBox MyFile.Name
    Next
End Sub
```

If you test this procedure on a directory with lots of files, and get tired of clicking OK, don't forget that you can break out of the code wih *Ctrl+Break*.

Arrays

Arrays are VBA variables that can hold more than one item of data. You declare an array by including parentheses after the array name. You place an integer within the parentheses, defining the number of elements in the array:

```
Dim Data(2)
```

You assign values to the elements of the array by indicating the element number as follows:

```
Data(0) = 1
Data(1) = 10
Data(2) = 100
```

The number of elements in the array depends on the array base. The default base is zero, which means that the first data element is item zero. Dim Data(2) declares a three element array if the base is zero. Alternatively, you can place the following statement in the declarations section at the top of your module to declare that arrays are one based:

```
Option Base 1
```

With a base of one, Dim Data(2) declares a two element array. Item zero does not exist. You can use the following procedure to test the effect of the Option Base statement:

```
Sub Array1()
    Dim Data(10) As Integer
    Dim Message As String, I As Integer

    For I = LBound(Data) To UBound(Data)
        Data(i) =I   NextI   Message = "Lower Bound = " & LBound(Data) & vbCr
    Message = Message & "Upper Bound = " & UBound(Data) & vbCr
    Message = Message & "Num Elements = " & WorksheetFunction.Count(Data) _
                 & vbCr
    Message = Message & "Sum Elements = " & WorksheetFunction.Sum(Data)
    MsgBox Message
End Sub
```

Array1 uses the LBound (lower bound) and UBound (upper bound) functions to determine the lowest and highest index values for the array. It uses the Count worksheet function to determine the number of elements in the array. If you run this code with Options Base 0, or no Options Base statement, in the declarations section of the module, it will show a lowest index number of zero and 11 elements in the array. With Options Base 1, it shows a lowest index number of one and 10 elements in the array. Note the use of the intrinsic constant vbCr, which contains a carriage return character. vbCr is used to break the message text to a new line.

If you want to make your array size independent of the Option Base statement, you can explicitly declare the lower bound as well as the upper bound as follows:

```
Dim Data(1 To 2)
```

Arrays are very useful for processing lists or tables of items. If you want to create a short list, you can use the Array function as follows:

```
Dim Data As Variant
Data = Array("North", "South", "East", "West")
```

You can then use the list in a For...Next loop. For example, you could open and process a series of workbooks called North.xls, South.xls, East.xls and West.xls:

```
Sub Array2()
    Dim Data As Variant, Wkb As Workbook
    Dim I As Integer

    Data = Array("North", "South", "East", "West")
    For I = LBound(Data) To UBound(Data)
        Set Wkb = Workbooks.Open(FileName:=Data(i) & ".xls")
        'Process data here
        Wkb.Close SaveChanges:=True
    NextIEnd Sub
```

Multi-Dimensional Arrays

So far we have only looked at arrays with a single dimension. You can actually define arrays with up to 60 dimensions, although few people would use more than two or three dimensions. The following statements declare two-dimensional arrays:

```
Dim Data(10,20)
Dim Data(1 To 10,1 to 20)
```

You can think of a two-dimensional array as a table of data. The last example defines a table with 10 rows and 20 columns.

Arrays are very useful in Excel for processing the data in worksheet ranges. It can be far more efficient to load the values in a range into an array, process the data and write it back to the worksheet, than to access each cell individually. The following procedure shows how you can assign the values in a range to a variant. The code uses the LBound and UBound functions to find the number of dimensions in Data. Note that there is a second parameter in LBound and UBound to indicate which index you are referring to. If you leave this parameter out, the functions refer to the first index.

```
Sub Array3()
    Dim Data As Variant, X As Variant
    Dim Message As String, I As Integer
    Data = Range("A1:A20").Value
    I = 1
    Do
        Message = "Lower Bound = " & LBound(Data, I) & vbCr
        Message = Message & "Upper Bound = " & UBound(Data, I) & vbCr
        MsgBox Message, , "Index Number = " &I
        I = I + 1
        On Error Resume Next
        X = UBound(Data, I)
        If Err.Number <> 0 Then Exit Do
        On Error GoTo 0
    Loop
    Message = "No: Non Blank Elements = " & WorksheetFunction.CountA(Data) & vbCr
    MsgBox Message
End Sub
```

The first time round the `Do...Loop`, `Array2` determines the upper and lower bounds of the first dimension of `Data`, as I has a value of one. It then increases the value of I to look for the next dimension. It exits the loop when an error occurs, indicating that no more dimensions exist.

By substituting different ranges into `Array2`, you can determine that the array created by assigning a range of values to a `Variant` is two-dimensional, even if there is only one row or one column in the range. You can also determine that the lower bound of each index is one, regardless of the `Option Base` setting in the declarations section.

Dynamic Arrays

When writing your code, it is sometimes not possible to determine the size of an array that will be required. For example, you might want to load the names of all the `.xls` files in the current directory into an array. You won't know in advance how many files there will be. One alternative is to declare an array that is big enough to hold the largest possible amount of data — but this would be inefficient. Instead, you can define a dynamic array and set its size when the procedure runs. You declare a dynamic array by leaving out the dimensions:

```
Dim Data()
```

You can declare the required size at run time with a `ReDim` statement, which can use variables to define the bounds of the indexes:

```
ReDim Data(iRows,iColumns)
ReDim Data(minRow to maxRow, minCol to maxCol)
```

`ReDim` will re-initialize the array and destroy any data in it, unless you use the `Preserve` keyword. `Preserve` is used in the following procedure that uses a `Do...Loop` to load the names of files into the dynamic array called `FNames`, increasing the upper bound of its index by one each time to accommodate the new name. The `Dir` function returns the first file name found that matches the wild card specification in `FType`. Subsequent usage of `Dir`, with no parameter, repeats the same specification, getting the next file that matches, until it runs out of files and returns a zero length string.

```
Sub FileNames()
    Dim FName As String
    Dim FNames() As String
    Dim FType As String
    Dim I As Integer

    FType = "*.xls"
    FName = Dir(FType)
    Do Until FName = ""
        I = I + 1
        ReDim Preserve FNames(1 To I)
        FNames(i) = FName
        FName = Dir
    Loop
    For I = 1 To UBound(FNames)
        MsgBox FNames(i)
    NextIEnd Sub
```

If you intend to work on the files in a directory, and save the results, it is a good idea to get all the file names first, as in the `FileNames` procedure, and use that list to process the files. It is not a good idea to rely on the `Dir` function to give you an accurate file list while you are in the process of reading and over-writing files.

Run Time Error Handling

When you are designing an application, you should try to anticipate any problems that could occur when the application is used in the real world. You can remove all the bugs in your code and have flawless logic that works with all permutations of conditions, but a simple operational problem could still bring your code crashing down with a less than helpful message displayed to the user. For example, if you try to save a workbook file to the floppy disk in the A: drive, and there is no disk in the A drive, your code will grind to a halt and display a message that will probably not mean anything to the average user.

If you anticipate this particular problem, you can set up your code to gracefully deal with the situation. VBA allows you to trap error conditions using the following statement:

```
On Error GoTo LineLabel
```

LineLabel is a marker that you insert at the end of your normal code, as shown below with the line label errTrap. Note that a colon follows the line label. The line label marks the start of your error recovery code and should be preceded by an Exit statement to prevent execution of the error recovery code when no error occurs.

```
Sub ErrorTrap1()
    Dim Answer As Long, MyFile As String
    Dim Message As String, CurrentPath As String

    On Error GoTo errTrap
    CurrentPath = CurDir$

    ChDrive "A"
    ChDrive CurrentPath
    ChDir CurrentPath
    MyFile = "A:\Data.xls"
    Application.DisplayAlerts = False
    ActiveWorkbook.SaveAs FileName:=MyFile
TidyUp:
    ChDrive CurrentPath
    ChDir CurrentPath
    Exit Sub
errTrap:
    Message = "Error No: = " & Err.Number & vbCr
    Message = Message & Err.Description & vbCr & vbCr
    Message = Message & "Please place a disk in the A: drive" & vbCr
    Message = Message & "and press OK" & vbCr & vbCr
    Message = Message & "Or press Cancel to abort File Save"
    Answer = MsgBox(Message, vbQuestion + vbOKCancel, "Error")
    If Answer = vbCancel Then Resume TidyUp
    Resume
End Sub
```

Once the On Error statement is executed, error trapping is enabled. If an error occurs, no message is displayed and the code following the line label is executed. You can use the Err object to obtain information about the error. The Number property of the Err object returns the error number and the Description property returns the error message associated with the error. You can use Err.Number to determine the error when it is possible that any of a number of errors could occur. You can incorporate Err.Description into your own error message, if appropriate.

In Excel 5 and 95, Err was not an object, but a function that returned the error number. As Number is the default property of the Err object, using Err, by itself, is equivalent to using Err.Number and the code from the older versions of Excel still works in Excel 2000.

The code in ErrorTrap1, after executing the On Error statement, saves the current directory drive and path into the variable CurrentPath. It then executes the ChDrive statement to try to activate the A drive. If there is no disk in the A drive, error 68 – Device unavailable – occurs and the error recovery code executes. For illustration purposes, the error number and description are displayed and the user is given the opportunity to either place a disk in the A drive, and continue, or abort the save. If the user wishes to stop, we branch back to TidyUp and restore the original drive and directory settings. Otherwise the Resume statement is executed. This means that execution returns to the statement that caused the error. If there is still no disk in the A drive, the error recovery code is executed again. Otherwise the code continues normally. The only reason for the ChDrive "A" statement is to test the readiness of the A drive, so the code restores the stored drive and directory path. The code sets the DisplayAlerts property of the Application object to False, before saving the active workbook. This prevents a warning if an old file called Data.xls is being replaced by the new Data.xls. (See Chapter 3 on the Application Object for more on DisplayAlerts.)

The Resume statement comes in three forms:

❑ Resume — causes execution of the statement that caused the error

❑ Resume Next — returns execution to the statement following the statement that caused the error, so the problem statement is skipped

❑ Resume LineLabel — jumps back to any designated line label in the code, so that you can decide to resume where you want

The following code uses Resume Next to skip the Kill statement, if necessary. The charmingly named Kill statement removes a file from disk. In the following code, we have decided to remove any file with the same name as the one we are about to save, so that there will be no need to answer the warning message about over-writing the existing file. The problem is that Kill will cause a fatal error if the file does not exist. If Kill does cause a problem, the error recovery code executes and we use Resume Next to skip Kill and continue with the SaveAs. The MsgBox is there for educational purposes only. You would not normally include it.

```
Sub ErrorTrap2()
    Dim MyFile As String, Message As String
    Dim Answer As String

    On Error GoTo errTrap

    Workbooks.Add
    MyFile = "C:\Data.xls"
    Kill MyFile
    ActiveWorkbook.SaveAs FileName:=MyFile
    ActiveWorkbook.Close
```

Continued on Following Page

```
      Exit Sub
errTrap:
    Message = "Error No: = " & Err.Number & vbCr
    Message = Message & Err.Description & vbCr & vbCr
    Message = Message & "File does not exist"
    Answer = MsgBox(Message, vbInformation, "Error")
    Resume Next
End Sub
```

On Error Resume Next

As an alternative to On Error GoTo, you can use:

```
On Error Resume Next
```

This statement causes errors to be ignored, so it should be used with caution. However, it has many uses. The following code is a re-work of ErrorTrap2:

```
Sub ErrorTrap3()
    Dim MyFile As String, Message As String

    Workbooks.Add
    MyFile = "C:\Data.xls"
    On Error Resume Next
    Kill MyFile
    On Error GoTo 0
    ActiveWorkbook.SaveAs FileName:=MyFile
    ActiveWorkbook.Close
End Sub
```

We use On Error Resume Next just before the Kill statement. If our C:\Data.xls does not exist, the error caused by Kill is ignored and execution continues on the next line. After all, we don't care if the file does not exist. That's the situation we are trying to achieve.

On Error GoTo 0 is used to turn normal VBA error handling on again. Otherwise, any further errors would be ignored. It is best not to try to interpret this statement, which appears to be directing error handling to line zero. Just accept that it works.

You can use On Error Resume Next to write code that would otherwise be less efficient. The following sub procedure determines whether a name exists in the active workbook.

```
Sub TestForName()
    If NameExists("SalesData") Then
        MsgBox "Name Exists"
    Else
        MsgBox "Name does not exist"
    End If
End Sub

Function NameExists(myName As String) As Boolean
    Dim X As String
    On Error Resume Next
    X = Names(myName).RefersTo
    If Err.Number <> 0 Then
        NameExists = False
    Err.Clear
    Else
        NameExists = True
    End If
End Function
```

TestForName calls the NameExists function, which uses On Error Resume Next to prevent a fatal error when it tries to assign the name's RefersTo property to a variable. There is no need for On Error GoTo 0 here, because error handling in a procedure is disabled when a procedure exits, although Err.Number is not cleared. If no error occurred, the Number property of the Err object is zero. If Err.Number has a non-zero value, an error occurred, which can be assumed to be because the name did not exist, so NameExists is assigned a value of False and the error is cleared. The alternative to this single pass procedure is to loop through all the names in the workbook, looking for a match. If there are lots of names, this can be a slow process.

Summary – the VBA Language

In this section you have seen those elements of the VBA language that enable you to write useful and efficient procedures. You have seen how to add interaction to your macros with the MsgBox and InputBox functions, how to use variables to store information and how to get help about VBA keywords. You have seen how to declare your variables and define their type and the effect on variable scope and lifetime of different declaration techniques. You have also used the block If and Select Case structures to perform tests and carry out alternative calculations, and Do...Loop and For...Next loops that allow you to efficiently repeat similar calculations. You have seen how arrays can be used, particularly with looping procedures. You have also seen how to use On Error statements to trap errors.

When writing VBA code for Excel, the easiest way to get started is to use the macro recorder. You can then modify that code, using the VB Editor, to better suit your own purposes and operate efficiently. Using the Object Browser and the Help screens and the reference section of this book, you can discover objects, methods and properties that can't be found with the macro recorder. Using the coding structures provided by VBA, you can efficiently handle large amounts of data and automate tedious processes.

You now have the knowledge required to move on to the next section, where you will find a rich set of practical examples showing you how to work with key Excel objects. You will draw on the experience of Excel experts who have shared their insights over many years of working with Excel and VBA, striving to harness the extraordinary power of this product. You will discover how to create your own user interface, setting up your own toolbars, menus and dialog boxes and embedding controls in your worksheets to enable yourself and others to work more productively.

The Application Object

The `Application` object sits at the top of the Excel object model hierarchy and contains all the other objects in Excel. It also acts as a catch-all area for properties and methods that do not fall neatly into any other object, but are necessary for programmatic control of Excel. There are `Application` properties that control screen updating and toggle alert messages, for example.

Many of the Application object's methods and properties are also members of <globals>, which can be found at the top of the list of classes in the Object Browser as shown in the screen opposite:

If a property or method is in <globals>, you can refer to that property or method without a preceding reference to an object. For example, the following two references are equivalent:

```
Application.ActiveCell
```

```
ActiveCell
```

However, you do need to be careful. It is easy to assume that frequently used `Application` object *properties*, such as `ScreenUpdating`, are globals when they are not. The following code is correct:

```
Application.ScreenUpdating = False
```

You will get unexpected results with the following:

```
ScreenUpdating = False
```

This code sets up a new variable and assigns the value `False` to it. You can easily avoid this error by having the line of code `Option Explicit` at the top of each module so that such references are flagged as undefined variables when your code is compiled.

> Remember that you can have `Option Explicit` automatically inserted in new modules if you use Tools | Options in the VB Editor window and, under the Editor tab, tick the Require Variable Declaration check box.

The "Active" Properties

The `Application` object provides many short cuts that allow you to refer to active objects without naming them explicitly. This makes it possible to discover what is currently active when your macro runs. It also makes it easy to write generalized code that can be applied to objects of the same type with different names.

The following `Application` object properties are global properties that allow you to refer to active objects:

ActiveCell
ActiveChart
ActivePrinter
ActiveSheet
ActiveWindow
ActiveWorkbook
Selection

If you have just created a new workbook and want to save it with a specific filename, using the `ActiveWorkbook` property is an easy way to return a reference to the new `Workbook` object:

```
Workbooks.Add
ActiveWorkbook.SaveAs Filename:="C:\Data.xls"
```

If you want to write a macro that can apply a bold format to the currently selected cells, you can use the `Selection` property to return a reference to the `Range` object containing the selected cells:

```
Selection.Font.Bold = True
```

Be aware that `Selection` will not refer to a `Range` object if another type of object, such as a `Shape` object, is currently selected or the active sheet is not a worksheet. You might want to build a check into a macro to ensure that a worksheet is selected before attempting to enter data into it.

```
If TypeName(ActiveSheet) <> "Worksheet" Or _
    TypeName(Selection) <> "Range" Then _
        MsgBox "You can only run this macro in a range", vbCritical
    Exit Sub
End If
```

Display Alerts

It can be annoying to have to respond to system alerts while a macro runs. For example, if a macro deletes a worksheet, an alert message appears and you have to press the OK button to continue. However, there is also the possibility of a user clicking the Cancel button, which would abort the delete operation and could adversely affect subsequent code where the delete operation was assumed to have been carried out.

You can suppress most alerts by setting the DisplayAlerts property to False, as follows. When you suppress an alert dialog box, the action that is associated with the default button in that box is automatically carried out:

```
Application.DisplayAlerts = False
ActiveSheet.Delete
Application.DisplayAlerts = True
```

It is not necessary to reset DisplayAlerts to True at the end of your macro as VBA does this automatically. However, it is usually a good idea, after suppressing a particular message, to turn the alerts back on so that any unexpected warnings do appear on screen.

DisplayAlerts is commonly used to suppress the warning that you are about to overwrite an existing file using File | Save As. When you suppress this warning, the default action is taken and the file is overwritten without interrupting the macro.

Screen Updating

It can be annoying to see the screen change and flicker while a macro is running. This happens with macros that select or activate objects and is typical of the code generated by the macro recorder.

> It is better to avoid selecting objects in VBA. It is seldom necessary to do this and your code will run faster if you can avoid selecting or activating objects. Most of the code in this book avoids selecting where possible.

If you want to freeze the screen while your macro runs, you use the following line of code:

```
Application.ScreenUpdating = False
```

The screen remains frozen until you assign the property a value of True, or when your macros finish executing and return control to the user interface. There is no need to restore ScreenUpdating to True, unless you want to display screen changes while your macros are still running.

There is one situation where it is a good idea to set ScreenUpdating to True while your macro is running. If you display a user form or built in dialog box while your macro is running, you should make sure screen updating is on before showing the object. If screen updating is off, and the user drags the user form around the screen, the user form will act as an eraser on the screen behind it. You can turn screen updating off again after showing the object.

> A beneficial side effect of turning off screen updating is that your code runs faster. It will even speed up code that avoids selecting objects, where little screen updating is required. Your code runs at maximum speed when you avoid selecting *and* turn off screen updating.

Evaluate

The Evaluate method can be used to calculate Excel worksheet formulas and generate references to Range objects. The normal syntax for the Evaluate method is as follows:

```
Evaluate("Expression")
```

There is also a short cut format you can use where you omit the quotes and place square brackets around the expression, as follows:

```
[Expression]
```

Expression can be any valid worksheet calculation, with or without the equal sign on the left, or it can be a reference to a range of cells. The worksheet calculations can include worksheet functions that are not made available to VBA through the WorksheetFunction object or they can be worksheet array formulas. You will find more information about the WorksheetFunction object later in this chapter.

For instance, the ISBLANK function, which you can use in your worksheet formulas, is not available to VBA through the WorksheetFunction object, because the VBA equivalent function IsEmpty provides the same functionality. All the same, you can use ISBLANK, if you need to. The following two examples are equivalent and return True if A1 is empty or False if A1 is not empty:

```
MsgBox Evaluate("=ISBLANK(A1)")
```

```
MsgBox [ISBLANK(A1)]
```

The advantage of the first technique is that you can generate the string value using code, which makes it very flexible. The second technique is shorter, but you can only change the expression by editing your code. The following procedure displays a True or False value to indicate whether the active cell is empty or not, and illustrates the flexibility of the first technique:

```
Sub IsActiveCellEmpty()
    Dim stFunctionName As String, stCellReference As String
    stFunctionName = "ISBLANK"
    stCellReference = ActiveCell.Address
    MsgBox Evaluate(stFunctionName & "(" & stCellReference & ")")
End Sub
```

Note that you cannot evaluate an expression containing variables using the second technique.

The following two lines of code show you two ways you can use `Evaluate` to generate a reference to a `Range` object and assign a value to that object:

```
Evaluate("A1").Value = 10
```

```
[A1].Value = 10
```

The first expression is unwieldy and is rarely used, but the second is a convenient way to refer to a `Range` object, although it is not very flexible. You can further shorten the expressions by omitting the `Value` property, as this is the default property of the `Range` object.

```
[A1] = 10
```

More interesting uses of `Evaluate` include returning the contents of a workbook's `Names` collection and efficiently generating arrays of values. The following code creates a hidden name to store a password. Hidden names cannot be seen in the **Insert | Name | Define** dialog box, so they are a convenient way to store information in a workbook without cluttering the user interface:

```
Names.Add Name:="PassWord", RefersTo:="Bazonkas", Visible:=False
```

You can then use the hidden data in expressions like the following:

```
UserInput = InputBox("Enter Password")
If UserInput = [PassWord] Then
...
```

The use of names for storing data is discussed in more detail in Chapter 6 on Names.

The following expression generates a `Variant` array with two dimensions, 100 rows and one column, containing the values from 101 to 200. This process is carried out more efficiently than using a `For...Next` loop:

```
RowArray = [ROW(101:200)]
```

Similarly, the following code assigns the values 101 to 200 to the range B1:B100, and again does it more efficiently than a `For...Next` loop:

```
[B1:B100] = [ROW(101:200)]
```

InputBox

VBA has an InputBox *function* that provides an easy way to prompt for input data. There is also the InputBox *method* of the Application object that produces a very similar dialog box for obtaining data, but which is more powerful. It allows you to control the type of data that must be supplied by the user and allows you to detect when the Cancel key is pressed.

If you have an unqualified reference to InputBox in your code, as follows, you are using the VBA InputBox function:

```
Answer = InputBox(prompt:="Enter range")
```

The user can only type data into the dialog box. It is not possible to point to a cell with the mouse. The return value from the InputBox function is always a string value and there is no check on what that string contains. If the user enters nothing, a zero length string is returned. If the user clicks the Cancel button, a zero length string is also returned. Your code cannot distinguish between no entry and the result of pressing Cancel.

The following example uses the Application object's InputBox method to prompt for a range:

```
Answer = Application.InputBox(prompt:="Enter range", Type:=8)
```

The Type parameter can take the following values, or any sum of the following values if you want to allow for multiple types.

Value of Type	Meaning
0	A formula
1	A number
2	Text (a string)
4	A logical value (True or False)
8	A cell reference, as a Range object
16	An error value, such as #N/A
64	An array of values

The user can point to cells with the mouse or type in data. If the input is of the wrong type, the InputBox method displays an error message and prompts for the data again. If the user clicks the Cancel button, the InputBox method returns a value of False.

If you assign the return value to a Variant, you can check to see if the value is False, for most return types, to detect a Cancel. If you are prompting for a range, the situation is not so simple. You need to use code like the following:

```
Sub GetRange()
    Dim Rng As Range

    On Error Resume Next
    Set Rng = Application.InputBox(prompt:="Enter range", Type:=8)
    If Rng Is Nothing Then
        MsgBox "Operation Cancelled"
    Else
        Rng.Select
    End If
End Sub
```

When you run this code, the output should look something like the following:

The problem is that you must use the Set statement to assign a range object to an object variable. If the user clicks **Cancel**, and a False value is returned, the Set fails and you get a run time error. Using the On Error Resume Next statement, you can avoid the run time error and then check to see if a valid range was generated. You know that the in-built type checking of the InputBox method ensures a valid range will be returned if the user clicks **OK**, so an empty range indicates that **Cancel** was pressed.

StatusBar

The StatusBar property allows you to assign a text string to be displayed at the left hand side of the Excel status bar at the bottom of the screen. This is an easy way to keep users informed of progress during a lengthy macro operation. It is a good idea to keep users informed, particularly if you have screen updating turned off and there is no sign of activity on the screen. Even though you have turned off screen updating, you can still display messages on the status bar.

The following code shows how you can use this technique in a looping procedure:

```
Sub ShowMessage()
    Dim i As Long
    For i = 0 To 10000000
        If i Mod 1000000 = 0 Then
            Application.StatusBar = "Processing Record " & i
        End If
    Next i
    Application.StatusBar = False
End Sub
```

At the end of your processing, you must set the `StatusBar` property to `False` so that it returns to normal operation. Otherwise, your last message will stay on the screen.

SendKeys

`SendKeys` allows you to send keystrokes to the currently active window. It is used to control applications that do not support any other form of communication, such as DDE (Dynamic Data Exchange) or OLE. It is generally considered a last resort technique.

The following example opens the Notepad application, which does not support DDE or OLE, and writes a line of data to the notepad document:

```
Sub SKeys()
    Dim ReturnValue
    ReturnValue = Shell("NOTEPAD.EXE", vbNormalFocus)
    AppActivate ReturnValue
    Application.SendKeys "Copy Data.xls c:\", True
    Application.SendKeys "~", True
    Application.SendKeys "%FABATCH~", True
End Sub
```

SKeys uses *Alt+FA* to perform a File | Save As and enters the file name as BATCH. The symbol `%` is used to represent *Alt* and `~` represents *Enter*. The symbol `^` is used to represent *Ctrl* and other special keys are specified by putting their names in braces, for example, the *Del* is represented by `{Del}` as shown in the example below.

You can also send keystrokes directly to Excel. The following procedure clears the VB Editor's Immediate window. If you have been experimenting in the Immediate window or using `Debug.Print` to write to the Immediate window, it can get cluttered with old information. This procedure switches focus to the Immediate window and sends *Ctrl+a* to select all the text in the window. The text is then deleted by sending *Del*.

```
Sub ImmediateWindowClear()
    Application.VBE.Windows.Item("Immediate").SetFocus
    Application.SendKeys "^a"
    Application.SendKeys "{Del}"
End Sub
```

OnTime

You can use the `OnTime` method to schedule a macro to run some time in the future. You need to specify the date and time for the macro to run and the name of the macro. If you use the `Wait` method of the `Application` object to pause a macro, all Excel activity, including manual interaction, is suspended. The advantage of `OnTime` is that it allows you to return to normal Excel interaction, including running other macros, while you wait for the scheduled macro to run.

Say you have an open workbook with links to `Data.xls`, which exists on your network server but is not currently open. At 3 p.m. you want to update the links to `Data.xls`. The following example schedules the `RefreshData` macro to run at 3 p.m., which is 15:00 hours using a 24 hour clock, on the current day. `Date` returns the current date and the `TimeSerial` function is used to add the necessary time:

```
Sub RunOnTime()
    Application.OnTime Date + TimeSerial(15, 0, 0), "RefreshData"
End Sub
```

The following `RefreshData` macro updates the links to `Data.xls` that exist in `ThisWorkbook` using the `UpdateLink` method. `ThisWorkbook` is a convenient way to refer to the workbook containing the macro:

```
Sub RefreshData()
    ThisWorkbook.UpdateLink Name:="C:\Data.xls", Type:=xlExcelLinks
End Sub
```

If you want to keep refreshing the data on a regular basis, you can make the macro run itself as follows:

```
Dim dtScheduledTime As Date

Sub RefreshData()
    ThisWorkbook.UpdateLink Name:="C:\Data.xls", Type:= xlExcelLinks
    dtScheduledTime = Now + TimeSerial(0, 1, 0)
    Application.OnTime dtScheduledTime, "RefreshData"
End Sub

Sub StopRefresh()
    Application.OnTime dtScheduledTime, "RefreshData", , False
End Sub
```

Once you run `RefreshData`, it will keep scheduling itself to run every minute. In order to stop the macro, you need to know the scheduled time, so the module level variable `dtScheduledTime` is used to store the latest scheduled time. `StopRefresh` sets the fourth parameter of `OnTime` to `False` to cancel the scheduled run of `RefreshData`.

> When you schedule a macro to run at a future time using the `OnTime` method, you must make sure that Excel keeps running in memory until the scheduled time occurs.

The `OnTime` method is also useful when you want to introduce a delay in macro processing to allow an event to occur that is beyond your control. For example, you might want to send data to another application through a DDE link and before waiting for a response from that application. To do this you would create two macros. The first macro sends the data and schedules the second macro, which processes the response, to run after sufficient time has passed. The second macro could keep running itself until it detected a change in the worksheet caused by the response from the external application.

OnKey

You can use the `OnKey` method to assign a macro procedure to a single keystroke or any combination of *Ctrl*, *Shift* and *Alt* with another key. You can also use the method to disable key combinations.

The following example shows how to assign the DownTen macro to the *Down Arrow* key. Once AssignDown has been run, the *Down Arrow* key will run the DownTen macro and move the cell pointer down ten rows instead of one.

```
Sub AssignDown()
    Application.OnKey "{Down}", "DownTen"
End Sub

Sub DownTen()
    ActiveCell.Offset(10, 0).Select
End Sub

Sub ClearDown()
    Application.OnKey "{Down}"
End Sub
```

ClearDown returns the DownArrow key to its normal function.

OnKey can be used to disable existing keyboard short cuts. You can disable the *Ctrl+c* short cut, normally used to copy, with the following code that assigns a null procedure to the key combination:

```
Sub StopCopyShortCut()
    Application.OnKey "^c", ""
End Sub
```

Note that a lower case *c* is used. If you used an upper case *C*, it would apply to *Ctrl+Shift+c*. Once again, you can restore the normal operation of *Ctrl+c* with the following code:

```
Sub ClearCopyShortCut()
    Application.OnKey "^c"
End Sub
```

> The key assignments made with the OnKey method apply to all open workbooks and only persist during the current Excel session.

Worksheet Functions

There are two sources of built-in functions that you can use directly in your Excel VBA code. One group of functions is part of the VBA language. The other group of functions is a subset of the Excel worksheet functions.

Excel and the Visual Basic language, in the form of VBA, were not merged until Excel 5. Each system independently developed its own functions, so there are inevitably some overlaps and conflicts between the two series of functions. For example, Excel has a DATE function and VBA also has a Date function. The Excel DATE function takes three input arguments (year, month and day) to generate a specific date. The VBA Date function takes no input arguments and returns the current date from the system clock. In addition, VBA has a DateSerial function that takes the same input arguments as the Excel DATE function and returns the same result as the Excel DATE function. Finally, Excel's TODAY function takes no arguments and returns the same result as the VBA Date function.

As a general rule, if a VBA function serves the same purpose as an Excel function, the Excel function is not made directly available to VBA macros (although, you can use the Evaluate method to access any Excel function, as pointed out previously in this chapter). There is also a special case regarding the Excel MOD function. MOD is not directly available in VBA, but VBA has a Mod operator that serves the same purpose. The following line of code uses the Evaluate method short cut and displays the day of the week as a number, using the Excel MOD function and the Excel TODAY function:

```
MsgBox [MOD(TODAY(),7)]
```

The same result can be achieved more simply with the VBA Date function and the Mod operator as follows:

```
MsgBox Date Mod 7
```

The Excel CONCATENATE function is also not available in VBA. You can use the & operator as a substitute, just as you can in an Excel worksheet formula. If you insist on using the CONCATENATE function in VBA, you can write code like the following:

```
Sub ConcatenateExample1()
    Dim X As String, Y As String
    X = "Jack "
    Y = "Smith"
    MsgBox Evaluate("CONCATENATE(""" & X & """,""" & Y & """)")
End Sub
```

On the other hand, you can avoid being absurd and get the same result with the following code:

```
Sub ConcatenateExample2()
    Dim X As String, Y As String
    X = "Jack "
    Y = "Smith"
    MsgBox X & Y
End Sub
```

The VBA functions, such as Date, DateSerial and IsEmpty can be used without qualification, as they are members of <globals>. For example, you can use the following:

```
StartDate = DateSerial(1999, 6, 1)
```

The Excel functions, such as VLookUp and Sum, are methods of the WorksheetFunction object and are used with the following syntax:

```
Total = WorksheetFunction.Sum(Range("A1:A10"))
```

For compatibility with Excel 5 and Excel 95, you can use Application rather than WorksheetFunction:

```
Total = Application.Sum(Range("A1:A10"))
```

For a complete list of the worksheet functions directly available in VBA, see the WorksheetFunction object in the reference section.

Caller

The `Caller` property of the `Application` object returns a reference to the object that called or executed a macro procedure. It had a wide range of uses in Excel 5 and Excel 95, where it was used with menus and controls on dialog sheets. From Excel 97 onwards, command bars and ActiveX controls on user forms have replaced menus and controls on dialog sheets. The `Caller` property does not apply to these new features.

`Caller` still applies to the Forms toolbar controls, drawing objects that have macros attached and user-defined functions. It is particularly useful in determining the cell that called a user-defined function. The following worksheet uses the `WorksheetName` function to display the name of the worksheet in B2.

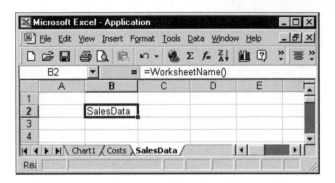

When used in a function, `Application.Caller` returns a reference to the cell that called the function, which is returned as a `Range` object. The following `WorksheetName` function uses the `Parent` property of the `Range` object to generate a reference to the `Worksheet` object containing the `Range` object. It assigns the `Name` property of the `Worksheet` object to the return value of the function. The `Volatile` method of the `Application` object forces Excel to recalculate the function every time the worksheet is recalculated, so that if you change the name of the sheet, the new name is displayed by the function.

```
Function WorksheetName()
    Application.Volatile
    WorksheetName = Application.Caller.Parent.Name
End Function
```

It would be a mistake to use the following code in the `WorksheetName` function:

```
WorksheetName = ActiveSheet.Name
```

If a recalculation takes place while a worksheet is active that is different to the one containing the formula, the wrong name will be returned to the cell.

Summary

In this chapter we have highlighted some of the more useful properties and methods of the Application object. Because Application is used to hold general-purpose functionality that does not fall clearly under other objects, it is easy to miss some of these very useful capabilities.

The following properties and methods have been covered:

- ❑ ActiveCell — contains a reference to the active cell
- ❑ ActiveChart — contains a reference to the active chart
- ❑ ActivePrinter — contains a reference to the active printer
- ❑ ActiveSheet — contains a reference to the active worksheet
- ❑ ActiveWindow — contains a reference to the active window
- ❑ ActiveWorkbook — contains a reference to the active workbook
- ❑ Caller — contains reference to the cell that called a macro
- ❑ DisplayAlerts — determines whether alert dialogs are displayed or not
- ❑ Evaluate — used to calculate Excel functions and generate Range objects
- ❑ InputBox — used to prompt a user for input
- ❑ OnKey — assigns a macro to a single keystroke, or a combination (with *Ctrl*, *Alt* etc.)
- ❑ OnTime — used to set the time for a macro to run
- ❑ ScreenUpdating — determines whether screen updating is turned on or off
- ❑ Selection — contains a reference to the selected range
- ❑ SendKeys — send keystrokes to the active window
- ❑ StatusBar — allows messages to be displayed on the status bar
- ❑ WorksheetFunction — contains the Excel functions available to VBA

This is but a small sample of the total number of properties and methods of the Application object — there are very nearly two hundred of them. A full list is given in the Reference section of this book.

Workbooks and Worksheets

In this chapter you will see how to create new Workbook objects and how to interact with the files that you use to store those workbooks. To do this, some basic utility functions will be presented. You will also see how to handle the Sheet objects within the workbook, and how some important features must be handled through the Window object. Finally, you will see how to synchronize your worksheets as you move from one worksheet to another.

The Workbooks Collection

The Workbooks collection consists of all the currently open Workbook objects in memory. You can add members to the Workbooks collection in a number of ways. You can create a new empty workbook based on the default properties of the Workbook object, or you can create a new workbook based on a template file. Finally, you can open an existing workbook file.

To create a new empty workbook based on the default workbook, use the Add method of the Workbooks collection:

```
Workbooks.Add
```

The new workbook will be the active workbook, so you can refer to it in the following code as ActiveWorkbook. If you immediately save the workbook, using the SaveAs method, you can give it a file name that can be used to refer to the workbook in later code, even if it is no longer active:

```
Workbooks.Add
ActiveWorkbook.SaveAs Filename:="C:\Data\SalesData1.xls"
Workbooks.Add
ActiveWorkbook.SaveAs Filename:="C:\Data\SalesData2.xls"
Workbooks("SalesData1.xls").Activate
```

However, a better technique is to use the return value of the Add method to create an object variable that refers to the new workbook. This provides a short cut way to refer to your workbook and you can keep track of a temporary workbook, without the need to save it:

```
Sub NewWorkbooks()
    Dim Wkb1 As Workbook
    Dim Wkb2 As Workbook

    Set Wkb1 = Workbooks.Add
    Set Wkb2 = Workbooks.Add
    Wkb1.Activate
End Sub
```

The Add method allows you to specify a template for the new workbook. The template does not need to be a file saved as a template, with an .xlt extension — it can be a normal workbook file with an .xls extension. The following code creates a new, unsaved workbook called SalesDataX, where X is a sequence number that increments as you create more workbooks based on the same template, in the same way that Excel creates workbooks called Book1, Book2 etc. when you create new workbooks through the user interface:

```
Set Wkb1 = Workbooks.Add(Template:="C:\Data\SalesData.xls")
```

To add an existing workbook file to the Workbooks collection, you use the Open method. Once again, it is a good idea to use the return value of the Open method to create an object variable that you can use later in your code to refer to the workbook:

```
Set Wkb1 = Workbooks.Open(Filename:="C:\Data\SalesData1.xls")
```

Getting a File Name from a Path

When you deal with workbooks in VBA, you often need to specify directory paths and file names. Some tasks require that you know just the path — for example, if you set a default directory. Some tasks require you to know just the file name — for example, if you want to activate an open workbook. Other tasks require both path and file name — for example, if you want to open an existing workbook file that is not in the active directory.

Once a workbook is open, there is no problem getting its path, getting its full path and file name, or just getting the file name. For example, the following code displays "SalesData1.xls" in the message box:

```
Set Wkb = Workbooks.Open(FileName:="C:\Data\SalesData1.xls")
MsgBox Wkb.Name
```

Wkb.Path returns "C:\Data" and Wkb.FullName returns "C:\Data\SalesData1.xls". However, if you are trying to discover whether a certain workbook is already open, and you have the full path information, you need to extract the file name from the full path to get the value of the Name property of the Workbook object. The following GetFileName function returns the name "SalesData1.xls" from the full path "C:\Data\SalesData1.xls":

```
Function GetFileName(stFullName As String) As String
    'GetFileName returns the file name, such as Cash.xls from
    'the end of a full path such as C:\Data\Project1\Cash.xls
    'stFullName is returned if no path separator is found
    Dim stPathSep As String        'Path Separator Character
    Dim iFNLength As Integer        'Length of stFullName
    Dim i As Integer
```

```
      stPathSep = Application.PathSeparator
      iFNLength = Len(stFullName)
      'Find last path separator character, if there is one
      For i = iFNLength To 1 Step -1
         If Mid(stFullName, i, 1) = stPathSep Then Exit For
      Next i
      GetFileName = Right(stFullName, iFNLength - i)
End Function
```

So that `GetFileName` works on the Macintosh as well as under Windows, the path separator character is obtained using the `PathSeparator` property of the `Application` object. This returns : on the Macintosh and \ under Windows. The `Len` function returns the number of characters in `stFullName` and the `For...Next` loop searches backwards from the last character in `stFullName`, looking for the path separator. If it finds one, it exits the `For...Next` loop, and the index i is equal to the character position of the separator. If it does not find a separator, i will have a value of zero when the `For...Next` loop is completed.

> When a `For...Next` loop is permitted to complete normally, the index variable will not be equal to the `Stop` value. It will have been incremented past the end value.

`GetFileName` uses the `Right` function to extract the characters to the right of the separator in `stFullName`. If there is no separator, all the characters from `stFullName` are returned. Once you have the file name of a workbook, you can use the following `IsWorkbookOpen` function to see if the workbook is already a member of the `Workbooks` collection:

```
Function IsWorkbookOpen(stName As String) As Boolean
      'IsWorkbookOpen returns True if stName is a member
      'of the Workbooks collection. Otherwise, it returns False
      'stName must be provided as a file name without path
      Dim Wkb As Workbook

      On Error Resume Next
      Set Wkb = Workbooks(stName)
      If Not Wkb Is Nothing Then
         IsWorkbookOpen = True
      End If
End Function
```

In the above code `IsWorkbookOpen` tries to assign a reference to the workbook to an object variable and then sees whether that attempt was successful or not. An alternative way to achieve the same result would be to search through the `WorkBooks` collection to see if any `Workbook` object had the name required. In the code above, the `On Error Resume Next` ensures that no run time error occurs when the workbook is not open. If the named document is found, `IsWorkbookOpen` returns a value of `True`. If you do not define the return value of a Boolean function, it will return `False`. In other words, if no open workbook of the given name is found, `False` is returned.

> You might prefer to use the following more lengthy but more explicit code to define the return value of `IsWorkbookOpen`. It is also easier to understand as it avoids the double negative. Despite this, my own preference is for the shorter code as presented above.

```
    If Wkb Is Nothing Then
        IsWorkbookOpen = False
    Else
        IsWorkbookOpen = True
    End If
```

The following code uses the user-defined functions GetFileName and IsWorkbookOpen functions described above. ActivateWorkbook is designed to activate the workbook file in the path assigned to the variable stFullName:

```
Sub ActivateWorkbook1()
    Dim stFullName As String
    Dim stFileName As String
    Dim Wkb As Workbook

    stFullName = "C:\Data\SalesData1.xls"
    stFileName = GetFileName(stFullName)
    If IsWorkbookOpen(stFileName) Then
        Set Wkb = Workbooks(stFileName)
        Wkb.Activate
    Else
        Set Wkb = Workbooks.Open(FileName:=stFullName)
    End If
End Sub
```

ActivateWorkbook first uses GetFileName to extract the workbook file name, SalesData1.xls, from stFullName and assigns it to stFileName. It uses IsWorkbookOpen to determine whether SalesData1.xls is currently open. If the file is open, it assigns a reference to the Workbook object to the Wkb object variable and activates the workbook. If the file is not open, it opens the file and assigns the return value of the Open method to Wkb. When the workbook is opened, it will automatically become the active workbook.

Files in the Same Directory

It is common practice to break up an application into a number of workbooks and keep the related workbook files in the same directory, including the workbook containing the code that controls the application. In this case, you could use the common directory name in your code when opening the related workbooks. However, if you "hard wire" the directory name into your code, you will have problems if the directory name changes or you copy the files to another directory on the same PC or another PC. You will have to edit the directory path in your macros.

To avoid maintenance problems in this situation, you can make use of ThisWorkbook.Path. ThisWorkbook is a reference to the workbook that contains the code. No matter where the workbook is located, the Path property of ThisWorkbook gives you the required path to locate the related files, as demonstrated in the following code:

```
Sub ActivateWorkbook2()
    Dim stPath As String
    Dim stFileName As String
    Dim stFullName As String
    Dim Wkb As Workbook
```

```
      stFileName = "SalesData1.xls"
   If IsWorkbookOpen(stFileName) Then
      Set Wkb = Workbooks(stFileName)
      Wkb.Activate
   Else
      stPath = ThisWorkbook.Path
      stFullName = stPath & "\" & stFileName
      Set Wkb = Workbooks.Open(FileName:= stFullName)
   End If
End Sub
```

Overwriting an Existing Workbook

When you want to save a workbook using the SaveAs method and using a specific file name, there is the possibility that a file with that name already exists on disk. If the file does already exist, the user receives an alert message and has to make a decision about overwriting the existing file. If you want, you can avoid the alert and take control programmatically.

If you want to overwrite the existing file every time, you can just suppress the alert with the following code:

```
Set Wkb1 = Workbooks.Add
Application.DisplayAlerts = False
Wkb1.SaveAs Filename:="C:\Data\SalesData1.xls"
Application.DisplayAlerts = True
```

If you want to check for the existing file and take alternative courses of action, you can use the Dir function. If this is a test that you need to perform often, you can create the following FileExists function:

```
Function FileExists(stFile As String) As Boolean
   If Dir(stFile) <> "" Then FileExists = True
End Function
```

The Dir function attempts to match its input argument against existing files. Dir can be used with wild cards under Windows for matches such as "*.xls." If it finds a match, it returns the first match found and can be called again without an input argument to get subsequent matches. Here, we are trying for an exact match that will either return the same value as the input argument or a zero length string if there is no match. The FileExists function has been declared to return a Boolean type value, and as I explained earlier, is set to the default value of False if no return value is defined. The If test assigns a value of True to the return value if Dir does not return a zero length string.

The following code shows how you can use the FileExists function to test for a specific file name and take alternative courses of action:

```
Sub TestForFile()
   Dim stFileName As String
   stFileName = "C:\Data\SalesData9.xls"
   If FileExists(stFileName) Then
      MsgBox stFileName & " exists"
   Else
      MsgBox stFileName & " does not exist"
   End If
End Sub
```

What you actually do in each alternative depends very much on the situation you are dealing with. One alternative could be to prompt the user for a new file name if the name already exists. Another approach could be to compute a new file name by finding a new sequence number to be appended to the end of the text part of the file name as shown here:

```
Sub CreateNextFileName()
    Dim Wkb1 As Workbook
    Dim i As Integer
    Dim stFileName As String

    Set Wkb1 = Workbooks.Add(Template:="C:\Data\SalesData.xls")
    i = 0
    Do
        i = i + 1
        stFileName = "C:\Data\SalesData" & i & ".xls"
    Loop While FileExists(stFileName)
    Wkb1.SaveAs FileName:= stFileName
End Sub
```

Here, the Do...Loop is repeated, increasing the value of i by one for each loop, as long as the file name generated exists. When i reaches a value for which there is no matching file name, the loop ends and the file is saved using the new name.

Saving Changes

You can close a workbook using the Close method of the Workbook object as shown:

```
ActiveWorkbook.Close
```

If changes have been made to the workbook, the user will be prompted to save the changes when an attempt is made to close the workbook. If you want to avoid this prompt, you can use several techniques, depending on whether you want to save the changes or not.

If you want to save changes automatically, you can specify this as a parameter of the Close method:

```
Sub CloseWorkbook()
    Dim Wkb1 As Workbook

    Set Wkb1 = Workbooks.Open(FileName:="C:\Data\SalesData1.xls")
    Range("A1").Value = Format(Date, "ddd mmm dd, yyyy")
    Range("A1").EntireColumn.AutoFit
    Wkb1.Close SaveChanges:=True
End Sub
```

If you don't want to save changes, you can set the SaveChanges parameter of the Close method to False.

Another situation that could arise is that you open and manipulate a workbook, and you want to leave the workbook open to view but you don't want to save those changes or be prompted to save the changes when you close the workbook or close Excel. In this situation, you can set the Saved property of the workbook to True and Excel will think that there are no changes to be saved. You should make doubly sure you would want to do this before you add this line of code:

```
ActiveWorkbook.Saved = True
```

The Sheets Collection

Within a `Workbook` object there is a `Sheets` collection whose members can be either `Worksheet` objects or `Chart` objects. For compatibility with older versions of Excel, they can also be Dialog Sheets, Excel4MacroSheets and Excel4InternationalMacroSheets. Excel 5 and Excel 95 included modules as part of the `Sheets` collection, but since Excel 97, modules have moved to the VB Editor.

> Modules in workbooks created under Excel 5 or Excel 95 are considered by Excel 2000 to belong to a hidden `Modules` collection and can still be manipulated by the code originally set up in the older versions.

`Worksheet` objects and `Chart` objects also belong to their own collections, the `Worksheets` collection and the `Charts` collection, respectively. The `Charts` collection only includes chart sheets, that is charts that are embedded in a worksheet are *not* members of the `Charts` collection. Charts embedded in worksheets are contained in `ChartObject` objects, which are members of the `ChartObjects` collection of the worksheet. See Chapter 8 for more details.

Worksheets

You can refer to a worksheet by its name or index number in the `Sheets` collection and the `Worksheets` collection. If you know the name of the worksheet you want to work on, it is appropriate, and usually safer, to use that name to specify the required member of the `Worksheets` collection. If you want to process all the members of the `Worksheets` collection, in a `For...Next` loop for example, you would ususally reference each worksheet by its index number.

The index number of a worksheet in the `Worksheets` collection can be different to the index number of the worksheet in the `Sheets` collection. In the following workbook, `Sheet1` can be referenced by any of the following:

```
ActiveWorkbook.Sheets("Sheet1")

ActiveWorkbook.Worksheets("Sheet1")

ActiveWorkbook.Sheets(2)

ActiveWorkbook.Worksheets(1)
```

There is a trap, however, concerning the Index property of the Worksheet object. The Index property of the Worksheet object returns the value of the index in the Sheets collection, not the Worksheets collection. The following code tells you that Worksheets(1) is Sheet1 with index 2, Worksheets(2) is Sheet2 with index 4 and Worksheets(3) is Sheet3 with index 5.

```
Sub WorksheetIndex()
    Dim i As Integer

    For i = 1 To ThisWorkbook.Worksheets.Count
        MsgBox ThisWorkbook.Worksheets(i).Name & " has Index = " & _
                            ThisWorkbook.Worksheets(i).Index
    Next i
End Sub
```

You should avoid using the Index property of the worksheet, if possible, as it leads to confusing code. The following example shows how you must use the worksheet Index as an index in the Sheets collection, not the Worksheets collection. The macro adds a new empty chart sheet to the left of every worksheet in the active workbook:

```
Sub InsertChartsBeforeWorksheets()
    Dim Wks As Worksheet

    For Each Wks In Worksheets
        Charts.Add Before:=Sheets(Wks.Index)
    Next Wks
End Sub
```

In most cases you can avoid using the worksheet Index property. The code above should have been written as follows:

```
Sub InsertChartsBeforeWorksheets2()
    Dim Wks As Worksheet

    For Each Wks In Worksheets
        Charts.Add Before:=Wks
    Next Wks
End Sub
```

Strangely enough, Excel will not allow you to add a new chart after the last worksheet, although it will let you move a chart after the last worksheet. If you want to insert chart sheets after each worksheet, you can use code like the following:

```
Sub InsertChartsAfterWorksheets()
    Dim Wks As Worksheet
    Dim Cht As Chart

    For Each Wks In Worksheets
        Set Cht = Charts.Add
        Cht.Move After:=Wks
    Next Wks
End Sub
```

Chart sheets are covered in more detail in Chapter 8.

Copy and Move

The Copy and Move methods of the Worksheet object allow you to copy or move one or more worksheets in a single operation. They both have two optional parameters that allow you to specify the destination of the operation. The destination can be either before or after a specified sheet. If you do not use one of these parameters, the worksheet will be copied or moved to a new workbook.

Copy and Move do not return any value or reference, so you have to rely on other techniques if you want to create an object variable referring to the copied or moved worksheets. This is not generally a problem as the first sheet created by a Copy operation, or the first sheet resulting from moving a group of sheets, will be active immediately after the operation.

Say you have a workbook like the following and want to add another worksheet for February — and then more worksheets for the following months. The numbers on rows 3 and 4 are the input data, but row 5 contains calculations to give the difference between rows 3 and 4. When you copy the worksheet, you would want to clear the input data from the copies but retain the headings and formulas.

The following code creates a new monthly worksheet that is inserted into the workbook after the latest month. It copies the first worksheet, removes any numeric data from it but leaves any headings or formulas in place and then renames the worksheet to the new month and year:

```
Sub NewMonth()
    'Copy the first worksheet in the active workbook
    'to create a new monthly sheet with name having format "mmm yyyy".
    'The first worksheet must have a name that is in a recognisable
    'date format.
    Dim Wks As Worksheet
    Dim dtFirstDate As Date
    Dim iFirstMonth As Integer
    Dim iFirstYear As Integer
    Dim iCount As Integer

    iCount = Worksheets.Count
    Worksheets(1).Copy After:=Worksheets(iCount)
    iCount = iCount + 1
    Set Wks = Worksheets(iCount)
    dtFirstDate = DateValue(Worksheets(1).Name)
    iFirstMonth = Month(dtFirstDate)
    iFirstYear = Year(dtFirstDate)
    Wks.Name = Format(DateSerial(iFirstYear, iFirstMonth + iCount - 1, 1), _
                                 "mmm yyyy")

    On Error Resume Next
    Wks.Cells.SpecialCells(xlCellTypeConstants, 1).ClearContents
End Sub
```

The result of the copy is as follows:

	A	B	C	D	E
1					
2					
3		Apples	Mangoes	Bananas	Lychees
4	Production				
5	Sales				
6		0	0	0	0
7					
8					
9					
10					

SheetCopy:1 [Group] — Jan2000 / Feb 2000

`NewMonth` first determines how many worksheets are in the workbook and then copies the current worksheet, appending it to the workbook. It updates the number of worksheets in `iCount` and creates an object variable `Wks` which refers to the copied sheet. It then uses the `DateValue` function to convert the name of the January worksheet to a date.

`NewMonth` extracts the month and year of the date into the two integer variables `iFirstMonth` and `iFirstYear` using the `Month` and `Year` functions. It then uses the `DateSerial` function to calculate a new date that follows on from the last one. This calculation is valid even when new years are created, as `DateSerial`, like the worksheet `DATE` function, treats month numbers greater than 12 as the appropriate months in the following year. `NewMonth` uses the VBA `Format` function to convert the new date into "mmm yyyy" format as a string. It assigns the text to the `Name` property of the new worksheet. Finally, `NewMonth` clears the contents of any cells containing numbers using the `SpecialCells` method to find the numbers. `SpecialCells` is discussed in more detail in the following chapter on the `Range` object. The `On Error` statement prevents a run time error when there is no numeric data to be cleared.

Grouping Worksheets

You can manually group the sheets in a workbook by clicking on a sheet tab then, holding down *Shift* or *Ctrl*, clicking on another sheet tab. *Shift* groups all the sheets between the two tabs. *Ctrl* adds just the new sheet to the group. You can also group sheets in VBA by using the `Select` method of the `Worksheets` collection in conjunction with the `Array` function. The following code groups the first, third and fifth worksheets and makes the third worksheet active.

```
Worksheets(Array(1, 3, 5)).Select
Worksheets(3).Activate
```

In addition to this, you can also create a group using the `Select` method of the `Worksheet` object. The first sheet is selected in the normal way. Other worksheets are added to the group by using the `Select` method while setting its `Replace` parameter to `False`:

```
Sub Groupsheets()
    Dim stNames(1 To 3) As String
    Dim i As Integer

    stNames(1) = "Sheet1"
    stNames(2) = "Sheet2"
    stNames(3) = "Sheet3"
    Worksheets(stNames(1)).Select
    For i = 2 To 3
        Worksheets(stNames(i)).Select Replace:=False
    Next i
End Sub
```

The above technique is particularly useful when the names have been specified by user input, via a multi-select list box, for example.

> One benefit of grouping sheets, when you group manually, is that any data inserted into the active sheet and any formatting applied to the active sheet is automatically copied to the other sheets in the group. Printer settings and other sheet level option changes are also applied to each member of the group. However, only the active sheet is affected when you apply changes to a grouped sheet using VBA code. If you want to change the other members of the group, you need to set up a For Each...Next loop and carry out the changes on each member.

The following code places the value 100 into the **A1** cell of worksheets with index numbers 1, 3 and 5 and bolds the numbers.

```
Sub FormatGroup()
    Dim shSheets As Sheets
    Dim Wks As Worksheet
    Set shSheets = Worksheets(Array(1, 3, 5))
    For Each Wks In shSheets
        Wks.Range("A1").Value = 100
        Wks.Range("A1").Font.Bold = True
    Next Wks
End Sub
```

The Window Object

In VBA, if you want to detect what sheets are currently grouped, you use the SelectedSheets property of the Window object. You might think that SelectedSheets should be a property of the Workbook object. However, that is not the case. SelectedSheets is a property of the Window object because you can open many windows on the same workbook and each window can have different groups, as the following screen shows.

There are many other common workbook and worksheet properties that you might presume to be properties of the `Workbook` object or the `Worksheet` object, but which are actually `Window` object properties. Some examples of these are `ActiveCell`, `DisplayFormulas`, `DisplayGridlines` and `DisplayHeadings` and `Selection`.

The following code determines which cells are selected on the active sheet, bolds them and then goes on to apply bold format to the corresponding ranges on the other sheets in the group:

```
Sub FormatSelectedGroup()
    Dim Sht As Object
    Dim stAddress As String

    stAddress = Selection.Address
    For Each Sht In ActiveWindow.SelectedSheets
        If TypeName(Sht) = "Worksheet" Then
            Sht.Range(stAddress).Font.Bold = True
        End If
    Next Sht
End Sub
```

The address of the selected range on the active sheet is captured in `stAddress` as a `String`. It is possible just to activate the selected sheets and apply bold format to the selected cells. Group mode ensures that the selections are the same on each worksheet. However, activating sheets is a slow process. By capturing the selection address as a string, you can generate references to the same range on other sheets using the `Range` property of the other sheets. The address is stored as a string in the form `"$B$2:$E$2,$A$3:$A$4"`, for example, and need not be a single contiguous block.

`FormatSelectedGroup` allows for the possibility that the user can include a chart sheet or another type of sheet in the group of sheets. It checks that the `TypeName` of the sheet is indeed `"Worksheet"` before applying the new format.

> It is necessary to `Dim Sht` as the generic `Object` type, if you want to allow it to refer to different sheet types. There is a `Sheets` collection in the Excel object model, but there is no `Sheet` object.

Synchronizing Worksheets

When you move from one worksheet in a workbook to another, the sheet you activate will be configured as it was when it was last active, that is the top left hand corner cell, the selected range of cells and the active cell will be in exactly the same positions as they were the last time the sheet was active, unless you are in Group mode. In Group mode, the selection and active cell are synchronized across the group. However, the top left hand corner cell is not synchronized in Group mode, and it is possible that you will not be able to see the selected cells and the active cell when you activate a worksheet.

If you want to synchronize your worksheets completely, even out of Group mode, you can add the following code to the `ThisWorkbook` module of your workbook:

```
Dim OldSheet As Object

Private Sub Workbook_SheetDeactivate(ByVal Sht As Object)
    'If the deactivated sheet is a worksheet, store a reference to it in
    'OldSheet
    If TypeName(Sht) = "Worksheet" Then Set OldSheet = Sht
End Sub

Private Sub Workbook_SheetActivate(ByVal NewSheet As Object)
    Dim lCurrentCol As Long
    Dim lCurrentRow As Long
    Dim stCurrentCell As String
    Dim stCurrentSelection As String

    On Error GoTo Fin
    If OldSheet Is Nothing Then Exit Sub
    If TypeName(NewSheet) <> "Worksheet" Then Exit Sub
    Application.ScreenUpdating = False
    Application.EnableEvents = False

    OldSheet.Activate      'Get the old worksheet configuration
    lCurrentCol = ActiveWindow.ScrollColumn
    lCurrentRow = ActiveWindow.ScrollRow
    stCurrentSelection = Selection.Address
    stCurrentCell = ActiveCell.Address

    NewSheet.Activate      'Set the new worksheet configuration
    ActiveWindow.ScrollColumn = lCurrentCol
    ActiveWindow.ScrollRow = lCurrentRow
    Range(stCurrentSelection).Select
    Range(stCurrentCell).Activate
Fin:
    Application.EnableEvents = True
End Sub
```

The `Dim` statement for `OldSheet` must be at the top of the module in the declarations area so that it is a module level variable that will retain its value while the workbook is open and can be accessed by the two event procedures. The `Workbook_SheetDeactivate` event procedure is used to store a reference to any worksheet that is deactivated. The `Deactivate` event occurs after another sheet is activated, so it is too late to store the active window properties. The procedure's `Sht` parameter refers to the deactivated sheet and its value is assigned to `OldSheet`.

The `Workbook_SheetActivate` event procedure executes after the `Deactivate` procedure. It has an `On Error` statement to ensure that, if an error occurs, there are no error messages displayed and that control jumps to the `Fin:` label where event processing is enabled, just in case event processing has been switched off. The first `If` tests check that `OldSheet` has been defined, indicating that a worksheet has been deactivated during the current session. The second `If` test checks that the active sheet is a worksheet. If either `If` test fails, the procedure exits. These tests allow for other types of sheets, such as charts, being deactivated or activated. Next, screen updating is turned off to minimize screen flicker. It is not possible to eliminate all flicker, because the new worksheet has already been activated and the user will get a brief glimpse of its old configuration before it is changed. Then, event processing is switched off so that no chain reactions occur. To get the data it needs, the procedure has to re-activate the deactivated worksheet, which would trigger the two event procedures again.

After reactivating the old worksheet, the ScrollRow (the row at the top of the screen), the ScrollColumn (the column at the left of the screen), the addresses of the current selection and the active cell are stored. The new worksheet is then reactivated and its screen configuration is set to match the old worksheet. As there is no Exit Sub statement before the Fin: label, the final statement is executed to make sure event processing is enabled again.

Summary

In this chapter, you have seen many techniques for handling workbooks and worksheets in your VBA code. You have been shown how to:

❑ Create new workbooks and open existing workbooks

❑ Handle saving workbook files and overwriting existing files.

❑ Move and copy worksheets and interact with Group mode.

You have also seen that you access some workbook and worksheet features through the Window object, and have been shown that you can synchronize your worksheets using workbook events procedures. See Chapter 9 for more discussion on this topic.

In addition, a number of utility macros have been presented including routines to check that a workbook is open, to extract a file name from the full file path and a simple macro that confirms that a file does indeed exist.

Using Ranges

The Range object is probably the one you will use most often in your VBA code. A Range object can be a single cell, a rectangular block of cells or the union of many rectangular blocks (a non-contiguous range). A Range object is contained within a Worksheet object.

The Excel object model does not support three-dimensional Range objects that span multiple worksheets. Every cell in a single Range object must be on the same worksheet. If you want to process 3D ranges, you must process a Range object in each worksheet separately.

Range Property

You can use the Range property of the Application object to refer to a Range object on the active worksheet, using the familiar A1 style of addressing. The following example refers to a Range object that is the B2 cell on the currently active worksheet:

```
Application.Range("B2")
```

It is important to note that the above reference to a Range object will cause an error if there is no worksheet currently active. For example, it will cause an error if you have a chart sheet active.

As the Range property of the Application object is a member of <globals>, you can omit the reference to the Application object, as follows:

```
Range("B2")
```

You can refer to more complex Range objects than a single cell. The following example refers to a single block of cells on the active worksheet:

```
Range("A1:D10")
```

And this code refers to a non-contiguous range of cells:

```
Range("A1:A10,C1:C10,E1:E10")
```

The Range property also accepts two arguments that refer to diagonally opposite corners of a range. This gives you an alternative way to refer to the A1:D10 range:

```
Range("A1","D10")
```

Range also accepts names that have been applied to ranges. If you have defined a range of cells with the name SalesData, you can use the name as an argument:

```
Range("SalesData")
```

The arguments can be objects as well as strings, which provides much more flexibility. For example, you might want to select every cell in column A from cell A1 down to a cell that has been assigned the name LastCell:

```
Range("A1",Range("LastCell")).Select
```

Short Cut Range References

You can also refer to a range by enclosing an A1 style range reference or a name in square brackets, which is a short cut form of the Evaluate method of the Application object. It is equivalent to using a single string argument with the Range property, but is shorter:

```
[B2]
[A1:D10]
[A1:A10,C1:C10,E1:E10]
[SalesData]
```

This short cut is convenient when you want to refer to an absolute range. However, it is not as flexible as the Range property as it cannot handle variable input as strings or object references.

Ranges on Inactive Worksheets

If you want to work efficiently with more than one worksheet at the same time, it is important to be able to refer to ranges on worksheets without having to activate those worksheets. Switching between worksheets is slow and code that does this is more complex than it need be and is harder to read and debug.

All our examples so far apply to the active worksheet, because they have not been qualified by any specific worksheet reference. If you want to refer to a range on a worksheet that is not active, simply use the Range property of the required Worksheet object:

```
Worksheets("Sheet1").Range("C10")
```

If the workbook containing the worksheet and range is not active, you need to further qualify the reference to the Range object as follows:

```
Workbooks("Sales.xls").Worksheets("Sheet1").Range("SalesData")
```

However, you need to be careful if you want to use the Range property as an argument to another Range property. Say you want to sum A1:A10 on Sheet1, while Sheet2 is the active sheet. You might be tempted to use the following code, which results in a run time error:

```
MsgBox WorksheetFunction.Sum(Sheets("Sheet1").Range(Range("A1"), _
    Range("A10")))
```

The problem is that `Range("A1")` and `Range("A10")` refer to the active sheet, `Sheet2`. You need to use more fully qualified properties:

```
MsgBox
WorksheetFunction.Sum(Sheets("Sheet1").Range(Sheets("Sheet1").Range("A1"), _
    Sheets("Sheet1").Range("A10")))
```

In this situation it is more elegant, and more efficient, to use a `With...End With` construct:

```
With Sheets("Sheet1")
    MsgBox WorksheetFunction.Sum(.Range(.Range("A1"), .Range("A10")))
End With
```

Range Property of a Range Object

The `Range` property is normally used as a property of the `Worksheet` object. You can also use the `Range` property of the `Range` object. In this case, it acts as a reference relative to the `Range` object itself. The following is a reference to the D4 cell:

```
Range("C3").Range("B2")
```

If you consider a virtual worksheet that has C3 as the top left hand cell, and B2 is one column across and one row down on the virtual worksheet, you arrive at D4 on the real worksheet. As this is obviously very confusing, it is best to avoid this type of referencing. The `Cells` property is a much better way to reference relatively. However, you will see this "Range in a Range" technique used in code generated by the macro recorder when you record relatively. For example, the following code was recorded when the active cell and the four cells to its right were selected while recording relatively:

```
ActiveCell.Range("A1:E1").Select
```

Cells Property

You can use the `Cells` property of the `Application`, `Worksheet` or `Range` objects to refer to the `Range` object containing all the cells in a `Worksheet` object or `Range` object. The following two lines of code each refer to a `Range` object that contains all the cells in the active worksheet:

```
ActiveSheet.Cells
```

```
Application.Cells
```

As the `Cells` property of the `Application` object is a member of <globals>, you can also refer to the `Range` object containing all the cells on the active worksheet as follows:

```
Cells
```

You can use the `Cells` property of a `Range` object as follows:

```
Range("A1:D10").Cells
```

However, this code achieves nothing as it simply refers to the original `Range` object it qualifies.

You can refer to a specific cell relative to the Range object by using the Item property of the Range object and specifying the relative row and column positions. The row parameter is always numeric. The column parameter can be numeric or you can use the column letters entered as a string. The following are both references to the Range object containing the B2 cell in the active worksheet:

```
Cells.Item(2,2)
Cells.Item(2,"B")
```

As the Item property is the default property of the Range object, you can omit it as follows:

```
Cells(2,2)
Cells(2,"B")
```

The numeric parameters are particularly useful when you want to loop through a series of rows or columns using an incrementing index number. The following example loops through rows 1 to10 and columns A to E in the active worksheet, placing values in each cell:

```
Sub FillCells()
    Dim i As Integer, j As Integer

    For i = 1 To 10
        For j = 1 To 5
            Cells(i, j).Value = i * j
        Next j
    Next i
End Sub
```

This is what you get:

Cells used in Range

You can use the `Cells` property to specify the parameters within the `Range` property to define a `Range` object. The following code refers to **A1:E10** in the active worksheet:

```
Range(Cells(1,1), Cells(10,5))
```

This type of referencing is particularly powerful because you can specify the parameters using numeric variables as shown in the previous looping example.

Ranges of Inactive Worksheets

As with the `Range` property, you can apply the `Cells` property to a worksheet that is not currently active:

```
Worksheets("Sheet1").Cells(2,3)
```

If you want to refer to a block of cells on an inactive worksheet using the `Cells` property, the same precautions apply as with the `Range` property. However, you must make sure you qualify the `Cells` property fully. If **Sheet2** is active and you want to refer to the range **A1:E10** on **Sheet1**, the following code will fail because the `Cells(1,1)` and `Cells(10,5)` are properties of the active worksheet:

```
Sheets("Sheet1").Range(Cells(1,1), Cells(10,5)).Font.Bold = True
```

A `With...End With` construct is an efficient way to incorporate the correct sheet reference:

```
With Sheets("Sheet1")
    .Range(.Cells(1, 1), .Cells(10, 5)).Font.Bold = True
End With
```

More on the Cells Property of the Range Object

The `Cells` property of a `Range` object provides a nice way to refer to cells relative to a starting cell or within a block of cells. The following refers to cell **F11**:

```
Range("D10:G20").Cells(2,3)
```

If you want to examine a range with the name `SalesData` and color any figure under 100 red, you can use code like the following:

```
Sub ColorCells()
    Dim rgSales As Range
    Dim i As Long, j As Long

    Set rgSales = Range("SalesData")
    For i = 1 To rgSales.Rows.Count
        For j = 1 To rgSales.Columns.Count
            If rgSales.Cells(i, j).Value < 100 Then
                rgSales.Cells(i, j).Font.ColorIndex = 3
            Else
                rgSales.Cells(i, j).Font.ColorIndex = 1
            End If
        Next j
    Next i
End Sub
```

This is the result:

	A	B	C	D	E	F	G	H
1	Jan	Feb	Mar	Apr	May	Jun	Jul	
2	13	104	70	183	97	10	174	
3	177	91	19	72	10	126	71	
4	177	111	127	33	145	150	164	
5	88	34	94	151	130	101	31	
6	7	106	126	116	157	1	61	
7	189	167	186	2	176	190	195	
8	47	188	36	141	77	130	193	
9	181	27	85	29	104	131	151	
10	5	182	120	103	181	48	134	
11	166	55	155	61	21	168	134	
12	24	121	172	124	103	145	132	
13	32	78	158	188	29	197	6	
14	166	53	45	131	47	191	38	
15	130	138	74	174	158	4	155	
16								
17								
18								

It is not, in fact, necessary to confine the referenced cells to the contents of the `Range` object. You can reference cells outside the original range. This means that you really only need to use the top left cell of the `Range` object as a starting point. This code refers to F11, as in the earlier example:

```
Range("D10").Cells(2,3)
```

You can also use a short cut version of this form of reference. The following is also a reference to cell F11:

```
Range("D10")(2,3)
```

Technically, this works because it is an allowable short cut for the `Item` property of the `Range` object, rather than the `Cells` property, as described previously:

```
Range("D10").Item(2,3)
```

It is even possible to use zero or negative subscripts, as long as you don't attempt to reference outside the worksheet boundaries. This can lead to some odd results. The following code refers to cell C9:

```
Range("D10")(0,0)
```

The following refers to B8:

```
Range("D10")(-1,-1)
```

The previous `Font.ColorIndex` example using `rgSales` can be written as follows, using this technique:

```
Sub ColorCells()
    Dim rgSales As Range
    Dim i As Long, j As Long

    Set rgSales = Range("SalesData")
    For i = 1 To rgSales.Rows.Count
        For j = 1 To rgSales.Columns.Count
            If rgSales(i, j).Value < 100 Then
                rgSales(i, j).Font.ColorIndex = 3
            Else
                rgSales(i, j).Font.ColorIndex = 1
            End If
        Next j
    Next i
End Sub
```

There is actually a small increase in speed, if you adopt this short cut. Running the second example, the increase is about 5% on my PC when compared to the first example.

Single Parameter Range Reference

The short cut range reference accepts a single parameter as well as two. If you are using this technique with a range with more than one row, and the index exceeds the number of columns in the range, the reference wraps within the columns of the range, down to the appropriate row.

The following refers to cell **E10**:

```
Range("D10:E11")(2)
```

The following refers to cell **D11**:

```
Range("D10:E11")(3)
```

The index can exceed the number of cells in the Range object and the reference will continue to wrap within the Range object's columns. The following refers to cell **D12**:

```
Range("D10:E11")(5)
```

Qualifying a Range object with a single parameter is useful when you want to step through all the cells in a range without having to separately track rows and columns. The ColorCells example can be further rewritten as follows, using this technique:

```
Sub ColorCells()
    Dim rgSales As Range
    Dim i As Long

    Set rgSales = Range("SalesData")
    For i = 1 To rgSales.Cells.Count
        If rgSales(i).Value < 100 Then
            rgSales(i).Font.ColorIndex = 3
        Else
            rgSales(i).Font.ColorIndex = 1
        End If
    Next i
End Sub
```

In the fourth and final variation on the ColorCells theme, you can step through all the cells in a range using a For Each...Next loop, if you do not need the index value of the For...Next loop for other purposes:

```
Sub ColorCells()
    Dim Rng As Range

    For Each Rng In Range("SalesData")
        If Rng.Value < 100 Then
            Rng.Font.ColorIndex = 5
        Else
            Rng.Font.ColorIndex = 1
        End If
    Next Rng
End Sub
```

Offset Property

The Offset property of the Range object returns a similar object to the Cells property, but is different in two ways. The first difference is that the Offset parameters are zero based, rather than 1 based, as the term "offset" implies. These examples both refer to the A10 cell:

```
Range("A10").Cells(1,1)
```

```
Range("A10").Offset(0,0)
```

The second difference is that the Range object generated by Cells consists of one cell. The Range object referred to by the Offset property of a range has the same number of rows and columns as the original range. The following refers to B2:C3:

```
Range("A1:B2").Offset(1,1)
```

Offset is useful when you want to refer to ranges of equal sizes with a changing base point. For example, you might have sales figures for January to December in B1:B12 and want to generate a three-month moving average from March to December in C3:C12. The code to achieve this is:

```
Sub MoveAvg()
    Dim Rng As Range
    Dim i As Long

    Set Rng = Range("B1:B3")
    For i = 3 To 12
        Cells(i, "C").Value = WorksheetFunction.Sum(rng) / 3
        Set Rng = Rng.Offset(1, 0)
    Next i
End Sub
```

The result of running the code is:

	A	B	C	D	E
1	Jan	100			
2	Feb	123			
3	Mar	115	113		
4	Apr	140	126		
5	May	120	125		
6	Jun	132	131		
7	Jul	124	125		
8	Aug	120	125		
9	Sep	115	120		
10	Oct	132	122		
11	Nov	143	130		
12	Dec	128	134		
13					
14					

Resize Property

You can use the `Resize` property of the `Range` object to refer to a range with the same top left hand corner as the original range, but with a different number of rows and columns. The following refers to D10:E10:

```
Range("D10:F20").Resize(1,2)
```

`Resize` is useful when you want to extend or reduce a range by a row or column. For example, if you have a data list, which has been given the name `Database`, and you have just added another row at the bottom, you need to redefine the name to include the extra row. The following code extends the name by the extra row:

```
With Range("Database")
    .Resize(.Rows.Count + 1).Name = "Database"
End With
```

When you omit the second parameter, the number of columns remains unchanged. Similarly, you can omit the first parameter to leave the number of rows unchanged. The following refers to A1:C10:

```
Range("A1:B10").Resize(, 3)
```

You can use the following code to search for a value in a list and, having found it, copy it and the two columns to the right to a new location. The code to do this is:

```
Sub FindIt()
    Dim Rng As Range

    Set Rng = Range("A1:A12").Find(What:="Jun", LookAt:=xlWhole, _
        LookIn:=xlValues)
    If Rng Is Nothing Then
        MsgBox "Data not found"
        Exit Sub
    Else
        Rng.Resize(1, 3).Copy Destination:=Range("G1")
    End If
End Sub
```

And this is the result:

The Find method does not act like the Edit | Find command. It returns a reference to the found cell as a Range object but it does not select the found cell. If Find does not locate a match, it returns a null object that you can test for with the Is Nothing expression. If you attempt to copy the null object, a run time error occurs.

SpecialCells Method

When you press the *F5* key in a worksheet, the Go To dialog box appears. You can then press the Special... button to show the following dialog box:

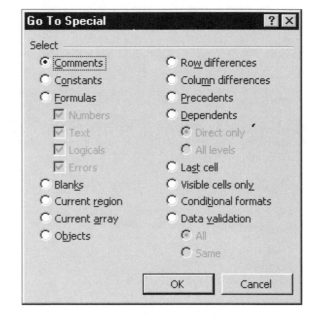

This dialog allows you to do a number of useful things, such as find the last cell in the worksheet or all the cells with numbers rather than calculations. You can carry out all of these operations in your VBA code. Some have their own methods, but most of them can be performed using the SpecialCells method of the Range object.

Last Cell

The following code determines the last row and column in the worksheet:

```
Set rgLast = Range("A1").SpecialCells(xlCellTypeLastCell)
LastRow = rngLast.Row
LastCol = rngLast.Column
```

The LastCell is considered to be the intersection of the highest numbered row in the worksheet that contains information and the highest numbered column in the worksheet that contains information. (Excel also includes cells that have contained information during the current session, even if you have deleted that information. The LastCell property is not reset until you save the worksheet.) Excel considers formatted cells and unlocked cells to contain information. As a result, you will often find the last cell well beyond the region containing data, especially if the workbook has been imported from another spreadsheet application such as Lotus 1-2-3. If you want to consider only cells that contain data in the form of numbers, text and formulas, you can use the following code:

```
Sub GetRealLastCell()
    Dim lRealLastRow As Long
    Dim lRealLastColumn As Long
    Range("A1").Select
    On Error Resume Next
    lRealLastRow = Cells.Find("*", Range("A1"), xlFormulas, , xlByRows, _
        xlPrevious).Row
    lRealLastColumn = Cells.Find ("*",Range("A1"), xlFormulas, , _
        xlByColumns, xlPrevious).Column
    Cells(lRealLastRow, lRealLastColumn).Select
End Sub
```

In this example, the `Find` method searches backwards from the **A1** cell (which means that Excel wraps around the worksheet and starts searching from the `LastCell` towards the A1 cell) to find the last row and column containing any characters. The `On Error Resume Next` statement is used to prevent a run time error when the spreadsheet is empty.

> Note that it is necessary to `Dim` the row number variables as `Long`, rather than `Integer` as integers can only be as high as about 32,000 and worksheets can contain 65,536 rows.

If you want to get rid of the extra rows containing formats, you should select the entire rows, by selecting their row numbers, and then use Edit | Delete to remove them. You can also select the unnecessary columns by their column letters, and delete them. At this point, the last cell will not be reset. You can save the worksheet to reset the last cell, or execute `ActiveSheet.UsedRange` in your code to perform a reset. The following code will remove extraneous rows and columns and reset the last cell:

```
Sub DeleteUnusedFormats()
    Dim lLastRow As Long, lLastColumn As Long
    Dim lRealLastRow As Long, lRealLastColumn As Long

    With Range("A1").SpecialCells(xlCellTypeLastCell)
        lLastRow = .Row
        lLastColumn = .Column
    End With
    lRealLastRow = Cells.Find("*", Range("A1"), xlFormulas, , xlByRows, _
        xlPrevious).Row
    lRealLastColumn = Cells.Find("*", Range("A1"), xlFormulas, , _
        xlByColumns, xlPrevious).Column
    If lRealLastRow < lLastRow Then
        Range(Cells(lRealLastRow + 1, 1), Cells(lLastRow, 1)).EntireRow.Delete
    End If
    If lRealLastColumn < lLastColumn Then
        Range(Cells(1, lRealLastColumn + 1), Cells(1, lLastColumn)) _
            .EntireColumn.Delete
    End If
    ActiveSheet.UsedRange 'Resets LastCell
End Sub
```

The `EntireRow` property of a `Range` object refers to a `Range` object that spans the entire spreadsheet i.e. columns 1 to 256 (or A to IV) on the rows contained in the original range. The `EntireColumn` property of a `Range` object refers to a `Range` object that spans the entire spreadsheet (rows 1 to 65536) in the columns contained in the original object.

Deleting Numbers

Sometimes it is useful to delete all the input data in a worksheet or template so that it is more obvious where new values are required. The following code deletes all the numbers in a worksheet, leaving the formulas intact:

```
On Error Resume Next
Cells.SpecialCells (xlCellTypeConstants, xlNumbers).ClearContents
```

> **The code above should be preceded by the** `On Error` **statement if you want to prevent a run time error when there are no numbers to be found.**

Excel considers dates as numbers and they will be cleared by the above code. If you have used dates as headings and want to avoid this, you can use the following code:

```
For Each Rng In Cells.SpecialCells(xlCellTypeConstants, xlNumbers)
    If Not IsDate(Rng.Value) Then Rng.ClearContents
Next Rng
```

CurrentRegion Property

If you have tables of data that are separated from surrounding data by at least one empty row and one empty column, you can select an individual table using the `CurrentRegion` property of any cell in the table. It is equivalent to the manual *Ctrl+** keyboard short cut. In the following worksheet, you could select the `Bananas` table by clicking on the A9 cell and pressing *Ctrl+**:

The same result can be achieved with the following code, given that cell **A9** has been named `Bananas`:

```
Range("Bananas").CurrentRegion.Select
```

This property is very useful for tables that change size over time. You can select all the months up to the current month as the table grows during the year, without having to change the code each month. Naturally, in your code, there is rarely any need to select anything. If you want to perform a consolidation of the fruit figures into a single table in a new sheet called `Consolidation`, and you have named the top left corner of each table with the product name, you can use the following code to achieve this:

```
Sub Consolidate()
    Dim vaProducts As Variant
    Dim rgCopy As Range 'Range to be copied
    Dim rgDestination As Range
    Dim i As Long

    Application.ScreenUpdating = False
    vaProducts = Array("Mangoes", "Bananas", "Lychees", "Rambutan")
    Set rgDestination = Worksheets("Consolidation").Range("B4")
    For i = LBound(vaProducts) To UBound(vaProducts)
        With Range(vaProducts(i)).CurrentRegion
            'Exclude headings from copy range
            Set rgCopy = .Offset(1, 1).Resize(.Rows.Count - 1, _
                .Columns.Count - 1)
        End With
        rgCopy.Copy
        If i = LBound(vaProducts) Then
            'Paste the first product values
            rgDestination.PasteSpecial xlPasteValues, _
                xlPasteSpecialOperationNone
        Else
            'Add the other product values
            rgDestination.PasteSpecial xlPasteValues, xlPasteSpecialOperationAdd
        End If
    Next i
    Application.CutCopyMode = False 'Clear the clipboard
End Sub
```

This gives the following output:

Screen updating is suppressed to cut out screen flicker and speed up the macro. The Array function is a convenient way to define relatively short lists of items to be processed. The LBound and UBound functions are used to avoid worrying about which Option Base has been set in the declarations section of the module. The code can be reused in other modules without a problem.

The first product is copied and its values are pasted over any existing values in the destination cells. The other products are copied and their values added to the destination cells. The clipboard is cleared at the end to prevent users accidentally carrying out another copy by pressing the *Enter* key.

End Property

The End property emulates the operation of *Ctrl+ArrowKey*. If you have selected a cell at the top of a column of data, *Ctrl+DownArrow* takes you to next item of data in the column that is before an empty cell. If there are no empty cells in the column, you go to the last data item in the column. If the cell after the selected cell is empty, you jump to the next cell with data, if there is one, or the bottom of the worksheet.

The following code selects the last data cell at the bottom of column A if there are no empty cells between it and A1:

```
Range("A1").End(xlDown).Select
```

To go in other directions, you use the constants xlUp, xlToLeft and xlToRight. If there are gaps in the data, and you want to select the last cell in column A, you can start from the bottom of the worksheet and go up, as long as A65536 is empty:

```
Range("A65536").End (xlUp).Select
```

In the section on rows, later in this chapter, you will see a way to avoid the A65536 reference and generalize the code above for different versions of Excel.

Selecting Ranges with End

You can select a range of cells from the active cell to the end of the same column with:

```
Range(ActiveCell, ActiveCell.End(xlDown)).Select
```

Say you have a table of data, starting at cell B3, which is separated from surrounding data by an empty row and an empty column. You can select the table, as long as it has continuous headings across the top and continuous data in the last column, using this line of code:

```
Range("B3", Range("B3").End(xlToRight).End(xlDown)).Select
```

The effect, in this case, is the same as using the CurrentRegion property, but End has many more uses as you will see in the following examples.

As usual, there is no need to select anything if you want to operate on a `Range` object in VBA. The following code copies the continuous headings across the top of Sheet1 to the top of Sheet2.

```
With Worksheets("Sheet1").Range("A1")
    .Range(.Cells(1), _
        .End(xlToRight)).Copy Destination:= Worksheets("Sheet2") .Range("A1")
End With
```

This code can be executed, no matter what sheet is active, as long as the workbook is active.

Summing a Range

Say you want to place a SUM function in the active cell to add the values of the cells below it, down to the next empty cell. You can do that with the following code:

```
With ActiveCell
    Set Rng = Range(.Offset(1), .Offset(1).End(xlDown))
    .Formula = "=SUM(" & Rng.Address & ")"
End With
```

The `Address` property of the `Range` object returns an absolute address by default. If you want to be able to copy the formula to other cells and sum the data below them, you can change the address to relative and perform the copy as follows:

```
With ActiveCell
    Set Rng = Range(.Offset(1), .Offset(1).End(xlDown))
    .Formula = "=SUM(" & Rng.Address(RowAbsolute:=False, _
                ColumnAbsolute:=False) & ")"
    .Copy Destination:=Range(.Cells(1), .Offset(1).End(xlToRight).Offset(-1))
End With
```

And this is what you get:

	A	B	C	D	E	F	G	H	I
1		Jan	Feb	Mar	Apr	May	Jun	Jul	
2	Total	1402	1455	1467	1508	1435	1592	1639	
3	Prod1	13	104	70	183	97	10	174	
4	Prod2	177	91	19	72	10	126	71	
5	Prod3	177	111	127	33	145	150	164	
6	Prod4	88	34	94	151	130	101	31	
7	Prod5	7	106	126	116	157	1	61	
8	Prod6	189	167	186	2	176	190	195	
9	Prod7	47	188	36	141	77	130	193	
10	Prod8	181	27	85	29	104	131	151	
11	Prod9	5	182	120	103	181	48	134	
12	Prod10	166	55	155	61	21	168	134	
13	Prod11	24	121	172	124	103	145	132	
14	Prod12	32	78	158	188	29	197	6	
15	Prod13	166	53	45	131	47	191	38	
16	Prod14	130	138	74	174	158	4	155	
17									
18									

Cell B2 = =SUM(B3:B16)

The end of the destination range is determined by dropping down a row from the SUM, finding the last data column to the right and popping back up a row.

Columns and Rows Properties

Columns and Rows are properties of the Application, Worksheet and Range objects. They return a reference to all the columns or rows in a worksheet or range. In each case, the reference returned is a Range object, but this Range object has some odd characteristics that might make you think there are such things as a "Column object" and a "Row object", which do not exist in Excel. They are useful when you want to count the number of rows or columns, or process all the rows or columns of a range.

Excel 97 increased the number of worksheet rows from the 16,384 in previous versions to 65,536. If you want to write code to detect the number of rows in the active sheet, you can use the Count property of Rows:

```
Rows.Count
```

This is useful if you need a macro that will work with all versions of Excel VBA, and detect the last row of data in a column, working from the bottom of the worksheet:

```
Cells(Rows.Count, "A").End(xlUp).Select
```

If you have a multi-column table of data in a range named Data, and you want to step through each row of the table making every cell in each row bold where the first cell is greater than 1000, you can use:

```
For Each rgRow In Range("Data").Rows
    If rgRow.Cells(1).Value > 1000 Then
        rgRow.Font.Bold = True
    Else
        rgRow.Font.Bold = False
    End If
Next rgRow
```

Which gives:

Curiously, you cannot replace rgRow.Cells(1) with rgRow(1), as you can with a normal Range object as it causes a run time error . It seems that there is something special about the Range object referred to by the Rows and Columns properties.

Areas

You need to be careful when using the Columns or Rows properties of non-contiguous ranges, such as those returned from the SpecialCells method when locating the numeric cells or blank cells in a worksheet, for example. Recall that a non-contiguous range consists of a number of separate rectangular blocks. If the cells are not all in one block, and you use the Rows.Count properties, you only count the rows from the first block. The following code generates an answer of 5, because only the first range, A1:B5, is evaluated:

```
Range("A1:B5,C6:D10,E11:F15").Rows.Count
```

The blocks in a non-contiguous range are Range objects contained within the Areas collection and can be processed separately. The following displays the address of each of the three blocks in the Range object, one at a time:

```
For Each Rng In Range("A1:B5,C6:D10,E11:F15").Areas
    MsgBox Rng.Address
Next Rng
```

The following code copies all the numeric constants in the active sheet to blocks in Sheet3, leaving an empty row between each block:

```
Sub CopyAreas()
    Dim Rng As Range, rgDestination As Range

    Set rgDestination = Worksheets("Sheet3").Range("A1")
    For Each Rng In Cells.SpecialCells(xlCellTypeConstants, _
                                       xlNumbers).Areas

        Rng.Copy Destination:=rgDestination
        ' Set next destination under previous block copied
        Set rgDestination = rgDestination.Offset(rng.Rows.Count + 1)
    Next Rng
End Sub
```

Which gives:

Union and Intersect Methods

Union and Intersect are methods of the Application object, but they can be used without preceding them with a reference to Application as they are members of <globals>. They can be very useful tools, as we shall see.

You use Union when you want to generate a range from two or more blocks of cells. You use Intersect when you want to find the cells that are common to two or more ranges, or in other words, where the ranges overlap. The following event procedure, entered in the module behind a worksheet, illustrates how you can apply the two methods to prevent a user selecting cells in two ranges B10:F20 and H10:L20. One use for this routine is to prevent a user from changing data in these two blocks:

```
Private Sub Worksheet_SelectionChange(ByVal Target As Range)
    Dim rgForbidden As Range

    Set rgForbidden = Union(Range("B10:F20"), Range("H10:L20"))
    If Intersect(Target, rgForbidden) Is Nothing Then Exit Sub
    Range("A1").Select
    MsgBox "You can't select cells in " & rgForbidden.Address, vbCritical
End Sub
```

The Worksheet_SelectionChange event procedure is triggered every time the user selects a new range in the worksheet associated with the module containing the event procedure. See Chapter 9 for more information on working with event procedures. The above code uses the Union method to define a forbidden range consisting of the two non-contiguous ranges. It then uses the Intersect method, in the If test, to see if the Target range, which is the new user selection, is within the forbidden range. Intersect returns Nothing if there is no overlap and the sub exits. If there is an overlap, the code in the two lines following the If test is executed — cell A1 is selected and a warning message is issued to the user.

Empty Cells

You have seen that if you want to step through a column or row of cells until you get to an empty cell, you can use the End property to detect the end of the block. Another way is to examine each cell, one at a time, in a loop structure and stop when you find an empty cell.

You can test for an empty cell with the VBA IsEmpty function.

In the spreadsheet shown opposite, you want to insert blank rows between each week to produce a report that is more readable.

The following macro compares dates, using the VBA `Weekday` function to get the week day as a number. By default, Sunday is day 1 and Saturday is day 7. If the macro finds today's day number is less than yesterday's, it assumes a new week has started and inserts a blank row:

```
Sub ShowWeeks()
    Dim dtToday, dtYesterday
    Range("A2").Select
    dtYesterday = Weekday(ActiveCell.Value)
    Do Until IsEmpty(ActiveCell.Value)
        ActiveCell.Offset(1, 0).Select
        dtToday = Weekday(ActiveCell.Value)
        If dToday < dYesterday Then
            ActiveCell.EntireRow.Insert
            ActiveCell.Offset(1, 0).Select
        End If
        dtYesterday = dtToday
    Loop
End Sub
```

The result is the following:

	A	B	C	D	E	F
1	**Date**	**Customer**	**Product**	**NumberSold**	**Price**	**Revenue**
2	Fri Jan 01, 1999	Kee	Apples	659	12.5	8237.5
3						
4	Tue Jan 05, 1999	Pradesh	Pears	195	18	3510
5	Wed Jan 06, 1999	Smith	Mangoes	928	20	18560
6	Wed Jan 06, 1999	Smith	Mangoes	608	20	12160
7	Fri Jan 08, 1999	Pradesh	Pears	191	18	3438
8						
9	Tue Jan 12, 1999	Roberts	Apples	605	12.5	7562.5
10	Thu Jan 14, 1999	Kee	Apples	785	12.5	9812.5
11						
12	Mon Jan 18, 1999	Kee	Oranges	167	15	2505
13	Mon Jan 18, 1999	Kee	Oranges	978	15	14670
14	Tue Jan 19, 1999	Kee	Pears	301	18	5418
15	Wed Jan 20, 1999	Smith	Apples	947	12.5	11837.5
16	Thu Jan 21, 1999	Smith	Mangoes	437	20	8740
17						
18	Mon Jan 25, 1999	Kee	Mangoes	972	20	19440
19	Tue Jan 26, 1999	Smith	Oranges	607	15	9105
20	Thu Jan 28, 1999	Kee	Mangoes	763	20	15260
21						
22	Mon Feb 01, 1999	Pradesh	Mangoes	50	20	1000
23	Mon Feb 01, 1999	Smith	Oranges	615	15	9225
24	Wed Feb 03, 1999	Kee	Mangoes	196	20	3920
25	Fri Feb 05, 1999	Roberts	Apples	13	12.5	162.5

Microsoft Excel - FruitSales

File Edit View Insert Format Tools Data Window Help

A92

Database / Backup /

Ready

Note that many users detect an empty cell by testing for a zero length string:

```
Do Until ActiveCell.Value = ""
```

This test works in most cases, and would have worked in the example above, had we used it. However, problems can occur if you are testing cells that contain formulas that can produce zero length strings, such as the following:

```
=IF(B2="Kee","Trainee","")
```

The zero length string test does not distinguish between an empty cell and a zero length string resulting from a formula. It is better practice to use the VBA IsEmpty function when testing for an empty cell.

Transferring Values between Arrays and Ranges

If you want to process all the data values in a range, it is much more efficient to assign the values to a VBA array and process the array rather than process the Range object itself. You can then assign the array back to the range.

You can assign the values in a range to an array very easily, as follows:

```
SalesData = Range("A2:F10000").Value
```

The transfer is very fast compared with stepping through the cells, one at a time. Note that this is quite different to creating an object variable referring to the range using:

```
Set rgSalesData = Range("A2:F10000")
```

The variable must have a Variant data type. VBA copies all the values in the range to the variable, creating an array with two dimensions. The first dimension represents the rows and the second dimension represents the columns so you can access the values by their row and column numbers in the array. To assign the value in the first row and second column of the array to Customer, use:

```
Customer = SalesData(1, 2)
```

> *When you assign the values in a range to a Variant, the indexes of the array that is created are always one based, not zero based, regardless of the Option Base setting in the declarations section of the module. Also, the array always has two dimensions, even if the range has only one row or one column. This preserves the inherent column and row structure of the worksheet in the array and is an advantage when you write the array back to the worksheet. If you assign the values in A1:A10 to SalesData, the first element is SalesData(1,1) and the last element is SalesData(10,1). If you assign the values in A1:E1 to SalesData, the first element is SalesData(1,1) and the last element is SalesData(1,5).*

You might want a macro that sums all the Revenues for Kee in our last example. The following macro uses the traditional method to directly test and sum the range of data:

```
Sub KeeTotal1()
    Dim dTotal As Double
    Dim i As Long

    With Range("A2:F73")
        For i = 1 To .Rows.Count
            If .Cells(i, 2) = "Kee" Then dTotal = dTotal + .Cells(i, 6)
        Next i
    End With
    MsgBox "Kee Total = " & Format(dTotal, "$#,##0")
End Sub
```

The following macro does the same job by first assigning the Range values to a Variant and processing the resulting array. The speed increase is very significant. It can be fifty times faster, which can be a great advantage if you are handling large ranges.

```
Sub KeeTotal2()
    Dim vaSalesData As Variant
    Dim dTotal As Double
    Dim i As Long

    vaSalesData = Range("A2:F73").Value
    For i = 1 To UBound(vaSalesData, 1)
        If vaSalesData(i, 2) = "Kee" Then dTotal = dTotal + vaSalesData(i, 6)
    Next i
    MsgBox "Kee Total = " & Format(dTotal, "$#,##0")
End Sub
```

You can also assign an array of values directly to a Range. Say you want to place a list of numbers in column G of the FruitSales.xls example above, containing a 10% discount on **Revenue** for customer **Kee** only. The following macro, once again, assigns the range values to a Variant for processing. It also sets up a dynamic array called Discount, which it ReDims to the number of rows in vaSalesData and one column, so that it retains a two dimensional structure like a range, even though there is only one column. After the values have been assigned to vaDiscount, vaDiscount is directly assigned to the range in column G. Note that it is necessary to specify the correct size of the range receiving the values, not just the first cell as in a worksheet copy operation:

```
Sub KeeDiscount()
    Dim vaSalesData As Variant
    Dim vaDiscount() As Variant
    Dim i As Long

    vaSalesData = Range("A2:F73").Value
    ReDim vaDiscount(1 To UBound(vaSalesData, 1), 1 To 1)
    For i = 1 To UBound(vaSalesData, 1)
        If vaSalesData(i, 2) = "Kee" Then
            vaDiscount(i, 1) = vaSalesData(i, 6) * 0.1
        End If
    Next i
    Range("G2").Resize(UBound(vaSalesData, 1), 1).Value = vaDiscount
End Sub
```

The outcome of this operation is:

	A	B	C	D	E	F	G
1	Date	Customer	Product	NumberSold	Price	Revenue	Kee Discount
2	Fri Jan 01, 1999	Kee	Apples	659	12.5	8237.5	823.75
3	Tue Jan 05, 1999	Pradesh	Pears	195	18	3510	
4	Wed Jan 06, 1999	Smith	Mangoes	928	20	18560	
5	Wed Jan 06, 1999	Smith	Mangoes	608	20	12160	
6	Fri Jan 08, 1999	Pradesh	Pears	191	18	3438	
7	Tue Jan 12, 1999	Roberts	Apples	605	12.5	7562.5	
8	Thu Jan 14, 1999	Kee	Apples	785	12.5	9812.5	981.25
9	Mon Jan 18, 1999	Kee	Oranges	167	15	2505	250.5
10	Mon Jan 18, 1999	Kee	Oranges	978	15	14670	1467
11	Tue Jan 19, 1999	Kee	Pears	301	18	5418	541.8
12	Wed Jan 20, 1999	Smith	Apples	947	12.5	11837.5	
13	Thu Jan 21, 1999	Smith	Mangoes	437	20	8740	
14	Mon Jan 25, 1999	Kee	Mangoes	972	20	19440	1944
15	Tue Jan 26, 1999	Smith	Oranges	607	15	9105	
16	Thu Jan 28, 1999	Kee	Mangoes	763	20	15260	1526
17	Mon Feb 01, 1999	Pradesh	Mangoes	50	20	1000	
18	Mon Feb 01, 1999	Smith	Oranges	615	15	9225	
19	Wed Feb 03, 1999	Kee	Mangoes	196	20	3920	392
20	Fri Feb 05, 1999	Roberts	Apples	13	12.5	162.5	
21	Tue Feb 09, 1999	Roberts	Apples	181	12.5	2262.5	
22	Wed Feb 10, 1999	Smith	Apples	605	12.5	7562.5	
23	Wed Feb 10, 1999	Pradesh	Mangoes	397	20	7940	
24	Thu Feb 11, 1999	Roberts	Oranges	851	15	12765	
25	Mon Feb 15, 1999	Kee	Apples	875	12.5	10937.5	1093.75
26	Mon Feb 15, 1999	Roberts	Oranges	13	15	195	

It is possible to use a one-dimension array for vaDiscount. However, if you assign the one-dimension array to a range, it will be assumed to contain a row of data, not a column. It is possible to get around this by using the worksheet Transpose function when assigning the array to the range. Say you have changed the dimensions of vaDiscount as follows:

```
ReDim vaDiscount(1 To Ubound(vaSalesData,1))
```

You could assign this version of vaDiscount to a column with:

```
Range("G2").Resize(UBound(vaSalesData, 1), 1).Value = WorkSheetFunction _
                                                    .Transpose(vaDiscount)
```

Deleting Rows

A very commonly asked question is "What is the best way to delete rows that I do not need from a spreadsheet?" Generally, the requirement is to find the rows that have certain text in a given column and remove those rows. The best solution depends on how large the spreadsheet is and how many items are likely to be removed.

Say that you want to remove all the rows that contain the text "Mangoes" in column B. One way to do this is to loop through all the rows and test every cell in column B. If you do this, it is better to test the last row first and work up the worksheet row by row. This is more efficient because Excel does not have to move any rows up that would later be deleted, which would not be the case if you worked from the top down. Also, if you work from the top down, you can't use a simple For...Next loop counter to keep track of the row you are on because, as you delete rows, the counter and the row numbers no longer correspond:

```
Sub DeleteRows1()
    Dim i As Long
    Application.ScreenUpdating = False
    For i = Cells(Rows.Count, "B").End(xlUp).Row To 1 Step -1
        If Cells(i, "B").Value = "Mangoes" Then Cells(i, "B").EntireRow.Delete
    Next i
End Sub
```

A good programming principal to follow is this: if there is an Excel spreadsheet technique you can utilize, it is likely to be more efficient than a VBA emulation of the same technique, such as the For...Next loop used here.

> Excel VBA programmers, especially when they do not have a strong background in the user interface features of Excel, often fall into the trap of writing VBA code to perform tasks that Excel can handle already. For example, you can write a VBA procedure to work through a sorted list of items, inserting rows with subtotals. You can also use VBA to execute the Subtotal method of the Range object. The second method is much easier to code and it executes in a fraction of the time taken by the looping procedure. It is much better to use VBA to harness the power built into Excel than to re-invent existing Excel functionality.

However, it isn't always obvious which Excel technique is the best one to employ. To locate the cells to be deleted, without having to examine every row using VBA code, a fairly obvious Excel contender is the Edit | Find command. The following code uses the Find method to reduce the number of cycles spent in VBA loops:

```
Sub DeleteRows2()
    Dim rgFoundCell As Range
    Application.ScreenUpdating = False
    Set rgFoundCell = Range("B:B").Find(what:="Mangoes")
    Do Until rgFoundCell Is Nothing
        rgFoundCell.EntireRow.Delete
        Set rgFoundCell = Range("B:B").FindNext
    Loop
End Sub
```

This code is faster than the first procedure when there are not many rows to be deleted. As the percentage increases, it becomes less efficient. Perhaps we need to look for a better Excel technique.

The fastest way to delete rows, that I am aware of, is provided by Excel's AutoFilter feature.

```
Sub DeleteRows3()
    Dim lLastRow As Long        'last row
    Dim Rng As Range

    Application.ScreenUpdating = False
    Rows(1).Insert              'Insert dummy row for dummy field name
    Range("B1").Value = "Temp"  'Insert dummy field name
    With ActiveSheet
        .UsedRange              'Reset Last Cell
        'Determine last row
        lLastRow = .Cells.SpecialCells(xlCellTypeLastCell).Row
        'Set Rng to the B column data rows
        Set Rng = Range("B1", Cells(lLastRow, "B"))
        'Filter the B column to show only the data to be deleted
        Rng.AutoFilter Field:=1, Criteria1:="Mangoes"
        'Delete the visible cells, including dummy field name
        Rng.SpecialCells(xlCellTypeVisible).EntireRow.Delete
        .UsedRange 'Reset the last cell
    End With
End Sub
```

This is a bit more difficult to code, but it is significantly faster than the other methods, no matter how many rows are to be deleted. To use AutoFilter, you need to have field names at the top of your data. A dummy row is first inserted above the data and a dummy field name supplied for column B. The AutoFilter is only carried out on column B, which hides all the rows except those that have the text "Mangoes".

The SpecialCells method is used to select only the visible cells in column B. This is extended to the entire visible rows and they are deleted, including the dummy field name row. The AutoFilter is automatically turned off when the dummy row is deleted.

Summary

In this chapter you have seen the most important properties and methods that you can use to manage ranges of cells in a worksheet. The emphasis has been on those techniques that are difficult or impossible to discover using the macro recorder. The properties and methods discussed were:

- ❑ Cells property
- ❑ Columns and Rows properties
- ❑ CurrentRegion property
- ❑ End property
- ❑ Offset property
- ❑ Range property
- ❑ Resize property
- ❑ SpecialCells method
- ❑ Union and Intersect methods

You have also seen how to assign a worksheet range of values to a VBA array for efficient processing and how to assign a VBA array of data to a worksheet range.

This chapter has also emphasized that it is very rarely necessary to select cells or activate worksheets, which the macro recorder invariably does as it can only record what you do manually. Activating cells and worksheets is a very time consuming process and should be avoided if you want your code to run at maximum speed.

The final examples show that it is usually best to utilize Excel's existing capabilities, tapping into the Excel object model, rather than write a VBA coded equivalent. And bear in mind, some Excel techniques are better than others. You might need to experiment to get the best code when speed is important.

Using Names

One of the most useful features in Excel is the ability to create names and they can be created using Insert | Name | Define. If the name refers to a range, you can create it by selecting the range and typing the name into the Name box at the left hand side of the Formula Bar. However, in Excel, names can refer to more than just ranges. A name can contain a number, text or a formula. Such a name has no visible location on the worksheet and can only be viewed in the Insert | Name | Define dialog box. Therefore, you can use names to store information in a workbook without having to place the data in a worksheet cell. Names can be declared hidden so that they don't appear in the Insert | Name | Define dialog box. This can be a useful way to keep the stored information unseen by users.

The normal use of names is to keep track of worksheet ranges. This is particularly useful for tables of data that vary in size. If you know that a certain name is used to define the range containing the data you want to work on, your VBA code can be much easier to write than it might otherwise be. It is also relatively simple, given a few basic techniques, to change the definition of a name to allow for changes that you make to the tables in your code.

The Excel object model includes a Names collection and a Name object that you can use in your VBA code. Names can be defined globally at the workbook level, or they can be local or worksheet specific. If you create local names, you can repeat the same name on more than one worksheet in the workbook. To make a Name object worksheet specific, you precede its Name property by the name of the worksheet and an exclamation mark. For example, you can type "Sheet1!Costs" into the top edit box of the Insert | Name | Define dialog box to define a name Costs that is local to Sheet1.

Define Name		? X
Names in workbook:		
Sheet1!Costs		OK
Costs	Sheet1	Close
Criteria	Sheet1	
Data		Add
Database		
Extract	Sheet1	Delete
HoldData		
Input		
ItemsInA		
StoreNumber		
StoreString		
Refers to:		
=Sheet1!$G$3		

When you display the Insert | Name | Define dialog box you see the global names in the workbook and the local names for the active worksheet. The local names are identified by the worksheet name to the right of the name. If a local name is the same as a global name, you will only see the local name.

A great source of confusion with names is that they also have names. You need to distinguish between a Name object and the Name property of that object. The following code returns a reference to a Name object in the Names collection:

```
Names("Data")
```

If you want to change the Name property of a Name object, you use code like the following:

```
Names("Data").Name = "NewData"
```

Having changed its Name property, you would now refer to this Name object as follows:

```
Names("NewData")
```

Global names and local names belong to the Names collection associated with the Workbook object. If you use a reference such as Application.Names or Names, you are referring to the Names collection for the active workbook. If you use a reference such as Workbooks("Data.xls").Names, you are referring to the Names collection for that specific workbook.

Local names, but not global names, also belong to the Names collection associated with the WorkSheet object to which they are local. If you use a reference such as Worksheets("Sheet1").Names or ActiveSheet.Names, you are referring to the local Names collection for that worksheet.

There is also another way to refer to names that refer to ranges. You can use the Name property of the Range object. More of this later.

Naming Ranges

You can create a global name that refers to a range using the Add method of the Workbook object's Names collection:

```
Names.Add Name:="Data", RefersTo:="=Sheet1!$D$10:$D$12"
```

It is important to include the equals sign in front of the definition and to make the cell references absolute, using the $ signs. You can omit the worksheet reference if you want the name to refer to the active worksheet.

```
Names.Add Name:="Data", RefersTo:="=$D$10:$D$12"
```

If the name already exists, it will be replaced by the new definition.

If you want to create a local name, you can use the following:

```
Names.Add Name:="Sheet1!Sales", RefersTo:="=Sheet1!$E$10:$E$12"
```

Alternatively, you can add the name to the Names collection associated with the worksheet, which only includes the names that are local to that worksheet:

```
Worksheets("Sheet1").Names.Add Name:="Costs", RefersTo:="=Sheet1!$F$10:$F$12"
```

Using the Name Property of the Range Object

There is a much simpler way to create a name that refers to a Range. You can directly define the Name property of the Range object:

```
Range("A1:D10").Name = "SalesData"
```

If you want the name to be local, you can include a worksheet name:

```
Range("F1:F10").Name = "Sheet1!Staff"
```

It is generally easier, in code, to work with Range objects in this way, than to have to generate the string address of a range, preceded by an equals sign that is required by the RefersTo property of the Add method of the Names collection. For example, if you created an object variable Rng and want to apply the name Data to it, you need to get the Address property of Rng and append it to an =:

```
Names.Add Name:="Data", RefersTo:="=" & Rng.Address
```

The alternative method is:

```
Rng.Name = "Data"
```

You cannot forget about the Add method, however, because it is the only way to create names that refer to numbers, formulas and strings, rather than ranges.

Special Names

Excel uses some names internally to track certain features. When you apply a print range to a worksheet, Excel gives that range the name Print_Area as a local name. If you set print titles, Excel creates the local name Print_Titles. If you use the Data | Filter | Advanced Filter feature to extract data from a list to a new range, Excel creates the local names Criteria and Extract.

In older versions of Excel, the name Database was used to name the range containing your data list (or database). Although it is no longer mandatory to use this name, Database is still recognized by some Excel features such as Advanced Filter.

> If you create a macro that uses the Data | Form feature to edit your data list, you will find that the macro does not work if the data list is not close to the A1 cell. You can rectify this by applying the name Database to your data list.

You need to be aware that Excel uses these names and, in general, you should avoid using them unless you want the side effects they can produce. For example, you can remove the print area by deleting the name `Print_Area`. The following two lines of code have the same effect if you have defined a print area:

```
ActiveSheet.PageSetup.PrintArea = ""
```

```
ActiveSheet.Names("Print_Area").Delete
```

To summarize, you need to take care when using the following names:

- ❏ Criteria
- ❏ Database
- ❏ Extract
- ❏ Print_Area
- ❏ Print_Titles

Storing Values in Names

The use of names to store data items has already been mentioned in chapter 3 on the `Application` object, specifically under the `Evaluate` method topic. Now for a bit more detail.

When you use a name to store numeric or string data, you should *not* precede the value of the `RefersTo` property with =. If you do, it will be taken as a formula. The following code stores a number and a string into `StoreNumber` and `StoreString`, respectively:

```
Dim X As Variant
X = 3.14159
Names.Add Name:="StoreNumber", RefersTo:=X
X = "Sales"
Names.Add Name:="StoreString", RefersTo:=X
```

This provides you with a convenient way to store the data you need in your VBA code from one Excel session to another, so that it does not disappear when you close Excel. When storing strings, you can store up to 255 characters.

You can retrieve the value in a name using the `Evaluate` method equivalent as follows:

```
X = [StoreNumber]
```

You can also store formulas into names. The formula must start with =. The following places the COUNTA function into a name:

```
Names.Add Name:="ItemsInA", RefersTo:="=COUNTA($A:$A)"
```

This name can be used in worksheet cell formulas to return a count of the number of items in column A:

Once again, you can use the `Evaluate` method equivalent to evaluate the name in VBA:

```
MsgBox [ItemsInA]
```

Storing Arrays

You can store the values in an array variable in a name just as easily as you can store a number or a label. The following code creates an array of numbers in `MyArray` and stores the array values in `MyName`:

```
Sub ArrayToName()
    Dim MyArray(1 To 200, 1 To 3)
    Dim i as Integer
    Dim j as Integer

    For i = 1 To 200
        For j = 1 To 3
            MyArray(i, j) = i + j
        Next j
    Next i
    Names.Add Name:="MyName", RefersTo:=MyArray
End Sub
```

> There is a limit to the size of an array that can be assigned to a name in Excel 2000. The maximum number of columns is 256 and the total number of elements in the array cannot exceed 5461.

The `Evaluate` method can be used to assign the values in a name that holds an array to a `Variant` variable. The following code assigns the contents of `MyName`, created in `ArrayToName`, to `MyArray` and displays the last element in the array:

```
Sub NameToArray()
    Dim MyArray As Variant
    MyArray = [MyName]
    MsgBox MyArray(200, 3)
End Sub
```

The array created by assigning a name containing an array to a variant is always one based, even if you have an Option Base 0 *statement in the declarations section of your module.*

Hiding Names

You can hide a name by setting its Visible property to False. You can do this when you create the name:

```
Names.Add Name:="StoreNumber", RefersTo:=x, Visible:=False
```

You can also hide the name after it has been created:

```
Names("StoreNumber").Visible = False
```

The effect is that the name cannot be seen by users in the Insert | Name | Define dialog box. It is not a highly secure way to conceal information. Anyone with VBA skills can detect the name. But it is an effective way to ensure that users are not confused by the presence of strange names.

You should also be aware that if, through the Excel user interface, a user creates a name object with a name property corresponding to your hidden name, the hidden name is destroyed. You can prevent this by protecting the worksheet.

Despite some limitations, hidden names do provide a nice way to store information in a workbook.

Working with Named Ranges

The following spreadsheet contains a data list in B4:D10 that has been given the name Database. There is also a data input area in B2:D2 that has been given the name Input.

If you want to copy the `Input` data to the bottom of the data list and increase the range referred to by the name `Database` to include the new row, you can use the following code:

```
Sub AddNewData()
    Dim lRows As Long

    With Range("Database")
        lRows = .Rows.Count + 1
        Range("Input").Copy Destination:=.Cells(lRows, 1)
        .Resize(lRows).Name = "Database"
    End With
End Sub
```

The output resulting from this code will be the same as the screenshot above but with the data "Shelley 26 F" in cells B11:D11. The range `Database` will now refer to B4:D11.

The variable `lRows` is assigned the count of the number of rows in `Database` plus one, to allow for the new record of data. `Input` is then copied. The destination of the copy is the B11 cell, which is defined by the `Cells` property of `Database`, being `lRows` down from the top of `Database`, in column 1 of `Database`. The `Resize` property is applied to `Database` to generate a reference to a `Range` object with one more row than `Database` and the `Name` property of the new `Range` object is assigned the name `Database`.

The nice thing about this code is that it is quite independent of the size or location of `Database` in the active workbook and the location of `Input` in the active workbook. `Database` can have seven or 7,000 rows. You can add more columns to `Input` and `Database` and the code still works without change. `Input` and `Database` can even be on different worksheets and the code will still work.

Searching for a Name

If you want to test to see if a name exists in a workbook, you can use the following function. It has been designed to work both as a worksheet function and as a VBA callable function, which makes it a little more complex than if it were designed for only one job:

```
Function IsNameInWorkbook(stName As String) As Boolean
    Dim X As String
    Dim Rng As Range

    Application.Volatile
    On Error Resume Next
    Set Rng = Application.Caller
    Err.Clear
    If Rng Is Nothing Then
        X = ActiveWorkbook.Names(stName).Name
    Else
        X = Rng.Parent.Parent.Names(stName).Name
    End If
    If Err.Number = 0 Then IsNameInWorkbook = True
End Function
```

IsNameInWorkbook has an input parameter stName, which is the required name as a string. The function has been declared volatile, so that it recalculates when it is used as a worksheet function and the referenced name is added or deleted. The function first determines if it has been called from a worksheet cell by assigning the Application.Caller property to Rng. If it has been called from a cell, Application.Caller returns a Range object that refers to the cell containing the function. If the function has not been called from a cell, the Set statement causes an error, which is suppressed by the preceding On Error Resume Next statement. That error, should it have occurred, is cleared because the function anticipates further errors that should not be masked by the first error.

Next, the function uses an If test to see if Rng is undefined. If so, the call was made from another VBA routine. In this case, the function attempts to assign the Name property of the Name object in the active workbook to the dummy variable X. If the name exists, this attempt succeeds and no error is generated. Otherwise an error does occur, but is once again suppressed by the On Error statement.

If the function has been called from a worksheet cell, the Else clause of the If test identifies the workbook containing Rng and attempts to assign the Name property of the required Name object to X. The parent of Rng is the worksheet containing Rng and the parent of that worksheet is the workbook containing Rng. Once again, an error will be generated if the name does not exist in the workbook.

Finally, IsNameInWorkbook checks the Number property of the Err object to see if it is zero. If it is, the return value of the function is set to True as the name does exist. If there is a non-zero error number, the function is left to return its default value of False as the name does not exist.

You could use IsNameInWorkbook in a spreadsheet cell as follows:

```
=IF(IsNameInWorkbook("John"),"John is ","John is not ")&"an existing name"
```

You could use the following procedure to ask the user to enter a name and determine its existence:

```
Sub TestName()
    If IsNameInWorkbook(InputBox("What Name")) Then
        MsgBox "Name exists"
    Else
        MsgBox "Name does not exist"
    End If
End Sub
```

Note that, if you are searching for a local name, you must include its sheet name, in the form Sheet1!Name, in the above examples.

If you invoke IsNameInWorkbook as a worksheet function and if the name "John" is present, you will get output like this:

```
Microsoft Excel - NameExists                                    _|□|×|
File  Edit  View  Insert  Format  Tools  Data  Window  Help      _|□|×|
```

D4 = =IF(isNameInWorkbook("John"),"John is ","John is not ")&"an existing name"

	A	B	C	D	E	F	G	H
1								
2								
3								
4				John is an existing name				
5								
6								

Sheet2 / Sheet3 \ Sheet1 /

Ready

Searching for the Name of a Range

The `Name` property of the `Range` object returns the name of the range, if the range has a name and the `RefersTo` property of the `Name` object corresponds exactly to the range. You might be tempted to display the name of a range `Rng` with the following code:

```
MsgBox Rng.Name
```

This code fails because the `Name` property of a `Range` object returns a `Name` object. What you want is the `Name` property of the `Name` object, so you must use:

```
MsgBox Rng.Name.Name
```

This code only works if `Rng` has a name. It will return a run time error if `Rng` does not have one. You can use the following code to display the name of the selected cells in the active sheet:

```
Sub TestNameOfRange()
    Dim nmName As Name
    On Error Resume Next
    Set nmName = Selection.Name
    If nmName Is Nothing Then
        MsgBox " Selection has no name"
    Else
        MsgBox nmName.Name
    End If
End Sub
```

If a range has more than one name, the first of the names, in alphabetical order, will be returned.

When this macro is run, the output will look something like this:

```
NameExists                                              _|□|×|
       A            B       C         D          E
 1  Data
 2  Sheet1!Jack
 3  Jack
 4  John              Microsoft Excel    ×
 5  Sheet3!Peg
 6                      Data
 7
 8                         [ OK ]
 9
10
11
   Sheet2 / Sheet3 / Sheet1 /
```

129

Determining which Names Overlap a Range

When you want to check the names that have been applied to ranges in a worksheet, it can be handy to get a list of all the names that are associated with the currently selected cells. You might be interested in names that completely overlap the selected cells, or names that partly overlap the selected cells. The following code lists all the names that completely overlap the selected cells of the active worksheet:

```
Sub SelectionEntirelyInNames()
    Dim stMessage As String
    Dim nmName As Name
    Dim rgNameRange As Range
    Dim Rng As Range
    On Error Resume Next
    For Each nmName In Names
        Set rgNameRange = Nothing
        Set rgNameRange = nmName.RefersToRange
        If Not rgNameRange Is Nothing Then
            If rgNameRange.Parent.Name = ActiveSheet.Name Then
                Set Rng = Intersect(Selection, rgNameRange)
                If Not Rng Is Nothing Then
                    If Selection.Address = Rng.Address Then
                        stMessage = stMessage & nmName.Name & vbCr
                    End If
                End If
            End If
        End If
    Next nmName
    If stMessage = "" Then
        MsgBox "The selection is not entirely in any name"
    Else
        MsgBox stMessage
    End If
End Sub
```

SelectionEntirelyInNames starts out by suppressing errors with On Error Resume Next. It then goes into a For Each...Next loop that processes all the names in the workbook. It sets rgNameRange to Nothing to get rid of any range reference left in it from one iteration of the loop to the next. It then tries to use the Name property of the current Name object as the name of a Range object and assign a reference to the Range object to rgNameRange. This will fail if the name does not refer to a range, so the rest of the loop is only carried out if a valid Range object has been assigned to rgNameRange.

The next If test checks that the range that rgNameRange refers to is on the active worksheet. The parent of rgNameRange is the worksheet containing rgNameRange. The inner code is only executed if the name of the parent worksheet is the same as the name of the active sheet. Rng is then assigned the intersect (the overlapping cells) of the selected cells and rgNameRange. If there is an overlap and Rng is not Nothing, the innermost If is executed. This final If checks that the overlapping range in Rng is identical to the selected range. If this is true, then the selected cells are contained entirely in rgNameRange and the Name property of the current Name object is added to any names already in stMessage. In addition, a carriage return character is appended, using the VBA intrinsic constant vbCr, so that each name is on a new line in stMessage.

When the For Each...Next loop terminates, the following If tests to see if there is anything in stMessage. If stMessage is a zero length string, MsgBox displays an appropriate message to say that no names were found. Otherwise, the list of found names in stMessage is displayed.

When this code is run in a spreadsheet with three named ranges — Data, Fred and Mary — you get the following result on running `SelectionEntirelyInNames`:

If you want to find out which names are overlapping the selected cells, regardless of whether they entirely contain the selected cells, you can remove the second innermost `If` test as in the following code:

```
Sub NamesOverlappingSelection()
    Dim stMessage As String
    Dim nmName As Name
    Dim rgNameRange As Range
    Dim Rng As Range

    On Error Resume Next
    For Each nmName In Names
        Set rgNameRange = Nothing
        Set rgNameRange = Range(nmName.Name)
        If Not rgNameRange Is Nothing Then
            If rgNameRange.Parent.Name = ActiveSheet.Name Then
                Set Rng = Intersect(Selection, rgNameRange)
                If Not Rng Is Nothing Then
                    stMessage = stMessage & nmName.Name & vbCr
                End If
            End If
        End If
    Next nmName
    If stMessage = "" Then
        MsgBox "No Names are overlapping the selection"
    Else
        MsgBox stMessage
    End If
End Sub
```

Note that `SelectionEntirelyInNames` and `NamesOverlappingSelection` use different techniques to assign the range referred to by the name to the object variable `rgNameRange`. The following statements are equivalent:

```
Set rgNameRange = nmName.RefersToRange
```

```
Set rgNameRange = Range(nmName.Name)
```

131

Summary

In this chapter I have presented an in-depth discussion of using names in Excel. You have seen how to:

❑ Use names to keep track of worksheet ranges

❑ Use names to store numeric and string data in a worksheet

❑ Make names hidden from the user if necessary

❑ Check for the presence of names in workbooks and in ranges

❑ Determine which names completely or partially overlap a selected range

Filtered Lists

In this chapter you will see how to set up VBA code to manage data in lists and code to filter information from lists. The features we will be looking at are:

❑ Data Form

❑ AutoFilter

❑ Advanced Filter

As always, you can use the macro recorder to generate some basic code for these operations. However, the recorded code needs modification to make it useful and the recorder can even generate erroneous code in some cases. You will see that dates can be a problem, if not handled properly, especially in an international setting.

Before you can apply Excel's list management tools, your data must be set up in a very specific way. The data must be structured like a database table, with headings at the top of each column, which are the field names, and the data itself must consist of single rows of information, which are the equivalent of database records. The following screen shows a typical list that holds information on the sales of fruit products:

	A	B	C	D	E	F	G
5	**Date**	**Customer**	**State**	**Product**	**NumberSold**	**Price**	**Revenue**
6	Jan 01, 1997	Roberts	NSW	Oranges	903	15	13545
7	Jan 01, 1997	Roberts	TAS	Oranges	331	15	4965
8	Jan 02, 1997	Smith	QLD	Mangoes	299	20	5980
9	Jan 06, 1997	Roberts	QLD	Oranges	612	15	9180
10	Jan 08, 1997	Roberts	VIC	Apples	907	12.5	11337.5
11	Jan 08, 1997	Pradesh	TAS	Pears	107	18	1926
12	Jan 10, 1997	Roberts	VIC	Apples	770	12.5	9625
13	Jan 14, 1997	Smith	NT	Apples	223	12.5	2787.5
14	Jan 14, 1997	Smith	VIC	Oranges	132	15	1980
15	Jan 15, 1997	Pradesh	QLD	Oranges	669	15	10035
16	Jan 17, 1997	Roberts	NSW	Mangoes	881	20	17620
17	Jan 21, 1997	Kee	SA	Pears	624	18	11232
18	Jan 22, 1997	Roberts	QLD	Mangoes	193	20	3860
19	Jan 23, 1997	Smith	SA	Mangoes	255	20	5100
20	Jan 27, 1997	Kee	QLD	Mangoes	6	20	120
21	Jan 27, 1997	Kee	VIC	Mangoes	311	20	6220
22	Jan 28, 1997	Roberts	NT	Oranges	9	15	135
23	Jan 28, 1997	Kee	TAS	Apples	706	12.5	8825
24	Jan 29, 1997	Kee	NT	Mangoes	441	20	8820
25	Jan 30, 1997	Kee	WA	Oranges	936	15	14040
26	Feb 03, 1997	Kee	NSW	Oranges	901	15	13515
27	Feb 04, 1997	Smith	NT	Oranges	631	15	9465
28	Feb 06, 1997	Pradesh	NT	Apples	181	12.5	2262.5
29	Feb 10, 1997	Kee	WA	Pears	748	18	13464
30	Feb 11, 1997	Roberts	WA	Mangoes	593	20	11860
31	Feb 12, 1997	Kee	QLD	Oranges	845	15	12675
32	Feb 13, 1997	Smith	NT	Apples	742	12.5	9275
33	Feb 17, 1997	Smith	NT	Mangoes	804	20	16080
34	Feb 18, 1997	Pradesh	VIC	Oranges	863	15	12945

Excel should never be considered a fully equipped database application. It is limited in the amount of data it can handle and it cannot efficiently handle multiple related database tables. However, Excel can work with other database applications to provide you with the data you need and it has some powerful tools, such as Data Form, AutoFilter, Advanced Filter, SubTotal and PivotTables, for analyzing, manipulating and presenting that data.

Data Form

Excel has a built-in form that you can use to view, find and edit data in a list. If you select a single cell in the list, or select the entire list, and click on Data | Form… you will see a form like the following:

If you record this process, you will get code like the following:

```
Range("B2").Select
ActiveSheet.ShowDataForm
```

If your list has its top left hand corner in A1, B1, A2 or B2, and you record selecting the top left hand corner and showing the Data Form, the recorded macro works. If your list starts in any cell outside the range A1:B2, and you record while selecting the top left hand corner and showing the Data Form, the recorded macro will give an error message when you try to run it. You can overcome this problem by applying the name Database to your list.

If you don't work entirely with US date and number formats, the Data
Form feature is quite dangerous, when displayed by VBA code using the
`ShowDataForm` method. The Data Form, when invoked by VBA,
displays dates and numbers only in US format. On the other hand, any
dates or numbers typed in by a user are interpreted according to the
regional settings in the Windows Control Panel, So if you set the date in
the British format (dd/mm/yyyy), when you use the Data Form, the dates
become corrupted. See Chapter 16 on International Issues for more
details.

AutoFilter

The AutoFilter feature is a very easy way to select data from a list, if you want an exact
match on a field such as `Customer`. All you need to do is click the drop down beside
the field and click on the required match, as shown below:

	A	B	C	D	E	F	G	H
5	Date ▼	Customer ▼	State ▼	Product ▼	NumberSold ▼	Price ▼	Revenue ▼	
11	Jan 08, 1997	(All)	TAS	Pears	107	18	1926	
15	Jan 15, 1997	(Top 10...)	QLD	Oranges	669	15	10035	
28	Feb 06, 1997	(Custom...)	NT	Apples	181	12.5	2262.5	
34	Feb 18, 1997	Kee	VIC	Oranges	863	15	12945	
45	Mar 06, 1997	Pradesh	NSW	Pears	92	18	1656	
		Roberts						
52	Mar 20, 1997	Smith	QLD	Oranges	769	15	11535	
		Pradesh						
54	Mar 24, 1997	Pradesh	SA	Apples	335	12.5	4187.5	
65	Apr 14, 1997	Pradesh	WA	Mangoes	99	20	1980	
71	Apr 22, 1997	Pradesh	VIC	Pears	434	18	7812	
76	Apr 28, 1997	Pradesh	TAS	Pears	30	18	540	
82	May 07, 1997	Pradesh	NSW	Oranges	240	15	3600	
83	May 07, 1997	Pradesh	NSW	Pears	687	18	12366	
86	May 13, 1997	Pradesh	VIC	Mangoes	286	20	5720	
96	May 27, 1997	Pradesh	SA	Apples	973	12.5	12162.5	
101	Jun 06, 1997	Pradesh	NT	Oranges	563	15	8445	
109	Jun 25, 1997	Pradesh	TAS	Oranges	466	15	6990	
111	Jun 26, 1997	Pradesh	QLD	Oranges	72	15	1080	
113	Jul 02, 1997	Pradesh	WA	Mangoes	389	20	7780	
116	Jul 07, 1997	Pradesh	TAS	Apples	695	12.5	8687.5	
119	Jul 14, 1997	Pradesh	NT	Mangoes	559	20	11180	
121	Jul 15, 1997	Pradesh	QLD	Mangoes	776	20	15520	
122	Jul 17, 1997	Pradesh	NT	Pears	599	18	10782	
123	Jul 21, 1997	Pradesh	WA	Oranges	850	15	12750	
124	Jul 23, 1997	Pradesh	SA	Oranges	448	15	6720	
126	Jul 29, 1997	Pradesh	NSW	Pears	68	18	1224	
129	Aug 04, 1997	Pradesh	SA	Oranges	260	15	3900	
132	Aug 11, 1997	Pradesh	NSW	Apples	682	12.5	8525	
135	Aug 18, 1997	Pradesh	NT	Mangoes	637	20	12740	
150	Sep 08, 1997	Pradesh	NSW	Pears	954	18	17172	
153	Sep 11, 1997	Pradesh	NSW	Apples	442	12.5	5525	

Database1

Custom AutoFilter

If you want something a bit more complex, such as a range of dates, you need to do a bit more work. The following screen shows how you can manually filter the data to show a particular month. You use Data | Filter | AutoFilter, click on the drop down button beside Date and choose Custom. You can then fill in the dialog box as shown:

> The format you use when you type in dates in the Custom AutoFilter dialog box depends on your regional settings. You can use a dd/mm/yy format if you work with UK settings or an mm/dd/yy format if you work with US settings. Some formats that are more international, such as yyyy-m-d, are also recognized.

Adding Combo Boxes

You can make it even easier for a user by placing controls in the worksheet to run AutoFilter. This also gives you the opportunity to do far more with the data than filter it. You could copy the filtered data to another worksheet and generate a report, you could chart the data or you could delete it. The following screen shows two ActiveX combo box controls that allow the user to select the month and year required:

The combo boxes have the default names of ComboBox1 and ComboBox2. To place list values into the combo boxes, you can enter the list values into a worksheet column and define the ListFillRange property of the ComboBox object as something like "=Sheet2!A1:A12". Alternatively, you can use the following Workbook_Open event procedure in the ThisWorkbook module of the workbook, to populate the combo boxes when the workbook is opened:

```
Private Sub Workbook_Open()
   Dim Months
   Dim Years
   Dim i As Integer

   Months = Array("Jan", "Feb", "Mar", "Apr", "May", "Jun", "Jul", "Aug", _
                                  "Sep","Oct", "Nov", "Dec")
   Years = Array(1997, 1998, 1999)
   For i = LBound(Months) To UBound(Months)
      Sheet1.ComboBox1.AddItem Months(i)
   Next i
   Sheet1.ComboBox2.List = WorksheetFunction.Transpose(Years)
End Sub
```

The AddItem method of the ComboBox object adds the Months array values to the ComboBbox1 list. To show an alternative technique, the worksheet Transpose function is used to convert the Years array from a row to a column and the values are assigned to the List property of ComboBox2.

Note that the programmatic name of Sheet1, which you can see in the **Project Explorer** window or the **Properties** window of the VB Editor, has been used to define the location of the combo boxes. Even though the name of the worksheet is Database, the programmatic name is still Sheet1, unless you change it at the top of the **Properties** window where it is identified by **(Name)**, rather than **Name**, as shown here:

In the code module behind the worksheet, the following code is entered

```
Private Sub ComboBox1_Click()
    Call FilterDates
End Sub

Private Sub ComboBox2_Click()
    Call FilterDates
End Sub
```

When you click on an entry in their drop down lists, each combo box executes the `FilterDates` procedure, which is described below. `FilterDates` can be in the same module, and declared `Private` if you do not want any other modules to be able to use it, or it can be in a standard code module if you want to use it as a general utility procedure.

So, how do you construct the `FilterDates` procedure? As we have shown in previous chapters, you can use the macro recorder to get something to start with, and then refine the code to make it more flexible and efficient. If you use the macro recorder to record the process of filtering the dates, you will get code like this:

```
Range("A6").Select
Selection.AutoFilter
Selection.AutoFilter Field:=1, Criteria1:=">=1/01/1999", Operator:=xlAnd, _
    Criteria2:="<1/02/1999"
```

As usual, the macro recorder selects ranges and produces redundant code. If your list has the name `Database`, you can reduce this code to:

```
Range("Database").AutoFilter Field:=1, Criteria1:=">=1/01/1999", _
    Operator:=xlAnd,Criteria2:="<1/02/1999"
```

You might also notice that the dates have been translated to the format of the regional settings – in this case that of Australia, which uses the UK format. The format generated by the recorder is `d/mm/yyyy`. Also note that the dates are formatted as text, rather than dates, because the criteria must include the logical operators.

Date Format Problems

Unfortunately, the above code does not perform as expected. When you run the recorded macro, the dates are interpreted by VBA as US dates in the format `mm/dd/yyyy`. The above code selects dates greater than or equal to Jan 1, 1999 and less than Jan 2, 1999. In other words, only Jan 1, 1999. To make this macro perform properly, you need to convert the dates to a US format. Of course, you will not have this problem with your recorded code if you work with US date formats, in your regional settings, in the first place.

> **Trying to make your VBA code compatible with dates in all language versions of Excel is very difficult. See the chapter on Programming for International Clients for more details.**

The following `FilterDates` procedure, which is executed from the `Click` event procedures of the combo boxes, and which computes the start date and end date required for the criteria of the `AutoFilter` method. `FilterDates` has been placed in the same module as the combo box event procedures and declared as `Private` so that it does not appear in the Tools | Macro | Macros dialog box:

```
Private Sub FilterDates()
    Dim iStartMonth As Integer
    Dim iStartYear As Integer
    Dim dtStartDate As Date
    Dim dtEndDate As Date
    Dim stStartCriterion As String
    Dim stEndCriterion As String

    iStartMonth = Me.ComboBox1.ListIndex + 1
    iStartYear = Me.ComboBox2.Value
    dtStartDate = DateSerial(iStartYear, iStartMonth, 1)
    dtEndDate = DateSerial(iStartYear, iStartMonth + 1, 1)
    stStartCriterion = ">=" & Format(dtStartDate, "mm/dd/yyyy")
    stEndCriterion = "<" & Format(dtEndDate, "mm/dd/yyyy")
    Range("Database").AutoFilter Field:=1, Criteria1:=stStartCriterion, _
                        Operator:=xlAnd, Criteria2:=stEndCriterion
End Sub
```

FilterDates assigns the values selected in the combo boxes to iStartMonth and iStartYear. The Me keyword has been used to refer to the sheet containing the code, rather than the programmatic name Sheet1. This means that you don't need to change the sheet name if you use the code in another sheet module. iStartMonth uses the ListIndex property of ComboBox1 to obtain the month as a number. As the ListIndex is zero based, 1 is added to give the correct month number. The DateSerial function translates the year and month numbers into a date and assigns the date to dtStartDate. The second DateSerial function calculates a date that is one month ahead of dtStartDate and assigns it to dtEndDate.

The Format function is used to turn dtStartDate and dtEndDate back into strings in the US date format of mm/dd/yyyy. The appropriate logical operators are placed in front and the resulting strings are assigned to stStartCriterion and stEndCriterion, respectively. FilterDates finally executes the AutoFilter method on the range Database, using the computed criteria.

Getting the Exact Date

There is another tricky problem with AutoFilter that occurs with dates in all language versions of Excel. The problem arises when you want to get an exact date, rather than a date within a range of dates. In this case, AutoFilter matches your date with the formatted appearance of the dates in the worksheet, not the underlying date values.

Excel holds dates as numeric values equal to the number of days since Jan 1, 1900. For example, Jan 1, 1999 is held as 36161. When you ask for dates greater than or equal to Jan 1, 1999, Excel looks for date serial numbers greater than or equal to 36161. However, when you ask for dates equal to Jan 1, 1999, Excel does not look for the numeric value of the date. Excel checks for the string value "Jan 1, 1999" as it appears formatted in the worksheet.

The following adaptation of FilterDate will handle an exact date match in our list, because stExactCriterion is assigned the date value, as a string in the format "mmm dd, yyyy" and the dates are formatted in the worksheet as mmm dd, yyyy:

```
Private Sub FilterExactDate()
    Dim iExactMonth As Integer
    Dim iExactYear As Integer
    Dim dtExactDate As Date
    Dim stExactCriterion As String

    iExactMonth = Sheet1.ComboBox1.ListIndex + 1
    iExactYear = Sheet1.ComboBox2.Value
    dtExactDate = DateSerial(iExactYear, iExactMonth, 1)
    stExactCriterion = Format(dtExactDate, "mmm dd, yyyy")
    Range("Database").AutoFilter Field:=1, Criteria1:=stExactCriterion
End Sub
```

The code below will give all the entries for the first of the month, as 1 is specified as the third parameter in the DateSerial function. To select any day of the month, a third combo box could be added to cell A2 and some code added to the Workbook_Open procedure to list the correct number of days for the month specified in cell B2.

Copying the Visible Rows

If you want to make it easy to create a new worksheet containing a copy of the filtered data, you can place an ActiveX command button at the top of the worksheet and enter the following Click event procedure in the worksheet module. This procedure copies the entire Database range, knowing that, by default, only the visible cells will be copied:

```
Private Sub CommandButton1_Click()
    Dim wsNew As Worksheet
    Dim stWksName As String
    Dim stMonth As String
    Dim stYear As String
    Dim wsDummyWks As Worksheet

    stMonth = Sheet1.ComboBox1.Value
    stYear = Sheet1.ComboBox2.Value
    On Error Resume Next
    stWksName = Format(DateValue(stYear & "-" & stMonth & "-1"), "mmm yyyy")
    Set wsDummyWks = Worksheets(stWksName)
    If Err.Number = 0 Then
        MsgBox "This data has already been copied"
        Exit Sub
    End If
    On Error GoTo 0
    Set wsNew = Worksheets.Add
    Range("Database").Copy Destination:=wsNew.Range("A1")
    wsNew.Columns("A:G").AutoFit
    wsNew.Name = stWksName
End Sub
```

The Click event procedure first calculates a name for the new worksheet in the format mmm yyyy. It then checks to see if this worksheet already exists by setting a dummy object variable to refer to a worksheet with the new name. If this does not cause an error, the worksheet already exists and the procedure issues a message and exits.

If there is no worksheet with the new name, the event procedure adds a new worksheet at the end of the existing worksheets. It copies the Database range to the new sheet and AutoFits the column widths to accommodate the copied data. The procedure then names the new worksheet.

Finding the Visible Rows

When you use AutoFilter, Excel simply hides the rows that do not match the current filters. If you want to process just the rows that are visible in your code, you need to look at each row in the list and decide if it is hidden or not. There is a trick to this. When referring to the `Hidden` property of a `Range` object, the `Range` object must be an entire row, extending from column A to column IV, or an entire column, extending from row 1 to row 65536. You can't use the `Hidden` property with a single cell or a 7 column row from the list shown below.

The following code checks each row that is visible on the screen and shades the background of any row that has an invalid `Revenue` calculation:

```
Private Sub CommandButton1_Click()
   Dim rgDB As Range
   Dim rgRow As Range
   Dim dNumberSold As Double
   Dim dPrice As Double
   Dim dRevenue As Double

   With Range("Database")
      Set rgDB = .Offset(1, 0).Resize(.Rows.Count - 1)
   End With
   For Each rgRow In rgDB.Rows
      If rgRow.EntireRow.Hidden = False Then
         dNumberSold = rgRow.Cells(5).Value
         dPrice = rgRow.Cells(6).Value
         dRevenue = rgRow.Cells(7).Value
         If Abs(dNumberSold * dPrice - dRevenue) > 0.000001 Then
            rgRow.Select
            MsgBox "Error in selected row"
            rgRow.Interior.ColorIndex = 15
         End If
      End If
   Next rgRow
End Sub
```

The `Click` event procedure for the command button first defines an object variable `rgDB` referring to the range named `Database`, excluding the top row containing the field names. It then uses a `For Each...Next` loop to process all the rows in `rgDB`. The first `If` test ensures that only rows that are not hidden are processed. The `dNumberSold`, `dPrice` and `dRevenue` values for the current row are assigned to variables and the second `If` tests that the `dRevenue` figure is within a reasonable tolerance of the product of `dNumberSold` and `dPrice`.

Because worksheet computations are done with binary representations of numbers to an accuracy of about 15 significant figures, it is not always appropriate to check that two numbers are equal to the last decimal point, especially if the input figures have come from other worksheet calculations. It is better to see if they differ by an acceptably small amount. Because the difference can be positive or negative, the Abs function is used to convert both positive and negative differences to a positive difference before comparison.

If the test shows an unacceptable difference, the row is selected and a message displayed. The row is also given a background color of light gray.

Advanced Filter

The most powerful way to filter data from a list is to use Advanced Filter. You can filter the list in place, like AutoFilter, or you can extract to a different location.

The extract location can be in the same worksheet, another worksheet in the same workbook or in another open workbook. When you use Advanced Filter, you specify your criteria in a worksheet range. An example of a `Criteria` range is shown in A1:C3 of the following screen. This worksheet is in a workbook called `Extract.xls`. The data list is in the same workbook `Database.xls` that we used in the AutoFilter examples:

The top row of the `Criteria` range contains the field names from the list that you want to filter on. You can have as many rows under the field names as you need. Criteria on different rows are combined using the `OR` operator. Criteria across a row are combined using the `AND` operator. You can also use computed criteria in the form of logical statements that evaluate to `True` or `False`. In the case of computed criteria, the top row of the `Criteria` range must be empty or contain a label that is not a field name in the list, such as `Calc` in this case.

When you create computed criteria, you can refer to the data list field names in your formulas, as you can see in the formula bar above the worksheet. The formula bar shows the contents of C2, which is as follows:

```
=AND(Database.xls!Date>=$D$2,Database.xls!Date<=$E$2)
```

The formula in C3 is identical to the formula in C2.

The criteria shown are the result of this filter:

```
(State=NSW AND Date>=Jan 1, 1999 AND Date<Mar 1, 1999) OR _
             (State=VIC AND Date>=Jan 1, 1999 AND Date<Mar 1, 1999)
```

As the data list is in the file Database.xls, the references to the Date field are entered as external references, in the same format you would use to refer to workbook names in another workbook. Because the field names are not workbook names, the formulas evaluate to a #NAME? error.

To facilitate the Advanced Filter, the data list in the Database.xls workbook has been named Database. In the Extract.xls workbook, A1:C3 has been named Criteria and A6:G6 has been named Extract. If you carry out the Advanced Filter manually, using Data | Filter | Advanced Filter, you see the following dialog box, where you can enter the names as shown:

To automate this process, the command button with the **Extract** caption runs the following Click event procedure:

```
Private Sub CommandButton1_Click()
    Dim rgDB As Range
    Dim rgCriteria As Range
    Dim rgExtract As Range

    Set rgDB = Workbooks("Database.xls").Worksheets("Database") _
        .Range("Database")
    Set rgCriteria = ThisWorkbook.Worksheets(1).Range("Criteria")
    Set rgExtract = ThisWorkbook.Worksheets(1).Range("Extract")
    rgDB.AdvancedFilter Action:=xlFilterCopy, CriteriaRange:=rgCriteria, _
        CopyToRange:=rgExtract
End Sub
```

The event procedure defines three object variables referring to the Database, Criteria and Extract ranges. It then runs the AdvancedFilter method of the Database Range object.

Summary

The Data Form feature makes it very easy to set up a data maintenance macro. However, you should apply the name Database to your data list if the top left hand corner of the list is not in the range A1:B2.

As you have seen, the AutoFilter and Advanced Filter features can be combined with VBA code to provide flexible ways for users to extract information from data lists. By teaming these features with ActiveX controls, such as combo boxes and command buttons, you can make them readily accessible to all levels of users. You can use the macro recorder to get an indication of the required methods and adapt the recorded code to accept input from the ActiveX controls.

However, you need to take care, if you work with non-US date formats. You need to bear in mind that VBA requires you to use US date formats when you compare ranges of dates using AutoFilter. If this interests you, you should check out Chapter 16, which deals with international programming issues.

Also, when you want to detect which rows have been hidden by AutoFilter, you need to be aware that the Hidden property of the Range object can only be applied to entire worksheet rows.

Advanced Filter provides the most powerful filtering in Excel. You can set up much more complex criteria with Advanced Filter than you can with AutoFilter and you can copy filtered data to a specified range. You can also use Advanced Filter to copy filtered data from one workbook to another.

Generating Charts

In this chapter we will see how you can use the macro recorder to discover what objects, methods and properties are required to manipulate charts. We will then improve and extend that code to make it more flexible and efficient. This chapter is designed to show you how to gain access to Chart objects in VBA code so that you can start to program the vast number of objects that Excel charts contain. You can find more information on these objects in the Reference section. We will look specifically at:

- ❑ Creating Chart objects on separate sheets
- ❑ Creating Chart objects embedded in a worksheet
- ❑ Editing data series in charts
- ❑ Defining series with arrays
- ❑ Defining chart labels linked to worksheet cells

You can create two types of charts in Excel, charts that occupy their own chart sheets and charts that are embedded in a worksheet. They can be manipulated in code in much the same way. The only difference is that, while the chart sheet is a Chart object in its own right, the chart embedded in a worksheet is contained by a ChartObject object. Each ChartObject on a worksheet is a member of the worksheet's ChartObjects collection. Chart sheets are members of the workbook's Charts collection.

Each ChartObject is a member of the Shapes collection, as well as a member of the ChartObjects collection. The Shapes collection provides you with an alternative way to refer to embedded charts. The macro recorder generates code that uses the Shapes collection rather than the ChartObjects collection.

Chart Sheets

If you want to create a new chart sheet called Mangoes, you can turn on the macro recorder while using the Chart Wizard to create a chart from the following data in cells A3:D7. In Step 2 of the Chart Wizard, choose the "Series in Rows" option. In Step 4 of the Chart Wizard, choose the "As new sheet" option and enter the name of the chart sheet as "Mangoes":

The following screen shows the chart created:

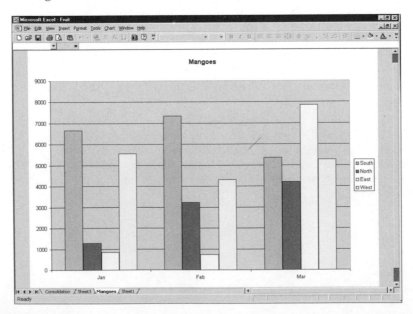

Using the Macro Recorder

The recorded macro should look like the following:

```
Charts.Add
ActiveChart.ChartType = xlColumnClustered
ActiveChart.SetSourceData Source:=Sheets("Sheet1").Range("A3:D7"), _
                                              PlotBy:= xlRows
ActiveChart.Location Where:=xlLocationAsNewSheet, Name:="Mangoes"

With ActiveChart
    .HasTitle = True
    .ChartTitle.Characters.Text = "Mangoes"
    .Axes(xlCategory, xlPrimary).HasTitle = False
    .Axes(xlValue, xlPrimary).HasTitle = False
End With
```

The recorded macro uses the Add method of the Charts collection to create a new chart. It defines the active chart's ChartType property, and then uses the SetSourceData method to define the ranges plotted. The macro uses the Location method to define the chart as a chart sheet and assign it a name. It sets the HasTitle property to True so that it can define the ChartTitle property. Finally, it sets the HasTitle property of the axes back to False, a step which is not necessary.

Adding a Chart Sheet Using VBA Code

The recorded code is reasonably good as it stands. However, it is more elegant to create an object variable, so that you have a simple and efficient short cut way to refer to the chart in subsequent code. You can also remove some of the redundant code and add a chart title that is linked to the worksheet. The following code incorporates these changes:

```
Sub AddChartSheet()
    Dim Cht As Chart

    Set Cht = Charts.Add
    With Cht
        .Name = "Mangoes"
        .ChartType = xlColumnClustered
        .SetSourceData Source:=Sheets("Sheet1").Range("A3:D7"), PlotBy:=xlRows
        .HasTitle = True
        .ChartTitle.Text = "=Sheet1!R3C1"
    End With
End Sub
```

The Location method has been removed, as it is not necessary. A chart sheet is produced by default. The Chart Wizard does not allow you to enter a formula to define a title in the chart, but you can separately record changing the chart title to a formula to discover that you need to set the Text property of the ChartTitle object equal to the formula. In the above code, the chart title has been defined as a formula referring to the A3 cell.

> When you enter a formula into a chart text element, it must be defined using the R1C1 addressing method, not the A1 addressing method.

Embedded Charts

When you create a chart embedded as a `ChartObject`, it is a good idea to name the `ChartObject` so that it can be easily referenced in later code. You can do this by manually selecting a worksheet cell, so that the chart is not selected, then holding down *Ctrl* and clicking the chart. This selects the `ChartObject`, rather than the chart, and you will see its name to the left of the formula bar at the top of the screen. This is how you can tell that you have selected the `ChartObject`: not only does its name appear on the formula bar, but you will also see white boxes at each corner of the embedded chart and the middle of each edge, as shown below. If you select the *chart*, rather than the `ChartObject`, you will see black boxes.

You can select and change the name of the `ChartObject` and press *Enter* to update it. The following embedded chart was created using the Chart Wizard. It was then dragged to its new location and its name changed to `MangoesChart`.

Using the Macro Recorder

If you select cells A3:D7 and turn on the macro recorder while creating the chart above, including moving the `ChartObject` to the required location and changing its name to `MangoesChart`, you will get code like the following:

```
Charts.Add
ActiveChart.ChartType = xlColumnClustered
ActiveChart.SetSourceData Source:=Sheets("Sheet1").Range("A3:D7"), _
                                          PlotBy:= xlRows
ActiveChart.Location Where:=xlLocationAsObject, Name:="Sheet1"
With ActiveChart
    .HasTitle = True
    .ChartTitle.Characters.Text = "Mangoes"
    .Axes(xlCategory, xlPrimary).HasTitle = False
    .Axes(xlValue, xlPrimary).HasTitle = False
End With
ActiveSheet.Shapes("Chart 30").IncrementLeft 65.25
ActiveSheet.Shapes("Chart 30").IncrementTop -54.75
ActiveWindow.Visible = False
Windows("Charts.xls").Activate
Range("F17").Select
ActiveSheet.Shapes("Chart 30").Select
Selection.Name = "MangoesChart"
```

The recorded macro is similar to the one that created a chart sheet, down to the definition of the chart title, except that it uses the Location method to define the chart as an embedded chart. Up to the End With, the recorded code is reusable. However, the code to relocate the ChartObject and change its name is not reusable. The code uses the default name applied to the ChartObject to identify the ChartObject. (Note that the recorder prefers to refer to a ChartObject as a Shape object, which is an alternative that we pointed out at the beginning of this chapter.) If you try to run this code again, or adapt it to create another chart, it will fail on the reference to Chart 30. How to refer to the ChartObject itself is not as obvious as how to refer to the active chart sheet.

Adding an Embedded Chart Using VBA Code

The following code uses the Parent property of the embedded chart to identify the ChartObject containing the chart:

```
Sub AddChart()
    Dim Cht As Chart

    ActiveSheet.ChartObjects.Delete
    Set Cht = Charts.Add
    Set Cht = Cht.Location(Where:=xlLocationAsObject, Name:="Sheet1")
    With Cht
        .ChartType = xlColumnClustered
        .SetSourceData Source:=Sheets("Sheet1").Range("A3:D7"), PlotBy:= xlRows
        .HasTitle = True
        .ChartTitle.Text = "=Sheet1!R3C1"
        With .Parent
            .Top = Range("F3").Top
            .Left = Range("F3").Left
            .Name = "MangoesChart"
        End With
    End With
End Sub
```

AddChart first deletes any existing ChartObjects. It then creates an object variable Cht to refer to the added chart. By default, the new chart is on a chart sheet, so the Location method is used to define the chart as an embedded chart.

> When you use the Location method of the Chart object, the Chart object is re-created and any reference to the original Chart object is destroyed. Therefore, it is necessary to assign the return value of the Location method to the Cht object variable so that it refers to the new Chart object.

AddChart defines the chart type, source data, and chart title. Again, the chart title has been assigned a formula referring to cell **A3**. Using the Parent property of the Chart object to refer to the ChartObject object, AddChart sets the Top and Left properties of the ChartObject to be the same as the Top and Left properties of cell **F3**. AddChart finally assigns the new name to the ChartObject so that it can be easily referenced in the future.

Editing Data Series

The SetSourceData method of the Chart object is the quickest way to define a completely new set of data for a chart. You can also manipulate individual series using the Series object, which is a member of the chart's SeriesCollection object. The following example is designed to show you how to access individual series.

We will take the `MangoesChart` and delete all the series from it, and then replace them with four new series, one at a time. The new chart will contain product information for a region nominated by the user. To make it easier to locate each set of product data, names have been assigned to each product range in the worksheet. For example, A3:D7 has been given the name `Mangoes`, corresponding to the label in A3. The final chart will be similar to the following:

The following code converts `MangoesChart` to include the new data:

```
Sub MangoesToRegion()
    Dim ctObject As ChartObject
    Dim Cht As Chart
    Dim scSeries As SeriesCollection
    Dim i As Integer
    Dim j As Integer
    Dim rgY As Range
    Dim rgX As Range
    Dim vaProducts As Variant
    Dim vaRegions As Variant
    Dim iRegion As Integer
    Dim vaAnswer As Variant

    vaProducts = Array("Mangoes", "Bananas", "Lychees", "Rambutan")
    vaRegions = Array("South", "North", "East", "West")

    'Determine that MangoesChart exists
    On Error Resume Next
    Set ctObject = Worksheets("Sheet1").ChartObjects("MangoesChart")
    If ctObject Is Nothing Then
        MsgBox "MangoesChart was not found - procedure aborted", vbCritical
        Exit Sub
    End If
    On Error GoTo 0
```

```
    'Get Region number
    Do
        vaAnswer = InputBox("Enter Region number (1 to 4)")
        If vaAnswer = "" Then Exit Sub
        If vaAnswer >= 1 And vaAnswer <= 4 Then
            Exit Do
        Else
            MsgBox "Region must be be 1, 2, 3 or 4", vbCritical
        End If
    Loop
    iRegion = CInt(vaAnswer)

    'Set up new chart
    Set Cht = ctObject.Chart
    Set scSeries = Cht.SeriesCollection
    'Delete all existing chart series
    For i = scSeries.Count To 1 Step -1
        scSeries(i).Delete
    Next i

    'Add Products for Region
    For i = LBound(vaProducts) To UBound(vaProducts)
        Set rgY = Range(vaProducts(i)).Offset(iRegion, 1).Resize(1, 3)
        Set rgX = Range(vaProducts(i)).Offset(0, 1).Resize(1, 3)
        With scSeries.NewSeries
            .Name = vaProducts(i)
            .Values = rgY
            .XValues = "=" & rgX.Address _
                (RowAbsolute:=True, _
                 ColumnAbsolute:=True, _
                 ReferenceStyle:=xlR1C1, _
                 External:=True)
        End With
    Next i
    Cht.ChartTitle.Text = vaRegions(iRegion - Array(0, 1)(1))
    ctObject.Name = "RegionChart"
End Sub
```

As MangoesToRegion is a fairly long procedure, we will examine it in sections. After
the variable declarations comes the following code:

```
    vaProducts = Array("Mangoes", "Bananas", "Lychees", "Rambutan")
    vaRegions = Array("South", "North", "East", "West")

    'Determine that MangoesChart exists
    On Error Resume Next
    Set ctObject = Worksheets("Sheet1").ChartObjects("MangoesChart")
    If ctObject Is Nothing Then
        MsgBox "MangoesChart was not found - procedure aborted", vbCritical
        Exit Sub
    End If
    On Error GoTo 0
```

MangoesToRegion first assigns the product names to vaProducts and the region
names to vaRegions. It then tries to set the ctObject object variable by assigning
the variable a reference to the ChartObject named MangoesChart. If this fails, the
procedure is aborted. As it is not the main point of the exercise, this section of code has
been kept very simple.

```
    'Get Region number
    Do
        vaAnswer = InputBox("Enter Region number (1 to 4)")
        If vaAnswer = "" Then Exit Sub
        If vaAnswer >= 1 And vaAnswer <= 4 Then
            Exit Do
        Else
            MsgBox "Region must be be 1, 2, 3 or 4", vbCritical
        End If
    Loop
    iRegion = CInt(Answer)
```

The user is then asked to enter the region number. The `Do...Loop` will continue until the user presses **Cancel**, presses **OK** without entering anything or enters a number between 1 and 4. If a number between 1 and 4 is entered, the value is converted to an integer value, using the `CInt` function, and assigned to `iRegion`.

```
'Set up new chart
Set Cht = ctObject.Chart
Set scSeries = Cht.SeriesCollection
'Delete all existing chart series
For i = scSeries.Count To 1 Step -1
    scSeries(i).Delete
Next i
```

Next, `Cht` is assigned a reference to the `chart` in the `ChartObject`. Then `scSeries` is assigned a reference to the `SeriesCollection` in the chart. The following `For...Next` loop deletes all the members of the collection. This is done backwards because if you delete the lower number series first, the item numbers of the higher series automatically decrease and there will be no series 3 when you try to delete it, which will cause a run time error.

```
'Add Products for Region
For i = LBound(vaProducts) To UBound(vaProducts)
    Set rgY = Range(vaProducts(i)).Offset(iRegion, 1).Resize(1, 3)
    Set rgX = Range(vaProducts(i)).Offset(0, 1).Resize(1, 3)
    With scSeries.NewSeries
        .Name = vaProducts(i)
        .Values = rgY
        .XValues = "=" & rgX.Address _
            (RowAbsolute:=True, _
             ColumnAbsolute:=True, _
             ReferenceStyle:=xlR1C1, _
             External:=True)
    End With
Next i
```

The following `For...Next` loop adds a new series to the chart for each product. The loop uses the `UBound` and `LBound` functions to avoid having to know the `Option Base` setting for the module. The range object `rgY` is assigned a reference to the chosen region data within the current product data.

`Range(vaProducts(i))` refers to the product table with the worksheet name corresponding to `vaProducts(i)`. `iRegion` is used as the row offset into the product data to refer to the correct region data. The column offset is one so that the name of the region is excluded from the data. `Resize` ensures that the data range has one row and three columns. The range object `rgX` is assigned a reference to the month names at the top of the product data table.

Following the `With` statement, `MangoesToRegion` uses the `NewSeries` method to add a new empty series to the chart. The `NewSeries` method returns a reference to the new series, which supplies the `With...End With` reference that is used by the lines between `With` and `End With`. The `Name` property of the series, which appears in the legend, is assigned the current product name.

The `Values` property of the new series is assigned a reference to `rgY`. The `XValues` property could have been assigned a direct reference to `rgX` in the same way. However, both properties can also be defined by a formula reference, as long as it is an external reference in the R1C1 style. This code has been written to show how this can be done, as it is necessary to do this with some other properties, such as the `ChartTitle` property when you want it to refer to a worksheet cell. The string value generated and assigned to the `Mangoes` series `XValues` property is:

```
=Sheet1!R3C2:R3C4
```

The final section of code is as follows:

```
Cht.ChartTitle.Text = vaRegions(iRegion - Array(0, 1)(1))
ctObject.Name = "RegionChart"
```

The `ChartTitle.Text` property is assigned the appropriate string value in the `vaRegions` array, using the value of `iRegion` as an index to the array. To avoid having to know the `Option Base` setting for the module, `Array(0,1)(1)` has been used to adjust the index value in `iRegion`, which ranges from 1 to 4. If the `Option Base` setting is zero, this expression returns a value of one, which adjusts the value of `iRegion` such that it ranges from 0 to 3. If the `Option Base` setting is one, the expression returns zero, which does not change the `iRegion` value so that it still has the range of 1 to 4. Another way to handle the `Option Base` is to use the following code:

```
Cht.ChartTitle.Text = vaRegions(iRegion - 1 + LBound(vaRegions))
```

The code finally changes the name of the `ChartObject` to `RegionChart`.

Defining Chart Series with Arrays

A chart series can be defined by assigning a VBA array to its `Values` property. This can come in handy if you want to generate a chart that is not linked to the original data. The chart can be distributed in a separate workbook that is independent of the source data.

The following screen shows a chart of the `Mangoes` data. You can see the definition of the first data series in the formula bar above the worksheet. The month names and the values on the vertical axis are defined by Excel arrays. The region names have been assigned as text to the series names.

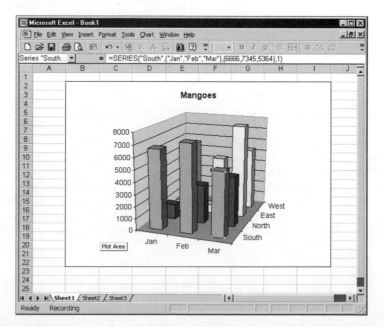

The 3D chart can be created using the following code:

```
Sub MakeArrayChart()
    Dim wsSource As Worksheet
    Dim rgSource As Range
    Dim Wkb As Workbook
    Dim Wks As Worksheet
    Dim Cht As Chart
    Dim seNewSeries As Series
    Dim i As Integer
    Dim vaSalesArray As Variant
    Dim vaMonthArray As Variant

    vaMonthArray = Array("Jan", "Feb", "Mar")
    Set wsSource = ThisWorkbook.Worksheets("Sheet1")
    Set rgSource = wsSource.Range("Mangoes")
    Set Wkb = Workbooks.Add
    Set Wks = Wkb.Worksheets(1)
    Set Cht = Wkb.Charts.Add
    Set Cht = Cht.Location(Where:=xlLocationAsObject, Name:="Sheet1")
    With Cht
        .ChartType = xl3DColumn
        For i = 1 To 4
            Set seNewSeries = .SeriesCollection.NewSeries
            vaSalesArray = rgSource.Offset(i, 1).Resize(1, 3).Value
            seNewSeries.Values = vaSalesArray
            seNewSeries.XValues = vaMonthArray
            seNewSeries.Name = rgSource.Cells(i + 1, 1).Value
        Next i
        .HasLegend = False
        .HasTitle = True
        .ChartTitle.Text = "Mangoes"
        With .Parent
            .Top = Wks.Range("B2").Top
            .Left = Wks.Range("B2").Left
            .Width = Wks.Range("B2:I22").Width
            .Height = Wks.Range("B2:I22").Height
            .Name = "ArrayChart"
        End With
    End With
End Sub
```

The first section of code in MakeArrayChart is as follows:

```
    vaMonthArray = Array("Jan", "Feb", "Mar")
    Set wsSource = ThisWorkbook.Worksheets("Sheet1")
    Set rgSource = wsSource.Range("Mangoes")
    Set Wkb = Workbooks.Add
    Set Wks = Wkb.Worksheets(1)
    Set Cht = Wkb.Charts.Add
    Set Cht = Cht.Location(Where:=xlLocationAsObject, Name:="Sheet1")
```

MakeArrayChart assigns the month names to vaMonthArray. This data could have come from the worksheet, if required, like the sales data. A reference to the worksheet that is the source of the data is assigned to wsSource. The Mangoes range is assigned to rgSource. A new workbook is created for the chart and a reference to it is assigned to Wkb. A reference to the first worksheet in the new workbook is assigned to Wks. A new chart is added to the Charts collection in Wkb and a reference to it assigned to Cht. The Location method converts the chart to an embedded chart and redefines Cht.

```
With Cht
    .ChartType = xl3DColumn
    For i = 1 To 4
        Set seNewSeries = .SeriesCollection.NewSeries
        vaSalesArray = rgSource.Offset(i, 1).Resize(1, 3).Value
        seNewSeries.Values = vaSalesArray
        seNewSeries.XValues = vaMonthArray
        seNewSeries.Name = rgSource.Cells(i + 1, 1).Value
    Next i
    .HasLegend = False
    .HasTitle = True
    .ChartTitle.Text = "Mangoes"
    With .Parent
        .Top = Wks.Range("B2").Top
        .Left = Wks.Range("B2").Left
        .Width = Wks.Range("B2:I22").Width
        .Height = Wks.Range("B2:I22").Height
        .Name = "ArrayChart"
    End With
End With
End Sub
```

In the `With...End With` structure, the `ChartType` property of `Cht` is changed to a 3D column type. The `For...Next` loop creates the four new series. Each time around the loop, a new series is created with the `NewSeries` method. The region data from the appropriate row is directly assigned to the variant `vaSalesArray` and `vaSalesArray` is immediately assigned to `Values` property of the new series.

`vaMonthArray` is assigned to the `XValues` property of the new series. The text in column A of the `Mangoes` range is assigned to the `Name` property of the new series.

The code then removes the chart legend, which is added by default, and sets the chart title. The final code operates on the `ChartObject`, which is the chart's parent, to place the chart exactly over B2:I22, and name the chart `ArrayChart`.

Chart Labels

In Excel, it is easy to add data labels to a chart, as long as the labels are based on the data series values or X-axis values. These options are available using Chart | Chart Options.

You can also enter your own text as labels, or you can enter formulas into each label to refer to cells, but this involves a lot of manual work. You would need to add standard labels to the series and then individually select each one and either replace it with your own text, or click in the formula bar and enter a formula. Alternatively, you can write a macro to do it for you.

The screen opposite shows a chart of sales figures for each month, with the name of the top salesperson for each month. The labels have been defined by formulas linked to row 4 of the worksheet, as you can see for Jenny in April. The formula in the formula bar points to cell E4.

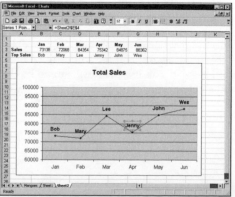

You can add the data label formulas using the following code:

```
Sub AddDataLabels()
    Dim seSales As Series
    Dim Pts As Points
    Dim Pt As Point
    Dim Rng As Range
    Dim i As Integer

    Set Rng = Range("B4:G4")
    Set seSales = ActiveSheet.ChartObjects(1).Chart.SeriesCollection(1)
    seSales.HasDataLabels = True
    Set Pts = seSales.Points
    For Each Pt In Pts
        i = i + 1
        Pt.DataLabel.Text = "=" & Rng.Cells(i).Address _
                (RowAbsolute:=True, _
                 ColumnAbsolute:=True, _
                 ReferenceStyle:=xlR1C1, _
                 External:=True)
        Pt.DataLabel.Font.Bold = True
        Pt.DataLabel.Position = xlLabelPositionAbove
    Next Pt
End Sub
```

The object variable Rng is assigned a reference to **B4:G4**. seSales is assigned a reference to the first, and only, series in the embedded chart and the HasDataLabels property of the series is set to True. The For Each...Next loop processes each point in the data series. For each point, the code assigns a formula to the Text property of the points data label. The formula refers to the worksheet cell as an external reference in R1C1 format. The data label is also made bold and the label positioned above the data point.

Summary

It is easy to create a programmatic reference to a chart on a chart sheet. The Chart object is a member of the Charts collection of the workbook. To reference a chart embedded in a worksheet, you need to be aware that the Chart object is contained in a ChartObject object that belongs to the ChartObjects collection of the worksheet.

You can move or resize an embedded chart by changing the Top, Left, Width and Height properties of the ChartObject. If you already have a reference to the Chart object, you can get a reference to the ChartObject object through the Parent property of the Chart object.

Individual series in a chart are Series objects and belong to the SeriesCollection object of the chart. You use the Delete method of the Series object to delete a series from a chart. You use the NewSeries method of the SeriesCollection object to add a new series to a chart.

You can assign a VBA array, rather than the more commonly used Range object, to the Values property of a Series object. This creates a chart that is independent of worksheet data and can be distributed without a supporting worksheet.

The data points in a chart are `Point` objects and belong to the `Points` collection of the `Series` object. Excel does not provide an easy way to link cell values to labels on series data points through the user interface. However, links can be easily established to data point labels using VBA code.

Event Procedures

Excel makes it very easy for you to write code that runs when a range of worksheet, chart sheet and workbook events occur. In previous chapters, we have already seen how to highlight the active row and column of a worksheet by placing code in the `Worksheet_SelectionChange` event procedure (Primer – Excel Object Model). This runs every time the user selects a new range of cells. We have also seen how to synchronize the worksheets in a workbook using the `Worksheet_Deactivate` and `Worksheet_Activate` events (see Chapter 4).

It is easy to create these workbook, chart sheet and worksheet events, because Excel automatically provides you with code modules for these objects. However, note that the chart events that are supplied automatically in a chart module apply only to chart sheets, not to embedded charts. If you want to write event procedures for embedded charts, you can do so, but it takes a bit more knowledge and effort. There are also many other high level events that can be accessed, for the `Application` object, for example. These events will be covered later on in Chapters 13 and 17 (Class Modules and Programming the VBE). Events associated with controls and forms will also be treated in their own chapters. In this chapter we will look, in more detail, at worksheet, chart and workbook events and related issues.

Worksheet Events

The following worksheet event procedures are available in the code module behind each worksheet:

```
Private Sub Worksheet_Activate()

Private Sub Worksheet_BeforeDoubleClick(ByVal Target As
Range, Cancel As Boolean)

Private Sub Worksheet_BeforeRightClick(ByVal Target As
Range, Cancel As Boolean)

Private Sub Worksheet_Calculate()

Private Sub Worksheet_Change(ByVal Target As Range)

Private Sub Worksheet_Deactivate()

Private Sub Worksheet_FollowHyperlink(ByVal Target As
Hyperlink)

Private Sub Worksheet_SelectionChange(ByVal Target As
Range)
```

You should use the drop down menus at the top of the code module to create the first and last lines of any procedure you want to use. For example, in a worksheet code module, you can select the Worksheet object from the left hand drop down list. This will generate the following lines of code:

```
Private Sub Worksheet_SelectionChange(ByVal Target As Range)

End Sub
```

The SelectionChange event is the default event for the Worksheet object. If you want a different event, select the event from the right hand drop down list.

As an alternative to using the drop downs, you can type the first line of the procedure yourself, but you can easily make mistakes. The arguments must correspond, in number, order and type with those shown above. You are permitted to use different parameter names, if you wish, but it is better to stick with the standard names to avoid confusion.

Most parameters must be declared with the ByVal keyword, which prevents your code passing back changes to the object or item referenced by assigning a new value to the parameter. If the parameter represents an object, you can change the object's properties and execute its methods, but you cannot pass back a change in the object definition by assigning a new object definition to the parameter.

Some event procedures are executed before the associated event occurs and have a Cancel parameter that is passed by reference. You can assign a value of True to the Cancel parameter to cancel the associated event. For example, you could prevent a user accessing the worksheet shortcut menu by canceling the RightClick event in the Worksheet_BeforeRightClick event procedure:

```
Private Sub Worksheet_BeforeRightClick(ByVal Target As Range, _
                                       Cancel As Boolean)
    Cancel = True
End Sub
```

Enable Events

It is important to turn off event handling in some event procedures to prevent a chain reaction occurring. For example, if a worksheet Change event procedure changes the worksheet, it will itself trigger the Change event and run itself again. The event procedure will change the worksheet again and trigger the Change event again, and so on. If only one event procedure is involved, Excel 2000 will usually detect the chain reaction and terminate it after some hundreds of cycles (whereas Excel 97 would stop after about 40). If more than one event procedure is involved, the process can continue indefinitely or until you press *Esc* or *Ctrl+Break* enough times to stop each process. For example, there could be a Calculation event procedure active as well as a Change event procedure. If both procedures change a cell that is referenced in a calculation, both events are triggered into an interactive chain reaction. That is, the first event triggers the second event, which triggers the first event again, and so on. The following Change event procedure makes sure that it does not cause a chain reaction by turning off event handling while it changes the worksheet. It is important to turn event handling back on again before the procedure ends:

```
Private Sub Worksheet_Change(ByVal Target As Range)
    Application.EnableEvents = False
    Range("A1").Value = 100
    Application.EnableEvents = True
End Sub
```

> **Application.EnableEvents = False** does not affect events outside
> the Excel object model. Events associated with ActiveX controls and user
> forms, for example, will continue to occur.

Worksheet Calculate

You could use the Worksheet_Calculate event to warn you, as you enter new data
assumptions into a forecast, when key results go outside their expected range of
values. In the following worksheet, you want to know when the profit figure in cell N8
exceeds 600 or is lower than 500:

The following event procedure runs every time the worksheet recalculates, checks cell
N8, which has been named FinalProfit, and generates messages if the figure goes
outside the required band of values:

```
Private Sub Worksheet_Calculate()
  Dim dProfit As Double

  dProfit = Sheet2.Range("FinalProfit").Value
  If dProfit > 600 Then
    MsgBox "Profit has risen to " & Format(dProfit, "#,##0.0")
  ElseIf dProfit < 500 Then
    MsgBox "Profit has fallen to " & Format(dProfit, "#,##0.0")
  End If
End Sub
```

Chart Events

The following chart event procedures are available in the code module behind each
chart:

```
Private Sub Chart_Activate()

Private Sub Chart_BeforeDoubleClick(ByVal ElementID As
XlChartItem, ByVal Arg1 As Long, ByVal Arg2 As Long,
Cancel As Boolean)
```

```
Private Sub Chart_BeforeRightClick(Cancel As Boolean)

Private Sub Chart_Calculate()

Private Sub Chart_Deactivate()

Private Sub Chart_DragOver()

Private Sub Chart_DragPlot()

Private Sub Chart_MouseDown(ByVal Button As
XlMouseButton, ByVal Shift As Long, ByVal x As Long,
ByVal y As Long)

Private Sub Chart_MouseMove(ByVal Button As
XlMouseButton, ByVal Shift As Long, ByVal x As Long,
ByVal y As Long)

Private Sub Chart_MouseUp(ByVal Button As XlMouseButton,
ByVal Shift As Long, ByVal x As Long, ByVal y As Long)

Private Sub Chart_Resize()

Private Sub Chart_Select(ByVal ElementID As XlChartItem,
ByVal Arg1 As Long, ByVal Arg2 As Long)

Private Sub Chart_SeriesChange(ByVal SeriesIndex As Long,
ByVal PointIndex As Long)
```

Before Double Click

Normally, when you double-click a chart element, you open the formatting dialog box
for the element. You could provide some short cut formatting by trapping the double-
click event and writing your own code.

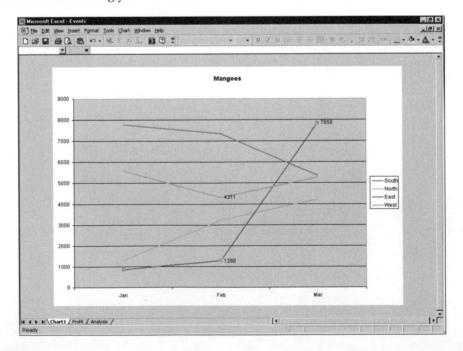

The following event procedure formats three chart elements when they are double-clicked. If, in the chart shown above, you double-click the legend, it is removed. If you double-click the chart area (around the outside of the plot area), the legend is displayed. If you double-click a series line with all points selected, it changes the color of the line. If a single point in the series is selected, the data label at the point is toggled on and off:

```
Private Sub Chart_BeforeDoubleClick(ByVal ElementID As XlChartItem, _
             ByVal Arg1 As Long, ByVal Arg2 As Long, Cancel As Boolean)
    Dim Srs As Series

    Select Case ElementID
        Case xlLegend
            Me.HasLegend = False
            Cancel = True
        Case xlChartArea
            Me.HasLegend = True
            Cancel = True
        Case xlSeries
            'Arg1 is the Series index
            'Arg2 is the Point index (-1 if the entire series is selected)
            Set Srs = Me.SeriesCollection(Arg1)
            If Arg2 = -1 Then
                With Srs.Border
                    If .ColorIndex = xlColorIndexAutomatic Then
                        .ColorIndex = 1
                    Else
                        .ColorIndex = (.ColorIndex Mod 56) + 1
                    End If
                End With
            Else
                With Srs.Points(Arg2)
                    .HasDataLabel = Not .HasDataLabel
                End With
            End If
            Cancel = True
    End Select
End Sub
```

The ElementID parameter returns an identifying number to indicate the element that was double clicked. You can use intrinsic constants, such as xlLegend, to determine the element. At the end of each case, Cancel is assigned True so that the default double-click event is cancelled and the formatting dialog box does not appear.

Note the use of the keyword Me to refer to the object associated with the code module. Using Me instead of Chart1 makes the code transportable to other charts.

If the chart element is a series, Arg1 contains the series index in the SeriesCollection and Arg2 contains the point index if a single point in the series has been selected. Arg2 is −1 if the whole series is selected. If the whole series is selected, the event procedure assigns 1 to the color index of the series border, if the color index is automatic. If the color index is not automatic, it increases the color index by 1. As there are only 56 colors available, the procedure uses the Mod operator, which divides the color index by 56 and gives the remainder, before adding 1. The only color index value that is affected by this is 56. 56 Mod 56 returns zero, which means that the next color index after 56 is 1.

If a single point is selected in the series, the procedure toggles the data label for the point. If the HasDataLabel property of the point is True, Not converts it to False. If the HasDataLabel property of the point is False, Not converts it to True.

Workbook Events

The following workbook event procedures are available:

```
Private Sub Workbook_Activate()

Private Sub Workbook_AddinInstall()

Private Sub Workbook_AddinUninstall()

Private Sub Workbook_BeforeClose(Cancel As Boolean)

Private Sub Workbook_BeforePrint(Cancel As Boolean)

Private Sub Workbook_BeforeSave(ByVal SaveAsUI As
Boolean, Cancel As Boolean)

Private Sub Workbook_Deactivate()

Private Sub Workbook_NewSheet(ByVal Sh As Object)

Private Sub Workbook_Open()

Private Sub Workbook_SheetActivate(ByVal Sh As Object)

Private Sub Workbook_SheetBeforeDoubleClick(ByVal Sh As
Object, ByVal Target As Range, Cancel As Boolean)

Private Sub Workbook_SheetBeforeRightClick(ByVal Sh As
Object, ByVal Target As Range, Cancel As Boolean)

Private Sub Workbook_SheetCalculate(ByVal Sh As Object)

Private Sub Workbook_SheetChange(ByVal Sh As Object,
ByVal Target As Range)

Private Sub Workbook_SheetDeactivate(ByVal Sh As Object)

Private Sub Workbook_SheetFollowHyperlink(ByVal Sh As
Object, ByVal Target As Hyperlink)

Private Sub Workbook_SheetSelectionChange(ByVal Sh As
Object, ByVal Target As Range)

Private Sub Workbook_WindowActivate(ByVal Wn As Window)

Private Sub Workbook_WindowDeactivate(ByVal Wn As Window)

Private Sub Workbook_WindowResize(ByVal Wn As Window)
```

Some of the workbook event procedures are the same as the worksheet and chart event procedures. The difference is that when you create these procedures (such as the Change event procedure) in a worksheet or chart, it applies to only that sheet. When you create a workbook event procedure (such as the SheetChange event procedure) it applies to all the sheets in the workbook.

One of the most commonly used workbook event procedures is the Open event procedure. This is used to initialize the workbook when it opens. You can use it to set the calculation mode, establish screen settings, alter the menu structure, decide what toolbars should appear or enter data into combo boxes or list boxes in the worksheets for example.

Similarly, the `Workbook_BeforeClose` event procedure can be used to tidy up when the workbook is closed. It can restore screen and menu settings, for example. It can also be used to prevent a workbook's closure by setting `Cancel` to `True`. The following event procedure will only allow the workbook to close if the figure in the cell named `FinalProfit` is between 500 and 600:

```
Private Sub Workbook_BeforeClose(Cancel As Boolean)
    Dim dProfit As Double

    dProfit = ThisWorkbook.Worksheets(1).Range("FinalProfit").Value
    If dProfit < 500 Or dProfit > 600 Then
        MsgBox "Profit must be in the range 500 to 600"
        Cancel = True
    End If
End Sub
```

> Note that if you assign `True` to `Cancel` in the workbook `BeforeClose` event procedure, you also prevent Excel closing.

Save Changes

If you want to make sure that all changes are saved when the workbook closes, but you don't want the user to be prompted to save changes, you can save the workbook in the `BeforeClose` event procedure. You can check to see if this is really necessary using the `Saved` property of the workbook, which will be `False` if there are unsaved changes.

```
Private Sub Workbook_BeforeClose(Cancel As Boolean)
    If Not ThisWorkbook.Saved Then
        ThisWorkbook.Save
    End If
End Sub
```

If, on the other hand, you want to throw away any changes to the workbook and you don't want users to be prompted to save changes in a workbook when they close it, you can set the `Saved` property of the workbook to `True` in the `BeforeClose` event procedure:

```
Private Sub Workbook_BeforeClose(Cancel As Boolean)
    ThisWorkbook.Saved = True
End Sub
```

This fools Excel into thinking that any changes have been saved.

Headers and Footers

A common need, in Excel, is to have information in the print header or footer that either comes from the worksheet cells, or is not available in the standard header and footer options. You might want to insert a company name that is part of the data in the worksheet and display the full path to the workbook file.

You can insert this information using the `BeforePrint` event procedure to ensure it is always up to date in reports. The following procedure puts the text in cell A1 of the worksheet named `Profit` in the left footer, clears the center footer and puts the full file name in the right footer. It applies the changes to every worksheet in the file:

```
Private Sub Workbook_BeforePrint(Cancel As Boolean)
    Dim Wks As Worksheet
    Dim stFullFileName As String
    Dim stCompanyName As String

    stCompanyName = Worksheets("Profit").Range("A1").Value
    stFullFileName = ThisWorkbook.FullName
    For Each Wks In ThisWorkbook.Worksheets
        With Wks.PageSetup
            .LeftFooter = stCompanyName
            .CenterFooter = ""
            .RightFooter = stFullFileName
        End With
    Next Wks
End Sub
```

The footer can be seen in a **Print Preview** as follows:

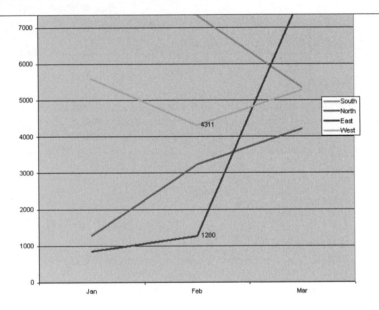

Walrus Enterprises   C:\Wrox\Chapter 9\Events.xls

Summary

In this section you have seen some useful examples of how to utilize event procedures to respond to user actions.

We have introduced you to the Worksheet, Chart, and Workbook events. And we've delved a little deeper into the following events:

```
Worksheet_Calculate

Chart_BeforeDoubleClick

Workbook_BeforeClose

Workbook_BeforePrint
```

VBA is essentially an event-driven language, a good knowledge of the events at your disposal can open up a whole new world of functionality you never knew existed.

To find out more, have a play with the Object Browser, and consult the object model in Appendix A.

Adding Controls

As we have already discussed in Chapter 2, you can add two different types of controls to Excel worksheets. You can use ActiveX controls, found on the **Control Toolbox** toolbar (see below), or the controls from the **Forms** toolbar. The **Forms** toolbar is an Excel 5 and Excel 95 feature, and provided controls for the dialog sheets used in those versions, as well as controls that can be embedded in a worksheet or chart. Dialog sheets have since been superseded by UserForms in Excel 97 and Excel 2000, and UserForms utilize the ActiveX controls.

The Control Toolbox

The **Forms** toolbar controls and dialog sheets are still supported in Excel, however. The **Forms** toolbar controls (shown below) even have some advantages over the ActiveX controls. If you want to place controls on a chart sheet, you can only use the **Forms** toolbar controls. However, each **Forms** toolbar control can only respond to a single event. In most cases, that event is the Click event – the edit box is an exception, responding to the Change event.

The Forms Toolbar

If you want to create controls and define their event procedures in your VBA code, as opposed to creating them manually, the **Forms** toolbar controls are easier to work with. A big advantage over an ActiveX control is that the event procedure for a **Forms** toolbar control can be placed in a standard module, can have any valid VBA procedure name, and can be created when you write the code for the application, before the control is created. You can create the control programmatically, when it is needed, and assign the procedure name to the OnAction property of the control. You can even assign the same procedure to more than one control. On the other hand, ActiveX event procedures must be placed in the class module behind the worksheet or user form in which they are embedded and must have a procedure name that corresponds with the name of the control and the name of the event. For example, the click event procedure for a control named Optionbutton1 must be as follows:

```
Sub OptionButton1_Click()
```

If you try to create an event procedure for an ActiveX control before the control exists, you will get compiler errors, so you have to create the event procedure programmatically. This is not an easy task. See Chapter 17 – Programming the VBE – for an example of adding an event procedure programmatically to a user form control.

ActiveX Controls

The following screen shows four types of ActiveX controls embedded in the worksheet (Controls.xls is available for download from www.wrox.com). The scrollbar in cells C3:F3 allows you to set the value in cell B3. The spin button in cell C4 increments the growth percentage in cell B4. The check box in cell B5 increases the tax rate in cell B16 from 30% to 33%, if it is checked. The option buttons in column I change the cost factor in cell B15 and also change the maximum and minimum values for the scrollbar.

A control can be linked to a worksheet cell so that the cell always displays the Value property of the control. None of the ActiveX controls shown above use a link cell, although the scrollbar could have been linked because its value is displayed in B3. Each control uses an event procedure to make its updates. This gives you far more flexibility than a simple cell link and removes the need to dedicate a worksheet cell to the task.

Scrollbar Control

The scrollbar uses the Change event and the Scroll event to assign the Value property of the scrollbar to cell B3. The maximum and minimum values of the scrollbar are set by the option buttons (we'll discuss that later):

```
Private Sub ScrollBar1_Change()
    Range("B3").Value = ScrollBar1.Value
End Sub

Private Sub ScrollBar1_Scroll()
    Range("B3").Value = ScrollBar1.Value
End Sub
```

The Change event procedure is triggered when you change the scrollbar value by clicking the scroll arrows, by clicking above or below the scroll box (or to the left or right if it is aligned horizontally), or by dragging the scroll box. However, there is a small glitch that occurs immediately after you change the option buttons. Dragging the scroll box does not trigger the change event on the first attempt. Utilizing the Scroll event procedure solves this problem.

The Scroll event causes continuous updating as you drag the scroll bar, so that you can see what figure you are producing as you drag, rather than after you have released the scroll bar. It might not be practical to use the Scroll event procedure in a very large worksheet in auto-recalculation mode because of the large number of recalculations it causes.

Spin Button Control

The spin button control uses the SpinDown and SpinUp events to decrease and increase the value in cell B4:

```
Private Sub SpinButton1_SpinDown()
   With Range("B4")
      .Value = WorksheetFunction.Max(0, .Value - 0.0005)
   End With
End Sub

Private Sub SpinButton1_SpinUp()
   With Range("B4")
       .Value = WorksheetFunction.Min(0.01, .Value + 0.0005)
   End With
End Sub
```

The Value property of the spin button is ignored. It is not suitable to be used directly as a percentage figure as the Value property can only be a long integer value. The events are used as triggers to run the code that operates directly on the value in B4. The growth figure is kept in the range of zero to 1 per cent. Clicking the down side of the spin button runs the SpinDown event procedure, which decreases the value in cell B4 by 0.05%. The worksheet Max function is used to ensure that the calculated figure does not become less than zero. The SpinUp event procedure increases the value in cell B4 by 0.05%. It uses the Min function to ensure that the calculated value does not exceed 1%.

Check Box Control

The check box control returns a True value when checked or False value if it is not checked. The Click event procedure that follows uses an If structure to set the value in cell B16:

```
Private Sub CheckBox1_Click()
   If CheckBox1.Value Then
      Range("B16").Value = 0.33
   Else
      Range("B16").Value = 0.3
   End If
End Sub
```

Each option button has code similar to the following:

```
Private Sub OptionButton1_Click()
   Call Options
End Sub
```

The processing for all the buttons is carried out in the following procedure:

```
Private Sub Options()
    Dim dCostFactor As Double
    Dim lScrollBarMax As Long
    Dim lScrollBarMin As Long

    Select Case True
        Case OptionButton1.Value
            dCostFactor = 0.63
            lScrollBarMin = 50000
            lScrollBarMax = 150000
        Case OptionButton2.Value
            dCostFactor = 0.74
            lScrollBarMin = 25000
            lScrollBarMax = 75000
        Case OptionButton3.Value
            dCostFactor = 0.57
            lScrollBarMin = 10000
            lScrollBarMax = 30000
        Case OptionButton4.Value
            dCostFactor = 0.65
            lScrollBarMin = 15000
            lScrollBarMax = 30000
    End Select
    Range("B15").Value = dCostFactor
    ScrollBar1.Min = lScrollBarMin
    ScrollBar1.Max = lScrollBarMax
    ScrollBar1.Value = lScrollBarMax
End Sub
```

The Select Case structure is used here in an unusual way. Normally you use a variable reference in the first line of a Select Case and use comparison values in the Case statements. Here, we have used the value True in the Select Case and referenced the option button Value property in the Case statements. This provides a nice structure for processing a set of option buttons where you know that only one can have a True value. Only one option button can be selected and have a value of True in the worksheet above because they all belong to the same group. As you add option buttons to a worksheet, the GroupName property of the button is set to the name of the worksheet – Profit, in this case. If you want two sets of unrelated option buttons, you need to assign a different GroupName to the second set.

Options uses the Select Case structure to carry out any processing that is different for each option button. The code following the End Select carries out any processing that is common to all the option buttons. This approach also works very well when the coding is more complex and also when the code is triggered by another control, such as a command button, rather than the option button events.

Forms Toolbar Controls

The following screen shows a **Forms** toolbar control that is being used to select a product name to be entered in column D. The control appears over any cell in column D that you double click. When you select the product, the product name is entered in the cell 'behind' the control, the price of the product is entered in column F on the same row, and the control disappears.

If you hover your mouse over the **Forms** toolbar button that creates the control shown above, the tooltip that pops up describes this control as a **Combo Box**. However, in the Excel object model, it is called a `DropDown` object, and it belongs to the `DropDowns` collection.

> The `DropDown` object is a hidden member of the Excel object model in Excel 2000. You will not find any help screens for this object and it will not normally appear in the Object Browser. You can make it visible in the Object Browser if you right-click in the Object Browser window and select Show Hidden Members from the shortcut menu. You can learn a lot about the Forms toolbar controls by using the Macro Recorder and the Object Browser, but you will need to have access to Excel 5 or Excel 95 to get full documentation on them.

The dropdown control is created by a procedure called from the following `BeforeDoubleClick` event procedure in the `SalesData` sheet, which has the programmatic name `Sheet2`:

```
Private Sub Worksheet_BeforeDoubleClick(ByVal Target As Range, _
                                        Cancel As Boolean)
    If Not Intersect(Target, Columns("D")) Is Nothing Then
        Call AddDropDown(Target)
        Cancel = True
    End If
End Sub
```

The event procedure checks that `Target` (the cell that was double-clicked) is in column D. If so, it then runs the `AddDropDown` procedure, passing `Target` as an input argument, and cancels the double-click event.

The following two procedures are in a standard module:

```
Sub AddDropDown(Target As Range)
    Dim ddBox As DropDown
    Dim vaProducts As Variant
    Dim i As Integer

    vaProducts = Array("Bananas", "Lychees", "Mangoes", "Rambutan")
    With Target
        Set ddBox = Sheet2.DropDowns.Add(.Left, .Top, .Width, .Height)
    End With
    With ddBox
        .OnAction = "EnterProdInfo"
        For i = LBound(vaProducts) To UBound(vaProducts)
            .AddItem vaProducts(i)
        Next i
    End With
End Sub

Private Sub EnterProdInfo()
    Dim vaPrices As Variant

    vaPrices = Array(15, 12.5, 20, 18)
    With Sheet2.DropDowns(Application.Caller)
        .TopLeftCell.Value = .List(.ListIndex)
        .TopLeftCell.Offset(0, 2).Value = vaPrices(.ListIndex - Array(0, 1)(1))
        .Delete
    End With
End Sub
```

AddDropDown is not declared Private, as it would not then be possible to call it from the Sheet2 code module. This would normally be a problem if you wanted to prevent users seeing the procedure in the **Tools | Macro | Macros** dialog box. However, because it has an input argument, it will not be shown in the dialog box, anyway. Also, it does not matter whether AddDropDown is placed in the Sheet2 module or a standard module. It will operate in either location.

AddDropDown uses the Add method of the DropDowns collection to create a new dropdown. It aligns the new control exactly with Target, giving it the same Left, Top, Width and Height properties as the cell. In the With...End With construction, the procedure defines the OnAction property of the dropdown to be the EnterProdInfo procedure. This means that EnterProdInfo will be run when an item is chosen from the dropdown. The For...Next loop uses the AddItem method of the dropdown to place the list of items in vaProducts into the dropdown list.

EnterProdInfo has been declared Private to prevent its appearance in the **Tools | Macro | Macros** dialog box. Although it is private, the dropdown can access it. EnterProdInfo could have been placed in the Sheet2 code module, but the OnAction property of the dropdown would have to be assigned "Sheet2.EnterProdInfo".

EnterProdInfo loads vaPrices with the prices corresponding to the products. It then uses Application.Caller to return the name of the dropdown control that called the OnAction procedure. It uses this name as an index into the DropDowns collection on Sheet2 to get a reference to the DropDown object itself. In the With...End With construction, EnterProdInfo uses the ListIndex property of the dropdown to get the index number of the item chosen in the dropdown list.

You cannot directly access the name of the chosen item in a DropDown object, unlike a ComboBox object that returns the name in its Value property. The Value property of a dropdown is the same as the ListIndex, which returns the numeric position of the item in the list. To get the item name from a dropdown, you use the ListIndex property as a one- based index to the List property of the dropdown. The List property returns an array of all the items in the list.

The TopLeftCell property of the DropDown object returns a reference to the Range object under the top left corner of the DropDown object. EnterProdInfo assigns the item chosen in the list to the Value property of this Range object. It then assigns the price of the product to the Range object that is offset two columns to the right of the TopLeftCell Range object.

EnterProdInfo also uses the ListIndex property of the dropdown as an index into the Prices array. The problem with this is that the dropdown list is always one-based, while the Array function list depends on the Option Base statement in the declarations section of the module. Array(0,1)(1) is used to reduce the ListIndex value by one if Option Base 0 is in effect or by zero if Option Base 1 is in effect.

> You can use the following code to ensure that the resulting array is zero based under Option Base 1 in Excel 2000:
>
> ```
> vaPrices = VBA.Array(15, 12.5, 20, 18)
> ```
>
> This technique does not work in Excel 5 and Excel 95 where the above expression is influenced by the Option Base statement.

Controls on Charts

The following screen shows a chart that contains a button to remove or add the profit series from the chart, which is based on the Profit Planner figures of the Profit sheet. The control is a **Forms** toolbar Button object belonging to the Buttons collection (remember ActiveX controls cannot be used in Charts) :

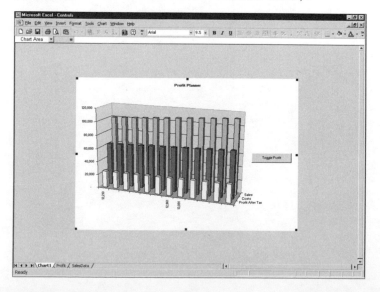

The code assigned to the OnAction property of the Button object is as follows:

```
Sub Button1_Click()
    With ActiveChart
        If .SeriesCollection.Count = 3 Then
            .SeriesCollection(1).Delete
        Else
            With .SeriesCollection.NewSeries
                .Name = Sheet1.Range("A13")
                .Values = Sheet1.Range("B13:M13")
                .XValues = Sheet1.Range("B12:M12")
                .PlotOrder = 1
            End With
        End If
    End With
End Sub
```

If the SeriesCollection.Count property is three, the first series is deleted. Otherwise a new series is added and the appropriate ranges assigned to it to show the profit after tax figures. The new series is added as the last series, which would plot behind the existing series, so the PlotOrder property of the new series is set to one to place it in front of the others.

Summary

In this chapter we have explained some of the differences between ActiveX controls embedded in worksheets and Forms toolbar controls embedded in worksheets and chart sheets, and we've also shown how to work with them. You have seen how scroll bars, spinner buttons, check boxes and option buttons can be used to execute macros that can harness the full power of VBA and that do not need to depend on a link cell.

You also have seen how Forms toolbar controls can be created and manipulated programmatically.

UserForms

UserForms are essentially user defined dialog boxes. You can use them to display information, and to allow the user to input new data or modify the displayed data. The MsgBox and InputBox functions provide simple tools to display messages and get input data, but UserForms take you to a new dimension. With these you can implement nearly all the features that you are accustomed to seeing in normal Windows dialog boxes.

You create a UserForm in the VB Editor window using Insert | UserForm. You add controls from the ToolBox in the same way that you add controls to a worksheet. If the ToolBox is not visible, use View | ToolBox.

UserForms can contain labels, text boxes, list boxes, combo boxes, command buttons and many other ActiveX controls. You have complete control over the placement of controls and can use as many controls as you need. Naturally, each control can respond to a wide variety of events.

Displaying a UserForm

To load a UserForm called UserForm1 into memory, without making it visible, you use the Load statement:

```
Load UserForm1
```

You can remove UserForm1 from memory using the UnLoad statement:

```
UnLoad UserForm1
```

To make UserForm1 visible, use the Show method of the UserForm object:

```
UserForm1.Show
```

If you show a UserForm that has not been loaded, it will be automatically loaded. You can use the Hide method to remove a UserForm from the screen without removing it from memory:

```
UserForm1.Hide
```

The following screenshot shows a simple UserForm in action. We will develop it over the course of this chapter. It has been designed to allow you to see the current values in B2:B6 and to make changes in those values. It is linked directly to the cells in the worksheet, which makes it very easy to set up with a minimum of VBA code:

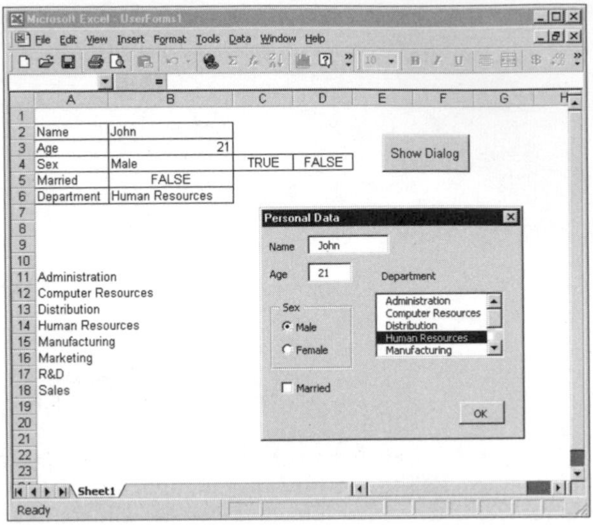

The ActiveX command button in the worksheet, with the caption Show Dialog contains the following event procedure:

```
Private Sub CommandButton1_Click()
    fmPersonal.Show
End Sub
```

The UserForm is modal by default. This means that the UserForm retains the focus until it is unloaded or hidden. The user cannot activate the worksheet or make menu choices until the UserForm disappears. We will discuss modeless UserForms, which do allow the user to perform other tasks while they are visible, later in this chapter. The following screen shows the UserForm in the VB Editor window:

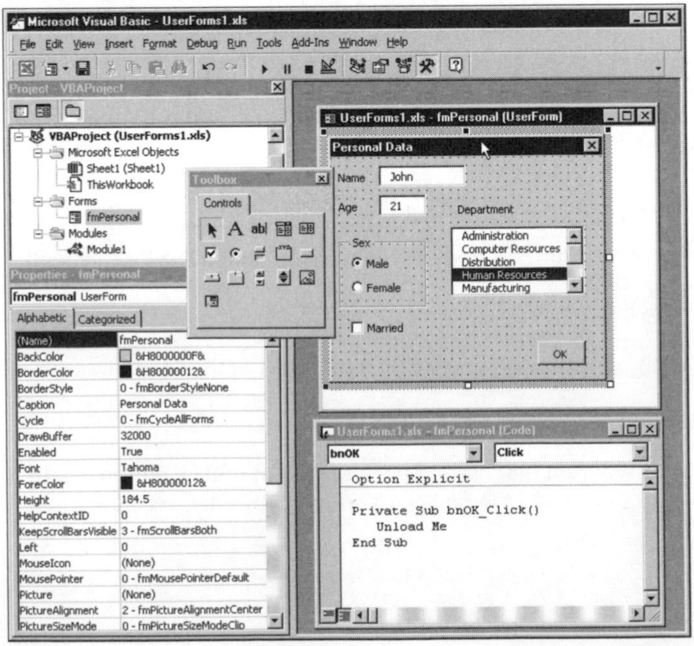

The name of the UserForm was changed from the default name `UserForm1` to `fmPersonal`. You do this in the first entry, (Name), in the **Properties** window. The `Caption` property is changed to `Personal Data`.

> It is a good idea to give your UserForms and controls descriptive names that identify what type of object they are and what their purpose is. The lower case two character prefix identifies the object type. For example, you use fm for a UserForm, sb for a scrollbar and tx for a text box. The capitalized words that follow identify the control's purpose. This makes it much easier to write and maintain the VBA code that manipulates these objects.

The controls were added from the **ToolBox**. There are two TextBox controls at the top of the form for name and age data. Their names were changed to `txName` and `txAge`. The `ControlSource` property of `txName` was entered as `Sheet1!B2` and the `ControlSource` property of `txAge` was entered as `Sheet1!B3`. When you assign a `ControlSource` property to a worksheet cell, the cell and the control are linked in both directions. Any change to the control affects the cell and any change to the cell affects the control. The following table shows the names of the main controls:

Control	Name	ControlSource
TextBox	txName	Sheet1!B2
TextBox	txAge	Sheet1!B3
OptionButton	opMale	Sheet1!C4
OptionButton	opFemale	Sheet1!D4
CheckBox	ckMarried	Sheet1!B5
ListBox	lsDepartment	Sheet1!B6
CommandButton	cmOK	

The descriptive titles on the form to the left of the TextBoxes and above the ListBox showing the departments are Label controls. The `Caption` properties of the Labels were changed to `Name`, `Age` and `Department`. The box around the OptionButton controls is a Frame control. Its `Caption` property was changed to `Sex`.

> When you want to have a frame around other controls, you must insert the frame first and then insert the controls into the frame.

The **Male** and **Female** option buttons can't be linked to **B4**. It is not appropriate to display the values of these controls directly, so an `IF` function in cell **B4** converts the `True` or `False` value in cell `C4` to the required `Male` or `Female` result. Although you only need to set cell `C4` to get the required result, you need to link both option buttons to separate cells if you want the buttons to display properly when the UserForm is shown. The `RowSource` property of `lsDepartment` was entered as `Sheet1!A11:A18`. It is good practice to create names for the linked cells and use those names in the ControlSource, rather than the cell references used here, but this extra step has been omitted to simplify our example.

The following `Click` event procedure was created for the button in the code module behind the UserForm:

```
Private Sub bnOK_Click()
    Unload Me
End Sub
```

Me is a shortcut keyword that refers to the `UserForm` object containing the code. If you want to access the control values later in your VBA code, you must use the `Hide` method, which leaves the UserForm in memory. Otherwise, the `Unload` statement removes the UserForm from memory and the control values are lost. You will see examples that use `Hide` shortly.

Clicking the x in the top right corner of the UserForm will also dismiss the UserForm. This unloads the UserForm so that it is removed from memory. We will see how to prevent this later.

Directly Accessing Controls in UserForms

Linking UserForm controls to cells is not always the best way to work. You can gain more flexibility by directly accessing the data in the UserForm. The following screen shows a revised version of our previous example. We want to display essentially the same UserForm, but we want to store the resulting data as shown. Sex will be stored as a single letter code, M or F. The `Department` name will be stored as a two-character code:

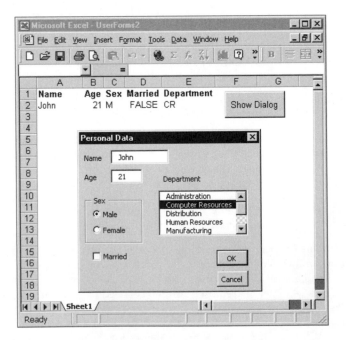

We have added a Cancel button to the UserForm so that any changes made can be discarded if the user wishes, rather than being automatically applied to the worksheet. The module behind `fmPersonal` now contains the following code:

```
Option Explicit
Public Cancelled As Boolean

Private Sub bnCancel_Click()
   Cancelled = True
   Me.Hide
End Sub

Private Sub bnOK_Click()
   Cancelled = False
   Me.Hide
End Sub
```

The `Public` variable `Cancelled` will provide a way to detect that the Cancel button has been pressed. If the OK button is pressed, `Cancelled` is assigned the value `False`. If the Cancel button is pressed, `Cancelled` is assigned a value of `True`. Both buttons hide fmPersonal so that it remains in memory. The following event procedure has also been added to the module behind `fmPersonal`:

```
Private Sub UserForm_Initialize()
   Dim vaDepartment As Variant
   Dim vaDeptCode As Variant
   Dim stDeptList() As String
   Dim i As Integer

   vaDepartment = VBA.Array("Administration", _
         "Computer Resources", _
         "Distribution", _
         "Human Resources", _
         "Manufacturing", _
         "Marketing", _
         "R&D", _
         "Sales")
   vaDeptCode = VBA.Array("AD", _
         "CR", _
         "DS", _
         "HR", _
         "MF", _
         "MK", _
         "RD", _
         "SL")
   ReDim stDeptList(0 To UBound(vaDepartment), 0 To 1)
   For i = 0 To UBound(vaDepartment)
      stDeptList(i, 0) = vaDeptCode(i)
      stDeptList(i, 1) = vaDepartment(i)
   Next i
   lsDepartment.List = stDeptList
End Sub
```

The `UserForm_Initialize` event occurs when the UserForm is loaded into memory. It does not occur when the form has been hidden and is shown again. It is used here to load `lsDepartment` with two columns of data. The first column contains the department codes and the second contains the department names to be displayed.

vaDepartment and vaDeptCode are assigned arrays in the usual way using the Array function, except that VBA.Array has been used to ensure that the arrays are zero based. stDeptList is a dynamic array and ReDim is used to dimension it to the same number of rows as in vaDepartment and two columns, once again zero based. The For...Next loop assigns the department codes and names to the two columns of stDeptList. stDeptList is then assigned directly to the List property of lsDepartment. If you prefer, you can maintain a table of departments and codes in a worksheet range and set the list box's RowSource property equal to the range.

When you have a multicolumn list box, you need to specify which column contains the data that will appear in a link cell and be returned in the control's Value property. This column is referred to as the bound column. The BoundColumn property of lsDepartment has been set to 1. This property is one based, so the bound column is the department code. The ColumnCount property has been set to 2, as there are two columns of data in the list. However, we only want to see the department names in the list box, so we want to hide the first column. We can do that by setting the column width of the first column to 0. To do this, we only need to enter a single 0 in the ColumnWidths property, rather than, for example, 0 ; 40 Entering a single 0 sets the first column to a width of 0 and leaves the second column to fill the list box width.

The following code has been placed in the module behind Sheet1:

```
Private Sub CommandButton1_Click()
    Dim rgData As Range
    Dim vaData As Variant

    ' first block of code here
    Set rgData = Range("Database").Rows(2)
    vaData = rgData.Value
    With fmPersonal
        .txName.Value = vaData(1, 1)
        .txAge.Value = vaData(1, 2)
        Select Case vaData(1, 3)
            Case "F"
                .opFemale.Value = True
            Case "M"
                .opMale.Value = True
        End Select
        .ckMarried.Value = vaData(1, 4)
        .lsDepartment.Value = vaData(1, 5)

        ' second block of code here
        .Show
        If Not .Cancelled Then

            ' third block of code here
            vaData(1, 1) = .txtName
            vaData(1, 2) = .txtAge
            Select Case True
                Case .opFemale.Value
                    vaData(1, 3) = "F"
                Case .opMale.Value
                    vaData(1, 3) = "M"
            End Select
            vaData(1, 4) = .ckMarried.Value
            vaData(1, 5) = .lsDepartment.Value

            rgData.Value = vaData
        End If
    End With
    Unload fmPersonal
End Sub
```

The code is in three blocks after the initial declaration statements. The first block loads the data from the worksheet into fmPersonal. The second block (only two lines) displays fmPersonal, then checks to see if the Cancel button is pressed. The third block copies the data in fmPersonal back to the worksheet.

At the start of the first block, rgData is assigned a reference to cells A2:E2. The range A1:E2 has been given the name Database, so Range("Database").Rows(2) refers to the required data range. The values in rgData are then assigned directly to the variant Data. This creates a two dimensional, one based array of values having one row and five columns. It is much more efficient to access the worksheet data in this way than to access each cell individually.

Most of the remaining code is within the With... End With structure, which makes it possible to use shorter and more efficient references to the controls, properties and methods associated with fmPersonal. The first reference to fmPersonal also causes fmPersonal to be loaded into memory, although it remains hidden at this point.

The Value properties of the controls on fmPersonal are then assigned the values in Data. The option buttons are an exception because the M and F code values need to be translated to True values as appropriate. It is only necessary to set one of the option buttons to True as the other will automatically be set to False. You can group option buttons by assigning them the same value in their GroupName property or by placing them in the same frame. The option buttons here do not have a value in their GroupName property. They are considered to be in the same group because they are in the same frame.

The Show method displays fmPersonal. Control then passes to fmPersonal until it is hidden, which occurs when the user presses the OK or Cancel button, or the x at the top of the UserForm. The user can also press *Esc* to activate the Cancel button because it has had its Cancel property set to True. The user can also press *Enter* to activate the OK button, as long as the Cancel button does not have the focus, because the OK button's Default property has been set to True. When fmPersonal is hidden, the Click event procedure regains control and it checks to see if the Cancel button was pressed. It does this by examining the value of the Public variable Cancelled on fmPersonal.

> The code modules behind UserForms (as well as those behind sheets and workbooks) are class modules. When you define a Public variable in a class module, the variable behaves as a property of the object associated with the class module. See Chapter 13 – Class Modules – for more details.

If Cancelled is False, the procedure loads the values of the controls back into vaData, translating the option button settings back into an F or M value and the values in vaData are directly assigned back to the worksheet. The final step is to unload fmPersonal from memory.

Stopping the Close Button

One problem with the above code is that, if the user clicks the x, which is the Close button at the top of fmPersonal, the event procedure does not exit. Instead, it transfers any changes back to the worksheet. This is because the default value for Cancelled is False. Normally, clicking the x would also unload the form and the code would fail when it tries to access the controls on the form. However, in this case the With...End With structure keeps fmPersonal in scope and fmPersonal is not unloaded until after the End With.

There are a number of simple ways in which the above problem could be corrected, but the following method gives you total control over that little x. You can use the QueryClose event of the UserForm object to discover what is closing the UserForm and cancel the event if necessary. Adding the following code to the fmPersonal module blocks the Close button exit:

```
Private Sub UserForm_QueryClose(iCancel As Integer, iCloseMode As Integer)
    If iCloseMode = vbFormControlMenu Then
        MsgBox "Please use only the OK or Cancel buttons", vbCritical
        iCancel = True
    End If
End Sub
```

The QueryClose event can be triggered in four ways. You can determine what caused the event by using the following intrinsic constants to test the CloseMode parameter:

Constant	Value	Reason for the event
vbFormControlMenu	0	The user clicked the x in the Control menu on the UserForm.
vbFormCode	1	The Unload statement was used to remove the UserForm from memory.
vbAppWindows	2	Windows is shutting down.
vbAppTaskManager	3	The application is being closed by the Windows Task Manager.

Maintaining a Data List

The code we have developed can now be extended to maintain a data list without too much extra effort. However, we will take a different approach to the last example. This time we will build all the code into fmPersonal, apart from the code behind the command button in the worksheet that shows the UserForm. The code behind the button now becomes the following:

```
Private Sub CommandButton1_Click()
    fmPersonal.Show
End Sub
```

It is really much easier to maintain a data list in a proper database application, such as Microsoft Access, but it can be done in Excel without too much trouble if your requirements are fairly simple.

If we are going to manage more than one row of data, we need to be able to add new rows, delete existing rows and be able to navigate through the rows. fmPersonal needs some extra controls as shown:

The scroll bar is a handy way to navigate through many records quickly. It also makes it easy to get to the last record or first record. It can also be used to go to the next or previous record. For variety, we have included buttons to go to the next and previous records as well. The New Record button adds a record to the end of the data list and initializes some of the values in the new record. The Delete button deletes the record that is currently showing in fmPersonal.

The code in fmPersonal is discussed below. It is important to note first that the following module level variables have been declared in the declarations section at the top of the fmPersonal code module:

```
Dim rgData As Range
Dim vaData As Variant
```

These variables are used in exactly the same way as they were used in the previous example except that the row referred to can vary. The object variable rgData is always set to the current row of data in the named range Database, which currently refers to A1:E18 in the worksheet shown above. vaData always holds the values from rgData as a VBA array.

The code from the command button event procedure in our previous example has been converted to two utility procedures that reside in fmPersonal's code module:

```
Private Sub LoadRecord()
    'Copy values in rgData from worksheet to vaData array
    vaData = rgData.Value
    'Assign array values to fmPersonal controls
    txName.Value = vaData(1, 1)
    txAge.Value = vaData(1, 2)
    Select Case vaData(1, 3)
        Case "F"
            opFemale.Value = True
        Case "M"
            opMale.Value = True
    End Select
    ckMarried.Value = vaData(1, 4)
    lsDepartment.Value = vaData(1, 5)
End Sub
```

Continued on Following Page

```
Private Sub SaveRecord()
    'Copy values from fmPersonal controls to Data array
    vaData(1, 1) = txName
    vaData(1, 2) = txAge
    Select Case True
        Case opFemale.Value
            vaData(1, 3) = "F"
        Case opMale.Value
            vaData(1, 3) = "M"
    End Select
    vaData(1, 4) = ckMarried.Value
    vaData(1, 5) = lsDepartment.Value
    'Assign Data array values to current record in Database
    rgData.Value = vaData
End Sub
```

Because the code is in the fmPersonal module, there is no need to refer to fmPersonal when referring to a control, so all controls are directly addressed in the code.

LoadRecord and SaveRecord are the only procedures that are tailored to the data list structure and the controls. As long as the data list has the name Database, none of the other code in fmPersonal needs to change if we decide to add more fields to the data list or remove fields. It also means that we can readily apply the same code to a completely different data list. All we have to do is redesign the UserForm controls and update LoadRecord and SaveRecord.

The key navigation device in fmPersonal is the scroll bar, which has been named sbNavigator. It is used by the other buttons when a change of record is required, as well as being available to the user directly. The Value property of sbNavigator corresponds to the row number in the range named Database. The minimum value of sbNavigator is fixed permanently at two, as the first record is the second row in Database. The maximum value is altered as needed by the other event procedures in fmPersonal so that it always corresponds to the last row in Database:

```
Private Sub sbNavigator_Change()
    'When Scollbar value changes, save current record and load
    'record number corresponding to scrollbar value
    Call SaveRecord
    Set rgData = Range("Database").Rows(sbNavigator.Value)
    Call LoadRecord
End Sub
```

When the user changes the sbNavigator.Value property (or when it is changed by other event procedures) the Change event fires and saves the current record in fmPersonal, redefines rgData to be the row in Database corresponding to the new value of sbNavigator.Value, and loads the data from that row into fmPersonal.

The UserForm_Initialize event procedure has been updated from the previous exercise to set the correct starting values for sbNavigator:

```
Private Sub UserForm_Initialize()
    'Sets up lsDepartment list values
    'and loads first record in Database
    Dim vaDepartment As Variant
    Dim vaDeptCode As Variant
    Dim stDeptList() As String
    Dim i As Integer

    vaDepartment = VBA.Array("Administration", _
            "Computer Resources", _
            "Distribution", _
```

```
            "Human Resources", _
            "Manufacturing", _
            "Marketing", _
            "R&D", _
            "Sales", _
            "None")
    vaDeptCode = VBA.Array("AD", _
            "CR", _
            "DS", _
            "HR", _
            "MF", _
            "MK", _
            "RD", _
            "SL", _
            "NA")
    ReDim stDeptList(0 To UBound(vaDepartment), 0 To 1)
    For i = 0 To UBound(vaDepartment)
        stDeptList(i, 0) = vaDeptCode(i)
        stDeptList(i, 1) = vaDepartment(i)
    Next i
    lsDepartment.List = stDeptList
    'Load 1st record in Database and initialise scrollbar
    With Range("Database")
        Set rgData = .Rows(2)
        Call LoadRecord
        sbNavigator.Value = 2
        sbNavigator.Max = .Rows.Count
    End With
End Sub
```

After initializing the lsDepartment List property, the code initializes rgData to refer to the second row of Database, row 2 being the first row of data under the field names on row 1, and loads the data from that row into fmPersonal. It then initializes the Value property of sbNavigator to 2 and sets the Max property of sbNavigator to the number of rows in Database. If the user changes the scroll bar, they can navigate to any row from row 2 through to the last row in Database.

The buttons captioned Next Record and Previous Record have been named bnNext and bnPrevious. The Click event procedure for bnNext is as follows:

```
Private Sub bnNext_Click()
    With Range("Database")
        If rgData.Row < .Rows(.Rows.Count).Row Then
            'Load next record only if not on last record
            sbNavigator.Value = sbNavigator.Value + 1
            'Note: Setting sbNavigator.Value runs its Change event procedure
        End If
    End With
End Sub
```

The If test checks that the current row number in Database is less than the last row number in Database to ensure that we don't try to go beyond the data. If there is room to move, the value of sbNavigator is increased by 1. This change triggers the Change event procedure for sbNavigator, which saves the current data, resets rgData and loads the next row's data.

The code for bnPrevious is similar to bnNext except that there is no need for the With...End With as we don't to keep repeating the reference to Range("Database"):

```
Private Sub bnPrevious_Click()
    If rgData.Row > Range("Database").Rows(2).Row Then
        'Load previous record if not on first record
        sbNavigator.Value = sbNavigator.Value - 1
        'Note: Setting sbNavigator.Value runs its Change event procedure
    End If
End Sub
```

The check is to ensure that we don't try to move to row numbers lower than the second row in Database. This and the bnNext check could have also been carried out using the Value, Max and Min properties of sbNavigator, but the method used in bnNext_Click shows you how to determine the row number of the last row in a named range, which is a technique that it is very useful to know. It is important to carry out these checks as trying to set the sbNavigator.Value property outside the Min to Max range causes a run time error.

The code for bnDelete is as follows:

```
Private Sub bnDelete_Click()
    'Deletes current record in fmPersonal

    If Range("Database").Rows.Count = 2 Then
        'Don't delete if only one record left
        MsgBox "You cannot delete every record", vbCritical
        Exit Sub
    ElseIf rgData.Row = Range("Database").Rows(2).Row Then
        'If on 1st record, move down one record and delete 1st record
        Set rgData = rgData.Offset(1)
        rgData.Offset(-1).Delete shift:=xlUp
        Call LoadRecord
    Else
        'If on other than 1st record, move to previous record before delete
        sbNavigator.Value = sbNavigator.Value - 1
        'Note: Setting sbNavigator.Value runs its Change event procedure
        rgData.Offset(1).Delete shift:=xlUp
    End If
    sbNavigator.Max = sbNavigator.Max - 1
End Sub
```

This procedure carries out the following actions:

It aborts if you try to delete the last remaining record in Database.
If you delete the first record, rgData is assigned a reference to the second record. SbNavigator.Value is not reset, as row 2 becomes row 1, once the original row 1 is deleted. LoadRecord is called to load the data in rgData into the UserForm.
If you delete a record that is not the first one, sbNavigator.Value is reduced by 1. This causes the previous record to be loaded into the UserForm.
At the end, the count of the number of rows in Database, held in sbNavigator.Max, is decreased by 1.

The code for bnNew is as follows:

```
Private Sub bnNew_Click()
    'Add new record at bottom of database
    Dim iRowCount As Integer

    With Range("Database")
        'Add extra row to name Database
        iRowCount = .Rows.Count + 1
        .Resize(iRowCount).Name = "Database"
        sbNavigator.Max = iRowCount
```

```
        sbNavigator.Value = iRowCount
        'Note: Setting sbNavigator.Value runs its Change event procedure
    End With
    'Set default values
    opMale.Value = True
    ckMarried = False
    lsDepartment.Value = "NA"
End Sub
```

This event procedure defines iRowCount to be one higher than the current number of rows in Database. It then generates a reference to a range with one more row than Database and redefines the name Database to refer to the larger range. It then assigns iRowCount to both the Max property of sbNavigator and the Value property of sbNavigator. Setting the Value property fires the Change event procedure for sbNavigator, which makes the new empty row the current row and loads the empty values into fmPersonal. Default values are then applied to some of the fmPersonal controls.

The only remaining code in fmPersonal is for the Click events of the OK and Cancel buttons as follows:

```
Private Sub bnOK_Click()
    'Save Current Record and unload fmPersonal
    Call SaveRecord
    Unload Me
End Sub

Private Sub bnCancel_Click()
    'Unload fmPersonal without saving current record
    Unload Me
End Sub
```

Both unload fmPersonal. Only the OK button saves any changes to the current record in the UserForm.

Modeless UserForms

For the first time in any version of Excel, Excel 2000 can show modeless UserForms. The modal UserForms that we have dealt with so far do not allow the user to change the focus away from the UserForm while it is being displayed. You cannot activate a worksheet, menu or toolbar, for example, until the UserForm has been hidden or unloaded from memory. If you have a procedure that uses the Show method to display a modal UserForm, that procedure cannot execute the code that follows the Show until the UserForm is hidden or unloaded.

A modeless UserForm does allow the user to activate worksheets, menus and toolbars. It floats in the foreground until it is hidden or unloaded. The procedure that uses the Show method to display a modeless UserForm immediately continues to execute the code that follows the Show. fmPersonal, from our previous example that maintains a data list, can easily be displayed modeless. All you need to do is change the code that displays it as follows:

```
Private Sub CommandButton1_Click()
    fmPersonal.Show vbModeless
End Sub
```

When the UserForm is modeless, you can carry on with other work while it is visible. You can even copy and paste data from text boxes on the UserForm to worksheet cells.

Progress Indicator

One feature that has been lacking in Excel is a good progress indicator that lets you show how much work has been done, and remains to be done, while a lengthy task is carried out in the background. You can display a message on the status bar using `Application.StatusBar` as discussed in Chapter 3, but this message is not very obvious.

You can set up a good progress indicator very easily using a modeless UserForm. The following screen shows a simple bar indicator that moves from left to right to give a graphic indication of progress:

The progress indicator is a normal UserForm with two label controls, one on top of the other, which have been given contrasting background colors. The `Caption` properties of both labels are blank.

This UserForm has been given the name `fmProgress`. The longer label is named `lbFixed`, as it extends over almost all the width of the UserForm and never changes. The shorter label, which is on top of the fixed label, is named `lbIndicate`. Initially, it is given a width of 0 and its width is gradually increased until it equals the width of the fixed label. The UserForm module contains the following procedure:

```
Public Sub pcProgress(iPerCent As Integer)
    lbIndicate.Width = iPerCent / 100 * lbFixed.Width
    DoEvents
End Sub
```

When you execute `pcProgress`, you pass a number between 0 and 100 as the input argument `iPerCent`. `pcProgress` sets the width of `lbIndicate` to `iPerCent` percent of the width of `lbFixed`. The `DoEvents` statement instructs the operating system to update the UserForm.

> *The operating system gives priority to the running macro and holds back on updating the modeless UserForm. DoEvents tells the operating system to stop the macro and complete any pending events. This technique often corrects problems with screen updating or where background tasks need to be completed before a macro can continue processing.*

The progress indicator can be used with a procedure like the following, which counts how many cells contain errors within a range:

```
Sub TakesAWhile()
    Dim Rng As Range
    Dim lErrorCount As Long

    For Each Rng In Range(Cells(1, 1), Cells(1000, 100))
        If IsError(Rng.Value) Then lErrorCount = errCount + 1
    Next Rng
    MsgBox "Error count = " & lErrorCount
End Sub
```

To incorporate the progress indicator, you can add the following code to the procedure:

```
Sub TakesAWhile()
  Dim Rng As Range
  Dim lCount As Long
  Dim lRows As Long
  Dim lErrorCount As Long

  lRows = 1000
  fmProgress.Show vbModeless
  For Each Rng In Range(Cells(1, 1), Cells(lRows, 100))
    If IsError(Rng.Value) Then lErrorCount = lErrorCount + 1
    If lCount Mod lRows = 0 Then
      fmProgress.pcProgress lCount / lRows
    End If
    lCount = lCount + 1
  Next Rng
  Unload fmProgress
  MsgBox "Error count = " & lErrorCount
End Sub
```

The changes include showing `fmProgress` as a modeless UserForm at the start. Within the `For Each...Next` loop, the variable `lCount` is used to count the loops. `lCount Mod lRows` has a value of zero when `lCount` is zero and every multiple of 1000 loops, so `fmProgress` is updated when `lCount` is zero and then at intervals of 1000 iterations. As this loop repeats 100,000 times, the `pcProgress` procedure in `fmProgress` is run 100 times with the input parameter varying from 0 to 99.

> When a class module (such as the module behind a UserForm) contains a public procedure, you can execute the procedure as a method of the object represented by the class module.

The time taken by the macro will vary according to your processor. For demonstration purposes, you can alter the time taken by the procedure by changing the value of `lRows`.

Variable UserForm Name

In all our examples of UserForms, we have referred to the UserForm by its programmatic name such as `fmProgress`. There can be situations where you need to run a number of different forms with the same code, or you don't know the programmatic name of the UserForm before the code is executed. In these cases you need to be able to assign the UserForm name to a variable and use the variable as an argument. The following code allows you to do this:

```
FormName = "fmPersonal"
VBA.UserForms.Add(FormName).Show
```

Summary

In this chapter you have seen how to work with UserForms. You have seen how to directly link controls on a form to a worksheet. You have seen how to use VBA code to access UserForm controls and copy data between the form and a worksheet. You have also seen how to prevent closure of a UserForm by modifying the code executed when the x button is pressed. You have seen how you can set up a form to maintain a data list and the difference between modal and modeless UserForms. You have seen how you can construct a progress indicator using a modeless UserForm.

12

Command Bars

Command bars were first introduced into Excel in Excel 97. Excel 5 and 95 supported menu bars and toolbars as separate object types. Short cut menus, or popups, such as those which appear when you right-click a worksheet cell, were a special type of menu bar. In the latest version of Excel, the "command bar" is a generic term which includes menu bars, toolbars, and short cut menus as sub-types of the `CommandBars` collection. In this chapter we will learn how to create and manipulate these useful tools using some simple VBA routines.

Toolbars, Menu Bars and Popups

The following screen shows the standard worksheet menu bar at the top of the Excel window:

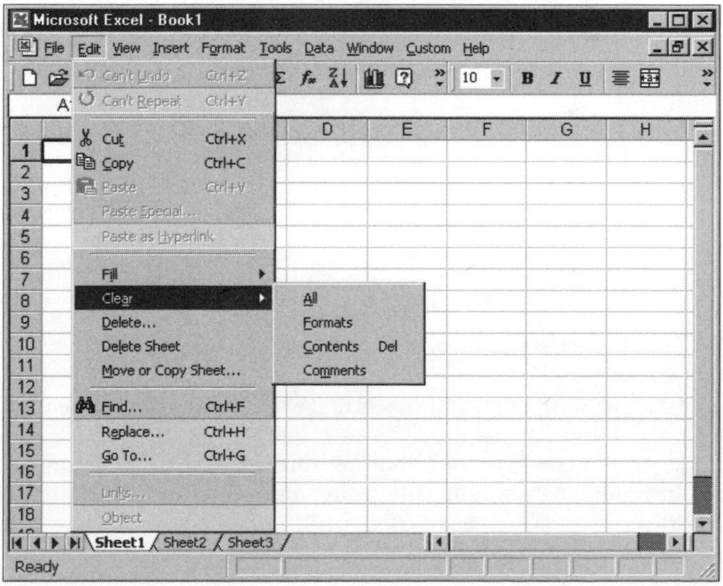

The worksheet menu bar contains menus, such as File and Edit. When you click on a menu, you see a list of commands. Cut and Copy are examples of commands on the Edit menu. Some commands have submenus, such as Clear, which can be highlighted to display another list of commands.

The following shows the Standard toolbar:

Toolbars contain buttons that can be clicked to carry out Excel commands, for example the button with the scissors icon carries out a Cut. Toolbars can also contain other types of objects such as the Zoom combo box two from the end of the Standard toolbar that allows you to select, or type in, a zoom factor, displayed as a percentage.

The following shows the short cut menu that appears when you right-click a worksheet cell:

This short cut menu contains commands that are related to cells, such as Copy.

All the objects on menu bars, toolbars and short cut menus are considered to be controls, including menus, submenus, commands and other special objects such as combo boxes.

Excel 2000 has nearly 100 different built-in command bars containing many thousands of controls. In addition, you can create your own command bars or tailor existing command bars to suit your needs. This can be accomplished manually using View | Toolbars | Customize…, or you can do it programmatically. You might be able to accomplish all the customization you need manually, including attaching command bars to workbooks, but some tasks can only be carried out using VBA code. For example, if you want to automatically remove or hide a command bar when its related workbook is closed or deactivated, you need to use VBA. If you want to add a custom menu to a built-in menu bar when a workbook is opened and remove it when the workbook is closed, you need VBA. Any time you want to dynamically change your command bars in response to user actions, you need VBA. Also, there are some types of controls, such as combo boxes, that can only be created and controlled using VBA.

When you create a command bar using VBA, you specify which of the three types it will be, using the appropriate parameters of the Add method of the CommandBars collection. You will see examples of this below. You can find out what type an existing command bar is by testing its Type property, which will return a numeric value equal to the value of one of the following intrinsic constants:

Constant	Command bar type
msoBarTypeNormal	Toolbar
msoBarTypeMenuBar	Menu Bar
msoBarTypePopup	Short Cut Menu

Controls on command bars also have a Type property similar to the mso... constants shown above. The control that is used most frequently has a Type property of msoControlButton, which represents a command such as the Copy command on the Edit menu of the worksheet menu bar, or a command button on a toolbar, such as the Cut button on the Standard toolbar. This type of control runs a macro or a built in Excel action when it is clicked.

The second most common control has a Type property of msoControlPopup. This represents a menu on a menu bar, such as the Edit menu on the worksheet menu bar, or a submenu on a menu, such as the Clear submenu on the Edit menu on the worksheet menu bar. This type of control contains its own Controls collection, to which you can add further controls.

Controls have an ID property. For built in controls, the ID property determines the internal action carried out by the control. When you set up a custom control, you assign the name of a macro to its OnAction property to make it execute that macro when it is clicked. Custom controls have an ID property of 1.

Many built in menu items and most built-in toolbar controls have a graphic image associated with them. The image is defined by the FaceId property. The ID and FaceId properties of built in commands normally have the same numeric value. You can assign the built-in FaceId values to your own controls, if you know what numeric value to use. You can determine these values using VBA, as you will see below.

Excel's Built-In Command Bars

Before launching into creating our own command bars, it will help to understand how the built in command bars are structured and find out just what is already available in Excel 2000. You can use the following code to list the existing command bars and any that you have added yourself. It lists the name of each command bar in column A and the names of the controls in the command bar's Controls collection in column B as shown in the following screen. The code does not attempt to display lower level controls that belong to controls such as the File menu on the worksheet menu bar, so the procedure has been named ListFirstLevelControls. The macro also shows the control's ID property value, in all cases, and its image and its FaceId property value when such an image exists. Note that some listed controls might not be visible on your own screen. For example, the Standard toolbar's &Mail Recipient button will not be visible if you do not have a mail system.

> Make sure you are in an empty worksheet when you run this macro and the following two examples. They contain tests to make sure they will not overwrite any data in the active sheet.

	CommandBar	Control	FaceID	ID
1	**CommandBar**	**Control**	**FaceID**	**ID**
2	Worksheet Menu Bar			
3		&File		30002
4		&Edit		30003
5		&View		30004
6		&Insert		30005
7		F&ormat		30006
8		&Tools		30007
9		&Data		30011
10		A&ction		30083
11		&Window		30009
12		&Help		30010
13	Chart Menu Bar			
14		&File		30002
15		&Edit		30003
16		&View		30004
17		&Insert		30005
18		F&ormat		30006
19		&Tools		30007
20		&Chart		30022
21		A&ction		30083
22		&Window		30009
23		&Help		30010
24	Standard			
25		&New	2520	2520
26		Open	23	23
27		&Save	3	3
28		&Mail Recipient	3738	3738
29		Print (Production)	2521	2521
30		&Set Print Area	364	364
31		Print Pre&view	109	109
32		&Spelling...	2	2
33		Cu&t	21	21

Here is the code to list the first level controls:

```
Sub ListFirstLevelControls()
    Dim cbCtl As CommandBarControl
    Dim cbBar As CommandBar
    Dim i As Integer
```

```
    If Not IsEmptyWorksheet(ActiveSheet) Then Exit Sub
    On Error Resume Next
    Application.ScreenUpdating = False
    Cells(1, 1).Value = "CommandBar"
    Cells(1, 2).Value = "Control"
    Cells(1, 3).Value = "FaceID"
    Cells(1, 4).Value = "ID"
    Cells(1, 1).Resize(1,4).Font.Bold = True
    i = 2
    For Each cbBar In CommandBars
        Application.StatusBar = "Processing Bar " & cbBar.Name
        Cells(i, 1).Value = cbBar.Name
        i = i + 1
        For Each cbCtl In cbBar.Controls
            Cells(i, 2).Value = cbCtl.Caption
            cbCtl.CopyFace
            If Err.Number = 0 Then
                ActiveSheet.Paste Cells(i, 3)
                Cells(i, 3).Value = cbCtl.FaceID
            End If
            Cells(i, 4).Value = cbCtl.ID
            Err.Clear
            i = i + 1
        Next cbCtl
    Next cbBar
    Range("A:B").EntireColumn.AutoFit
    Application.StatusBar = False
End Sub
```

> This example, and the two following examples can take a long time to complete. If you only want to see part of the output, press *Ctrl+Break* after a minute or so to interrupt the macro, click Debug and then Run | Reset.

`ListFirstLevelControls` first checks that the active sheet is an empty worksheet using the `IsEmptyWorksheet` function that is shown below. It then uses `On Error Resume Next` to avoid run time errors when it tries to access control images that do not exist. In the outer `For Each...Next` loop, it assigns a reference to each command bar to `cbBar`, shows the `Name` property of the command bar on the Status Bar so you can track what it is doing, and places the `Name` in the A column of the current row, defined by `i`.

The inner `For Each...Next` loop processes all the controls on `cbBar`, placing the `Caption` property of each control in column B. It then attempts to use the `CopyFace` method of the control to copy the control's image to the clipboard. If this does not create an error, it pastes the image to column C and places the value of the `FaceId` property in the same cell. It places the `ID` property of the control in column D. It clears any errors, increments `i` by one and processes the next control.

The `IsEmptyWorksheet` function, shown below, checks that the input parameter object `Sht` is a worksheet. If so, it checks that the count of entries in the used range is 0. If both checks succeed, it returns `True`. Otherwise, it issues a warning message and the default return value, which is `False`, is returned:

```
Function IsEmptyWorksheet(Sht As Object) As Boolean
    If TypeName(Sht) = "Worksheet" Then
        If WorksheetFunction.CountA(Sht.UsedRange) = 0 Then
            IsEmptyWorksheet = True
            Exit Function
        End If
    End If
    MsgBox "Please make sure that an empty worksheet is active"
End Function
```

Third Level Controls

The following screen and code take the previous procedure to greater levels of detail. Any controls with the Type property equal to msoControlPopup are examined to see what controls are contained within them. The information on sub controls is indented across the worksheet. The code lists the first, second and third levels of controls, when they exist. For example, the File | Print Area | Set Print Area command, which is at the third level, will be listed. The code could easily allow for four levels of containment, but the built in controls of type msoControlPopup do not go beyond the second level and, therefore, controls contained in them do not go beyond the third level.

Here is the code to list the third level controls:

```
Sub ListThirdLevelControls()
    Dim cbCtl As CommandBarControl
    Dim subCtl As CommandBarControl
    Dim subsubCtl As CommandBarControl
    Dim cbBar As CommandBar
    Dim i As Integer

    If Not IsEmptyWorksheet(ActiveSheet) Then Exit Sub
    On Error Resume Next
    Application.ScreenUpdating = False
    i = 1
    For Each cbBar In CommandBars
        Application.StatusBar = "Processing Bar " & cbBar.Name
        Cells(i, 1).Value = cbBar.Name
        i = i + 1
        For Each cbCtl In cbBar.Controls
            Cells(i, 2).Value = cbCtl.Caption
            cbCtl.CopyFace
            If Err.Number = 0 Then
                ActiveSheet.Paste Cells(i, 3)
                Cells(i, 3).Value = cbCtl.FaceID
            End If
            Err.Clear
            i = i + 1
            If cbCtl.Type = msoControlPopup Then
                For Each subCtl In cbCtl.Controls
                    Cells(i, 3).Value = subCtl.Caption
                    subCtl.CopyFace
                    If Err.Number = 0 Then
                        ActiveSheet.Paste Cells(i, 4)
                        Cells(i, 4).Value = subCtl.FaceID
```

```
            End If
            Err.Clear
            i = i + 1
            If subCtl.Type = msoControlPopup Then
                For Each subsubCtl In subCtl.Controls
                    Cells(i, 4).Value = subsubCtl.Caption
                    subsubCtl.CopyFace
                    If Err.Number = 0 Then
                        ActiveSheet.Paste Cells(i, 5)
                        Cells(i, 5).Value = subsubCtl.FaceID
                    End If
                    Err.Clear
                    i = i + 1
                Next subsubCtl
            End If
        Next subCtl
      End If
    Next cbCtl
  Next cbBar
  Range("A:D").EntireColumn.AutoFit
  Application.StatusBar = False
End Sub
```

The code in `ListThirdLevelControls` nests nearly identical sets of the inner `For Each...Next` loop from `ListFirstLevelControls`. The object variables used are necessarily different and the column numbers a further indented in each nested loop.

Only controls of type `msoControlPopup` are investigated in depth by this macro. There are many other types of toolbar controls that contain control collections that will not be exposed by this macro. See the reference section for a list of other types.

FaceIds

The following code gives you a table of the built in button faces. There are over 5,500 faces, a number that will probably increase with updates to Excel 2000. Note that many `FaceId` values represent blank images and that the same images appear repeatedly as the numbers get higher:

Here is the code to all the `FaceIds`:

```
Sub ListAllFaces()
    Dim i As Integer
    Dim j As Integer
    Dim k As Integer
    Dim cbCtl As CommandBarControl
    Dim cbBar As CommandBar

    If Not IsEmptyWorksheet(ActiveSheet) Then Exit Sub
    On Error Resume Next
    Application.ScreenUpdating = False
    Set cbBar = CommandBars.Add(Position:=msoBarFloating, _
        MenuBar:=False, temporary:=True)
    Set cbCtl = cbBar.Controls.Add(Type:=msoControlButton, _
        temporary:=True)
    k = 1
    Do While Err.Number = 0
        For j = 1 To 10
            i = i + 1
            Application.StatusBar = "FaceID = " & i
            cbCtl.FaceID = i
            cbCtl.CopyFace
            If Err.Number <> 0 Then Exit For
            ActiveSheet.Paste Cells(k, j + 1)
            Cells(k, j).Value = i
        Next j
        k = k + 1
    Loop
    Application.StatusBar = False
    cbBar.Delete
End Sub
```

> Note that when you run this macro your computer may well freeze for a few minutes. The CPU has to do a lot of hard work!

`ListAllFaces` creates a temporary toolbar, `cbBar`, using the `Add` method of the `CommandBars` collection. The toolbar is declared temporary, which means that it will be deleted when you exit Excel, if it has not already been deleted. `cbBar` is declared to be floating, rather than docked at an edge of the screen or a popup. It is also declared *not* to be a menu bar, which means that `cbBar` will be a toolbar. A temporary control is added to `cbBar` using the `Add` method of the `Controls` collection for the command bar, and assigned to `cbCtl`.

The `Do...Loop` continues looping until there are no more valid `FaceId` values and an error occurs. The `Do...Loop` increments k, which represents the row numbers in the worksheet. On every row, j is incremented from 1 to 10. j represents the columns of the worksheet. The value of i is increased by one for every iteration of the code in the `For...Next` loop. i represents the `FaceId`. The `FaceId` property of `cbCtl` is assigned the value of i, and the resulting image is copied to the worksheet. When an error occurs, the `For` loop exits and the test on the `Do` loop ensures that it exits as well.

> The information you have gathered with the last three exercises is not available in any standard Office 2000 documentation. It will be valuable data when you want to modify the existing command bar structures or alter command bar behavior, and as a guide to the built in button faces at your disposal.

Creating New Menus

If you want to provide a user with extra functionality without removing any of the standard commands, you can add a new menu to the existing worksheet menu bar. The following screen shows a new menu called Custom, inserted between the Window and Help menus:

The code to create this menu follows:

```
Public Sub AddCustomMenu()
    Dim cbWSMenuBar As CommandBar
    Dim muCustom As CommandBarControl
    Dim iHelpIndex As Integer

    Set cbWSMenuBar = CommandBars("Worksheet Menu Bar")
    iHelpIndex = cbWSMenuBar.Controls("Help").Index
    Set muCustom = cbWSMenuBar.Controls.Add(Type:=msoControlPopup, _
                                            Before:=iHelpIndex_
                                            Temporary := True)
    With muCustom
        .Caption = "&Custom"
        With .Controls.Add(Type:=msoControlButton)
            .Caption = "&Show Data Form"
            .OnAction = "ShowDataForm"
        End With
        With .Controls.Add(Type:=msoControlButton)
            .Caption = "&Print Data List"
            .OnAction = "PrintDataList"
        End With
        With .Controls.Add(Type:=msoControlButton)
            .Caption = "Sort Names &Ascending"
            .BeginGroup = True
            .OnAction = "SortList"
            .Parameter = "Asc"
        End With
        With .Controls.Add(Type:=msoControlButton)
            .Caption = "Sort Names &Descending"
            .OnAction = "SortList"
            .Parameter = "Dsc"
        End With
    End With
End Sub
```

AddCustomMenu creates an object variable cbWSMenuBar referencing the worksheet menu bar. If you want to add a menu before an existing menu, you need to know the index number of that menu. You can determine the Index property of the control as shown.

AddCustomMenu uses the Add method of the menu bar's Controls collection to add the new menu. The Type property is declared msoControlPopup so that other controls can be attached to the menu. The Before parameter places the new menu just before the Help menu. If you do not specify the position, it will be placed at the end of the menu bar. The Caption property of the new menu is assigned &Custom. The & does not appear in the menu, it causes an underscore to be placed under the character it precedes and indicates that you can activate this menu from the keyboard with *Alt+C*.

The Add method of the new menus Controls collection is then used to add four commands to the menu. They are all of type msoControlButton so they can each run a macro. Each is given an appropriate Caption property, including short cut keys indicated with an &. The OnAction property of each command is assigned the name of the macro it is to run. The first of the sort menu items has its BeginGroup property set to True. This places the dividing line above it to mark it as the beginning of a different group. Both sort commands are assigned the same OnAction macro, but also have their Parameter property assigned text strings which distinguish them.

The Parameter property is a holder for a character string. You can use it for any purpose. Here it is used to hold the strings "Asc", for ascending, and "Dsc", for descending. As you will see below, the SortList procedure will access the strings to determine the sort order required.

The OnAction Macros

The macro assigned to the OnAction property of the Show Data Form menu item is as follows:

```
Private Sub ShowDataForm()
    fmPersonal.Show
End Sub
```

It displays the exactly the same data form the previous chapter on UserForms. The macro assigned to the Print Data List menu item is as follows:

```
Private Sub PrintDataList()
    Range("Database").PrintPreview
End Sub
```

PrintDataList shows a print preview of the list, from which the user can elect to print the list or not.

The macro assigned to the Sort menu items is as follows:

```
Private Sub SortList()
    Dim iAscDsc As Integer

    Select Case CommandBars.ActionControl.Parameter
        Case "Asc"
            iAscDsc = xlAscending
        Case "Dsc"
            iAscDsc = xlDescending
    End Select
    Range("Database").Sort Key1:=Range("A2"), Order1:=iAscDsc, Header:=xlYes
End Sub
```

SortList uses the ActionControl property of the CommandBars collection to get a reference to the command bar control that caused SortList to execute. This is similar to Application.Caller, used in user-defined functions to determine the Range object that executed the function. Knowing the control object that called it, SortList can examine the control's Parameter property to get further information. If the Parameter value is "Asc", SortList assigns an ascending sort. If the Parameter value is "Dsc", it assigns a descending sort. Controls also have a Tag property that can be used, in exactly the same way as the Parameter property, to hold another character string. You can use the Tag property as an alternative to the Parameter property, or you can use it to hold supplementary data.

Deleting a Menu

Built in and custom controls can be deleted using the control's Delete method. The following macro deletes the Custom menu:

```
Public Sub RemoveCustomMenu()
    Dim cbWSMenuBar As CommandBar

    On Error Resume Next
    Set cbWSMenuBar = CommandBars("Worksheet Menu Bar")
    cbWSMenuBar.Controls("Custom").Delete
End Sub
```

On Error is used in case the menu has already been deleted.

> You can use a built in command bar's Reset method to make the entire command bar revert to its default layout and commands. This is not a good idea if users have customized their command bars, or use workbooks or add-ins that customize their command bars, as all customization will be lost.

The following event procedures should be added to the ThisWorkbook module to add the custom menu when the workbook is opened and delete when the workbook is closed:

```
Private Sub Workbook_BeforeClose(Cancel As Boolean)
    Call RemoveCustomMenu
End Sub

Private Sub Workbook_Open()
    Call AddCustomMenu
End Sub
```

It is important to recognize that command bar changes are permanent. If
you do not remove the Custom menu in this example, it will stay in the
Excel worksheet menu bar during the current session and future
sessions. Trying to use this menu with another workbook active could
cause unexpected results.

Creating a Toolbar

If you are creating a simple toolbar with buttons and drop downs, you can do it
manually. However, there are more complex controls, such as those of type
`msoControlEdit`, `msoControlDropdown` and `msoControlComboBox`, which you
can only fully manipulate in VBA code. The following toolbar contains three controls.
The first is of type `msoControlButton` and, in this case, displays the user form for
the data list:

The second control is of type `msoControlPopup` and displays two controls of type
`msoControlButton`:

The third control is of type `msoControlDropdown` and applies an AutoFilter on Department:

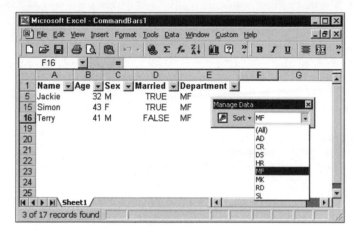

The following code creates the toolbar:

```
Public Sub CreateToolbar()
    'Get rid of any existing toolbar called Manage Data
    On Error Resume Next
    CommandBars("Manage Data").Delete
    On Error GoTo 0

    'Create new toolbar
    With CommandBars.Add(Name:="Manage Data")
        With .Controls.Add(Type:=msoControlButton)
            .OnAction = "ShowDataForm"
            .FaceID = 264
            .TooltipText = "Show Data Form"
        End With
        With .Controls.Add(Type:=msoControlPopup)
            .Caption = "Sort"
            .TooltipText = "Sort Ascending or Descending"
            With .Controls.Add(Type:=msoControlButton)
                .Caption = "Sort Ascending"
                .FaceID = 210
                .OnAction = "SortList"
                .Parameter = "Asc"
            End With
            With .Controls.Add(Type:=msoControlButton)
                .Caption = "Sort Decending"
                .FaceID = 211
                .OnAction = "SortList"
                .Parameter = "Dsc"
            End With
        End With
        With .Controls.Add(Type:=msoControlDropdown)
            .AddItem "(All)"
            .AddItem "AD"
            .AddItem "CR"
            .AddItem "DS"
            .AddItem "HR"
            .AddItem "MF"
            .AddItem "MK"
            .AddItem "RD"
            .AddItem "SL"
            .OnAction = "FilterDepartment"
            .TooltipText = "Select Department"
        End With
        .Visible = True
    End With
End Sub
```

The toolbar itself is very simple to create. CreateToolbar uses the Add method of the CommandBars collection and accepts all the default parameter values apart from the Name property. The first control button is created in much the same way as a menu item, using the Add method of the Controls collection. It is assigned an OnAction macro, a FaceId, and a tool tip.

The second control is created as type msoControlPopup. It is given the Caption of Sort and a tool tip. It is then assigned two controls of its own, of type msoControlButton. They, in turn are assigned the SortList macro and Parameter values as well as FaceIds and captions.

Finally the control of type msoControlDropdown is added. Its dropdown list is populated with department codes and its OnAction macro is FilterDepartment. It is also given a tool tip. The last action is to set the toolbar's Visible property to True to display it.

The FilterDepartment macro follows:

```
Sub FilterDepartment()
    Dim stDept As String

    With CommandBars.ActionControl
        stDept = .List(.ListIndex)
    End With
    If stDept = "(All)" Then
        Range("Database").Parent.AutoFilterMode = False
    Else
        Range("Database").AutoFilter Field:=5, Criteria1:=stDept
    End If
End Sub
```

A dropdown control has a List property that is an array of its list values and a ListIndex property that is the index number of the current list value. The ActionControl property of the CommandBars object, which refers to the currently active control, is a quick way to reference the control and access the List and ListIndex properties to get the department code required. The code is then used to perform the appropriate AutoFilter operation. If the (All) option is chosen, the AutoFilterMode property of the worksheet that is the parent of the Database Range object is set to False, removing the AutoFilter dropdowns and showing any hidden rows.

It is a good idea to run CreateToolbar from the Workbook_Open event procedure and to delete the toolbar in the Workbook_BeforeClose event procedure. The toolbar will remain permanently in Excel if it is not deleted and will give unexpected results when its buttons are pressed when other workbooks are active. If you do refer to CommandBars directly in workbook event procedures, you need to qualify the reference with Application:

```
Application.CommandBars("Manage Data").Delete
```

PopUp Menus

Excel's built in short cut menus are included in the command bar listing created by the macro, ListFirstLevelControls, which we saw earlier in this chapter. The following modified version of this macro shows only the command bars of type msoBarTypePopup:

	A	B	C	D
1	CommandBar	Control	FaceID	ID
2	Query and Pivot			
3		Forma&t Report...	5473	5473
4		Pivot&Chart	3789	3789
5		&Wizard...	457	457
6		&Refresh Data	459	459
7		C&lient-Server Settings...	3988	3988
8		&Select		30252
9		For&mulas		30254
10		Fi&eld Settings...	460	460
11		Table &Options...	1604	1604
12		Show &Pages...	461	461
13	PivotChart Menu			
14		Fi&eld Settings...	460	460
15		&Options...	1604	1604
16		&Refresh Data	459	459
17		&Hide PivotChart Field Buttons	3956	3956
18		For&mulas		30254
19		Remo&ve Field	5416	5416
20	Workbook tabs			
21		Popups	957	957
22		Sheet1	957	957

The code to display the popups is shown below:

```
Sub ListPopups()
    Dim cbCtl As CommandBarControl
    Dim cbBar As CommandBar
    Dim i As Integer

    On Error Resume Next
    Application.ScreenUpdating = False
    Cells(1, 1).Value = "CommandBar"
    Cells(1, 2).Value = "Control"
    Cells(1, 3).Value = "FaceId"
    Cells(1, 4).Value = "ID"
    i = 2
    For Each cbBar In CommandBars
        Application.StatusBar = "Processing Bar " & cbBar.Name
        If cbBar.Type = msoBarTypePopup Then
            Cells(i, 1).Value = cbBar.Name
            i = i + 1
            For Each cbCtl In cbBar.Controls
                Cells(i, 2).Value = cbCtl.Caption
                cbCtl.CopyFace
                If Err.Number = 0 Then
                    ActiveSheet.Paste Cells(i, 3)
                    Cells(i, 3).Value = cbCtl.FaceID
                End If
                Cells(i, 4).Value = cbCtl.ID
                Err.Clear
                i = i + 1
            Next cbCtl
        End If
    Next cbBar
    Range("A:B").EntireColumn.AutoFit
    Application.StatusBar = False
End Sub
```

The listing is identical to `ListFirstLevelControls`, apart from the introduction of a block `If` structure that processes only command bars of type `msoBarTypePopup`. If you peruse the listing produced by `ListPopups`, you will find you can identify the common short cut menus. For example, there are command bars named Cell, Row, and Column that correspond to the short cut menus that pop up when you right click a worksheet cell, row number or column letter.

> You might be confused about the fact that the Cell, Row and Column command bars are listed twice. The first set is for a worksheet in normal view. The second set is for a worksheet in page break view.
>
> Another tricky one is the Workbook tabs command bar. This is not the short cut you get when you click on an individual worksheet tab. It is the short cut for the workbook navigation buttons to the left of the worksheet tabs. The short cut for the tabs is the Ply command bar. I can only assume this is some type of obscure American joke that is not decipherable to Australians.

Having identified the short cut menus, you can tailor them to your own needs using VBA code. For example, the following screen shows a modified Cell command bar that includes an option to Clear All:

The Clear All control was added using the following code:

```
Public Sub AddShortCut()
    Dim cbBar As CommandBar
    Dim cbCtl As CommandBarControl
    Dim lIndex As Long

    Set cbBar = CommandBars("Cell")
    lIndex = cbBar.Controls("Clear Contents").Index
    Set cbCtl = cbBar.Controls.Add(Type:=msoControlButton, ID:=1964, _
                                    Before:=lIndex)
    cbCtl.Caption = "Clear &All"
End Sub
```

`AddShortCut` starts by assigning a reference to the `Cell` command bar to `cbBar`.

> If you want to refer to the Cell command bar that is shown in page
> break view in Excel 2000, you can use its Index property:
>
> ```
> Set cbBar = CommandBars(26)
> ```
>
> You need to take care here, if you want code compatible with Excel 97. In
> Excel 97, the Index property of the Cell command bar in page break
> view is 24. You can use the following code in both versions:
>
> ```
> Set cbBar = CommandBars(CommandBars("Cell").Index + 3)
> ```

AddShortCut records the Index property of the Clear Contents control in
lIndex, so that it can add the new control before the Clear Contents control.
AddShortCut uses the Add method of the Controls collection to add the new
control to cbBar, specifying the ID property of the built-in Edit | Clear | All menu
item on the worksheet menu bar.

> *The* Add *method of the* Controls *collection allows you to specify the* ID
> *property of a built-in command. The listing from*
> ListThirdLevelControls *allows you to determine that the* ID
> *property, which is the same as the* FaceId *property, of the* Edit | Clear | All
> *menu item, is 1964.*

The built-in Caption property for the newly added control is All, so AddShortCut
changes the Caption to be more descriptive.

> *You can safely leave the modified* Cell *command bar in your* CommandBars
> *collection. It is not tied to any workbook and does not depend on having access*
> *to macros in a specific workbook.*

Showing Popup Command Bars

If you want to display a short cut menu without having to right-click on a cell, or chart
etc., you can create code to display the short cut in a number of ways. For example,
you might like to display the short cut Cell command bar from the keyboard, using
Ctrl+Shift+c. You can do this using the following code:

```
Sub SetShortCut()
    Application.OnKey "^+c", "ShowCellShortCut"
End Sub

Private Sub ShowCellShortCut()
    CommandBars("Cell").ShowPopup x:=0, y:=0
End Sub
```

ShowCellShortCut uses the ShowPopup method to display the Cell short cut menu
at the top left corner of the screen. The parameters are the x and y screen coordinates
for the top left of the menu.

You can also create a popup menu from scratch. The following popup appears when you right-click inside the range named `Database`. Outside the range, the normal Cell popup menu appears:

The following code created the pop up menu:

```
Sub MakePopup()
    With CommandBars.Add(Name:="Data Popup", Position:=msoBarPopup)
        With .Controls.Add(Type:=msoControlButton)
            .OnAction = "ShowDataForm"
            .FaceID = 264
            .Caption = "Data Form"
            .TooltipText = "Show Data Form"
        End With
        With .Controls.Add(Type:=msoControlButton)
            .Caption = "Sort Ascending"
            .FaceID = 210
            .OnAction = "SortList"
            .Parameter = "Asc"
        End With
        With .Controls.Add(Type:=msoControlButton)
            .Caption = "Sort Decending"
            .FaceID = 211
            .OnAction = "SortList"
            .Parameter = "Dsc"
        End With
    End With
End Sub
```

The code is similar to the code that created the custom menu and toolbar in previous examples. The difference is that, when the popup is created by the Add method of the CommandBars collection, the Position parameter is set to msoBarPopup. The Name property here is set to Data Popup.

You can display the pop up with the following BeforeRightClick event procedure in the code module behind the worksheet:

```
Private Sub Worksheet_BeforeRightClick(ByVal Target As Range, _
                                       Cancel As Boolean)
    If Not Intersect(Range("Database"), Target) Is Nothing Then
        CommandBars("Data Popup").ShowPopup
        Cancel = True
    End If
End Sub
```

When you right-click the worksheet, the event procedure checks to see if Target is within Database. If so, it displays **Data Popup** and cancels the right-click event. Otherwise the normal **Cell** short cut menu appears.

Disabling Command Bars

Command bars have an Enabled property and a Visible property. If a command bar is enabled, and it is not of type msoBarTypePopup, it appears in the **Tools | Customize** dialog box. If it is checked in the **Tools | Customize** dialog box, it is visible on the screen.

You cannot set the Visible property of a command bar to True unless the Enabled property is also set to True. Setting the Visible property of an enabled command bar of type msoBarTypeNormal to False removes it from the screen. Setting the worksheet menu bar's Visible property to False does not work. Excel treats it as a special case and insists on showing it when a worksheet is active. The only way to remove the worksheet menu is to set its Enabled property to False.

The following code removes any visible toolbars and the worksheet menu bar from the screen:

```
Sub RemoveToolbarsAndWorksheetMenuBar()
    Dim cbBar As CommandBar

    For Each cbBar In CommandBars
        If cbBar.Enabled And cbBar.Type = msoBarTypeNormal Then
            cbBar.Visible = False
        End If
    Next cbBar
    CommandBars("Worksheet Menu Bar").Enabled = False
    Application.OnKey "%-", ""
End Sub
```

And this is what the screen looks like:

	A	B	C	D	E	F	G
1	Name	Age	Sex	Married	Department		
2	Warren	45	M	FALSE	HR		
3	Wacka	39	F	TRUE	RD		
4	Terry	41	M	FALSE	MF		
5	Simon	43	F	TRUE	MF		
6	Sheila	38	F	TRUE	MK		
7	Sally	21	M	FALSE	CR		
8	Molly	47	F	FALSE	HR		
9	Len	42	F	TRUE	RD		
10	Kim	55	F	TRUE	SL		
11	Kielly	40	M	FALSE	AD		
12	Kendal	43	F	TRUE	HR		
13	John	44	F	TRUE	DS		
14	Joan	37	F	TRUE	MK		
15	Jackie	32	M	TRUE	MF		
16	Harry	46	M	TRUE	HR		
17	Francine	23	M	TRUE	MK		
18	Bill	36	M	FALSE	SL		

Microsoft Excel - CommandBars1

D7 = FALSE

Sheet1

Ready

> The final action carried out by
> `RemoveToolbarsAndWorksheetMenuBar` is to disable the *Alt+-* key
> combination that displays the workbook window's control menu. If you
> don't do this when you remove the worksheet menu bar, the user can still
> access the control menu using *Alt+-*, and then use the cursor movement
> keys to make a phantom copy of the worksheet menu bar slowly appear.

You can restore the worksheet menu bar and the Standard and Formatting toolbars,
with the following code, assuming the toolbars have not had their `Enabled` property
set to `False`:

```
Sub RestoreToolbarsAndWorksheetMenuBar()
    CommandBars("Worksheet Menu Bar").Enabled = True
    Application.OnKey "%-"
    CommandBars("Standard").Visible = True
    CommandBars("Formatting").Visible = True
End Sub
```

Disabling Shortcut Access to Customize

If you want to stop users making changes to your custom command bars or built in
command bars, you can prevent access to the customization dialog box and toolbar
with the following code. The code could be placed in the `Personal.xls` workbook so
that it is automatically applied at the beginning of an Excel session:

```
Private Sub Workbook_Open()
    'Code to customize command bars goes here…
    Application.CommandBars("Tools").Controls("Customize...").Enabled = False
    Application.CommandBars("Toolbar List").Enabled = False
End Sub
```

The second last line of the code disables the Tools | Customize menu item. The last line
of the code disables the short cut menu that appears when you right click a command
bar and also disables the View | Toolbars menu item. Because the code is in a
workbook event procedure, the reference to `Application` is required.

> *Note the syntax in the above code. We have been able to treat the* Tools
> *control on the worksheet menu bar as if it were a command bar itself. If you
> search the table generated by* `ListThirdLevelControls`, *you will find a
> command bar called* Built-in Menus. *The controls on this command bar can be
> directly addressed as command bars.*

> *The* Toolbar List *command bar was introduced in Excel 97 Service Release 1.
> You cannot use this command bar in earlier releases of Excel 97 — it is a
> special hidden command bar. Like the* Built-in Menus *command bar controls,*
> `ToolBar List` *has no* `Index` *property in the* `CommandBars` *collection,
> although it can be addressed by its* `Name` *property.*

If you only want to protect some command bars, you can use the `Protect` property of
the command bars. The following code applies all protection options to the Standard
toolbar. You can omit the constants for any options that are not wanted:

```
Sub ProtectToolbar()
    CommandBars("Standard").Protection = msoBarNoCustomize + _
                                         msoBarNoResize + _
                                         msoBarNoMove + _
                                         msoBarNoChangeVisible + _
                                         msoBarNoChangeDock + _
                                         msoBarNoVerticalDock + _
                                         msoBarNoHorizonaldock
End Sub
```

You can remove the protection with:

```
Sub UnProtectToolbar()
    CommandBars("Standard").Protection = msoBarNoProtection
End Sub
```

Summary

In this chapter you have seen how the Excel 2000 command bars are structured and learned how to create:

❑ Lists of the built-in control images with their ID and FaceId properties,

❑ An entire list of the FaceIds that are available,

❑ A complete list of popup menu items .

You have also seen how to create your own command bars and how to add controls to your command bars. The differences between the three types of command bars, that is toolbars, menu bars and popup menus, have been described and methods of creating them programmatically have been presented. In addition, you have been shown how to enable and disable command bars and controls and how to protect command bars so that users cannot change them.

13

Class Modules

Class modules are used in VBA to create your own customized objects. Most VBA users will never have to create their own objects because Excel already provides all of the objects they need. However, there are occasions when class modules can be very useful. You can use them to trap application events, embedded chart events and events associated with ActiveX controls as you will see below.

In this chapter, we will create some simple (if not terribly useful) objects, to get the idea of how class modules work. Then we will apply the principles to some more useful examples. You are already familiar with Excel's built-in objects, such as the Worksheet object, and you know that objects often belong to collections such as the Worksheets collection. You also know that objects have properties and methods, such as the Name property and the Copy method of the Worksheet object. Using a class module, you can create your own "blueprint" for a new object, such as an Employee object. You can define properties and methods for the object, such as a rate property that records the employee's current rate of pay, and a training method that consumes resources and increases the employee's skills. You can also create a new collection for the object, such as the Employees collection. The class module is a plan for the objects you want to create. From it you can create instances of your object. For example, Mary, Jack and Anne could be instances of an Employee object, all belonging to the Employees collection.

You might not be aware of it, but you have been using some class modules already. The modules behind worksheets, charts, workbooks and UserForms are class modules. However, they are special types of class module that behave a little differently to those you create yourself. They are designed specifically to support the object with which they are associated, give you access to the event procedures for that object and they cannot be deleted without deleting the associated object.

Creating Your Own Objects

Let's proceed with creating the Employee object we have talked about. You want to store the employee's name, hours worked per week and rate of pay. From this information, you want to calculate the employee's weekly pay. You can create an Employee object with three properties to hold the required data and with a method that calculates the weekly pay.

To do this, you create a class module as shown in the top right of the following screen. The class module has been named `clsEmployee`:

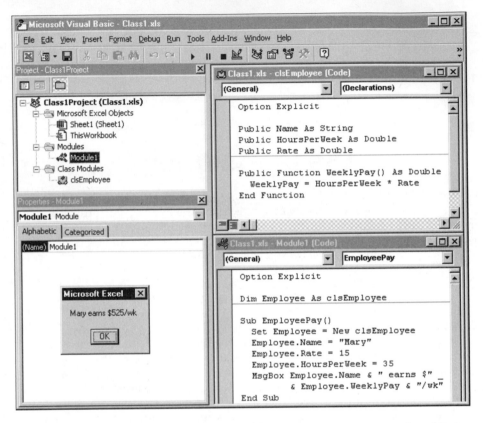

The class module declares three public variables — `Name`, `HoursPerWeek` and `Rate` — which are the properties of the `Employee` object. There is also one a public function, `WeeklyPay`. Recall, that any public function or sub procedure in the class module behaves as a method of the object. A function is a method that can generate a return value. A sub is a method that does not return a value.

The code in the standard module (at the bottom right of the screen) generates an employee object from the `clsEmployee` blueprint. The module declares `Employee` as a `clsEmployee` type. The `EmployeePay` sub procedure uses the `Set` statement to assign a new instance of `clsEmployee` to `Employee`, i.e. `Set` creates the new object. The sub then assigns values to the three properties of the object, before generating the message that appears in the message box at the bottom left of the screen. To form the message, it accesses the `Name` property of the `Employee` object and executes the `WeeklyPay` method of the `Employee` object.

An alternative way of setting up the standard code module, when you only need to create a single instance of the object variable, is as follows:

```
Dim Employee As New clsEmployee

Sub EmployeePay()
    Employee.Name = "Mary"
    Employee.Rate = 15
    Employee.HoursPerWeek = 35
    MsgBox Employee.Name & " earns $" & Employee.WeeklyPay & "/wk"
End Sub
```

Here, the keyword New is used on the declaration line. In this case, the Employee object is automatically created when it is first referenced in the code.

Property Procedures

If your properties are defined by public variables, they are read/write properties. They can be directly accessed and can be directly assigned new values, as we have seen above. If you want to perform checks or calculations on properties, you use Property Let and Property Get procedures to define the properties in your class module, instead of using public variables. Property Get procedures allow the class module to control the way in which properties are accessed. Property Let procedures allow the class module to control the way in which properties can be assigned values. For example, say you want to break up the employee hours into normal time and overtime, where the value of overtime is anything over 35 hours. You want to have an HoursPerWeek property, which includes both normal and overtime hours that can be read and can be assigned new values. You want the class module to split the hours into normal and overtime and set up two properties, NormalHours and OverTimeHours that can be read, but cannot be directly assigned new values. You can set up the following code in your class module:

```
Class2.xls - clsEmployee (Code)
(General)                              NormalHours [PropertyGet]

    Public Name As String
    Private NormalHrs As Double
    Private OverTimeHrs As Double
    Public Rate As Double

    Public Function WeeklyPay() As Double
        WeeklyPay = NormalHrs * Rate + OverTimeHrs * Rate * 1.5
    End Function

    Property Let HoursPerWeek(Hours As Double)
        NormalHrs = WorksheetFunction.Min(35, Hours)
        OverTimeHrs = WorksheetFunction.Max(0, Hours - 35)
    End Property

    Property Get HoursPerWeek() As Double
        HoursPerWeek = NormalHours + OverTimeHours
    End Property

    Property Get NormalHours() As Double
        NormalHours = NormalHrs
    End Property

    Property Get OverTimeHours() As Double
        OverTimeHours = OverTimeHrs
    End Property
```

HoursPerWeek is no longer declared as a variable in the declarations section. Instead, two new private variables have been added — NormalHrs and OverTimeHrs. HoursPerWeek is now defined by a Property Let procedure, which processes the input when you assign a value to the HoursPerWeek property. It breaks the hours into normal time and overtime. The Property Get procedure for HoursPerWeek returns the sum of normal and overtime hours when you access the property value.

NormalHours and OverTimeHours are defined only by Property Get procedures that return the values in the Private variables, NormalHrs and OverTimeHrs, respectively. This makes the properties NormalHours and OverTimeHours read-only. There is no way they can be assigned values apart from through the HoursPerWeek property.

The WeeklyPay function has been updated to calculate pay as normal hours at the standard rate and overtime hours at 1.5 times the standard rate. You can change the standard module code as follows to generate the message shown:

```
Dim Employee As New clsEmployee

Sub EmployeePay()
    Employee.Name = "Mary"
    Employee.Rate = 15
    Employee.HoursPerWeek = 45
    MsgBox Employee.Name & " earns $" _
           & Employee.WeeklyPay & "/wk" _
           & " including " & Employee.OverTimeHours _
           & " hrs overtime"
End Sub
```

Microsoft Excel

Mary earns $750/wk including 10 hrs overtime

OK

Creating Your Own Collections

Now that you have an Employee object, you will want to have many employee objects and what better way is there to organize them, but in a collection. VBA has a Collection object that you can use as follows, in a standard module:

```
Option Explicit
    Dim Employees As New Collection

Sub AddEmployees()
    Dim Employee As clsEmployee
    Dim lCount As Long

    For lCount = 1 To Employees.Count
        Employees.Remove 1
    Next lCount

    Set Employee = New clsEmployee
    Employee.Name = "Mary"
    Employee.Rate = 15
    Employee.HoursPerWeek = 45
    Employees.Add Employee, Employee.Name
```

```
    Set Employee = New clsEmployee
    Employee.Name = "Jack"
    Employee.Rate = 14
    Employee.HoursPerWeek = 35
    Employees.Add Employee, Employee.Name

    MsgBox "Number of Employees =  " & Employees.Count
    MsgBox "Employees(2).Name = " & Employees(2).Name
    MsgBox "Employees("""Jack""").Rate = " & Employees("Jack").Rate
    For Each Employee In Employees
        MsgBox Employee.Name & " earns $" & Employee.WeeklyPay
    Next Employee
End Sub
```

At the top of the standard module, we declare Employees to be a new collection. The AddEmployees procedure uses the Remove method of the collection in the For...Next loop to remove any existing objects. It keeps removing the first object in the collection, because as soon as you remove it, the second object automatically becomes the first object, and so on — hence the .Remove 1 statement. This step is normally not necessary, as the collection is initialized empty. It is only here to demonstrate the Remove method and also allow you to run the procedure more than once without doubling up the items in the collection.

AddEmployees creates the first employee, Mary, and uses the Add method of the collection to place the Mary object in the collection. The first parameter of the Add method is a reference to the object itself. The second parameter, which is optional, is an identifying key that can be used to reference the object later. In this case we have used the Employees collection's Name property. The same procedure is used with Jack.

> If you supply a key value for each member of the collection, the keys must be unique. You will get a runtime error when you attempt to add a new member to the collection with a key value that is already in use. Using a person's name as the key is not recommended as people can have the same name. Use a unique identifier, such as a Social Security number.

The MsgBox statements illustrate that you can reference the collection in the same ways you can reference Excel's built-in collections. For instance the Employees collection has a Count property. You can reference a member of the collection by position or by the key, if you have entered a key value.

Class Module Collection

You can also set up your collection in a class module. There are advantages and disadvantages in doing this. The advantages are that you get much more control over interaction with the collection, you can prevent direct access to the collection, and the code is encapsulated into a single module that makes it more transportable and easier to maintain. The disadvantages are that it takes more work to set up the collection, and that you lose some of the short cut ways to reference members of the collection and the collection itself.

The following screen shows the contents of a class module `clsEmployees`:

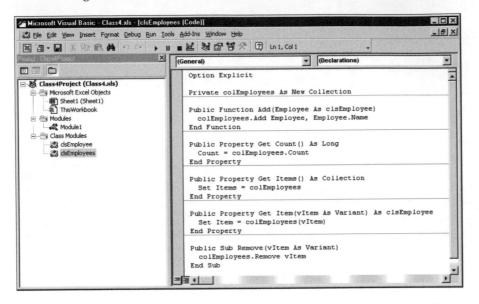

When the collection is in its own class module, you can no longer directly use the collection's four methods (Add, Count, Item, and Remove) in your standard module. You need to set up your own methods and properties in the class module, even if you have no intention of modifying the collections methods. On the other hand, you have control over what you choose to implement and what you choose to modify and what you present as a method and what you present as a property.

In `clsEmployees`, Function Add, Sub Remove, Property Get Item, and Property Get Count pass on most of the functionality of the collection's methods. There is one new feature in the Property Get Items procedure. Whereas Property Get Item passes back a reference to a single member of the collection, Property Get Items passes back a reference to the entire collection. This is to provide the capability to use the collection in a For Each...Next loop.

The standard module code is now as follows:

```
Option Explicit
Dim Employees As New clsEmployees

Sub AddEmployees()
    Dim Employee As clsEmployee
    Dim lCount As Long
    Dim Names As Variant
    Dim Rates As Variant
    Dim Hours As Variant

    Names = Array("Mary", "Jack", "Anne", "Harry")
    Rates = Array(15, 14, 20, 17)
    Hours = Array(45, 35, 40, 40)

    For lCount = 1 To Employees.Count
        Employees.Remove 1
    Next lCount
```

```
    For lCount = LBound(Names) To UBound(Names)
        Set Employee = New clsEmployee
        Employee.Name = Names(lCount)
        Employee.Rate = Rates(lCount)
        Employee.HoursPerWeek = Hours(lCount)
        Employees.Add Employee
        Set Employee = Nothing
    Next lCount

    MsgBox "Number of Employees =  " & Employees.Count
    MsgBox "Employees.Item(2).Name = " & Employees.Item(2).Name
    MsgBox "Employees.Item(""Jack"").Rate = " & Employees.Item("Jack").Rate
    For Each Employee In Employees.Items
        MsgBox Employee.Name & " earns $" & Employee.WeeklyPay
    Next Employee
End Sub
```

Employees is declared to be an instance of clsEmployees. The code that follows
defines three arrays as a convenient way to make it clear what data is being used. As
before, the collection is cleared of objects and then a For...Next loop adds the four
employees to the collection. As one small convenience, we no longer need to specify
the key value when using the Add method of the Employees collection. The Add
method code in clsEmployees does this for us.

The second, third and fourth MsgBox statements show the new properties needed to
reference the collection and its members. You need to use the Item property to
reference a member and the Items property to reference the whole collection.

Trapping Application Events

You can use a class module to trap application events. Most of these events are the
same as the workbook events, but they apply to all open workbooks, not just the
particular workbook that contains the event procedures. For example, in a workbook
there is a BeforePrint event that is triggered when you print anything in that
workbook. At the application level, there is a WorkbookBeforePrint event that is
triggered when any open workbook prints.

To see the application events, you first insert a class module into your project. The
class module can have any valid module name. The one shown in the screenshot below
has been named clsAppEvents. You then type in the following variable declaration
at the top of the module:

```
Public WithEvents xlApp As Application
```

The object variable name, xlApp, can be any valid variable name, as long as you use it
consistently in code that refers to the class module, as a property of the class. The
WithEvents key word causes the events associated with the application object to be
exposed. You can now choose xlApp from the left hand side drop down at the top of
the module and then use the right hand side drop down to see the event list as follows:

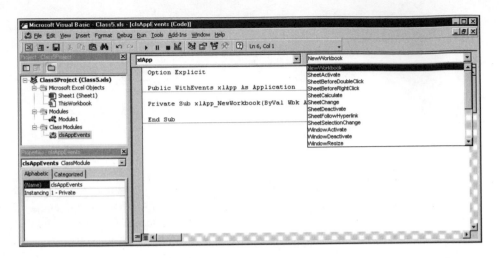

We will choose the WorkbookBeforePrint event and extend the event procedure that was presented in the chapter on events, using the following code in clsAppEvents:

```
Private Sub xlApp_WorkbookBeforePrint(ByVal Wbk As Workbook, _
                                      Cancel As Boolean)
    Dim Wks As Worksheet
    Dim stFullFileName As String
    Dim stCompanyName As String

    With Wbk
        stCompanyName = "Execuplan Consulting"
        stFullFileName = .FullName
        For Each Wks In .Worksheets
            With Wks.PageSetup
                .LeftFooter = stCompanyName
                .CenterFooter = ""
                .RightFooter = stFullFileName
            End With
        Next Wks
    End With
End Sub
```

Unlike sheet and workbook class modules, the event procedures you place in your own class modules do not automatically function. You need to create an instance of your class module and assign the Application object to the xlApp property of the new object. The following code must be set up in a standard module:

```
Public xlApplication As New clsAppEvents

Sub TrapApplicationEvents()
    Set xlApplication.xlApp = Application
End Sub
```

All you need to do now is execute the TrapApplicationEvents procedure. The WorkbookBeforePrint event procedure will then run when you use any **Print** or **Preview** commands, until you close the workbook containing the event procedure.

> It is possible to terminate application event trapping during the current session. Any action that resets module level variables and public variables will terminate application event processing, as the class module instance will be destroyed. Actions that can cause this include editing code in the VB Editor and executing the End statement in VBA code.
>
> There have been (relatively rare) cases, in previous versions of Excel, where bugs in Excel have caused variables to reset. It would be wise to expect that bugs could also exist in Excel 2000.

If you want to enable application event processing for all Excel sessions, you can place your class module and standard module code in Personal.xls and execute TrapApplicationEvents in the Workbook_Open event procedure. You could even transfer the code in TrapApplicationEvents to the Workbook_Open event procedure. However, you must keep the Public declaration of xlApplication in a standard module.

To illustrate, you can place the following code in the declarations section of a standard module:

```
Public xlApplication As New clsAppEvents
```

You can place the following event procedure in the ThisWorkbook module:

```
Private Sub Workbook_Open()
    Set xlApplication.xlApp = Application
End Sub
```

Embedded Chart Events

If you want to trap events for a chart embedded in a worksheet, you use a process similar to the process for trapping application events. First insert a new class module in your project, or you could use the same class module that you used for the application events. You place the following declaration at the top of the class module:

```
Public WithEvents Cht As Chart
```

We will set up the same BeforeDoubleClick event procedure that we used in the chapter on Event Procedures for a chart sheet. The class module should be as follows:

```
Public WithEvents Cht As Chart

Private Sub cht_BeforeDoubleClick(ByVal ElementID As XlChartItem, _
        ByVal Arg1 As Long, ByVal Arg2 As Long, Cancel As Boolean)
    Dim Srs As Series

    Select Case ElementID
        Case xlLegend
            ActiveChart.HasLegend = False
            Cancel = True
        Case xlChartArea
            ActiveChart.HasLegend = True
            Cancel = True
        Case xlSeries
            'Arg1 is the Series index
```

```
        'Arg2 is the point index (-1 if the entire series is selected)
        Set Srs = ActiveChart.SeriesCollection(Arg1)
        If Arg2 = -1 Then
            With Srs.Border
                If .ColorIndex = xlColorIndexAutomatic Then
                    .ColorIndex = 1
                Else
                    .ColorIndex = (.ColorIndex Mod 56) + 1
                End If
            End With
        Else
            With Srs.Points(Arg2)
                .HasDataLabel = Not .HasDataLabel
            End With
        End If
        Cancel = True
    End Select
End Sub
```

This code allows you to double click the chart legend to make it disappear, or double click in the Chart Area to make it re-appear. If you double click a series line, it changes color. If you select a point in a series, by clicking on it, and then double click it, it will toggle the data label on and off for that point. For more details see Chapter 9 on Event Procedures.

Say your chart is contained in a `ChartObject` named `Chart Area` in a worksheet called `Mangoes` and you have named your class module `clsChartEvents`. In your standard module, you enter the following:

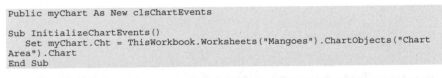

```
Public myChart As New clsChartEvents

Sub InitializeChartEvents()
    Set myChart.Cht = ThisWorkbook.Worksheets("Mangoes").ChartObjects("Chart
Area").Chart
End Sub
```

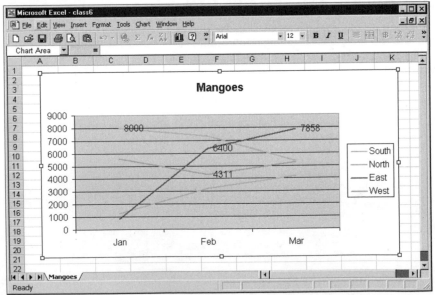

After executing `InitializeChartEvents`, you can double click the series, points and legend to run the `BeforeDoubleClick` event procedure.

230

A Collection of UserForm Controls

When you have a number of the same type of control on a form, you often write almost identical event procedures for each one. For example, say you want to be able to double click the label to the left of each of the text boxes in the following user form to clear the text box and set the focus to the text box. You would normally write four, almost identical, event procedures, one for each label control:

```
Fruit Prices                    [X]

    Bananas      [   15  ]

    Lychees      [  12.5 ]

    Mangoes      [   20  ]
                            [  OK   ]
    Rambutan     [   18  ]  [ Cancel ]
```

Using a class module, you can write a single generic event procedure to apply to all the label controls, or just those that need the procedure. The label controls and text boxes in the user form have been given corresponding names as follows:

Label	Text Box
lbBananas	txBananas
lbychees	txLychees
lbMangoes	txMangoes
lbRambutan	txRambutan

The following code is entered in a class module clsControlEvents:

```
Public WithEvents Lbl As MSForms.Label
Public Frm As UserForm

Private Sub Lbl_DblClick(ByVal Cancel As MSForms.ReturnBoolean)
    Dim stProduct As String
    Dim stTextBoxName As String

    Product = Mid(Lbl.Name, 3)
    stTextBoxName = "tx" & stProduct
    With Frm.Controls(stTextBoxName)
        .Text = ""
        .SetFocus
    End With
End Sub
```

Lbl is declared with events as a user form label. Frm is declared to be the user form. The generic DblClick event procedure for Lbl uses the Mid function to get the product name starting with the third character of the label name, removing the "lb" identifier. It converts this to the text box name by appending "tx" in front of the product name.

231

The With...End With structure identifies the text box object by using the text box name as an index into the Controls collection of the user form. It sets the Text property of the text box to a zero length string and uses the SetFocus method to place the cursor in the text box.

The following code is entered into the class module behind the UserForm:

```
Dim colLabels As New Collection

Private Sub UserForm_Initialize()
    Dim Ctl As MSForms.Control
    Dim obEvents As clsControlEvents

    For Each Ctl In Me.Controls
        If TypeOf Ctl Is MSForms.Label Then
            Set obEvents = New clsControlEvents
            Set obEvents.Lbl = Ctl
            Set obEvents.Frm = Me
            colLabels.Add obEvents
        End If
    Next Ctl
End Sub
```

colLabels is declared as a new collection to hold the objects that will be created from the clsControlEvents class module. In the user form Initialize event procedure, the label controls are associated with instances of clsControlEvents.

The For Each...Next loop processes all the controls on the form. When it identifies a control that is a label, using the TypeOf key word to identify the control type, it creates a new instance of clsControlEvents and assigns it to ctlEvents. The Lbl property of the new object is assigned a reference to the control and the Frm property is assigned a reference to the user form. The new object is then added to the colLabels collection.

When the user form is loaded into memory, the Initialize event runs and connects the label controls to instances of the class module event procedure. Double-clicking any label clears the text box to the right and sets the focus to that text box, ready for new data to be typed in.

Referencing Classes across Projects

When you want to run macros in another workbook, you can use Tools | References in the VB Editor window to create a reference to the other workbook's VBA project. The reference shows as a special entry in the Project Explorer as shown on the following screen:

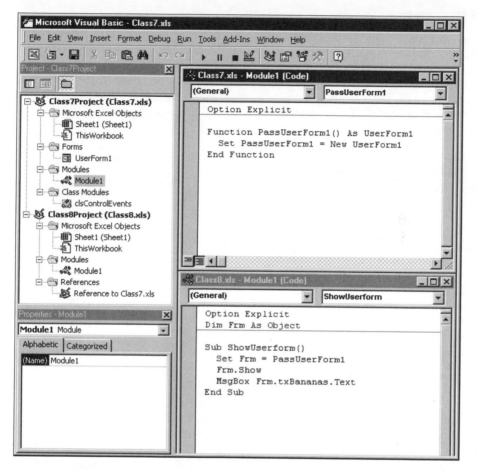

Class8.xls has a reference to Class7.xls, which contains the UserForm from our previous example. The reference allows you to run procedures in standard modules in Class7.xls from standard modules in Class8.xls. However, the reference does not allow you to create instances of class modules or UserForms in the referenced workbook.

However, there is a way to get around this, which is illustrated in the above screen. For example, you can indirectly access a UserForm in the referenced workbook if that workbook has a function that returns a reference to the UserForm. There is an example of this type of function in the top right hand corner of the above screen. PassUserForm1, in Class7.xls, is a function that assigns a new instance of UserForm1 to its return value. In Class8.xls, Frm is declared as a generic Object type. ShowUserform assigns the return value of PassUserForm1 to Frm. Frm can then be used to show the UserForm and access its control values, as long as the UserForm is hidden, not unloaded.

Summary

Class module are used to create a blueprint for a new object, such as the Employee object that was presented in this chapter. Function and Sub procedures are used in the class module to create methods for the object. Public variables declare the properties for the object. However, if you need to take programmatic control when a property is assigned a value, you can define the property using a Property Let procedure. In addition, Property Get procedures allow you to control access to property values.

To use the code in your class module, you create one or more instances of your object. For example, you can create Mary and Jack as instances of an Employee object. You can further customize your objects by creating your own collection, where you add all the instances of your object.

Class modules are not used to create objects to the same extent in Excel VBA as they are used in a stand-alone programming language such as Visual Basic. This is because Excel already contains the objects that most Excel programmers want to use. However, Excel programmers can use class modules to trap application level events, such as the WorkbookBeforePrint event that allows you to control the printing of all open workbooks. Class modules also make it possible to write a single event procedure that can be used by many instances of a particular object, such as a text box control on a UserForm.

Addins

If you want to make your workbook invisible to the user in the Excel window, you can turn it into an **Addin** file. An Addin can be loaded into memory using File | Open, but it generally makes more sense to access it via Tools | Add-Ins…. Either way, the file does not appear in the Excel Application window, but the macros it contains can be executed from the user interface and user defined functions it contains can be used in worksheet calculations. The Addin's macros can be attached to menu commands and toolbar buttons, and the Addin can communicate with the user through UserForms and VBA functions such as `InputBox` and `MsgBox`.

There is a misconception about Addins. It is widely believed that an Addin is a compiled version of a workbook. In most programming languages, compilation involves translating the readable programming code into machine language that is not decipherable by you and I. This is *not* the case with an Excel Addin. In fact, all that happens is that the workbook is hidden from the user interface. The Addin's worksheets and charts can no longer be seen by anyone. Its code modules can still be viewed, as normal, in the VB Editor window and remain complete with comments as well as code.

However, the Office 2000 Developer Addition does make it is possible to create a compiled version of an Addin. This is referred to as a COM (Component Object Model) Addin. It is beyond the scope of this book to explain COM Addins in detail, but you will find a description of how to convert an Excel Addin, which has been designed to run in the VB Editor, to a COM Addin in Chapter 17 on Programming the VBE.

> For this chapter, we have taken the `CommandBars1.xls` file that we used in Chapter 12 on Command Bars, saved it as `AddIn1.xls`, prior to converting it to `Addin1.xla`, and adapted the code to make it suitable for an Addin. We have removed the code on popup menus as it is not relevant and we have changed the name of Sheet1 to `Database`.
>
> Although it is not necessary to give an Addin file name an `.xla` extension, it is a good idea to do so. It identifies the file as an Addin and ensures that the Addin icon appears against the file in the Windows File Manager. The conversion of a workbook file to an Addin file is covered below.

Hiding the Code

You cannot stop users from seeing a standard workbook's name, or an Addin's name, in the Project Explorer window. However, you can stop users from expanding the workbook's name, or Addin's name, to view the component modules and user forms and the code they contain.

You prevent access to your code by putting a password on the VBA project. Select the project and use Tools | <ProjectName> Properties (where ProjectName is the name of your particular project) to see the following screen:

After you have entered the password twice and clicked OK, you need to save the file, close it and reopen it to see the effect. The top file, VBETools.xla has been password protected and cannot be expanded (by pressing the + to its left, or by double-clicking it) unless you supply the password. You are prompted for the password when you try to expand the project.

> It is a common misconception that Excel's passwords cannot be broken. There are programs available that can decipher the file, workbook and worksheet passwords, as well as the VBA project passwords for all previous versions of Excel. It seems likely that Excel 2000's passwords will suffer the same fate, although there is some hope. The Excel 97 file password has proven a difficult nut to crack if it contains more than just a few characters.

Creating an Addin

Converting a workbook to an Addin is a trivial exercise, on the face of it. Make sure that a worksheet is active in your workbook, use the Excel window File | Save As and scroll to the bottom of the dropdown labeled Save as type: and choose Microsoft Excel Add-In (*.xla). Excel 2000 automatically positions you in a special Addins folder, although there is no requirement that you use it. The advantage of this method is that you do not overwrite the original .xls file and you create a file with the .xla extension that distinguishes it as an Addin to the operating system.

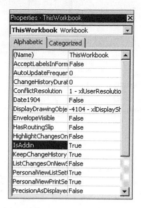

An easier way to create an Addin is to change the IsAddin property of ThisWorkbook to True in the Properties window:

The disadvantage of this method is that you change the original .xls file to an Addin, but its .xls extension remains unchanged and, when you save the file, you are not warned that you are replacing a workbook file with an Addin file. If you want to change the file extension to .xla, you can exit from Excel to remove the Addin from memory, and change it manually using the Windows Explorer.

If you have just converted a workbook to an Addin by changing its IsAddin property and saving it, or you have loaded the Addin using File | Open, *there is no obvious way to close the file from the menus without closing Excel. One way to close the Addin is to go to the Immediate window and type in code that uses the Close method, treating the Addin as a member of the Workbooks collection:*

```
Workbooks("Addin1.xls").Close
```

Addins do not have an Index property value in the Workbooks collection and are not included in the Count property of the Workbooks collection, but they can be addressed by name as members of the Workbooks collection.

Another method you can use to close an Addin is to click on the file name in the recently used file list at the bottom of the Excel File *menu while holding down Shift. You might get a message about overwriting the copy in memory (depending on whether it has changed or not) and then you will get a message about not being able to open an Addin for editing (a hangover from previous versions). Click* OK *and the Addin will be removed from memory.*

Code Changes

In most cases you need to make some changes to the VBA code that was written for a standard workbook, to make it suitable for an Addin. This is particularly true if you reference data within your Addin workbook. Most Excel programmers write code that assumes that the workbook is the active workbook and that the worksheet is the active sheet. Nothing is active in an Addin. Your code must explicitly reference the Addin workbook and worksheet. For example, in our chapters on UserForms and on command bars, our code assumed that it was dealing with the active workbook, using statements like the following:

```
With Range("Database")
    Set rgData = .Rows(2)
    Call LoadRecord
    sbNavigator.Value = 2
    sbNavigator.Max = .Rows.Count
End With
```

This code only works if the workbook containing the name Database is active. In your Addin code, you need to include a reference to the workbook and worksheet. You could say:

```
With Workbooks("Addins1.xls").Sheets("Database").Range("Database")
```

A more useful way to refer to the workbook containing the code is to use the ThisWorkbook property of the Application object that refers to the workbook containing the code. This makes the code much more flexible. You can save the workbook under any file name and the code still works:

```
With ThisWorkbook.Sheets("Database").Range("Database")
```

You can also use the programmatic name for the sheet that you see in the project explorer:

```
With ThisWorkbook.Sheet1.Range("Database")
```

> You can edit both the workbook's programmatic name and the sheet's programmatic name in the Properties window. If you change the sheet's programmatic name, you must also change your code. If you change the workbooks programmatic name, you can use the new name if you wish, but ThisWorkbook remains a valid reference, as it is a property of the Application object and a member of <globals>.

If you want to be able to ignore the sheet name, to allow the name Database to exist on any sheet, you can use the following construction:

```
With ThisWorkbook.Names("Database").RefersToRange
```

Saving Changes

Another potential problem with an Addin that contains data is that changes to the data will not be saved automatically at the end of an Excel session. For example, Addin1.xla allows users to edit the data in the range Database, so it is essential to save those changes before the Addin is closed. It is one of the nice things about Addins that users are never bothered with prompts about saving changes. Therefore, you need to ensure that data is saved, if this is necessary, by setting up a procedure in your VBA code. One way to do this is to add the following code to the Workbook_BeforeClose event procedure:

```
If Not ThisWorkbook.Saved Then ThisWorkbook.Save
```

> This technique does not work in Excel 5 or Excel 95. They do not allow you to save an Addin file.

Interface Changes

You need to bear in mind that the Addin's sheets will not be visible and you will not see the names of the Addin's macros in the Tools | Macro | Macros dialog box. You need to create menus, toolbars or command buttons in other workbooks to execute your macros. Luckily, we have already built in a menu and toolbar interface in our Addin1.xla application.

It is also a good idea to make all your code as robust as possible. You should allow for abnormal events such as system crashes that could upset your code. The CommandBars1.xls application adds a menu and a toolbar to Excel when it is opened. In doing this, CommandBars1.xls assumes that it was successful in deleting the same menu and toolbar when it was last closed. This might not always be the case.

CommandBars1.xls used the following code to add a new menu:

```
Set cbMenuBar = CommandBars("Worksheet Menu Bar")
iHelpIndex = cbMenuBar.Controls("Help").Index
Set muCustom = cbMenuBar.Controls.Add(Type:=msoControlPopup, _
    Before:=iHelpIndex)
With muCustom
    .Caption = "&Custom"
```

If the old menu still exists, you get two copies of the new menu in the worksheet menu bar. It is safer to do an extra delete before adding the new menu, as follows, using On Error Resume Next to mask the run time error that occurs if the old menu does not exist:

```
Set cbMenuBar = CommandBars("Worksheet Menu Bar")
On Error Resume Next
cbMenuBar.Controls("Custom").Delete
On Error GoTo 0
iHelpIndex = cbMenuBar.Controls("Help").Index
Set muCustom = cbMenuBar.Controls.Add(Type:=msoControlPopup, _
    Before:=iHelpIndex)
With muCustom
    .Caption = "&Custom"
```

Similarly, with the new toolbar the following code is used in CommandBars1.xls:

```
With CommandBars.Add(Name:="Manage Data")
```

If the old toolbar still exists, this causes a run time error. It is better to delete the old toolbar before trying to add the new one:

```
On Error Resume Next
CommandBars("Manage Data").Delete
On Error GoTo 0
With CommandBars.Add(Name:="Manage Data")
```

Finally, CommandBars1.xls had the data list visible on the screen, so the results of an AutoFilter were obvious. The data list is not visible when it is in an Addin so you need another way to show the results of a filter. We have adapted the Next and Previous buttons on the user form fmPersonal to show only the filtered data. The Addin user interface appears as follows on the screen:

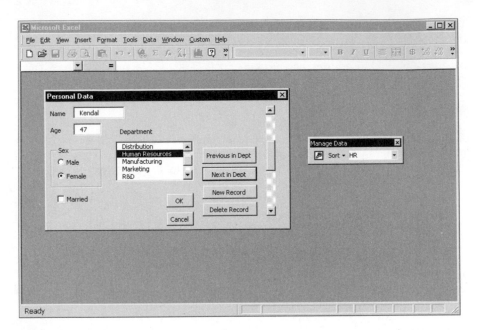

The captions on the Next and Previous buttons have been changed to Next in Dept and Previous in Dept. The code in the Click event procedure of the two buttons has been re-written to show only the rows in the data that are not hidden by the AutoFilter. The operating procedure for these buttons might not be clear to users, so we will include an explanatory screen that displays when the Addin is installed, as you will see below.

Installing an Addin

An Addin can be opened from the worksheet File menu, as has been mentioned. However, you get better control over an Addin if you install it using Tools | Add-Ins, which displays the following dialog box:

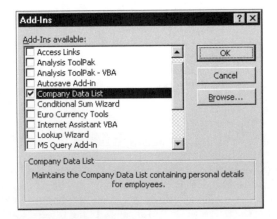

The Company Data List Addin is the Addin1.xla file. If it does not already appear in the list, you can click the Browse... button to locate it.

The friendly title and description are provided by filling in the workbook's Properties. If you have already converted the workbook to an Addin, you can set its `IsAddin` property to `False` to make the workbook visible in the Excel window and use File | Properties to display the following dialog box:

The Title: and Comments: boxes supply the information for the Tools | Add-Ins dialog box. When you have added the required information, you can set the `IsAddin` property back to `True` and save the file.

If you change the Addin workbook properties after adding it to the Tools | Add-Ins *dialog box, the friendly text will not appear. You need to remove the Addin from the list and add it back again. The removal process is covered below.*

Once the Addin is visible in the Tools | Add-Ins dialog box, you can install and uninstall the Addin by checking and un-checking the check box beside the Addin's description. When it is installed, it is loaded into memory and becomes visible in the VB Editor window and will be automatically loaded in future Excel sessions. When it is uninstalled, it is removed from memory and is no longer visible in the VB Editor window and will no longer be loaded in future Excel sessions.

AddinInstall Event

There are two special events that are triggered when you install and uninstall an Addin. The following code, in the `ThisWorkbook` module, shows how to display a user form when the Addin is installed.

```
Private Sub Workbook_AddinInstall()
    fmInstall.Show
End Sub
```

The user form displays the following information for the user:

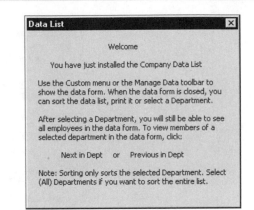

Data List

Welcome

You have just installed the Company Data List

Use the Custom menu or the Manage Data toolbar to show the data form. When the data form is closed, you can sort the data list, print it or select a Department.

After selecting a Department, you will still be able to see all employees in the data form. To view members of a selected department in the data form, click:

Next in Dept   or   Previous in Dept

Note: Sorting only sorts the selected Department. Select (All) Departments if you want to sort the entire list.

Removing an Addin from the Addin's List

There is no easy way to remove an Addin from the Tools | Add-Ins dialog box. One way you can do this is to move the Addin file from its current folder using the Windows Explorer, before opening Excel. The following message will appear when you open Excel:

Microsoft Excel

'C:\WINDOWS\Application Data\Microsoft\AddIns\AddIns.xla' could not be found. Check the spelling of the file name, and verify that the file location is correct.

If you are trying to open the file from your list of most recently used files on the File menu, make sure that the file has not been renamed, moved, or deleted.

OK

Open the Tools | Add-Ins dialog box and click the check box against the Addin's entry. You will get the following message:

Microsoft Excel

Cannot find add-in 'C:\WINDOWS\Application Data\Microsoft\AddIns\AddIns.xla'. Delete from list?

Yes   No

Click Yes and the Addin will be deleted from the list.

The Code for Addin1.xla

The code for Addin1.xla is very similar, but not identical, to that of CommandBars1.xls and the main differences have already been outlined in the text above. It is therefore not being presented in full in this chapter. However, it can be downloaded from the Wrox web site, along with most of the macros presented in this book.

The code for the Addin is contained in a text file called "Chapter 14 Addin.txt" and consists of the code for two UserForms: fmPersonal and fmInstall, and a standard module, modCommandBars. Finally, a short section of code containing the Workbook_AddinInstall, Workbook_Open and Workbook_BeforeClose event procedures is to be included in the ThisWorkbook code module.

Summary

You can provide users with all the power of VBA customization, without cluttering the Excel screen with a workbook, by creating an Addin. Workbook files can be easily converted to Addin files, just be changing the .xls extension to .xla and making some changes to the code. Once a file is an Addin, it is no longer visible in the Excel window — its sheets still exist, and can be used by the Addin, but are not displayed. You can still see the Addin file in the Project Explorer in the VB Editor window. However, a password can be applied to lock the VBA project and prevent users viewing or editing the projects modules and UserForms, just as you can lock the VBA project of a normal workbook.

An Addin application can be accessed by users through menu commands, toolbar controls or controls embedded in workbooks, though you cannot use popup menus. It can obtain and display information through functions such as MsgBox and InputBox and through UserForms. A workbook based application usually needs some redesign in this area before it can be converted to an Addin application.

Although Addin files can be opened in the same way as workbooks, they work best when added to the Addins listed in the Tools | Add-Ins dialog box. Once added, they can be installed and uninstalled using the same dialog box. If they are installed, they will open automatically in every Excel session.

15

Interacting with other Office Applications

The Office 2000 application programs: Excel, Word, Powerpoint, Outlook and Access all use the same VBA language. Once you understand VBA in Excel, you know how to use VBA in all the other applications. Where these applications differ is in their object models. To work with a particular application, you need to be familiar with its object model.

One of the really nice things about the common VBA language is that all the Office 2000 applications are able to expose their objects to each other, and you can program interaction between all of the applications from any one of them. To work with Word objects from Excel, for example, you only need to establish a link to Word and then you have access to its objects as if you were programming with VBA in Word itself. This chapter explains how to create the link in a number of different ways and presents some simple examples of programming the other application. In all cases, the code is written in Excel 2000 VBA, but it could easily be modified for any other Office application. The code is equally applicable to products outside Office that support the VBA language. These include other Microsoft products such as Visual Basic and SQL Server. There is also a growing list of non-Microsoft products that can be programmed in the same way.

We will not attempt to give detailed explanations of the objects, methods and properties of the other Office applications used in the following examples. Our aim is to show how to establish communication with them, not to study their object models. You can learn about their object models in the other Wrox publications in the Office 2000 series, namely: Word 2000 VBA Programmers Reference by Duncan MacKenzie and Outlook 2000 VBA Programmers Reference by Dwayne Gifford. In addition, Wrox Press has published a comprehensive beginner's guide to Access VBA programming, complete with compact disk: Beginning Access 2000 VBA by Rob Smith and Dave Sussman.

Establishing the Connection

Once a connection with an Office application has been made, its objects are exposed for automation through a type library. There are two ways to establish such a connection between the application in which you are programming and the target application's type library. They are referred to as late binding and early binding. In either case, you establish the connection by creating an object variable that refers to the target application or a specific object in the target application. You can then proceed to use the properties and methods of the object referred to by the object variable.

In **late binding**, you create an object that refers to the Office application *before* you make a link to the Office application's type library. In earlier versions of the Office applications it was necessary to use late binding and you will still see it used, because it has some advantages over early binding. One advantage is that you can write code that can detect the presence or absence of the required type library on the PC running your code and link to different versions of applications based on decisions made as the code executes.

The disadvantage of late binding is that the type library for the target application is not accessed when you are writing your code. Therefore, you get no help information regarding the application, you cannot reference the intrinsic constants in the application and, when the code is compiled, the references to the target application may not be correct, as they cannot be checked. The links are only fully resolved when you try to execute the code and this takes time. It is also possible that coding errors may be detected at this point that cause your program to fail.

Early binding is supported by all the Office 2000 applications. Code that uses early binding executes faster than code using late binding. The target application's type library is present when you write your code. Therefore, more syntax and type checking can be performed, and more linkage details can be established, before the code executes. It is also easier to write code for early binding because you can see the objects, methods and properties of the target application in the Object Browser and, as you write your code, you will see automatic tips appear, such as a list of related properties and methods after you type an object reference. You can also use the intrinsic constants defined in the target application.

Late Binding

The following code creates an entry in the Outlook calendar. The code uses the late binding technique:

```
Sub MakeOutlookAppointment()
    'Example of Outlook automation using late binding
    'Creates an appointment in Outlook
    Dim olApp As Object 'Reference to Outlook
    Dim olAppointment As Object 'Reference to Outlook Appointment
    Const olAppointmentItem = 1 'Outlook intrinsic constants not available

    'Create link to Outlook
    Set olApp = CreateObject("Outlook.Application")
    Set olAppointment = olApp.CreateItem(olAppointmentItem)
```

```
    'Set details of appointment
    With olAppointment
        .Subject = "Discuss Whitefield Contract"
        .Start = DateSerial(99, 2, 25) + TimeSerial(9, 30, 0)
        .End = DateSerial(99, 2, 25) + TimeSerial(11, 30, 0)
        .ReminderPlaySound = True
        .Save
    End With
    'Exit Outlook
    olApp.Quit
    'Release object variable
    Set olApp = Nothing
End Sub
```

The basic technique in programming another application is to create an object variable referring to that application. The object variable in this case is olApp. You then use olApp (as you would use the Application object in Excel) to refer to objects in the external application's object model. In this case, the CreateItem method of Outlook's Application object is used to create a reference to a new AppointmentItem object. Because Outlook's intrinsic constants are not available in the case of late binding, you need to define your own constants, such as olAppointmentItem here, or substitute the value of the constant as the parameter value. We go on to use the properties and methods of the Appointment object in the With...End With structure. Note the times have been defined using the DateSerial and TimeSerial functions to avoid ambiguity or problems in an international context. See chapter 16 for more details.

The declarations of olApp and olAppointment as the generic Object type forces VBA to use late binding. VBA cannot resolve all the links to Outlook until it executes the CreateObject function.

The CreateObject input argument defines the application name and class of object to be created. Outlook is the name of the application and Application is the class. Many applications allow you to create objects at different levels in the object model. Excel allows you to create, from other applications, WorkSheet or Chart objects, for example, using Excel.WorkSheet or Excel.Chart as the input parameter of the CreateObject function.

It is good programming practice to close the external application when you are finished with it and set the object variable to Nothing. This releases the memory used by the link and the application.

If you run this macro nothing will happen in Excel at all. However, open up Outlook and in the Calendar you will find that the appointment has been added for the morning of February 25!

Early Binding

If you want to use early
binding, you need to
establish a reference to
the type library of the
external application in
your VBA project. You do
this from the VB Editor
by selecting **Tools** |
References, which
displays this dialog box:

Once you have a reference to an application, you can declare your object variables as
the correct type. For example, you could declare `olEntry` as an `AddressEntry` type
as follows:

```
Dim olEntry As AddressEntry
```

VBA will search through the type libraries, in the order shown from the top down, to
find references to object types. If the same object type is present in more than one
library, it will use the first one found. You can select a library and click the **Priority**
buttons to move it up or down the list to change the order in which libraries are
searched.

The following example uses early binding. It lists all the names of the entries in the
Outlook Contacts folder, placing them in column **A** of the active worksheet:

```
Sub DisplayOutlookContactNames()
    'Example of Outlook automation using early binding
    'Lists all the Contact names from Outlook in the A column
    'of the active sheet
    Dim olApp As Outlook.Application
    Dim olNameSpace As Outlook.NameSpace
    Dim olAddresslist As AddressList
    Dim olEntry As AddressEntry
    Dim i As Long

    'Create link to Outlook
    Set olApp = New Outlook.Application
    Set olNameSpace = olApp.GetNamespace("MAPI")
    Set olAddresslist = olNameSpace.AddressLists("Contacts")
    For Each olEntry In olAddresslist.AddressEntries
        i = i + 1
        'Enter contacts in A column of active sheet
        Cells(i, 1).Value = olEntry.Name
    Next
    'Exit Outlook
    olApp.Quit
    'Release object variable
    Set olApp = Nothing
End Sub
```

Here, we directly declare olApp to be an Outlook.Application type. The other Dim statements also declare object variables of the type we need. If the same object name is used in more than one object library, you can precede the object name by the name of the application, rather than depend on the priority of the type libraries. We have done this with Outlook.NameSpace to illustrate the point. The New keyword is used when assigning a reference to Outlook.Application to olApp to create a new instance of Outlook.

The fact that we declare the variable types correctly makes VBA use early binding. You could use the CreateObject function to create the olApp object variable, instead of the New keyword, without affecting the early binding. However, it is more efficient to use New.

Opening a Document in Word

If you want to open a file created in another Office application, you can use the GetObject function to directly open the file. However, it is just as easy to open an instance of the application and open the file from the application. We will look at another use of GetObject shortly.

> If you are not familiar with the Word object model, you can use the Word macro recorder to discover which objects, properties and methods you need to use to perform a Word task that you can do manually.

The following code copies an embedded Excel chart to the clipboard. It then starts a new instance of Word, opens an existing Word document and pastes the chart to the end of the document. As the code uses early binding, you must establish a reference to the Word 9 object library:

```
Sub CopyChartToWordDocument()
    'Example of Word automation using early binding
    'Copies chart from workbook and appends it to existing Word document
    Dim wdApp As Word.Application

    'Copy embedded chart
    ThisWorkbook.Sheets(1).ChartObjects(1).Chart.ChartArea.Copy

    'Establish link to Word
    Set wdApp = New Word.Application
    With wdApp
        'Open Word document
        .Documents.Open Filename:="C:\Clients\Wrox\OtherApps\Chart.doc"
        With .Selection
            'Go to end of document and insert paragraph
            .EndKey Unit:=wdStory
            .TypeParagraph
            'Paste chart
            .PasteSpecial Link:=False, DataType:=wdPasteOLEObject, _
                    Placement:=wdInLine, DisplayAsIcon:=False
        End With
        .ActiveDocument.Save
        'Exit Word
        .Quit
    End With
    'Release object variable
    Set wdApp = Nothing
End Sub
```

The New keyword creates a new instance of Word, even if Word is already open. The Open method of the Documents collection is used to open the existing file. The following code selects the end of the document, enters a new empty paragraph and pastes the chart. The document is then saved and the new instance of Word is closed.

Accessing an Active Word Document

Say you are working in Excel, creating embedded charts. You also have Word open with a document active, into which you want to paste the charts you are creating, one under the other. You can copy the currently active chart in Excel to the document using the following code. There is no need to establish a reference to Word if you declare wdApp as an Object type and VBA will use late binding. On the other hand, you can establish a reference to Word, declare wdApp as a Word.Application type and VBA will use early binding. In this example we are using early binding:

```
Sub CopyChartToOpenWordDocument()
    'Example of Word automation using late binding
    'Copies active chart from workbook and appends it to
    ' a currently open Word document

    Dim wdApp As Word.Application

    'Copy active chart
    ActiveChart.ChartArea.Copy

    'Establish link to open instance of Word
    Set wdApp = GetObject(, "Word.Application")
    With wdApp.Selection
       'Go to end of document and insert paragraph
       .EndKey Unit:=wdStory
       .TypeParagraph
       'Paste chart
       .PasteSpecial Link:=False, DataType:=wdPasteOLEObject, _
            Placement:=wdInLine, DisplayAsIcon:=False
    End With
    'Release object variable
    Set wdApp = Nothing
End Sub
```

The GetObject function has two input parameters. Both are optional. The first parameter can be used to specify a file to be opened. The second can be used to specify the application program to open. If you do not specify the first parameter, GetObject assumes you want to access a currently open instance of Word. If you specify a zero length string as the first parameter, GetObject assumes you want to open a new instance of Word.

You can use GetObject, with no first parameter, as in the code above, to access a current instance of Word that is in memory. However, if there is no current instance of Word running, GetObject with no first parameter causes a run time error.

Creating a New Word Document

Say you want to use a current instance of Word, if one exists or if there is no current instance, you want to create one. The following code shows how to do this. Again, we are using early binding:

```
Sub CopyChartToAnyWordDocument()
    'Example of Word automation using early binding
    'Copies active chart from workbook and appends it to
    ' a currently open Word document, if there is one.
    'If not, opens new instance of Word
    Dim wdApp As Word.Application
```

```
         'Copy active chart
         ActiveChart.ChartArea.Copy

         On Error Resume Next
         'Try to establish link to open instance of Word
         Set wdApp = GetObject(, "Word.Application")
         'If this fails, open Word
         If wdApp Is Nothing Then
             Set wdApp = GetObject("", "Word.Application")
             With wdApp
                 'Add new document
                 .Documents.Add
                 'Make Word visible
                 .Visible = True
             End With
         End If
         On Error GoTo 0
         With wdApp.Selection
             'Go to end of document and insert paragraph
             .EndKey Unit:=wdStory
             .TypeParagraph
             'Paste chart
             .PasteSpecial Link:=False, DataType:=wdPasteOLEObject, _
                 Placement:=wdInLine, DisplayAsIcon:=False
         End With
         'Release object variable
         Set wdApp = Nothing
End Sub
```

If there is no current instance of Word, using GetObject with no first argument causes a run time error and the code then uses GetObject with a zero length string as the first argument, which opens a new instance of Word, and then creates a new document. The code also makes the new instance of Word visible, unlike our previous examples where the work was done behind the scenes without showing the Word window. The chart is then pasted at the end of the Word document. At the end of the procedure, the object variable wdApp is released, but the Word window is accessible on the screen so that you can view the result.

Access and DAO

If you want to copy data from Access to Excel, you can establish a reference to the Access object library and use the Access object model. However, this is overkill because you don't really need most of the functionality in Access. You can also use ADO (ActiveX Data Objects), which is Microsoft's latest technology for programmatic access to relational databases, and many other forms of data storage. However, another simple and efficient way to get to Access data is provided by DAO (Data Access Objects). As a DAO link to an Access file is simpler to set up than an ADO link, we will use it here.

The screen opposite shows an Access table named Sales that is in an Access database file FruitSales.mdb.

ID	Date	Customer	State	Product	NumberSold	Price	Revenue
1	Jan 01, 1997	Roberts	NSW	Oranges	903	15	13545
2	Jan 01, 1997	Roberts	TAS	Oranges	331	15	4965
3	Jan 02, 1997	Roberts	QLD	Mangoes	299	20	5980
4	Jan 06, 1997	Roberts	QLD	Oranges	612	15	9180
5	Jan 08, 1997	Roberts	VIC	Apples	907	12.5	11337.5
6	Jan 08, 1997	Pradesh	TAS	Pears	107	18	1926
7	Jan 10, 1997	Roberts	VIC	Apples	770	12.5	9625
8	Jan 14, 1997	Smith	NT	Apples	223	12.5	2787.5
9	Jan 14, 1997	Smith	VIC	Oranges	132	15	1980
10	Jan 15, 1997	Pradesh	QLD	Oranges	669	15	10035
11	Jan 17, 1997	Roberts	NSW	Mangoes	881	20	17620
12	Jan 21, 1997	Kee	SA	Pears	624	18	11232
13	Jan 22, 1997	Roberts	QLD	Mangoes	193	20	3860
14	Jan 23, 1997	Smith	SA	Mangoes	255	20	5100
15	Jan 27, 1997	Kee	QLD	Mangoes	6	20	120
16	Jan 27, 1997	Kee	VIC	Mangoes	311	20	6220
17	Jan 28, 1997	Roberts	NT	Oranges	9	15	135
18	Jan 28, 1997	Kee	TAS	Apples	706	12.5	8825
19	Jan 29, 1997	Kee	NT	Mangoes	441	20	8820

Sales : Table

Record: 1 of 499

The following code uses DAO to open a recordset based on the Sales table. It uses early binding, so a reference to the DAO object library is required:

```
Sub GetSalesDataViaDAO()
    'Example of DAO automation using early binding
    'Copies Sales table from Access database to new worksheet
    Dim daoApp As DAO.DBEngine
    Dim dbSales As DAO.Database
    Dim rsSales As DAO.Recordset
    Dim i As Integer
    Dim Wks As Worksheet
    Dim iCount As Integer

    'Establish link to DAO
    Set daoApp = New DAO.DBEngine
    'Open Access database file
    Set dbSales = daoApp.OpenDatabase _
        ("C:\Clients\Wrox\OtherApps\FruitSales.mdb")
    'Open recordset based on Sales Table
    Set rsSales = dbSales.OpenRecordset("Sales")
    'Add new worksheet to active workbook
    Set Wks = Worksheets.Add
    iCount = rsSales.Fields.Count
    'Enter field names across ow 1
    For i = 0 To iCount - 1
        Wks.Cells(1, i + 1).Value = rsSales.Fields(i).Name
    Next

    'Copy entire recordset data to worksheet, starting in A2
    Wks.Range("A2").CopyFromRecordset rsSales

    'Format worksheet dates in A column
    Wks.Columns("B").NumberFormat = "mmm dd, yyyy"
    'Bold row 1 and fit columns to largest entry
    With Wks.Range("A1").Resize(1, iCount)
        .Font.Bold = True
        .EntireColumn.AutoFit
    End With

    'Release object variables
    Set rsSales = Nothing
    Set dbSales = Nothing
    Set daoApp = Nothing
End Sub
```

The code opens the Access database file, creates a recordset based on the Sales table, and assigns a reference to the recordset to rsSales. A new worksheet is added to the Excel workbook and the field names in rsSales are assigned to the first row of the new worksheet. The code uses the CopyFromRecordSet method of the Range object to copy the records in rsSales to the worksheet, starting in cell A2. CopyFromRecordSet is a very fast way to copy the data compared to a looping procedure that copies record by record.

Summary

To automate the objects in another application, you create an object variable referring to the target application or an object in the application. You can use early binding or late binding to establish the link between VBA and the other application's objects. Early binding requires that you establish a reference to the target applications type library and you must declare any object variables that refer to the target objects using their correct type. If you declare the object variables as the generic Object type, VBA uses late binding.

Early binding produces code that executes faster than late binding and you can get information on the target applications objects using the Object Browser and the short cut tips that automatically appear as you type your code. Syntax and type checking is also performed as you code, so you are less likely to get errors when the code executes than with late binding where these checks cannot be done until the code is run.

You must use the `CreateObject` or `GetObject` function to create an object variable reference to the target application when using late binding. You can use the same functions when early binding, but it is more efficient to use the `New` keyword. However, if you want to test for an open instance of another application at run time, `GetObject` can be usefully employed with early binding.

16

International Issues

Introduction

If you think that your application may be used internationally, it has to work with any choice of Windows Regional Setting, on any language version of Windows and with any language choice for the Excel user interface.

If you are very lucky, all your potential users will have exactly the same settings as your development machine and you don't need to worry about international issues. However, a more likely scenario is that you do not even know who all your users are going to be, let alone where in the world they will live, or the settings they will use.

Any bugs in your application that arise from the disregarding or ignoring of international issues will not occur on your development machine unless you explicitly test for them. However, they will be found immediately by your clients.

The combination of Regional Settings and Excel language is called the user's 'locale' and the aim of this chapter is to show you how to write locale-independent VBA applications. In order to do this, we include an explanation of the features in Excel that deal with locale related issues and highlight areas within Excel where locale support is absent or limited. Workarounds are provided for most of these limitations, but some are so problematic that the only solution is to not use the feature at all.

The Rules provided in this chapter should be included in your coding standards and used by you and your colleagues. It is easy to write locale-independent code from scratch; it is much more difficult to make existing code compatible with the many different locales in the world today.

Changing Windows Regional Settings and the Office 2000 UI Language

During this chapter, the potential errors will be demonstrated by using the following three locales:

Setting	US	UK	Norway
Decimal Separator	.	.	,
Thousand Separator	,	,	.
Date order	mm/dd/yyyy	dd/mm/yyyy	dd.mm.yyyy
Date separator	/	/	.
Example number: 1234.56	1,234.56	1,234.56	1.234,56
Example date: Feb 10, 1999	02/10/1999	10/02/1999	10.02.1999
Windows and Excel Language	English	English	Norwegian
The text for the Boolean True	True	True	Sann

The regional settings are changed using the Regional Settings applet in Windows Control Panel, while the Office 2000 language is changed using the "Microsoft Office Language Settings" program provided with the Office 2000 Language Packs. Unfortunately, the only way to change the Windows language is to install a new version from scratch.

When testing your application, it is a very good idea to use some fictional regional settings, such as having # for the thousand separator, ! for the decimal separator and a YMD date order. It is then very easy to determine if your application is using your settings or some internal default. For completeness, you should also have a machine in your office with a different language version of Windows than the one you normally use.

Responding to Regional Settings and the Windows Language

This section explains how to write applications that work with different regional settings and Windows language versions, which should be considered the absolute minimum requirement.

Identifying the User's Regional Settings and Windows Language

Everything you need to know about your user's Windows Regional Settings and Windows Language version is found in the Application.International property. The online help lists all of the items which can be accessed, though you are unlikely to use more than a few of them. The most notable are:

XlCountryCode — The language version of Excel (or of the currently active Office language)

XlCountrySetting — The Windows regional settings location.

XlDateOrder — the choice of MDY, DMY or YMD order to display dates.

Note that there is no constant that enables us to identify which language version of Windows is installed (but we can get than information from the Windows API if required).

Note that "Windows Regional Settings" is abbreviated to WRS in the rest of this chapter and are also described as 'local' settings.

VBA Conversion Functions from an International Perspective

The online help files explain the use of VBA's conversion functions in terms of converting between different data types. This section explains their behaviour when converting to and from strings in different locales.

Implicit Conversion

This is the most common form of type conversion used in VBA code and forces the VBA interpreter to convert the data using whichever format it thinks is most appropriate. A typical example of this code is:

```
Dim dtMyDate As Date
dtMyDate = DateValue("Jan 1, 1999")
MsgBox "This first day of this year is " & dtMyDate
```

When converting a number to a string, VBA in Office 2000 uses the WRS to supply either a date string in the user's 'ShortDate' format, the number formatted according to the WRS, or the text for True or False in the WRS language. This is fine, if you want the output as a locally formatted string. If, however, your code assumes you've got a US-formatted string, it will fail. Of course, if you develop using US formats, you won't notice the difference (though your client will).

There is a much bigger problem with using implicit conversion if you are writing code for multiple versions of Excel. In previous versions, the number formats used in the conversion were those appropriate for the Excel language being used at run-time (i.e. buried within the Excel object library), which may be different to both US and local formats, and were not affected by changing the WRS.

Be very careful with the data types returned from, and used by, Excel and VBA functions. For example, Application.GetOpenFilename returns a Variant containing the Boolean value False if the user cancels, or a String containing the text of the selected file. If you set this to a String variable, the Boolean False will be converted to a string in the user's WRS language, and may not equal the string "False" that you may be comparing it to. To avoid these problems, use the Object Browser to check the function's return type and parameter types, then make sure to match them, or explicitly convert them to your variable's data type. Applying this recommendation gives us (at least) three solutions to using Application.GetOpenFilename:

Typical code running in Norway:

```
Dim stFile As String
stFile = Application.GetOpenFilename()
If stFile = "False" Then
    ...
```

If the user cancels, `GetOpenFilename` returns a variable containing the Boolean value `False`. Excel converts it to a string to put in our variable, using the Windows Language. In Norway, the string will contain "Usann". If this is compared to the string "False", which doesn't match, so the code assumes that a file was retrieved name and the subsequent program crashes.

Solution 1:

```
Dim vaFile As Variant
vaFile = Application.GetOpenFileName()
If vaFile = False Then      'Compare using the same data types
    ...
```

Solution 2:

```
Dim vaFile As Variant
vaFile = Application.GetOpenFileName()
If CStr(vaFile) = "False" Then      'Explicit conversion with CStr() always
                                    'gives a US Boolean string
    ...
```

Solution 3:

```
Dim vaFile As Variant
vaFile = Application.GetOpenFileName()
If TypeName(vaFile) = "Boolean" Then      'Got a Boolean, so must have
                                          'cancelled
    ...
```

Note that in all three cases, the key point is that we are matching the data type returned by `GetOpenFilename` (a `Variant`) with our variable.

Date literals

When coding in VBA, you can write dates using a format of `#01/01/1999#`, which is obviously Jan 1, 1999. But what is `#02/01/1999#`? Is it Jan 2 or Feb 1? Well, it is actually Feb 1, 1999. This is because when coding in Excel 2000, we do so in American English, regardless of any other settings we may have, and hence we must use US-formatted date literals (i.e. mm/dd/yyyy format).

What happens if you happen to be Norwegian or British and try typing in your local date format (which you *will* do at some time, usually near a deadline)? If you type in a Norwegian-formatted date literal, `#02.01.1999#`, you get a syntax error which at least alerts you to the mistake you made. However, if you type in date in a UK format (dd/mm/yyyy format) things get a little more interesting. VBA recognizes the date, and so doesn't no give an error, but 'sees' that you have the day and month the wrong way round; it swaps them for you. So, typing in dates from Jan 10, 1999 to Jan 15, 1999 results in:

You Typed	VBA Shows	Meaning
10/1/1999	10/1/1999	Oct 1, 1999
11/1/1999	11/1/1999	Nov 1, 1999
12/1/1999	12/1/1999	Dec 1, 1999
13/1/1999	1/13/1999	Jan 13, 1999
14/1/1999	1/14/1999	Jan 14, 1999
15/1/1999	1/15/1999	Jan 15, 1999

If these literals are sprinkled through your code, you will not notice the errors.

It is much safer to avoid using date literals and use the VBA functions `DateSerial(Year, Month, Day)` or `DateValue(DateString)`, where `DateString` is a non-ambiguous string such as "Jan 1, 1999". Both of these functions return the corresponding `Date` number.

IsNumeric(), IsDate()

These two functions test if a string can be evaluated as a number or date according to the WRS and Windows language version. You should always use these functions before trying to convert a string to another data type. Note that we don't have an `IsBoolean()` function, or functions to check if a string is a US-formatted number or date. `IsNumeric()` does not recognise a `%` character on the end of a number and `IsDate()` does not recognise days of the week.

CStr()

This is the function most used by VBA in implicit data type conversions. It converts a `Variant` to a `String`, formatted according to the WRS. When converting a `Date` type, the 'ShortDate' format is used, as defined in the WRS. Note that when converting Booleans, the resulting text is the English "True" or "False" and is not dependent on any Windows settings. Compare this with the implicit conversion of Booleans, whereby `MsgBox "I am " & True` results in the `True` being displayed in the WRS language (i.e. "I am Sann" in Norwegian Regional Settings).

CDbl(), CSng(), CLng(), CInt(), CByte(), CCur() & CDec()

All of these can convert a string representation of a number into a numeric data type (as well as converting different numeric data types into each other). The string must be formatted according to WRS. These functions do not recognise date strings or `%` characters

CDate(), DateValue()

These methods can convert a string to a `Date` data type (`CDate` can also convert other data types to the `Date` type). The string must be formatted according to WRS and use the Windows language for month names. It does not recognise the names for the days of the week, giving a `Type Mismatch` error. If the year is not specified in the string, it uses the current year.

CBool()

CBool() can converts a string to a Boolean value. Contrary to all the other Cxxx() conversion functions, the string must be the English "True" or "False". Hence, CBool("" & True) will give a Type Mismatch error, while CBool(CStr(True)) will work as you would expect.

Format()

Converts a number or date to a string, using a number format supplied in code. The number format must use US symbols (m, d, s etc), but results in a string formatted according to WRS (i.e. with the correct decimal, thousand and date separators) and the WRS language (for the weekday and month names). For example, the code:

```
MsgBox Format(DateSerial(1999, 1, 1), "dddd dd/mm/yyyy")
```

will result in "Friday 01/01/1999" in the US, but "Fredag 01.01.1999" when with Norwegian settings. If you omit the number format string, it behaves exactly the same as the CStr function (even though online help says it behaves like Str()), including the strange handling of Boolean values, where Format(True) always results in the English "True".

FormatCurrency(), FormatDateTime(), FormatNumber(), FormatPercent()

These functions added in Excel 2000 provide the same functionality as the Format function, but use parameters to define the specific resulting format instead of a custom format string. They correspond to standard options in Excel's Format | Cells | Number dialog, while the Format() function corresponds to the Custom option.

Str()

Converts a number, date or Boolean to a US-formatted string, regardless of the WRS, Windows language or Office language version. When converting a positive number, it adds a space on the left. When converting a decimal fraction, it does not add a leading zero. The following function is a variation on Str() which removes the space and adds the zero.

sNumToUS()

This function converts a number, date or Boolean variable to a US-formatted string. There is an additional parameter that can be used to return a string using Excel's DATE() function, which would typically be used when constructing .Formula strings.

```
Function sNumToUS(vValue As Variant, Optional bUseDATEFunction) As String
' **********************************************************
' *
' * Function Name: sNumToUS
' *
' * Input:     vValue - a variant containing the number to convert.
' *               Can be:
' *                    a number  - converted to a string with US formats
' *                    a date    - converted to a string in mm/dd/yyyy format
' *                    a Boolean - the strings "True" or "False"
' *
' *               bUseDATEFunction - an optional Boolean for handling dates
' *               False (or missing) - returns a date string in mm/dd/yyyy format
' *               True              - returns a date as DATE(yyyy,mm,dd)
' *
' * Output:    The input as a string in US regional format
' *
' * Purpose:   Explicitly converts an item to a string in US regional formats
' *
' **********************************************************

    Dim sTmp As String

    'Don't accept strings or arrays as input
    If TypeName(vValue) = "String" Then Exit Function
    If Right(TypeName(vValue), 2) = "()" Then Exit Function

    If IsMissing(bUseDATEFunction) Then bUseDATEFunction = False

    'Do we want it returned as Excel's DATE() function
    '(which we can't do with strings)?
    If bUseDATEFunction Then

        'We do, so build the Excel DATE() function string
        sTmp = "DATE(" & Year(vValue) & "," & Month(vValue) & "," & _
        Day(vValue) & ")"
    Else
        'Is it a date type?
        If TypeName(vValue) = "Date" Then
            sTmp = Format(vValue, "mm""/""dd""/""yyyy")
        Else
            'Convert number to string in US format and remove leading space
            sTmp = Trim(Str(vValue))

            'If we have fractions, we don't get a leading zero, so add one.
            If Left(sTmp, 1) = "." Then sTmp = "0" & sTmp
            If Left(sTmp, 2) = "-." Then sTmp = "-0" & Mid(sTmp, 2)
        End If
    End If

    'Return the US formatted string
    sNumToUS = sTmp
End Function
```

Val()

This is the most common function that I've seen used to convert from strings to numbers. It actually only converts a US-formatted numerical string to a number. All the other string-to-number conversion functions try to convert the entire string to a number and raise an error if they can't. Val(), however, works from left to right until it finds a character that it doesn't recognise as part of a number. Many characters typically found in numbers, such as $ and commas, are enough to stop it recognising the number. Val() does not recognise US-formatted date strings.

`Val()` also has the dubious distinction of being the only one of VBA's conversion functions to take a specific data type for its input. While all the others use `Variants`, `Val()` accepts only a `String`. This means that anything you pass to `Val()` is converted to a string (implicitly, i.e. according to the WRS and Windows language), before being evaluated according to US formats!

The use of `Val()` can have the following unwanted side-effects (otherwise known as bugs), which are *very* difficult to detect in code that is running fine on your own machine, but which would fail on another machine with different WRS. Here `myDate` is a `Date` variable containing Feb 10, 1999 and `myDbl` is a `Double` containing 1.234.

Expression	US	UK	Norway
Val(myDate)	2	10	10.02 (or 10.2)
Val(myDbl)	1.234	1.234	1
Val(True)	0 (=False)	0 (=False)	0 (=False)

Application.Evaluate

While not normally considered to be a conversion function, `Application.Evaluate` is the only way to convert a US-formatted date string to a date number. The following two functions `IsDateUS()` and `DateValueUS()` are wrapper functions which use this method.

IsDateUS()

The built-in `IsDate()` function validates a string against the Windows Regional Settings. This function provides us with a way to check if a string contains a US-formatted date.

```
Function IsDateUS(sDate As String) As Boolean

' ********************************************************
' *
' * Function Name:    IsDateUS
' *
' * Input:            sDate - a string containing a US-formatted date
' *
' * Output:           Returns True if the string contains a valid US date,
' *                   False if not
' *
' * Purpose:          Checks if a given string can be recognised as a date
' *                   according to US formats
' *
' ********************************************************

    IsDateUS = Not IsError(Application.Evaluate("DATEVALUE(""" & _
               sDate & """)"))
End Function
```

DateValueUS()

The VBA `DateValue()` function converts a string formatted according to the Windows Regional Settings to a `Date` type. This function converts a string containing a US-formatted date to a `Date` type. If the string can not be recognized as a US-formatted date, it returns an `Error`.

```
Function DateValueUS(sDate As String) As Variant
' ********************************************************
' *
' * Function Name:    DateValueUS
' *
' * Input:            sDate - a string containing a US-formatted date
' *
' * Output:           Returns the date value of the given string, in a Variant
' *
' * Purpose:          Converts a US-formatted date string to a date number
' *
' ********************************************************

    DateValueUS = Application.Evaluate("DATEVALUE(""" & sDate & """)")
End Function
```

Interacting with Excel

VBA and Excel are two different programs that have had very different upbringings.
VBA speaks American. Excel also speaks American. However, Excel can also speak in
its user's language if they have the appropriate Windows settings and Office language
pack installed. On the other hand VBA knows only a little about Windows settings,
even less about Office 2000 language packs. So, we can either do some awkward
coding to teach VBA how to speak to Excel in the user's language, or we can just let
them converse in American. I very much recommend the latter.

Unfortunately, most of the newer features in Excel are not multilingual. Some only
speak American, while others only speak in the user's language. We can use the
American-only features if we understand their limitations; the others are best avoided.
All of them are documented later in the chapter.

Sending Data to Excel

By far the best way to get numbers, dates, Booleans and strings into Excel cells is to do
so in their native format. Hence, the following code works perfectly, regardless of
locale:

```
Sub SendToExcel()
    Dim dtDate As Date, dNumber As Double, bBool As Boolean, _
        stString As String

    dtDate = DateSerial(1999, 2, 13)
    dNumber = 1234.567
    bBool = True
    stString = "Hello World"

    Range("A1").Value = dtDate
    Range("A2").Value = dNumber
    Range("A3").Value = bBool
    Range("A4").Value = stString
End Sub
```

There is a boundary layer between VBA and Excel. When VBA passes a variable
through the boundary, Excel does its best to interpret it according to its own rules. If
the VBA and Excel data types are mutually compatible the variable passes straight
through unhindered. The problems start when Excel forces us to pass it numbers, dates
or Booleans within strings, or when we choose to do so ourselves. The answer to the
latter situation is easy — don't do it! Whenever you have a string representation of
some other data type, if it is possible, always explicitly convert it to the data type you
want Excel to store, before passing it to Excel.

Excel requires string input in the following circumstances:

- Setting the formula for a cell, chart series, conditional format or pivot table calculated field.
- Specifying the `RefersTo` formula for a defined name.
- Specifying an AutoFilter criteria.
- Passing a formula to `ExecuteExcel4Macro`.
- Setting the number format of a cell, style, chart axis, pivot table field.
- The number format used in the VBA `Format()` function.

In these cases, we have to ensure that the string that VBA sends to Excel is in US-formatted text — i.e. we use English language formulas and US regional settings. If the string is built within the code, we must be very careful to explicitly convert all our variables to US-formatted strings.

Take this simple example:

```
Sub SetLimit(dLimit As Double)
    ActiveCell.Formula = "=IF(A1<" & dLimit & ",1,0)"
End Sub
```

We are setting a cell's formula based on a parameter supplied from another routine. Note that the formula is being constructed in the code and we are using US language and regional settings (i.e. the English `IF()` and using a comma for the list separator). When used with different values for `dLimit` in different locales, we get the following results:

DLimit	US	UK	Norway
100	Works fine	Works fine	Works fine
100.23	Works fine	Works fine	Run-Time Error 1004

It fails when run in Norway with any non-integer value for `dLimit`. This is because we are implicitly converting the variable to a string, which you'll recall uses the Windows Regional Settings number formats. The resulting string that we're passing to Excel is:

```
=IF(A1<100,23,1,0)
```

This fails because the `IF()` function does not have four parameters. If we change the line to read:

```
ActiveCell.Formula = "=IF(A1<" & Str(dLimit) & ",1,0)"
```

The function will work correctly, as `Str()` forces a conversion to a US-formatted string.

If we try the same routine with a `Date` instead of a `Double`, we come across another problem. The text that is passed to Excel (e.g. for Feb 13, 1999) is:

```
=IF(A1<02/13/1999,1,0)
```

While this is a valid formula, Excel interprets the date as a set of divisions, so the formula is equivalent to:

```
=IF(A1<0.0000077,1,0)
```

This is unlikely to ever be true! To avoid this, we have to convert the `Date` data type to a `Double`, and from that to a string:

```
Sub SetLimit(dtLimit As Date)
    ActiveCell.Formula = "=IF(A1<" & Str(CDbl(dtLimit)) & ",1,0)"
End Sub
```

The function is then the correct (but less readable):

```
=IF(A1<36221,1,0)
```

To maintain readability, we should convert dates to Excel's `DATE()` function, to give:

```
=IF(A1<DATE(1999,2,13),1,0)
```

This is also achieved by the `sNumToUS()` function presented earlier on in the chapter.

If you call the `SetLimit` procedure with a value of 100.23 and look at the cell that the formula was put into, you'll see that Excel has converted the US string into the local language and regional settings. In Norway, for example, the cell actually shows:

```
=HVIS(A1<100,23;1;0)
```

This translation also applies to number formats. Whenever we set a number format within VBA, we can give Excel a format string which uses US characters (such as 'd' for day, 'm' for month and 'y' for year). When applied to the cell (or style or chart axis), or used in the Format() function, Excel translates these characters to the local versions. For example, the following code results in a number format of dd/mm/åååå when we check it using Format, Cells, Number in Norwegian Windows:

```
ActiveCell.NumberFormat = "dd/mm/yyyy"
```

This ability of Excel to translate US strings into the local language and formats makes it easy for developers to create locale-independent applications. All we have to do is code in American and ensure that we explicitly convert our variables to US-formatted strings before passing them to Excel.

Reading Data from Excel

When reading a cell's value, using it's `.Value` property, the data type which Excel provides to VBA is determined by a combination of the cell's value and its formatting. For example, the number 3000 could reach VBA as a `Double`, a `Currency` or a `Date` (March 18, 1908). The only international issue that concerns us here, is if the cell's value is read directly into a string variable — the conversion will be done implicitly and you may not get what you expect (particularly if the cell contains a Boolean value).

As well as when sending data to Excel, the translation between US and local functions and formats occurs when reading data from Excel. This means that a cell's `.Formula` or `.NumberFormat` property is given to us in English and with US number and date formatting, regardless of the user's choice of language or regional settings.

While for most applications, it is much simpler to read and write using US formulas and formats, we will sometimes need to read exactly what the user is seeing (i.e. in their choice of language and regional settings). This is done by using the `xxxLocal` versions of many properties, which return (and interpret) strings according to the user's settings. They are typically used when displaying a formula or number format on a UserForm and are discussed in the following section.

The Rules for Working with Excel

1. Pass values to Excel in their natural format if possible (i.e. don't convert dates / numbers / Booleans to strings if you don't have to). If you have strings, convert them yourself before passing them to Excel.

2. When you have to convert numbers and dates to strings for passing to Excel (such as in criteria for AutoFilter or `.Formula` strings), *always explicitly convert the data* to a US-formatted string, using `Trim(Str(MyNumber))`, or the `sNumToUS()` function shown earlier on, for all number and date types. Excel will then use it correctly and convert it to the local number/date formats.

3. Avoid using `Date` literals (e.g. `#1/3/1999#`) in your code. It is better to use the VBA `DateSerial()`, or the Excel `DATE()` functions, which are not ambiguous.

4. If possible, use the date number instead of a string representation of a date. Numbers are much less prone to ambiguity (though not immune).

5. When writing formulas in code to be put into a cell (using the `.Formula` property), create the string using English functions. Excel will translate them to the local Office language for you.

6. When setting number formats or using the `Format()` function, use US formatting characters, e.g. `ActiveCell.NumberFormat = "dd mmm yyyy"`. Excel will translate these to the local number format for you.

7. When reading information from a worksheet, using `.Formula`, `.NumberFormat` etc, Excel will supply it using English formulas and US format codes, regardless of the local Excel language.

Interacting with your Users

The golden rule when displaying data to your users, or getting data from them, is to always respect their choice of Windows Regional Settings and Office UI Language. They should not be forced to enter numbers dates, formulas and/or number formats according to US settings, just because it's easier for you to develop.

Paper Sizes

One of the most annoying things for a user is to print a report from your application, then discover that their printer does not recognise the paper sizes used in your templates. If you use templates for your reports, you should always change the paper size to the user's default size. This can easily be determined by creating a new workbook and reading off the paper size from the `PageSetup` object.

Displaying Data

Excel does a very good job of displaying worksheets according to the user's selection of regional settings and language. When displaying data in UserForms or dialog sheets, however, we have to do all the formatting ourselves.

As discussed above, Excel 2000 converts number and dates to strings according to the WRS by default. This means that we can write code like:

```
tbNumber.Text = dNumber
```

and be safe in the knowledge that Excel will display it correctly. There are two problems with this approach:

1.   Dates will get the default 'ShortDate' format, which may not include 4 digits for the year and will not include a time component. To force a 4-digit year and include a time, use the sFormatDate() function shown later. It may be better, though, to use a less ambiguous date format on UserForms, such as the 'mmm dd, yyyy' format used throughout this book.

2.   Previous versions of Excel did not use the Windows Regional Settings for their default formats. If you are creating applications for use in older versions of Excel, you can't rely on the correct behavior.

The solution is simple – just use the Format() function. This tells VBA to convert the number to a locally-formatted string and works in all versions of Excel from 5.0:

```
tbNumber.Text = Format(dNumber)
```

Interpreting Data

Your users will want to type in dates and numbers according to their choice of regional settings and your code must validate those entries accordingly and maybe display meaningful error messages back to the user. This means that you have to use the Cxxx() conversion functions and the IsNumeric() and IsDate() validation functions. Unfortunately, these functions all have their problems (such as not recognising the % sign at the end of a number) which require some working around. An easy solution is to the use bWinToNum() and bWinToDate() functions shown later in this chapter to perform the validation, conversion and error prompting for you. The validation code for a UserForm will typically be done in the OK button's Click event, and be something like:

```
Private Sub bnOK_Click()
    Dim dResult As Double

    'Validate the number as display an error
    If bWinToNum(tbNumber.Text, dResult, True) Then
        'It was valid, so store the number
        Sheet1.Range("A1").Value = dResult
    Else
        'An error, so set the focus back and quit the routine
        tbNumber.SetFocus
        Exit Sub
    End If

    'All OK and stored, so hide the userform
    Me.Hide
End Sub
```

The xxxLocal Properties

Up until now, we have said that you have to interact with Excel using English language functions and the default US formats. Now we present an alternative situation where your code interacts with the user in his or her own language using the appropriate regional settings. How then, can your program take something typed in by the user (such as a number format or formula) and send it straight to Excel, or display an Excel formula in a message box in the user's own language?

Microsoft have anticipated this requirement and have provided us with local versions of most of the functions we need. They have the same name as their US equivalent, with the word "Local" on the end (such as FormulaLocal, NumberFormatLocal etc). When we use these functions, Excel does not perform any language or format coercion for us. The text we read and write is exactly how it appears to the user. Nearly all of the functions that return strings or have string arguments have local equivalents. The following table lists them all and the objects to which they apply:

Applies To	These versions of the functions use and return strings according to US number and date formats and English text	These versions of the functions use and return locally-formatted strings and in the language used for the Office UI (or Windows version – see later)
Number/string conversion	Str()	CStr()
Number/string conversion	Val()	CDbl() etc.
Name, Style, Command Bar	.Name	.NameLocal
Range, Chart Series	.Formula	.FormulaLocal
Range, Chart Series	.FormulaR1C1	.FormulaR1C1Local
Range, Style, Chart Data Label, Chart Axes Label	.NumberFormat	.NumberFormatLocal
Range	.Address	.AddressLocal
Range	.AddressR1C1	.AddressR1C1Local
Defined Name	.RefersTo	.RefersToLocal
Defined Name	.RefersToR1C1	.RefersToR1C1Local
Defined Name	.Category	.CategoryLocal

The Rules for Working with your Users

1. When converting a number or date to a text string for displaying to your users, or setting it as the `.Caption` or `.Text` properties of controls, explicitly convert numbers and dates to text according to the WRS, using `Format(myNum)`, or `CStr(MyNum)`.

2. When converting dates to strings, Excel does *not* rearrange the date part order, so `Format(MyDate, "dd/mm/yyyy")` will always give a DMY date order (but will show the correct date separator). Use `Application.International(xlDateOrder)` to determine the correct date order — as used in the `sFormatDate()` function shown later, or use one of the standard date formats (e.g. ShortDate)

3. If possible, use locale-independent date formats, such as `Format(MyDate, "mmm dd, yyyy")`. Excel will display month names according to the user's WRS language.

4. When evaluating date or number strings which have been entered by the user, use `CDate()` or `CDbl()`, to convert the string to a date/number. These will use the WRS to interpret the string. Note that `CDbl()` does not handle the `%` character if the user has put one at the end of the number.

5. Always validate numbers and dates entered by the user before trying to convert them. See then `bWinToNum()` and `bWinToDate()` functions later for an example.

6. When displaying information about Excel objects, use the `xxxLocal` properties (where they exist) to display it in your user's language and formats.

7. Use the `xxxLocal` properties when setting the properties of Excel objects with text provided by the user (which we must assume is in their native language and format).

Features that don't play by the Rules

The `xxxLocal` functions discussed in the previous section were all introduced during the original move from XLM functions to VBA in Excel 5.0. They cover most of the more common functions that a developer is likely to use. There were, however a number of significant omissions in the original conversion and new features have been added to Excel since then with almost complete disregard for international issues.

This section guides you through the maze of inconsistency, poor design and omission that you'll find hidden within the following of Excel 2000's features. This table shows the methods, properties and functions in Excel which are sensitive to the user's locale, but which do not behave according to the Rules we have stated above:

Applies To	US Version	Local Version
Opening a text file	OpenText()	OpenText()
Application	.ShowDataForm	.ShowDataForm
Worksheet / Range		.Paste / .PasteSpecial
Pivot Table calculated fields and items		.Formula
Conditional formats		.Formula
QueryTables (Web Queries)		.Refresh
Worksheet functions		=TEXT()
Range	.Value	
Range	.FormulaArray	
Range	.AutoFilter	.AutoFilter
Range		.AdvancedFilter
Application	.Evaluate	
Application	.ConvertFormula	
Application	.ExecuteExcel4Macro	

Fortunately, workarounds are available for most of these issues. There are a few, however, that should be completely avoided.

OpenText()

Workbooks.OpenText is the VBA equivalent of opening a text file in Excel by using File | Open. It opens the text file, parses it to identify numbers, dates, Booleans and strings and stores the results in worksheet cells. It is discussed in more detail elsewhere in the book. Of relevance to this chapter is the method Excel uses to parse the data file (and how it has changed over the past few versions). In Excel 5, the text file was parsed according to your Windows Regional Settings when opened from the user interface, but according to US formats when opened in code. In Excel 97, this was changed to always use these settings from both the UI and code. Unfortunately, this meant that there was no way to open a US-formatted text file with any confidence that the resulting numbers were correct. Since Excel 5, we have been able to specify the date order to be recognised, on a column-by-column basis, which works very well for numeric dates (e.g. 01/02/1999).

New to Excel 2000 is the Advanced button on the Text Import Wizard, and the associated DecimalSeparator and ThousandSeparator parameters of the OpenText() method. These allow us to specify the separators that Excel should use to identify numbers and are welcome additions. It is slightly disappointing to see that we can not specify the general date order in the same way.

Unfortunately, while Microsoft are to be congratulated for fixing the number format problems, they did not take the opportunity to fix the language issues. Throughout this book, we have stated that the best way to handle date strings is to use unambiguous formats that include the month name (e.g. Feb 1, 1999). The OpenText() method is the one place in Excel development where that advice should not be followed. This is because in OpenText(), Excel only recognises the month names according to your selected Windows Regional Setting language — English month names are not recognized if you have WRS set to Norwegian. The advice for text files is to store them as numeric dates (e.g. 01/02/1999) and use the OpenText() parameters to tell Excel which data order to recognise.

The other language-related issue is in the recognition, or otherwise, of Boolean values. You'll recall that all the VBA string/Boolean conversion functions worked with the English text "True" and "False" and were not dependant on the WRS language or the Office UI language. When opening text files, Excel uses the Office UI Language translations of "True" and "False" to identify Booleans. Hence, while "True" and "False" will be recognised when using an English UI, only "Sann" and "Usann" will be recognised as Booleans when using a Norwegian UI.

To summarise, OpenText() recognises:

- ❑ Numbers according to the separators we specify (defaulting to the WRS)
- ❑ Numeric date formats according to the date order we specify (by column)
- ❑ Textual dates according to the WRS language
- ❑ Boolean strings according to the Office UI language

While OpenText() is a vast improvement from earlier versions of Excel, it can still only be used reliably if the text file does not contain textual dates (use 01/02/1999 instead of Feb 1, 1999) or Boolean texts (use 1/0 instead of True/False).

ShowDataForm()

Using ActiveSheet.ShowDataForm is exposing yourself to one of the most dangerous of Excel's international issues. ShowDataForm is the VBA equivalent of the Data | Form menu item. It displays a standard dialog which allows the user to enter and change data in an Excel list/database. When run by clicking the Data | Form menu, the dates and numbers are displayed according to the WRS and changes made by the user are interpreted according to the WRS, which fully complies with the user-interaction rules above.

When run from code, using ActiveSheet.ShowDataForm, Excel displays dates and numbers according to US formats but interprets them according to WRS. Hence, if you have a date of Feb 10, 1999, shown in the worksheet in the dd/mm/yyyy order of 10/02/1999, Excel will display it on the data form as 2/10/1999. If you change this to the 11th (2/11/1999), Excel will store Nov 2, 1999 in the sheet! Similarly, if you are using Norwegian number formats, a number of 1-decimal-234 will be displayed on the form as 1.234. Change that to read 1.235 and Excel stores 1235, one thousand times too big!

Fortunately there is an easy workaround for this if your routine only has to work with Excel 2000 or Excel 97. Instead of using ShowDataForm, you can select the first cell in the range, then execute the Data | Form menu item itself:

```
Sub ShowForm()
    ActiveSheet.Range("A1").Select
    RunMenu 860   '860 is the CommandBarControl ID of the Data, Form menu item
End Sub
```

The following RunMenu routine executes a given menu item, as if it had been clicked by the user. In this case, the data form behaves correctly.

RunMenu()

This routine will run a menu item, given its CommandBar.Control ID (e.g. 860 is the ID for the Data | Form menu item).

```
Sub RunMenu(iMenuID As Long)
' *****************************************************
' * Function Name:   RunMenu
' *
' * Input/Output:    iMenuID - The control ID of the menu item to be run
' *
' * Purpose:         Runs a specified menu item, simulating clicking on it
' *
' *****************************************************

    Dim oCtrl As CommandBarButton

    'Ignore any errors (such as the menu ID not valid)
    On Error Resume Next

    'Create our own temporary commandbar to hold the control
    With Application.CommandBars.Add

        'Add the control and execute it
        .Controls.Add(ID:=iMenuID).Execute

        'Then delete our temporary menu bar
        .Delete
    End With

End Sub
```

Pasting Text

When pasting text from other applications into Excel, it is parsed according to the WRS. We have no way to tell Excel the number and date formats and language to recognise. The only workaround is to use a DataObject to retrieve the text from the clipboard, parse it yourself in VBA, then write the result to the sheet.

PivotTable Calculated Fields and Items and Conditional Format Formulas

If you are used to using the .Formula property of a range or chart series, you'll know that it returns and accepts formula strings that use English functions and US number formats. There is an equivalent .FormulaLocal property which returns and accepts formula strings as they appear on the sheet (i.e. using the Office UI language and WRS number formats).

Pivot table calculated fields and items and conditional formats also have a .Formula property, but for these objects, it returns and accepts formula strings as they appear to the user, i.e. it behaves in the same way as the .FormulaLocal property of a Range object. This means that to set the formula for one of these objects, we need to construct it in the Office UI language, and according to the WRS!

A workaround for this is to use the cell's own .Formula and .FormulaLocal properties to convert between the formats, as shown in the ConvertFormulaLocale() function below.

ConvertFormulaLocale()

This function converts a formula string between US and local formats and languages.

```
Function ConvertFormulaLocale(sFormula As String, bUSToLocal As Boolean) _
            As String
' ********************************************************
' * Function Name:    ConvertFormulaLocale
' *
' * Input/Output:     sFormula    - The text of the formula to convert from
' *                   bUSToLocal - True to convert US to Local
' *                                False to convert Local to US
' *
' *                   Returns the text of the formula according to local
' *                   settings.
' *
' * Purpose:          Converts a formula string between US and local formats
' *
' ********************************************************

   On Error GoTo ERR_BAD_FORMULA

   'Use a cell that is likely to be empty!
   'This should be changed to suit your own situation
   With ThisWorkbook.Worksheets(1).Range("IU1")
      If bUSToLocal Then
         .Formula = sFormula
         ConvertFormulaLocale = .FormulaLocal
      Else
         .FormulaLocal = sFormula
         ConvertFormulaLocale = .Formula
      End If

      .ClearContents
   End With

   ERR_BAD_FORMULA:

End Function
```

Web Queries

While the concept behind Web Queries is an excellent one, they have been implemented with complete disregard to international issues. When the text of the web page is parsed by Excel, all the numbers and dates are interpreted according to your Windows Regional Settings. This means that if a European web page is opened in the US, or a US page is opened in Europe, it is likely that the numbers will be wrong. For example, if the web page contains the text 1.1, it will appear as 1st Jan on a computer running Norwegian Windows. Web queries cannot be used reliably in a multinational application.

=TEXT() Worksheet Function

The TEXT() worksheet function converts a number to a string, according to a specified format. The format string has to use formatting characters defined by the Windows Regional Settings. Hence, if you use =TEXT(NOW(),"dd/mm/yyyy"), you will get "01/02/yyyy" on Norwegian Windows, since Excel will only recognise 'å' as the Norwegian number-format character used for years. Excel does not translate the number-format characters when it opens the file on a different platform. A workaround for this is to create a defined name that reads the number format from a specific cell, then use that definition within the TEXT() function. For example, if you format cell **A1** with the date format to use throughout your sheet, you can click on Insert | Name | Define and define a name as:

```
Name:          DateFormat
Refers To:     =GET.CELL(7,$A$1)
```

Then use =TEXT(Now(),DateFormat) elsewhere in the sheet. The GET.CELL() function is an Excel 4 macro function — which Excel 2000 lets us use within define names, though not on the worksheet. This is equivalent to, but much more powerful than the =CELL() worksheet function. The 7 in the example tells GET.CELL() to return the number-format string for the cell.

> *The XLM functions are documented in the* MACROFUN.HLP *and* XLMACR8.HLP *files, available from Microsoft's web site.*

Range.Value and Range.FormulaArray

These two properties of a range only break the rules by not having local equivalents. The strings passed to (and returned by) them are in US format. Use the ConvertFormulaLocale() function shown above to convert between US and local versions of formulas.

Range.AutoFilter

The AutoFilter method of a Range object is a very curious beast. We are forced to pass it strings for its filter criteria and hence must be aware of its string handling behaviour. The criteria string consists of an operator (=, >, <, >= etc.) followed by a value. If no operator is specified, the "=" operator is assumed. The key issue is that when using the "=" operator, AutoFilter performs a textual match, while using any other operator results in a match by value. This gives us problems when trying to locate exact matches for dates and numbers. If we use "=", Excel matches on the text that is displayed in the cell, i.e. the formatted number. As the text displayed in a cell will change with different regional settings and Windows language version, it is impossible for us to create a criteria string that will locate an exact match in all locales.

There is a workaround for this problem. When using any of the other filter criteria, Excel plays by the rules and interprets the criteria string according to US formats. Hence, a search criterion of ">=02/01/1999" will find all dates on or after 1st Feb, 1999, in all locales. We can use this to match an exact date by using two AutoFilter criteria. The following code will give an exact match on 1st Feb, 1999 and will work in any locale:

```
Range("A1:D200").AutoFilter 2, ">=02/01/1999", xlAnd, "<=02/01/1999"
```

Range.AdvancedFilter

The AdvancedFilter method does play by the rules, but in a way that may be undesirable. The criteria used for filtering are entered on the worksheet in the criteria range. In a similar way to AutoFilter, the criteria string includes an operator and a value. Note that when using the "=" operator, AdvancedFilter correctly matches by value and hence differs from AutoFilter in this respect. As this is entirely within the Excel domain, the string must be formatted according to the Windows Regional Settings to work, which gives us a problem when matching on dates and numbers. An advanced filter search criterion of ">1.234" will find all numbers greater then 1.234 in the US, but all numbers greater than 1234 when run in Norway. A criterion of ">02/03/1999" will find all dates after 3rd Feb in the US, but after 2nd March in Europe. The only workarounds are to populate the criteria strings from code, before running the AdvancedFilter method, or to use a calculated criteria string, using the =TEXT() trick mentioned above. Instead of a criterion of ">=02/03/1999", to find all dates on or after 3rd Feb, 1999, we could use the formula:

```
=">="&TEXT(DATE(1999,2,3),DateFormat)
```

Here DateFormat is the defined name introduced above that returns a local date format. If the date is an integer (i.e. does not contain a time component), we could also just use the criteria string ">=36194" and hope that the user realises that 36194 is actually 3rd Feb, 1999.

Application.Evaluate, Application.ConvertFormula and Application.ExecuteExcel4Macro

These functions all play by the rules, in that we must use US-formatted strings. They do not, however, have local equivalents. To evaluate a formula that the user may have typed into a UserForm (or convert it between using relative to absolute cell ranges), we need to convert it to US before passing it to Application.Evaluate or Application.ConvertFormula The Application.ExecuteExcel4Macro function is used to execute XLM-style functions. One of the most common uses of it is to call the XLM PAGE.SETUP() function, which is much faster than the VBA equivalent. This takes many parameters, including strings, numbers and Booleans. Be very careful to explicitly convert all these parameters to US-formatted strings and avoid the temptation to shorten the code by omitting the Str() around each one.

Responding to Office 2000 Language Settings

One of the major advances in Office 2000 is that there is a single set of executables, with a set of plug-in language packs (whereas in previous versions, each language was a different executable, with its own set of bugs). This makes it very easy for a user of Office to have their own choice of language for the user interface, help files etc. In fact, if a number of people share the same computer, each person can run the Office applications in a different language.

As developers of Excel applications, we must respect the user's language selection and do as much as we can to present our own user interface in their choice of language.

Where does the text come from?

There are three factors that together determine the text seen by the Office user:

Regional Settings Location

The Regional Settings location is chosen on the first tab (called **Regional Settings**) of the Control Panel **Regional Settings** applet and defines:

❑ The day and month names shown in Excel cells for long date formats,

❑ The day and month names returned by the VBA Format() function,

❑ The month names recognized by the VBA CDate() function and when typing dates into Excel directly,

❑ The month names recognized by the Text Import Wizard and the VBA OpenText() method,

❑ The number format characters used in the =TEXT() worksheet function,

❑ The text resulting from the implicit conversion of Boolean values to strings, that is:
   "I am " & True.

Office UI Language Settings

The Office User Interface language can be selected by using the "Microsoft Office Language Settings" applet, installed with Office 2000 and defines:

❑ The text displayed on Excel's menus and dialog boxes,

❑ The text for the standard buttons on Excel's message boxes,

❑ The text displayed in Excel's cells for Boolean values,

❑ The text for Boolean values recognized by the Text Import Wizard, the VBA OpenText() method and when typing directly into Excel,

❑ The default names for worksheets in a new workbook,

❑ The local names for command bars.

Language Version of Windows

By this, I mean the basic language version of Windows itself. This choice defines:

The text for the standard buttons in the VBA MsgBox function (i.e. when using the vbMsgBoxStyles constants). Hence, while the text of the buttons on Excel's built-in messages respond to the Office UI language, the text of the buttons on our own messages respond to the Windows language. Note that the only way to discover the Windows language is with a Windows API call.

There are some things in Office 2000 which are 100% (US) English, and don't respond to any changes in Windows language, regional settings or Office UI language, namely:

> The text resulting from the explicit conversion of Boolean values to strings, i.e. all of `Str(True)`, `CStr(True)` and `Format(True)` result in "True". Hence, the only way to convert a Boolean variable to the same string that Excel displays for it, is to enter it into a cell, then read the cell's `.FormulaLocal` property!

> The text of Boolean strings recognized by `CBool()`.

Identifying the Office UI Language Settings

The first step to creating a multilingual application is to identify the user's settings. We can identify the language chosen in Windows Regional Settings by using `Application.International(xlCountrySetting)`, which returns a number that corresponds approximately to the country codes used by the telephone system (e.g. 1 is the USA, 44 is the UK, 47 is Norway etc). We can also use `Application.International(xlCountryCode)` to retrieve the user interface language using the same numbering system. This method has worked well in previous versions of Excel, where there were only 30 or so languages from which to choose your copy of Office.

Office 2000 has changed things a little. By moving all the language configuration into separate language packs, Microsoft can support many more languages with relative ease. If you use the Object Browser to look at the `msoLanguageID` constants defined in the Office object library, you'll see that there are over 180 languages and dialects listed!

To find out the exact Office UI language, we can use:

```
Application.LanguageSettings.LanguageID(msoLanguageIDUI)
```

Creating a Multilingual Application

How far to go?

When developing a multilingual application, you have to balance a number of factors, including:

- ❑ The time and cost spent developing the application,
- ❑ The time and cost spent translating the application,
- ❑ The time and cost spent testing the translated application,
- ❑ The increased sales from having a translated version,
- ❑ Improved ease-of-use, and hence reduced support costs,
- ❑ The requirement for multi-lingual support,
- ❑ Should you create language-specific versions, or use add-on language packs?

You also have to decide how much of the application to translate, and which languages to support:

- ❑ Translate nothing,
- ❑ Translate only the packaging and promotional documentation,
- ❑ Enable the code to work in a multilingual environment (e.g. month names etc),
- ❑ Translate the user interface (menus, dialogs, screens and messages),
- ❑ Translate the help files, examples and tutorials,
- ❑ Customize the application for each location (e.g. to use local data feeds),
- ❑ Support left-to-right languages only,
- ❑ Support right-to-left languages (and hence redesign your UserForms),
- ❑ Support Double-Byte-Character-Set languages (e.g. Japanese).

The decision on how far to go will depend to a large extent on your users, your budget, and the availability of translators.

A Suggested Approach

It is doubtful that creating a single Excel application to support all 180+ Office languages will make economic sense, but the time spent in making your application support a few of the more common languages will often be a wise investment. This will, of course, depend on your users and whether support for a new language is preferable to new features!

The approach that I take is to write the application to support multiple languages and provide the user with the ability to switch between the installed languages or conform to their choice of Office UI Language. I develop the application in English, then have it translated into one or two other languages depending on my target users. I will only translate it into other languages if there is sufficient demand.

How to Store String Resources

When creating multilingual applications, we cannot hard-code *any* text strings that will be displayed to the user; we must look them up in a **string resource**. The easiest form of string resource is a simple worksheet table. Give all your text items a unique identifier and store them in a worksheet, one row per identifier and one column for each supported language. You can then look up the ID and return the string in the appropriate language using a simple VLOOKUP() function. You will need to do the same for all your menu items, worksheet contents and UserForm controls. The following code is a simple example, which assumes you have a worksheet called shLanguage that contains a lookup table which has been given a name of rgTranslation. It also assumes you have a public variable to identify which column to read the text from. The variable would typically be set in an Options type screen. Note that the code shown below is not particularly fast and is shown as an example. A faster (and more complex) routine would read the entire column of IDs and selected language texts into two static VBA arrays, then work from those; only reading in a new array when the language selection was changed.

```
Public iLanguageCol As Integer

Sub Test()
    iLanguageCol = 2
    MsgBox GetText(1001)
End Sub

Function GetText(lTextID As Long) As String
    Dim vaTest As Variant
    Static rgLangTable As Range

    'Set an object to point to the string resource table (once)
    If rgLangTable Is Nothing Then
       Set rgLangTable = ThisWorkbook.Worksheets("shLanguage") _
          .Range("rgTranslation")
    End If

    'If the language choice is not set, assume the first language in our table
    If iLanguageCol < 2 Then iLanguageCol = 2

    'Try to locate and read off the required text
    vaTest = Application.VLookup(lTextID, rgLangTable, iLanguageCol)

    'If we got some text, return it
    If Not IsError(vaTest) Then GetText = vaTest
End Function
```

Many of your messages will be constructed at runtime. For example, you may have code to check that a number is within certain boundaries:

```
If iValue <= iMin Or iValue >= iMax Then
    MsgBox "The number must be greater than " & CStr(iMin) & _
           " and less than " & CStr(iMax) & "."
End If
```

This would mean that we have to store two text strings with different IDs in our resource sheet, which is both inefficient and much harder to translate. In the example given, we would probably not have a separate translation string for the full stop. Hence, the maximum value would always come at the end of the sentence, which may not be appropriate for many languages. A better approach is to store the combined string with placeholders for the two numbers, and substitute the numbers at runtime:

```
If iValue < iMin Or iValue > iMax Then
    MsgBox ReplaceHolders( _
                "The number must be greater than %0 and less than %1.", _
                                     CStr(iMin), CStr(iMax))
End If
```

The translator (who may not understand your program) can construct a correct sentence, inserting the values at the appropriate points. The ReplaceHolders() function is shown later.

Working in a Multilingual Environment

Allow Extra Space

It is a fact that most other languages use longer words than the English equivalents. When designing our UserForms and worksheets, we must allow extra room for the non-English text to fit in the controls and cells. A good rule-of-thumb is to make your controls 1.5 times the width of the English text.

Using Excel's Objects

The names that Excel gives to its objects when they are created often depend on the user's choice of Office UI Language. For example, when creating a blank workbook using `Workbooks.Add`, it will not always be called "Book*n*", and the first worksheet in it will not always be called "Sheet1". With the German UI, for example, they are called "Mappe*n*" and "Tabelle1" respectively. Instead of referring to these objects by name, you should create an object reference as they are created, then use that object elsewhere in your code:

```
Dim Wkb As Workbook, Wks As Worksheet

Set Wbk = Workbooks.Add
Set Wks = Wkb.Worksheets(1)
```

Working with `CommandBarControls` can also be problematic. For example, you may want to add a custom menu item to the bottom of the **Tools** menu of the worksheet menu bar. In an English-only environment, you may write something like:

```
Sub AddHelloButton()
    Dim cbTools As CommandBarPopup
    Dim cbCtl As CommandBarButton

    Set cbTools = Application.CommandBars("Worksheet Menu Bar") _
        .Controls("Tools")

    Set cbCtl = cbTools.CommandBar.Controls.Add(msoControlButton)

    cbCtl.Caption = "Hello"
    cbCtl.OnAction = "MyRoutine"
End Sub
```

This code will fail if your user has a UI language other than English. While Excel recognises English names for command bars themselves, it does not recognise English names for the controls placed on them. In this example, the "Tools" dropdown menu is not recognised. The solution is to identify `CommandBar.Controls` by their ID and use `FindControl` to locate them. 30007 is the ID of the **Tools** popup menu:

```
Sub AddHelloButton()
    Dim cbTools As CommandBarPopup
    Dim cbCtl As CommandBarButton

    Set cbTools = Application.CommandBars("Worksheet Menu
Bar").FindControl(ID:=30007)

    Set cbCtl = cbTools.CommandBar.Controls.Add(msoControlButton)

    cbCtl.Caption = "Hello"
    cbCtl.OnAction = "MyRoutine"
End Sub
```

Using SendKeys

In the best of cases, the use of `SendKeys` should be avoided if at all possible. It is most often used to send key combinations to Excel, in order to activate a menu item or navigate a dialog box. It works by matching the menu item or dialog control accelerator keys, in the same way that you can use *Alt+key* combinations to navigate Excel using the keyboard. When used in a non-English version of Excel, it is highly unlikely that the key combinations in the `SendKeys` string will match up with the menus and dialogs, having potentially disastrous results.

For example, SendKeys "%DB" will bring up the Subtotals dialog in English Excel, but will Quit Excel when run with the German UI. Instead of using SendKeys to trigger menu items, you should use the RunMenu routine presented earlier in this chapter to execute a menu item by its CommandBarControl ID.

The Rules for Developing a Multilingual Application

1. Decide early in the analysis phase the level of multilingual support that you are going to provide, then stick to it.

2. Do not include any text strings within your code. Always look them up in a table.

3. Never construct sentences by concatenating separate text strings, as the foreign language version is unlikely to use the same word order. Instead use place-holders in your text and replace the place-holder at runtime.

4. When constructing UserForms, always make the controls bigger than you need for the English text; most other languages use longer words.

5. Do not try to guess the name that Excel gives to objects that you create in code. For example, when creating a new workbook, the first sheet will not always be "Sheet1".

6. Do not refer to command bar controls by their caption. While you can refer to command bars themselves by their English name, you must refer to the menu items by their ID (for built-in items) or tag (for custom items).

7. Do not use SendKeys

Some Helpful Functions

In addition to some of the custom functions already presented, such as RunMenu and IsDateUS, here are some more functions that I have found to be very useful when creating multinational applications. Note that the code has been written to be compatible with all versions of Excel from 5.0 to 2000 and hence avoids the use of newer VBA constructs (such as giving optional parameters specific data types).

bWinToNum()

This method checks if a string contains a number formatted according to the Windows Regional Settings and converts it to a Double. The function returns True or False to indicate the success of the validation, and optionally displays an error message to the user. It is best used as a wrapper function when validating numbers entered by a user, as shown in the 'Interacting with your users' section above.

```
Function bWinToNum(ByVal sWinString As String, _
                   ByRef dResult As Double, _
                   Optional bShowMsg) As Boolean
```

Continued on Following Page

```
' ********************************************************
' * Function Name:    bWinToNum
' *
' * Input/Output:     sWinString    String to be converted
' *                   dResult       The converted number, set to zero if
' *                                 the number is not valid or empty
' *                   bShowMsg      Optional.  True (or missing) to show
' *                                 an error message.
' *                                 False to suppress the error message.
' * Purpose:                        Function to convert a number string in Windows
' *                                 format to a number
' ********************************************************

    Dim dFrac As Double

    ' Take a copy of the string to play with
    sWinString = Trim(sWinString)
    dFrac = 1

    If IsMissing(bShowMsg) Then bShowMsg = True
    If sWinString = "-" Then sWinString = "0"
    If sWinString = "" Then sWinString = "0"

    ' Check for percentage, strip it out and remember to divide by 100
    If InStr(1, sWinString, "%") > 0 Then
        dFrac = dFrac / 100
        sWinString = Application.Substitute(sWinString, "%", "")
    End If
    ' Are we left with a number string in windows format?
    If IsNumeric(sWinString) Then
        ' If so, convert it to a number and return success
        dResult = CDbl(sWinString) * dFrac
        bWinToNum = True
    Else
        ' If not, display a message, return zero and failure
        If bShowMsg Then MsgBox "This entry was not recognised as a number," _
            & Chr(10) & "according to your Windows Regional Settings.", vbOKOnly
        dResult = 0
        bWinToNum = False
    End If

End Function
```

bWinToDate()

This provides the same functionality as bWinToNum(), but for dates instead of numbers.

```
Function bWinToDate(ByVal sWinString As String, _
                ByRef dResult As Double, _
                Optional bShowMsg) As Boolean
' ********************************************************
' * Function Name:    bWinToDate
' *
' * Input/Output:     sWinString    -String to be converted
' *                   dResult       -The converted number, set to zero if the
' *                                 number is not valid, or empty
' *                   bShowMsg      -Optional
' *                             .  True (or missing) to show
' *                                   an error  message.
' *                                 False to suppress the error message.
' *
' * Purpose:                        Function to Convert a date string in
' *                                 Windows' format to a date
' ********************************************************
```

```
      If IsMissing(bShowMsg) Then bShowMsg = True

      If sWinString = "" Then
          ' An empty string gives a valid date of zero
          dResult = 0
          bWinToDate = True

      ElseIf IsDate(sWinString) Then
          ' We got a proper date, so convert it to a Double
          ' (i.e. the internal date number)
          dResult = CDbl(CDate(sWinString))
          bWinToDate = True
      Else
          ' If not, display a message, return zero and failure
          If bShowMsg Then MsgBox "This entry was not recognised as a date," & _
              Chr(10) & according to your Windows Regional Settings.", vbOKOnly
          dResult = 0
          bWinToDate = False
      End If

End Function
```

sFormatDate()

This function formats a date according to the Windows Regional Settings, using a 4-digit year and optionally including a time string in the result.

```
Function sFormatDate(dDate As Date, Optional bTimeReq) As String
' ******************************************************
' * Function Name:        sFormatDate
' *
' * Input:                dDate    - The Excel date number
' *                       bTimeReq - Optional. True to include the time string
' *                                           in the result
' *
' * Output:               Returns the date formatted as a string according to
' *                                Windows settings and with a 4-digit year
' *
' * Purpose:              Format a date for display.
' *
' ******************************************************

    Dim sDate As String

    If IsMissing(bTimeReq) Then bTimeReq = False

    Select Case Application.International(xlDateOrder)
        Case 0        'month-day-year
          sDate = Format$(dDate, "mm/dd/yyyy")
        Case 1        'day-month-year
          sDate = Format$(dDate, "dd/mm/yyyy")
        Case 2        'year-month-day
          sDate = Format$(dDate, "yyyy/mm/dd")
    End Select

    If bTimeReq Then sDate = sDate & " " & Format$(dDate, "hh:mm:ss")

    sFormatDate = sDate

End Function
```

ReplaceHolders()

This function replaces the placeholders in a string with values provided to it.

```
Function ReplaceHolders(ByVal sString As String, ParamArray avReplace()) _
     As String
' **************************************************
' * Function Name:    ReplaceHolders
' *
' * Input/Output:     sString   - The text to replace the placeholders in
' *                   avReplace - A list of items to replace the placeholders
' *
' *                   Returns the original text, with the placeholders
' *                   substituted with the values
' *
' * Purpose:          To substitute the placeholders in a string with
' *                   their values
' *
' **************************************************

   Dim i As Integer

   'Work backwards, so we don't replace %10 with our %1 text
   For i = UBound(avReplace) To LBound(avReplace) Step -1
       sString = Application.Substitute(sString, "%" & i, _
           avReplace(i - LBound(avReplace)))
   Next

   ReplaceHolders = sString

End Function
```

Summary

It is possible to create an Excel application that will work on every installation of Excel in the world and support all 180-plus Office languages, but it is unlikely to be economically viable.

If you have a limited set of users and you are able to dictate their Language and Windows Regional Settings, you can create your application without worrying about international issues. Even if this is the case, you should get into the habit of creating locale-independent code. The requirement for locale-independence should be included in your analysis, design and coding standards. It is much, much easier and cheaper to write locale-independent code at the onset than to rework an existing application.

At a minimum, your application should work regardless of the user's choice of Windows Regional Settings or Windows or Office UI Language. You should be able to achieve this by following the rules listed in this chapter.

The following Excel features don't play by the rules and have to be treated very carefully:

> OpenText
>
> ShowDataForm
>
> Pasting text from other applications
>
> The .Formula property in all its guises
>
> <range>.Value
>
> <range>.FormulaArray
>
> <range>.AutoFilter
>
> <range>.AdvancedFilter
>
> The =TEXT() worksheet function
>
> Application.Evaluate
>
> Application.ConvertFormula
>
> Application.ExecuteExcel4Macro

There are also some features in Excel that you may have to avoid completely:

> Web Queries
>
> SendKeys
>
> Using True and False in imported text files

Programming the VBE

Introduction

Up until now, the book has focused on writing VBA procedures to automate Excel. While writing the code, you have been working in the Visual Basic Editor (VBE), otherwise known as the Visual Basic Integrated Design Environment (VBIDE).

There is an object library provided with Office 2000 that is shown as **Microsoft Visual Basic for Applications Extensibility 5.3** in the VBE's **Tools | References** list. The objects in this library and their methods, properties and events enable us to:

- ❑ Program the VBE itself, to create useful Addins to assist you in our development efforts and automate many of your development tasks

- ❑ Programmatically create, delete and modify the code, UserForms and references in your own and other workbooks.

This chapter explains how to write code to automate the VBE itself by walking you through the development of a VBE toolkit. You will then add a few utilities to the toolkit that demonstrate how to programmatically manipulate code, UserForms and references. For simplicity, most of the code examples in this chapter have not been provided with error handling.

> The completed toolkit Addin, can be found as 'VBE Tools 2000.exe' on my web site at www.BMSLtd.co.uk or on the Wrox Press web site at www.wrox.com. The Project has been protected to prevent accidental changes and to stop Excel expanding its modules in the Project Explorer. The password to unprotect the project is the letter 'a', without the quotes.

Identifying VBE Objects in Code

All the objects that form the VBE and their properties and methods are contained in their own object library. You need to create a reference to this library before you can use the objects, by switching to the VBE, selecting the menu item **Tools | References**, checking the **VBA Extensibility** library and clicking OK. In code, this library is referred to as the **VBIDE** object library.

The full VBIDE object model is documented in the References section of this book. The more important objects are summarised below:

The VBE Object

The top-level object of the Visual Basic Editor is known as the VBE object and is itself a property of the Excel Application object. Hence, to create an object variable to refer to the VBE, we need code like:

```
Dim obVBE As VBIDE.VBE

Set cbVBE = Application.VBE
```

The VBProject Object

This object is the container for all the 'program' aspects of a workbook, including UserForms, modules, class modules and the code behind each worksheet and the workbook itself. Each VBProject corresponds to one of the top-level items in the Project Explorer. A specific VBProject object can be located either by iterating through the VBE's VBProjects collection, or through the VBProject property of a workbook.

To find the VBProject that corresponds to the workbook Book1.xls, the following code can be used:

```
Dim obVBP As VBIDE.VBProject

Set obVBP = Workbooks("Book1.xls").VBProject
```

When creating Addins for the VBIDE itself, it often needs to know which project is currently highlighted in the Project Explorer. This is given by the ActiveVBProject property of the VBE:

```
Dim obVBP As VBIDE.VBProject

Set obVBP = Application.VBE.ActiveVBProject
```

> Note that the ActiveVBProject is the project that the user is editing within the VBE. It is not related in any way to the ActiveWorkbook given by Excel. In fact with the Office 2000 Developer Edition, it is possible to create self-contained VB Projects that are not part of an Excel workbook.

The VBComponent Object

The UserForms, modules and class modules and the code modules behind the worksheets and workbook are all VBComponent objects. Each VBComponent object corresponds to one of the lower-level items in the Project Explorer tree. A specific VBComponent can be located through the VBComponents collection of a VBProject. Hence, to find the VBComponent that represents the UserForm1 form in Book1.xls, code like this can be used:

```
Dim obVBC As VBIDE.VBComponent

Set obVBC = Workbooks("Book1.xls").VBProject.VBComponents("UserForm1")
```

The name of the VBComponent that contains the code behind the workbook, worksheets and charts is given by the CodeName property of the related Excel object (i.e. the workbook, worksheet or chart object). Hence, to find the VBComponent for the code behind the workbook (i.e. where code can be written to hook into workbook events), this code can be used:

```
Dim obVBC As VBIDE.VBComponent

With Workbooks("Book1.xls")
    Set obVBC = .VBProject.VBComponents(.CodeName)
End With
```

And for a specific worksheet:

```
Dim obVBC As VBIDE.VBComponent

With Workbooks("Book1.xls")
    Set obVBC = .VBProject.VBComponents(.Worksheets("Sheet1").CodeName)
End With
```

Note that the name of the workbook's VBComponent is usually called "ThisWorkbook" in the Project Explorer. **Do not be tempted to rely on this name**. If your user has chosen a different language for the Office User Interface, it will be different. The name can also be easily changed by the user in the VBE. For this reason, **DO NOT** use code like:

```
Dim obVBC As VBIDE.VBComponent

With Workbooks("Book1.xls")
    Set obVBC = .VBProject.VBComponents("ThisWorkbook")
End With
```

When developing Addins for the VBE, you often need to know the VBComponent that the user is editing (i.e. the one highlighted in the Project Explorer). This is given by the SelectedVBComponent property of the VBE:

```
Dim obVBC As VBIDE.VBComponent

Set obVBC = Application.VBE.SelectedVBComponent
```

Each VBComponent has a Properties collection, corresponding approximately to the list shown in the Properties Window of the VBE when a VBComponent is selected in the Project Explorer. One of these is the "Name" Property, shown in the following test routine:

```
Sub ShowNames()
    With Application.VBE.SelectedVBComponent
        Debug.Print .Name & ": " & .Properties("Name")
    End With
End Sub
```

For most VBComponents, the text returned by .Name and .Properties("Name") is the same. However, for the VBComponents that contain the code behind workbooks, worksheets and charts, .Properties("Name") gives the name of the Excel object (i.e. the workbook, worksheet or chart). You can use this to find the Excel object that corresponds to the item that the user is working on in the VBE, or the Excel workbook that corresponds to the ActiveVBProject. The code for doing this is shown later in this chapter.

The CodeModule Object

All of the VBA code for a VBComponent is contained within its CodeModule object. Through this object you can programmatically read, add, change and delete lines of code. There is only ever one CodeModule for a VBComponent. In Office 2000, every type of VBComponent has a CodeModule, though this may not be the case in future. For example, you may get a tool to help design, execute and debug SQL Queries that only has a graphical interface, like MS Query, but does not have any code behind it.

The CodePane Object

This object gives us access to the user's view of a CodeModule. Through this object, you can identify such items as the section of a CodeModule that is visible on the screen, the text that the user has selected etc. You can identify which CodePane is currently being edited by using the VBE's ActiveCodePane property:

```
Dim obCP As VBIDE.CodePane

Set obCP = Application.VBE.ActiveCodePane
```

The Designer Object

Some VBComponents (such as UserForms) present both code and a graphical interface to the developer. While the code is accessed through the CodeModule and CodePane objects, the Designer object gives you access to the graphical part. In the standard versions of Office 2000, UserForms are the only components with a graphical interface for you to control. However, the Office 2000 Developer Edition includes a number of other items (such as the Data Connection Designer), which have graphical interfaces; these too are exposed to use through the Designer object.

Starting Up

There is very little difference in Excel 2000 between a normal workbook and an Addin. The code and UserForms can be modified in the same manner and they both offer the same level of protection (i.e. locking the Project from view). The two advantages of using an Addin to hold your tools are that it is invisible within the Excel User Interface, and that it can be loaded using Excel's Tools | Add-Ins menu. This chapter uses the term 'Addin' to mean a container for tools that you're adding to Excel/VBE. In fact, during the development of the Addin, you will actually keep the file as a standard workbook, only converting it to an Addin at the end.

Most Addins have a common structure, and the one we will develop in this chapter will be no exception:

- ❑   A startup module to trap the opening and closing of the Addin
- ❑   Some code to add our menu items to the commandbars on opening and remove them when closing
- ❑   For the VBE, a class module to handle the menu items' Click events
- ❑   Some code to perform your menus' actions.

Start with a new workbook and delete all of the worksheets apart from the first. Press *Alt+F11* to switch to the VBE, find your workbook in the Project Explorer. Select the VBProject entry for it. In the Properties Window, change the project's name to 'aaVBETools2000' (no quotes). The name starts with the prefix 'aa' so that it always appears at the top of the Project Explorer, nicely out of the way of any other projects you may be developing.

Add a new module to the project, give it the name of modCommon and type in the following code, which runs when the workbook is opened and closed:

```
Option Explicit
Option Compare Text

'The Addin ID is used to identify our menus, making it easy to remove them
Public Const psAddinID As String = "VBETools"

'The Addin title is shown on various message boxes
Public Const psAddinTitle As String = "Excel VBE Tools 2000"

''''''''''''''''''''''''''''''''''''''
' Subroutine: Auto_Open
'
' Purpose:    Adds our menus and menuitems to the VBE and sets up the objects
'             to trap the command bar events for the new controls
'
Sub Auto_Open()
    SetUpMenus
End Sub

''''''''''''''''''''''''''''''''''''''
' Subroutine: Auto_Close
'
' Purpose:    Removes our menus and menu items from the VBE
'

Sub Auto_Close()
    RemoveMenus
End Sub
```

The Auto_Open and Auto_Close procedures just call some other routines (which will be created in the following section) to add and remove the menus and menu items to/from the VBE command bars. A global constant has also been defined to uniquely identify our Addin's menus and another to use as a standard title for the Addin's message boxes.

Adding Menu Items to the VBE

The VBE uses the same command bar code as the rest of the Office suite, so the procedure for adding your own menus to the VBE is very little different to that documented in Chapter 12 of this book.

There is one major difference, which is how to run your routine when the menu item is clicked. When adding menu items to Excel, we set the CommandBarButton's OnAction property to the name of the procedure to run. In the VBE, CommandBarButtons still have an OnAction property, but it is ignored.

Instead of the simple OnAction, MS has provided the VBE developer with a specific type of object to handle events in CommandBars, unsurprisingly called CommandBarEvents. It has no properties or methods and only one event, the Click event. By using this event object, you can trap the Click event for any of the menu items within the VBE, either the built-in ones or user-defined ones, and decide in code whether to handle the click ourselves, ignore it completely, or let it pass through to the VBE's normal menu handling. While we only have the Click event in Office 2000 VBE, I predict that we'll be able to respond to many more command bar related events in future versions (such as BeforeDropdown, ItemAdded, ItemRemoved etc).

In order to use the CommandBarEvents, you need an object declared WithEvents to pass them to and a class module to put it in, so add a class module to the project, give it the name of CBarEvents and type in the following code:

```
'Object to trap the CommandBar events (i.e. clicking)
Public WithEvents cbBtnEvents As CommandBarEvents

'''''''''''''''''''''''''''''''''''''
' Subroutine: cbBtnEvents_Click
'
' Purpose:    Handles clicking on the commandbar control
'

Private Sub cbBtnEvents_Click(ByVal obCommandBarControl As Object, _
        bHandled As Boolean, bCancelDefault As Boolean)

    On Error Resume Next    'In case the routine is wrong/doesn't exist

    'Run the routine given by the commandbar control's OnAction property
    Application.Run obCommandBarControl.OnAction

    'We handled it OK
    bHandled = True
    bCancelDefault = True
End Sub
```

The key things to note here are:

❑ An object, cbBtnEvents, is declared to receive the CommandBar events for the menu item.

❑ The Click event is trapped for the cbBtnEvents object (the only one exposed by it!)

❑ The Click event passes the cbCommandBarControl object (i.e. the menu item or toolbar button) that was clicked.

We are simply running the routine stored in the control's OnAction property, which normally has no effect in the VBE. This code is simulating the behavior that occurs when adding menu items to Excel's menus.

Table-Driven Menu Creation

Very few professional Excel developers write code to add their menu items one-by-one. Most of us use a table-driven approach, whereby we fill out a table with information about the menu items we want to add, then have a routine which generates all the menu items based on this table. The same technique will be used here.

The first thing that is needed is a table for the menu information. Back in Excel, rename the worksheet to `MenuTable` and fill out the sheet as shown below:

	A	B	C	D	E	F	G	H
1	App / VBE	CommandBar	Sub Control ID	Type	Caption	Position	Begin Group	BuiltIn ID
2	VBE	Menu Bar	30002	1	&New Workbook	1		1
3	VBE	Standard		1	&New Workbook	3		1
4								

	I	J	K			L	M	N	O
1	Procedure	FaceID	ToolTip			Popup1	Popup2	Popup3	etc_
2	FileNewBook	18	Create a new workbook						
3	FileNewBook	18	Create a new workbook						
4									

The columns of the `MenuTable` are:

Col	Title	Description
A	App / VBE	Either 'App' to add items to Excel's menus or 'VBE' to add them to the VBE.
B	Command Bar	The name of the top-level command bar to add our menu to. See below for a list of valid names and the parts of the VBE to which they apply.
C	Sub Control ID	The ID number of a built-in pop-up bar to add our menu to. For example, 30002 is the ID of the File popup menu.
D	Type	The type of control to add: 1 for a normal button, 10 for a popup etc. These correspond to the `msoControl...` types listed in the Object Browser.
E	Caption	The text to use for the menu item.
F	Position	The position in the command bar to add the menu item. Leave this blank to add the menu to the end of the bar.
G	Begin Group	`True` or `False` to specify whether to place a separator line before the item.
H	BuiltIn ID	If we're adding a built-in menu item, this is the ID of that menu. Use 1 for all custom menus items.
I	Procedure	The name of the procedure to run when the menu item is clicked.
J	FaceID	The ID number of the built-in tool face to use for the menu. This can also be the name of a picture in the worksheet to use for the button face. 18 is the number for the standard New icon.
K	ToolTip	The text of the pop-up tooltip to show for the button.
L -	Popup1 – n	If we add our own popup menus, this is the caption of the custom popup to add further menu items to. See later for an example of its use. We can include as many levels of popup as we like, by simply adding more columns – the code will detect the extra columns.

The names for each of the top-level command bars in the VBE (i.e. the names to use in column B of the menu table) are shown in the following table. Note that Excel will always recognise these names, regardless of the user's choice of language for the Office User Interface. The same is not true for the menu items placed on these toolbars. The only language-independent way to locate specific built-in menu items is to use their ID number. A routine to list the ID numbers of built-in menu items is provided in Chapter 12.

Name	Description
Menu Bar	The normal VBE menu bar.
Standard	The normal VBE toolbar.
Edit	The VBE edit toolbar, containing useful code-editing tools.
Debug	The VBE debug toolbar, containing typical debugging tools.
UserForm	The VBE UserForm toolbar, containing useful form-editing tools.
MSForms	The popup menu for a UserForm (shown when you right-click the UserForm background).
MSForms Control	The popup menu for a normal control on a UserForm.
MSForms Control Group	The popup menu that appears when you right-click a group of controls on a UserForm.
MSForms MPC	The popup menu for the Multi-Page Control.
MSForms Palette	The popup menu that appears when you right-click a tool in the Control Toolbox.
MSForms Toolbox	The popup menu that appears when you right-click one of the tabs at the top of the Control Toolbox.
MSForms DragDrop	The popup menu that appears when you use the right mouse button to drag a control between tabs in the Control Toolbox, or on to a UserForm.
Code Window	The popup menu for a code window.
Code Window (Break)	The popup menu for a code window, when in Break (debug) mode.
Watch Window	The popup menu for the Watch window.
Immediate Window	The popup menu for the Immediate window.
Locals Window	The popup menu for the Locals window.
Project Window	The popup menu for the Project Explorer.

Name	Description
Project Window (Break)	The popup menu for the Project Explorer, when in Break mode.
Object Browser	The popup menu for the Object Browser.
Property Browser	The popup menu for the Properties window.
Docked Window	The popup menu that appears when you right-click the title bar of a docked window.

As this sheet will be referred to a number of times in code, it is a good idea to give it a meaningful 'code name', such as shMenuTable. To do this, locate and select the sheet in the Project Explorer window in the VBE, probably shown as Sheet1 (MenuTable), and change its name in the Properties window. It should now be shown as shMenuTable (MenuTable) in the Project Explorer. Using the code name allows you to refer directly to that sheet as an object, so the following two lines are equivalent:

```
Debug.Print ThisWorkbook.Worksheets("MenuTable").Name
```

```
Debug.Print shMenuTable.Name
```

The code to create the menus from this table is shown below. The code should be copied into a new module called modSetupBars:

At the top of the module, a number of constants are declared, which correspond to each column of the menu table and you will use these throughout your code. If the menu table structure changes, all you need to do is renumber these constants — you don't need to search through the code:

```
Option Explicit
Option Compare Text

'Constants for the columns in the commandbar creation table
Const miTABLE_APP_VBE          As Integer = 1
Const miTABLE_COMMANDBAR_NAME  As Integer = 2
Const miTABLE_CONTROL_ID       As Integer = 3
Const miTABLE_CONTROL_TYPE     As Integer = 4
Const miTABLE_CONTROL_CAPTION  As Integer = 5
Const miTABLE_CONTROL_POSITION As Integer = 6
Const miTABLE_CONTROL_GROUP    As Integer = 7
Const miTABLE_CONTROL_BUILTIN  As Integer = 8
Const miTABLE_CONTROL_PROC     As Integer = 9
Const miTABLE_CONTROL_FACEID   As Integer = 10
Const miTABLE_CONTROL_TOOLTIP  As Integer = 11
Const miTABLE_POPUP_START      As Integer = 12
```

You need to create one instance of our menu event handler class for every menu item that you add to the VBE menus. They each need to be stored in a global or module-level variable, to ensure they are not destroyed by Excel when the procedure finishes (i.e. by going out of scope). Using a standard Collection object is the easiest way to store all the instances of the class:

```
'Define a collection to store the menu item click event handlers
Dim mcolBarEvents As New Collection
```

The routine to actually set up the menus is called from our Addin's `Auto_Open` procedure:

```
''''''''''''''''''''''''''''''''''''''
' Subroutine: SetUpMenus
'
' Purpose:    Adds the menus to the VBE Edit menu and sets up the objects to
'             trap the command bar events for the new controls
'
Sub SetUpMenus()
    Dim rgRow As Range
    Dim cbAllBars As CommandBars
    Dim cbBar As CommandBar
    Dim cbBtn As CommandBarControl
    Dim cbBarEvents As CBarEvents
    Dim iBuiltInID As Integer, iPopUpCol As Integer, vaData As Variant

    On Error Resume Next    'Just ignore errors in the table definition

    'Remove all of our menus to before adding them.
    'This ensures we don't get any duplicated menus
    RemoveMenus

    'Loop through each row of our menu generation table
    For Each rgRow In shMenuTable.Cells(1).CurrentRegion.Rows
        'Ignore the header row
        If rgRow.Row > 1 Then
            'Read the row into an array of the cells' values
            vaData = rgRow.Value

            Set cbBar = Nothing
```

A single routine can be used to add menu items to both the Excel and VBE menus. The only difference is the `CommandBars` collection that is looked in – Excel's or the VBE's:

```
            'Get the collection of all command bars, either in the VBE or Excel
            If vaData(1, miTABLE_APP_VBE) = "VBE" Then
                Set cbAllBars = Application.VBE.CommandBars
            Else
                Set cbAllBars = Application.CommandBars
            End If

            'Try to find the commandbar we want
            Set cbBar = cbAllBars.Item(vaData(1, miTABLE_COMMANDBAR_NAME))

            'Did we find it - if not, we must be adding one!
            If cbBar Is Nothing Then
                Set cbBar = cbAllBars.Add(Name:=vaData _
                    (1, miTABLE_COMMANDBAR_NAME), temporary:=True)
            End If
```

If you want to look for a built-in popup menu to add your control to, you can recursively search for it in the `CommandBars` collection. For example, if you wanted to add a menu item to the Format | Make same size menu, you can just give it the ID of the Make same size menu (32790).

```
'If set, locate the built-in popup menu bar (by ID) to add our
'control to. e.g. Menu Bar > Edit
If Not IsEmpty(vaData(1, miTABLE_CONTROL_ID)) Then
   Set cbBar = cbBar.FindControl(ID:=vaData(1,_
            miTABLE_CONTROL_ID), Recursive:=True).CommandBar
End If

'Loop through the PopUp name columns to navigate
'down the menu structure
For iPopUpCol = miTABLE_POPUP_START To UBound(vaData, 2)
   'If set, navigate down the menu structure to the next popup menu
   If Not IsEmpty(vaData(1, iPopUpCol)) Then
      Set cbBar = cbBar.Controls(vaData(1, iPopUpCol)).CommandBar
   End If
Next

'Get the ID number if we're adding a built-in control
iBuiltInID = vaData(1, miTABLE_CONTROL_BUILTIN)

'If it's empty, set it to 1, indicating a custom control
If iBuiltInID = 0 Then iBuiltInID = 1

'Now add our control to the command bar, passing the procedure
'to run as the control's parameter
If IsEmpty(vaData(1, miTABLE_CONTROL_POSITION)) Or vaData _
      (1, miTABLE_CONTROL_POSITION) > cbBar.Controls.Count Then
   Set cbBtn = cbBar.Controls.Add(Type:=vaData_
      (1 miTABLE_CONTROL_TYPE), ID:=iBuiltInID, temporary:=True)
Else
   Set cbBtn = cbBar.Controls.Add(Type:=vaData_
      (1, miTABLE_CONTROL_TYPE),ID:=iBuiltInID, temporary:=True, _
         before:=vaData(1, miTABLE_CONTROL_POSITION))
End If

'Set the rest of button's properties
With cbBtn
   .Caption = vaData(1, miTABLE_CONTROL_CAPTION)
   .BeginGroup = vaData(1, miTABLE_CONTROL_GROUP)
   .TooltipText = vaData(1, miTABLE_CONTROL_TOOLTIP)
```

You can either use one of the standard Office tool faces, by supplying the numeric FaceID, or provide your own picture to use. To use your own picture, just give the name of the Picture object in the FaceID column of the menu table.

```
'The FaceID can be empty for a blank button, the number
'of a standard button face, or the name of a picture object
'on the sheet, which contains the picture to use.
If Not IsEmpty(vaData(1, miTABLE_CONTROL_FACEID)) Then
   If IsNumeric(vaData(1, miTABLE_CONTROL_FACEID)) Then
      'A numeric face ID, so use it
      .FaceId = vaData(1, miTABLE_CONTROL_FACEID)
   Else
      'A textual face ID, so copy the picture to the button
      shMenuTable.Shapes(vaData(1, miTABLE_CONTROL_FACEID))_
            .CopyPicture
      .PasteFace
   End If
End If
```

It is a good idea to set a property of all your menu items that identifies it as one of yours. If you use the `.Tag` property to do this, you can use the `FindControl` method of the `CommandBars` object to locate all of your menu items, without having to remember exactly where you added them. This is done in the `RemoveMenus` procedure later in the module:

```
            'Set the button's tag to identify it as one we created.
            'This way, we can still find it if the user moves or renames it
            .Tag = psAddinID

            'Set the control's OnAction property.  This only really has an
            'effect on the Excel menus, but we can use it in the VBE to say
            'which routine to run in the Click event handler
            'Surround the workbook name with quote marks, in case the name
            'includes spaces
            .OnAction = "'" & ThisWorkbook.Name & "'!" & _
                vaData(1, miTABLE_CONTROL_PROC)
        End With
```

This is the code that sets up the menu event handler. A new instance of our event handler class is created, the `cbBtnEvents` object defined in it is linked to the `CommandBarEvents` associated with the menu item that was created (`cbBtn`), and then this new instance of the class is added to the module-level collection:

```
            'We only need to handle events for custom controls in the VBE
            If iBuiltInID = 1 And vaData(1, miTABLE_APP_VBE) = "VBE" Then
                'Create a new instance of our button event-handling class
                Set cbBarEvents = New CBarEvents

                'Tell the class to hook into the events for this button
                Set cbBarEvents.cbBtnEvents = Application.VBE.Events _
                                        .CommandBarEvents(cbBtn)

                'And add the event handler to our collection of handlers
                mcolBarEvents.Add cbBarEvents
            End If
        End If
    Next
End Sub
```

When the Addin is closed, you need to run some code to remove your menus from the VBE. Some developers just use `CommandBars.Reset`, but this removes all other customizations from the command bars as well as their own. It is much better behaviour to locate all the menu items and command bars that were created for your Addin and delete them. This takes two routines. The first removes all the menus from a specific `CommandBars` collection, by searching for its `Tag`:

```
Private Sub RemoveMenusFromBars(cbBars As CommandBars)
    Dim cbCtl As CommandBarControl

    'Ignore errors while deleting our menu items
    On Error Resume Next

    'Using the application or VBE CommandBars ...
    With cbBars
        'Find a CommandBarControl with our tag
        Set cbCtl = .FindControl(Tag:=psAddinID)

        'Loop until we didn't find one
        Do Until cbCtl Is Nothing
            'Delete the one we found
            cbCtl.Delete
```

```
            'Find the next one
            Set cbCtl = .FindControl(Tag:=psAddinID)
        Loop
    End With
End Sub
```

The second removal routine calls the first to remove the menu items from the Excel command bars and the VBE command bars, removes any custom bars that might have been created, and clears the module-level collection of event handlers:

```
Sub RemoveMenus()
    Dim cbBar As CommandBar, rgRow As Range, stBarName As String

    'Ignore errors while deleting our menu items and commandbars
    On Error Resume Next

    'Delete our menu items from the Excel and VBE commandbars
    RemoveMenusFromBars Application.CommandBars
    RemoveMenusFromBars Application.VBE.CommandBars

    'Loop through each row of our menu generation table
    For Each rgRow In shMenuTable.Cells(1).CurrentRegion.Rows
        'Ignore the header row
        If rgRow.Row > 1 Then
            stBarName = rgRow.Cells(1, miTABLE_COMMANDBAR_NAME)

            Set cbBar = Nothing
            'Find the command bar, either in the VBE or Excel
            If rgRow.Cells(1, miTABLE_APP_VBE) = "VBE" Then
                Set cbBar = Application.VBE.CommandBars(stBarName)
            Else
                Set cbBar = Application.CommandBars(stBarName)
            End If
            'If we found it, delete it if it is not a built-in bar
            If Not cbBar Is Nothing Then
                If Not cbBar.BuiltIn Then
                    'Only delete blank command bars - in case two Addins
                    'added menu items to the same custom bar
                    If cbBar.Controls.Count = 0 Then cbBar.Delete
                End If
            End If
        End If
    Next

    'Clear down all our menu click event handlers
    Set mcolBarEvents = Nothing
End Sub
```

> You now have a complete template, which can be used as the basis for any
> Excel or VBE Addin (or just in a normal workbook where you want to modify
> the menu structure).

Looking at the completed menu table in our worksheet, we have two lines that will add a New button to the File menu and Standard toolbar, to run a procedure called FileNewBook:

	A	B	C	D	E	F	G	H
1	App / VBE	CommandBar	Sub Control ID	Type	Caption	Position	Begin Group	Builtin ID
2	VBE	Menu Bar	30002	1	&New Workbook	1		1
3	VBE	Standard		1	&New Workbook	3		1
4								

	I	J	K	L	M	N	O
1	Procedure	FaceID	ToolTip	Popup1	Popup2	Popup3	etc...
2	FileNewBook	18	Create a new workbook				
3	FileNewBook	18	Create a new workbook				
4							

Let's add this procedure, then test the Addin! Add a new module called modMenuFile and copy in the following code. We will be adding more file-related routines to this module later.

> **Note that the complete file is available for download from the web — 'VBE Tools 2000.exe' from** www.BMSLtd.co.uk **or** www.wrox.com.

```
'''''''''''''''''''''''''''''''''''''
' Subroutine: FileNewBook
'
' Purpose:    Create a new workbook
'
Sub FileNewBook()
    'Just ignore any errors
    On Error Resume Next

    'Create a new workbook
    Application.Workbooks.Add

    'Refresh the VBE display
    With Application.VBE.MainWindow
        .Visible = False
        .Visible = True
    End With
End Sub
```

This just adds a new blank workbook and refreshes the VBE display. Note that the VBE Project Explorer does not always update correctly when workbooks are added and removed through code. The easiest way to refresh the VBE display is to hide and then reshow the main VBE window.

First, check that the Addin compiles, using the Debug | Compile menu. If any compile errors are highlighted, check your code against the listings above. To run the Addin, click on Tools | Macros, select the Auto_Open procedure and click the Run button. If all goes well, a New menu item will be added to the VBE File menu and a standard New icon will appear on the VBE toolbar, just to the left of the Save icon:

When you click the button, a new workbook will be created in Excel and you will see its VBProject added to the Project Explorer. Congratulations, you have programmed the VBE!

Displaying Built-In Dialogs, UserForms and Messages

The ability to save a workbook from the VBE is built in to Office 2000, but you have also added the ability to create new workbooks. For a full complement of file operations, you need to add routines to open and close workbooks as well. Adding a "Most Recently Used" list to the VBE is left as an exercise for the reader!

By the end of this chapter, you'll have functionality within the VBE to:

❏ Create a new workbook

❏ Open an existing workbook

❏ Save a workbook (this is built into the VBE)

❏ Close a workbook

❏ Display a workbook's Properties dialog

For the Open routine, another menu item will be added to the File menu, and another standard button to the toolbar. For the Close routine, an item will once again be added to the File menu, but it will also be added to the Project Explorer popup menu, allowing you to close a VBProject by right-clicking on it in the Project Explorer. The following additions to the menu table will achieve this:

	A	B	C	D	E	F	G	H
1	App / VBE	CommandBar	Sub Control ID	Type	Caption	Position	Begin Group	Builtin ID
2	VBE	Menu Bar	30002	1	&New Workbook	1		1
3	VBE	Standard		1	&New Workbook	3		1
4	VBE	Menu Bar	30002	1	&Open Workbook	2		1
5	VBE	Standard		1	&Open Workbook	4		1
6	VBE	Menu Bar	30002	1	Close &Workbook	3		1
7	VBE	Project Window		1	Close &Workbook			1
8	VBE	Menu Bar	30002	1	Workbook Proper&ties	4		1
9	VBE	Project Window		1	Workbook Proper&ties			1

	I	J	K	L	M	N	O
1	Procedure	FaceID	ToolTip	Popup1	Popup2	Popup3	etc_
2	FileNewBook	18	Create a new workbook				
3	FileNewBook	18	Create a new workbook				
4	FileOpenBook	23	Open a workbook				
5	FileOpenBook	23	Open a workbook				
6	FileCloseBook		Close the workbook containing the active project				
7	FileCloseBook		Close the workbook containing the active project				
8	FileBookProps		Workbook Properties				
9	FileBookProps		Workbook Properties				

Note that the Close menu does not have a standard image, so the FaceID column has been left empty and by not specifying a position, it is added to the bottom of the Project Explorer popup menu.

To accurately simulate Excel's functionality, a test should be made to see if the *Shift* key is held down when the menu button is clicked, and turn off any events if this is the case. Unfortunately, if the user holds down the *Shift* key when a workbook is opened in the VBE, the routine will stop dead (see MS KnowledgeBase article Q175223 for the gory details). The best that can be done is to use the *Ctrl* key for the same effect. Back in the modCommon module, add the following declaration at the top:

```
'Windows API call to see if the Shift, Ctrl and/or Alt keys are pressed
Private Declare Function GetAsyncKeyState Lib "user32" _
    (ByVal vKey As Long) As Integer
```

This is telling VBA about a function available in Windows — see Chapter 18 on Programming with the Windows API for more information about these calls. At the bottom of the modCommon module, add the following function:

```
''''''''''''''''''''''''''''''''''''
' Subroutine: fnGetShiftCtrlAlt
'
' Purpose:    Uses a Windows API call to detect if the shift, ctrl and/or
'             alt keys are pressed

Function fnGetShiftCtrlAlt() As Integer
    Dim iKeys As Integer

    Const VK_SHIFT As Long = &H10
    Const VK_CONTROL As Long = &H11
    Const VK_ALT As Long = &H12

    'Check to see if the Shift, Ctrl and Alt keys are pressed
    If GetAsyncKeyState(VK_SHIFT) <> 0 Then iKeys = iKeys + 1
    If GetAsyncKeyState(VK_CONTROL) <> 0 Then iKeys = iKeys + 2
    If GetAsyncKeyState(VK_ALT) <> 0 Then iKeys = iKeys + 4

    fnGetShiftCtrlAlt = iKeys
End Function
```

For the Open routine, Excel's GetOpenFilename method will be used to retrieve the name of a file, and then open it. If the user holds down the *Shift* key, the application events will be turned off, so that he or she can open the workbook without triggering any other code — either within the workbook being opened, or Excel's own Workbook_Open event. If the user is not holding down the *Shift* key, an attempt would be made to run any Auto_Open routines in the workbook.

Whenever a dialog is used that would normally be shown in the Excel window (including the built-in dialogs, any UserForms and even MsgBox and InputBox calls), Excel automatically switches to its own window to show the dialog. When developing applications for the VBE, however, we really want the dialog to appear within the VBE window, not Excel's. The easiest way to achieve this effect is to hide the Excel window before showing the dialog, then unhide it afterwards.

```
''''''''''''''''''''''''''''''''''''''''
' Subroutine: FileOpenBook
'
' Purpose:    Opens an existing workbook
'
Sub FileOpenBook()
    Dim vaFile As Variant, bCtrl As Boolean
    Dim Wbk As Workbook

    'Use our error handler to display a message if something goes wrong
    On Error GoTo ERR_HANDLER

    'Check if the Ctrl key is held down (1=Shift, 2=Ctrl, 4=Alt)
    bCtrl = (fnGetShiftCtrlAlt And 2) = 2

    'Hide Excel, so the Open dialog appears in the VBE
    Application.Visible = False

    'Get the filename to open (or False if cancelled)
    vaFile = Application.GetOpenFilename
```

```
    'Make Excel visible again
    Application.Visible = True

    'If the user didn't cancel, open the workbook, adding it to Excel's MRU
    If Not (vaFile = False) Then
        If bCtrl Then
            'If the user held the Ctrl key down, we should disable events and
            'not update links
            Application.EnableEvents = False

            Set Wbk = Workbooks.Open(Filename:=vaFile, updatelinks:=0, _
                    AddToMru:=True)

            'Enable events again
            Application.EnableEvents = True
        Else
            'Shift not held down, so open the book normally and run Auto_Open
            Set Wbk = Workbooks.Open(Filename:=vFile, AddToMru:=True)
            Wbk.RunAutoMacros xlAutoOpen
        End If
    End If

    'Refresh the VBE display
    With Application.VBE.MainWindow
        .Visible = False
        .Visible = True
    End With

    Exit Sub

ERR_HANDLER:

    'Display the error message (in the VBE Window) and end the routine.
    Application.Visible = False

    MsgBox "An Error has occurred." & vbCrLf & _
            Err.Number & ": " & Err.Description, vbOKOnly, psAddinTitle

    Application.Visible = True
End Sub
```

The `Close` routine presents us with a new challenge. We are adding a **Close Workbook** menu item to the popup menu for the Project Explorer and hence need to determine which `VBProject` was clicked. The `ActiveVBProject` property of the VBE provides this, but a way is needed to get from the `VBProject` object to the workbook containing it. The method for doing this was described in the 'Identifying VBE Objects' section at the start of this chapter and the code is shown below. Add it to the `modCommon` module, along with the `Auto_Open` and `Auto_Close` routines, as you will be needing it again:

```
Function fnActiveProjectBook() As Workbook
    Dim obVBP As VBIDE.VBProject, obVBC As VBIDE.VBComponent
    Dim stName As String

    'If any errors occur (e.g. the project is locked), assume we can't find
    'the workbook
    On Error GoTo ERR_CANT_FIND_WORKBOOK

    'Get the VBProject that is active in the VBE
    Set obVBP = Application.VBE.ActiveVBProject

    If obVBP.Protection = vbext_pp_locked Then
        'If the project is locked, it must have been saved, so we can read its
        'file name.
```

Continued on Following Page

```
           'Note that this is new to Excel 2000
           stName = obVBP.Filename

           'Strip off the path
           If InStrRev(stName, "\") <> 0 Then
               stName = Mid(stName, InStrRev(stName, "\") + 1)

               'If it's the name of a workbook, we found it!
               '(it could be the name of a VBE project)
               If fnIsWorkbook(stName) Then
                   Set fnActiveProjectBook = Workbooks(stName)
                   Exit Function
               End If
           End If
       Else
           'Loop through all the VB Components in the project.
           'The 'ThisWorbook' component exposes the name of the workbook, but the
           'component may not be called "ThisWorkbook"!

           For Each obVBC In obVBP.VBComponents
               'Only need to check Document types (i.e. Excel objects)
               If obVBC.Type = vbext_ct_Document Then

                   'Get the underlying name of the component
                   stName = obVBC.Properties("Name")

                   'Is it the name of an open workbook
                   If fnIsWorkbook(stName) Then

                       'Yes it is, but is it the correct one?
                       If Workbooks(stName).VBProject Is obVBP Then

                           'We found it!
                           Set fnActiveProjectBook = Workbooks(stName)
                           Exit Function
                       End If
                   End If
               End If
           Next
       End If

PTR_CANT_FIND:

   'We didn't find the workbook, so display an error message in the VBE
   Application.Visible = False
   MsgBox "Unable to identify the workbook for this project.", _
       vbOKOnly, psAddinTitle
   Application.Visible = True

   Set fnActiveProjectBook = Nothing
   Exit Function

ERR_CANT_FIND_WORKBOOK:

   'We had an error, so we can't find the workbook.
   'Continue with the clean-up code.
   Resume PTR_CANT_FIND
End Function
```

Note that the Excel window is being hidden before displaying our error message before being "unhidden" afterwards. The following routine is needed to check if the result is the name of a workbook:

```
Function fnIsWorkbook(stBook As String) As Boolean
   Dim stName As String

   'Use inline error handling to check for a workbook
   On Error Resume Next
```

```
      Err.Clear
      stName = Workbooks(stBook).Name
      fnIsWorkbook = (Err.Number = 0)
End Function
```

Now that you can get the workbook that corresponds to the active VB Project, you can use it in our Close routine, which should be added to the modMenuFile module:

```
'''''''''''''''''''''''''''''''''''''''''
' Subroutine: FileCloseBook
'
' Purpose:    Closes the workbook containing the active VB Project
'

Sub FileCloseBook()
    Dim Wbk As Workbook, bCtrl As Boolean

    'Use our error handler to display a message if something goes wrong
    On Error GoTo ERR_HANDLER

    'Try to get the workbook containing the active VB Project
    Set Wbk = fnActiveProjectBook

    'If we didn't find it, just quit
    If Wbk Is Nothing Then Exit Sub

    'Check if the Ctrl key is held down (1=Shift, 2=Ctrl, 4=Alt)
    bCtrl = (fnGetShiftCtrlAlt And 2) = 2

    If bCtrl Then
        'Ctrl key is held down, so disable events and don't run Auto_Close
        'Disable events, so we we don't run anything in the workbook if it
        'is closed
        Application.EnableEvents = False

        'Close the workbook - Excel will ask to save changes etc.
        Wbk.Close

        'Enable events again
        Application.EnableEvents = True
    Else
        'Normal close so run any Auto_Close macros and close the workbook
        Wbk.RunAutoMacros xlAutoClose
        Wbk.Close
    End If

    Exit Sub

ERR_HANDLER:

    'Display the error message (in the VBE Window) and end the routine.
    Application.Visible = False

    MsgBox "An Error has occurred." & vbCrLf & _
            Err.Number & ": " & Err.Description, vbOKOnly, psAddinTitle

    Application.Visible = True
End Sub
```

The last workbook-related tool to be defined displays the File Properties dialog for the active VB Project's workbook. One of the main uses for the workbook properties is to provide the information shown in the Tools | Add-Ins dialog. The list box shows the Addin's title from its Properties dialog, while the description shown when an Addin is selected, is obtained from its Comments box.

Excel's built-in Properties dialog can be used for this, but we cannot tell it which workbook to show the properties for — the active workbook is used. Therefore any Addins need to be temporarily converted to normal workbooks and "unhidden" if they are hidden. After showing the Properties dialog, the workbooks must be converted back to Addins:

```
'''''''''''''''''''''''''''''''''''''
' Subroutine: FileBookProps
'
' Purpose:    Displays the workbook properties dialog for the active
'             VB Project
'

Sub FileBookProps()
    Dim Wbk As Workbook, bAddin As Boolean, bVis As Boolean

    'Just ignore any errors
    On Error Resume Next

    'Try to get the workbook containing the active VB Project
    Set Wbk = fnActiveProjectBook

    'If we didn't find it, just quit
    If Wbk Is Nothing Then Exit Sub

    'Hide the Excel window, so the dialog seems to appear within the
    'VBE environment
    Application.Visible = False

    'Using the workbook...
    With Wbk
        'If it is an Addin, convert it to a normal workbook temporarily
        bAddin = .IsAddin
        .IsAddin = False

        'Make sure its window is visible
        bVis = .Windows(1).Visible
        .Windows(1).Visible = True

        'Display the Workbook Properties dialog
        Application.Dialogs(xlDialogProperties).Show

        'Restore the workbook's visibility and Addin Status
        .Windows(1).Visible = bVis
        .IsAddin = bAddin
    End With

    'Make Excel visible again
    Application.Visible = True
End Sub
```

To test the Addin so far, just run the Auto_Open routine using Tools | Macros to recreate our menu items, then check that each item works as intended!

Working with Code

So far in this chapter, you have been working at a fairly high level in the VBIDE and Excel object models (i.e. limiting ourselves to the VBProject and Workbook objects), to add typical file operations to the Visual Basic environment. You now have the ability to create new workbooks (and hence their VB Projects), open existing workbooks, change a workbook's properties, save and close workbooks from within the VBE.

In this section, we will plunge to the lowest level of the VBE object model and learn how to work with the user's code. We will limit ourselves to detecting the line of code the user is editing (and even identifying the selected characters within that line), and getting information about the procedure, module and project containing that line of code. We will leave adding and changing code until the next section, where we'll be creating a UserForm, adding some buttons to it and adding code to handle the buttons' events.

To demonstrate how to identify the code that the user is working on, right-click access will be added to a print routine, with individual buttons to print the current selection, current procedure, module or project. First some additional lines will be added to our menu table:

	A	B	C	D	E	F	G	H
1	App l VBE	CommandBar	Sub Control ID	Type	Caption	Position	Begin Group	Builtin ID
2	VBE	Menu Bar	30002	1	&New Workbook	1		1
3	VBE	Standard		1	&New Workbook	3		1
4	VBE	Menu Bar	30002	1	&Open Workbook	2		1
5	VBE	Standard		1	&Open Workbook	4		1
6	VBE	Menu Bar	30002	1	Close &Workbook	3		1
7	VBE	Project Window		1	Close &Workbook			1
8	VBE	Menu Bar	30002	1	Workbook Proper&ties	4		1
9	VBE	Project Window		1	Workbook Proper&ties			1
10	VBE	Code Window		10	P&rint	4		
11	VBE	Code Window		1	&Selected Text	1		1
12	VBE	Code Window		1	&Procedure	2		1
13	VBE	Code Window		1	&Module	3		1
14	VBE	Code Window		1	Pro&ject	4		1

	I	J	K	L	M	N	O
1	Procedure	FaceID	ToolTip	Popup1	Popup2	Popup3	etc...
2	FileNewBook	18	Create a new workbook				
3	FileNewBook	18	Create a new workbook				
4	FileOpenBook	23	Open a workbook				
5	FileOpenBook	23	Open a workbook				
6	FileCloseBook		Close the workbook containing the active project				
7	FileCloseBook		Close the workbook containing the active project				
8	FileBookProps		Workbook Properties				
9	FileBookProps		Workbook Properties				
10							
11	CodePrintSel	3518	Print selected text	P&rint			
12	CodePrintProc	2564	Print current procedure	P&rint			
13	CodePrintMod	472	Print current module	P&rint			
14	CodePrintProj	2557	Print all modules in the project	P&rint			

By now, you should be realising exactly why a table-driven menu creator is being used — it is much easier to add a few lines to a spreadsheet table than to add code to `CreateMenus` and `RemoveMenus` routines.

The first thing to note is that we're adding our own cascading menu to the Code Window popup menu (type 10 is a custom popup menu), then adding four menu items to the cascading menu, each of which has its own face ID. The result is:

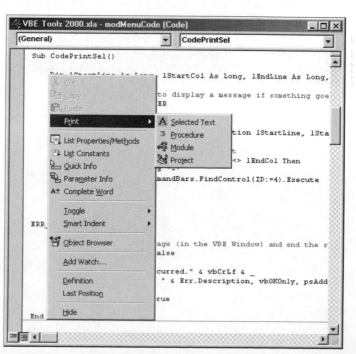

The code for the four printing routines will be placed into their own module, so add a new module to the project called modMenuCode.

Unfortunately, the VBIDE object model does not include a Print method for any of its objects. To provide right-click printing, there are three options:

❑   Show the VBE's Print dialog and operate it using SendKeys

❑   Copy the code to a worksheet range and print it from there

❑   Copy the code to a private instance of Word, reformat to show the Excel reserved words etc. in their correct colours and then print it from Word.

For the sake of simplicity, option 1 will be implemented. The main problem that this presents is how to select the **Selected Text**, **Module** or **Project** option buttons on the Print dialog, using SendKeys, especially as the **Selected Text** option is only enabled when some text is actually selected.

The answer is to identify if any text is selected, then send the appropriate number of *DownArrow* keys to the dialog to select either the <u>Module</u> or <u>Project</u> options. If we could rely on our users only ever having an English user-interface language, we could send *Alt+M* or *Alt+J* keystrokes — sending *DownArrow*s works with any choice of user interface language.

The code for the **Selected Text** menu item is the simplest and is presented below. All that is required is to do is identify if the user has actually selected anything and if so, to send some keystrokes to the Print dialog to print it:

```
Option Explicit

'''''''''''''''''''''''''''''''''''''
' Subroutine: CodePrintSel
'
' Purpose:    Print the current selection
'
Sub CodePrintSel()
    Dim lStartLine As Long, lStartCol As Long, lEndLine As Long, _
        lEndCol As Long

    'Get the current selected text
    Application.VBE.ActiveCodePane.GetSelection lStartLine, lStartCol, _
        lEndLine, lEndCol

    'If there's something selected, print it
    If lStartLine <> lEndLine Or lStartCol <> lEndCol Then
        Application.SendKeys "{ENTER}"
        Application.VBE.CommandBars.FindControl(ID:=4).Execute
    End If
End Sub
```

The main items to note are:

The ActiveCodePane property of the VBE is being used to identify which module the user is editing.

The variables sent to the GetSelection method are sent ByRef and actually get filled by the method. After the call to GetSelection, they contain the start and ending line numbers and start and ending columns of the currently selected text. It should be noted that while *none* of the methods in the Excel object model change the value of the variables passed to it, this technique is quite common in the VBIDE object model and is getting more common in Windows applications generally.

A simple *Enter* keystroke is sent to the keyboard buffer. Then the VBE Print dialog is immediately shown by running the File | Print menu item (ID = 4) directly. This technique of running menu items directly was introduced in the previous chapter on International Issues, in connection with the RunMenu routine presented there. By default (if some text is selected), when the VBE Print dialog is shown, the **Selected Text** option is selected, so this does not need to be changed.

To print the current module and project, very similar code can be used. The only difference is to check if any text is selected (i.e. if the **Selected Text** option in the **Print** dialog is enabled), then send a number of {DOWN} keystrokes to the dialog to select the correct option. Both of these routines can be added to the modMenuCode module:

```
'''''''''''''''''''''''''''''''''''''''''''
' Subroutine: CodePrintMod
'
' Purpose:    Print the current module
'

Sub CodePrintMod()
    Dim lStartLine As Long, lStartCol As Long, lEndLine As Long, _
        lEndCol As Long

    'Get the current selection
    Application.VBE.ActiveCodePane.GetSelection lStartLine, lStartCol, _
        lEndLine, lEndCol

    If lStartLine <> lEndLine Or lStartCol <> lEndCol Then
        'If there's something selected, make sure the 'Module' item is selected
        Application.SendKeys "{DOWN}{ENTER}"
    Else
        'If there's nothing selected, the 'Module' item is selected by default
        Application.SendKeys "{ENTER}"
    End If

    Application.VBE.CommandBars.FindControl(ID:=4).Execute
End Sub

'''''''''''''''''''''''''''''''''''''''''''
' Subroutine: CodePrintProj
'
' Purpose:    Print the current project
'
Sub CodePrintProj()
    Dim lStartLine As Long, lStartCol As Long, lEndLine As Long, _
        lEndCol As Long
```

Continued on Following Page

```
'Get the current selection
Application.VBE.ActiveCodePane.GetSelection lStartLine, lStartCol, _
    lEndLine, lEndCol

'Make sure the 'Project' item is selected
If lStartLine <> lEndLine Or lStartCol <> lEndCol Then
    Application.SendKeys "{DOWN}{DOWN}{ENTER}"
Else
    Application.SendKeys "{DOWN}{ENTER}"
End If

Application.VBE.CommandBars.FindControl(ID:=4).Execute
End Sub
```

The code to print the current procedure is slightly more complex, as the Print dialog does not have a Current Procedure option. The steps we need to perform are:

Identify and store away the user's current selection

Identify the procedure (or declaration lines) containing the user's selection

Expand the selection to encompass the full procedure (or all the declaration lines)

Show the Print dialog to print this expanded selection

Restore the user's original selections

Doing this on some PCs raises an interesting issue — the final step of restoring the user's original selection sometimes gets run before the Print dialog has been shown! This is presumably because the printing is done on a separate thread of execution and Excel 2000 is having a timing problem. The easy fix is to include a DoEvents statement immediately after showing the Print dialog, to let the print routine carry out its task.

```
''''''''''''''''''''''''''''''''''''''''''
' Subroutine: CodePrintProc
'
' Purpose:    Print the current procedure

Sub CodePrintProc()
    Dim lStartLine As Long, lStartCol As Long, lEndLine As Long, _
        lEndCol As Long
    Dim lProcType As Long, stProcName As String, lProcStart As Long, _
        lProcEnd As Long

    With Application.VBE.ActiveCodePane
        'Get the current selection, so we know what to print and can
        'restore it later
        .GetSelection lStartLine, lStartCol, lEndLine, lEndCol

        With .CodeModule
            If lStartLine <= .CountOfDeclarationLines Then
                'We're in the declarations section
                lProcStart = 1
                lProcEnd = .CountOfDeclarationLines
```

```
        Else
            'We're in a procedure, so find its start and end
            stProcName = .ProcOfLine(lStartLine, lProcType)
            lProcStart = .ProcStartLine(stProcName, lProcType)
            lProcEnd = lProcStart + .ProcCountLines(stProcName, lProcType)
        End If
    End With

    'Select the text to print
    .SetSelection lProcStart, 1, lProcEnd, 0

    'Print it
    Application.SendKeys "{ENTER}"
    Application.VBE.CommandBars.FindControl(ID:=4).Execute

    'The VBE Printing code is on another thread, so we need to
    'let it do its stuff before setting the selection back.
    DoEvents

    'And select the original text again
    .SetSelection lStartLine, lStartCol, lEndLine, lEndCol
    End With
End Sub
```

The main item to note in this code is that the ProcOfLine method accepts the start line as an input, fills the lProcType variable with a number to identify the procedure type (i.e. Sub, Function, Property Let, Property Get etc) and returns the name of the procedure. The procedure type and name are used to find the start of the procedure (using ProcStartLine) and the number of lines within the procedure (ProcCountLines), which are then selected and printed.

Working with UserForms

The code examples presented in this chapter so far have been extending the VBE, to provide additional tools for the developer. In this section, we move our attention to programmatically creating and manipulating UserForms, adding controls and adding procedures to the UserForm's code module, to handle the controls' events. While the example provided in this section continues to extend the VBE, the same code and techniques can be applied in end-user applications, including:

Adding UserForms to workbooks created by the application

Sizing the UserForm and moving and sizing its controls to make the best use of the available screen space

Adding code to handle events in UserForms created by the application

Changing the controls shown on an existing UserForm in response to user input

Creating UserForms on-the-fly, as they are needed (for example, when the number and type of controls on the UserForm will vary significantly depending on the data to be shown)

The techniques will be demonstrated by writing code to add a UserForm to the active project, complete with standard-sized OK and Cancel buttons and code to handle the buttons' Click events and the UserForm's QueryClose event. The UserForm's size will be set to 2/3 of the width and height of the Excel window and the OK and Cancel buttons' position will be adjusted accordingly.

The example shown here is the difficult way to achieve the desired result and is intended to be an educational, rather than a practical, example. The easy way to add a standardised UserForm is to create it manually and export it to disk as a .frm file. When you need to include it in another project, just import it again. The only advantage with doing it through code is that the UserForm can be given a size appropriate to the user's screen resolution and size and position its controls correctly.

Start by adding another row to the menu table, which should now look like:

	A	B	C	D	E	F	G	H
1	App / VBE	CommandBar	Sub Control ID	Type	Caption	Position	Begin Group	BuiltIn ID
2	VBE	Menu Bar	30002	1	&New Workbook	1		1
3	VBE	Standard		1	&New Workbook	3		1
4	VBE	Menu Bar	30002	1	&Open Workbook	2		1
5	VBE	Standard		1	&Open Workbook	4		1
6	VBE	Menu Bar	30002	1	Close &Workbook	3		1
7	VBE	Project Window		1	Close &Workbook			1
8	VBE	Menu Bar	30002	1	Workbook Prope&rties	4		1
9	VBE	Project Window		1	Workbook Prope&rties			1
10	VBE	Code Window		10	P&rint	4		
11	VBE	Code Window		1	&Selected Text	1		1
12	VBE	Code Window		1	&Procedure	2		1
13	VBE	Code Window		1	&Module	3		1
14	VBE	Code Window		1	Pro&ject	4		1
15	VBE	Standard	32806	1	&Standard Form	2		1
16								

	I	J	K		L	M	N	O
1	Procedure	FaceID	ToolTip		Popup1	Popup2	Popup3	etc...
2	FileNewBook	18	Create a new workbook					
3	FileNewBook	18	Create a new workbook					
4	FileOpenBook	23	Open a workbook					
5	FileOpenBook	23	Open a workbook					
6	FileCloseBook		Close the workbook containing the active project					
7	FileCloseBook		Close the workbook containing the active project					
8	FileBookProps		Workbook Properties					
9	FileBookProps		Workbook Properties					
10								
11	CodePrintSel	3518	Print selected text		P&rint			
12	CodePrintProc	2564	Print current procedure		P&rint			
13	CodePrintMod	472	Print current module		P&rint			
14	CodePrintProj	2557	Print all modules in the project		P&rint			
15	FormNewUserform	581	Insert standardised UserForm					
16								

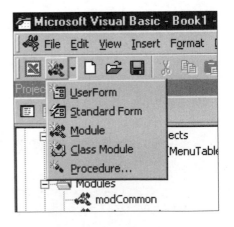

The result of this addition will be the Standard Form item:

Add a new module for this routine, called `modMenuForm` and copy in the code below:

```
Option Explicit
Option Compare Text

'Window API call to freeze a window
'It does the same as Application.ScreenUpdating, but for the VBE
Private Declare Function LockWindowUpdate Lib "user32" _
    (ByVal hwndLock As Long) As Long
```

`Application.ScreenUpdating` does not affect the VBE and this routine results in quite a lot of screen activity. A simple Windows API call can be used to freeze the VBE window at the start of the routine and unfreeze it at the end. See the next chapter on Programming with the Windows API for more information about using this and other API functions.

```
''''''''''''''''''''''''''''''''''''''''''
' Subroutine: FormNewUserform
'
' Purpose:    Creates a new userform, adding standard OK and Cancel buttons
'             and code to handle their events
'
Sub FormNewUserform()
    Dim obVBC As VBIDE.VBComponent, fmFrmDesign As UserForm, lLine As Long
    Dim cbBtn As CommandBarButton, cbPopup As CommandBarPopup
```

Microsoft's Windows design guidelines recommend a gap of 6 points (approximately 4 pixels) between buttons and between a button and the edge of a form.

```
    Const dGap As Double = 6
```

This is one of the more complex routines in the Addin, so some error handling code will be added to it. Every routine in this chapter should really be given similar error-handling code.

```
    'Use our error handler to display a message if something goes wrong
    On Error GoTo ERR_HANDLER
```

Use the Windows API call to freeze the VBE's window. Note that `HWnd` is a hidden property of the `MainWindow` object. To display the hidden properties for an object, open the Object Browser, right-click in its window and click the **Show Hidden Members** item.

```
    'Freeze the VBE window - same as Application.ScreenUpdating = False
    LockWindowUpdate Application.VBE.MainWindow.HWnd
```

The `VBComponent` object (`obVBC` in the code) provides the 'canvas' (i.e. background) of the UserForm, its `Properties` collection and its `CodeModule`. When a new UserForm is added to a project, a `VBComponent` object is passed back that contains the form. The `VBComponent`'s `Properties` collection can be used to change the size (as shown here), colour, font, caption etc. of the form's background.

```
    'Add a new userform to the active VB Project
    Set obVBC = Application.VBE.ActiveVBProject.VBComponents _
                .Add(vbext_ct_MSForm)

    'Set the form's height and width to 2/3 that of the Excel application.
    obVBC.Properties("Width") = Application.UsableWidth * 2 / 3
    obVBC.Properties("Height") = Application.UsableHeight * 2 / 3
```

The VBComponent's Designer object provides access to the *content* of the UserForm and is responsible for the area inside the form's borders and below its title bar. In this code, two controls are added to the normal blank UserForm, to provide standard OK and Close buttons. The name to use for the control (Forms.CommandButton.1 in this case) can be found by adding the control from Excel's Control Toolbox to a worksheet, then examining the resulting =EMBED() function:

```
'Get the UserForm's Designer
Set fmFrmDesign = obVBC.Designer

'Use the designer to add the standard controls
With fmFrmDesign
    'Add an OK button, according to standard Windows size
    With .Controls.Add("Forms.CommandButton.1", "bnOK")
        .Caption = "OK"
        .Default = True
        .Height = 18
        .Width = 54
    End With

    'Add a Cancel button, according to standard Windows size
    With .Controls.Add("Forms.CommandButton.1", "bnCancel")
        .Caption = "Cancel"
        .Cancel = True
        .Height = 18
        .Width = 54
    End With
```

This could be extended to add list boxes, labels, check boxes etc. From this point on, you could just as easily be working with an existing UserForm, changing its size and the position and size of its controls to make the best use of the available screen resolution. The code below just moves the OK and Cancel buttons to the bottom-right corner of the UserForm, without adjusting their size. The same technique can be used to move and size all of a UserForm's controls.

```
'Move the OK and Cancel buttons to the bottom-right of the UserForm,
'with a standard-width gap around and between them
With .Controls("bnOK")
    .Top = fmFrmDesign.InsideHeight - .Height - dGap
    .Left = fmFrmDesign.InsideWidth - .Width * 2 - dGap * 2
End With

With .Controls("bnCancel")
    .Top = fmFrmDesign.InsideHeight - .Height - dGap
    .Left = fmFrmDesign.InsideWidth - .Width - dGap
End With
End With
```

Now that buttons have been added to the UserForm at the correct place (i.e. bottom-right hand corner), some code can be added to the UserForm's module to handle the buttons' and UserForm's events. In this example, the code is being added from strings.

Alternatively, the code could be kept in a separate text file and imported into the UserForm's module.

We'll first add simple code for the **OK** and **Cancel** buttons' `Click` events. Code like this could be used to create the routine:

```
.AddFromString "Sub bnOK_Click()"
```

However, if `CreateEventProc` is used, all of the procedure's parameters are filled in on our behalf. There is very little difference between the two techniques:

```
' Now add some code to the userform's code module
With obVBC.CodeModule
    'Add the code for the OK button's Click event
    lLine = .CreateEventProc("Click", "bnOK")
    .InsertLines lLine, "'Standard OK button handler"
    .ReplaceLine lLine + 2, "    mbOK = True" & vbCrLf & "    Me.Hide"

    'Add the code for the Cancel button's Click event
    .AddFromString vbCrLf & _
            "'Standard Cancel button handler" & vbCrLf & _
            "Private Sub bnCancel_Click()" & vbCrLf & _
            "    mbOK = False" & vbCrLf & _
            "    Me.Hide" & vbCrLf & _
            "End Sub"
```

Note that the `CreateEventProc` adds the 'Private Sub...' line, the 'End Sub' line and a space between them. **DO NOT** type this into the Addin:

```
Private Sub bnOK_Click()

End Sub
```

It returns the number of the line in the module where the 'Private Sub...' was added, which is then used to insert a comment line and to replace the default blank line with the code. The code for the UserForm's `QueryClose` event is the same as that of the **Cancel** button, so some code will be added just to call the `bnCancel_Click` routine:

```
    'Add the code for the UserForm's Close event - just call
    'the Cancel code
    lLine = .CreateEventProc("QueryClose", "UserForm")
    .InsertLines lLine, "    'Standard Close handler, treat same as Cancel"
    .ReplaceLine lLine + 2, "bnCancel_Click"

    'And close the code window that was automatically opened by Excel
    'when we created the event procedures
    .CodePane.Window.Close
End With

'Unfreeze the VBE window - same as Application.ScreenUpdating = True
LockWindowUpdate 0&

Exit Sub
```

The standard error handler unfreezes the window, displays the error message and closes. Such error handling should be added to all the routines in the Addin.

```
ERR_HANDLER:

    'Unfreeze the VBE window - same as Application.ScreenUpdating = True
    LockWindowUpdate 0&

    'Display the error message (in the VBE Window) and end the routine.
    Application.Visible = False

    MsgBox "An Error ocurred while creating the standard userform." & _
        vbCrLf & Err.Number & ": " & Err.Description, vbOKOnly, psAddinTitle

    Application.Visible = True
End Sub
```

The Addin is now complete. Switch back to Excel and save the workbook as an Addin (at the bottom of the list of available file types), with an .xla extension. Then use Tools | Add-Ins to install it.

Working with References

One of the major enhancements in recent versions of VBA is the ability to declare a reference to an external object library (using the Tools | References dialog), then use the objects defined in that library as if they were built in to Excel. In this chapter, for example, you have been using the objects defined in the VBA Extensibility library without thinking about where they came from.

The term for this is 'early binding', so named because we are binding the external object library to our application at design-time. Using early binding gives the following benefits:

❑ The code is much faster, as all the links between the libraries have been checked and compiled

❑ The New operator can be used to create instances of the external objects

❑ All of the constants defined in the object library can be utilized, thus avoiding numerous 'magic numbers' throughout the code

❑ Excel displays the Auto List Members, Auto Quick Info and Auto Data Tips information for the objects while the application is being developed

This has been explained in more detail in Chapter 15 on Interacting with Other Office Applications.

There is, however, one major disadvantage. If you try to run your application on a computer that does not have the external object library installed, you will get a compile-time error which cannot be trapped using standard error-handling techniques — usually showing a perfectly valid line of code as being the culprit. Excel will display the error when it runs some code in a module, which contains:

❑ An undeclared variable in a procedure — and you didn't use Option Explicit

❑ A declaration of a type defined in the missing object library

❑ A constant defined in the missing object library

❑ A call to a routine, object, method or property defined in the missing object library

The VBIDE `References` collection provides a method of checking that all the application's references are functioning correctly, and that all the required external object libraries are installed and are the correct version. The code to check this should be put in your `Auto_Open` routine and the module that contains the `Auto_Open` must not contain any code that uses the external object libraries. Typical `Auto_Open` code is:

```
Sub Auto_Open()
    Dim obRef As Object, bBroken As Boolean, stDescn As String

    For Each obRef In ThisWorkbook.VBProject.References
        'Is the link broken?
        If obRef.IsBroken Then
            'Some broken links don't have descriptions, so ignore the error
            On Error Resume Next
            stDescn = "<Not known>"
            stDescn = obRef.Description
            On Error GoTo 0

            'Display a message, asking the user to install the missing item
            MsgBox "Missing reference to:" & vbCrLf & _
                "    Name: " & stDescn & vbCrLf & _
                "    Path: " & obRef.FullPath & vbCrLf & _
                "Please reinstall this file."

            bBroken = True
        End If
    Next

    'If everything present and correct, carry on with the initialising code
    If Not bBroken Then
        '...Continue to open
    End If
End Sub
```

COM Addins

The Addin in this chapter was created as an Excel workbook, which means that we can only use it when we are developing in Excel. The VBIDE is a common component to all of the Office 2000 applications (including Access, Outlook and FrontPage) and it would be nice if we could have access to all of our utilities, regardless of which Office application we're developing in. Obviously, we cannot open an Excel workbook while developing in Word.

Office 2000 introduces a new Addin technology called COM Addins. These are DLLs created in any language that can produce Component Object Model DLLs (such as Visual Basic's ActiveX DLLs). A full description of COM Addins is beyond the scope of this book, but this section should be enough of an introduction to get you started.

By using COM Addins, it is possible to develop a single program that can be loaded by, and work in, all of the Office applications, including the VBIDE.

The Office 2000 Developer Edition (ODE) includes tools to assist in the creation of COM Addins, by enabling the Office developer to create and compile ActiveX DLLs from within the VBIDE. In effect, Microsoft is including a version of Visual Basic 6 within the ODE.

If you have a copy of the ODE, converting the VBE Tools 2000 worksheet Addin into a COM Addin is easy:

Within the Excel VBE, create a new project of type "Addin Project".

Fill out the Add In designer to show:

Display the code module for the Designer and copy in the following code:

```
'The COM Addin equivalent of Auto_Open
Private Sub AddinInstance_OnConnection(ByVal Application As Object, _
          ByVal ConnectMode As AddInDesignerObjects.ext_ConnectMode, _
          ByVal AddInInst As Object, custom() As Variant)

   'We're given the VBE instance that started us, so remember it
   Set obVBE = Application

   'Set up our menus
   SetUpMenus
End Sub

'The COM Addin equivalent of Auto_Close
Private Sub AddinInstance_OnDisconnection(ByVal RemoveMode As _
          AddInDesignerObjects.ext_DisconnectMode, custom() As Variant)

   'Remove our menus
   RemoveMenus
End Sub
```

Copy all the modules from the workbook project to this project

Add the declaration of the obVBE object to the modCommon module:

```
Public obVBE As Object
```

Change all occurrences of Application.VBE to use the public obVBE instead

Change the menu creation code, to store the menu information within the project, instead of the worksheet, typically using an array of comma-separated strings:

```
Dim stMenuTable(1 To 14) As String
   Sub SetUpMenus()

   stMenuTable(1) = "VBE,Menu Bar,30002,1,&New Workbook,1,,1," & _
                    "FileNewBook,18,Create a new workbook,,,,"

   stMenuTable(2) = "VBE,Standard,,1,&New Workbook,3,,1," & _
                    "FileNewBook,18,Create a new workbook,,,,"
   'etc.
   For iRow = LBound(stMenuTable) To UBound(stMenuTable)
      vaData = Split(stMenuTable(iRow), ",")

      'etc.
End Sub
```

Compile and use it!

Summary

The *Microsoft Visual Basic for Applications Extensibility 5.3* object library provides a rich set of objects, properties, methods and events for controlling the Visual Basic Editor itself.

Using these objects, developers can create their own labour-saving Addins to help in their daily development tasks.

Many end-user applications can also utilize these objects to manipulate their own code modules, UserForms and references, to provide a feature-rich, flexible and robust set of functionality.

The example Addin developed in this chapter can be downloaded from www.BMSLtd.co.uk.

Programming with the Windows API

Introduction to The Windows API

Visual Basic for Applications is a high-level language that provides us with a rich, powerful, yet quite simple set of functionality for controlling the Office suite of products, as well as many other applications. We are insulated, some would say protected, from the "mundane minutiae" of Windows programming that, say, a C++ programmer has to contend with.

The price we pay for this protection is an inability to investigate and control many elements of the Windows platform. We can, for example, use `Application.International` to read most of the Windows Regional Settings and read the screen dimensions from `Application.UsableWidth` and `.UsableHeight`, but that's about it. All the Windows-related items are properties of the `Application` object and are listed in the Reference section of the book.

The Windows platform includes a vast amount of functionality that is not normally accessible from VBA, from identifying the system colours to creating a temporary file. Some of the functionality has been exposed in VBA but only to a limited extent, such as creating and using an Internet connection (e.g. we can open a page from the Internet using `Workbooks.Open "<URL>"`, but we can't just download it to disk).

There are times when we need to go beyond the limits of VBA and delve into the files that contain the low-level procedures provided, and used, by Windows. The Windows Operating System is made up of a large number of separate files, mostly dynamic link libraries (DLLs), each containing code to perform a discrete set of inter-related functions. Dynamic link libraries are files that contain functions that can be called by other Windows programs or other DLLs. They can not be 'run' like a program themselves.

These files are collectively known as the Windows Application Programming Interface, or Windows API. Some of the most common files you'll use in the Windows API are:

File	Function Group(s)
USER32.EXE	User-interface functions (such as managing windows, the keyboard, clipboard etc)
KERNEL32.DLL	File and system-related functions (such as managing programs)
GDI32.DLL	Graphics and display functions
SHELL32.DLL	Windows shell functions (such as handling icons and launching programs)
COMDLG32.DLL	Standard Windows dialog functions.
ADVAPI32.DLL	Registry and NT Security functions
MPR.DLL and NETAPI32.DLL	Network functions
WININET.DLL	Internet functions
WINMM.DLL	Multimedia functions
WINSPOOL.DRV	Printing functions

This chapter explains how to use the functions contained in these files in your VBA applications and includes a number of useful examples. All of the Windows API functions are documented in the 'Platform SDK' section of the MSDN library at: http://msdn.microsoft.com/library/default.htm, which can be thought of as the on-line help for the Windows API.

Anatomy of an API Call

Before we can use the procedures contained in the Windows DLLs, we need to tell the VBA interpreter where they can be found, the parameters they take and what they return. We do this using the Declare statement, which VBA help shows as:

```
[Public | Private] Declare Sub name Lib "libname" [Alias "aliasname"]
[([arglist])]
```

```
[Public | Private] Declare Function name Lib "libname" [Alias "aliasname"]
[([arglist])] [As type]
```

The VBA Help gives a good explanation of the syntax of these statements, but does not include any examples. The following is the declaration used to find the Windows TEMP directory:

```
Private Declare Function GetTempPath Lib "kernel32" _
        Alias "GetTempPathA" ( _
        ByVal nBufferLength As Long, _
        ByVal lpBuffer As String) As Long
```

This tells VBA that:

> The function in the code is going to be referred to as `GetTempPath`
>
> The procedure can be found in `kernel32.dll`
>
> It goes by the name of `GetTempPathA` in the DLL (case sensitive)
>
> It takes two parameters, a `Long` and a `String` (more about these later)
>
> It returns a `Long`

The declarations for most of the more common API functions can be found in the file `win32api.txt`. The Developer version of Office 2000 (and Office 97) and any of the more recent versions of Visual Basic include this file and a small API Viewer applet to help locate the declarations. At the time of writing, the text file can be downloaded from the 'Free Stuff' page of the Office Developer section of Microsoft's web site, `http://www.microsoft.com/officedev/o-free.htm`, or directly from `http://www.microsoft.com/OfficeDev/Articles/Exe/Win32api.exe`

Interpreting C-Style Declarations

The MSDN library is the best source for information about the functions in the Windows API, but is primarily targeted towards C and C++ programmers and displays the function declarations using C notation. The `win32api.txt` file contains most of the declarations for the core Windows functions in VBA notation, but has not been updated to include some of the newer Windows DLLs (such as the OLE functions in `olepro32.dll` and the Internet functions in `WinInet.dll`). It is usually possible to convert the C notation to a VBA `Declare` statement, using the method shown below.

The declaration shown in MSDN for the `GetTempPath` function (at `http://msdn.microsoft.com/library/sdkdoc/winbase/filesio_78fc.htm`) is:

```
DWORD GetTempPath(
    DWORD nBufferLength,    // size, in characters, of the buffer
    LPTSTR lpBuffer         // pointer to buffer for temp. path
    );
```

This should be read as:

```
<Return data type> <Function name>(
    <Parameter data type> <Parameter name>,
    <Parameter data type> <Parameter name>,
    );
```

Rearranging the C-style declaration to a VBA `Declare` statement gives:

```
Declare Function <Our Name> Lib "???" Alias "GetTempPath" ( _
        nBufferLength As DWORD, _
        lpBuffer As LPTSTR _
        ) As DWORD
```

On the Windows platform, there are two types of character sets. The ANSI character set has been the standard for many years and uses one byte to represent one character, which only gives 255 characters available at any time. To provide simultaneous access to a much wider range of characters (e.g. Far Eastern alphabets), the Unicode character set was introduced. This allocates two bytes for each character, allowing for 65,535 characters. To provide the same functionality for both character sets, the Windows API includes two versions of all the functions that involve strings, denoted by the 'A' suffix for the ANSI version and 'W' for the Unicode (or Wide) version. VBA always uses ANSI strings, so we will always be using the 'A' version of the functions – in this case `GetTempPathA`. The C-style declarations also use different names for their data types, which we need to convert. While not an exhaustive list, the following table shows the most common data types:

C Data Type	VBA Declaration
BOOL	ByVal <Name> As Long
BYTE	ByVal <Name> As Byte
BYTE *	ByRef <Name> As Byte
Char	ByVal <Name> As Byte
char _huge *	ByVal <Name> As String
char FAR *	ByVal <Name> As String
char NEAR *	ByVal <Name> As String
DWORD	ByVal <Name> As Long
HANDLE	ByVal <Name> As Long
HBITMAP	ByVal <Name> As Long
HBRUSH	ByVal <Name> As Long
HCURSOR	ByVal <Name> As Long
HDC	ByVal <Name> As Long
HFONT	ByVal <Name> As Long
HICON	ByVal <Name> As Long
HINSTANCE	ByVal <Name> As Long
HLOCAL	ByVal <Name> As Long
HMENU	ByVal <Name> As Long
HMETAFILE	ByVal <Name> As Long
HMODULE	ByVal <Name> As Long
HPALETTE	ByVal <Name> As Long
HPEN	ByVal <Name> As Long
HRGN	ByVal <Name> As Long
HTASK	ByVal <Name> As Long
HWND	ByVal <Name> As Long
Int	ByVal <Name> As Long

C Data Type	VBA Declaration
int FAR *	ByRef <Name> As Long
LONG	ByVal <Name> As Long
LPARAM	ByVal <Name> As Long
LPCSTR	ByVal <Name> As String
LPCTSTR	ByVal <Name> As String
LPSTR	ByVal <Name> As String
LPTSTR	ByVal <Name> As String
LPVOID	ByRef <Name> As Any
LRESULT	ByVal <Name> As Long
UINT	ByVal <Name> As Integer
UINT FAR *	ByRef <Name> As Integer
WORD	ByVal <Name> As Integer
WPARAM	ByVal <Name> As Integer
Otherwise	It is a probably a user-defined type, which you need to define.

Some API definitions on the MSDN also include the IN and OUT identifiers. If the VBA type is shown in the table as 'ByVal <Name> As Long', it should be changed to 'ByRef . . .' for the OUT parameters.

Note that strings are *always* passed ByVal to API functions. This is because VBA uses its own storage mechanism for strings, which the C DLLs do not understand. By passing the string ByVal, VBA converts its own storage structure into one that the DLLs can use.

Putting these into the declaration, gives:

```
Declare Function GetTempPath Lib "???" _
       Alias "GetTempPathA" ( _
       ByVal nBufferLength As Long, _
       ByVal lpBuffer As String _
       ) As Long
```

The only thing that the declaration doesn't tell you is the DLL that contains the function. Looking at the bottom of the MSDN page, the 'QuickInfo' section includes the line:

```
Import Library: Use kernel32.lib.
```

Which tells you that the file is in kernel32.dll, giving the final declaration of:

```
Declare Function GetTempPath Lib "kernel32.dll" _
       Alias "GetTempPathA" ( _
       ByVal nBufferLength As Long, _
       ByVal lpBuffer As String _
       ) As Long
```

This is the same as that shown in the `win32api.txt` file, which should be your first reference point for all API function definitions.

> **Warning: Using an incorrect function declaration is likely to crash Excel. When developing with API calls, save your work as often as possible.**

Constants, Structures, Handles and Classes

Most of the API functions include arguments that accept a limited set of predefined constants. For example, to get information about the operating system's capabilities, you can use the `GetSystemMetrics` function:

```
Declare Function GetSystemMetrics Lib "user32" ( _
        ByVal nIndex As Long) As Long
```

The value that you pass in the `nIndex` argument tells the function which metric you want to be given and must be one of a specific set of constants that the function knows about. The applicable constants are listed in the MSDN documentation, but their values are often not shown. Fortunately, the `win32api.txt` file contains most of the constants that you are likely to need. There are over 80 constants for `GetSystemMetrics` including `SM_CXSCREEN` and `SM_CYSCREEN` to retrieve the screen's dimensions:

```
Const SM_CXSCREEN As Long = 0    'Screen width
Const SM_CYSCREEN As Long = 1    'Screen height

Private Declare Function GetSystemMetrics Lib "user32"_
            (ByVal nIndex As Long) As Long

Sub ShowScreenDimensions()
    Dim lScreenX As Long, lScreenY As Long

    'Get the screen's dimensions
    lScreenX = GetSystemMetrics(SM_CXSCREEN)
    lScreenY = GetSystemMetrics(SM_CYSCREEN)

    MsgBox "Screen resolution is " & lScreenX & "x" & lScreenY
End Sub
```

Many of the Windows API functions pass information using **structures**, which is the C term for a User-Defined Type. For example, the `GetWindowRect` function is used to return the size of a window, and is defined as:

```
Declare Function GetWindowRect Lib "user32" ( _
        ByVal hwnd As Long, _
        lpRect As RECT) As Long
```

The `lpRect` parameter is a `RECT` structure that is filled in by the `GetWindowRect` function with the window's dimensions. The `RECT` structure is defined on MSDN as:

```
typedef struct tagRECT {
    LONG left;
    LONG top;
    LONG right;
    LONG bottom;
} RECT;
```

This can be converted to a VBA User-Defined Type using the same data-type conversion shown in the previous section, giving:

```
Type RECT
    Left As Long
    Top As Long
    Right As Long
    Bottom As Long
End Type
```

The UDT definitions for most of the common structures are also included in the win32api.txt file.

The first parameter of the GetWindowRect function is shown as 'hwnd' (read as 'H-wind'), and represents a handle to a window. A handle is simply a pointer to an area of memory that contains information about the object being pointed to (in this case, a window). Handles are allocated dynamically by Windows and are unlikely to be the same between sessions. You cannot, therefore, hard-code the handle number in your code, but must use other API functions to give you the handle you need. For example, to obtain the dimensions of the Excel window, you need to get the Excel window's hwnd. The API function FindWindow gives it to you:

```
Public Declare Function FindWindow Lib "user32" _
       Alias "FindWindowA" (_
       ByVal lpClassName As String, _
       ByVal lpWindowName As String) As Long
```

This function looks through all the open windows until it finds one with the class name and caption that you ask for.

There are many different types of window in Windows applications, ranging from Excel's application window, to the windows used for dialog sheets, UserForms, list boxes or buttons. Each type of window has a unique identifier, known as its **class**. Some common class names in Excel are:

Window	Class name
Excel's main window	XLMAIN
Excel worksheet	EXCEL7
Excel UserForm	ThunderDFrame (in Excel 2000)
	ThunderXFrame (in Excel 97)
Excel dialog sheet	bosa_sdm_xl9 (in Excel 2000)
	bosa_sdm_xl8 (in Excel 97)
	bosa_sdm_xl (in Excel 5 and 95)
Excel status bar	EXCEL4

The FindWindow function uses this class name and the window's caption to find the window.

> Note that the class names for some of Excel's standard items have changed with every release of Excel. You therefore need to include version checking in your code to determine which class name to use:
>
> ```
> Select Case Val(Application.Version)
>
> Case Is >= 9      'Use Excel 2000 class names
>
> Case Is >= 8      'Use Excel 97 class names
>
> Case Else         'Use Excel 5/95 class names
>
> End Select
> ```
>
> This gives us a forward-compatibility problem. It would be nice if we could write code with a reasonable amount of confidence that it will work in the next version of Excel, but we don't know what the class names are going to be.

Putting these items together, you can use the following code to find the location and size of the Excel main window:

```
Type RECT
    Left As Long
    Top As Long
    Right As Long
    Bottom As Long
End Type

Declare Function FindWindow Lib "user32" _
       Alias "FindWindowA" ( _
       ByVal lpClassName As String, _
       ByVal lpWindowName As String) As Long

Declare Function GetWindowRect Lib "user32" ( _
       ByVal hWnd As Long, _
       lpRect As RECT) As Long

Sub ShowExcelWindowSize()
   Dim hWnd As Long, uRect As RECT

   'Get the handle on Excel's main window
   hWnd = FindWindow("XLMAIN", Application.Caption)

   'Get the window's dimensions into the RECT structure
   GetWindowRect hWnd, uRect

   'Display the result
   MsgBox "The Excel window has the following dimensions:" & _
          vbCrLf & " Left: " & uRect.Left & _
          vbCrLf & " Right: " & uRect.Right & _
          vbCrLf & " Top: " & uRect.Top & _
          vbCrLf & " Bottom: " & uRect.Bottom & _
          vbCrLf & " Width: " & (uRect.Right - uRect.Left) & _
          vbCrLf & " Height: " & (uRect.Bottom - uRect.Top)

End Sub
```

Size the Excel window to cover a portion of the screen and run the
`ShowExcelWindowSize` routine. You should be given a message box showing the
window's dimensions. Now try it with Excel maximized – you may get negative
values for the top and left. This is because the `GetWindowRect` function returns the
size of the Excel window, measuring around the edge of its borders. When maximised,
the borders are off the screen, but still part of the window.

What If Something Goes Wrong?

One of the hardest parts of working with the windows API functions is identifying the
cause of any errors. If an API call fails for any reason, it *should* return some indication
of failure (usually a zero result from the function) and register the error with
Windows. you should then be able to use the VBA function `Err.LastDLLError` to
retrieve the error code and use the `FormatMessage` API function to retrieve the
descriptive text for the error:

```
'Windows API declaration to get the API error text
Private Declare Function FormatMessage Lib "kernel32" _
        Alias "FormatMessageA" ( _
        ByVal dwFlags As Long, _
        lpSource As Any, _
        ByVal dwMessageId As Long, _
        ByVal dwLanguageId As Long, _
        ByVal lpBuffer As String, _
        ByVal nSize As Long, _
        Arguments As Long) As Long

'Constant for use in the FormatMessage API function
Private Const FORMAT_MESSAGE_FROM_SYSTEM As Long = &H1000

Sub ShowExcelWindowSize()
    'Define some variables to use in the API calls
    Dim hWnd As Long, uRect As RECT

    'Get the handle on Excel's main window
    hWnd = FindWindow("XLMAIN", Application.Caption)

    If hWnd = 0 Then
        'An error occured, so get the text of the error
        MsgBox LastDLLErrText(Err.LastDllError)
    Else
        'Etc.
    End If
End Sub

Function LastDLLErrText(ByVal lErrorCode As Long) As String
    Dim sBuff As String * 255, iAPIResult As Long

    'Get the text of the error and return it
    iAPIResult = FormatMessage(FORMAT_MESSAGE_FROM_SYSTEM, 0&, _
        lErrorCode, 0, sBuff, 255, 0)

    LastDLLErrText = Left(sBuff, iAPIResult)
End Function
```

Unfortunately, this technique does not always work. For example, if you change the
class name to `XLMAINTEST` in the `FindWindow` function call, you may expect to get an
error message of 'Unable to find window'. This is the case on Windows NT 4, but
when using `FindWindow` under Windows 98, the error information is not populated
and you get the standard message 'The operation completed successfully'. In most
cases, you do get some error information, as will be seen in the next section.

Wrapping API Calls in Class Modules

If you need to use lots of API calls in your application, your code can get very messy, very quickly. Most developers prefer to encapsulate the API calls within class modules, providing a number of benefits:

❑   The API declarations and calls are removed from your core application code.

❑   The class module can perform a number of initialisation and clean-up tasks, improving your system's robustness.

❑   Many of the API functions take a large number of parameters, most of which are not used in your situation. The class module need expose only those properties that need to be changed by your calling routine.

❑   Class modules can be stored as text files, providing a self-contained set of functionality that is easy to reuse in future projects.

The code below is an example of a class module for working with temporary files, allowing the calling code to:

❑   Create a temporary file in the Windows default TEMP directory

❑   Create a temporary file in a user-specified directory

❑   Retrieve the path and file name of the temporary file

❑   Retrieve the text of any errors that may have occurred while creating the temporary file

❑   Delete the temporary file after use

Create a class module called CTempFile and copy in the code below:

```
Option Explicit

'Windows API declaration to find the Windows Temporary directory
Private Declare Function GetTempPath Lib "kernel32" _
        Alias "GetTempPathA" ( _
        ByVal nBufferLength As Long, _
        ByVal lpBuffer As String) As Long

'Windows API declaration to create, and return the name of,
'a temporary filename
Private Declare Function GetTempFileName Lib "kernel32" _
        Alias "GetTempFileNameA" ( _
        ByVal lpszPath As String, _
        ByVal lpPrefixString As String, _
        ByVal wUnique As Long, _
        ByVal lpTempFileName As String) As Long

'Windows API declaration to get the text for an API error code
Private Declare Function FormatMessage Lib "kernel32" _
        Alias "FormatMessageA" ( _
        ByVal dwFlags As Long, _
        lpSource As Any, _
        ByVal dwMessageId As Long, _
        ByVal dwLanguageId As Long, _
        ByVal lpBuffer As String, _
        ByVal nSize As Long, _
        Arguments As Long) As Long
```

```
'Constant for use in the FormatMessage API function
Const FORMAT_MESSAGE_FROM_SYSTEM As Long = &H1000

'Variables to store the path, file and error messsage
Dim stTempPath As String
Dim stTempFile As String
Dim stErrMsg As String
Dim bTidyUp As Boolean
```

One advantage of using a class module is that you can perform some operations when the class is initialized. In this case, you will identify the default Windows TEMP directory. The temporary file will be created in this directory, unless the calling code tells you otherwise

```
Private Sub Class_Initialize()
    'Define some variables to use in the API calls
    Dim stBuff As String * 255, lAPIResult As Long

    'Call the Windows API function to get the TEMP path
    lAPIResult = GetTempPath(255, stBuff)

    If lAPIResult = 0 Then
        'An error occured, so get the text of the error
        stErrMsg = LastDLLErrText(Err.LastDllError)
    Else
        'Store the TEMP path
        stTempPath = Left(stBuff, lAPIResult)
    End If
End Sub
```

This is the routine to create the temporary file, returning its name (including the path). In its simplest use, the calling routine can just call this one method to create a temporary file.

```
Public Function CreateFile() As String
    'Define some variables to use in the API calls
    Dim stBuff As String * 255, lAPIResult As Long

    'Try to get a temporary file name (also creates the file)
    lAPIResult = GetTempFileName(stTempPath, "", 0, stBuff)

    If lAPIResult = 0 Then
        'An error occured, so get the text of the error
        stErrMsg = LastDLLErrText(Err.LastDllError)
    Else
        'Created a temp file OK, so store the file and "OK" error message
        stTempFile = Left(stBuff, InStr(1, stBuff, Chr(0)) - 1)
        stErrMsg = "OK"
        bTidyUp = True

        CreateFile = stTempFile
    End If
End Function
```

In a class module, you can expose a number of properties that allow the calling routine to retrieve and modify the temporary file creation. For example, you may want to enable the calling program to set which directory to use for the temporary file. You could extend this to make the property read-only after the file has been created, raising an error in that case. The use of Property procedures in class modules is described in more detail in chapter 13.

```
'Show the TEMP path as a property of the class
Public Property Get Path() As String
   'Return the path, without the final '\'
   Path = Left(stTempPath, Len(stTempPath) - 1)
End Property

'Allow the user to change the TEMP path
Public Property Let Path(stNewPath As String)
   stTempPath = stNewPath
   If Right(stTempPath, 1) <> "\" Then
      stTempPath = stTempPath & "\"
   End If
End Property
```

You can also give the calling routine read-only access to the temporary file's name and full name (i.e. including the path):

```
'Show the temporary file name as a property
Public Property Get Name() As String
   Name = Mid(stTempFile, Len(stTempPath) + 1)
End Property

'Show the full name (directory and file) as a property
Public Property Get FullName() As String
   FullName = stTempFile
End Property
```

Give the calling program read-only access to the error messages.

```
'Show the error message as a property of the class
Public Property Get ErrorText() As String
   ErrorText = stErrMsg
End Property
```

You'll also allow the calling program to delete the temporary file after use.

```
'Delete the temporary file
Public Sub Delete()
   On Error Resume Next  'In case it has already been deleted
   Kill stTempFile
   bTidyUp = False
End Sub
```

By default, you will delete the temporary file that you created when the class is destroyed. The calling application may not want you to, so provide some properties to that effect.

```
'Whether or not to delete the temp file when the
'class is deleted
Public Property Get TidyUpFiles() As Boolean
   TidyUpFiles = bTidyUp
End Property

'Allow the user to prevent the deletion of his/her own files
Public Property Let TidyUpFiles(bNew As Boolean)
   bTidyUp = bNew
End Property
```

In the class's Terminate code, you'll delete the temporary file, unless told not to. This code is run when the instance of the class is destroyed. If declared within a procedure, this will be when the class variable goes out of scope at the end of the procedure. If declared at a module level, it will occur when the workbook is closed.

```
Private Sub Class_Terminate()
   If bTidyUp Then Delete
End Sub
```

This is the same function you saw in the previous section, to retrieve the text associated with a Windows API error code.

```
'Get the text associated with a Windows API error code
Private Function LastDLLErrText(ByVal lErrorCode As Long) As String
   Dim stBuff As String * 255, lAPIResult As Long

   'Get the text of the error and return it
   lAPIResult = FormatMessage(FORMAT_MESSAGE_FROM_SYSTEM, _
           0&, lErrorCode, 0, stBuff, 255, 0)

   LastDLLErrText = Left(stBuff, lAPIResult)
End Function
```

Once this class module is included in a project, the calling routine does not need to know anything about any of the API functions you're using:

```
Sub Test1()
   Dim obTempFile As New CTempFile

   If obTempFile.CreateFile = "" Then
      MsgBox "An error occured while creating the temp file:" & _
          vbCrLf & obTempFile.ErrorText
   Else
      MsgBox "Temporary file " & obTempFile.FullName & " created"
   End If
End Sub
```

This results in a message like:

Temporary file C:\WINDOWS\TEMP\5024.TMP created

Note that the temporary file is created during the call to CreateFile. When the procedure ends, the variable obTempFile goes out of scope and hence is destroyed by VBA. The Terminate event in the class module ensures the temporary file is deleted – the calling procedure does not need to know about any clean-up routines.

You can force an error by specifying a non-existent directory for the temp file:

```
Sub Test2()
   Dim obTempFile As New CTempFile

   'Tell the class to use a non-existent path
   obTempFile.Path = "C:\NoSuchPath"

   If obTempFile.CreateFile = "" Then
      MsgBox "An error occured while creating the temp file:" & _
          Chr(10) & obTempFile.ErrorText
   Else
      MsgBox "Temporary file " & obTempFile.FullName & " created"
   End If
End Sub
```

This time, you get a meaningful error message:

Microsoft Excel
An error occured while creating the temp file:
The directory name is invalid.
OK

Some Example Classes

This section provides a number of common API calls to include in your projects. Note that in each case the function and constant definitions must be put in the `Declarations` section at the top of a module.

A High-Resolution Timer Class

When testing your code, it is a good idea to time the various routines, in order to identify and eliminate any bottlenecks. VBA includes two functions that can be used as timers:

The `Now` function returns the current time and has a resolution of about 1 second. The `Timer` function returns the number of milliseconds since midnight, with a resolution of approximately 10 milliseconds.

Neither of these are accurate enough to time VBA routines, unless the routine is repeated many times.

Most modern PCs include a high-resolution timer, which updates many thousands of times per second, accessible through API calls. you can wrap these calls in a class module to provide easy access to a high-resolution timer.

Class module *CHighResTimer:*

```
Option Explicit

'How many times per second is the counter updated?
Private Declare Function QueryFrequency Lib "kernel32" _
        Alias "QueryPerformanceFrequency" ( _
        lpFrequency As Currency) As Long

'What is the counter's value
Private Declare Function QueryCounter Lib "kernel32" _
        Alias "QueryPerformanceCounter" ( _
        lpPerformanceCount As Currency) As Long
```

Note that the `win32api.txt` file shows these definitions using the 'LARGE_INTEGER' data type, but they are defined as `Currency` above. The LARGE_INTEGER is a 64-bit data type, usually made up of two Longs. The VBA Currency data type also uses 64-bits to store the number, so you can use it in place of a LARGE_INTEGER. The only differences are that the `Currency` data type is scaled down by a factor of 10,000 and that VBA can perform standard maths operations with `Currency` variables.

```
'Variables to store the counter information
Dim cyFrequency As Currency
Dim cyOverhead As Currency
Dim cyStarted As Currency
Dim cyStopped As Currency
```

The API call itself takes a small amount of time to complete. For accurate timings, you should take this delay into account. you find this delay and the counter's frequency in the class's `Initialize` routine:

```
Private Sub Class_Initialize()
    Dim cyCount1 As Currency, cyCount2 As Currency

    'Get the counter frequency
    QueryFrequency cyFrequency

    'Call the hi-res counter twice, to check how long it takes
    QueryCounter cyCount1
    QueryCounter cyCount2

    'Store the call overhead
    cyOverhead = cyCount2 - cyCount1
End Sub

Public Sub StartTimer()
    'Get the time that you started
    QueryCounter cyStarted
End Sub

Public Sub StopTimer()
    'Get the time that you stopped
    QueryCounter cyStopped
End Sub

Public Property Get Elapsed() As Double
    Dim cyTimer As Currency

    'Have you stopped or not?
    If cyStopped = 0 Then
        QueryCounter cyTimer
    Else
        cyTimer = cyStopped
    End If

    'If you have a frequency, return the duration, in seconds
    If cyFrequency > 0 Then
        Elapsed = (cyTimer - cyStarted - cyOverhead) / cyFrequency
    End If
End Property
```

When you calculate the elapsed time, both the timer and the frequency contain values that are a factor of 10,000 too small. As the numbers are divided, the factors cancel out to give a result in seconds.

The High-Resolution Timer class can be used in a calling routine like:

```
Sub Test3()
    Dim i As Long
    Dim obTimer As New CHighResTimer

    obTimer.StartTimer

    For i = 1 To 10000
    Next i

    obTimer.StopTimer

    Debug.Print "10000 iterations took " & obTimer.Elapsed & " seconds"
End Sub
```

Freeze a UserForm

When working with UserForms, the display may be updated whenever a change is made to the form, such as adding an item to a list box, or enabling/disabling controls. Application.ScreenUpdating has no effect on UserForms; this class provides a useful alternative.

Class module *CFreezeForm*:

```
Option Explicit

'Find a window
Private Declare Function FindWindow Lib "user32" _
        Alias "FindWindowA" ( _
        ByVal lpClassName As String, _
        ByVal lpWindowName As String) As Long

'Freeze the window to prevent continuous redraws
Private Declare Function LockWindowUpdate Lib "user32" ( _
        ByVal hwndLock As Long) As Long

Public Sub Freeze(oForm As UserForm)
    Dim hWnd As Long

    'Get a handle to the userform window,
    'using the class name appropriate for the XL version
    If Val(Application.Version) >= 9 Then
        hWnd = FindWindow("ThunderDFrame", oForm.Caption)
    Else
        hWnd = FindWindow("ThunderXFrame", oForm.Caption)
    End If

    'If you got a handle, freeze the window
    If hWnd > 0 Then LockWindowUpdate hWnd
End Sub

'Allow the calling routine to unfreeze the userform
Public Sub UnFreeze()
    LockWindowUpdate 0
End Sub

'If they forget to unfreeze the form, do it at the end
'of the calling routine (when you go out of scope)
Private Sub Class_Terminate()
    UnFreeze
End Sub
```

To demonstrate this in action, create a new UserForm and add a list box and a command button. Add the following code for the command button's Click event:

```
Private Sub CommandButton1_Click()
    Dim i As Integer

    For i = 1 To 1000
        ListBox1.AddItem "Item " & i
        DoEvents
    Next i
End Sub
```

The DoEvents line forces the UserForm to redraw, to demonstrate the problem. In more complicated routines, the UserForm may redraw itself without using DoEvents. To prevent the redrawing, you can modify the routine to use the CFreezeForm class as shown below:

```
Private Sub CommandButton1_Click()
    Dim obFF As New CFreezeForm, i As Integer
    'Freeze the userform
    obFF.Freeze Me

    For i = 1 To 1000
        ListBox1.AddItem "Item " & i
        DoEvents
    Next i
End Sub
```

This is obviously much easier than including a number of API calls in every function. The class's `Terminate` event ensures that the UserForm is unfrozen when the `obFF` object variable goes out of scope at the end of the procedure. Like using `Application.ScreenUpdating = False` in Excel, freezing a UserForm in this way can have a dramatic performance improvement. For example, the first (non-frozen) version takes approximately 5½ seconds to fill the list box, while the second (frozen) version of the routine takes approximately 2 seconds.

A System Info Class

The classic use of a class module and API functions is to provide all the information about the Windows environment that you cannot get at using VBA alone. The following properties are typical components of such a `CSysInfo` class.

> Note that the declarations for the constants and API functions used in these procedures must all be placed together at the top of the class module. For clarity, they are shown here with the corresponding routines.

Obtaining the Screen Resolution (in pixels):

```
Option Explicit

Private Const SM_CYSCREEN As Long = 1   'Screen height
Private Const SM_CXSCREEN As Long = 0   'Screen width

Private Declare Function GetSystemMetrics Lib "user32" ( _
        ByVal nIndex As Long) As Long

Public Property Get ScreenHeight() As Long
   ScreenHeight = GetSystemMetrics(SM_CYSCREEN)
End Property

Public Property Get ScreenWidth() As Long
   ScreenWidth = GetSystemMetrics(SM_CXSCREEN)
End Property
```

Obtaining the Color Depth (in bits):

```
Private Declare Function GetDC Lib "user32" ( _
        ByVal hwnd As Long) As Long

Private Declare Function GetDeviceCaps Lib "Gdi32" ( _
        ByVal hDC As Long, _
        ByVal nIndex As Long) As Long

Private Declare Function ReleaseDC Lib "user32" ( _
        ByVal hwnd As Long, _
        ByVal hDC As Long) As Long

Private Const BITSPIXEL = 12

Public Property Get ColourDepth() As Integer
   Dim hDC As Long

   'A device context is the canvas on which a window is drawn
   hDC = GetDC(0)
   ColourDepth = GetDeviceCaps(hDC, BITSPIXEL)
   ReleaseDC 0, hDC
End Property
```

Reading the User's Login ID

```
Private Declare Function GetUserName Lib "advapi32.dll" _
      Alias "GetUserNameA" ( _
      ByVal lpBuffer As String, _
      ByRef nSize As Long) As Long

Public Property Get UserName() As String
   Dim stBuff As String * 255, lAPIResult As Long
   Dim lBuffLen As Long

   lBuffLen = 255

   'The second parameter, lBuffLen is both In and Out.
   '  On the way in, it tells the function how big the string buffer is
   '  On the way out, it tells us how long the user name is
   '  (including a terminating Chr(0))
   lAPIResult = GetUserName(stBuff, lBuffLen)

   'If you got something, return the text of the user name
   If lBuffLen > 0 Then UserName = Left(stBuff, lBuffLen - 1)
End Property
```

Reading the Computer's Name

```
Private Declare Function GetComputerName Lib "kernel32" _
      Alias "GetComputerNameA" ( _
      ByVal lbbuffer As String, _
      nsize As Long) As Long

Public Property Get ComputerName() As String
   Dim stBuff As String * 255, lAPIResult As Long
   Dim lBuffLen As Long

   lBuffLen = 255
   lAPIResult = GetComputerName(stBuff, lBuffLen)
   If lBuffLen > 0 Then ComputerName = Left(stBuff, lBuffLen)
End Property
```

These can be tested by using the following routine (in a normal module):

```
Sub Test4()
   Dim obSysInfo As New CSysInfo

   Debug.Print "Screen Height = " & obSysInfo.ScreenHeight
   Debug.Print "Screen Width = " & obSysInfo.ScreenWidth
   Debug.Print "Colour Depth = " & obSysInfo.ColourDepth
   Debug.Print "User name = " & obSysInfo.UserName
   Debug.Print "Computer name = " & obSysInfo.ComputerName
End Sub
```

Other Examples

You are not forced to put all your API calls into class modules. This section
demonstrates a few examples where the API calls would typically be used within a
normal module.

Hide a UserForm's Close Button

Put the following code in a UserForm's code module to remove its close button — the
x in the top-right corner of the form. Be careful to provide another way for the user to
close the form.

```
'Find the userform's Window
Private Declare Function FindWindow Lib "user32" _
        Alias "FindWindowA" ( _
        ByVal lpClassName As String, _
        ByVal lpWindowName As String) As Long

'Get the current window style
Private Declare Function GetWindowLong Lib "user32" _
        Alias "GetWindowLongA" ( _
        ByVal hWnd As Long, _
        ByVal nIndex As Long) As Long

'Set the new window style
Private Declare Function SetWindowLong Lib "user32" _
        Alias "SetWindowLongA" ( _
        ByVal hWnd As Long, _
        ByVal nIndex As Long, _
        ByVal dwNewLong As Long) As Long

Const GWL_STYLE = -16
Const WS_SYSMENU = &H80000

Private Sub UserForm_Initialize()
   Dim hWnd As Long, lStyle As Long

   'Which type of userform
   If Val(Application.Version) >= 9 Then
      hWnd = FindWindow("ThunderDFrame", Me.Caption)
   Else
      hWnd = FindWindow("ThunderXFrame", Me.Caption)
   End If

   'Get the current window style and turn off the Close button
   lStyle = GetWindowLong(hWnd, GWL_STYLE)
   SetWindowLong hWnd, GWL_STYLE, (lStyle And Not WS_SYSMENU)
End Sub
```

Change Excel's Icon

When developing an application that takes over the entire Excel interface, you can use the following code to give Excel your own icon:

```
'Get the handle for a window
Declare Function FindWindow Lib "user32" _
        Alias "FindWindowA" ( _
        ByVal lpClassName As String, _
        ByVal lpWindowName As String) As Long

'Extract an icon from a file
Declare Function ExtractIcon Lib "shell32.dll" _
        Alias "ExtractIconA" ( _
        ByVal hInst As Long, _
        ByVal lpszExeFileName As String, _
        ByVal nIconIndex As Long) As Long

'Send a Windows message
Declare Function SendMessage Lib "user32" _
        Alias "SendMessageA" ( _
        ByVal hWnd As Long, _
        ByVal wMsg As Long, _
        ByVal wParam As Integer, _
        ByVal lparam As Long) As Long

'Windows message types
Const WM_SETICON = &H80

Sub SetExcelIcon(stIconPath As String)
   Dim A As Long, hWnd As Long, hIcon As Long
```

Continued on Following Page

```
    'Get the handle of the Excel window
    hWnd = FindWindow("XLMAIN", Application.Caption)

    'Get the icon from the source file
    hIcon = ExtractIcon(0, stIconPath, 0)

    '1 means invalid icon source, 0 means no icons in source
    If hIcon > 1 Then
        'Set the big (32x32) and small (16x16) icons
        SendMessage hWnd, WM_SETICON, True, hIcon
        SendMessage hWnd, WM_SETICON, False, hIcon
    End If
End Sub
```

```
Sub TestExcelIcon()
    SetExcelIcon "c:\MyDir\MyIcon.ico"
End Sub
```

Play a wav file

Excel does not include a built-in method of playing sounds. This is a simple API call to play a `.wav` file. The `uFlags` argument is not used in this example, but can be used to play the sound asynchronously or in a continuous loop.

```
Declare Function sndPlaySound Lib "winmm.dll" _
        Alias "sndPlaySoundA" ( _
        ByVal lpszSoundName As String, _
        ByVal uFlags As Long) As Long

Sub PlayWav(stWavFileName As String)
    sndPlaySound stWavFileName, 0
End Sub
```

```
Sub TestWav()
    PlayWav "c:\MyDir\MySound.wav"
End Sub
```

Summary

The functions defined in the Windows API provide a valuable and powerful extension to the VBA developer's tool set. The `win32api.txt` file provides the VBA definitions for most of the core functions. The definitions for the remaining functions can be converted from the C-style versions shown in the online MSDN library.

Class modules enable the user to encapsulate both the API definitions and their use into simple chunks of functionality that are easy to use and reuse in VBA applications. A number of example classes and routines have been provided in this chapter to get you started using the Windows API functions within your applications. These include:

- ❑ Creating a TEMP file
- ❑ High resolution timer
- ❑ Freeze a UserForm
- ❑ Getting system information
- ❑ Hiding the **Close** Button on a UserForm
- ❑ Changing Excel's icon
- ❑ Playing a `.wav` file

Excel 2000 Object Model

Common Properties with Collections and Associated Objects

Most of the objects in the Excel Object Model have objects with associated collections. The collection object is usually the plural form of the associated object. For example, the Worksheets collection holds a collection of Worksheet objects. For simplicity, each object and associated collection will be grouped together under the same heading.

In most cases the purpose of the collection object is only to hold a collection of the same objects. The common properties and methods of the collection objects are listed below. Only unique properties, methods or events will be mentioned in each object section.

Common Collection Properties

Name	Returns	Description
Application	Application	Read Only. Returns a reference to the owning Application of the current object. Excel in this case.
Count	Long	Read Only. Returns the number of objects in the collection.
Creator	Long	Read Only. Returns a Long number that describes whether the object was created in Excel or not.
Parent	Object	The Parent object is the owning object of the collection object. For example, Workbooks.Parent returns a reference to the Application object.

Common Collection Methods

Name	Returns	Parameters	Description
Item	Single	Index As Variant	Returns the object from the collection with the Index value specified by the Index parameter. The Index value may also specify a unique string key describing one of the objects in the collection.

Common Object Properties

Objects also have some common properties. To avoid redundancy the common properties and methods of all objects are listed below. They will be mentioned in each object description as existing but are only defined here.

Name	Returns	Description
Application	Application	Read Only. Returns a reference to the owning Application of the current object – Excel in this case.
Creator	Long	Read Only. Returns a Long number that describes whether the object was created in Excel or not.
Parent	Object	Read Only. The owning object of the current object. For example Characters.Parent may return a reference to a Range object, since a Range object is one of the possible owners of a Characters object.

Excel Objects and Their Properties, Methods and Events

The objects are listed in alphabetical order. Each object has a general description of the object and possible parent objects. This is followed by a table format of each of the object's properties, methods and events. The last section of each object describes some code examples of the object's use.

Addin Object and the Addins Collection

The Addins collection holds all of the Addin objects available to Excel. Each Addin object represents an Addin shown in Excel's Add-Ins dialog box under the Tools | Add-Ins... menu. The Addin must be installed (AddIn.Installed = True) to be able to use it in the current session. Examples of available Addin objects in Excel include the Analysis Toolpack, the MS Query Addin, and the Conditional Sum Wizard.

The Add method of the Addins collection can be used to add a new Addin to the collection. The Add method requires a FileName to be specified (usually with a XLL or XLA file extension). The Count property of the Addins collection returns the number of Addins that are available for use by the current Excel session.

Addin Common Properties

The Application, Creator, and Parent properties are defined at the beginning of this Appendix.

Addin Properties

Name	Returns	Description
FullName	String	Read Only. Returns the full path and filename of the associated Addin.
Installed	Boolean	Set / Get whether the Addin can be used in the current session.
Name	String	Read Only. Returns the filename of the Addin.
Path	String	Read Only. Returns the full file path of the associated Addin.
Title	String	Read Only. This hidden property returns the string shown in the Addin Manager dialog box.

Example: AddIn Object and the AddIns Collection

This example ensures that the Analysis Toolpack is installed:

```
Sub UseAnalysisToolpack()
    Dim oAddin As AddIn

    'Make sure the Analysis Toolpack is installed
    For Each oAddin In AddIns
        If oAddin.Name = "ANALYS32.XLL" Then
            oAddin.Installed = True
        End If
    Next
End Sub
```

Note that instead of looping through the Addins collection, you could follow the on-line help and use:

```
AddIns("Analysis Toolpak").Installed = True
```

Unfortunately, this approach may not work with a non-English User-Interface language, if the Addin's title has been localised.

Adjustments Object

The `Adjustments` object holds a collection of numbers used to move the adjustment 'handles' of the parent Shape object. Each `Shape` object can have up to 8 different adjustments. Each specific adjustment handle can have one or two adjustments associated with it depending on if it can be moved both horizontally and vertically (two) or in just one dimension. Adjustment values are between 0 and 1 and hence are percentage adjustments – the absolute magnitude of a 100% change is defined by the shape being adjusted.

Adjustments Common Properties

The `Application`, `Creator`, and `Parent` properties are defined at the beginning of this Appendix.

Adjustments Properties

Name	Returns	Description
Count	Long	Read Only. Returns the number of adjustments values associated with the parent Shape object.
Item	Single	Parameters: Index As Long. Set / Get the adjustment value or values indicated by the Index parameter.

Example: Adjustments Object

This example draws a block arrow on the sheet, then modifies the dimensions of the arrow head:

```
Sub AddArrow()
    Dim oShp As Shape

    'Add an arrow head to the sheet
    Set oShp = ActiveSheet.Shapes.AddShape( _
            msoShapeRightArrow, 10, 10, 100, 50)

    'Set the 'head' of the arrow to start 30% of the way across
    'and the 'shaft' to start 40% of the way down.
    oShp.Adjustments(1) = 0.3      'Left/right
    oShp.Adjustments(2) = 0.4      'Up/down
End Sub
```

Application Object

The `Application` object is the root object of the Excel Object Model. All the other objects in the Excel Object Model can only be accessed through the `Application` object. Many objects, however, are globally available. For example, the `ActiveSheet` property of the `Application` object is also available globally. That means that the active WorkSheet can be accessed by at least two ways: `Application.ActiveSheet` and `ActiveSheet`.

The `Application` object holds most of the application level attributes that can be set through the <u>T</u>ools | <u>O</u>ptions menu in Excel. For example, the `DefaultFilePath` is equivalent to the `Default File Location` text box in the **General** tab of the **Options** dialog box.

> *Many of the* `Application` *object's properties and methods are equivalent to things that can be set with the* **Options** *dialog box.*

The `Application` object is also used when automating Excel from another application, such as Word 2000. The `CreateObject` function, `GetObject` function or the `New` keyword can be used to create a new instance of an Excel `Application` object from another application. Please refer to Chapter 15 for examples of automation from another application.

The `Application` object can also expose events. However, Application events are not automatically available for use. The following three steps must be completed before Application events can be used:

1. Create a new class module, say called `cAppObject`, and declare a `Public` object variable in a class, say called `AppExcel`, to respond to events. For example:

```
Public WithEvents AppExcel As Excel.Application
```

2. Now the `Application` object events will be available in the class for the `AppExcel` object variable. Write the appropriate event handling code in the class. For example if you wanted a message to appear whenever a worksheet is activated then you could write the following:

```
Private Sub AppExcel_SheetActivate(ByVal Sh As Object)
    'display worksheet name
    MsgBox "The " & Sh.Name & " sheet has just been activated."
End Sub
```

3. Finally, in a procedure in a standard module instantiate the class created above with a current `Application` object:

```
Private App As New cAppObject 'class with the above code snippets
Sub AttachEvents()
    Set App.AppExcel = Application
End Sub
```

The `EnableEvents` property of the `Application` object must also be set to `True` for events to trigger at the appropriate time.

Application Common Properties

The `Application`, `Creator`, and `Parent` properties are defined at the beginning of this Appendix.

Application Properties

Name	Returns	Description
`ActiveCell`	`Range`	Read Only. Returns the cell in the active sheet where the cursor is located.
`ActiveChart`	`Chart`	Read Only. Returns the currently selected chart in the active workbook. If no chart is currently selected `Nothing` is returned.
`ActivePrinter`	`String`	Set / Get the name of the printer currently being used.
`ActiveSheet`	`Object`	Read Only. Returns the currently active sheet in the active workbook.
`ActiveWindow`	`Window`	Read Only. Returns the currently selected Excel window, if any.
`ActiveWorkbook`	`Workbook`	Read Only. Returns the workbook that is currently active, if any.
`AddIns`	`AddIns`	Read Only. Returns the collection of Addins currently available for use in Excel.
`AlertBefore Overwriting`	`Boolean`	Set / Get whether a message pops up any time an attempt to overwrite nonblank cells by a drag-and-drop operation is made.
`AltStartupPath`	`String`	Set / Get the alternate startup file location folder for Excel.
`AnswerWizard`	`Answer Wizard`	Read Only. Returns an object allowing manipulation of the Answer Wizard.
`AskToUpdateLinks`	`Boolean`	Set / Get whether the user is prompted to update links whenever a workbook with links is opened.
`Assistant`	`Assistant`	Read Only. Returns an object allowing manipulation of the Office Assistant.
`AutoCorrect`	`Auto Correct`	Read Only. Returns an object allowing modification of Excel's AutoCorrect features.

Name	Returns	Description
AutoPercentEntry	Boolean	Set / Get whether Excel automatically adds a % sign when typing a number into a cell that has a Percentage format applied.
Build	Long	Read Only. Returns the exact build number of Excel.
CalculateBefore Save	Boolean	Set / Get whether workbooks are calculated before they are saved to disk. This assumes that formula calculation is not set to automatic (Calculation property).
Calculation	xl Calculation	Set / Get when calculations are made automatically, manually, or semi-automatically.
Calculation Version	Long	Read Only. Returns the Excel version and calculation engine version used when the file was last saved.
Caller	Variant	Read Only. Parameters: [Index]. Returns information describing what invoked the current Visual Basic code (e.g. cell function, document event).
CanPlaySounds	Boolean	Read Only. Returns whether sound notes are heard in Excel. Property unused in Excel 2000.
CanRecordSounds	Boolean	Read Only. Returns whether sound notes can be recorded in Excel. Property unused in Excel 2000.
Caption	String	Set / Get the caption that appears in the main Excel window.
CellDragAndDrop	Boolean	Set / Get whether dragging and dropping cells is possible.
Cells	Range	Read Only. Returns all the cells in the active sheet.

Table Continued on Following Page

Name	Returns	Description
Charts	Sheets	Read Only. Returns all the charts in the active workbook.
ClipboardFormats	Variant	Read Only. Parameters: [Index]. Returns an array of format values (xlClipboardFormat) that are currently in the clipboard.
Columns	Range	Read Only. Returns all the columns in the currently active sheet.
COMAddIns	COMAddIns	Read Only. Returns the collection of installed COM Addins.
CommandBars	CommandBars	Read Only. Returns the collection of command bars available to Excel.
CommandUnderlines	xlCommand Underlines	Set / Get how commands are underlined in Excel. Used only on Macintosh systems.
ConstrainNumeric	Boolean	Set / Get whether only numbers and punctuation marks are recognized by handwriting recognition. Used only by Windows for Pen Computing.
ControlCharacters	Boolean	Set / Get whether control characters are displayed for right-to-left languages. (Language support must be installed).
CopyObjectsWith Cells	Boolean	Set / Get whether objects (such as embedded objects) can be cut, copied, and sorted along with cell data.
Cursor	xlMouse Pointer	Set / Get which mouse pointer is seen in Microsoft Excel.
CursorMovement	Long	Set / Get what type of cursor is used: visual or logical.

Name	Returns	Description
CustomListCount	Long	Read Only. Returns the number of custom and built-in lists used in Excel (e.g. Monday, Tuesday, Wednesday…).
CutCopyMode	xlCutCopyMode	Set / Get whether a cut or copy operation is currently happening.
DataEntryMode	Long	Set / Get whether locked cells can be edited (xlOff for editing allowed, xlOn for editing of unlocked cells only, xlStrict for editing of unlocked cells only that can not be canceled by pressing Escape).
DDEAppReturnCode	Long	Read Only. Returns the result (confirmation/error) of the last DDE message sent by Excel.
DefaultFilePath	String	Set / Get the default folder used when opening files.
DefaultSaveFormat	xlFileFormat	Set / Get the default file format used when saving files.
DefaultSheet Direction	Long	Set / Get which direction new sheets will appear in Excel.
DefaultWebOptions	DefaultWeb Options	Read Only. Returns an object allowing manipulation of the items associated with the **Web Options** dialog.
Dialogs	Dialogs	Read Only. Returns a collection of all the built-in dialog boxes.
DisplayAlerts	Boolean	Set / Get whether the user is prompted by typical Excel messages (e.g. '**Save Changes to Workbook?**') or no prompts appear and the default answer is always chosen.

Table Continued on Following Page

Name	Returns	Description
DisplayClipboard Window	Boolean	Set / Get whether the Clipboard window is displayed. Used in Microsoft Office Macintosh Edition.
DisplayComment Indicator	xlComment DisplayMode	Set / Get how Excel displays cell comments and indicators.
DisplayExcel4Menus	Boolean	Set / Get whether Excel display Excel 4.0 menus.
DisplayFormulaBar	Boolean	Set / Get whether the formula bar is displayed.
DisplayFullScreen	Boolean	Set / Get whether the Excel is in full screen mode.
DisplayNoteIndicator	Boolean	Set / Get whether comments inserted into cells have a little note indicator at the top right corner of the cell.
DisplayRecentFiles	Boolean	Set / Get whether the most recently opened files are displayed under the File menu.
DisplayScrollBars	Boolean	Set / Get whether scroll bars are displayed for all open workbooks in the current session.
DisplayStatusBar	Boolean	Set / Get whether the status bar is displayed.
EditDirectlyInCell	Boolean	Set / Get whether existing cell text can be modified directly in the cell. Note that cell text can still be overwritten directly.
EnableAnimations	Boolean	Set / Get whether adding and deleting cells, rows, and columns are animated.

Name	Returns	Description
EnableAutoComplete	Boolean	Set / Get whether the AutoComplete feature is enabled.
EnableCancelKey	xlEnable CancelKey	Set / Get how an Excel macro reacts when the user tries to interrupt the macro (e.g. *Ctrl-Break*). This can be used to disable any user interruption, send any interruption to the error handler, or to just stop the code (default). **USE WITH CARE!**
EnableEvents	Boolean	Set / Get whether events are triggered for any object in the Excel Object Model that supports events.
EnableSound	Boolean	Set / Get whether sounds are enabled for Excel.
Excel4IntlMacroSheets	Sheets	Read Only. Returns the collection of sheets containing Excel 4 International macros.
Excel4MacroSheets	Sheets	Read Only. Returns the collection of sheets containing Excel 4 macros.
ExtendList	Boolean	Set / Get whether formatting and formulas are automatically added when adding new rows or columns to existing lists of rows or columns.
FeatureInstall	MsoFeature Install	Set / Get how Excel reacts when an Excel feature is accessed that is not installed (through the interface or programmatically).

Table Continued on Following Page

Name	Returns	Description
FileConverters	Variant	Read Only. Parameters: [Index1], [Index2]. Returns an array of all the file converters available in Excel.
FileFind	IFind	Returns an object that can be used to search for files. Used in Microsoft Office Macintosh Edition.
FileSearch	FileSearch	Read Only. Returns an object that can be used to search for files.
FixedDecimal	Boolean	Set / Get whether any numbers entered in the future will have the decimal points specified by FixedDecimalPlaces
FixedDecimalPlaces	Long	Set / Get the decimals places used for any future numbers.
Height	Double	Set / Get the height of Excel's main application window. The value cannot be set if the main window is maximized or minimized.
IgnoreRemote Requests	Boolean	Set / Get whether remote requests through DDE are ignored.
Interactive	Boolean	Set / Get whether Excel accepts keyboard and mouse input.
International	Variant	Read Only. Parameters: [Index]. Returns international settings for Excel. Use the xlApplicationInternational constants as one of the values of Index.

Name	Returns	Description
Iteration	Boolean	Set / Get whether Excel will iterate through and calculate all the cells in a circular reference trying to resolve the circular reference. Use with `MaxIterations` and `MaxChange`.
LanguageSettings	LanguageSettings	Read Only. Returns an object describing the language settings in Excel.
Left	Double	Set / Get the left edge of Excel's main application window. The value cannot be set if the main window is maximized or minimized.
LibraryPath	String	Read Only. Returns the directory where Addins are stored.
MailSession	Variant	Read Only. Returns the hexadecimal mail session number or `Null` if mail session is active.
MailSystem	xlMailSystem	Read Only. Returns what type of mail system is being used by the computer (e.g. `xlMapi`, `xlPowerTalk`).
MathCoprocessor Available	Boolean	Read Only. Returns whether a math coprocessor is available.
MaxChange	Double	Set / Get the minimum change between iterations of a circular reference before iterations stop.
MaxIterations	Long	Set / Get the maximum number of iterations allowed for circular references before iterations stop.

Table Continued on Following Page

Name	Returns	Description
MemoryFree	Long	Read Only. Returns how much free memory (in bytes) Excel can use.
MemoryTotal	Long	Read Only. Returns how much total memory (in bytes) is available to Excel (including memory in use).
MemoryUsed	Long	Read Only. Returns how much memory (in Bytes) Excel is using.
MouseAvailable	Boolean	Read Only. Returns whether the mouse is available.
MoveAfterReturn	Boolean	Set / Get whether the current cell changes when the user hits *ENTER*.
MoveAfterReturn Direction	xlDirection	Set / Get which direction the cursor will move when the user hits *ENTER* changing the current cell.
Name	String	Read Only. Returns "Microsoft Excel".
Names	Names	Read Only. Returns the collection of defined names in an active workbook.
NetworkTemplates Path	String	Read Only. Returns the location on the network where the Excel templates are kept, if any.
ODBCErrors	ODBCErrors	Read Only. Returns the collection of errors returned by the most recent query or PivotTable report that had an ODBC connection.
ODBCTimeout	Long	Set / Get how long, in seconds, an ODBC connection will be kept before timing out.

Name	Returns	Description
OLEDBErrors	OLEDBErrors	Read Only. Returns the collection of errors returned by the most recent query or PivotTable report that had an OLE DB connection.
OnWindow	String	Set / Get the procedure that is executed every time a window is activated by the end user.
OperatingSystem	String	Read Only. Returns the name and version of the operating system.
OrganizationName	String	Read Only. Returns the organization name as seen in the About Microsoft Excel dialog box.
Path	String	Read Only. Returns the path where Excel is installed.
PathSeparator	String	Read Only. Returns a backslash ("\") on a PC or a colon ":" on a Macintosh.
PivotTable Selection	Boolean	Set / Get whether pivot tables use structured selection. For example, when selecting a Row field title the associated data is selected with it.
Previous Selections	Variant	Read Only. Parameters: [Index]. Returns an array of the last four ranges or named areas selected by using Name dialog box or Goto feature.
ProductCode	String	Read Only. Returns the GUID for Excel.
PromptForSummary Info	Boolean	Set / Get whether the user is prompted to enter summary information when trying to save a file.
Range	Range	Read Only. Parameters: Cell1, [Cell2]. Returns a Range object containing all the cells specified by the parameters.

Table Continued on Following Page

Name	Returns	Description
RecentFiles	RecentFiles	Read Only. Returns the collection of recently opened files.
RecordRelative	Boolean	Read Only. Returns whether recorded macros use relative cell references (True) or absolute cell references (False).
ReferenceStyle	xlReference Style	Set / Get how cells are referenced: Letter-Number (e.g.A1, A3) or RowNumber-ColumnNumber (e.g. R1C1, R3C1).
Registered Functions	Variant	Read Only. Parameters: [Index1], [Index2] . Returns the array of functions and function details relating to external DLLs or code resources. Using Addins will add external DLLs to your workbook.
RollZoom	Boolean	Set / Get whether scrolling with a scroll mouse will zoom instead of scroll.
Rows	Range	Read Only. Returns all the rows in the active sheet.
ScreenUpdating	Boolean	Set / Get whether Excel updates its display while a procedure is running. This property can be used to speed up procedure code by turning off screen updates (setting the property to False) during processing. Use with the ScreenRefresh method to manually refresh the screen.
Selection	Object	Read Only. Returns whatever object is currently selected (e.g. sheet, chart).
Sheets	Sheets	Read Only. Returns the collection of sheets in the active workbook.
SheetsInNew Workbook	Long	Set / Get how many blank sheets are put in a newly created workbook.

Name	Returns	Description
ShowChartTip Names	Boolean	Set / Get whether charts show the tip names over data points.
ShowChartTip Values	Boolean	Set / Get whether charts show the tip values over data points.
ShowToolTips	Boolean	Set / Get whether tool tips are shown in Excel.
ShowWindowsIn Taskbar	Boolean	Set / Get whether each workbook is visible on the taskbar (True) or only one Excel item is visible in the taskbar (False).
StandardFont	String	Set / Get what font is used as the standard Excel font.
StandardFont Size	Double	Set / Get what font size is used as the standard Excel font size (in points).
StartupPath	String	Read Only. Returns the folder used as the Excel startup folder.
StatusBar	Variant	Set / Get the status bar text. Returns False if Excel has control of the status bar. Set to False to give control of the status bar to Excel.
TemplatesPath	String	Read Only. Returns the path to the Excel templates.
ThisWorkbook	Workbook	Read Only. Returns the workbook that contains the currently running VBA code.
Top	Double	Set / Get the top of Excel's main application window. The value cannot be set if the main window is maximized or minimized.
TransitionMenu Key	String	Set / Get what key is used to bring up Excel's menu. The Forward slash key ("/") is the default.
TransitionMenu KeyAction	Long	Set / Get what happens when the Transition Menu Key is pressed. Either Excel menus appear (xlExcelMenu) or Lotus help dialog box (xlLotusHelp) appears.

Table Continued on Following Page

Name	Returns	Description
TransitionNavig Keys	Boolean	Set / Get whether the Transition Navigation Keys are active. These provide different key combinations for moving and selecting within a worksheet.
UsableHeight	Double	Read-Only. Returns the vertical space available in Excel's main window, in points, that is available to a sheet's Window. The value will be 1 if there is no space available.
UsableWidth	Double	Read-Only. Returns the horizontal space available in Excel's main window, in points, that is available to a sheet's Window. This property's value will be invalid if no space is available. Check the value of the UsableHeight property to check to see if there is any space available (>1).
UserControl	Boolean	Read-Only. True if the current Excel session was started by a user, and False if the Excel session was started programmatically.
UserLibraryPath	String	Read Only. Returns the location of Excel's COMAddins.
UserName	String	Set / Get the user name in Excel. Note that this is the name shown in the General tab of the Options dialog box and NOT the current user's network ID or the name shown in the Excel splash screen.
Value	String	Read Only. Returns "Microsoft Excel".
VBE	VBE	Read Only. Returns an object allowing manipulation of the Visual Basic editor.
Version	String	Read Only. Returns the version of Excel.
Visible	Boolean	Set / Get whether Excel is visible to the user.

Name	Returns	Description
Width	Double	Set / Get the width of Excel's main application window. The value cannot be set if the main window is maximized or minimized.
Windows	Windows	Read Only. Returns all the Windows open in the current Excel session.
WindowsForPens	Boolean	Read Only. Returns whether Excel is running in a Windows for Pen Computing environment.
WindowState	xlWindow State	Set / Get whether the window is maximized, minimized, or in a normal state.
Workbooks	Workbooks	Read Only. Returns all the open workbooks (not including Addins) in the current Excel session.
WorksheetFunction	Worksheet Function	Read Only. Returns an object holding all the Excel's worksheet functions that can be used in VBA.
Worksheets	Sheets	Read Only. Returns all the worksheets in the active workbook.

Application Methods

Name	Returns	Parameters	Description
Activate MicrosoftApp		Index As xlMS Application	Activate an application specified by xlMSApplication. Opens the application if it is not open. Acts in a similar manner as the GetObject function in VBA.
AddChartAuto Format		Chart, Name As String, [Description]	Adds the formatting and legends of the Chart specified by the parameter to the custom chart types.

Table Continued on Following Page

Name	Returns	Parameters	Description
AddCustom List		ListArray, [ByRow]	Adds the array of strings specified by ListArray to Excel's custom lists. The ListArray may also be a cell range.
Calculate			Calculates all the formulas in all open workbooks that have changed since the last calculation. Only applicable if using manual calculation.
Calculate Full			Calculates all the formulas in all open workbooks. Forces recalculation of every formula in every workbook, regardless of whether or not it has changed since the last calculation.
Centimeters ToPoints	Double	Centimeters As Double	Converts the Centimeters parameter to points where 1 cm = 28.35 points.
Check Spelling	Boolean	Word As String, [Custom Dictionary], [IgnoreUpper case]	Checks the spelling of the Word parameter and returns True if the spelling is correct or False if there are errors.

Name	Returns	Parameters	Description
Convert Formula	Variant	Formula, FromReference Style As xlReference Style, [ToReference Style], [ToAbsolute], [RelativeTo]	Converts the Formula parameter between R1C1 references and A1 references and returns the converted formula. Also can change the Formula parameter between relative references and absolute references using the ToReferenceStyle parameter and the xlReferenceStyle constants.
DDEExecute		Channel As Long, String As String	Sends a Command to an application using DDE through the given Channel number. The properties starting with DDE are associated with the older technology, Dynamic Data Exchange, which was used to share data between applications.
DDEInitiate	Long	App As String, Topic As String	Returns a channel number to use for DDE given an application name and the DDE topic.
DDEPoke		Channel As Long, Item, Data	Sends Data to an item in an application using DDE through the given Channel number.

Table Continued on Following Page

Name	Returns	Parameters	Description
DDERequest	Variant	Channel As Long, Item As String	Returns information given a specific DDE channel and a requested item.
DDETerminate		Channel As Long	Closes the specified DDE channel.
DeleteChart AutoFormat		Name As String	Deletes the custom chart type specified by the Name parameter.
DeleteCustom List		ListNum As Long	Deletes the custom list specified by the list number. The first four lists are built-in to Excel and cannot be removed.
DoubleClick			Trigged by a double-click to the active cell in the active sheet.
Evaluate	Variant	Name	Evaluates the Name string expression as if it were entered into a worksheet cell.
ExecuteExcel 4Macro	Variant	String As String	Executes the Excel 4 macro specified by the String parameter and returns the results.
FindFile	Boolean		Shows the Open dialog box allowing the user to choose a file to open. True is returned if the file opens successfully.
GetCustom ListContents	Variant	ListNum As Long	Returns the custom list specified by the ListNum parameter as an array of strings.

Name	Returns	Parameters	Description
GetCustom ListNum	Long	ListArray	Returns the list number for the custom list that matches the given array of strings. A zero is returned if nothing matches.
GetOpen Filename	Variant	[FileFilter], [FilterIndex], [Title], [ButtonText], [MultiSelect]	The **Open** dialog box is displayed with the optional file filters, titles, and button texts specified by the parameters. The filename and path are returned from this method call. Optionally can return an array of filenames if the MultiSelect parameter is True. Does not actually open the file.
Get Phonetic	String	[Text]	Returns the phonetic text of the Japanese characters in the Text parameter. If no Text parameter is specified then an alternate phonetic text of the previous Text parameter is returned.
GetSaveAs Filename	Variant	[InitialFilen ame], [FileFilter], [FilterIndex], [Title], [ButtonText]	The **Save As** dialog box is displayed with the optional default file name, file filters, titles, and button texts specified by the parameters. The filename and path are returned from this method call. Does not actually save the file.

Table Continued on Following Page

Name	Returns	Parameters	Description
Goto		[Reference], [Scroll]	Selects the object specified by the Reference parameter and activates the sheet containing that object. The Reference parameter can be a cell, range, or the name of a VBA procedure. The Scroll parameter, if set to True, will scroll the selected object to the top left corner of the Excel window.
Help		[HelpFile], [HelpContextID]	Displays the help topic specified by the HelpContextID parameter in the help file HelpFile.
InchesTo Points	Double	Inches As Double	Converts the Inches parameter to points and returns the new value. (1 inch = 72 points).
InputBox	Variant	Prompt As String, [Title], [Default], [Left], [Top], [HelpFile], [HelpContextID], [Type]	Displays a simple input box very similar to standard VBA one. However, the [Type] parameter can be used to set the return type to a formula (0), number (1), text (2), Boolean (4), cell reference (8), an error value (16), or an array of values (64).

Name	Returns	Parameters	Description
Intersect	Range	Arg1 As Range, Arg2 As Range, [Arg3], ... [Arg30]	Returns the intersection or overlap of the ranges specified by the parameters as a Range object.
Macro Options		[Macro], [Description], [HasMenu], [MenuText], [HasShortcut Key], [ShortcutKey], [Category], [StatusBar], [HelpContext ID], [HelpFile]	Allows modification of macro attributes such as the name, description, shortcut key, category and associated help file. Equivalent to the Macro Options dialog box.
MailLogoff			Logs off the current MAPI mail session (e.g. Exchange, Outlook)
MailLogon		[Name], [Password], [DownloadNew Mail]	Logs on to the default MAPI mail client (e.g. Exchange, Outlook). Credentials such as name and password can be specified.
NextLetter	Workbook		Used in Macintosh systems with PowerTalk mail extensions to open the oldest unread workbook from the In Tray. Generates an error in Windows.

Table Continued on Following Page

Name	Returns	Parameters	Description
OnKey		Key As String, [Procedure]	Executes the procedure specified by the Procedure parameter whenever the keystroke or key combination described in the Key parameter is pressed.
OnRepeat		Text As String, Procedure As String	Specify the text to appear by the Edit | Repeat menu item and the procedure to run when the user chooses Edit | Repeat.
OnTime		EarliestTime, Procedure As String, [LatestTime], [Schedule]	Choose a procedure to run at the time specified by the EarliestTime parameter. Use the LatestTime parameter to specify a time range.
OnUndo		Text As String, Procedure As String	Specify the text to appear by the Edit | Undo menu item and the procedure to run when the user chooses Edit | Undo.
Quit			Shuts down Microsoft Excel.
RecordMacro		[BasicCode], [xlmCode]	If the user is currently recording a macro, running this statement will put the code specified in the BasicCode parameter into the currently recording macro.

Name	Returns	Parameters	Description
RegisterXLL	Boolean	Filename As String	Loads the code resource specified by the `Filename` parameter and registers all the functions and procedures in that code resource.
Repeat			Repeats the last user action made. Must be the first line of a procedure.
Run	Variant	[Macro], [Arg1], [Arg2], ... [Arg30]	Runs the macro or procedure specified by the `Macro` parameter. Can also run Excel 4.0 macros with this method.
SaveWorkspace		[Filename]	Saves the current workspace to the `Filename` parameter.
SendKeys		Keys, [Wait]	Sends the keystrokes in the `Keys` parameter to Microsoft Excel user interface.
SetDefault Chart		[FormatName], [Gallery]	Set the default chart type added when programmatically adding a chart. The `FormatName` parameter can be a built-in chart type or a custom chart type name.
Undo			Undoes the last action done with the user interface.

Name	Returns	Parameters	Description
Union	Range	Arg1 As Range, Arg2 As Range, [Arg3], . . . [Arg30]	Returns the union of the ranges specified by the parameters.
Volatile		[Volatile]	Sets the function that currently contains this statement to be either volatile (Volatile parameter to True) or not. A volatile function will be recalculated whenever the sheet containing it is calculated, even if its input values have not changed.
Wait	Boolean	Time	Pauses the macro and Excel until the time in the Time parameter is reached.

Application Events

Name	Parameters	Description
NewWorkbook	Wb As Workbook	Triggered when a new workbook is created. The new workbook is passed into the event.
SheetActivate	Sh As Object	Triggered when a sheet is activated (brought up to front of the other sheets). The activated sheet is passed into the event.
SheetBefore DoubleClick	Sh As Object, Target As Range, Cancel As Boolean	Triggered when a sheet is about to be double-clicked. The sheet and the potential double-click spot are passed into the event. The double-click action can be canceled by setting the Cancel parameter to True.

Name	Parameters	Description
SheetBeforeRight Click	Sh As Object, Target As Range, Cancel As Boolean	Triggered when a sheet is about to be right-clicked. The sheet and the potential right-click spot are passed into the event. The right-click action can be canceled by setting the Cancel parameter to True.
SheetCalculate	Sh As Object	Triggered when a sheet is recalculated passing in the recalculated sheet.
SheetChange	Sh As Object, Target As Range	Triggered when a range on a sheet is changed, for example by clearing the range, entering data, deleting rows or columns, pasting data etc. **NOT** triggered when inserting rows/columns.
SheetDeactivate	Sh As Object	Triggered when a sheet loses focus. Passes in the sheet.
SheetFollow Hyperlink	Sh As Object, Target As Hyperlink	Triggered when the user clicks on a hyperlink on a sheet. Passes in the sheet and the clicked hyperlink.
SheetSelection Change	Sh As Object, Target As Range	Triggered when the user selects a new cell in a worksheet. Passes in the new range and the sheet where the change occurred.
WindowActivate	Wb As Workbook, Wn As Window	Triggered when a workbook window is activated (brought up to the front of other workbook windows). The workbook and the window are passed in.
WindowDeactivate	Wb As Workbook, Wn As Window	Triggered when a workbook window loses focus. The related workbook and the window are passes in.
WindowResize	Wb As Workbook, Wn As Window	Triggered when a workbook window is resized. The resized workbook and window are passed into the event. Not triggered when Excel is resized.

Table Continued on Following Page

Name	Parameters	Description
Workbook Activate	Wb As Workbook	Triggered when a workbook is activated (brought up to the front of other workbook windows). The workbook is passed in.
WorkbookAddin Install	Wb As Workbook	Triggered when an Addin is added to Excel that is also a workbook. The Addin workbook is passed into the event.
WorkbookAddin Uninstall	Wb As Workbook	Triggered when an Addin is removed to Excel that is also a workbook. The Addin workbook is passed into the event.
WorkbookBefore Close	Wb As Workbook, Cancel As Boolean	Triggered just before a workbook is closed. The workbook is passed into the event. The closure can be canceled by setting the Cancel parameter to True.
Workbook BeforePrint	Wb As Workbook, Cancel As Boolean	Triggered just before a workbook is printed. The workbook is passed into the event. The printing can be canceled by setting the Cancel parameter to True.
Workbook BeforeSave	Wb As Workbook, SaveAsUI As Boolean, Cancel As Boolean	Triggered just before a workbook is saved. The workbook is passed into the event. The saving can be canceled by setting the Cancel parameter to True. If the SaveAsUI is set to True then the **Save As** dialog box appears.
Workbook Deactivate	Wb As Workbook	Triggered when a workbook loses focus. The related workbook and the window are passed in.
Workbook NewSheet	Wb As Workbook, Sh As Object	Triggered when a new sheet is added to a workbook. The workbook and new sheet are passed into the event
WorkbookOpen	Wb As Workbook	Triggered when a workbook is opened. The newly opened workbook is passed into the event.

Example: Application Object

This example demonstrates how to use `Application.GetOpenFilename` to get the name of a file to open. The key to using this function is to assign its return value to a `Variant` data type:

```
Sub UsingGetOpenFilename()
    Dim sFilter As String
    Dim vaFile As Variant

    'Build a filter list.  If you omit the space before the first comma,
    'Excel will not display the pattern, (*.New)
    sFilter = "New Files (*.New) ,*.new," & _
              "Old Files (*.Old) ,*.old," & _
              "All Files (*.*) ,*.*"

    'Display the File Open dialog, putting the result in a Variant
    vaFile = Application.GetOpenFilename(FileFilter:=sFilter, FilterIndex:=1, _
                        Title:="Open a New or Old File", MultiSelect:=False)

    'Did the user cancel?
    If vaFile <> False Then
        MsgBox "You want to open " & vaFile
    End If
End Sub
```

The `Application` object is used to store and retrieve custom sort orders:

```
Sub UsingACustomSortOrder()
    Dim vaSortList As Variant
    Dim iListNum As Integer
    Dim bAdded As Boolean

    'Sort the products in this order
    vaSortList = Array("Oranges", "Mangoes", "Apples", "Pears")

    'Get the number of this custom sort, if it exists.
    iListNum = Application.GetCustomListNum(vaSortList)

    'If it doesn't exist, we get zero, NOT an error
    If iListNum = 0 Then
        'Create a custom list for this sort order
        Application.AddCustomList vaSortList

        'And retrieve its number (the last one!)
        iListNum = Application.CustomListCount

        'Remember that we added it - delete it after use
        bAdded = True
    End If

    'Sort the range using this custom list.  Note that we have to
    'add 1 to the list number, as 'ordercustom:=1' means to use the
    'standard sort order (which is not a custom list)
    ActiveCell.CurrentRegion.Sort key1:=ActiveCell, _
                        ordercustom:=iListNum + 1, header:=xlYes

    'If we added the list, remove it.
    If bAdded Then Application.DeleteCustomList iListNum
End Sub
```

Chapter 3 in the first section of this book contains more examples of using the `Application` object

Areas Collection

The `Areas` collection holds a collection of `Range` objects. Each `Range` object represents a block of cells (e.g. A1:A10) or a single cell. The `Areas` collection can hold many ranges from different parts of a workbook. The parent of the `Areas` Collection is the `Range` object.

Areas Common Properties

The `Application`, `Creator`, and `Parent` properties are defined at the beginning of this Appendix.

Areas Properties

Name	Returns	Description
Count	Long	Read Only. Returns the number of `Range` objects that are contained in the area.
Item	Range	Parameter: `Index As Long`. Returns a single `Range` object in the `Areas` collection. The `Index` parameter corresponds to the order of the ranges selected.

Example: Areas Collection

When using a `Range` containing a number of different areas, we cannot use code like `rgRange.Cells(20).Value` if the twentieth cell is not inside the first area in the range. This is because Excel only looks at the first area, implicitly doing `rgRange.Areas(1).Cells(20).Value`, as this example shows – with a function to provide a workaround:

```
Sub TestMultiAreaCells()
    Dim oRNg As Range

    'Define a multi-area range
    Set oRNg = Range("D2:F5,H2:I5")

    'The 12th cell should be F5.
    MsgBox "Rng.Cells(12) is " & oRNg.Cells(12).Address & _
            vbCrLf & "Rng.Areas(1).Cells(12) is " & _
                oRNg.Areas(1).Cells(12).Address & _
        vbCrLf & "MultiAreaCells(Rng, 12) is " & _
                MultiAreaCells(Rng, 12).Address

    'The 13th cell of the multi-area range should be H2,
    'i.e. the first cell in the second area.
    MsgBox "Rng.Cells(13) is " & oRNg.Cells(13).Address & _
            vbCrLf & "Rng.Areas(1).Cells(13) is " & _
                oRNg.Areas(1).Cells(13).Address & _
        vbCrLf & "MultiAreaCells(Rng, 13) is " & _
                MultiAreaCells(Rng, 13).Address
End Sub

Function MultiAreaCells(oRange As Range, iCellNum As Long) As Range
    Dim iTotCells As Long, oArea As Range

    'Loop through all the areas in the range,
    'starting again from the first if we run out
    Do
```

```
        For Each oArea In oRange.Areas
            'Is the cell we want in this area?
            If iTotCells + oArea.Cells.Count >= iCellNum Then

                'Yes - return it and exit the function
                Set MultiAreaCells = oArea.Cells(iCellNum - iTotCells)
                Exit Function
            Else
                'No - count up the cells we've checked and carry on
                iTotCells = iTotCells + oArea.Cells.Count
            End If
        Next
    Loop
End Function
```

AutoCorrect Object

The AutoCorrect object represents all of the functionality of the Excel's AutoCorrect features.

AutoCorrect Common Properties

The Application, Creator, and Parent properties are defined at the beginning of this Appendix.

AutoCorrect Properties

Name	Returns	Description
CapitalizeNames OfDays	Boolean	Set / Get whether the first letter of days of the weeks are capitalized.
CorrectCapsLock	Boolean	Set / Get whether typing mistakes made with leaving the Caps Lock on is automatically corrected.
CorrectSentence Cap	Boolean	Set / Get whether the first letter of a sentence is capitalized if accidentally left in small case.
ReplaceText	Boolean	Set / Get whether Excel will automatically replace certain words with words from the AutoCorrect list.
TwoInitial Capitals	Boolean	Set / Get whether Excel will automatically change the second letter of a word to lowercase if the first letter is uppercase.

AutoCorrect Methods

Name	Returns	Parameters	Description
Add Replacement	Variant	What As String, Replacement As String	Adds a word (the What parameter) that will be automatically replaced with another word (the Replacement parameter) to the ReplacementList list array.
Delete Replacement	Variant	What As String	Deletes a word from the ReplacementList list so that it does not get replaced with another word automatically.
Replacement List	Variant	[Index]	Returns a multidimensional array of strings. The first column of the array holds the word that will be changed and the second column holds the replaced text. The Index parameter can be used to return an array containing a single word and its replacement.

Example: AutoCorrect Object

This example uses the AutoCorrect object to find the replacement to use for a given word:

```
Sub TestAutoCorrect()
    MsgBox "'(c)' is replaced by " & UseAutoCorrect("(c)")
End Sub

Function UseAutoCorrect(ByVal sWord As String) As String
    Dim i As Integer
    Dim vaRepList As Variant
    Dim sReturn As String

    'Default to returning the word we were given
    sReturn = sWord

    'Get the replacement list into an arrary
    vaRepList = Application.AutoCorrect.ReplacementList
```

```
   'Go through the replacement list
   For i = LBound(vaRepList) To UBound(vaRepList)
      'Do we have a match?
      If vaRepList(i, 1) = sWord Then

          'Return the replacement text
          sReturn = vaRepList(i, 2)

          'Jump out of the loop
          Exit For
      End If
   Next

   'Return the word, or its replacement if it has one
   UseAutoCorrect = sReturn
End Function
```

AutoFilter Object

The `AutoFilter` object provides the functionality equivalent to the AutoFilter feature in Excel. This object can programmatically filter a range of text for specific types of rows, hiding the rows that do not meet the filter criteria. Examples of filters include Top 10 rows in the column, rows matching specific values, and non-blank cells in the row. Using the Data | Filter | AutoFilter submenu in Excel can access this feature. The parent of the `AutoFilter` object is the `Worksheet` object (implying that a worksheet can have only one AutoFilter).

The `AutoFilter` object is used with the AutoFilter method of the `Range` object and the `AutoFilterType` property of the `Worksheet` object.

AutoFilter Common Properties

The `Application`, `Creator`, and `Parent` properties are defined at the beginning of this Appendix.

AutoFilter Properties

Name	Returns	Description
Filters	Filters	Read Only. Returns the collection of filters associated with the range that was autofiltered (e.g. non-blank rows)
Range	Range	Read Only. Returns the group of cells that have an AutoFilter applied to it.

Example: AutoFilter Object

This example demonstrates how to use the `AutoFilter`, `Filters` and `Filter` objects, by displaying the complete set of auto-filters currently in use:

```
Sub ShowAutoFilterCriteria()
   Dim oAF As AutoFilter, oFlt As Filter
   Dim sField As String
   Dim sCrit1 As String, sCrit2 As String
   Dim sMsg As String, i As Integer
```

```
    'Check if the sheet is filtered at all
    If ActiveSheet.AutoFilterMode = False Then
        MsgBox "The sheet does not have an AutoFilter"
        Exit Sub
    End If

    'Get the sheet's AutoFilter object
    Set oAF = ActiveSheet.AutoFilter

    'Loop through the Filters of the AutoFilter
    For i = 1 To oAF.Filters.Count

        'Get the field name from the first row
        'of the AutoFilter range
        sField = oAF.Range.Cells(1, i).Value

        'Get the Filter object
        Set oFlt = oAF.Filters(i)

        'If it is on...
        If oFlt.On Then

            'Get the standard filter criteria
            sMsg = sMsg & vbCrLf & sField & oFlt.Criteria1

            'If it's a special filter, show it
            Select Case oFlt.Operator
                Case xlAnd
                    sMsg = sMsg & " And " & sField & oFlt.Criteria2

                Case xlOr
                    sMsg = sMsg & " Or " & sField & oFlt.Criteria2

                Case xlBottom10Items
                    sMsg = sMsg & " (bottom 10 items)"

                Case xlBottom10Percent
                    sMsg = sMsg & " (bottom 10%)"

                Case xlTop10Items
                    sMsg = sMsg & " (top 10 items)"

                Case xlTop10Percent
                    sMsg = sMsg & " (top 10%)"

            End Select
        End If
    Next

    If sMsg = "" Then
        'No filters are applied, so say so
        sMsg = "The range " & oAF.Range.Address & " is not filtered."
    Else
        'Filters are applied, so show them
        sMsg = "The range " & oAF.Range.Address & " is filtered by:" & sMsg
    End If

    'Display the message
    MsgBox sMsg
End Sub
```

Axis Object and the Axes Collection

The Axes collection represents the all of Axes in an Excel chart. Each Axis object is equivalent to an axis in an Excel chart (e.g. X axis, Y axis, etc). The parent of the Axes collection is the Chart object. Besides the typical properties and methods associated with a collection object, the Axes collection also has a Count property that returns the number of Axis objects in the collection. Also, unlike most other collections, the Item method of the Axes collection has two parameters: Type and AxisGroup. Use one of the xlAxisType constants for the Type parameter (xlValue, xlCategory, or xlSeriesAxis). The optional second parameter, AxisGroup, can take one of the xlAxisGroup constants (xlPrimary or xlSecondary).

Axis Common Properties

The Application, Creator, and Parent properties are defined at the beginning of this Appendix.

Axis Properties

Name	Returns	Description
AxisBetween Categories	Boolean	Set / Get whether the value axis crosses the category axis between categories (as in Column charts) or aligned with the category label (as in Line charts).
AxisGroup	xlAxisGroup	Read Only. Returns whether the current axis is of the primary group (xlPrimary) or the secondary group (xlSecondary).
AxisTitle	AxisTitle	Read Only. Returns an object manipulating the axis title properties.
BaseUnit	xlTimeUnit	Set / Get what type of base units to have for a category axis. Use with BaseUnitIsAuto property. Fails on a value axis.
BaseUnitIsAuto	Boolean	Set / Get whether the Excel automatically chooses the base units for a category axis. Fails on a value axis.
Border	Border	Read Only. Returns the border's properties around the selected axis.
CategoryNames	Variant	Set / Get the category names for the axis as a string array.

Name	Returns	Description
CategoryType	xlCategory Type	Set / Get what type of axis to make the category axis. Fails on a value axis.
Crosses	xlAxisCrosses	Set / Get where one axis crosses with the other axis: at the minimum value, maximum value, Excel automatic, or some custom value.
CrossesAt	Double	Set / Get what value the other axis crosses the current one. Use when the Crosses property is xlAxisCrossesCustom.
DisplayUnit	xlDisplayUnit	Set / Get what sort of unit to display for the axis (e.g. xlThousands)
DisplayUnit Custom	Double	Set / Get the value to display units if the DisplayUnit property is set to xlCustom.
DisplayUnit Label	DisplayUnit Label	Read Only. Returns an object that to manipulate a unit label for an axis.
HasDisplayUnit Label	Boolean	Set / Get whether a display unit label created using the DisplayUnit or DisplayUnitCustom property is visible on the axis.
HasMajor Gridlines	Boolean	Set / Get whether major gridlines are displayed on the axis.
HasMinor Gridlines	Boolean	Set / Get whether minor gridlines are displayed on the axis
HasTitle	Boolean	Set / Get whether the axis has a title.
Height	Double	Read Only. Returns the height of the axis.

Name	Returns	Description
Left	Double	Read Only. Returns the position of the axis from the left edge of the chart.
Major Gridlines	Gridlines	Read Only. Returns an object to manipulate major gridline formatting associated.
MajorTickMark	xlTickMark	Set / Get how the major ticks should look like (e.g. inside the axis, outside the axis).
MajorUnit	Double	Set / Get what the value is between major blocks of a unit.
MajorUnitIsAuto	Boolean	Set / Get whether the value of MajorUnit is set automatically.
MajorUnitScale	xlTimeUnit	Set / Get what type to set for the major units.
MaximumScale	Double	Set / Get what the maximum value is for the axis.
MaximumScaleIs Auto	Boolean	Set / Get whether the maximum value for the axis is determined automatically.
MinimumScale	Double	Set / Get what the minimum value is for the axis.
MinimumScaleIs Auto	Boolean	Set / Get whether the minimum value for the axis is determined automatically.
MinorGridlines	Gridlines	Read Only. Returns an object to manipulate major gridline formatting associated.
MinorTickMark	xlTickMark	Set / Get how the minor ticks should look like (e.g. inside the axis, outside the axis).
MinorUnit	Double	Set / Get what the value is between minor blocks of a unit.
MinorUnitIsAuto	Boolean	Set / Get whether the value of MinorUnit is set automatically.
MinorUnitScale	xlTimeUnit	Set / Get what scale to set for the minor units.

Table Continued on Following Page

Name	Returns	Description
ReversePlotOrder	Boolean	Set / Get whether the unit values on the axis should be reversed.
ScaleType	xlScaleType	Set / Get the type of scale to use for the units: Linear or Logarithmic.
TickLabelPosition	xlTickLabel Position	Set / Get the position that the tick marks will appear in relation to the axis (e.g. low, high)
TickLabels	TickLabels	Read Only. Returns an object to manipulate properties of the tick labels of an axis.
TickLabelSpacing	Long	Set / Get how often to display the tick labels.
TickMarkSpacing	Long	Set / Get how often to display tick marks on an axis. Fails on a value axis.
Top	Double	Read Only. Returns the top of the axis in relation to the top edge of the chart.
Type	xlAxisType	Set / Get the type of axis (xlCategory, xlSeriesAxis, or xlValue).
Width	Double	Read Only. Returns the width of the axis.

Axis Methods

Name	Returns	Parameters	Description
Delete	Variant		Deletes the axis from the axes collection.
Select	Variant		Selects the axis on the chart.

Example: Axis Object and the Axes Collection

This example sets the labels for the X axis (independently of the data that's plotted) and applies some formatting.

```
Sub FormatXAxis()
    Dim oCht As Chart, oAxis As Axis

    'Get the first embedded chart on the sheet
    Set oCht = ActiveSheet.ChartObjects(1).Chart

    'Get it's X axis
    Set oAxis = oCht.Axes(xlCategory)

    'Format the X axis
    With oAxis
        .CategoryNames = Array("Item 1", "Item 2", "Item 3")
        .TickLabels.Orientation = 45
        .AxisBetweenCategories = True
        .ReversePlotOrder = False
        .MinorTickMark = xlTickMarkNone
        .MajorTickMark = xlTickMarkCross
    End With
End Sub
```

AxisTitle Object

The `AxisTitle` object contains the formatting and words associated with a chart axis title. The parent of the `AxisTitle` object is the `Axis` object. The `AxisTitle` object is used in coordination with the `HasTitle` property of the parent `Axis` object. The `HasTitle` property must be True for a child `AxisTitle` object to exist.

AxisTitle Common Properties

The `Application`, `Creator`, and `Parent` properties are defined at the beginning of this Appendix.

AxisTitle Properties

Name	Returns	Description
AutoScaleFont	Variant	Set / Get whether the font size will change automatically if the parent chart changes sizes.
Border	Border	Read Only. Returns the border's properties around the selected axis title.
Caption	String	Set / Get the axis title's text.
Characters	Characters	Read Only. Parameters: [Start], [Length] . Returns an object containing all the characters in the axis title. Allows manipulation on a character-by-character basis.

Table Continued on Following Page

Name	Returns	Description
Fill	ChartFill Format	Read Only. Returns an object containing fill formatting options for the chart axis title.
Font	Font	Read Only. Returns an object containing Font options for the chart axis title.
Horizontal Alignment	Variant	Set / Get how you want the axis title horizontally aligned. Use the xlAlign constants.
Interior	Interior	Read Only. Returns an object containing options to format the area in the chart title text area (e.g. interior color).
Left	Double	Set / Get the distance from the left edge of the axis title text area to the chart's left edge.
Name	String	Read Only. Returns the name of the axis title object.
Orientation	Variant	Set / Get the angle of the text for the axis title. The value can be in degrees (from –90 to 90) or one of the xlOrientation constants.
ReadingOrder	Long	Set / Get how the text is read (from left to right or right to left). Only applicable in appropriate languages.
Shadow	Boolean	Set / Get whether the axis title has a shadow effect.
Text	String	Set / Get the axis title's text.
Top	Double	Set / Get the distance from the top edge of the axis title text area to the chart's top edge.
Vertical Alignment	Variant	Set / Get how you want the axis title horizontally aligned. Use the xlVAlign constants.

AxisTitle Methods

Name	Returns	Parameters	Description
Delete	Variant		Deletes the axis title from the axis.
Select	Variant		Selects the axis title on the chart.

Example: AxisTitle Object

This example ensures the X axis has a title and sets the X axis title's caption and formatting:

```
Sub FormatXAxisTitle()
    Dim oCht As Chart, oAT As AxisTitle

    'Get the first embedded chart on the sheet
    Set oCht = ActiveSheet.ChartObjects(1).Chart

    'Give the X axis a title
    oCht.Axes(xlCategory).HasTitle = True

    'Get the title
    Set oAT = oCht.Axes(xlCategory).AxisTitle

    'Format the title
    With oAT
        .AutoScaleFont = False
        .Caption = "X Axis Title"
        .Font.Bold = True
    End With
End Sub
```

Border Object and the Borders Collection

The Borders collection contains the properties associated with four borders around the parent object. Parent objects of the Borders collection are the Range and the Style object. A Borders collection always has four borders. Use the xlBordersIndex constants with the Item property of Borders collection to access one of the Border objects in the collection.

Each Border object corresponds to a side or some sides of a border around a parent object. Some objects only allow access to all four sides of a border as a whole (e.g. left side of border can not be accessed independently). The following objects are parents of the Border object (not the Borders collection): Axis, AxisTitle, ChartArea, ChartObject, ChartTitle, DataLabel, DataTable, DisplayUnitLabel, Downbars, DropLines, ErrorBars, Floor, GridLines, HiLoLines, LeaderLines, Legend, LegendKey, OleObject, PlotArea, Point, Series, SeriesLines, TrendLine, UpBars, and Walls. The following collections are also possible parents of the Border object: DataLabels, ChartObjects, and OleObjects.

The Borders collection has a few properties besides the typical collection attributes. They are listed in the following table.

Borders Collection Properties

Name	Returns	Description
Color	Variant	Set / Get the color for all four of the borders in the collection. Use the RGB function to set the color.
ColorIndex	Variant	Set / Get the color for all four of the borders in the collection. Use the index number of a color in the current color palette to set the Color value.
Count	Long	Read Only. Returns the number of Border objects in the collection. Always returns four.
LineStyle	Variant	Set / Get the style of line to use for the borders (e.g. xlDash). Use the xlLineStyle constants to set the value.
Value	Variant	Set / Get the style of line to use for the borders (e.g. xlDash). Use the xlLineStyle constants to set the value. Same as LineStyle.
Weight	Variant	Set / Get how thick to make the borders in the collection (e.g. xlThin, xlThick). Use the xlBorderWeight constants.

Border Common Properties

The Application, Creator, and Parent properties are defined at the beginning of this Appendix.

Border Properties

Name	Returns	Description
Color	Variant	Set / Get the color for a border. Use the RGB function to set the color.
ColorIndex	Variant	Set / Get the color for a border. Use the index number of a color in the current color palette to set the color value.
LineStyle	Variant	Set / Get the style of line to use for a border (e.g xlDash). Use the xlLineStyle constants to set the value.
Weight	Variant	Set / Get how thick to make the border (e.g. xlThin, xlThick). Use the xlBorderWeight constants.

Example: Border Object and the Borders Collection

Applies a 3D effect to a range:

```
Sub TestFormat3D()
    'Format the selected range as 3D sunken
    Format3D Selection
End Sub

Sub Format3D(oRange As Range, Optional bSunken As Boolean = True)
    'Using the range...
    With oRange
        'Surround it with a white border
        .BorderAround Weight:=xlMedium, Color:=RGB(255, 255, 255)

        If bSunken Then
            'Sunken, so make the left and top dark-grey
            .Borders(xlEdgeLeft).Color = RGB(96, 96, 96)
            .Borders(xlEdgeTop).Color = RGB(96, 96, 96)
        Else
            'Raised, so make the right and bottom dark-grey
            .Borders(xlEdgeRight).Color = RGB(96, 96, 96)
            .Borders(xlEdgeBottom).Color = RGB(96, 96, 96)
        End If
    End With
End Sub
```

CalculatedFields Collection

See the 'PivotField Object, PivotFields Collection and the CalculatedFields Collection' section.

CalculatedItems Collection

See the 'PivotItem Object, PivotItems Collection, and the CalculatedItems Collection' section.

CalloutFormat Object

The `CalloutFormat` object corresponds to the line callouts on shapes. The parent of the `CalloutFormat` object is the `Shape` object.

CalloutFormat Common Properties

The `Application`, `Creator`, and `Parent` properties are defined at the beginning of this Appendix.

CalloutFormat Properties

Name	Returns	Description
Accent	msoTriState	Set / Get whether a vertical accent bar is used to separate the callout box from the line.
Angle	msoCalloutAngle Type	Set / Get the angle of the callout line in relation to the callout box.

Table Continued on Following Page

Name	Returns	Description
AutoAttach	msoTriState	Set / Get whether a callout line automatically changes where it is attached to on callout box depending on the where the line is pointing (left or right of the callout box).
AutoLength	msoTriState	Read Only. Return whether the callout line changes size automatically if the multi-segment callout box is moved.
Border	msoTriState	Set / Get whether the callout box has a border around it.
Drop	Single	Read Only. Returns the distance from the callout box to the spot where the callout line is pointing.
DropType	msoCalloutDrop Type	Read Only. Returns the spot on the callout box that attaches to the callout line.
Gap	Single	Set / Get the distance between the callout line end and the callout box.
Length	Single	Read Only. Returns the length of the first part of a callout line. AutoLength must be False.
Type	msoCalloutType	Set / Get the type of line callout used.

CalloutFormat Methods

Name	Returns	Parameters	Description
AutomaticLength			Sets the AutoLength property to True.
CustomDrop		Drop As Single	Uses the Drop parameter to set the distance from the callout box to the spot where the callout line is pointing.

Name	Returns	Parameters	Description
CustomLength		Length As Single	Sets the length of the first part of a callout line to the Length parameter and sets AutoLength to False.
PresetDrop		DropType As msoCallout DropType	Sets the spot on the callout box that attaches to the callout line using the DropType parameter.

Example: CalloutFormat Object

This example applies the same formatting to all the callouts in a worksheet:

```
Sub FormatAllCallouts()
    Dim oShp As Shape
    Dim oCF As CalloutFormat

    'Loop through all the shapes in the sheet
    For Each oShp In ActiveSheet.Shapes

        'Is this a callout?
        If oShp.Type = msoCallout Then

            'Yes - set its text box to autosize
            oShp.TextFrame.AutoSize = True

            'Get the CalloutFormat object
            Set oCF = oShp.Callout

            'Format the callout
            With oCF
                .Gap = 0
                .Border = msoFalse
                .Accent = msoTrue
                .Angle = msoCalloutAngle30
                .PresetDrop msoCalloutDropCenter
            End With
        End If
    Next
End Sub
```

Characters Object

The Characters object allows access to individual characters in a string of text. Characters can have some of the visual properties modified with this object. Possible parents of the Characters object are the AxisTitle, ChartTitle, DataLabel, and the Range object. Each of the parent objects can use the Characters([Start], [Length]) property to access a part of their respective texts. The Start parameter can specify which character to start at and the Length parameter can specify how many to take from the Start position.

Characters Common Properties

The `Application`, `Creator`, and `Parent` properties are defined at the beginning of this Appendix.

Characters Properties

Name	Returns	Description
Caption	String	Set / Get the full string contained in the Characters object.
Count	Long	Read Only. Returns the number of characters in the object.
Font	Font	Read Only. Returns an object allowing manipulation of the character's font.
Phonetic Characters	String	Set / Get the phonetic characters contained in the Characters object.
Text	String	Set / Get the full string contained in the Characters object.

Characters Methods

Name	Returns	Parameters	Description
Delete	Variant		Delete the characters in the collection.
Insert	Variant	String As String	Replaces the characters in the collection with the specified string

Example: Characters Object

This example formats all the capital letters in the active cell in red with 16 point bold text:

```
Sub FormatCellCapitals()
    Dim sText As String
    Dim oChars As Characters
    Dim i As Integer

    'Get the text of the active cell
    sText = ActiveCell.Text

    'Loop through the text
    For i = 1 To Len(sText)
        'Is this character a capital letter?
        If Asc(Mid(sText, i, 1)) > 64 And Asc(Mid(sText, i, 1)) < 91 Then

            'Yes, so get the Characters object
            Set oChars = ActiveCell.Characters(i, 1)
```

```
              'Format the Characters object in Red, 16pt Bold.
          With oChars
              .Font.Color = RGB(255, 0, 0)
              .Font.Size = 16
              .Font.Bold = True
          End With
      End If
   Next
End Sub
```

Chart Object and the Charts Collection

The `Charts` collection holds the collection of chart sheets in a workbook. The `Workbook` object is always the parent of the `Charts` collection. The `Charts` collection only holds the chart sheets. Individual charts can also be embedded in worksheets and dialog sheets. The `Chart` objects in the `Charts` collection can be accessed using the `Item` property. Either the name of the chart can be specified as a parameter to the `Item's` parameter or an index number describing the position of the chart in the workbook (from left to right).

The `Chart` object allows access to all of the attributes of a specific chart in Excel. This includes chart formatting, chart types, and other charting properties. The `Chart` object also exposes events that can be used programmatically.

The `Charts` collection has a few properties and methods besides the typical collection attributes. These are listed in the following table.

Charts Collection Properties and Methods

Name	Returns	Description
Count	Long	Read Only. Returns the number of charts in the collection.
HPageBreaks	HPage Breaks	Read Only. Returns a collection holding all the horizontal page breaks associated with the `Charts` collection.
VPageBreaks	VPage Breaks	Read Only. Returns a collection holding all the vertical page breaks associated with the `Charts` collection.
Visible	Variant	Set / Get whether the charts in the collection are visible. Also can set this to `xlVeryHidden` to not allow a user to make the charts in the collection visible.

Table Continued on Following Page

Name	Returns	Description
Copy		Method. Parameters: [Before], [After].
		Adds a new copy of the currently active chart to the position specified at the Before or After parameters.
Delete		Method. Deletes all the charts in the collection.
Move		Method. Parameters: [Before], [After].
		Moves the current chart to the position specified by the parameters.
PrintOut		Method. Parameters: [From], [To], [Copies], [Preview], [ActivePrinter], [PrintToFile], [Collate], [PrToFileName].
		Prints out the charts in the collection. The printer, number of copies, collation, and whether a print preview is desired can be specified with the parameters. Also, the sheets can be printed to a file with using the PrintToFile and PrToFileName parameters. The From and To parameters can be used to specify the range of printed pages.
PrintPreview		Method. Parameters: [EnableChanges]. Displays the current chart in the collection in a print preview mode. Set the EnableChanges parameter to False to disable the Margins and Setup buttons, hence not allowing the viewer to modify the chart's page setup.
Select		Method. Parameters: [Replace]. Selects the current chart in the collection.

Chart Common Properties

The `Application`, `Creator`, and `Parent` properties are defined at the beginning of this Appendix.

Chart Properties

Name	Returns	Description
Area3DGroup	Chart Group	Read Only. Returns a `ChartGroup` object containing the area chart group for a 3-D chart.
AutoScaling	Boolean	Set / Get whether Excel will stretch a 3-D chart to match its 2-D chart equivalent. `RightAngleAxes` must be `true`.
Bar3DGroup	Chart Group	Read Only. Returns a `ChartGroup` object containing the bar chart group for a 3-D chart.
BarShape	XlBar Shape	Set / Get the basic shape used in 3D bar or column charts (e.g. box, cylinder, pyramid, etc)
ChartArea	ChartArea	Read Only. Returns the part of a chart containing axes, titles, legends, and formatting properties.
ChartTitle	Chart Title	Read Only. Returns an object manipulating the chart title's properties. Use with the `HasTitle` property.
ChartType	XlChart Type	Set / Get what the type of chart is. This property determines what other chart properties are valid. For example, if the `ChartType` is set to `xl3DBarClustered` then the `Bar3DGroup` property can be used to access the chart group properties.
CodeName	String	Read Only. Returns the programmatic name of the chart set at design time in the VBA editor.
Column3DGroup	Chart Group	Read Only. Returns a `ChartGroup` object containing the column chart group for a 3-D chart.
Corners	Corners	Read Only. Returns an object holding all the corners of a 3D chart.

Table Continued on Following Page

Name	Returns	Description
DepthPercent	Long	Set / Get the percentage that a 3D chart depth (y-axis) is in relation to it's width (x-axis).
DisplayBlanks As	XlDisplay BlanksAs	Set / Get how blank cells are treated when plotting data in a chart. (e.g xlNotPlotted, xlZero, or xlInterpolated).
Elevation	Long	Set / Get what angle of elevation, in degrees, the viewer sees a 3D chart. Valid degrees vary depending on the type of 3D chart.
Floor	Floor	Read Only. Returns an object with the formatting properties of the floor (base) of a 3D chart.
GapDepth	Long	Set / Get the percentage depth of a data series in relation to the marker width.
HasAxis	Variant	Parameters: [Index1], [Index2]. Set / Get whether an axes exist for the chart. The parameters can be used to specify the axis type (using the xlAxisType constants with the first parameter) and the axis group (using the xlAxisGroup constants with the second parameter).
HasDataTable	Boolean	Set / Get whether a data table is associated (and therefore displayed). Use with the DataTable property.
HasLegend	Boolean	Set / Get whether the chart has a legend. Use with the Legend property.
HasPivotFields	Boolean	Set / Get whether PivotChart controls are displayed for the PivotChart. Can only set to True if using a PivotChart report.
HasTitle	Boolean	Set / Get whether the chart has a title. Use with the ChartTitle property.

Name	Returns	Description
Hyperlinks	Hyperlinks	Read Only. Returns the collection of hyperlinks associated with the chart.
Index	Long	Read Only. Returns the spot in the parent collection that the current chart is located.
Legend	Legend	Read Only. Returns the formatting properties for a Legend. Use with the HasLegend property.
Line3DGroup	ChartGroup	Read Only. Returns a ChartGroup object containing the line chart group for a 3-D chart.
Name	String	Set / Get the name of the chart.
Next	Object	Read Only. Returns the next sheet in the workbook (from left to right) as an object.
PageSetup	PageSetup	Read Only. Returns an object to manipulate the page setup properties for the chart.
Perspective	Long	Sets the perspective, in degrees, that a 3D chart will be viewed as if the RightAngleAxes property is set to False.
Pie3DGroup	ChartGroup	Read Only. Returns a ChartGroup object containing the pie chart group for a 3-D chart.
PivotLayout	PivotLayout	Read Only. Returns an object to manipulate the location of fields for a PivotChart report.
PlotArea	PlotArea	Read Only. Returns an object to manipulate formatting, gridlines, data markers and other visual items for the area where the chart is actually plotted. Inside the chart area.
PlotBy	XlRowCol	Set / Get whether columns in the original data are used as individual data series (xlColumns) or if the rows in the original data are used as data series (xlRows).

Table Continued on Following Page

Name	Returns	Description
Previous		Read Only. Returns the previous sheet in the workbook (from right to left) as an object.
Protect Contents	Boolean	Read Only. Returns whether the chart and everything in it is protected from changes.
ProtectData	Boolean	Set / Get whether the source data can be redirected for a chart.
ProtectDrawing Objects	Boolean	Read Only. Returns whether the shapes in the chart can be modified (ProtectDrawingObjects = False).
Protect Formatting	Boolean	Set / Get whether formatting can be changed for a chart.
ProtectGoal Seek	Boolean	Set / Get whether the user can modify the points on a chart with a mouse action.
ProtectionMode	Boolean	Read Only. Returns whether protection has been applied to the user interface. Even if a chart has user interface protection on, any VBA code associated with the chart can still be accessed.
Protect Selection	Boolean	Set / Get whether parts of a chart can be selected and if shapes can be put into a chart.
RightAngleAxes	Variant	Set / Get whether axes are fixed at right angles for 3D charts even if the perspective of the chart changes.
Rotation	Variant	Set / Get what angle of rotation around the z-axis, in degrees, the viewer sees on a 3D chart. Valid degrees vary depending on the type of 3D chart.
Scripts	Scripts	Read Only. Returns the collection of VBScript code associated with a chart (typically to later use on Web pages).
Shapes	Shapes	Read Only. Returns all the shapes contained by the chart.

Name	Returns	Description
SizeWithWindow	Boolean	Set / Get whether chart sheets automatically change sizes to match the window size.
SurfaceGroup	ChartGroup	Read Only. Returns a ChartGroup object containing the surface chart group for a 3-D chart.
Visible	XlSheet Visibility	Set / Get whether the chart is visible or not. The Visible property can also be set to xlVeryHidden to make the chart inaccessible to the end user.
Walls	Walls	Read Only. Returns an object to manipulate the formatting of the walls on a 3D chart.
WallsAnd Gridlines2D	Boolean	Set / Get whether gridlines and walls are drawn in a 2D manner on a 3D bar charts, 3D stacked area charts, and 3D clustered column charts.

Chart Methods

Name	Returns	Parameters	Description
Activate			Activates the chart making it the ActiveChart.
Apply CustomType		ChartType As XlChartType, [TypeName]	Changes the chart type to the one specified in the ChartType parameter. If the ChartType is xlUserDefined then the second parameter can specify the custom chart type name.

Table Continued on Following Page

Name	Returns	Parameters	Description
ApplyData Labels		Type As XlDataLabelsType, [LegendKey], [AutoText], [HasLeaderLines]	Sets the point labels for a chart. The Type parameter specifies whether no label, a value, a percentage of the whole, or a category label is shown. The legend key can appear by the point by setting the LegendKey parameter to True.
AreaGroups	Object	[Index]	Returns either a single area chart group (ChartGroup) or a collection of area chart groups (ChartGroups) for a 2D chart.
Axes	Object	Type, AxisGroup As XlAxisGroup	Returns the Axis object or the Axes collection for the associated chart. The type of axis and the axis group can be specified with the parameters.
BarGroups	Object	[Index]	Returns either a single bar chart group (ChartGroup) or a collection of bar chart groups (ChartGroups) for a 2D chart.

Name	Returns	Parameters	Description
Chart Groups	Object	[Index]	Returns either a single chart group (ChartGroup) or a collection of chart groups (ChartGroups) for a chart.
Chart Objects	Object	[Index]	Returns either a single embedded chart (ChartObject) or a collection of embedded charts (ChartObjects) in a chart.
Chart Wizard		[Source], [Gallery], [Format], [PlotBy], [CategoryLabels], [SeriesLabels], [HasLegend], [Title], [CategoryTitle], [ValueTitle], [ExtraTitle]	A single method to modify the key properties associated with a chart. Specify the properties that you want to change. The Source specifies the data source. Gallery specifies the chart type. Format can specify one of the 10 built-in chart auto-formats. The rest of the parameters set up how the source will be read, the source of category labels, the source of the series labels, whether a legend appears, and the titles of the chart and the axis. If Source is not specified this method can only be used if the sheet containing the chart is active.

Table Continued on Following Page

Name	Returns	Parameters	Description
Check Spelling		[Custom Dictionary], [IgnoreUppercase], [AlwaysSuggest], [SpellLang]	Checks the spelling of the text in the chart. A custom dictionary can be specified (CustomDictionary), all UPPERCASE words can be ignored (IgnoreUppercase), and Excel can be set to display a list of suggestions (AlwaysSuggest).
Column Groups	Object	[Index]	Returns either a single column chart group (ChartGroup) or a collection of column chart groups (ChartGroups) for a 2D chart.
Copy		[Before], [After]	Adds a new copy of the chart to the position specified at the Before or After parameters.
Copy Picture		[Appearance As XlPictureAppearance], [Format As XlCopyPictureFormat], [Size As XlPictureAppearance]	Copies the chart into the clipboard as a picture. The Appearance parameter can be used to specify whether the picture is copied as it looks on the screen or when printed. The Format parameter can specify the type of picture that will be put into the clipboard. The Size parameter is used with chart sheets to describe the size of the picture.

Name	Returns	Parameters	Description
Create Publisher		Edition, Appearance As XlPicture Appearance, Size As XlPicture Appearance, [ContainsPICT], [ContainsBIFF], [ContainsRTF], [ContainsVALU]	Used on the Macintosh to create an image of the chart in a standard format. Equivalent to CopyPicture on the PC.
Delete			Deletes the chart.
Deselect			Unselects the chart object.
Doughnut Groups	Object	[Index]	Returns either a single doughnut chart group (ChartGroup) or a collection of doughnut chart groups (ChartGroups) for a 2D chart.
Evaluate	Variant	Name	Evaluates the Name string expression as if it were entered into a worksheet cell.
Export	Boolean	Filename As String, [FilterName], [Interactive]	Saves the chart as a picture (JPEG or GIF format) at the name specified by Filename.

Table Continued on Following Page

Name	Returns	Parameters	Description
GetChart Element		x As Long, y As Long, ElementID As Long, Arg1 As Long, Arg2 As Long	Returns what is located at the coordinates x and y of the chart. Only the first two parameters are sent. Variables must be put in the last three parameters. After the method is run the last three parameters can be checked for return values. The ElementID parameter will return one of the XlChartItem parameters. The Arg1 and Arg2 parameters may or may not hold data depending on the type of element.
Line Groups	Object	[Index]	Returns either a single line chart group (ChartGroup) or a collection of line chart groups (ChartGroups) for a 2D chart.
Location	Chart	Where As XlChartLocation, [Name]	Moves the chart to the location specified by the Where and Name parameters. The Where can specify if the chart is moving to become a chart sheet or an embedded object.

Name	Returns	Parameters	Description
Move		[Before], [After]	Moves the chart to the position specified by the parameters.
OLE Objects	Object	[Index]	Returns either a single OLE Object (OLEObject) or a collection of OLE objects (OLEObjects) for a chart.
Paste		[Type]	Pastes the data or pictures from the clipboard into the chart. The Type parameter can be used to specify if only formats, formulas or everything is pasted.
PieGroups	Object	[Index]	Returns either a single pie chart group (ChartGroup) or a collection of pie chart groups (ChartGroups) for a 2D chart.
PrintOut		[From], [To], [Copies], [Preview], [ActivePrinter], [PrintToFile], [Collate], [PrToFileName]	Prints out the chart. The printer, number of copies, collation, and whether a print preview is desired can be specified with the parameters. Also, the sheets can be printed to a file by using the PrintToFile and PrToFileName parameters. The From and To parameters can be used to specify the range of printed pages.

Table Continued on Following Page

Name	Returns	Parameters	Description
Print Preview		[EnableChanges]	Displays the current chart in the collection in a print preview mode. Set the EnableChanges parameter to False to disable the Margins and Setup buttons, hence not allowing the viewer to modify the page setup.
Protect		[Password], [DrawingObjects], [Contents], [Scenarios], [UserInterface Only]	Protects the chart from changes. A case sensitive Password can be specified. Also, whether shapes are protected (DrawingObjects), the entire contents are protected (Contents), and whether the only the user interface is protected (UserInterfaceOnly).
Radar Groups	Object	[Index]	Returns either a single radar chart group (ChartGroup) or a collection of radar chart groups (ChartGroups) for a 2D chart.
Refresh			Refresh the chart with the data source.

Name	Returns	Parameters	Description
SaveAs		Filename As String, [FileFormat], [Password], [WriteRes Password], [ReadOnly Recommended], [CreateBackup], [AddToMru], [TextCodepage], [TextVisual Layout]	Saves the current chart into a new workbook with the file name specified by the Filename parameter. A file format, password, write-only password, creation of backup files, and other properties of the saved file can be specified with the parameters.
Select		[Replace]	Selects the chart.
Series Collection	Object	[Index]	Returns either a single series (Series) or a collection of series (SeriesCollection) for a chart.
Set Background Picture		FileName As String	Sets the chart's background to the picture specified by the FileName parameter.
SetSource Data		Source As Range, [PlotBy]	Sets the source of the chart's data to the range specified by the Source parameter. The PlotBy parameter uses the XlRowCol constants to choose whether rows or columns of data will be plotted.
Unprotect		[Password]	Deletes the protection set up for a chart. If the chart was protected with a password, the password must be specified now.

Table Continued on Following Page

Name	Returns	Parameters	Description
XYGroups	Object	[Index]	Returns either a single scatter chart group (ChartGroup) or a collection of scatter chart groups (ChartGroups) for a 2D chart.

Chart Events

Name	Parameters	Description
Activate		Triggered when a chart is made to have focus.
Before Double Click	ElementID As XlChartItem, Arg1 As Long, Arg2 As Long, Cancel As Boolean	Triggered just before a user double-clicks on a chart. The element that was double-clicked in the chart is passed in to event procedure as ElementID. The Arg1 and Arg2 parameters may or may not hold values depending on the ElementID. The double-click action can be canceled by setting the Cancel parameter to True.
Before Right Click	Cancel As Boolean	Triggered just before a user right-clicks on a chart. The right-click action can be canceled by setting the Cancel parameter to True.
Calculate		Triggered after new or changed data is plotted on the chart.
Deactivate		Triggered when the chart loses focus.
DragOver		Triggered when a cell range is dragged on top of a chart. Typically used to change the mouse pointer or give a status message.
DragPlot		Triggered when a cell range is dropped onto a chart. Typically used to modify chart attributes.

Name	Parameters	Description
MouseDown	Button As XlMouseButton, Shift As Long, x As Long, y As Long	Triggered when the mouse button is pressed down on a chart. Which mouse button is pressed is passed in with the Button parameter. The Shift parameter holds information regarding the state of the *Shift, Ctrl,* and *Alt* keys. The x and y parameters hold the x and y coordinates of the mouse pointer.
MouseMove	Button As XlMouseButton, Shift As Long, x As Long, y As Long	Triggered when the mouse is moved on a chart. Which mouse button is pressed is passed in with the Button parameter. The Shift parameter holds information regarding the state of the *Shift, Ctrl,* and *Alt* keys. The x and y parameters hold the x and y coordinates of the mouse pointer.
MouseUp	Button As XlMouseButton, Shift As Long, x As Long, y As Long	Triggered when the mouse button is released on a chart. Which mouse button is pressed is passed in with the Button parameter. The Shift parameter holds information regarding the state of the *Shift, Ctrl,* and *Alt* keys. The x and y parameters hold the x and y coordinates of the mouse pointer.
Resize		Triggered when the chart is resized.
Select	ElementID As XlChartItem, Arg1 As Long, Arg2 As Long	Triggered when one of the elements in a chart is selected. The element that was selected in the chart is passed in to event procedure as ElementID. The Arg1 and Arg2 parameters may or may not hold values depending on the ElementID.
Series Change	SeriesIndex As Long, PointIndex As Long	Triggered when the value of a point on a chart is changed. SeriesIndex returns the location of the series in the chart series collection. PointIndex returns the point location in the series.

Example: Chart Object and the Charts Collection

This example creates a 3D chart from the table containing the active cell, formats it and saves a picture of it as a .jpg image.

```
Sub CreateAndExportChart()
    Dim oCht As Chart

    'Create a new (blank) chart
    Set oCht = Charts.Add

    'Format the chart
    With oCht
        .ChartType = xl3DColumnStacked

        'Set the data source and plot by columns
        .SetSourceData Source:=Selection.CurrentRegion, PlotBy:=xlColumns

        'Create a new sheet for the chart
        .Location Where:=xlLocationAsNewSheet

        'Size and shape matches the window it's in
        .SizeWithWindow = True

        'Turn of stretching of chart
        .AutoScaling = False

        'Set a title up
        .HasTitle = True
        .ChartTitle.Caption = "Main Chart"

        'No titles for the axes
        .Axes(xlCategory).HasTitle = False
        .Axes(xlSeries).HasTitle = False
        .Axes(xlValue).HasTitle = False

        'Set the 3D view of the chart
        .RightAngleAxes = False
        .Elevation = 50       'degrees
        .Perspective = 30 'degrees
        .Rotation = 20        'degrees
        .HeightPercent = 100

        'No data labels should appear
        .ApplyDataLabels Type:=xlDataLabelsShowNone

        'Save a picture of the chart as a jpg image
        .Export "c:\" & .Name & ".jpg", "jpg", False
    End With
End Sub
```

ChartArea Object

The ChartArea object contains the formatting options associated with a chart area. For 2D charts ChartArea includes the axes, axes titles and chart titles. For 3D charts ChartArea includes the chart title and its legend. The part of the chart where data is plotted (plot area) is not part of the ChartArea object. Please see the PlotArea object for formatting related to the plot area. The parent of the ChartArea is always the Chart object.

ChartArea Common Properties

The Application, Creator, and Parent properties are defined at the beginning of this Appendix.

ChartArea Properties

Name	Returns	Description
AutoScaleFont	Variant	Set / Get whether the font size changes in the ChartArea whenever the Chart changes sizes.
Border	Border	Read Only. Returns the border's attributes around the selected chart area.
Fill	ChartFill Format	Read Only. Returns an object to manipulate the fill attributes of the chart area.
Font	Font	Read Only. Returns access to Font properties such as Type and Size.
Height	Double	Set / Get the height of the chart area in points.
Interior	Interior	Read Only. Returns an object containing options to format the inside area of the chart area (e.g. interior color).
Left	Double	Set / Get the left edge of the chart area in relation to the chart in points.
Name	String	Read Only. Returns the name of the chart area.
Shadow	Boolean	Set / Get whether a shadow effect appears around the chart area.
Top	Double	Set / Get the top edge of the chart area in relation to the chart in points.
Width	Double	Set / Get the width of the chart area in points.

ChartArea Methods

Name	Returns	Parameters	Description
Clear	Variant		Clears the chart area.
Clear Contents	Variant		Clears the data from the chart area without affecting formatting.

Name	Returns	Parameters	Description
Clear Formats	Variant		Clears the formatting from the chart area without affecting the data.
Copy	Variant		Copies the chart area into the clipboard.
Select	Variant		Activates and selects the chart area.

Example: ChartArea Object

Apply formatting to the chart area:

```
Sub FormatChartArea()
    Dim oCA As ChartArea

    Set oCA = Charts(1).ChartArea

    With oCA
        .Border.LineStyle = xlContinuous
        .Fill.PresetTextured msoTextureCanvas
        .Fill.Visible = msoTrue
    End With
End Sub
```

ChartColorFormat Object

The ChartColorFormat object describes a color of the parent ChartFillFormat. For example, the ChartFillFormat object contains a BackColor property that returns a ChartColorFormat object to set the color.

ChartColorFormat Common Properties

The Application, Creator, and Parent properties are defined at the beginning of this Appendix.

ChartColorFormat Properties

Name	Returns	Description
RGB	Long	Read Only. Returns the red-green-blue value associated with color.
SchemeColor	Long	Set / Get the color of ChartColorFormat using an index value corresponding to the current color scheme.
Type	Long	Read Only. Returns whether the color is an RGB, mixed, or scheme type.

Example: ChartColorFormat Object

This example sets a chart's fill pattern to built-in colour number 6, then displays the RGB values for the colour.

```
Sub SetChartColorFormat()
    Dim oCCF As ChartColorFormat

    With Charts(3).PlotArea.Fill
        'Make sure we're using a Fill pattern
        .Visible = True

        'Get the ChartColorFormat for the ForeColor
        Set oCCF = .ForeColor

        'Set it to built-in colour #6
        oCCF.SchemeColor = 6

        'Read off colour 6's RGB values
        MsgBox "ForeColor #6 RGB is:" & vbCrLf & _
        "Red = " & ((oCCF.RGB And &HFF0000) / &H10000) & vbCrLf & _
        "Green = " & ((oCCF.RGB And &HFF00) / &H100) & vbCrLf & _
        "Blue = " & ((oCCF.RGB And &HFF))
    End With
End Sub
```

ChartFillFormat Object

The `ChartFillFormat` object represents the fill formatting associated its parent object. This object allows manipulation of foreground colors, background colors and patterns associated with the parent object.

ChartFillFormat Common Properties

The `Application`, `Creator`, and `Parent` properties are defined at the beginning of this Appendix.

ChartFillFormat Properties

Name	Returns	Description
BackColor	ChartColor Format	Read Only. Returns the background color through the `ChartColorFormat` object.
ForeColor	ChartColor Format	Read Only. Returns the foreground color through the `ChartColorFormat` object.
Gradient ColorType	msoGradient ColorType	Read Only. Returns what type of gradient fill color concept is used
Gradient Degree	Single	Read Only. Returns how dark or light the gradient fill is.
Gradient Style	msoGradient Style	Read Only. Returns the orientation of the gradient that is used.

Table Continued on Following Page

Name	Returns	Description
Gradient Variant	Long	Read Only. Returns the variant used for the gradient from the center.
Pattern	msoPatternType	Read Only. Returns the pattern used for the fill, if any.
Preset Gradient Type	msoPreset GradientType	Read Only. Returns the type of gradient that is used.
Preset Texture	msoPreset Texture	Read Only. Returns the non-custom texture of the fill.
Texture Name	String	Read Only. Returns the custom texture name of the fill.
Texture Type	msoTextureType	Read Only. Returns whether the texture is custom, preset, or mixed.
Type	msoFillType	Set / Get how transparent the fill is. From 0 (opaque) to 1 (clear)
Visible	msoTriState	Read Only. Returns if the fill is a texture, gradient, solid, background, picture or mixed.

ChartFillFormat Methods

Name	Returns	Parameters	Description
OneColor Gradient		Style As msoGradientStyle, Variant As Long, Degree As Single	Set the style, variant and degree for a one-color gradient fill.
Patterned		Pattern As msoPatternType	Set the pattern for a fill.
Preset Gradient		Style As msoGradientStyle, Variant As Long, PresetGradientType As msoPresetGradientType	Choose the style, variant, and preset gradient type for a gradient fill.
Preset Textured		PresetTexture As msoPresetTexture	Set the preset texture for a fill.

Name	Returns	Parameters	Description
Solid			Set the fill to a solid color.
TwoColor Gradient		Style As msoGradientStyle, Variant As Long	Set the style for a two-color gradient fill.
User Picture		[PictureFile], [PictureFormat], [PictureStackUnit], [PicturePlacement]	Set the fill to the picture in the PictureFile format.
User Textured		TextureFile As String	Set the custom texture for a fill with the TextureFile format.

Example: ChartFillFormat Object

```
Sub FormatPlotArea()
    Dim oCFF As ChartFillFormat

    'Get the ChartFillFormat for the plot area
    Set oCFF = ActiveSheet.ChartObjects(1).Chart.PlotArea.Fill

    'Format the fill area
    With oCFF
        .TwoColorGradient Style:=msoGradientDiagonalUp, Variant:=1
        .Visible = True
        .ForeColor.SchemeColor = 6
        .BackColor.SchemeColor = 7
    End With
End Sub
```

ChartGroup Object and the ChartGroups Collection

The ChartGroups collection holds all the plotting information associated with the parent chart. A chart can have more than one ChartGroup associated with it. For example, a single chart can contain both a line and a bar chart associated with it. The ChartGroups property of the Chart object can be used to access the ChartGroups collection. Also, the PieGroups and LineGroups properties of the Chart object will also return only chart groups of pie chart types and line chart types, respectively. Besides the typical properties associated with a collection, the ChartGroups collection also has a Count property that returns the number of ChartGroup objects in the collection. The parent of the ChartGroups collection or the ChartGroup object is the Chart object.

The ChartGroup object includes all of the plotted points associated a particular chart type. A ChartGroup can hold many series of points (each column or row of the original data). Each series can contain many points (each cell of the original data).

A Chart can contain more then one ChartGroup associated with it. The Bar3DGroup, Column3DGroup, Line3DGroup, Pie3DGroup, and the SurfaceGroup properties of the Chart object can be used to access a particular chart group of the corresponding chart type. The AreaGroups, BarGroups, ColumnGroups, DoughnutGroups, LineGroups, PieGroups, RadarGroups, and XYGroups methods of the Chart object can be used to return either a ChartGroup object or a ChartGroups collection.

ChartGroup Common Properties

The Application, Creator, and Parent properties are defined at the beginning of this Appendix.

ChartGroup Properties

Name	Returns	Description
AxisGroup	XlAxis Group	Set / Get whether the chart group is primary or secondary.
Bubble Scale	Long	Set / Get the percentage increase in the size of bubbles from the default size. Valid values from 0 to 300 percent. Valid only for bubble chart group.
Doughnut HoleSize	Long	Set / Get how large the hole in a doughnut chart group is. The value is a percentage of the size of the chart. Valid values from 10 to 90 percent. Valid only on doughnut chart groups.
DownBars	DownBars	Read Only. Returns an object to manipulate the formatting options of down bars on a line chart group. Valid only on line chart groups. Use with the HasUpDownBars property.
DropLines	DropLines	Read Only. Returns an object to manipulate the formatting options of drop lines on a line or area chart group. Valid only on line or area chart groups. Use with the HasDropLines property.
FirstSlice Angle	Long	Set / Get what angle to use for the first slice of a pie or doughnut chart groups (the first data point plotted on the chart).

Name	Returns	Description
GapWidth	Long	Set / Get how big to make the gap between the columns of different data series. Also, when dealing with Bar of Pie charts or Pie of Pie charts, the GapWidth describes the distance from the main chart to the secondary chart (when the ChartType is xlPieOfPie or xlBarOfPie for the parent chart).
Has 3Dshading	Boolean	Set / Get whether 3D shading is applied to the chart group visuals.
HasDrop Lines	Boolean	Set / Get whether the chart group has drop lines. Use with the DownLines property.
HasHiLo Lines	Boolean	Set / Get whether the chart group has high-low lines. Use with the HiLoLines property.
HasRadar AxisLabels	Boolean	Set / Get whether axis labels are put on a radar chart. Valid only for radar chart groups.
HasSeries Lines	Boolean	Set / Get whether the chart group has series lines. Use with the SeriesLines property.
HasUpDown Bars	Boolean	Set / Get whether the chart group has up and down bars. Use with the DownBars and UpBars property.
HiLoLines	HiLoLines	Read Only. Returns an object to manipulate the formatting of high-low lines in a line chart. Valid only for line charts.
Index	Long	Read Only. Returns the spot in the parent collection that the current ChartGroup object is located.
Overlap	Long	Set / Get whether bars and columns in a series will overlap each other or have a gap between them. A value from −100 to 100 can be specified where −100 will put a gap between each bar / column equal to the bar / column width and 100 will stack the bars / columns on top of each other. Valid only for 2D bar and column chart groups.

Table Continued on Following Page

Name	Returns	Description
RadarAxis Labels	TickLabels	Read Only. Returns an object to manipulate the formatting and labels associated with radar axis labels. Valid only for radar chart groups.
SecondPlot Size	Long	Set / Get the percentage of size the secondary part of a Pie of Pie or Bar of Pie chart group as a percentage of the main Pie.
Series Lines	Series Lines	Read Only. Returns an object to manipulate the formatting associated with the series lines in a chart group. A series line connects same series of data appearing in a stacked column chart groups, stacked bar chart groups, Pie of Pie chart groups, or Bar of Pie chart groups. Use with the HasSeriesLines property.
Show Negative Bubbles	Boolean	Set / Get whether bubbles with negative data values are shown. Valid only on bubble chart groups.
Size Represents	XlSize Represents	Set / Get whether the value of the data points are represented by the size or the area of bubbles on a bubble chart group. Valid only on bubble chart groups.
SplitType	XlChart SplitType	Set / Get how the two charts in Pie of Pie chart group and Bar of Pie chart group are split up. For example, the chart can be split by percentage of value (xlSplitByPercentValue) or be split by value (xlSplitByValue).
SplitValue	Variant	Set / Get the value that will be combined in the main pie chart but split up in the secondary chart in a Pie of Pie or Bar of Pie chart group.
UpBars	UpBars	Returns an object to manipulate the formatting options of up bars on a line chart group. Valid only on line chart groups. Use with the HasUpDownBars property.
VaryBy Categories	Boolean	Set / Get whether different colors are assigned to different categories in a single series of a chart group. The chart can only contain a single data series for this to work.

ChartGroup Methods

Name	Returns	Parameters	Description
Series Collection	Object	[Index]	Returns either a single series (Series) or a collection of series (SeriesCollection) for a chart.

Example: ChartGroup Object and the ChartGroups Collection

These set the gap width of all column groups in the chart to 10% and set each column to have a different colour

```
Sub FormatColumns()
    Dim oCht As Chart
    Dim oCG As ChartGroup

    For Each oCG In Charts(1).ColumnGroups
        oCG.GapWidth = 10
        oCG.VaryByCategories = True
    Next
End Sub
```

ChartObject Object and the ChartObjects Collection

The ChartObjects collection holds all of the embedded Chart objects in a worksheet, chart sheet, or dialog sheet. This collection does not include the actual chart sheets themselves. Chart sheets can be accessed through the Charts collection. Each Chart in the ChartObjects collection is accessed through the ChartObject object. The ChartObject acts as a wrapper for the embedded chart itself. The Chart property of the ChartObject is used to access the actual chart. The ChartObject object also contains properties to modify the formatting of the embedded chart (e.g. Height, Width).

The ChartObjects collection contains many properties besides the typical collection attributes. These properties are listed below.

ChartObjects Collection Properties and Methods

Name	Returns	Description
Border	Border	Read Only. Returns the border's properties around the collection of chart objects.
Count	Long	Read Only. Returns the number of ChartObject objects in the collection.
Enabled	Boolean	Set / Get whether any macros associated with each ChartObject object in the collection can be triggered by the user.

Table Continued on Following Page

Name	Returns	Description
Height	Double	Set / Get the height of the ChartObject in the collection if there is only one object in the collection.
Interior	Interior	Read Only. Returns an object containing options to format the inside area of all the Chart objects in the collection (e.g. interior color).
Left	Double	Set / Get the distance from the left edge of the ChartObject to the left edge of the parent sheet. This property only works if there is only one ChartObject in the collection.
Locked	Boolean	Set / Get whether the ChartObject is locked when the parent sheet is protected. This property only works if there is only one ChartObject in the collection.
Placement	Variant	Set / Get how the ChartObject object is anchored to the sheet (e.g. free floating, move with cells). Use the XlPlacement constants to set this property. This property only works if there is only one ChartObject in the collection.
Print Object	Boolean	Set / Get whether the embedded chart on the sheet will be printed when the sheet is printed. This property only works if there is only one ChartObject in the collection.
Rounded Corners	Boolean	Set / Get whether the corners of the embedded chart is rounded (True) or right angles (False). This property only works if there is only one ChartObject in the collection.
Shadow	Boolean	Set / Get whether a shadow appears around the embedded chart. This property only works if there is only one ChartObject in the collection.
Shape Range	Shape Range	Read Only. Returns the ChartObjects in the collection as Shape objects.
Top	Double	Set / Get the distance from top edge of the ChartObject to the top of the parent sheet. This property only works if there is only one ChartObject object in the collection.
Visible	Boolean	Set / Get whether all the ChartObject objects in the collection are visible.

Name	Returns	Description
Width	Double	Set / Get the width of the ChartObject in the collection if there is only one ChartObject object in the collection.
Add	Chart Object	Method. Parameters: Left As Double, Top As Double, Width As Double, Height As Double. Adds a ChartObject to the collection of ChartObjects. The position of the new ChartObject can be specified by using the Left, Top, Width, and Height parameters.
BringTo Front	Variant	Method. Brings all the ChartObject objects in the collection to the front of all the other objects.
Copy	Variant	Method. Copies all the ChartObject objects in the collection into the clipboard.
Copy Picture	Variant	Method. Parameters: [Appearance As XlPictureAppearance], [Format As XlCopyPictureFormat], [Size As XlPictureAppearance]. Copies the Chart objects in the collection into the clipboard as a picture. The Appearance parameter can be used to specify whether the picture is copied as it looks on the screen or when printed. The Format parameter can specify the type of picture that will be put into the clipboard.
Cut	Variant	Method. Cuts all the ChartObject objects in the collection into the clipboard.
Delete	Variant	Method. Deletes all the ChartObject objects in the collection into the clipboard.
Duplicate		Method. Duplicates all the ChartObject objects in the collection into the parent sheet. (e.g. if you had two ChartObject objects in the parent sheet and used this method then you would have four ChartObject objects).
Select	Variant	Method. Parameters: [Replace]. Selects all the ChartObject objects in the collection.
SendTo Back	Variant	Method. Brings the ChartObject objects in the collection to the back of other objects.

ChartObject Common Properties

The Application, Creator, and Parent properties are defined at the beginning of this Appendix.

ChartObject Properties

Name	Returns	Description
Border	Border	Read Only. Returns the border's properties around the embedded chart.
Bottom RightCell	Range	Read Only. Returns the single cell range located under the lower-right corner of the ChartObject.
Chart	Chart	Read Only. Returns the actual chart associated with the ChartObject.
Enabled	Boolean	Set / Get whether a macro associated with the ChartObject is capable of being triggered.
Height	Double	Set / Get the height of embedded chart.
Index	Long	Read Only. Returns the position of the ChartObject among the parent collection.
Interior	Interior	Read Only. Returns an object containing options to format the inside area of the chart object (e.g. interior color).
Left	Double	Set / Get the distance from left edge of the ChartObject to the left edge of the parent sheet
Locked	Boolean	Set / Get whether the ChartObject is locked when the parent sheet is protected.
Name	String	Set / Get the name of the ChartObject.
Placement	Variant	Set / Get how the ChartObject object is anchored to the sheet (e.g. free floating, move with cells). Use the XlPlacement constants to set this property.
Print Object	Boolean	Set / Get whether the embedded chart on the sheet will be printed when the sheet is printed.
Protect Chart Object	Boolean	Set / Get whether the embedded chart can change sizes, be moved, or deleted from the parent sheet.
Rounded Corners	Boolean	Set / Get whether the corners of the embedded chart is rounded (True) or right angles (False).
Shadow	Boolean	Set / Get whether a shadow appears around the embedded chart.
Shape Range	Shape Range	Read Only. Returns the ChartObject as a Shape object.
Top	Double	Set / Get the distance from top edge of the ChartObject to the top of the parent sheet.

Name	Returns	Description
TopLeft Cell	Range	Read Only. Returns the single cell range located above the top-left corner of the ChartObject.
Visible	Boolean	Set / Get whether the ChartObject object is visible.
Width	Double	Set / Get the width of embedded chart.
ZOrder	Long	Read Only. Returns the position of the embedded chart among all the other objects on the sheet. The ZOrder also matches the location of the ChartObject in the parent collection.

ChartObject Methods

Name	Returns	Parameters	Description
Activate	Variant		Makes the embedded chart the active chart.
BringTo Front	Variant		Brings the embedded chart to the front of all the other objects on the sheet. Changes the ZOrder.
Copy	Variant		Copies the embedded chart into the clipboard.
Copy Picture	Variant	[Appearance As XlPicture Appearance], [Format As XlCopyPicture Format], [Size As XlPicture Appearance]	Copies the Chart object into the clipboard as a picture. The Appearance parameter can be used to specify whether the picture is copied as it looks on the screen or when printed. The Format parameter can specify the type of picture that will be put into the clipboard. The Size parameter is used when dealing with chart sheets to describe the size of the picture.

Table Continued on Following Page

Name	Returns	Parameters	Description
Cut	Variant		Cuts the embedded chart into the clipboard.
Delete	Variant		Deletes the embedded chart from the sheet.
Duplicate			Duplicates the embedded chart and places the duplicate in the same parent sheet.
Select	Variant	[Replace]	Sets focus to the embedded chart.
SendTo Back	Variant		Sends the embedded object to the back of the other objects on the sheet.

Example: ChartObject Object and the ChartObjects Collection

This example creates .jpg images from all the embedded charts in the active worksheet:

```
Sub ExportChartObjects()
    Dim oCO As ChartObject

    For Each oCO In ActiveSheet.ChartObjects
        'Export the chart as a jpg image, giving it the
        'name of the embedded object
        oCO.Chart.Export "c:\" & oCO.Name & ".jpg", "jpg"
    Next
End Sub
```

ChartTitle Object

The ChartTitle object contains all of the text and formatting associated with a chart's title. The parent of the ChartTitle object is the Chart object. This object is usually used along with the HasTitle property of the parent Chart object.

ChartTitle Common Properties

The Application, Creator, and Parent properties are defined at the beginning of this Appendix.

ChartTitle Properties

Name	Returns	Description
AutoScale Font	Variant	Set / Get whether the font size will change automatically if the parent chart changes sizes.

Name	Returns	Description
Border	Border	Read Only. Returns the border's properties around the selected chart title.
Caption	String	Set / Get the chart title's text.
Characters	Characters	Read Only. Parameters: [Start], [Length]. Returns an object containing all the characters in the chart title. Allows manipulation on a character-by-character basis.
Fill	ChartFill Format	Read Only. Returns an object containing fill formatting options for the chart title.
Font	Font	Read Only. Returns an object containing Font options for the chart title.
Horizontal Alignment	Variant	Set / Get how the chart title is horizontally aligned. Use the xlAlign constants.
Interior	Interior	Read Only. Returns an object containing options to format the area in the chart title text area (e.g. interior color).
Left	Double	Set / Get the distance from the left edge of the chart title text area to the chart's left edge.
Name	String	Read Only. Returns the name of the chart title object.
Orientation	Variant	Set / Get either the angle of the text for the chart title. The value can be in degrees (from –90 to 90) or one of the XlOrientation constants.
ReadingOrder	Long	Set / Get how the text is read (from left to right or right to left). Only applicable in appropriate languages.
Shadow	Boolean	Set / Get whether the chart title has a shadow effect.
Text	String	Set / Get the chart title's text.
Top	Double	Set / Get the distance from the top edge of the chart title text area to the chart's top edge.

Table Continued on Following Page

Name	Returns	Description
Vertical Alignment	Variant	Set / Get how you want the chart title horizontally aligned. Use the xlVAlign constants.

ChartTitle Methods

Name	Returns	Parameters	Description
Delete	Variant		Deletes the chart title from the chart.
Select	Variant		Selects the chart title on the chart.

Example: ChartTitle Object

This example adds a chart title to a chart and formats it:

```
Sub AddAndFormatChartTitle()
    Dim oCT As ChartTitle

    'Make sure the chart has a title
    Charts(1).HasTitle = True

    'Get the ChartTitle object
    Set oCT = Charts(1).ChartTitle

    'Format the chart title
    With oCT
        .Caption = "Hello World"
        .Font.Name = "Times New Roman"
        .Font.Size = 16
        .Characters(1, 1).Font.Color = RGB(255, 0, 0)
        .Characters(7, 1).Font.Color = RGB(255, 0, 0)
        .Border.LineStyle = xlContinuous
        .Border.Weight = xlThin
        .Shadow = True
    End With
End Sub
```

ColorFormat Object

The ColorFormat object describes a single color used by the parent object. Possible parents of the ColorFormat object are the FillFormat, LineFormat, ShadowFormat, and ThreeDFormat objects.

ColorFormat Common Properties

The Application, Creator, and Parent properties are defined at the beginning of this Appendix.

ColorFormat Properties

Name	Returns	Description
RGB	Long	Read Only. Returns the red-green-blue value associated with color.

Name	Returns	Description
Scheme Color	Integer	Set / Get the color of the `ColorFormat` using an index value corresponding to the current color scheme.
Type	`msoColor Type`	Read Only. Returns whether the color is an RGB, mixed, or scheme type.

Example: ColorFormat Object

Set the `ForeColor` of a shape's fill effect:

```
Sub FormatShapeColour()
    Dim oShp As Shape
    Dim oCF As ColorFormat

    Set oShp = ActiveSheet.Shapes(1)
    Set oCF = oShp.Fill.ForeColor
    oCF.SchemeColor = 53
End Sub
```

Comment Object and the Comments Collection

The `Comments` collection holds all of the cell comments in the parent `Range` object. Each `Comment` object represents a single cell comment.

Comment Common Properties

The `Application`, `Creator`, and `Parent` properties are defined at the beginning of this Appendix.

Comment Properties

Name	Returns	Description
Author	String	Read Only. Returns the name of the person who created the comment.
Shape	Shape	Read Only. Returns the comment box as a `Shape` object allowing manipulation of the comment box.
Visible	Boolean	Set / Get whether the comment is visible all the time (`True`) or only when the user hovers over the cell containing the comment.

Comment Methods

Name	Returns	Parameters	Description
Delete			Deletes the comment from the cell.

Name	Returns	Parameters	Description
Next	Comment		Returns the next cell comment in the parent collection.
Previous	Comment		Returns the previous cell comment in the parent collection.
Text	String	[Text], [Start], [Overwrite]	Sets the text associated with the comment. The Text parameter is used to set the comment text. Use the Start parameter to specify the starting point for Text in the existing comment. Set the Overwrite parameter to True to overwrite existing text.

Example: Comment Object and the Comments Collection

This example removes the user name added by Excel at the start of the comment and formats the comment to make it more readable.

```
Sub FormatComments()
    Dim oComment As Comment, i As Integer

    'Loop through all the comments in the sheet
    For Each oComment In ActiveSheet.Comments

        'Using the text of the comment...
        With oComment.Shape.TextFrame.Characters

            'Find and remove the user name inserted by Excel
            i = InStr(1, .Text, ":" & vbLf)
            If i > 0 Then
                .Text = Mid(.Text, i + 2)
            End If

            'Increase the font size
            With .Font
                .Name = "Arial"
                .Size = 10
                .Bold = False
            End With
        End With

        'Make the text frame auto-fit
        oComment.Shape.TextFrame.AutoSize = True
    Next
End Sub
```

ConnectorFormat Object

The ConnectorFormat object represents the connector line used between shapes. This connector line connects two shapes together. If either of shapes are moved the connector automatically re-adjusts so the shapes still look visually connected. The parent of a ConnectorFormat object is the Shape object.

ConnectorFormat Common Properties

The Application, Creator, and Parent properties are defined at the beginning of this Appendix.

ConnectorFormat Properties

Name	Returns	Description
Begin Connected	msoTri State	Read Only. Returns whether the beginning of the connector has a shape attached. Use with BeginConnectedShape.
Begin Connected Shape	Shape	Read Only. Returns the shape that is connected to the beginning of the connector. Use with BeginConnected.
Begin Connection Site	Long	Read Only. Returns which connection site (connection spot) on the shape that the beginning of the connector is connected to. Use with BeginConnected.
End Connected	msoTri State	Read Only. Returns whether the end of the connector has a shape attached. Use with BeginConnectedShape.
End Connected Shape	Shape	Read Only. Returns the shape that is connected to the end of the connector. Use with EndConnected.
End Connection Site	Long	Read Only. Returns which connection site (connection spot) on the shape that the end of the connector is connected to. Use with EndConnected.
Type	mso Connector Type	Set / Get what type of connector is being used (e.g. msoConnectorStraight, msoConnectorCurve).

ConnectorFormat Methods

Name	Returns	Parameters	Description
Begin Connect		ConnectedShape As Shape, ConnectionSite As Long	Sets the beginning of the connector to the shape specified by the ConnectedShape parameter at the connection site specified by the ConnectionSite parameter.

Name	Returns	Parameters	Description
Begin Disconnect			Disconnects the shape that was at the beginning of the connection. This method does not move the connection line.
EndConnect		ConnectedShape As Shape, ConnectionSite As Long	Sets the end of the connector to the shape specified by the ConnectedShape parameter at the connection site specified by the ConnectionSite parameter.
End Disconnect			Disconnects the shape that was at the end of the connection. This method does not move the connection line.

Example: ConnectorFormat Object

This example formats all fully-connected connectors as curved lines

```
Sub FormatConnectors()
    Dim oShp As Shape
    Dim oCF As ConnectorFormat

    'Loop through all the Shapes in the sheet
    For Each oShp In ActiveSheet.Shapes

        'Is it a Connector?
        If oShp.Connector Then

            'Yes, so get the ConnectorFormat object
            Set oCF = oShp.ConnectorFormat

            'If the connector is connected at both ends,
            'make it a curved line.
            With oCF
                If .BeginConnected And .EndConnected Then
                    .Type = msoConnectorCurve
                End If
            End With
        End If
    Next
End Sub
```

ControlFormat Object

The ControlFormat object contains properties and methods used to manipulate Excel controls such as textboxes and listboxes. This object's parent is always the Shape object.

ControlFormat Common Properties

The Application, Creator, and Parent properties are defined at the beginning of this Appendix.

ControlFormat Properties

Name	Returns	Description
DropDown Lines	Long	Set / Get how many lines are displayed in the drop down part of a combo box. Valid only if the control is a combo box.
Enabled	Boolean	Set / Get whether the control is enabled.
Large Change	Long	Set / Get the value that is added or subtracted every time the user clicks inside the scroll bar area for a scroll box. Valid only if the control is a scroll box.
Linked Cell	String	Set / Get the range where the results of the control is placed.
List Count	Long	Read Only. Returns the number of items in the list box of combo box. Valid only for list box and combo box controls.
List Fill Range	String	Set / Get the range that contains the items for a list box or combo box. Valid only for list box and combo box controls.
List Index	Long	Set / Get the item that is currently selected in the list box or combo box. Valid only for list box and combo box controls.
Locked Text	Boolean	Set / Get whether the control text can be changed if the workbook is locked.
Max	Long	Set / Get the maximum value allowed for a scroll bar or spinner. Valid only on a control that is a scroll bar or spinner.
Min	Long	Set / Get the minimum value allowed for a scroll bar or spinner. Valid only on a control that is a scroll bar or spinner.

Table Continued on Following Page

Name	Returns	Description
Multi Select	Long	Set / Get how a list box acts to user selection. The property can be set to xlNone (only one item can be selected), xlSimple (each item the user clicks on is added to the selection), or xlExtended (the user has to hold down the Ctrl key to select multiple items). Valid only on list boxes.
Print Object	Boolean	Set / Get whether the control will be printed when the sheet is printed.
Small Change	Long	Set / Get the value that is added or subtracted every time the user clicks on the arrow button associated with the scroll bar. Valid only if the control is a scroll box.
Value	Long	Set / Get the value of the control.

ControlFormat Methods

Name	Returns	Parameters	Description
AddItem		Text As String, [Index]	Adds the value of the Text parameter into a list box or combo box. Valid only for list box and combo box controls.
List	Variant	[Index]	Set / Get the string list array associated with a combo box or list box. Can also Set / Get individual items in the list box or combo box if the Index parameter is specified. Valid only for list box and combo box controls.
Remove AllItems			Removes all the items from a list box or combo box. Valid only for list box and combo box controls.

Name	Returns	Parameters	Description
Remove Item		Index As Long, [Count]	Removes the item specified by the Index parameter from a list box or combo box. Valid only for list box and combo box controls.

Example: ControlFormat Object

This example resets all the list boxes, dropdowns, scrollbars, spinners and checkboxes on the sheet:

```
Sub ResetFormControls()
    Dim oShp As Shape
    Dim oCF As ControlFormat

    'Loop through all the shapes in the sheet
    For Each oShp In ActiveSheet.Shapes

        'Is this a Forms control?
        If oShp.Type = msoFormControl Then

            'Yes, so get the ControlFormat object
            Set oCF = oShp.ControlFormat

            'Reset the control as appropriate
            Select Case oShp.FormControlType
                Case xlListBox, xlDropDown
                    oCF.RemoveAllItems

                Case xlSpinner, xlScrollBar
                    oCF.Value = oCF.Min

                Case xlCheckBox
                    oCF.Value = xlOff

            End Select
        End If
    Next
End Sub
```

Corners Object

The Corners object represents the corners of a 3D chart. The parent of the Corners object is the Chart object. The parent chart must be a 3D chart. Individual corners cannot be accessed.

Corners Common Properties

The Application, Creator, and Parent properties are defined at the beginning of this Appendix.

Corners Properties

Name	Returns	Description
Name	String	Read Only. Returns the name of the Corners object – usually "Corners".

Corners Methods

Name	Returns	Parameters	Description
Select	Variant		Sets the corners on the chart.

Example: Corners Object

No example – its only method is to select it, which is not particularly useful!

CubeField Object and the CubeFields Collection

The CubeFields collection holds all of the PivotTable report fields based on an OLAP cube. Each CubeField object represents a measure or hierarchy field from the OLAP cube. The parent of the CubeFields collection is the PivotTable object.

The CubeFields collection contains a Count property besides the typical collection attributes. The Count property returns the number of objects in the collection.

CubeField Common Properties

The Application, Creator, and Parent properties are defined at the beginning of this Appendix.

CubeField Properties

Name	Returns	Description
Caption	String	Read Only. Returns the text label to use for the cube field.
Cube FieldType	XlCube FieldType	Read Only. Returns whether the cube field is hierarchy field (xlHierarchy) or a measure field (xlMeasure)
DragToColumn	Boolean	Set / Get whether the field can be dragged to a column position. False for measure fields.
DragToData	Boolean	Set / Get whether the field can be dragged to the data position.
DragToHide	Boolean	Set / Get whether the field can be dragged off the PivotTable report and therefore hidden.

Name	Returns	Description
DragToPage	Boolean	Set / Get whether the field can be dragged to the page position. False for measure fields.
DragToRow	Boolean	Set / Get whether the field can be dragged to a row position. False for measure fields.
HiddenLevels	Long	Set / Get the top levels of the hierarchy cube field that are hidden. Set the value to 0 before setting it a value greater then 0 (displays all the levels then hide some).
Name	String	Read Only. Returns the name of the field.
Orientation	XlPivot Field Orientation	Set / Get the where the field is located in the PivotTable report.
Position	Long	Set / Get the position number of the hierarchy field among all the fields in the same orientation.
Treeview Control	Treeview Control	Read Only. Returns an object allowing manipulation of the cube on an OLAP PivotTable report.
Value	String	Read Only. Returns the name of the field.

CustomView Object and the CustomViews Collection

The CustomViews collection holds the list of custom views associated with a workbook. Each CustomView object holds the attributes associated with a workbook custom view. A custom view holds settings such as window size, window position, column widths, hidden columns, and print settings of a workbook. The parent object of the CustomViews collection is the Workbook object. The CustomViews collection has two other properties besides the typical collection attributes. The Count property returns the number of CustomView objects in the collection. The Add method adds a custom view to the CustomViews collection. The Add method accepts a name for the view with the ViewName parameter. Optionally the Add method accepts whether print settings are included (PrintSettings) and whether hidden rows and columns are included (RowColSettings).

CustomView Common Properties

The `Application`, `Creator`, and `Parent` properties are defined at the beginning of this Appendix.

CustomView Properties

Name	Returns	Description
Name	String	Read Only. Returns the name of the custom view.
Print Settings	Boolean	Read Only. Returns whether print settings are included in the custom view.
RowCol Settings	Boolean	Read Only. Returns whether hidden rows and columns are included in the custom view.

CustomView Methods

Name	Returns	Parameters	Description
Delete			Deletes the custom view.
Show			Shows the custom view and the settings associated with it.

Example: CustomView Object and the CustomViews Collection

Display all the custom views in the workbook as a screen-show, pausing for 2 seconds between each one:

```
Sub ShowCustomView()
    Dim oCV As CustomView

    'Cycle through all the custom views in the sheet
    'that contain row/column information
    For Each oCV In ActiveWorkbook.CustomViews

        If oCV.RowColSettings Then
            oCV.Show
        End If

        'Pause for 2 seconds between each view
        Application.Wait Now + TimeValue("00:00:02")
    Next
End Sub
```

DataLabel Object and the DataLabels Collection

The `DataLabels` collection holds all the labels for individual points or trendlines in a data series. Each series has only one `DataLabels` collection. The parent of the `DataLabels` collection is the `Series` object. Each `DataLabel` object represents a single data label for a trendline or a point. The `DataLabels` collection is used with the `HasDataLabels` property of the parent `Series` object.

The DataLabels collection has a few properties and methods besides the typical collection attributes. They are listed in the following table.

DataLabels Collection Properties and Methods

Name	Returns	Description
AutoScale Font	Variant	Set / Get whether the font size will change automatically if the parent chart changes sizes.
AutoText	Boolean	Set / Get whether Excel will generate the data label text automatically.
Border	Border	Read Only. Returns the border's properties around the data label collection.
Count	Long	Read Only. Returns the number of data labels in the collection.
Fill	ChartFill Format	Read Only. Returns an object containing fill formatting options for the data labels in the collection.
Font	Font	Read Only. Returns an object containing Font options for the data labels in the collection.
Horizontal Alignment	Variant	Set / Get how the data labels are horizontally aligned. Use the xlAlign constants.
Interior	Interior	Read Only. Returns an object containing options to format the inside area of the data labels in the collection (e.g. interior color).
Name	String	Read Only. Returns the name of the collection.
Number Format	String	Set / Get the numeric formatting to use if the data labels are numeric values or dates.
NumberFormat Linked	Boolean	Set / Get whether the same numerical format used for the cells containing the chart data is used by the data labels.
NumberFormat Local	Variant	Set / Get the name of the numeric format being used by the data labels in the language being used by the user.

Table Continued on Following Page

Name	Returns	Description
Orientation	Variant	Set / Get the angle of the text for the data labels. The value can be in degrees (from –90 to 90) or one of the XlOrientation constants.
Position	XlData Label Position	Set / Get where the data labels are going to be located in relation to points or trendlines.
ReadingOrder	Long	Set / Get how the text is read (from left to right or right to left). Only applicable in appropriate languages.
Shadow	Boolean	Set / Get whether the data labels have a shadow effect.
ShowLegend Key	Boolean	Set / Get whether the key being used in the legend, usually a specific color, will show along with the data label.
Type	Variant	Set / Get what sort of data label to show for the collection (e.g. labels, percent, values)
Vertical Alignment	Variant	Set / Get how you want the data labels horizontally aligned. Use the xlVAlign constants.
Delete	Variant	Method. Deletes the data labels.
Select	Variant	Method. Selects the data labels on the chart.

DataLabel Common Properties

The Application, Creator, and Parent properties are defined at the beginning of this Appendix.

DataLabel Properties

Name	Returns	Description
AutoScale Font	Variant	Set / Get whether the font size will change automatically if the parent chart changes sizes.
AutoText	Boolean	Set / Get whether Excel will generate the data label text automatically.

Name	Returns	Description
Border	Border	Read Only. Returns the border's properties around the data label.
Caption	String	Set / Get the data label text.
Characters	Characters	Read Only. Parameters: [Start], [Length]. Returns an object that represents a range of characters within the text.
Fill	ChartFill Format	Read Only. Returns an object containing fill formatting options for the data label.
Font	Font	Read Only. Returns an object containing Font options for the data label.
Horizontal Alignment	Variant	Set / Get how the data labels are horizontally aligned. Use the xlAlign constants.
Interior	Interior	Read Only. Returns an object containing options to format the inside area of the data label (e.g. interior color).
Left	Double	Set / Get the distance from the left edge of the data label to the parent chart's left edge.
Name	String	Read Only. Returns the name of the data label.
NumberFormat	String	Set / Get the numeric formatting to use if the data label is a numeric value or a date.
NumberFormat Linked	Boolean	Set / Get whether the same numerical format used for the cells containing the chart data is used by the data label.
NumberFormat Local	Variant	Set / Get the name of the numeric format being used by the data label in the language being used by the user.
Orientation	Variant	Set / Get the angle of the text for the data label. The value can be in degrees (from –90 to 90) or one of the XlOrientation constants.
Position	XlData Label Position	Set / Get where the data label is going to be located in relation to points or trendlines.

Table Continued on Following Page

Name	Returns	Description
ReadingOrder	Long	Set / Get how the text is read (from left to right or right to left). Only applicable in appropriate languages.
Shadow	Boolean	Set / Get whether the data label has a shadow effect.
ShowLegend Key	Boolean	Set / Get whether the key being used in the legend, usually a specific color, will show along with the data label.
Text	String	Set / Get the data label text.
Top	Double	Set / Get the distance from the top edge of the data label to the parent chart's top edge.
Type	Variant	Set / Get what sort of data label to show (e.g. labels, percent, values).
Vertical Alignment	Variant	Set / Get how you want the data label horizontally aligned. Use the xlVAlign constants.

DataLabel Methods

Name	Returns	Parameters	Description
Delete	Variant		Deletes the data label.
Select	Variant		Selects the data label on the chart.

Example: DataLabel Object and the DataLabels Collection

This example adds data labels to all the points on the chart, using the column to the left of the X values range:

```
Sub AddDataLabels()
    Dim oSer As Series
    Dim vaSplits As Variant
    Dim oXRng As Range
    Dim oLblRng As Range
    Dim oLbl As DataLabel

    'Loop through all the series in the chart
    For Each oSer In Charts(1).SeriesCollection

        'Get the series formula and split it into its
        'constituent parts (Name, X range, Y range, order)
        vaSplits = Split(oSer.Formula, ",")

        'Get the X range
        Set oXRng = Range(vaSplits(LBound(vaSplits) + 1))

        'Get the column to the left of the X range
        Set oLblRng = oXRng.Offset(0, -1)
```

```
        'Show data labels for the series
        oSer.ApplyDataLabels

        'Loop through the points
        For i = 1 To oSer.Points.Count

            'Get the DataLabel object
            Set oLbl = oSer.Points(i).DataLabel

            'Set its text and alignment
            With oLbl
                .Caption = oLblRng.Cells(i)
                .Position = xlLabelPositionAbove
            End With
        Next
    Next
End Sub
```

DataTable Object

A DataTable object contains the formatting options associated with a chart's data table. The parent of the DataTable object is the Chart object.

DataTable Common Properties

The Application, Creator, and Parent properties are defined at the beginning of this Appendix.

DataTable Properties

Name	Returns	Description
AutoScale Font	Variant	Set / Get whether the font size will change automatically if the parent chart changes sizes.
Border	Border	Read Only. Returns the border's properties around the data table.
Font	Font	Read Only. Returns an object containing Font options for the data table.
HasBorder Horizontal	Boolean	Set / Get whether the data table has horizontal cell borders.
HasBorder Outline	Boolean	Set / Get whether the data table has border around the outside.
HasBorder Vertical	Boolean	Set / Get whether the data table has vertical cell borders.
ShowLegend Key	Boolean	Set / Get whether the legend key is shown along with the data table contents.

DataTable Methods

Name	Returns	Parameters	Description
Delete			Delete the data table.
Select			Selects the data table on the chart.

Example: DataTable Object

Adds a data table to a chart and formats it to only have vertical lines between the values:

```
Sub FormatDataTable()
   Dim oDT As DataTable

   'Display the data table
   Charts(1).HasDataTable = True

   'Get the DataTable object
   Set oDT = Charts(1).DataTable

   'Format the data table to only have vertical lines
   With oDT
      .HasBorderOutline = False
      .HasBorderHorizontal = False
      .HasBorderVertical = True
   End With
End Sub
```

DefaultWebOptions Object

Allows programmatic changes to items associated with the default settings of the Web Options dialog. These options include what Excel does when opening an HTML page and when saving a sheet as an HTML page.

DefaultWebOptions Common Properties

The Application, Creator, and Parent properties are defined at the beginning of this Appendix.

DefaultWebOptions Properties

Name	Returns	Description
AllowPNG	Boolean	Set / Get whether Portable Network Graphics Format PNG is allowed as an output format. PNG is a file format for the lossless, portable, well-compressed storage of images.
AlwaysSave InDefault Encoding	Boolean	Set / Get whether Web pages are always saved in the default encoding.
CheckIf OfficeIs HTMLEditor	Boolean	Set / Get whether Office is the default web editor for Office created pages.

Name	Returns	Description
Download Components	Boolean	Set / Get whether Office components are downloaded to the end user's machine when viewing Excel files in a web browser.
Encoding	mso Encoding	Set / Get the type of encoding to save a document as.
Folder Suffix	String	Read Only. Returns what the suffix name is for the support directory created when saving an Excel document as a web page. Language dependent.
Fonts	WebPage Fonts	Read Only. Returns a collection of possible web type fonts.
Load Pictures	Boolean	Set / Get whether images are loaded when opening up an Excel file.
LocationOf Components	String	Set / Get the URL or path that contains the Office Web components needed to view documents in a web browser.
OrganizeIn Folder	Boolean	Set / Get whether supporting files are organized in a folder.
PixelsPer Inch	Long	Set / Get how dense graphics and table cells should be when viewed on a web page.
RelyOnCSS	Boolean	Set / Get whether Cascading Style Sheets (CSS) is used for font formatting.
RelyOnVML	Boolean	Set / Get whether image files are not created when saving a document with drawn objects. Vector Markup Language is used to create the images on the fly. VML is an XML-based format for high-quality vector graphics on the Web.
SaveHidden Data	Boolean	Set / Get whether all hidden data is saved in the web page along with the regular data.
ScreenSize	msoScreen Size	Set / Get the target monitor's screen size.
Update LinksOn Save	Boolean	Set / Get whether links are updated every time the document is saved.
UseLong FileNames	Boolean	Set / Get whether long file names are used whenever possible.

Example: DefaultWebOptions Object

This example shows how to open a web page, without loading the pictures.

```
Sub OpenHTMLWithoutPictures()
    Dim bLoadImages As Boolean
    Dim oDWO As DefaultWebOptions

    'Get the Default Web options
    Set oDWO = Application.DefaultWebOptions

    'Remember whether to load pictures
    bLoadImages = oDWO.LoadPictures

    'Tell Excel not to load pictures, for faster opening
    oDWO.LoadPictures = False

    'Open a web page, without pictures
    Workbooks.Open "http://www.wrox.com"

    'Resetore the setting
    oDWO.LoadPictures = bLoadImages
End Sub
```

Dialog Object and the Dialogs Collection

The Dialogs collection represents the list of dialog boxes that are built-in to Excel.
The XlBuiltinDialog constants are used to access an individual Dialog object in
the Dialogs collection. A Dialog object represents a single built-in Excel dialog box.
Each Dialog object will have additional custom properties depending on what type
of Dialog object it is. Besides the typical collection attributes, the Dialogs collection
also has a Count property that returns the number of Dialog objects in the
collection.

Dialog Common Properties

The Application, Creator, and Parent properties are defined at the beginning of
this Appendix.

Dialog Methods

Name	Returns	Parameters	Description
Show	Boolean	[Arg1], [Arg2], . . . [Arg30]	Displays and executes the dialog box settings. True is returned if the user chose OK and False is returned if the user chose Cancel. The arguments to pass depends on the dialog box.

Example: Dialog Object and the Dialogs Collection

```
Sub ShowPrinterSelection()
    'Show printer selection dialog
    Application.Dialogs(xlDialogPrinterSetup).Show
End Sub
```

DisplayUnitLabel Object

The DisplayUnitLabel object contains all of the text and formatting associated with the label used for units on axes. For example, if the values on an axis are in the millions it would be messy to display such large values on the axis. Using a unit label such as 'Millions' would allow much smaller numbers to be used. The parent of the DisplayUnitLabel object is the Axis object. This object is usually used along with the HasDisplayUnit property of the parent Axis object.

DisplayUnitLabel Common Properties

The Application, Creator, and Parent properties are defined at the beginning of this Appendix.

DisplayUnitLabel Properties

Name	Returns	Description
AutoScaleFont	Variant	Set / Get whether the font size will change automatically if the parent chart changes sizes.
Border	Border	Read Only. Returns the border's properties around the unit label.
Caption	String	Set / Get the unit label's text.
Characters	Characters	Read Only. Parameters: [Start], [Length]. Returns an object containing all the characters in the unit label. Allows manipulation on a character-by-character basis.
Fill	ChartFill Format	Read Only. Returns an object containing fill formatting options for the unit label.
Font	Font	Read Only. Returns an object containing Font options for the unit label.
Horizontal Alignment	Variant	Set / Get how you want the unit label horizontally aligned. Use the xlAlign constants.
Interior	Interior	Read Only. Returns an object containing options to format the area in the unit label text area (e.g. interior color).

Table Continued on Following Page

Name	Returns	Description
Left	Double	Set / Get the distance from the left edge of the unit label text area to the chart's left edge.
Name	String	Read Only. Returns the name of the DisplayUnitLabel object.
Orientation	Variant	Set / Get the angle of the text for the unit label. The value can be in degrees (from –90 to 90) or one of the XlOrientation constants.
Reading Order	Long	Set / Get how the text is read (from left to right or right to left). Only applicable in appropriate languages.
Shadow	Boolean	Set / Get whether the unit label has a shadow effect.
Text	String	Set / Get the unit label's text.
Top	Double	Set / Get the distance from the top edge of the unit label text area to the chart's top edge.
Vertical Alignment	Variant	Set / Get how you want the unit label horizontally aligned. Use the xlVAlign constants.

DisplayUnitLabel Methods

Name	Returns	Parameters	Description
Delete	Variant		Deletes unit label from the axis.
Select	Variant		Selects the unit label on the chart.

Example: DisplayUnitLabel Object

```
Sub AddUnitLabel()
    Dim oDUL As DisplayUnitLabel

    'Format the Y axis to have a unit label
    With Charts(1).Axes(xlValue)
        .DisplayUnit = xlThousands
        .HasDisplayUnitLabel = True

        'Get the unit label
        Set oDUL = .DisplayUnitLabel
    End With

    'Format the unit label
    With oDUL
        .Caption = "Thousands"
        .Font.Name = "Arial"
        .VerticalAlignment = xlCenter
    End With
End Sub
```

DownBars Object

The DownBars object contains formatting options for down bars on a chart. The parent of the DownBars object is the ChartGroup object. To see if this object exists use the HasUpDownBars property of the ChartGroup object.

DownBars Common Properties

The Application, Creator, and Parent properties are defined at the beginning of this Appendix.

DownBars Properties

Name	Returns	Description
Border	Border	Read Only. Returns the border's properties around the down bars
Fill	ChartFill Format	Read Only. Returns an object containing fill formatting options for the down bars.
Interior	Interior	Read Only. Returns an object containing options to format the inside area of the down bars (e.g. interior color).
Name	String	Read Only. Returns the name of the down bars.

DownBars Methods

Name	Returns	Parameters	Description
Delete	Variant		Deletes the down bars.
Select	Variant		Selects the down bars in the chart.

DropLines Object

The DropLines object contains formatting options for drop lines in a chart. The parent of the DropLines object is the ChartGroup object. To see if this object exists use the HasDropLines property of the ChartGroup object.

DropLines Common Properties

The Application, Creator, and Parent properties are defined at the beginning of this Appendix.

DropLines Properties

Name	Returns	Description
Border	Border	Read Only. Returns the border's properties around the drop lines.
Name	String	Read Only. Returns the name of the drop lines.

DropLines Methods

Name	Returns	Parameters	Description
Delete	Variant		Deletes the drop lines.
Select	Variant		Selects the drop lines in the chart.

Example: DropLines Object

```
Sub AddAndFormatDropLines()
    Dim oDLine As DropLines

    'Show the drop lines
    Charts(1).ChartGroups(1).HasDropLines = True

    'Get the DropLines object
    Set oDLine = Charts(1).ChartGroups(1).DropLines

    'Format the drop lines
    With oDLine
        .Border.Weight = xlMedium
        .Border.LineStyle = xlDash
        .Border.ColorIndex = 3
    End With
End Sub
```

ErrorBars Object

The ErrorBars object contains formatting options for error bars in a chart. The parent of the Errors object is the SeriesCollection object.

ErrorBars Common Properties

The Application, Creator, and Parent properties are defined at the beginning of this Appendix.

ErrorBars Properties

Name	Returns	Description
Border	Border	Read Only. Returns the border's properties around the error bars.
EndStyle	XlEnd StyleCap	Set / Get the style used for the ending of the error bars.
Name	String	Read Only. Returns the name of the error bars.

ErrorBars Methods

Name	Returns	Parameters	Description
Clear Formats	Variant		Clears the formatting set on the error bar.
Delete	Variant		Deletes the error bars.
Select	Variant		Selects the error bars in the chart.

Example: ErrorBars Object

```
Sub AddAndFormatErrorBars()
    Dim oSer As Series
    Dim oErrBars As ErrorBars

    'Add error bars to the first series (at +/- 10% of the value)
    Set oSer = Charts(1).SeriesCollection(1)
    oSer.ErrorBar xlY, xlErrorBarIncludeBoth, xlErrorBarTypePercent, 10

    'Get the ErrorBars object
    Set oErrBars = oSer.ErrorBars

    'Format the error bars
    With oErrBars
        .Border.Weight = xlThick
        .Border.LineStyle = xlContinuous
        .Border.ColorIndex = 7
        .EndStyle = xlCap
    End With
End Sub
```

FillFormat Object

The FillFormat object represents the fill effects available for shapes. For example, a FillFormat object defines solid, textured, and patterned fill of the parent shape. A FillFormat object can only be access through the parent Shape object.

FillFormat Common Properties

The Application, Creator, and Parent properties are defined at the beginning of this Appendix.

FillFormat Properties

Name	Returns	Description
BackColor	Color Format	Read Only. Returns the background color through the ColorFormat object.
ForeColor	Color Format	Read Only. Returns the foreground color through the ColorFormat object.
Gradient ColorType	mso Gradient ColorType	Read Only. Returns what type of gradient fill color concept is used.

Table Continued on Following Page

Name	Returns	Description
Gradient Degree	Single	Read Only. Returns how dark or light the gradient fill is.
Gradient Style	mso Gradient Style	Read Only. Returns the orientation of the gradient that is used.
Gradient Variant	Integer	Read Only. Returns the variant used for the gradient from the center.
Pattern	mso Pattern Type	Read Only. Returns the pattern used for the fill, if any.
Preset GradientType	msoPreset Gradient Type	Read Only. Returns the type of gradient that is used.
Preset Texture	msoPreset Texture	Read Only. Returns the non-custom texture of the fill.
TextureName	String	Read Only. Returns the custom texture name of the fill.
TextureType	mso Texture Type	Read Only. Returns whether the texture is custom, preset, or mixed.
Transparency	Single	Set / Get how transparent the fill is. From 0 (opàque) to 1 (clear).
Type	msoFill Type	Read Only. Returns if the fill is a texture, gradient, solid, background, picture or mixed.
Visible	msoTri State	Set / Get whether the fill options are visible in the parent shape.

FillFormat Methods

Name	Returns	Parameters	Description
OneColor Gradient		Style As msoGradientStyle, Variant As Integer, Degree As Single	Set the style, variant and degree for a one color gradient fill.
Patterned		Pattern As msoPatternType	Set the pattern for a fill.

Name	Returns	Parameters	Description
Preset Gradient		Style As msoGradientStyle, Variant As Integer, PresetGradientType As msoPreset GradientType	Choose the style, variant, and preset gradient type for a gradient fill.
Preset Textured		PresetTexture As msoPresetTexture	Set the preset texture for a fill.
Solid			Set the fill to a solid color.
TwoColor Gradient		Style As msoGradientStyle, Variant As Integer	Set the style for a two-color gradient fill.
User Picture		PictureFile As String	Set the fill to the picture in the PictureFile format.
User Textured		TextureFile As String	Set the custom texture for a fill with the TextureFile format.

Example: FillFormat Object

```
Sub FormatShape()
    Dim oFF As FillFormat

    'Get the Fill format of the first shape
    Set oFF = ActiveSheet.Shapes(1).Fill

    'Format the shape
    With oFF
        .TwoColorGradient msoGradientFromCorner, 1
        .ForeColor.SchemeColor = 3
        .BackColor.SchemeColor = 5
    End With
End Sub
```

Filter Object and the Filters Collection

The Filters collection holds all of the filters associated with the specific parent AutoFilter. Each Filter object defines a single filter for a single column in an autofiltered range. The parent of the Filters collection is the AutoFilter object.

The Filters collection has one other property besides the typical collection attributes. The Count property returns the number of Filter objects in the collection.

Filter Common Properties

The Application, Creator, and Parent properties are defined at the beginning of this Appendix.

Filter Properties

Name	Returns	Description
Criteria1	Variant	Read Only. Returns the first criteria defined for the filter (e.g. ">=5")
Criteria2	Variant	Read Only. Returns the second criteria for the filter if defined.
On	Boolean	Read Only. Returns whether the filter is in use.
Operator	XlAuto Filter Operator	Read Only. Returns what sort of operator has been defined for the filter (e.g. xlTop10Items).

Example: Filter Object and the Filters Collection

See the AutoFormat object for an example of using the Filter object and the Filters collection.

Floor Object

The Floor object contains formatting options for the floor area of a 3D chart. The parent of the Floor object is the Chart object.

Floor Common Properties

The Application, Creator, and Parent properties are defined at the beginning of this Appendix.

Floor Properties

Name	Returns	Description
Border	Border	Read Only. Returns the border's properties around the floor of the 3D chart.
Fill	ChartFill Format	Read Only. Returns an object containing fill formatting options for the floor of a 3D chart.
Interior	Interior	Read Only. Returns an object containing options to format the inside area of the chart floor (e.g. interior color).

Name	Returns	Description
Name	String	Read Only. Returns the name of the Floor object.
Picture Type	Variant	Set / Get how an associated picture is displayed on the floor of the 3D chart (e.g. stretched, tiled). Use the XlPictureType constants.

Floor Methods

Name	Returns	Parameters	Description
Clear Formats	Variant		Clears the formatting made on the Floor object.
Paste			Pastes the picture in the clipboard into the Floor object.
Select	Variant		Selects the floor on the parent chart.

Example: Floor Object

```
Sub FormatFloor()
    Dim oFlr As Floor

    'Get the chart's Floor
    Set oFlr = Charts(1).Floor

    'Format the floor in white marble
    With oFlr
        .Fill.PresetTextured msoTextureWhiteMarble
        .Fill.Visible = True
    End With
End Sub
```

Font Object

The Font object contains all of the formatting attributes related to fonts of the parent including font type, size and color. Possible parents of the Font object are the AxisTitle, Characters, ChartArea, ChartTitle, DataLabel, Legend, LegendEntry, Range, Style and TickLabels objects. Also, the DataLabels collection is another possible parent of the Font object.

Font Common Properties

The Application, Creator, and Parent properties are defined at the beginning of this Appendix.

Font Properties

Name	Returns	Description
Background	Variant	Set / Get the type of background used behind the font text (xlBackgroundAutomatic, xlBackgroundOpaque, and xlBackgroundTransparent). Use the XlBackground constants. Valid only for text on charts.
Bold	Variant	Set / Get whether the font is bold.
Color	Variant	Set / Get the color of the font. Use the RGB function to create the color value.
ColorIndex	Variant	Set / Get the color of the font. Use the XlColorIndex constants or an index value in the current color palette.
FontStyle	Variant	Set / Get what style to apply to the font (e.g. "Bold").
Italic	Variant	Set / Get whether the font is italic.
Name	Variant	Set / Get the name of the font.
OutlineFont	Variant	Set / Get whether the font is an outline font. Not used in Windows.
Shadow	Variant	Set / Get whether the font is a shadow font. Not used in Windows.
Size	Variant	Set / Get the font size of the font.
Strikethrough	Variant	Set / Get whether the font has a strikethrough effect.
Subscript	Variant	Set / Get whether the font characters look like a subscript.
Superscript	Variant	Set / Get whether the font characters look like a superscript.
Underline	Variant	Set / Get whether the font is underlined.

Example: Font Object

```
Sub FormatCellFont()
    Dim oFont As Font

    'Get the font of the currently selected range
    Set oFont = Selection.Font

    'Format the font
    With oFont
        .Name = "Times New Roman"
        .Size = 16          'Points
```

```
        .ColorIndex = 5      'Blue
        .Bold = True
        .Underline = xlSingle
    End With
End Sub
```

FormatCondition Object and the FormatConditions Collection

The FormatConditions collection contains the conditional formatting associated with the particular range of cells. The Parent of the FormatConditions collection is the Range object. Up to three FormatCondition objects can be contained in the FormatConditions collection. Each FormatCondition object represents some formatting that will be applied if the condition is met.

The FormatConditions collection has one property and two methods besides the typical collection attributes. The Count property returns how many FormatCondition objects are in the collection. The Add method can be used to add a formatting condition to the collection. The Type parameter must be specified (XlFormatConditionType constants) and the condition may be specified with the Operator, Formula1, and Formula2 parameters.

Name	Returns	Description
Count	Long	Read Only. Returns the number of objects in the collection.
Add	Format Condition	Method. Parameters: Type As XlFormatConditionType, [Operator], [Formula1], [Formula2] .
Delete		Method.

FormatCondition Common Properties

The Application, Creator, and Parent properties are defined at the beginning of this Appendix.

FormatCondition Properties

Name	Returns	Description
Borders	Borders	Read Only. Returns a collection holding all of the individual border attributes for the formatting condition.
Font	Font	Read Only. Returns an object containing Font options for the formatting condition.

Table Continued on Following Page

Name	Returns	Description
Formula1	String	Read Only. Returns the value that the cells must contain or an expression or formula evaluating to True/False. If the formula or expression evaluates to True then the formatting is applied.
Formula2	String	Read Only. Returns the value that the cells must contain or an expression evaluating to True/False. Valid only if the Operator property is xlBetween or xlNotBetween.
Interior	Interior	Read Only. Returns an object containing options to format the inside area for the formatting condition (e.g. interior color).
Operator	Long	Read Only. Returns the operator to apply to the Formula1 and Formula2 property. Use the XlFormatConditionOperator constants.
Type	Long	Read Only. Returns whether the FormatCondition is applying formatting based on cell values or a formula. Use the XlFormatConditionType constants.

FormatCondition Methods

Name	Returns	Parameters	Description
Delete			Deletes the formatting condition.
Modify		Type As XlFormatConditionType, [Operator], [Formula1], [Formula2]	Modifies the formatting condition. Since all the properties are read only, this is the only way to modify the format condition.

Example: FormatCondition Object and the FormatConditions Collection

```
Sub AddConditionalFormat()
   Dim oFC As FormatCondition

   'Remove any existing conditions
   For Each oFC In Selection.FormatConditions
      Selection.FormatConditions(1).Delete
   Next

   'Add first condition
   Set oFC = Selection.FormatConditions.Add(Type:=xlCellValue, _
            Operator:=xlLess, Formula1:="10")
   With oFC
      .Font.ColorIndex = 2                    'white
      .Font.Bold = True
```

```
      .Interior.Pattern = xlSolid
      .Interior.Color = RGB(255, 0, 0)      'red
   End With

   'Add second condition
   Set oFC = Selection.FormatConditions.Add(Type:=xlCellValue, _
         Operator:=xlBetween, Formula1:="10", Formula2:="40")
   With oFC
      .Font.Color = RGB(0, 255, 0)
      .Font.Bold = False
      .Interior.Pattern = xlNone
   End With

   'Add third condition
   Set oFC = Selection.FormatConditions.Add(Type:=xlCellValue, _
         Operator:=xlGreater, Formula1:="40")
   With oFC
      .Font.Color = RGB(0, 0, 255)
      .Font.Bold = True
      .Interior.Pattern = xlNone
   End With
End Sub
```

FreeformBuilder Object

The FreeformBuilder object is used by the parent Shape object to create new 'free hand' shapes. The BuildFreeform method of the Shape object is used to return a FreeformBuilder object.

FreeformBuilder Common Properties

The Application, Creator, and Parent properties are defined at the beginning of this Appendix.

FreeformBuilder Methods

Name	Returns	Parameters	Description
AddNodes		SegmentType As msoSegmentType, EditingType As msoEditingType, X1 As Single, Y1 As Single, [X2], [Y2], [X3], [Y3]	This method adds a point in the current shape being drawn. A line is drawn from the current node being added to the last node added. SegmentType describes the type of line to add between the nodes. X1, Y1, X2, Y2, X3, Y3 is used to define the position of the current node being added. The coordinates are taken from the upper left corner of the document.

Table Continued on Following Page

Name	Returns	Parameters	Description
Convert ToShape	Shape		Converts the nodes added above into a shape object.

Example: FreeformBuilder Object

```
Sub MakeArch()
    Dim oFFB As FreeformBuilder

    'Create a new freeform builder
    Set oFFB = ActiveSheet.Shapes.BuildFreeform(msoEditingCorner, 100, 300)

    'Add the lines to the builder
    With oFFB
        .AddNodes msoSegmentLine, msoEditingAuto, 100, 200
        .AddNodes msoSegmentCurve, msoEditingCorner, 150, 150, 0, 0, 200, 200
        .AddNodes msoSegmentLine, msoEditingAuto, 200, 300
        .AddNodes msoSegmentLine, msoEditingAuto, 100, 300

        'Convert it to a shape
        .ConvertToShape
    End With
End Sub
```

Gridlines Object

The Gridlines object contains formatting properties associated with the major and minor gridlines on a chart's axes. The gridlines are an extension of the tick marks seen in the background of a chart allowing the end user to more easily see what a chart object's value is. The parent of the Gridlines object is the Axis object. To make sure the object is valid and to create the Gridlines object use the HasMajorGridlines and HasMinorGridlines properties of the Axis object first.

Gridlines Common Properties

The Application, Creator, and Parent properties are defined at the beginning of this Appendix.

Gridlines Properties

Name	Returns	Description
Border	Border	Read Only. Returns the border's properties around the gridlines.
Name	String	Read Only. Returns the name of the Gridlines object.

Gridlines Methods

Name	Returns	Parameters	Description
Delete	Variant		Deletes the Gridline object.

Name	Returns	Parameters	Description
Select	Variant		Selects the gridlines on the chart.

Example: Gridlines Object

```
Sub FormatGridlines()
    Dim oGL As Gridlines

    'Make sure the Y axis has gridlines
    With Charts(1).Axes(xlValue)
        .HasMajorGridlines = True

        'Get the Gridlines object for the major gridlines
        Set oGL = .MajorGridlines
    End With

    'Format the gridlines
    With oGL
        .Border.ColorIndex = 5
        .Border.LineStyle = xlDash
        .Border.Weight = xlThin
    End With
End Sub
```

GroupShapes Collection

The GroupShapes collection holds all of shapes that make up a grouped shape. The GroupShapes collection holds a collection of Shape objects. The parent of the GroupShapes object is the Shape object.

The GroupShapes collection only has one property besides the typical collection attributes. The Count property returns the number of Shape objects in the GroupShapes collection.

HiLoLines Object

The HiLoLines object contains formatting attributes for a chart's high-low lines. The parent of the HiLoLines object is the ChartGroup object. High-low lines connect the largest and smallest points on a 2D line chart group.

HiLoLines Common Properties

The Application, Creator, and Parent properties are defined at the beginning of this Appendix.

HiLoLines Properties

Name	Returns	Description
Border	Border	Read Only. Returns the border's properties around the high-low lines.
Name	String	Read Only. Returns the name of the HiLoLines object.

HiLoLines Methods

Name	Returns	Parameters	Description
Delete	Variant		Deletes the high-low lines.
Select	Variant		Selects the high-low lines on the chart.

Example: HiLoLines Object

```
Sub AddAndFormatHiLoLines()
    Dim oHLL As HiLoLines

    'Add hi-lo lines to the first group
    Charts(1).ChartGroups(1).HasHiLoLines = True

    'Get the HiLoLines object
    Set oHLL = Charts(1).ChartGroups(1).HiLoLines

    'Format the lines
    With oHLL
        .Border.Weight = xlMedium
        .Border.LineStyle = xlContinuous
        .Border.ColorIndex = 3
    End With
End Sub
```

HPageBreak Object and the HPageBreaks Collection

The HPageBreaks collection contains all of the horizontal page breaks in the printable area of the parent object. Each HPageBreak object represents a single horizontal page break for the printable area of the parent object. Possible parents of the HPageBreaks collection are the WorkSheet and the Chart objects. The HPageBreaks collection contains one property and one method besides the typical collection attributes. The Count property returns the number of HPageBreak objects in the collection. The Add method is used to add a HPageBreak object to the collection (and horizontal page break to the sheet). The Add method has a Before parameter to specify the range above where the horizontal page break will be added.

HPageBreak Common Properties

The Application, Creator, and Parent properties are defined at the beginning of this Appendix.

HPageBreak Properties

Name	Returns	Description
Extent	XlPageBreak Extent	Read Only. Returns whether the horizontal page break is full screen or only for the print area.

Name	Returns	Description
Location	Range	Set / Get the cell that the horizontal page break is located. The top edge of the cell is the location of the page break.
Type	XlPageBreak	Set / Get whether the page break is automatic or manually set.

HPageBreak Methods

Name	Returns	Parameters	Description
Delete			Deletes the page break.
DragOff		Direction As XlDirection, RegionIndex As Long	Drags the page break out of the printable area. The Direction parameter specifies the direction the page break is dragged. The RegionIndex parameter specifies which print region the page break is being dragged out of.

Example: HPageBreak Object and the HPageBreaks Collection

```
Sub AddHPageBreaks()
    Dim oCell As Range

    'Loop through all the cells in the first column of the sheet
    For Each oCell In ActiveSheet.UsedRange.Columns(1).Cells

        'If the font size is 16, add a page break above the cell
        If oCell.Font.Size = 16 Then
            ActiveSheet.HPageBreaks.Add oCell
        End If
    Next
End Sub
```

Hyperlink Object and the Hyperlinks Collection

The Hyperlinks collection represents the list of hyperlinks in a worksheet or range. Each Hyperlink object represents a single hyperlink in a worksheet or range. The Hyperlinks collection has an Add, and Delete method besides the typical collection properties and methods. The Add method takes the text or graphic that is to be converted into a hyperlink (Anchor) and the URL address or filename (Address) and creates a Hyperlink object. The Delete method deletes the hyperlinks in the collection. The Hyperlinks collection also has a Count property that returns the number of Hyperlink objects in the collection.

Hyperlink Common Properties

The Application, Creator, and Parent properties are defined at the beginning of this Appendix.

Hyperlink Properties

Name	Returns	Description
Address	String	Set / Get the file name or URL address of the hyperlink.
Email Subject	String	Set / Get the email subject line if the address is an email address.
Name	String	Read Only. Returns whether the ExtraInfo property needs to be filled.
Range	Range	Read Only. Returns the name of the hyperlink.
ScreenTip	String	Read Only. Returns the spot in the document where the hyperlink is.
Shape	Shape	Set / Get the text that appears when the mouse hovers over the hyperlink.
SubAddress	String	Read Only. Returns the shape associated with the hyperlink, if any.
TextTo Display	String	Set / Get the spot in the target location that the hyperlink points to.
Type	Long	Set / Get the target location of the HTML frame of the Address

Hyperlink Methods

Name	Returns	Parameters	Description
AddTo Favorites			Adds the Address property to the Favorites folder.
CreateNew Document		Filename As String, EditNow As Boolean, Overwrite As Boolean	Creates a new document with the FileName name from the results of the hyperlink's address. Set the EditNow property to True to open up the document in the appropriate editor. Set Overwrite to True to overwrite any existing document with the same name.
Delete			Deletes the Hyperlink object.

Name	Returns	Parameters	Description
Follow		[NewWindow], [AddHistory], [ExtraInfo], [Method], [HeaderInfo]	Opens up the target document specified by the Address property. Setting NewWindow to True opens up a new window with the target document. Set AddHistory to True to display the item in history folder. Use the Method parameter to choose if the ExtraInfo property is sent as a Get or a Post.

Example: Hyperlink Object and the Hyperlinks Collection

This example creates a hyperlink-based 'Table of Contents' worksheet:

```
Sub CreateHyperlinkTOC()
    Dim oBk As Workbook
    Dim oShtTOC As Worksheet, oSht As Worksheet
    Dim iRow As Integer

    Set oBk = ActiveWorkbook

    'Add a new sheet to the workbook
    Set oShtTOC = oBk.Worksheets.Add

    With oShtTOC
        'Add the title to the sheet
        .Range("A1").Value = "Table of Contents"

        'Add Mail and web hyperlinks
        .Hyperlinks.Add .Range("A3"), "mailto:Me@MyISP.com", _
                    TextToDisplay:="Email your comments"
        .Hyperlinks.Add .Range("A4"), "http://www.wrox.com", _
                    TextToDisplay:="Visit Wrox Press"
    End With

    'Loop through the sheets in the workbook
    'adding location hyperlinks
    iRow = 6
    For Each oSht In oBk.Worksheets
        If oSht.Name <> oShtTOC.Name Then
            oShtTOC.Hyperlinks.Add oShtTOC.Cells(iRow, 1), "", _
                    SubAddress:="'" & oSht.Name & "'!A1", _
                    TextToDisplay:=oSht.Name
            iRow = iRow + 1
        End If
    Next
End Sub
```

Interior Object

The Interior object contains the formatting options associated with the inside area of the parent object. Possible parents of the Interior object are the AxisTitle, ChartArea, ChartObject, ChartTitle, DataLabel, DownBars, Floor, FormatCondition, Legend, LegendKey, OLEObject, PlotArea, Point, Range, Series, Style, Upbars and Walls objects. The ChartObjects, DataLabels, and OLEObjects collections also are possible parents of the Interior object.

Interior Common Properties

The `Application`, `Creator`, and `Parent` properties are defined at the beginning of this Appendix.

Interior Properties

Name	Returns	Description
Color	Variant	Set / Get the color of the interior. Use the RGB function to create the color value.
ColorIndex	Variant	Set / Get the color of the interior. Use the XlColorIndex constants or an index value in the current color palette.
InvertIf Negative	Variant	Set / Get whether the color in the interior of the parent object is inverted if the values are negative.
Pattern	Variant	Set / Get the pattern to use for the interior of the parent object. Use one of the XlPattern constants.
Pattern Color	Variant	Set / Get the color of the interior pattern. Use the RGB function to create the color value.
Pattern ColorIndex	Variant	Set / Get the color of the interior pattern. Use the XlColorIndex constants or an index value in the current color palette.

Example: Interior Object

```
Sub FormatRange()
    Dim oInt As Interior

    'Get the interior of the current selection
    Set oInt = Selection.Interior

    'Format the interior in solid yellow
    '(colour depends on the workbook palette)
    With oInt
        .Pattern = xlSolid
        .ColorIndex = 6
    End With
End Sub
```

LeaderLines Object

The `LeaderLines` object contains the formatting attributes associated with leader lines on charts connecting data labels to the actual points. The parent of the `LeaderLines` object is the `Series` object. Use the `HasLeaderLines` property of the `Series` object to create a `LeaderLines` object and make sure one exists.

LeaderLines Common Properties

The `Application`, `Creator`, and `Parent` properties are defined at the beginning of this Appendix.

LeaderLines Properties

Name	Returns	Description
Border	Border	Read Only. Returns the border's properties around the leader lines.

LeaderLines Methods

Name	Returns	Parameters	Description
Delete			Deletes the LeaderLines object.
Select			Selects the leader lines on the chart.

Example: LeaderLines Object

```
Sub AddAndFormatLeaderLines()
    Dim oLL As LeaderLines

    'Using the first series of the PIE chart
    With Charts(1).SeriesCollection(1)

        'Add labels with leader lines (if required)
        .ApplyDataLabels HasLeaderLines:=True

        'Position the labels
        .DataLabels.Position = xlLabelPositionBestFit

        'Get the LeaderLines Object.  If all labels are
        'in their default position, this will give an error
        Set oLL = .LeaderLines
    End With

    'Format the leader lines
    With oLL
        .Border.LineStyle = xlContinuous
        .Border.ColorIndex = 5
    End With
End Sub
```

Legend Object

The Legend object contains the formatting options and legend entries for a particular chart. The parent of the Legend object is the Chart object. Use the HasLegend property of the Chart object to create a Legend object and to make sure one exists.

Legend Common Properties

The Application, Creator, and Parent properties are defined at the beginning of this Appendix.

Legend Properties

Name	Returns	Description
Auto Scale Font	Variant	Set / Get whether the font size will change automatically if the parent chart changes sizes.

Table Continued on Following Page

Name	Returns	Description
Border	Border	Read Only. Returns the border's properties around the legend.
Fill	ChartFill Format	Read Only. Returns an object containing fill formatting options for the legend of a chart.
Font	Font	Read Only. Returns an object containing Font options for the legend text.
Height	Double	Set / Get the height of the legend box.
Interior	Interior	Read Only. Returns an object containing options to format the inside area of a legend (e.g. interior color).
Left	Double	Set / Get the distance from the left edge of the legend box to the left edge of the chart containing the legend.
Name	String	Read Only. Returns the name of the Legend object.
Position	XlLegend Position	Set / Get the position of the legend on the chart (e.g. xlLegendPositionCorner, xlLegendPositionLeft).
Shadow	Boolean	Set / Get whether the legend has a shadow effect.
Top	Double	Set / Get the distance from the top edge of the legend box to the top edge of the chart containing the legend.
Width	Double	Set / Get the width of the legend box.

Legend Methods

Name	Returns	Parameters	Description
Clear	Variant		Deletes the legend.
Delete	Variant		Deletes the legend.
Legend Entries	Object	[Index]	Returns either one LegendEntry object or a LegendEntries collection depending if an Index parameter is specified. Contains all the legend text and markers.
Select	Variant		Selects the legend on the chart.

Example: Legend Object

```
Sub PlaceLegend()
    Dim oLgnd As Legend

    'Make sure the chart has a legend
    Charts(1).HasLegend = True

    'Get the Legend
    Set oLgnd = Charts(1).Legend

    'Position and format the legend
    With oLgnd
        .Position = xlLegendPositionRight
        .Border.LineStyle = xlNone
        .AutoScaleFont = False
    End With
End Sub
```

LegendEntry Object and the LegendEntries Collection

The LegendEntries collection contains the collection of entries in a legend. Each LegendEntry object represents a single entry in a legend. This consists of the legend entry text and the legend entry marker. The legend entry text is always the associated series name or trendline name. The parent of the LegendEntries collection is the Legend object.

The LegendEntries collection contains one property besides the typical collection attributes. The Count property returns the number of LegendEntry objects in the collection.

LegendEntry Common Properties

The Application, Creator, and Parent properties are defined at the beginning of this Appendix.

LegendEntry Properties

Name	Returns	Description
Auto Scale Font	Variant	Set / Get whether the font size will change automatically if the parent chart changes sizes.
Font	Font	Read Only. Returns an object containing Font options for the legend entry text.
Height	Double	Read Only. Returns the height of the legend entry.
Index	Long	Read Only. Returns the position of the LegendEntry in the LegendEntries collection.
Left	Double	Read Only. Returns the distance from the left edge of the legend entry box to the left edge of the chart.

Table Continued on Following Page

Name	Returns	Description
Legend Key	Legend Key	Read Only. Returns an object containing formatting associated with the legend entry marker.
Top	Double	Read Only. Returns the distance from the top edge of the legend entry box to the top edge of the chart.
Width	Double	Read Only. Returns the width of the legend entry.

LegendEntry Methods

Name	Returns	Parameters	Description
Delete	Variant		Deletes the LegendEntry object.
Select	Variant		Selects the legend entry on the chart.

Example: LegendEntry Object and the LegendEntries Collection

```
Sub FormatLegendEntries()
   Dim oLE As LegendEntry

   'Make sure the chart has a legend
   Charts(1).HasLegend = True

   'Loop through all the legend entries
   For Each oLE In Charts(1).Legend.LegendEntries

      'Format each entry with a different font style
      With oLE
         .Font.Size = 10 + .Index * 4
         .Font.Bold = (.Index Mod 2) = 0
         .Font.ColorIndex = .Index
      End With
   Next
End Sub
```

LegendKey Object

The LegendKey object contains properties and methods to manipulate the formatting associated with a legend key entry marker. A legend key is a visual representation, such as a color, that identifies a specific series or trendline.

LegendKey Common Properties

The Application, Creator, and Parent properties are defined at the beginning of this Appendix.

LegendKey Properties

Name	Returns	Description
Border	Border	Read Only. Returns the border's properties around the legend key.

Name	Returns	Description
Fill	Chart Fill Format	Read Only. Returns an object containing fill formatting options for the legend key of a series or trendline in a chart.
Height	Double	Read Only. Returns the height of the legend entry key.
Interior	Interior	Read Only. Returns an object containing options to format the inside area of the legend key (e.g. interior color).
InvertIf Negative	Boolean	Set / Get whether the color in the legend key is inverted if the values are negative.
Left	Double	Read Only. Returns the distance from the left edge of the legend key entry box to the left edge of the chart.
Marker Background Color	Long	Set / Get the color of the legend key background. Use the RGB function to create the color value.
Marker Background ColorIndex	XlColor Index	Set / Get the color of the legend key background. Use the XlColorIndex constants or an index value in the current color palette.
Marker Foreground Color	Long	Set / Get the color of the legend key foreground. Use the RGB function to create the color value.
Marker Foreground ColorIndex	XlColor Index	Set / Get the color of the legend key foreground. Use the XlColorIndex constants or an index value in the current color palette.
MarkerSize	Long	Set / Get the size of the legend key marker.
Marker Style	XlMarker Style	Set / Get the type of marker to use as the legend key (e.g. square, diamond, triangle, picture, etc.)
Picture Type	Long	Set / Get how an associated picture is displayed on the legend (e.g. stretched, tiled). Use the XlPictureType constants.
Picture Unit	Long	Set / Get how many units a picture represents if the PictureType property is set to xlScale.

Table Continued on Following Page

Name	Returns	Description
Shadow	Boolean	Set / Get whether a shadow effect appears around the legend entry key.
Smooth	Boolean	Set / Get whether the legend key has smooth curving enabled.
Top	Double	Read Only. Returns the distance from the top edge of the legend entry key box to the top edge of the chart.
Width	Double	Read Only. Returns the width of the legend entry key box.

LegendKey Methods

Name	Returns	Parameters	Description
Clear Formats	Variant		Clears the formatting made on the LegendKey object.
Delete	Variant		Deletes the LegendKey object.
Select	Variant		Selects the legend key on the parent chart.

Example: LegendKey Object

```
Sub FormatLegendKeys()
    Dim oLE As LegendEntry
    Dim oLK As LegendKey

    'Make sure the chart has a legend
    Charts(1).HasLegend = True

    'Loop through all the legend entries
    For Each oLE In Charts(1).Legend.LegendEntries

        'Get the legend key for the entry
        Set oLK = oLE.LegendKey

        'Format each legend key with a different colour and size
        With oLK
            .MarkerForegroundColor = oLE.Index
            .MarkerSize = oLE.Index * 2 + 1
        End With
    Next
End Sub
```

LineFormat Object

The LineFormat object represents the formatting associated with the line of the parent Shape object. The Line property of the Shape object is used to access the LineFormat object. The LineFormat object is commonly used to change line properties such as arrowhead styles and directions.

LineFormat Common Properties

The `Application`, `Creator`, and `Parent` properties are defined at the beginning of this Appendix.

LineFormat Properties

Name	Returns	Description
BackColor	ColorFormat	Read Only. Returns an object allowing manipulation of the background color of the line.
Begin Arrowhead Length	msoArrowhead Length	Set / Get the arrowhead length on the start of the line.
Begin Arrowhead Style	msoArrowhead Style	Set / Get how the arrowhead looks on the start of the line.
Begin Arrowhead Width	msoArrowhead Width	Set / Get the arrowhead width on the start of the line.
DashStyle	msoLineDash Style	Set / Get the style of the line.
EndArrowhead Length	msoArrowhead Length	Set / Get the arrowhead length on the end of the line.
EndArrowhead Style	msoArrowhead Style	Set / Get how the arrowhead looks on the end of the line.
EndArrowhead Width	msoArrowhead Width	Set / Get the arrowhead width on the end of the line.
ForeColor	ColorFormat	Read Only. Returns an object allowing manipulation of the background color of the line.
Pattern	msoPattern Type	Set / Get the pattern used on the line.
Style	msoLineStyle	Set / Get the line style.
Transparency	Single	Set / Get how transparent (1) or opaque (0) the line is.
Visible	msoTriState	Set / Get whether the line is visible.
Weight	Single	Set / Get how thick the line is.

Example: LineFormat Object

```
Sub AddAndFormatLine()
    Dim oShp As Shape
    Dim oLF As LineFormat
```

```
'Add a line shape
Set oShp = ActiveSheet.Shapes.AddLine(100, 100, 200, 250)

'Get the line format object
Set oLF = oShp.Line

'Set the line format
With oLF
    .BeginArrowheadStyle = msoArrowheadOval
    .EndArrowheadStyle = msoArrowheadTriangle
    .EndArrowheadLength = msoArrowheadLong
    .EndArrowheadWidth = msoArrowheadWide
    .Style = msoLineSingle
End With
End Sub
```

LinkFormat Object

The LinkFormat object represents the linking attributes associated with an OLE object or picture. The LinkFormat object is associated with a Shape object. Only Shape objects that are valid OLE objects can access the LinkFormat object.

LinkFormat Common Properties

The Application, Creator, and Parent properties are defined at the beginning of this Appendix.

LinkFormat Properties

Name	Returns	Description
Auto Update	Boolean	Set / Get whether the parent Shape object is updated whenever the source file changes or when the parent object is opened.
Locked	Boolean	Set / Get whether the parent Shape object does not update itself against the source file.

LinkFormat Methods

Name	Returns	Parameters	Description
Update			Updates the parent Shape object with the source file data.

Example: LinkFormat Object

```
Sub UpdateShapeLinks()
    Dim oShp As Shape
    Dim oLnkForm As LinkFormat

    'Loop through all the shapes in the sheet
    For Each oShp In ActiveSheet.Shapes

        'Is it a linked shape?
        If oShp.Type = msoLinkedOLEObject Or oShp.Type = msoLinkedPicture Then

            'Yes, so get the link format
            Set oLnkForm = oShp.LinkFormat
```

```
            'and update the link
            oLnkForm.Update
        End If
    Next
End Sub
```

Mailer Object

The Mailer object is used on the Macintosh to mail Excel files using the PowerTalk Mailer.

Mailer Common Properties

The Application, Creator, and Parent properties are defined at the beginning of this Appendix.

Mailer Properties

Name	Returns	Description
BCC Recipients	Variant	Set / Get the list of blind copies.
CC Recipients	Variant	Set / Get the list of carbon copies.
Enclosures	Variant	Set / Get the list of enclosures.
Received	Boolean	Read Only. Returns whether the mail message was received.
SendDate Time	Date	Read Only. Returns the date and time the message was sent.
Sender	String	Read Only. Returns the name of the mail message sender.
Subject	String	Set / Get the subject line of the mail message.
To Recipients	Variant	Set / Get the array of recipient names.
Which Address	Variant	Set / Get the address that the mail message originates from.

Name Object and the Names Collection

The Names collection holds the list of named ranges in a workbook. Each Name object describes a range of cells in a workbook that can be accessed by the name. Some Name objects are built-in (e.g. Print_Area) and others are user defined. The parent of the Names collection can be the WorkBook, Application, and Worksheet object. The Name object can also be accessed through the Range object.

The Names collection has an Add method besides the typical collection attributes. The Add method adds a Name object to the collection. The parameters of the Add method correspond to the properties of the Name object.

Name Common Properties

The Application, Creator, and Parent properties are defined at the beginning of this Appendix.

Name Properties

Name	Returns	Description
Category	String	Set / Get the category of the Name in the language used to create the macro. Valid only if the Name is a custom function or command.
Category Local	String	Set / Get the category of the Name in the language of the end user. Valid only if the Name is a custom function or command.
Index	Long	Read Only. Returns the spot that Name is located in the Names collection.
MacroType	XlXLM MacroType	Set / Get if the Name refers to command, function, or just a range.
Name	String	Set / Get the name of the Name object in the language of the macro.
Name Local	String	Set / Get the name of the Name object in the language of the end user.
RefersTo	Variant	Set / Get the range text that the Name refers to in the language of the macro and in A1 notation style.
RefersTo Local	Variant	Set / Get the range text that the Name refers to in the language of the user and in A1 notation style.
RefersToR 1C1	Variant	Set / Get the range text that the Name refers to in the language of the macro and in R1C1 notation style.
RefersTo R1C1 Local	Variant	Set / Get the range text that the Name refers to in the language of the user and in R1C1 notation style.
RefersTo Range	Range	Read Only. Returns the range that the Name refers to.
Shortcut Key	String	Set / Get the shortcut key to trigger a Microsoft Excel 4.0 macro associated with a Name.

Name	Returns	Description
Value	String	Set / Get the range text that the Name refers to in the language of the macro and in A1 notation style.
Visible	Boolean	Set / Get whether the name of the Name object appears in the Names Dialog box in Excel.

Name Methods

Name	Returns	Parameters	Description
Delete			Deletes the Name object from the collection.

Example: Name Object and the Names Collection

```
Sub DeleteInvalidNames()
    Dim oName As Name

    'Loop through all the names in the active workbook
    For Each oName In ActiveWorkbook.Names

        'Is it an invalid name?
        If InStr(1, oName.RefersTo, "#REF") > 0 Then

        'Yes, so log it
        Debug.Print "Deleted name " & oName.Name & " - " & oName.RefersToLocal

            'and delete it from the collection
            oName.Delete
        End If
    Next
End Sub
```

ODBCError Object and the ODBCErrors Collection

The ODBCErrors collection contains a list of errors that occurred by the most recent query using an ODBC connection. Each ODBCError object contains information describing an error that occurred on the most recent query using an ODBC connection. If the most recent query against an ODBC source did not generate any errors then the collection is empty.

The ODBCErrors collection has a Count property besides the typical collection attributes. The Count property returns the number of ODBCError objects in the collection.

ODBCError Common Properties

The Application, Creator, and Parent properties are defined at the beginning of this Appendix.

ODBCError Properties

Name	Returns	Description
ErrorString	String	Read Only. Returns the error string generated from the ODBC connection.
SqlState	String	Read Only. Returns the SQL state error generated from the ODBC connection.

Example: ODBCError Object and the ODBCErrors Collection

```
Sub CheckODBCErrors()
    Dim oErr As ODBCError
    Dim sMsg As String

    'Continue after errors
    On Error Resume Next

    'Don't show logon prompts etc
    Application.DisplayAlerts = False

    'Update an ODBC query table
    ActiveSheet.QueryTables(1).Refresh

    'Any errors?
    If Application.ODBCErrors.Count = 0 Then

        'No, so all OK
        MsgBox "Updated OK"
    Else
        'Yes, so list them all
        sMsg = "The following error(s) occured during the update"

        For Each oErr In Application.ODBCErrors
            sMsg = sMsg & vbCrLf & oErr.ErrorString & " (" & oErr.SqlState & ")"
        Next

        MsgBox sMsg
    End If
End Sub
```

OLEDBError Object and the OLEDBErrors Collection

The OLEDBErrors collection contains a list of errors that occurred by the most recent query using an OLE DB provider. Each OLEDBError object contains information describing an error that occurred on the most recent query using an OLE DB provider. If the most recent query against an OLE DB provider did not generate any errors then the collection is empty.

The OLEDBErrors collection has a Count property besides the typical collection attributes. The Count property returns the number of OLEDBError objects in the collection.

OLEDBError Common Properties

The Application, Creator, and Parent properties are defined at the beginning of this Appendix.

OLEDBError Properties

Name	Returns	Description
Error String	String	Read Only. Returns the error string generated from the OLE DB provider.
Native	Long	Read Only. Returns a provider specific error number describing the error.
Number	Long	Read Only. Returns the error number describing the error.
SqlState	String	Read Only. Returns the SQL state error generated from the OLE DB provider.
Stage	Long	Read Only. Returns the stage of an error generated from the OLE DB provider.

Example: OLEDBError Object and the OLEDBErrors Collection

```
Sub CheckOLEDbErrors()
    Dim oErr As OLEDBError
    Dim sMsg As String

    'Continue after errors
    On Error Resume Next

    'Don't show logon prompts etc
    Application.DisplayAlerts = False

    'Update an OLE DB pivot table
    ActiveSheet.PivotTables(1).Refresh

    'Any errors?
    If Application.OLEDBErrors.Count = 0 Then

        'No, so all OK
        MsgBox "Updated OK"
    Else
        'Yes, so list them all
        sMsg = "The following error(s) occured during the update"

        For Each oErr In Application.OLEDBErrors
            sMsg = sMsg & vbCrLf & oErr.ErrorString & " (" & oErr.SqlState & ")"
        Next

        MsgBox sMsg
    End If
End Sub
```

OLEFormat Object

The OLEFormat object represents all of attributes associated with an OLE object or ActiveX object for linking. Linking characteristics are taken care of by the LinkFormat object. The Shape object is the parent of the OLEFormat object. The parent Shape object must be a linked or embedded object to be able to use this object.

OLEFormat Common Properties

The Application, Creator, and Parent properties are defined at the beginning of this Appendix.

OLEFormat Properties

Name	Returns	Description
Object	Object	Read Only. Returns a reference to the parent OLE object.
ProgId	String	Read Only. Returns the ProgId of the parent OLE object.

OLEFormat Methods

Name	Returns	Parameters	Description
Activate			Activates and opens the parent OLE object.
Verb		[Verb]	Performs an action on the parent OLE object that triggers a reaction in the OLE object (e.g. xlOpen).

Example: OLEFormat Object

```
Sub PrintEmbeddedWordDocuments1()
    Dim oShp As Shape
    Dim oOF As OLEFormat

    'Loop through all the shapes in the sheet
    For Each oShp In ActiveSheet.Shapes

        'Is it an embedded object
        If oShp.Type = msoEmbeddedOLEObject Then

            'Get the embedded object's format
            Set oOF = oShp.OLEFormat

            'Is it a Word document?
            If oOF.ProgId Like "Word.Document*" Then

                'Yes, so print the Word document.
                'The first .Object gives us the generic
                'OLEObject contained in the Shape.
                'The second .Object gives us the Word object
                'contained within the OLEObject
                oOF.Object.Object.PrintOut
            End If
        End If
    Next
End Sub
```

OLEObject Object and the OLEObjects Collection

The OLEObjects collection holds all the ActiveX controls, linked OLE Objects and embedded OLE objects on a worksheet or chart. An OLE Object represents an ActiveX control, a linked OLE object, or an embedded OLE object on a worksheet or chart.

The OLEObjects collection has many properties and methods besides the typical collection attributes. These are listed in the following table.

OLEObjects Collection Properties and Methods

Name	Returns	Description
AutoLoad	Boolean	Set / Get whether the OLE object is automatically loaded when the workbook is opened. Not valid for ActiveX controls. Usually set to False. This property only works if there is one OLEObject in the collection.
Border	Border	Read Only. Returns the border's properties around the OLE object. This property only works if there is one OLEObject in the collection.
Count	Long	Read Only. Returns the number of OLEObject objects in the collection.
Enabled	Boolean	Set / Get whether the OLEObject is enabled. This property only works if there is one OLEObject in the collection.
Height	Double	Set / Get the height of OLEObject frame. This property only works if there is one OLEObject in the collection.
Interior	Interior	Read Only. Returns an object containing options to format the inside area of the OLE object (e.g. interior color). This property only works if there is one OLEObject in the collection.
Left	Double	Set / Get the distance from the left edge of the OLEObject frame to the left edge of the sheet. This property only works if there is one OLEObject in the collection.
Locked	Boolean	Set / Get whether editing will be possible when the parent sheet is protected. This property only works if there is one OLEObject in the collection.
Placement	Variant	Set / Get how the OLEObject object is anchored to the sheet (e.g. free floating, move with cells). Use the XlPlacement constants to set this property. This property only works if there is one OLEObject in the collection.
Print Object	Boolean	Set / Get whether the OLEObject on the sheet will be printed when the sheet is printed. This property only works if there is one OLEObject in the collection.

Table Continued on Following Page

Name	Returns	Description
Shadow	Boolean	Set / Get whether a shadow appears around the OLE object. This property only works if there is one OLEObject in the collection.
Shape Range	Shape Range	Read Only. Returns the OLE object as a Shape object. This property only works if there is one OLEObject in the collection.
Source Name	String	Set / Get the link source name of the OLE object. This property only works if there is one OLEObject in the collection.
Top	Double	Set / Get the distance from top edge of the OLE object to the top of the parent sheet. This property only works if there is one OLEObject in the collection.
Visible	Boolean	Set / Get whether all the OLEObjects in the collection are visible.
Width	Double	Set / Get the width of the OLE object frame. This property only works if there is one OLEObject in the collection.
ZOrder	Long	Read Only. Returns the position of the OLE object among all the other objects on the sheet. This property only works if there is one OLEObject in the collection.
Add	OLE Object	Method. Parameters: [ClassType], [Filename], [Link], [DisplayAsIcon], [IconFileName], [IconIndex], [IconLabel], [Left], [Top], [Width], [Height]. Adds an OLE object to the collection of OLEObjects. The position of the new OLE Object can be specified by using the Left, Top, Width and Height parameters. The type of OLEObject (ClassType) or its location (FileName) can be specified as well. The other parameters have equivalent OLEObject properties.
BringTo Front	Variant	Method. Brings all the OLE objects in the collection to the front of all the other objects.
Copy	Variant	Method. Copies all the OLE objects in the collection into the clipboard.

Name	Returns	Description
Copy Picture	Variant	Method. Parameters: [Appearance As XlPictureAppearance], [Format As XlCopyPictureFormat], [Size As XlPictureAppearance]. Copies the OLE objects in the collection into the clipboard as a picture. The Appearance parameter can be used to specify whether the picture is copied as it looks on the screen or when printed. The Format parameter can specify the type of picture that will be put into the clipboard.
Cut	Variant	Method. Cuts all the OLE objects in the collection into the clipboard.
Delete	Variant	Method. Deletes all the OLEObject objects in the collection into the clipboard.
Duplicate		Method. Duplicates all the OLEObject objects in the collection into the parent sheet.
Select	Variant	Method. Parameters: [Replace]. Selects all the OLEObject objects in the collection.
SendTo Back	Variant	Method. Brings the OLEObject objects in the collection to the back of other objects.

OLEObject Common Properties

The Application, Creator, and Parent properties are defined at the beginning of this Appendix.

OLEObject Properties

Name	Returns	Description
AltHTML	String	Set / Get what HTML to use when the document is saved as a web page instead of embedding the OLE control.
AutoLoad	Boolean	Set / Get whether the OLE object is automatically loaded when the workbook is opened. Not valid for ActiveX controls. Usually set the False.
Auto Update	Boolean	Set / Get whether the OLE object is automatically updated when the source changes. Valid only for linked objects (OLEType=xlOLELink).

Table Continued on Following Page

Name	Returns	Description
Border	Border	Read Only. Returns the border's properties around the OLE object.
Bottom RightCell	Range	Read Only. Returns the single cell range located under the lower-right corner of the OLE Object
Enabled	Boolean	Set / Get whether the OLEObject is enabled.
Height	Double	Set / Get the height of OLEObject frame.
Index	Long	Read Only. Returns the spot in the collection where the current OLEObject is located.
Interior	Interior	Read Only. Returns an object containing options to format the inside area of the OLE object (e.g. interior color).
Left	Double	Set / Get the distance from the left edge of the OLEObject frame to the left edge of the sheet.
Linked Cell	String	Set / Get the range that receives the value from the results of the OLE object.
ListFill Range	String	Set / Get the range that holds the values used by an ActiveX list box.
Locked	Boolean	Set / Get whether editing will be possible when the parent sheet is protected.
Name	String	Set / Get the name of the OLE object.
Object		Read Only. Returns access to some of the properties and methods of the underlying object in the OLE object.
OLEType	Variant	Read Only. Returns the type OLE object: xlOLELink or xlOLEEmbed. Use the XlOLEType constants.
Placement	Variant	Set / Get how the OLEObject object is anchored to the sheet (e.g. free floating, move with cells). Use the XlPlacement constants to set this property.
Print Object	Boolean	Set / Get whether the OLEObject on the sheet will be printed when the sheet is printed.
ProgId	String	Read Only. Returns the programmatic identifier associated with the OLE object (e.g. "Excel.Application").
Shadow	Boolean	Set / Get whether a shadow appears around the OLE object.

Name	Returns	Description
Shape Range	Shape Range	Read Only. Returns the OLE object as a Shape object.
Source Name	String	Set / Get the link source name of the OLE object.
Top	Double	Set / Get the distance from top edge of the OLE object to the top of the parent sheet.
TopLeft Cell	Range	Read Only. Returns the single cell range located above the top-left corner of the OLE object.
Visible	Boolean	Set / Get whether the OLEObject is visible
Width	Double	Set / Get the width of the OLE object frame.
ZOrder	Long	Read Only. the position of the OLE object among all the other objects on the sheet.

OLEObject Methods

Name	Returns	Parameters	Description
Activate	Variant		Sets the focus and activates the OLE object.
BringTo Front	Variant		Brings the OLE object to the front of all the other objects.
Copy	Variant		Copies the OLE object into the clipboard.
Copy Picture	Variant	[Appearance As XlPicture Appearance], [Format As XlCopyPicture Format], [Size As XlPictureAppe arance]	Copies the OLE object into the clipboard as a picture. The Appearance parameter can be used to specify whether the picture is copied as it looks on the screen or when printed. The Format parameter can specify the type of picture that will be put into the clipboard
Cut	Variant		Cuts the OLE object into the clipboard.

Table Continued on Following Page

Name	Returns	Parameters	Description
Delete	Variant		Deletes the OLEObject object into the clipboard.
Duplicate			Duplicates the OLEObject object into the parent sheet.
Select	Variant	[Replace]	Selects the OLEObject object.
SendTo Back	Variant		Brings the OLEObject object to the back of other objects.
Update	Variant		Updates the OLE object link if applicable.
Verb	Variant	Verb As XlOLEVerb	Performs an action on the parent OLE object that triggers a reaction in the OLE object (e.g. xlOpen).

OLEObject Events

Name	Parameters	Description
GotFocus		Triggered when the OLE object gets focus.
LostFocus		Triggered when the OLE object loses focus.

Example: OLEObject Object and the OLEObjects Collection

```
Sub PrintEmbeddedWordDocuments2()
    Dim oOLE As OLEObject

    'Loop through all the shapes in the sheet
    For Each oOLE In ActiveSheet.OLEObjects

        'Is it a Word document?
        If oOLE.ProgId Like "Word.Document*" Then

            'Yes, so print the Word document.
            oOLE.Object.PrintOut
        End If
    Next
End Sub
```

Outline Object

The Outline object represents the outline feature in Excel. The parent of the Outline object is the WorkSheet object.

Outline Common Properties

The `Application`, `Creator`, and `Parent` properties are defined at the beginning of this Appendix.

Outline Properties

Name	Returns	Description
Automatic Styles	Boolean	Set / Get whether the outline has styles automatically assigned by Excel.
Summary Column	XlSummary Column	Set / Get whether the summary columns are to the left (xlLeft) or the right (xlRight) of the detail columns.
Summary Row	XlSummary Row	Set / Get whether the summary rows are above (xlAbove) or below (xlBelow) the detail rows.

Outline Methods

Name	Returns	Parameters	Description
Show Levels	Variant	[RowLevels], [ColumnLevels]	Show the detail of rows and columns at a higher level as specified by the RowLevels and ColumnLevels parameters, respectively. The rest of the detail for the other levels is hidden.

Example: Outline Object

```
Sub ShowOutlines()
   Dim oOutl As Outline

   'Group some rows
   ActiveSheet.Range("4:5").Group

   'Get the Outline object
   Set oOutl = ActiveSheet.Outline

   'Format the outline display
   With oOutl
      .ShowLevels 1
      .SummaryRow = xlSummaryAbove
   End With
End Sub
```

PageSetup Object

The `PageSetup` object contains the functionality of the **Page Setup** dialog box. Possible parents of the `PageSetup` object are the `Chart` and `Worksheet` object.

PageSetup Common Properties

The `Application`, `Creator`, and `Parent` properties are defined at the beginning of this Appendix.

PageSetup Properties

Name	Returns	Description
BlackAnd White	Boolean	Set / Get whether worksheet items will be printed in black and white only. Not valid when parents are `Chart` objects.
BottomMargin	Double	Set / Get the bottom margin of the page in points.
CenterFooter	String	Set / Get the text for the center part of the footer.
CenterHeader	String	Set / Get the text for the center part of the header.
Center Horizontally	Boolean	Set / Get whether the worksheet or chart will be horizontally centered on the page.
Center Vertically	Boolean	Set / Get whether the worksheet or chart will be vertically centered on the page.
ChartSize	XlObjectSize	Set / Get how the chart is scaled to fit one page (`xlFullPage` or `xlFitToPage`) or the same way it appears on the screen (`xlScreenSize`). Not valid when parents are `Worksheet` objects.
Draft	Boolean	Set / Get whether graphics will be printed. `True` means graphics will not be printed.
FirstPage Number	Long	Set / Get which number will be used as the first page number. Use `xlAutomatic` to have Excel choose this (default).
FitToPages Tall	Variant	Set / Get how many pages tall the sheet will be scaled to. Setting this property to `False` will mean the `FitToPagesWide` property will be used.

Name	Returns	Description
FitToPages Wide	Variant	Set / Get how many pages wide the sheet will be scaled to. Setting this property to False will mean the FitToPagesTall property will be used.
FooterMargin	Double	Set / Get the distance from the page bottom to the footer of the page in points.
HeaderMargin	Double	Set / Get the distance from the page top to the header of the page in points.
LeftFooter	String	Set / Get the text for the left part of the footer.
LeftHeader	String	Set / Get the text for the left part of the header.
LeftMargin	Double	Set / Get the left margin of the page in points.
Order	XlOrder	Set / Get the manner that Excel numbers pages for large worksheets (e.g. xlDownTheOver, xlOverThenDown). Not valid for parents that are Chart objects.
Orientation	XlPage Orientation	Set / Get the page orientation: xlLandscape or xlPortrait.
PaperSize	XlPaper Size	Set / Get the paper size (e.g. xlPaperLetter, xlPaperLegal, etc)
PrintArea	String	Set / Get the range on a worksheet that will be printed. If this property is set to False then the entire sheet is printed. Not valid for parents that are Chart objects.
Print Comments	XlPrint Location	Set / Get how comments are printed or if they are at all (e.g. xlPrintInPlace, xlPrintNoComments).
Print Gridlines	Boolean	Set / Get whether cell gridlines are printed for a worksheet. Not valid for parents that are Chart objects.

Table Continued on Following Page

Name	Returns	Description
Print Headings	Boolean	Set / Get whether row and column headings are printed.
PrintNotes	Boolean	Set / Get whether notes attached the cells are printed at the end as endnotes. Not valid if parents are Chart objects.
PrintTitle Columns	String	Set / Get which columns to repeat on the left side of every printed page.
PrintTitle Rows	String	Set / Get which rows to repeat on the top of every page.
RightFooter	String	Set / Get the text for the right part of the footer.
RightHeader	String	Set / Get the text for the right part of the header.
RightMargin	Double	Set / Get the right margin of the page in points.
TopMargin	Double	Set / Get the top margin of the page in points.
Zoom	Variant	Set / Get the percentage scaling that will occur for the worksheet. Not valid for parents that are Chart objects. (10 to 400 percent).

PageSetup Methods

Name	Returns	Parameters	Description
Print Quality	Variant	[Index]	Set / Get the print quality. The Index parameter can be used to specify horizontal (1) or vertical (2) print quality.

Example: PageSetup Object

```
Sub SetUpPage()
    Dim oPS As PageSetup

    'Get the sheet's PageSetup object
    Set oPS = ActiveSheet.PageSetup

    'Set up the page
    With oPS
        'Set the paper size to the local default
        .PaperSize = fnLocalPaperSize
        .Orientation = xlPortrait
        'etc.
    End With
End Sub
```

```
Function fnLocalPaperSize() As XlPaperSize

    'Remember the paper size when we've read it
    Static iPaperSize As XlPaperSize

    'Is it set?
    If iPaperSize = 0 Then

        'No, so create a new workbook and read off the paper size
        With Workbooks.Add
            iPaperSize = .Worksheets(1).PageSetup.PaperSize
            .Close False
        End With
    End If

    'Return the paper size
    fnLocalPaperSize = iPaperSize
End Function
```

Pane Object and the Panes Collection

The Panes collection allows manipulation of the different panes of a window. A Pane object is equivalent to single pane of a window. The parent object of the Panes collection is the Window object. Besides the typical collection properties and methods the Panes collection has a Count property. The Count property returns the number of Pane objects in the collection.

Pane Common Properties

The Application, Creator, and Parent properties are defined at the beginning of this Appendix.

Pane Properties

Name	Returns	Description
Index	Long	Read Only. Returns the spot in the collection where Pane object is located.
Scroll Column	Long	Set / Get which column number is the leftmost column in the pane window.
Scroll Row	Long	Set / Get which row number is the top row in the pane window.
Visible Range	Range	Read Only. Returns the cell range that is visible in the pane.

Pane Methods

Name	Returns	Parameters	Description
Activate	Boolean		Activates the pane.

Table Continued on Following Page

Name	Returns	Parameters	Description
Large Scroll	Variant	[Down], [Up], [ToRight], [ToLeft]	Causes the document to scroll a certain direction a screen-full at a time as specified by the parameters.
Scroll IntoView		Left As Long, Top As Long, Width As Long, Height As Long, [Start]	Scrolls the spot specified by the Left, Top, Width, and Height parameters to either the upper-left corner of the pane (Start = True) or the lower-right corner of the pane (Start = False). The Left, Top, Width, and Height parameters are specified in points.
Small Scroll	Variant	[Down], [Up], [ToRight], [ToLeft]	Causes the document to scroll a certain direction a document line at a time as specified by the parameters.

Example: Pane Object and the Panes Collection

```
Sub ScrollActivePane()
    Dim oPane As Pane
    Dim oRNg As Range

    'The range to show in the pane
    Set oRNg = Range("G3:J10")

    'Get the active pane
    Set oPane = Application.ActiveWindow.ActivePane

    'Scroll the pane to show the range in the top-left corner
    oPane.ScrollColumn = oRNg.Column
    oPane.ScrollRow = oRNg.Row
End Sub
```

Parameter Object and the Parameters Collection

The Parameters collection holds the list of parameters associated with a query table. If no parameters exist then the collection has no Parameter objects inside of it. Each Parameter object represents a single parameter for a query table. The parent of the Parameters collection is the QueryTable object.

The Parameters collection has a few extra properties and methods besides the typical collection attributes. They are listed in the table below.

Parameters Collection Properties and Methods

Name	Returns	Description
Count	Long	Read Only. Returns the number of `Parameter` objects in the collection.
Add	Parameter	Method. Parameters: `Name As String`, `[iDataType]`. Adds a parameter to the collection creating a new query parameter for the parent query table. The type of parameter can be specified by `iDataType`. Use the `XlParamaterDataType` constants for `iDataType`.
Delete		Method. Deletes the parameters in the collection.

Parameter Common Properties

The `Application`, `Creator`, and `Parent` properties are defined at the beginning of this Appendix.

Parameter Properties

Name	Returns	Description
DataType	XlParameter DataType	Set / Get the data type of the parameter.
Name	String	Set / Get the name of the parameter.
Prompt String	String	Read Only. Returns the prompt that is displayed to the user when prompted for a parameter value.
Refresh OnChange	Boolean	Set / Get whether the query table results are refreshed when the parameter value changes.
Source Range	Range	Read Only. Returns the range of text that contains the parameter value.
Type	XlParameter Type	Read Only. Returns the type of parameter (e.g. `xlConstant`, `xlPrompt`, or `xlRange`). `XlConstant` means that the `Value` parameter has the value of the parameter. `XlPrompt` means that the user is prompted for the value. `XlRange` means that the value defines the cell range that contains the value.
Value	Variant	Read Only. Returns the parameter value.

Parameter Methods

Name	Returns	Parameters	Description
SetParam		Type As XlParameterType, Value	Set / Get the type of the parameter and the value of the parameter.

Example: Parameter Object and the Parameters Collection

```
Sub UpdateQuery()
    Dim oParam As Parameter

    'Using the Query Table...
    With ActiveSheet.QueryTables(1)

        'Get the first parameter
        Set oParam = .Parameters(1)

        'Set its value
        oParam.SetParam xlConstant, "Company"

        'Refresh the query
        .Refresh
    End With
End Sub
```

Phonetic Object and the Phonetics Collection

The Phonetics collection holds all of the phonetic text in a range. The Phonetic object represents a single phonetic text string. The parent of the Phonetics object is the Range object.

The Phonetics collection has a few properties and methods besides the typical collection attributes. They are listed in the following table.

Phonetics Collection Properties and Methods

Name	Returns	Description
Alignment	Long	Set / Get the alignment for the phonetic text. Use the XlPhoneticAlignment constants.
Character Type	Long	Set / Get the type of phonetic text to use. Use the XLPhoneticCharacterType constants.
Count	Long	Read Only. Returns the number of Phonetic objects in the collection.
Font	Font	Read Only. Returns an object containing Font options for the text in the Phonetics collection.
Length	Long	Read Only. Returns the number of phonetic text characters starting from the Start parameter.

Name	Returns	Description
Start	Long	Read Only. Returns what the position is that represents the first character of the phonetic text strings. Valid only if there is only one Phonetic object in the collection.
Text	String	Set / Get the phonetic text. Valid only if there is only one Phonetic object in the collection.
Visible	Boolean	Set / Get whether the phonetic text is visible to the end user. Valid only if there is only one Phonetic object in the collection.
Add		Method. Parameters: Start As Long, Length As Long, Text As String. Adds a Phonetic object to the collection at the cell specified by the parent Range object.
Delete		Method. Deletes all the Phonetic objects in the collection.

Phonetic Common Properties

The Application, Creator, and Parent properties are defined at the beginning of this Appendix.

Phonetic Properties

Name	Returns	Description
Alignment	Long	Set / Get the alignment for the phonetic text. Use the XlPhoneticAlignment constants.
Character Type	Long	Set / Get the type of phonetic text to use. Use the XLPhoneticCharacterType constants.
Font	Font	Read Only. Returns an object containing Font options for the phonetic text.
Text	String	Set / Get the phonetic text.
Visible	Boolean	Set / Get whether the phonetic text is visible to the end user.

PictureFormat Object

The PictureFormat object allows manipulation of the picture properties of the parent Shape object.

PictureFormat Common Properties

The `Application`, `Creator`, and `Parent` properties are defined at the beginning of this Appendix.

PictureFormat Properties

Name	Returns	Description
Brightness	Single	Set / Get the brightness of the parent shape (0 to 1 where 1 is the brightest).
ColorType	msoPicture ColorType	Set / Get the type of color setting of the parent shape.
Contrast	Single	Set / Get the contrast of the parent shape (0 to 1 where 1 is the greatest contrast).
CropBottom	Single	Set / Get how much is cropped off the bottom.
CropLeft	Single	Set / Get how much is cropped off the left.
CropRight	Single	Set / Get how much is cropped off the right.
CropTop	Single	Set / Get how much is cropped off the top.
Transparency Color	Long	Set / Get the color used for transparency.
Transparent Background	msoTri State	Set / Get whether transparent colors appear transparent.

PictureFormat Methods

Name	Returns	Parameters	Description
Increment Brightness		Increment As Single	Increases the brightness by the Increment value.
Increment Contrast		Increment As Single	Increases the contrast by the Increment value.

Example: PictureFormat Object

```
Sub SetPictureFormat()
    Dim oShp As Shape
    Dim oPF As PictureFormat

    For Each oShp In ActiveSheet.Shapes
        If oShp.Type = msoPicture Then

            'Get the PictureFormat
            Set oPF = oShp.PictureFormat
```

```
        'Format the picture
        With oPF
            .TransparentBackground = msoTrue
            .TransparencyColor = RGB(255, 0, 0)
            .ColorType = msoPictureWatermark
        End With
    End If
    Next
End Sub
```

PivotCache Object and the PivotCaches Collection

The PivotCaches collection holds the collection of memory 'caches' holding the data associated with a PivotTable report. Each PivotCache object represents a single memory cache for a PivotTable report. The parent of the PivotCaches collection is the Workbook object. As well a possible parent of the PivotCache object is the PivotTable object.

The PivotCaches has a Count property and Add method besides the typical collection attributes. The Count property returns the number of items in the collection. The Add method takes a SourceType constant (from the XlPivotTableSourceType constants) and SourceData to add a PivotCache to the collection.

PivotCache Common Properties

The Application, Creator, and Parent properties are defined at the beginning of this Appendix.

PivotCache Properties

Name	Returns	Description
Background Query	Boolean	Set / Get if the processing of queries in a PivotTable report is done asynchronously. False for OLAP data sources.
Command Text	Variant	Set / Get the SQL command used to retrieve data.
Command Type	XlCmd Type	Set / Get the type of CommandText (e.g. xlCmdSQL, xlCmdTable).
Connection	Variant	Set / Get either the OLE DB connection string, the ODBC string, Web data source, path to a text file, or path to a database.
EnableRefr esh	Boolean	Set / Get whether the PivotTable cache data can be refreshed. Always False for OLAP data sources.
Index	Long	Read Only. Returns the spot in the collection for the specific cache.

Table Continued on Following Page

Name	Returns	Description
Local Connection	String	Set / Get the connection string to an offline cube file. Blank for non-OLAP data sources. Use with `UseLocalConnection`.
Maintain Connection	Boolean	Set / Get whether the connection to the data source does not close until the workbook is closed. Valid only against an OLE DB source.
MemoryUsed	Long	Read Only. Returns the amount of bytes used by the `PivotTable` cache.
Optimize Cache	Boolean	Set / Get whether the `PivotTable` cache is optimized when it is built. Always `False` for OLE DB data sources.
QueryType	xlQuery Type	Read Only. Returns the type of connection associated with the query table. (e.g. `xlOLEDBQuery`, `xlDAOQuery`, `xlTextImport`).
Record Count	Long	Read Only. Returns the number of records in the `PivotTable` cache.
Recordset		Set / Get the recordset used as the data source for the `PivotTable` cache.
Refresh Date	Date	Read Only. Returns the date the cache was last refreshed.
Refresh Name	String	Read Only. Returns the name of the person who last refreshed the cache.
RefreshOn FileOpen	Boolean	Set / Get whether the `PivotTable` cache is refreshed when the workbook is opened.
Refresh Period	Long	Set / Get how long (minutes) between automatic refreshes from the data source. Set to 0 to disable.
Save Password	Boolean	Set / Get whether an ODBC connection password is saved with the query table.
SourceData	Variant	Set / Get the data source for the `PivotTable` report.
UseLocal Connection	Boolean	Set / Get if the `LocalConnection` property is used to set the data source. `False` means the `Connection` property is used. Allows you to store some data sources offline.

PivotCache Methods

Name	Returns	Parameters	Description
Create Pivot Table	Pivot Table	Table Destination, [TableName], [ReadData]	Creates a `PivotTable` report that is based on the current `PivotCache` object. The `TableDestination` parameter specifies where the new `PivotTable` report will be located. A `TableName` can also be specified. Set `ReadData` to `True` to fill the cache with all the records from the external database. Set `ReadData` to `True` to only retrieve some of the data.
Refresh			Refreshes the data in the `PivotTable` cache with the latest copy of the external data. Set the `BackgroundQuery` parameter to `True` to get the data to refresh asynchronously.
Reset Timer			Resets the time for the automatic refresh set by `RefreshPeriod` property.

Example: PivotCache Object and the PivotCaches Collection

```
Sub RefreshPivotCache()
    Dim oPC As PivotCache

    Set oPC = ActiveWorkbook.PivotCaches(1)

    With oPC
        'Refresh in the foreground
        .BackgroundQuery = False

        'Only refresh if the data is over 1 hour old
        If .RefreshDate < Now - TimeValue("01:00:00") Then
            .Refresh
        End If
    End With
End Sub
```

PivotField Object, PivotFields Collection and the CalculatedFields Collection

The `PivotFields` collection holds the collection of fields associated with the parent `PivotTable` report. The `CalculatedFields` collection holds the collection of calculated fields associated with the parent `PivotTable` report. Each `PivotField` object represents single field in a `PivotTable` report. The parent of the `PivotFields` and `CalculatedFields` collection is the `PivotTable` object.

The PivotFields and CalculatedFields collections have one extra property besides the typical collection attributes. The Count property returns the number of fields in the parent collection. The CalculatedFields collection also has an Add method that adds a new calculated field to the collection given a Name and a Formula.

PivotField Common Properties

The Application, Creator, and Parent properties are defined at the beginning of this Appendix.

PivotField Properties

Name	Returns	Description
Auto ShowCount	Long	Read Only. Returns the number of top or bottom items that are automatically displayed in the PivotTable field.
Auto ShowField	String	Read Only. Returns the name of the data field used to figure out what top or bottom items to show automatically for a PivotTable field.
Auto ShowRange	Long	Read Only. Returns either xlTop if the top items are shown automatically or xlBottom if the bottom items are shown.
AutoShowType	Long	Read Only. Returns either xlAutomatic if AutoShow is True or xlManual if AutoShow is disabled.
Auto SortField	String	Read Only. Returns the data field name that will be used to sort the PivotTable field automatically.
Auto SortOrder	Long	Read Only. Returns one of the XLSortOrder constants specifying the automatic sort order type used for the field.
BaseField	Variant	Set / Get the base field used for a calculation. Data fields only.
BaseItem	Variant	Set / Get the base item in the base field used for a calculation. Data fields only.
Calculation	XlPivotField Calculation	Set / Get the type of calculation to do on the data field.

Name	Returns	Description
Caption	String	Set / Get the text label to use for the field.
ChildField	PivotField	Read Only. Returns the child field of the current field, if any.
ChildItems	Variant	Read Only. Parameters: [Index]. Returns an object or collection containing a single PivotTable item (PivotItem) or group of PivotTable items (PivotItems) associated with the field.
CubeField	CubeField	Read Only. Returns the cube field that the current PivotTable field comes from.
CurrentPage	Variant	Set / Get the current page showing for the page field. Page fields only.
Current PageName	String	Set / Get the displayed page of the PivotTable report.
DataRange	Range	Read Only. Returns a range containing the data or items in the field.
DataType	XlPivotField DataType	Read Only. Returns the data type of the PivotTable field.
DragToColumn	Boolean	Set / Get whether the field can be dragged to a column position.
DragToData	Boolean	Set / Get whether the field can be dragged to the data position.
DragToHide	Boolean	Set / Get whether the field can be dragged off the PivotTable report and therefore hidden.
DragToPage	Boolean	Set / Get whether the field can be dragged to the page position.
DragToRow	Boolean	Set / Get whether the field can be dragged to a row position.
DrilledDown	Boolean	Set / Get whether the PivotTable field can be drilled down.
Formula	String	Set / Get the formula associated with field, if any.

Table Continued on Following Page

Name	Returns	Description
Function	Xl Consolidation Function	Set / Get the type of function used to summarize the PivotTable field.
GroupLevel	Variant	Read Only. Returns how the field is placed within a group of fields.
HiddenItems	Variant	Read Only. Parameters: [Index]. Returns an object or collection containing a single hidden PivotTable item (PivotItem) or group of hidden PivotTable items (PivotItems) associated with the field.
IsCalculated	Boolean	Read Only. Returns whether the PivotTable field is calculated.
LabelRange	Range	Read Only. Returns the cell range containing the field's label.
Layout BlankLine	Boolean	Set / Get whether a blank row is added just after the current row field.
LayoutForm	XlLayout FormType	Set / Get how the items will appear in the field.
Layout PageBreak	Boolean	Set / Get whether a page break is inserted after each field.
Layout Subtotal Location	xLSubtototal LocationType	Set / Get the location for the field subtotals as compared to the current field.
MemoryUsed	Long	Read Only. Returns the number of bytes of computer memory being used for the field.
Name	String	Set / Get the name of the field.
NumberFormat	String	Set / Get the format used for numbers in the field.
Orientation	XlPivot Field Orientation	Set / Get the where the field is located in the PivotTable report.
ParentField	PivotField	Read Only. Returns the parent field of the current field, if any.

Name	Returns	Description
ParentItems	Variant	Read Only. Parameters: [Index]. Returns an object or collection containing a single parent PivotTable item (PivotItem) or group of parent PivotTable items (PivotItems) associated with the field.
Position	Variant	Set / Get the position number of the field among all the fields in the same orientation.
ServerBased	Boolean	Set / Get whether only items that match the page field selection are retrieved from the external data source.
ShowAllItems	Boolean	Set / Get whether all items in the field are displayed.
SourceName	String	Read Only. Returns the name of the source data for the field.
SubtotalName	String	Set / Get the label used for the subtotal column or row for this field.
Subtotals	Variant	Parameters: [Index]. Set / Get the subtotals displayed for the field.
TotalLevels	Variant	Read Only. Returns the total number of fields in the current field group.
Value	String	Set / Get the name of the field.
VisibleItems	Variant	Read Only. Parameters: [Index]. Returns an object or collection containing a single visible PivotTable item (PivotItem) or group of visible PivotTable items (PivotItems) associated with the field.

PivotField Methods

Name	Returns	Parameters	Description
AutoShow		Type As Long, Range As Long, Count As Long, Field As String	Set the number of top or bottom items to display for a row, page, or column field. Type describes whether the items are shown as xlAutomatic or xlManual. Range is the location to start showing items. Count is the number of items to show for the field. Field is the base data field name.
AutoSort		Order As Long, Field As String	Sets the field to automatically sort based on the Order specified (using XlSortOrder constants) and the base data Field.
Calculated Items	Calculated Items		Returns the group of calculated PivotTable items associated with the field.
Delete			Deletes the PivotField object.
PivotItems	Variant	[Index]	Returns an object or collection containing a single PivotTable item (PivotItem) or group of PivotTable items (PivotItems) associated with the field.

Example: PivotField Object, PivotFields Collection and the CalculatedFields

```
Sub AddField()
    Dim oPT As PivotTable
    Dim oPF As PivotField

    Set oPT = ActiveSheet.PivotTables(1)

    Set oPF = oPT.CalculatedFields.Add("Total", "=Price * Volume")
```

```
    oPF.Orientation = xlDataField
End Sub
```

PivotFormula Object and the PivotFormulas Collection

The PivotFormulas collection holds the formulas associated with the PivotTable. Each PivotFormula object represents a formula being used in a PivotTable report. The parent of the PivotFormulas collection is the PivotTable object.

The PivotFormulas collection has a Count property and an Add method besides the typical collection attributes. The Count property returns the number of items in the collection. The Add method takes a Formula string and adds a PivotFormula to the collection.

PivotFormula Common Properties

The Application, Creator, and Parent properties are defined at the beginning of this Appendix.

PivotFormula Properties

Name	Returns	Description
Formula	String	Set / Get the formula associated with the table. Use the A1-style reference notation.
Index	Long	Read Only. Returns the order that the formulas in the parent collection will be processed.
Value	String	Set / Get the formula associated with the table.

PivotFormula Methods

Name	Returns	Parameters	Description
Delete			Deletes the formula from the parent collection.

PivotItem Object, PivotItems Collection, and the CalculatedItems Collection

The PivotItems collection holds the collection of individual data entries in a field. The CalculatedItems collection holds the collection of individual calculated entries in a field. Each PivotItem object represents a single entry in a data field. The parent of the PivotItems and CalculatedItems collections is the PivotField object.

The PivotItems and Calculated items have one extra property besides the typical collection attributes. The Count property returns the number of objects in the collection. Also, the Add method of the PivotItems collection adds another item to the collection (only a Name is required). The Add method of the CalculatedItems collection adds another item to the collection but requires a Name and a Formula to be specified.

PivotItem Common Properties

The Application, Creator, and Parent properties are defined at the beginning of this Appendix.

PivotItem Properties

Name	Returns	Description
Caption	String	Set / Get the label text associated with the item.
ChildItems	Variant	Read Only. Parameters: [Index]. Returns an object or collection containing a single PivotTable item (PivotItem) or group of PivotTable items (PivotItems) associated with the item.
DataRange	Range	Read Only. Returns a range containing the data or items in the item.
Drilled Down	Boolean	Set / Get whether the PivotTable item can be drilled down.
Formula	String	Set / Get the formula associated with item, if any.
Is Calculated	Boolean	Read Only. Returns whether the item was calculated is a data item.
LabelRange	Range	Read Only. Returns the cell range containing the field's item.
Name	String	Set / Get the name of the item.
ParentItem	Pivot Item	Read Only. Returns the parent item of the current item, if any.
Parent ShowDetail	Boolean	Read Only. Returns whether the current item is being show because the one of the item's parents is set to show detail.
Position	Long	Set / Get the position number of the item among all the items in the same orientation.
Record Count	Long	Read Only. Returns the number of records in the PivotTable cache that contain the item.

Name	Returns	Description
ShowDetail	Boolean	Set / Get whether the detail items are being displayed.
Source Name	Variant	Read Only. Returns the name of the source data for the item.
Value	String	Set / Get the name of the specified item.
Visible	Boolean	Set / Get whether the item is visible.

PivotItem Methods

Name	Returns	Parameters	Description
Delete			Deletes the item from the collection.

Example: PivotItem Object, PivotItems Collection, and the CalculatedItems Collection

```
Sub ShowPivotItemData()
    Dim oPT As PivotTable
    Dim oPI As PivotItem

    'Get the pivot table
    Set oPT = ActiveSheet.PivotTables(1)

    'Get the pivot item
    Set oPI = oPT.PivotFields("Product").PivotItems("Oranges")

    'Show all the source data rows for that pivot item
    oPI.ShowDetail = True
End Sub
```

PivotLayout Object

The PivotLayout object describes how the fields of a PivotChart are placed in the parent chart. Either the Chart object or the ChartGroup object is the parent of the PivotChart object.

PivotLayout Common Properties

The Application, Creator, and Parent properties are defined at the beginning of this Appendix.

PivotLayout Properties

Name	Returns	Description
Column Fields		Read Only. Parameters: [Index]. Returns an object or collection containing the PivotTable field (PivotField) or PivotTable fields (PivotFields) associated with the columns of the PivotChart.

Table Continued on Following Page

Name	Returns	Description
Cube Fields	Cube Fields	Read Only. Returns the collection of cube fields associated with the `PivotChart`.
Data Fields		Read Only. Parameters: `[Index]`. Returns an object or collection containing the `PivotTable` field (`PivotField`) or `PivotTable` fields (`PivotFields`) associated with the data fields of the `PivotChart`.
Hidden Fields		Read Only. Parameters: `[Index]`. Returns an object or collection containing the `PivotTable` field (`PivotField`) or `PivotTable` fields (`PivotFields`) associated with the hidden fields of the `PivotChart`.
Inner Detail	String	Set / Get the name of the field that will show the detail when the `ShowDetail` property is `True`.
Page Fields		Read Only. Parameters: `[Index]`. Returns an object or collection containing the `PivotTable` field (`PivotField`) or `PivotTable` fields (`PivotFields`) associated with the page fields of the `PivotChart`.
Pivot Cache	Pivot Cache	Read Only. Returns the `PivotChart`'s data cache.
Pivot Fields		Read Only. Parameters: `[Index]`. Returns an object or collection containing the `PivotTable` field (`PivotField`) or `PivotTable` fields (`PivotFields`) associated with the fields of the `PivotChart`
Pivot Table	Pivot Table	Read Only. Returns the `PivotTable` associated with the `PivotChart`.
Row Fields		Read Only. Parameters: `[Index]`. Returns an object or collection containing the `PivotTable` field (`PivotField`) or `PivotTable` fields (`PivotFields`) associated with the rows of the `PivotChart`.
Visible Fields		Read Only. Parameters: `[Index]`. Returns an object or collection containing the `PivotTable` field (`PivotField`) or `PivotTable` fields (`PivotFields`) associated with the visible fields of the `PivotChart`.

PivotLayout Methods

Name	Returns	Parameters	Description
Add Fields		[RowFields], [ColumnFields], [PageFields], [AppendField]	Adds row, column, and page fields to a PivotChart report. RowFields, ColumnFields, and PageFields can hold a single string field name or an array of string field names. Set AppendField to True to add the fields to the chart. Set AppendField to False to replace the fields in the chart.

Example: PivotLayout Object

```
Sub SetPivotLayout()
    Dim oPL As PivotLayout

    'Get the pivot layout
    Set oPL = Charts(1).PivotLayout

    'Show sales of Oranges by region
    With oPL
        .AddFields RowFields:="Region", PageFields:="Product"
        .PageFields("Product").CurrentPage = "Oranges"
    End With
End Sub
```

PivotTable Object and the PivotTables Collection

The PivotTables collection contains the collection of PivotTables in the parent worksheet. Each PivotTable object in the collection allows manipulation and creation of Excel PivotTables. The parent of the PivotTables collection is the Worksheet object.

The PivotTables collection has a Count property and an Add method besides the typical collection attributes. The Count property returns the number of PivotTable objects in the collection. The Add method takes a new PivotTable cache (containing the data) and the destination single cell range determining the upper-left corner of the PivotTable report to create a new PivotTable report. The name of the new PivotTable report can also be specified in the Add method.

PivotTable Common Properties

The Application, Creator, and Parent properties are defined at the beginning of this Appendix.

PivotTable Properties

Name	Returns	Description
CacheIndex	Long	Set / Get the index number pointing to the PivotTable cache of the current PivotTable.
Column Fields	Object	Read Only. Parameters: [Index]. Returns an object or collection containing the PivotTable field (PivotField) or PivotTable fields (PivotFields) associated with the columns of the PivotTable.
Column Grand	Boolean	Set / Get whether grand totals are shown for columns in the PivotTable.
Column Range	Range	Read Only. Returns the range of cells containing the column area in the PivotTable report.
CubeFields	Cube Fields	Read Only. Returns the collection of cube fields associated with the PivotTable report.
DataBody Range	Range	Read Only. Returns the range of cells containing the data area of the PivotTable report.
DataFields	Object	Read Only. Parameters: [Index]. Returns an object or collection containing the PivotTable field (PivotField) or PivotTable fields (PivotFields) associated with the data fields of the PivotTable.
DataLabel Range	Range	Read Only. Returns the range of cells that contain the labels for the data fields in the PivotTable report.
Display Error String	Boolean	Set / Get whether the string in the ErrorString property is displayed in cells that contain errors.
Display NullString	Boolean	Set / Get whether the string in the NullString property is displayed in cells that contain null values.
Enable Drilldown	Boolean	Set / Get whether drilldown in the PivotTable report is enabled.
EnableFiel dDialog	Boolean	Set / Get whether the PivotTable Field dialog box is displayed when the user double-clicks a PivotTable field.

Name	Returns	Description
Enable Wizard	Boolean	Set / Get whether the PivotTable Wizard is available.
Error String	String	Set / Get the string that is displayed in cells that contain errors. Use with the DisplayErrorString property.
GrandTotal Name	String	Set / Get the string label that will be displayed on the grand total column or row heading of a PivotTable report. Default is "Grand Total"
HasAuto Format	Boolean	Set / Get whether the PivotTable report is automatically re-formatted when the data is refreshed or the fields are moved around.
Hidden Fields	Object	Read Only. Parameters: [Index]. Returns an object or collection containing the PivotTable field (PivotField) or PivotTable fields (PivotFields) associated with the hidden fields of the PivotTable.
Inner Detail	String	Set / Get the name of the field that will show the detail when the ShowDetail property is True.
Manual Update	Boolean	Set / Get whether the PivotTable report is only recalculated manually.
Merge Labels	Boolean	Set / Get whether the outer-row item, column item, subtotal, and grand total labels of a PivotTable report have merged cells.
Name	String	Set / Get the name of the PivotTable report.
NullString	String	Set / Get the string that is displayed in cells that contain null strings. Use with the DisplayNullString property.
Page FieldOrder	Long	Set / Get how new page fields are added to a PivotTable report's layout. Use the xlOrder constants.
PageFields	Object	Read Only. Parameters: [Index]. Returns an object or collection containing the PivotTable field (PivotField) or PivotTable fields (PivotFields) associated with the page fields of the PivotTable.

Table Continued on Following Page

Name	Returns	Description
Page FieldStyle	String	Set / Get the style used for a page field area in a PivotTable.
PageField WrapCount	Long	Set / Get how many page fields are in each column or row of the PivotTable report.
PageRange	Range	Read Only. Returns the range containing the page area in the PivotTable report.
Page RangeCells	Range	Read Only. Returns the range containing the page fields and item drop-down lists in the PivotTable report.
Pivot Formulas	Pivot Formulas	Read Only. Returns the collection of formulas used in the PivotTable report.
Pivot Selection	String	Set / Get the data and label selection in the PivotTable using the standard PivotTable report selection format. For example, to select the data and label for the Country equal to 'Canada' then the string would be "Country[Canada]".
Preserve Formatting	Boolean	Set / Get whether formatting of the PivotTable report is preserved when the report is changed, sorted, pivoted, refreshed or recalculated.
Print Titles	Boolean	Set / Get whether the print title set on the PivotTable report are printed whenever the parent worksheet is printed.
Refresh Date	Date	Read Only. Returns the date that the PivotTable report data was refreshed last.
Refresh Name	String	Read Only. Returns the name of the user who last refreshed the PivotTable report data.
Repeat ItemsOn Each Printed Page	Boolean	Set / Get whether row, column, and item labels appear on the first row of each page when the PivotTable report is printed.
RowFields		Read Only. Parameters: [Index]. Returns an object or collection containing the PivotTable field (PivotField) or PivotTable fields (PivotFields) associated with the rows of the PivotTable.

Name	Returns	Description
RowGrand	Boolean	Set / Get whether grand totals are shown for rows in the PivotTable.
RowRange	Range	Read Only. Returns the range of cells containing the row area in the PivotTable report.
SaveData	Boolean	Set / Get whether the PivotTable report data is saved with the workbook.
Selection Mode	XlPT Selection Mode	Set / Get how the PivotTable report selection mode is set (e.g. xlLabelOnly)
SmallGrid	Boolean	Set / Get whether a two by two grid is used for a newly created PivotTable report (True) or a blank stencil outline (False).
SourceData	Variant	Set / Get the source of the PivotTable report data. Can be a cell reference, an array, multiple ranges, and another PivotTable report. Not valid to use with OLE DB data sources.
Subtotal HiddenPage Items	Boolean	Set / Get whether hidden page fields are included in row and column subtotals, block totals, and grand totals.
Table Range1	Range	Read Only. Returns the range containing the whole PivotTable report, not including page fields.
Table Range2	Range	Read Only. Returns the range containing the whole PivotTable report, with page fields.
TableStyle	String	Set / Get the PivotTable report body style.
Tag	String	Set / Get a string to be saved with the PivotTable report (e.g. a description of the PivotTable report).
Vacated Style	String	Set / Get the style to use for vacated cells when a PivotTable report is refreshed.
Value	String	Set / Get the name of the PivotTable report.
Visible Fields		Read Only. Parameters: [Index]. Returns an object or collection containing the PivotTable field (PivotField) or PivotTable fields (PivotFields) associated with the visible fields of the PivotTable.

PivotTable Methods

Name	Returns	Parameters	Description
AddFields	Variant	[RowFields], [Column Fields], [Page Fields], [AddToTable]	Adds row, column, and page fields to a PivotTable report. The RowFields, ColumnFields, and PageFields can hold a single string field name or an array of string field names. Set AddToTable to True to add the fields to the report. Set AddToTable to False to replace the fields in the report.
Calculated Fields	Calculated Fields		Returns the collection of calculated fields in the PivotTable Report.
Format		Format As xlPivot FormatType	Set the PivotTable report format to the predefined style specified in the Format parameter.
GetData	Double	Name As String	Get the value of a specific cell in the PivotTable report. The Name parameter must be in the standard PivotTable report selection format.

Name	Returns	Parameters	Description
List Formulas			Creates a separate worksheet with the list of all the calculated PivotTable items and fields.
Pivot Cache	Pivot Cache		Returns a data cache associated with the current PivotTable.
Pivot Fields	Object	[Index]	Returns an object or collection containing the PivotTable field (PivotField) or PivotTable fields (PivotFields) associated with the fields of the PivotTable.
Pivot Select		Name As String, Mode As XlPT Selection Mode	Selects the part of the PivotTable specified by Name parameter in the standard PivotTable report selection format. Mode decides which part of the PivotTable to select (e.g. xlBlanks).

Table Continued on Following Page

Name	Returns	Parameters	Description
Pivot Table Wizard		[SourceType], [SourceData], [Table Destination], [TableName], [RowGrand], [ColumnGrand], [SaveData], [HasAuto Format], [AutoPage], [Reserved], [Background Query], [Optimize Cache], [PageField Order], [PageField WrapCount], [ReadData], [Connection]	Creates a PivotTable report. The SourceType uses the XLPivotTableSourceTyp e constants to specify the type of SourceData being used for the PivotTable. The TableDestination holds the range in the parent worksheet that report will be placed. TableName holds the name of the new report. Set RowGrand or ColumnGrand to True to show grand totals for rows and columns, respectively. Set HasAutoFormat to True for Excel to format the report automatically when it is refreshed or changed. Use the AutoPage parameter to set if a page field is created for consolidation automatically. Set BackgroundQuery to True for Excel to query the data source asynchronously. Set OptimizeCache to True for Excel to optimize the cache when it is built. Use the PageFieldOrder with the xlOrder constants to set how new page fields are added to the report. Use the PageFieldWrapCount to set the number of page fields in each column or row. Set ReadData to True to copy the data from the external database into a cache. Finally, use the Connection parameter to specify an ODBC connection string for the PivotTable's cache.

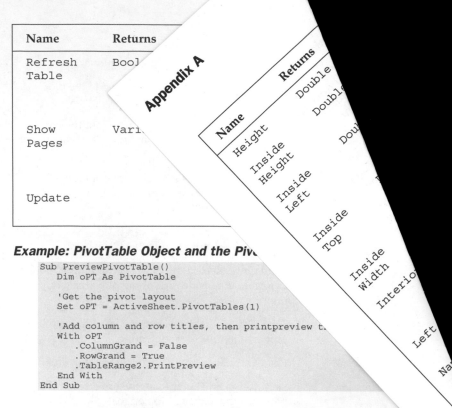

Name	Returns
Refresh Table	Bool
Show Pages	Vari
Update	

Example: PivotTable Object and the Piv

```
Sub PreviewPivotTable()
    Dim oPT As PivotTable

    'Get the pivot layout
    Set oPT = ActiveSheet.PivotTables(1)

    'Add column and row titles, then printpreview t.
    With oPT
        .ColumnGrand = False
        .RowGrand = True
        .TableRange2.PrintPreview
    End With
End Sub
```

PlotArea Object

The PlotArea object contains the formatting options associated with the plot of the parent chart. For 2D charts the PlotArea includes trendlines, data markers, gridlines, data labels, and the axis labels – but not titles. For 3D charts the PlotArea includes the walls, floor, axes, axis titles, tick-marks and all of the items mentioned for the 2D charts. The area surrounding the plot area is the chart area. Please see the ChartArea object for formatting related to the chart area. The parent of the PlotArea is always the Chart object.

PlotArea Common Properties

The Application, Creator, and Parent properties are defined at the beginning of this Appendix.

PlotArea Properties

Name	Returns	Description
Border	Border	Read Only. Returns the border's properties around the plot area.
Fill	ChartFill Format	Read Only. Returns an object containing fill formatting options for a chart's plot area.

Table Continued on Following Page

		Description
		Set / Get the height of the chart plot area.
		Read Only. Returns the height inside the plot area that does not include the axis labels.
	...le	Read Only. Returns the distance from the left edge of the plot area, not including axis labels, to the chart's left edge.
	...ouble	Read Only. Returns the distance from the left edge of the plot area, not including axis labels, to the chart's left edge.
	Double	Read Only. Returns the width inside the plot area that does not include the axis labels.
...r	Interior	Read Only. Returns an object containing options to format the inside area of the plot area (e.g. interior color).
	Double	Set / Get the distance from the left edge of the plot area to the chart's left edge.
...ne	String	Read Only. Returns the name of the plot area.
...op	Double	Set / Get the distance from the top edge of the plot area to the chart's top edge.
Width	Double	Set / Get the width of the chart plot area.

PlotArea Methods

Name	Returns	Parameters	Description
Clear Formats	Variant		Clears any formatting made to the plot area.
Select	Variant		Selects the plot area on the chart.

Example: PlotArea Object

This example uses the PlotArea object to make all the charts in the workbook have the same size and position plot area, regardless of the formatting of the axes (e.g. different fonts and number scales).

```
Sub MakeChartAreasSameSizeAsFirst()
    Dim oCht As Chart, oPA As PlotArea
    Dim dWidth As Double, dHeight As Double
    Dim dTop As Double, dLeft As Double

    'Get the dimensions of the inside of the
    'plot area of the first chart
    With Charts(1).PlotArea
        dWidth = .InsideWidth
```

```
         dHeight = .InsideHeight
         dLeft = .InsideLeft
         dTop = .InsideTop
   End With

   'Loop through the charts in the workbook
   For Each oCht In Charts

      'Get the PlotArea
      Set oPA = oCht.PlotArea

      'Size and move the plot area
      With oPA
         If .InsideWidth > dWidth Then
            'Too big, make it smaller
            .Width = .Width - (.InsideWidth - dWidth)
         Else
            'Too small, move it left and make bigger
            .Left = .Left - (dWidth - .InsideWidth)
            .Width = .Width + (dWidth - .InsideWidth)
         End If

         If .InsideHeight > dHeight Then
            'Too big, make it smaller
            .Height = .Height - (.InsideHeight - dHeight)
         Else
            'Too small, move it left and make bigger
            .Top = .Top - (dHeight - .InsideHeight)
            .Height = .Height + (dHeight - .InsideHeight)
         End If

         'Set the position of the inside of the plot area
         .Left = .Left + (dLeft - .InsideLeft)
         .Top = .Top + (dTop - .InsideTop)
      End With
   Next
End Sub
```

Point Object and the Points Collection

The `Points` collection holds all of the data points of a particular series of a chart. In fact, a chart (`Chart` object) can have many chart groups (`ChartGroups` / `ChartGroup`) that can contain many series (`SeriesCollection` / `Series`), which, in turn, can contain many points (`Points` / `Point`). A `Point` object describes the particular point of a series on a chart. The parent of the `Points` collection is the `Series` object.

The `Points` collection contains a `Count` property besides the typical collection attributes. The `Count` property returns the number of `Point` objects in the collection.

Point Common Properties

The `Application`, `Creator`, and `Parent` properties are defined at the beginning of this Appendix.

Point Properties

Name	Returns	Description
ApplyPict ToEnd	Boolean	Set / Get whether pictures are added to the end of the point.

Table Continued on Following Page

Name	Returns	Description
ApplyPict ToFront	Boolean	Set / Get whether pictures are added to the front of the point.
ApplyPict ToSides	Boolean	Set / Get whether pictures are added to the sides of the point.
Border	Border	Read Only. Returns the border's properties around the point.
DataLabel	Data Label	Read Only. Returns an object allowing to manipulate the data label attributes (e.g. formatting, text). Use with HasDataLabel.
Explosion	Long	Set / Get how far out a slice (point) of a pie or doughnut chart will explode out. 0 for no explosion.
Fill	Chart Fill Format	Read Only. Returns an object containing fill formatting options for a point.
HasData Label	Boolean	Set / Get whether the point has a data label. Use with DataLabel.
Interior	Interior	Read Only. Returns an object containing options to format the inside area of the point (e.g. interior color).
InvertIf Negative	Boolean	Set / Get whether the point's color will be inverted if the point value is negative.
Marker Background Color	Long	Set / Get the color of the point marker background. Use the RGB function to create the color value.
Marker Background ColorIndex	XlColor Index	Set / Get the color of the point marker background. Use the XlColorIndex constants or an index value in the current color palette.
Marker Foreground Color	Long	Set / Get the color of the point marker foreground. Use the RGB function to create the color value.
Marker Foreground ColorIndex	XlColor Index	Set / Get the color of the point marker foreground. Use the XlColorIndex constants or an index value in the current color palette.
MarkerSize	Long	Set / Get the size of the point key marker.

Name	Returns	Description
Marker Style	XlMarker Style	Set / Get the type of marker to use as the point key (e.g. square, diamond, triangle, picture, etc.)
Picture Type	XlChart Picture Type	Set / Get how an associated picture is displayed on the point (e.g. stretched, tiled). Use the XlPictureType constants.
Picture Unit	Long	Set / Get how many units a picture represents if the PictureType property is set to xlScale.
Secondary Plot	Boolean	Set / Get if the point is on the secondary part of a Pie of Pie chart of a Bar of Pie chart.
Shadow	Boolean	Set / Get whether the point has a shadow effect.

Point Methods

Name	Returns	Parameters	Description
Apply Data Labels	Variant	Type As XlData LabelsType, [LegendKey], [AutoText]	Applies the data label properties specified by the parameters to the point. The Type parameter specifies whether no label, a value, a percentage of the whole, or a category label is shown. The legend key can appear by the point by setting the LegendKey parameter to True.
Clear Formats	Variant		Clears the formatting made to a point.
Copy	Variant		Cuts the point and places it in the clipboard.
Delete	Variant		Deletes the point.
Paste	Variant		Pastes the picture in the clipboard into the current point so it becomes the marker.
Select	Variant		Selects the point on the chart.

Example: Point Object and the Points Collection

```
Sub ExplodePie()
    Dim oPt As Point

    'Get the first data point in the pie chart
    Set oPt = Charts(1).SeriesCollection(1).Points(1)

    'Add a label to the first point only and
    'set it away from the pie
    With oPt
        .ApplyDataLabels xlDataLabelsShowLabelAndPercent
        .Explosion = 20
    End With
End Sub
```

PublishObject Object and the PublishObjects Collection

The PublishObjects collection holds all of the things in a workbook that have been saved to a Web Page. Each PublishObject object contains items from a workbook that have been saved to a Web page and may need some occasional refreshing of values on the Web page side. The parent of the PublishObjects collection is the Workbook object.

The PublishObjects collection has a few properties and methods besides the typical collection attributes. The unique attributes are listed in the following table.

PublishObjects Properties and Methods

Name	Returns	Description
Count	Long	Read Only. Returns the number of PublishObject objects in the collection.
Add	Publish Object	Method. Parameters: SourceType As XlSourceType, Filename As String, [Sheet], [Source], [HtmlType], [DivID], [Title]. Adds a PublishObject to the collection.
Delete		Method. Deletes the PublishObject objects from the collection.
Publish		Method. Publishes all the items associated with the PublishObject objects to a Web page.

PublishObject Common Properties

The Application, Creator, and Parent properties are defined at the beginning of this Appendix.

PublishObject Properties

Name	Returns	Description
DivID	String	Read Only. Returns the id used for the <DIV> tag on a web page.
Filename	String	Set / Get the URL or path that the object will be saved to as a Web page.
Html Type	XlHtml Type	Set / Get what type of web page to save (e.g. xlHtmlStatic, xlHtmlChart). Pages saved as other then xlHtmlStatic needs special ActiveX components.
Sheet	String	Read Only. Returns the Excel sheet that will be saved as a web page.
Source	String	Read Only. Returns the specific item, like range name, chart name, or report name from the base type specified by the SourceType property.
Source Type	XlSource Type	Read Only. Returns the type of source being published (e.g. xlSourceChart, xlSourcePrintArea, etc)
Title	String	Set / Get the Web page title for the published Web page.

PublishObject Methods

Name	Returns	Parameters	Description
Delete			Deletes the PublishObject object.
Publish		[Create]	Publishes the source items specified by the PublishObject as a Web file. Set the Create parameter to True to overwrite existing files. False will append to the existing web page with the same name, if any.

Example: PublishObject Object and the PublishObjects Collection

```
Sub UpdatePublishedCharts()
    Dim oPO As PublishObject

    For Each oPO In ActiveWorkbook.PublishObjects
        If oPO.SourceType = xlSourceChart Then
            oPO.Publish
        End If
    Next
End Sub
```

QueryTable Object and the QueryTables Collection

The `QueryTables` collection holds the collection of data tables created from an external data source. Each `QueryTable` object represents a single table in a worksheet filled with data from an external data source. The external data source can be an ODBC source, an OLE DB source, a text file, a Data Finder, a Web based query, or a DAO / ADO recordset. The parent of the `QueryTables` collection is the `Worksheet` object.

The `QueryTables` collection has a few properties and methods not typical of a collection. These atypical attributes are listed below.

QueryTables Properties and Methods

Name	Returns	Description
Count	Long	Read Only. Returns the number of items in the collection.
Add	QueryTable	Method. Parameters: `Connection`, `Destination As Range`, `[Sql]`. Adds a `QueryTable` to the collection. The `Connection` parameter can specify the ODBC or OLE DB connection string, another `QueryTable` object, a DAO or ADO recordset object, a Web-based query, a Data Finder string, or a text file name. The `Destination` parameter specifies the upper-left corner that the query table results will be placed. The `SQL` parameter can specify the SQL for the connection, if applicable.

QueryTable Common Properties

The `Application`, `Creator`, and `Parent` properties are defined at the beginning of this Appendix.

QueryTable Properties

Name	Returns	Description
Adjust ColumnWidth	Boolean	Set / Get whether the column widths automatically adjust to best fit the data every time the query table is refreshed.
Background Query	Boolean	Set / Get if the query table processing is done asynchronously.
CommandText	Variant	Set / Get the SQL command used to retrieve data.

Name	Returns	Description
CommandType	XlCmd Type	Set / Get the type of ComandText (e.g. xlCmdSQL, xlCmdTable).
Connection	Variant	Set / Get either the OLE DB connection string, the ODBC string, Web data source, path to a text file, or path to a database.
Destination	Range	Read Only. Returns the upper-left corner cell that the query table results will be placed.
EnableEditing	Boolean	Set / Get whether the query table data can be edited or only refreshed (False).
EnableRefresh	Boolean	Set / Get whether the query table data can be refreshed.
Fetched RowOverflow	Boolean	Read Only. Returns whether the last query table refresh retrieved more rows than available on the worksheet.
FieldNames	Boolean	Set / Get whether the field names from the data source become column headings in the query table.
FillAdjacent Formulas	Boolean	Set / Get whether formulas located to the right of the query table will update automatically when the query table data is refreshed.
Maintain Connection	Boolean	Set / Get whether the connection to the data source does not close until the workbook is closed. Valid only against an OLE DB source.
Name	String	Set / Get the name of the query table.
Parameters	Parameters	Read Only. Returns the parameters associated with the query table.
PostText	String	Set / Get the post message sent to the Web server to return data from a Web query.
Preserve ColumnInfo	Boolean	Set / Get whether column location, sorting and filtering does not disappear when the data query is refreshed.

Table Continued on Following Page

Name	Returns	Description
Preserve Formatting	Boolean	Set / Get whether common formatting associated with the first five rows of data are applied to new rows in the query table.
QueryType	xlQuery Type	Read Only. Returns the type of connection associated with the query table. (e.g. xlOLEDBQuery, xlDAOQuery, xlTextImport)
Recordset		Read Only. Returns a recordset associated with the data source query.
Refreshing	Boolean	Read Only. Returns whether an asynchronous query is currently in progress.
Refresh OnFileOpen	Boolean	Set / Get whether the query table is refreshed when the workbook is opened.
RefreshPeriod	Long	Set / Get how long (minutes) between automatic refreshes from the data source. Set to 0 to disable.
RefreshStyle	XlCell Insertion Mode	Set / Get how worksheet rows react when data rows are retrieved from the data source. Worksheet cells can be overwritten (xlOverwriteCells), cell rows can be partial inserted / deleted as necessary (xlInsertDeleteCells), or only cell rows that need to be added are added (xlInsertEntireRows).
ResultRange	Range	Read Only. Returns the cell range containing the results of the query table.
RowNumbers	Boolean	Set / Get whether a worksheet column is added to the left of the query table containing row numbers.
SaveData	Boolean	Set / Get whether query table data is saved with the workbook.
SavePassword	Boolean	Set / Get whether an ODBC connection password is saved with the query table.

Name	Returns	Description
TextFile Column DataTypes	Variant	Set / Get the array of column constants representing the data types for each column. Use the XlColumnDataType constants. Used only when QueryType is xlTextImport.
Text FileComma Delimiter	Boolean	Set / Get whether a comma is the delimiter for text file imports into a query table. Used only when QueryType is xlTextImport and for a delimited text file.
TextFile Consecutive Delimiter	Boolean	Set / Get whether consecutive delimiters (e.g. " , , , ") are treated as a single delimeter. Used only when QueryType is xlTextImport.
TextFile Decimal Separator	String	Set / Get the type of delimeter to use to define a decimal point. Used only when QueryType is xlTextImport.
TextFileFixed ColumnWidths	Variant	Set / Get the array of widths that correspond to the columns. Used only when QueryType is xlTextImport and for a fixed width text file.
TextFileOther Delimiter	String	Set / Get the character that will be used to delimit columns from a text file. Used only when QueryType is xlTextImport and for a delimited text file.
TextFileParse Type	XlText Parsing Type	Set / Get the type of text file that is being imported: xlDelimited or xlFixedWidth. Used only when QueryType is xlTextImport.
TextFile Platform	XlPlatform	Set / Get the which code pages to use when importing a text file (e.g. xlMSDOS, xlWindows). Used only when QueryType is xlTextImport.
TextFile PromptOn Refresh	Boolean	Set / Get whether the user is prompted for the text file to use to import into a query table every time the data is refreshed. Used only when QueryType is xlTextImport. The prompt does not appear on the initial refresh of data.

Table Continued on Following Page

Name	Returns	Description
TextFile Semicolon Delimiter	Boolean	Set / Get whether the semicolon is the text file delimiter for importing text files. Used only when QueryType is xlTextImport and the file is a delimited text file.
TextFileSpace Delimiter	Boolean	Set / Get whether the space character is the text file delimiter for importing text files. Used only when QueryType is xlTextImport and the file is a delimited text file.
TextFileStart Row	Long	Set / Get which row number to start importing from a text file. Used only when QueryType is xlTextImport.
TextFileTab Delimiter	Boolean	Set / Get whether the tab character is the text file delimiter for importing text files. Used only when QueryType is xlTextImport and the file is a delimited text file.
TextFileText Qualifier	XlText Qualifier	Set / Get which character will be used to define string data when importing data from a text file. Used only when QueryType is xlTextImport.
TextFile Thousands Separator	String	Set / Get which character is used as the thousands separator in numbers when importing from a text file (e.g.",").
Web Consecutive Delimiters AsOne	Boolean	Set / Get whether consecutive delimiters are treated as a single delimiter when importing data from a Web page. Used only when QueryType is xlWebQuery.
WebDisable Date Recognition	Boolean	Set / Get whether data that looks like dates are parsed as text when importing Web page data. Used only when QueryType is xlWebQuery.
WebFormatting	xlWeb Formatting	Set / Get whether to keep any of the formatting when importing a Web page (e.g. xlAll, xlNone). Used only when QueryType is xlWebQuery.

Name	Returns	Description
WebPre FormattedText ToColumns	Boolean	Set / Get whether HTML data with the <PRE> tag is parsed into columns when importing Web pages. Used only when QueryType is xlWebQuery.
WebSelection Type	xlWeb Selection Type	Set / Get what data from a Web page is imported. Either all tables (xlAllTables), the entire page (xlEntirePage), or specified tables (xlSpecifiedTables). Used only when QueryType is xlWebQuery.
WebSingle BlockText Import	Boolean	Set / Get whether all the Web page data with the <PRE> tags are imported all at once. Used only when QueryType is xlWebQuery.
WebTables	String	Set / Get a comma-delimited list of all the table names that will be imported from a Web page. Used only when QueryType is xlWebQuery and WebSelectionType is xlSpecifiedTables.

QueryTable Methods

Name	Returns	Parameters	Description
Cancel Refresh			Cancels an asynchronously running query table refresh.
Delete			Deletes the query table.
Refresh	Boolean	[Background Query]	Refreshes the data in the query table with the latest copy of the external data. Set the BackgroundQuery parameter to True to get the data to refresh asynchronously.
Reset Timer			Resets the time for the automatic refresh set by RefreshPeriod property.

Example: QueryTable Object and the QueryTables Collection

```
Sub UpdateAllWebQueries()
    Dim oQT As QueryTable

    For Each oQT In ActiveSheet.QueryTables
        If oQT.QueryType = xlWebQuery Then
            oQT.BackgroundQuery = False
            oQT.Refresh
        End If
    Next
End Sub
```

Range Object

The Range object is one of the more versatile objects in Excel. A range can be a single cell, a column, a row, a contiguous block of cells, or a non-contiguous range of cells. The main parent of a Range object is the Worksheet object. However, most of the objects in the Excel Object Model use the Range object. The Range property of the Worksheet object can be used to choose a certain range of cells using the Cell1 and Cell2 parameters.

Range Common Properties

The Application, Creator, and Parent properties are defined at the beginning of this Appendix.

Range Properties

Name	Returns	Description
AddIndent	Variant	Set / Get whether text in a cell is automatically indented if the text alignment in a cell is set to equally distribute.
Address	String	Read Only. Parameters: RowAbsolute, ColumnAbsolute, ReferenceStyle As XlReferenceStyle, [External], [RelativeTo]. Returns the address of the current range as a string in the macro's language. The type of address (reference, absolute, A1 reference style, R1C1 reference style) is specified by the parameters.
AddressLocal	String	Read Only. Parameters: RowAbsolute, ColumnAbsolute, ReferenceStyle As XlReferenceStyle, [External], [RelativeTo]. Returns the address of the current range as a string in the user's language. The type of address (reference, absolute, A1 reference style, R1C1 reference style) is specified by the parameters.

Name	Returns	Description
Areas	Areas	Read Only. Returns an object containing the different non-contiguous ranges in the current range.
Borders	Borders	Read Only. Returns all the individual borders around the range. Each border side can be accessed individual in the collection.
Cells	Range	Read Only. Returns the cells in the current range. The Cells property will return the same range as the current range.
Characters	Characters	Read Only. Parameters: [Start], [Length]. Returns all the characters in the current range, if applicable.
Column	Long	Read Only. Returns the column number of the first column in the range.
Columns	Range	Read Only. Returns a range of the columns in the current range.
ColumnWidth	Variant	Set / Get the column width of all the columns in the range. Returns Null if the columns in the range have different widths.
Comment	Comment	Read Only. Returns an object representing the range comment, if any.
Count	Long	Read Only. Returns the number of cells in the current range.
CurrentArray	Range	Read Only. Returns a Range object that represents the array associated with the particular cell range, if the cell is part of an array.
Current Region	Range	Read Only. Returns the current region that contains the Range object. A region is defined as an area that is surrounded by blank cells.
Dependents	Range	Read Only. Returns the dependents of a cell on the same sheet as the range.
Direct Dependents	Range	Read Only. Returns the direct dependents of a cell on the same sheet as the range.

Table Continued on Following Page

Name	Returns	Description
Direct Precedents	Range	Read Only. Returns the direct precedents of a cell on the same sheet as the range.
End	Range	Read Only. Parameters: `Direction As XlDirection`. Returns the cell at end of the region containing the `Range` object. Which end of the region is specified by the `Direction` parameter.
EntireColumn	Range	Read Only. Returns the full worksheet column(s) occupied by the current range.
EntireRow	Range	Read Only. Returns the full worksheet row(s) occupied by the current range.
Font	Font	Read Only. Returns an object containing Font options for the text in the range.
Format Conditions	Format Conditions	Read Only. Returns an object holding conditional formatting options for the current range.
Formula	Variant	Set / Get the formula in the cells of the range.
FormulaArray	Variant	Set / Get the array formula of the cells in the range.
Formula Hidden	Variant	Set / Get whether the formula will be hidden if the workbook / worksheet is protected.
FormulaLabel	XlFormula Label	Set / Get the type of formula label to use for the specified range.
FormulaLocal	Variant	Set / Get the formula of the range in the language of the user using the A1 style references.
FormulaR1C1	Variant	Set / Get the formula of the range in the language of the macro using the R1C1 style references.
Formula R1C1Local	Variant	Set / Get the formula of the range in the language of the user using the R1C1 style references.
HasArray	Variant	Read Only. Returns whether a single cell range is part of an array formula.

Name	Returns	Description
HasFormula	Variant	Read Only. Returns whether all the cells in the range contain formulas (True). If only some of the cells contain formulas then Null is returned.
Height	Variant	Read Only. Returns the height of the range.
Hidden	Variant	Set / Get whether the cells in the range are hidden. Only works if the range contains whole columns or rows.
Horizontal Alignment	Variant	Set / Get how the cells in the range are horizontally aligned. Use the xlHAlign constants.
Hyperlinks	Hyperlinks	Read Only. Returns the collection of hyperlinks in the range.
ID	String	Set / Get the ID used for the range if the worksheet is saved as a Web page.
IndentLevel	Variant	Set / Get the indent level for the range.
Interior	Interior	Read Only. Returns an object containing options to format the inside area of the range if applicable (e.g. interior color).
Left	Variant	Read Only. Returns the distance from the left edge of the left-most column in the range to the left edge of Column A.
ListHeader Rows	Long	Read Only. Returns the number of header rows in the range.
Location InTable	XlLocation InTable	Read Only. Returns the location of the upper-left corner of the range.
Locked	Variant	Set / Get whether cells in the range can be modified if the sheet is protected. Returns Null if only some of the cells in the range are locked.
MergeArea	range	Read Only. Returns a range containing the merged range of the current cell range.
MergeCells	Variant	Set / Get whether the current range contains merged cells.
Name	Variant	Set / Get the Name object that contains the name for the range.

Table Continued on Following Page

Name	Returns	Description
Next	Range	Read Only. Returns the next range in the sheet.
NumberFormat	Variant	Set / Get the number format associated with the cells in the range. Null if all the cells don't have the same format.
NumberFormat Local	Variant	Set / Get the number format associated with the cells in the range in the language of the end user. Null if all the cells don't have the same format.
Offset	Range	Read Only. Parameters: [RowOffset], [ColumnOffset]. Returns the cell as a Range object that is the offset from the current cell as specified by the parameters. A positive RowOffset offsets the row downward. A negative RowOffset offsets the row upward. A positive ColumnOffset offsets the column to the right and a negative ColumnOffset offsets the column to the left.
Orientation	Variant	Set / Get the text orientation for the cell text. A value from –90 to 90 degrees can be specified, or use an XlOrientation constant.
Outline Level	Variant	Set / Get the outline level for the row or column range.
PageBreak	Long	Set / Get how page breaks are set in the range. Use the xlPageBreak constants.
Phonetic	Phonetic	Read Only. Returns the Phonetic object associated with the cell range.
Phonetics	Phonetics	Read Only. Returns the Phonetic objects in the range.
PivotField	PivotField	Read Only. Returns the PivotTable field associated with the upper-left corner of the current range.
PivotItem	PivotItem	Read Only. Returns the PivotTable item associated with the upper-left corner of the current range.

Name	Returns	Description
PivotTable	PivotTable	Read Only. Returns the PivotTable report associated with the upper-left corner of the current range.
Precedents	Range	Read Only. Returns the range of precedents of the current cell range on the same sheet as the range.
Prefix Character	Variant	Read Only. Returns the character used to define the type of data in the cell range. E.g. " ` " for a text label.
Previous	Range	Read Only. Returns the previous range in the sheet.
QueryTable	QueryTable	Read Only. Returns the query table associated with the upper-left corner of the current range.
Range	Range	Read Only. Parameters: Cell1, [Cell2]. Returns a Range object as defined by the Cell1 and optionally Cell2 parameters. The cell references used in the parameters are relative to the range. For example Range.Range ("A1") would return the first column in the parent range but not necessarily the first column in the worksheet.
Reading Order	Long	Set / Get whether the text is from right-to-left (xlRTL), left-to-right (xlLTR), or context sensitive (xlContext).
Resize	Range	Read Only. Parameters: [RowSize], [ColumnSize]. Returns a new resized range as specified by the RowSize and ColumnSize parameters.
Row	Long	Read Only. Returns the row number of the first row in the range.
RowHeight	Variant	Set / Get the height of the rows in the range. Returns Null if the rows in the range have different row heights.
Rows	Range	Read Only. Returns a Range object containing the rows of the current range.

Table Continued on Following Page

Name	Returns	Description
ShowDetail	Variant	Set / Get if all the outline levels in the range are expanded. Applicable only if a summary column or row is the range.
Shrink ToFit	Variant	Set / Get whether the cell text will automatically shrink to fit the column width. Returns Null if the rows in the range have different ShrinkToFit properties.
SoundNote	SoundNote	Property is kept for backwards compatibility only.
Style	Variant	Read Only. Returns the Style object associated with the range.
Summary	Variant	Read Only. Returns whether the range is an outline summary row or column.
Text	Variant	Read Only. Returns the text associated with a range cell.
Top	Variant	Read Only. Returns the distance from the top edge of the top-most row in the range to the top edge of Row A.
Use Standard Height	Variant	Set / Get whether the row height is the standard height of the sheet. Returns Null if the rows in the range contain different heights.
Use Standard Width	Variant	Set / Get whether the column width is the standard width of the sheet. Returns Null if the columns in the range contain different widths.
Validation	Validation	Read Only. Returns the data validation for the current range.
Value	Variant	Set / Get the value of a cell or an array of cells depending on the contents of the Range object.
Value2	Variant	Set / Get the value of a cell or an array of cells depending on the contents of the Range object. No Currency or Date types are returned by Value2.
Vertical Alignment	Variant	Set / Get how the cells in the range are vertically aligned. Use the xlVAlign constants.

Name	Returns	Description
Width	Variant	Read Only. Returns the height of the range.
Worksheet	Worksheet	Read Only. Returns the worksheet that has the Range object.
WrapText	Variant	Set / Get whether cell text wraps in the cell. Returns Null if the cells in the range contain different text wrap properties.

Range Methods

Name	Returns	Parameters	Description
Activate	Variant		Selects the range cells.
AddComment	Comment	[Text]	Adds the text specified by the parameter to the cell specified in the range. Must be a single cell range.
Advanced Filter	Variant	Action As XlFilter Action, [Criteria Range], [CopyToRange] , [Unique]	Copies or filters the data in the current range. The Action parameter specifies whether a copy or filter is to take place. CriteriaRange optionally specifies the range containing the criteria. CopyToRange specifies the range that the filtered data will be copied to (if Action is xlFilterCopy).

Table Continued on Following Page

Name	Returns	Parameters	Description
ApplyNames	Variant	Names, Ignore Relative Absolute, UseRowColumn Names, OmitColumn, OmitRow, Order As XlApplyNames Order, [AppendLast]	Applies defined names to the formulas in a range. For example, if a cell contained =$A$1*100 and $A$1 was given the name "TopLeft", you could apply the "TopLeft" name to the range, resulting in the formula changing to =TopLeft*100. Note that there is no 'UnApplyNames' method.
ApplyOutline Styles	Variant		Applies the outline styles to the range.
AutoComplete	String	String As String.	Returns and tries to AutoComplete the word specified in the String parameter. Returns the complete word if found. Returns an empty string if no word or more then one word is found.
AutoFill	Variant	Destination As Range, Type As XlAutoFill Type.	Uses the current range as the source to figure out how to AutoFill the range specified by the Destination parameter. The Type parameter can also be used to specify the type of fill to use (e.g. xlFillCopy, xlFillDays).
AutoFilter	Variant	Field, Criteria1, Operator As XlAutoFilter Operator, [Criteria2], [VisibleDrop Down].	Creates an auto-filter on the data in the range. See the AutoFilter object for details on the parameters.

Name	Returns	Parameters	Description
AutoFit	Variant		Changes the column widths in the range to best fit the data in the cells. The range must contain full rows or columns.
AutoFormat	Variant	Format As XlRangeAuto Format, [Number], [Font], [Alignment], [Border], [Pattern], [Width].	Formats the range using the format specified by the Format parameter. The other parameters are Boolean indicators to specify: if numbers are formatted appropriately (Number), Fonts applied (Font), alignments applied (Alignment), border formats applied (Border), pattern formats applied (Pattern), and if row / column widths are applied from the autoformat.
AutoOutline	Variant		Creates an outline for the range.
BorderAround	Variant	LineStyle, Weight As XlBorder Weight, ColorIndex As XlColor Index, [Color].	Creates a border around the range with the associated line style (LineStyle), thickness (Weight), and color (ColorIndex).
Calculate	Variant		Calculates all the formulas in the range.

Table Continued on Following Page

Name	Returns	Parameters	Description
Check Spelling	Variant	[Custom Dictionary], [Ignore Uppercase], [Always Suggest], [SpellLang]	Checks the spelling of the text in the range. A custom dictionary can be specified (CustomDictionary), all UPPERCASE words can be ignored (IgnoreUppercase), and Excel can be set to display a list of suggestions (AlwaysSuggest).
Clear	Variant		Clears the text in the cells of the range.
Clear Comments			Clears all the comments in the range cells.
Clear Contents	Variant		Clears the formulas and values in a range.
ClearFormats	Variant		Clears the formatting in a range.
ClearNotes	Variant		Clears comments from the cells in the range.
ClearOutline	Variant		Clears the outline used in the current range.
Column Differences	Range	Comparison	Returns the range of cells that are different to the cell specified by the Comparison parameter.
Consolidate	Variant	[Sources], [Function], [TopRow], [Left Column], [Create Links]	Consolidates the source array of range reference strings in the Sources parameter and returns the results to the current range. The Function parameter can be used to set the consolidation function. Use the xlConsolidationFunction constants.

Name	Returns	Parameters	Description
Copy	Variant	[Destination]	Copies the current range to the range specified by the parameter or to the clipboard if no destination is specified.
CopyFrom Recordset	Long	Data As Recordset, [MaxRows], [MaxColumns]	Copies the records from the ADO or DAO recordset specified by the Data parameter into the current range. The recordset can't contain OLE objects
CopyPicture	Variant	[Appearance As XlPicture Appearance], [Format As XlCopyPicture Format], [Size As XlPicture Appearance].	Copies the range into the clipboard as a picture. The Appearance parameter can be used to specify whether the picture is copied as it looks on the screen or when printed. The Format parameter can specify the type of picture that will be put into the clipboard.
CreateNames	Variant	[Top], [Left], [Bottom], [Right].	Creates a named range for the items in the current range. Set Top to True to make the first row hold the names for the ranges below. Set Bottom to True to use the bottom row as the names. Set Left or Right to True to make the left or right column contain the Names, respectively.

Table Continued on Following Page

Name	Returns	Parameters	Description
Create Publisher	Variant	Edition, Appearance As XlPicture Appearance, [Contains PICT], [Contains BIFF], [Contains RTF], [Contains VALU]	Creates a publisher based on the range. Available only on the Macintosh with System 7 or later.
Cut	Variant	[Destination]	Cuts the current range to the range specified by the parameter, or to the clipboard if no destination is specified.
DataSeries	Variant	Rowcol, Type As XlData SeriesType, Date As XlDataSeries Date, [Step], [Stop], [Trend].	Creates a data series at the current range location.
Delete	Variant	[Shift]	Deletes the cells in the current range and optionally shifts the cells in the direction specified by the Shift parameter. Use the XlDeleteShiftDir ection constants for the Shift parameter.
DialogBox	Variant		Displays a dialog box defined by an Excel 4.0 macro sheet.

Name	Returns	Parameters	Description
Edition Options	Variant	Type As XlEdition Type, Option As XlEdition Options Option, Name, Reference, Appearance As XlPicture Appearance, ChartSize As XlPicture Appearance, [Format].	Used on the Macintosh. EditionOptions set how the range should act when being used as the source (publisher) or target (subscriber) of the link. Editions are basically the same as Windows' DDE links.
FillDown	Variant		Copies the contents and formatting from the top row into the rest of the rows in the range.
FillLeft	Variant		Copies the contents and formatting from the rightmost column into the rest of the columns in the range.
FillRight	Variant		Copies the contents and formatting from the leftmost column into the rest of the columns in the range.
FillUp	Variant		Copies the contents and formatting from the bottom row into the rest of the rows in the range.
Find	Range	What, After, LookIn, LookAt, SearchOrder, Search Direction As XlSearch Direction, [MatchCase], [MatchByte]	Looks through the current range for the text of data type specified by the What parameter. Use a single cell range in the After parameter to choose the starting position of the search. Use the LookIn parameter to decide where the search is going to take place.

Table Continued on Following Page

Name	Returns	Parameters	Description
FindNext	Range	[After]	Finds the next instance of the search criteria defined with the Find method.
Find Previous	Range	[Before]	Finds the previous instance of the search criteria defined with the Find method.
Function Wizard	Variant		Displays the Function Wizard for the upper-left cell of the current range.
GoalSeek	Boolean	Goal, ChangingCell As Range	Returns True if the value specified by the Goal parameter is returned when changing the ChangingCell cell range.
Group	Variant	[Start], [End], [By], [Periods]	Either demotes the outline in the range or groups the discontinuous ranges in the current Range object.
Insert	Variant	[Shift]	Inserts the equivalent rows or columns in the range into the range's worksheet.
Insert Indent		InsertAmount As Long	Indents the range by the amount specified by the InsertAmount parameter.
Justify	Variant		Evenly distributes the text in the cells from the current range.
ListNames	Variant		Pastes the names of all the named ranges in the current range, starting at the top-left cell in the range.

Name	Returns	Parameters	Description
Merge		[Across]	Merges the cells in the range. Set the Across parameter to True to merge each row as a separate cell.
Navigate Arrow	Variant	[Toward Precedent], [Arrow Number], [LinkNumber]	Moves through the tracer arrows in a workbook from the current range, returning the range of cells that make up the tracer arrow destination. Tracer arrows must be turned on. Use the ShowDependents and ShowPrecendents methods.
Note Text	String	[Text], [Start], [Length]	Set / Get the cell notes associated with the cell in the current range.
Parse	Variant	[ParseLine], [Destination]	Parses the string specified by the ParseLine parameter and returns it to the current range parsed out by column. Optionally can specify the destination range with the Destination parameter. The ParseLine string should be in the "[ColumnA][ColumnB]" format.
Paste Special	Variant	Paste As XlPasteType, Operation As XlPasteSpecia lOperation, [SkipBlanks], [Transpose]	Pastes the range from the clipboard into the current range. Use the Paste parameter to choose what to paste (e.g. formulas, values). Use the Operation parameter to specifiy what to do with the paste. Set SkipBlanks to True to not have blank cells in the clipboard's range pasted. Set Transpose to True to transpose columns with rows.

Table Continued on Following Page

Name	Returns	Parameters	Description
PrintOut	Variant	[From], [To], [Copies], [Preview], [Active Printer], [PrintTo File], [Collate], [PrToFile Name]	Prints out the charts in the collection. The printer, number of copies, collation, and whether a print preview is desired can be specified with the parameters. Also, the sheets can be printed to a file with using the PrintToFile and PrToFileName parameters. The From and To parameters can be used to specify the range of printed pages.
Print Preview	Variant	[Enable Changes]	Displays the current range in a print preview. Set the EnableChanges parameter to False to disable the Margins and Setup buttons, hence not allowing the viewer to modify the page setup.
Remove Subtotal	Variant		Removes subtotals from the list in the current range.
Replace	Boolean	What, Replacement, [LookAt], [Search Order], [MatchCase], [MatchByte].	Finds the text specified by the What parameter in the range. Replaces the found text with the Replacement parameter. Use the SearchOrder parameters with the xlSearchOrder constants to choose whether the search occurs by rows or by columns.

Name	Returns	Parameters	Description
Row Differences	Range	Comparison.	Returns the range of cells that are different to the cell specified by the Comparison parameter.
Run	Variant	[Arg1], [Arg2], ... [Arg30]	Runs the Excel 4.0 macro specified by the current range. The potential arguments to the macro can be specified with the Argx paramteters.
Select	Variant		Selects the cells in the range.
SetPhonetic			Create a Phonetic object for each cell in the range.
Show	Variant		Scrolls the Excel window to display the current range. This only works if the range is a single cell.
Show Dependents	Variant	[Remove]	Displays the dependents for the current single cell range using tracer arrows.
ShowErrors	Variant		Displays the source of the errors for the current range using tracer arrows.
Show Precedents	Variant	[Remove]	Displays the precedents for the current single cell range using tracer arrows.

Table Continued on Following Page

Name	Returns	Parameters	Description
Sort	Variant	Key1, Order1 As XlSort Order, Key2, Type, Order2 As XlSort Order, Key3, Order3 As XlSortOrder, Header As XlYesNoGuess, OrderCustom, MatchCase, Orientation As XlSort Orientation, SortMethod As XlSortMethod	Sorts the cells in the range. If the range contains only one cell then the active region is searched. Use the Key1, Key2, and Key3 parameters to set which columns will be the sort columns. Use the Order1, Order2, and Order3 parameters to set the sort order. Use the Header parameter to set whether the first row contains headers. Set the MatchCase parameter to True to sort data and to treat upper case and lower case characters differently. Use the Orientation parameter to choose whether rows are sorted or columns are sorted. Finally, the SortMethod parameter is used to set sort method for other languages (e.g. xlStroke or xlPinYin). Use the SortSpecial method for sorting in East Asian languages.

Name	Returns	Parameters	Description
SortSpecial	Variant	SortMethod As XlSortMethod, Key1, Order1 As XlSort Order, Type, Key2, Order2 As XlSort Order, Key3, Order3 As XlSortOrder, Header As XlYesNoGuess, OrderCustom, MatchCase, Orientation As XlSort Orientation.	Sorts the data in the range using East Asian sorting methods. The parameters are the same as the Sort method.
SpecialCells	Range	Type As XlCellType, [Value].	Returns the cells in the current range that contain some special attribute as defined by the Type parameter. For example, if Type is xlCellTypeBlanks then a Range object containing all of the empty cells are returned.
SubscribeTo	Variant	Edition As String, Format As XlSubscribeTo Format.	Only valid on the Macintosh. Defines the source of a link that the current range will contain.

Table Continued on Following Page

Name	Returns	Parameters	Description
Subtotal	Variant	GroupBy As Long, Function As XlConsolidation Function, TotalList, Replace, PageBreaks, SummaryBelowData As XlSummaryRow	Creates a subtotal for the range. If the range is a single cell then a subtotal is created for the current region. The GroupBy parameter specifies the field to group (for subtotaling). The Function parameter describes how the fields will be grouped. The TotalList parameter uses an array of field offsets that describe the fields that will be subtotaled. Set the Replace parameter to True to replace existing subtotals. Set the PageBreaks to True for page breaks to be added after each group. Use the SummaryBelowData parameter to choose where the summary row will be added.
Table	Variant	[RowInput], [ColumnInput].	Creates a new data table at the current range.

Name	Returns	Parameters	Description
Text ToColumns	Variant	[Destination], [DataType As XlTextParsing Type], [TextQualifier As XlText Qualifier], [Consecutive Delimiter], [Tab], [Semicolon], [Comma], [Space], [Other], [OtherChar], [FieldInfo], [Decimal Separator], [Thousands Separator].	Parses text in cells into several columns. The Destination specifies the range that the parsed text will go into. The DataType parameter can be used to choose whether the text is delimited or fixed width. The TextQualifier parameter can specify which character denotes string data when parsing. Set the Consecutive Delimiter to True for Excel to treat consecutive delimiters as one. Set the Tab, Semicolon, Comma, or Space parameter to True to use the associated character as the delimiter. Set the Other parameter to True and specify an OtherChar to use another character as the delimiter. FieldInfo takes a two-dimensional array containing more parsing information. The DecimalSeparator and Thousands Separator can specify how numbers are treated when parsing.

Name	Returns	Parameters	Description
Ungroup	Variant		Either promotes the outline in the range or ungroups the range in a PivotTable report.
UnMerge			Splits up a merged cell into single cells.

Example: Range Object

See Chapter 5 for examples of working with the Range object.

RecentFile Object and the RecentFiles Collection

The RecentFiles collection holds the list of recently modified files. Equivalent to the files listed under the File menu in Excel. Each RecentFile object represents one of the recently modified files. RecentFiles has a few attributes besides the typical collection ones. The Maximum property can be used to set or return the maximum number of files that Excel will 'remember' modifying. The value can range from 0 to 9. The Count property returns the number of RecentFile objects in the collection. The Add method is used to add a file (with the Name parameter) to the collection.

RecentFile Common Properties

The Application, Creator, and Parent properties are defined at the beginning of this Appendix.

RecentFile Properties

Name	Returns	Description
Index	Long	Read Only. Returns the spot in the collection that the current object is located.
Name	String	Read Only. Returns the name of the recently modified file.
Path	String	Read Only. Returns the file path of the recently modified file.

RecentFile Methods

Name	Returns	Parameters	Description
Delete			Deletes the object from the collection.
Open	Workbook		Opens up the recent file and returns the opened workbook

Example: RecentFile Object and the RecentFiles Collection

```
Sub CheckRecentFiles()
   Dim oRF As RecentFile

   'Remove any recent files that refer to the floppy drive
   For Each oRF In Application.RecentFiles
      If Left(oRF.Path, 2) = "A:" Then
         oRF.Delete
      End If
   Next
End Sub
```

RoutingSlip Object

The RoutingSlip object represents the properties and methods of the routing slip of an Excel document. The parent object of the RoutingSlip object is the Workbook object. The HasRoutingSlip property of the Workbook object has to set to True before the RoutingSlip object can be manipulated.

RoutingSlip Common Properties

The Application, Creator, and Parent properties are defined at the beginning of this Appendix.

RoutingSlip Properties

Name	Returns	Description
Delivery	XlRoutingSlip Delivery	Set / Get how the delivery process will proceed.
Message	Variant	Set / Get the body text of the routing slip message.
Recipients	Variant	Parameters: [Index]. Returns the list of recipient names to send the parent workbook to.
ReturnWhen Done	Boolean	Set / Get whether the message is returned to the original sender.
Status	XlRoutingSlip Status	Read Only. Returns the current status of the routing slip.

Name	Returns	Description
Subject	Variant	Set / Get the subject text for the routing slip message.
Track Status	Boolean	Set / Get whether the message is sent to the original sender each time the message is forwarded.

RoutingSlip Methods

Name	Returns	Parameters	Description
Reset	Variant		Reset the routing slip.

Scenario Object and the Scenarios Collection

The Scenarios collection contains the list of all the scenarios associated with a worksheet. Each Scenario object represents a single scenario in a worksheet. A scenario holds the list of saved cell values that can later be substituted into the worksheet. The parent of the Scenarios collection is the Worksheet object. The Scenarios collection has a few extra properties and methods besides the typical collection attributes. These are listed in the following table.

Scenarios Properties and Methods

Name	Returns	Description
Count	Long	Read Only. Returns the number of Scenario objects in the collection.
Add	Scenario	Method. Parameters: Name As String, ChangingCells, [Values], [Comment], [Locked], [Hidden]. Adds a scenario to the collection. The Name parameter specifies the name of the scenario.
Create Summary	Variant	Method. Parameters: ReportType As XlSummaryReportType, [ResultCells]. Creates a worksheet containing a summary of all the scenarios of the parent worksheet. The ReportType parameter can specify the report type. The ResultCells parameter can be a range of cells containing the formulas related to the changing cells.
Merge	Variant	Method. Parameters: Source. Merges the scenarios in the Source parameter into the current worksheet.

Scenario Common Properties

The `Application`, `Creator`, and `Parent` properties are defined at the beginning of this Appendix.

Scenario Properties

Name	Returns	Description
Changing Cells	Range	Read Only. Returns the range of cells in the worksheet that will have values plugged in for the specific scenario.
Comment	String	Set / Get the scenario comment.
Hidden	Boolean	Set / Get whether the scenario is hidden.
Index	Long	Read Only. Returns the spot in the collection that the current `Scenario` object is located.
Locked	Boolean	Set / Get whether the scenario cannot be modified when the worksheet is protected.
Name	String	Set / Get the name of the scenario.
Values	Variant	Read Only. Parameters: `[Index]`. Returns an array of the values to plug in to the changing cells for this particular scenario.

Scenario Methods

Name	Returns	Parameters	Description
Change Scenario	Variant	Changing Cells, [Values]	Changes which set of cells in the worksheet are able to change for the scenario. Optionally can choose new values for the scenario.
Delete	Variant		Deletes the `Scenario` object from the collection.
Show	Variant		Shows the scenario results by putting the scenario values into the worksheet.

Example: Scenario Object and the Scenarios Collection

```
Sub GetBestScenario()
    Dim oScen As Scenario
    Dim oBestScen As Scenario
    Dim dBestSoFar As Double

    'Loop through the scenarios in the sheet
    For Each oScen In ActiveSheet.Scenarios
```

```
    'Show the secnario
    oScen.Show

    'Is it better?
    If Range("Result").Value > dBestSoFar Then
        dBestSoFar = Range("Result").Value

        'Yes - remember it
        Set oBestScen = oScen
    End If
Next

  'Show the best scenario
  oBestScen.Show

  MsgBox "The best scenario is " & oBestScen.Name
End Sub
```

Series Object and the SeriesCollection Collection

The SeriesCollection collection holds the collection of series associated with a chart group. Each Series object contains a collection of points associated with a chart group in a chart. For example, a simple line chart contains a series (Series) of points brought in from the originating data. Since some charts can have many series plotted on the same chart, the SeriesCollection is used to hold that information. The parent of the SeriesCollection is the ChartGroup. The SeriesCollection has a few attributes that are not typical of a collection. These are listed in the following table.

SeriesCollection Properties and Methods

Name	Returns	Description
Add	Series	Method. Parameters: Source, Rowcol As XlRowCol, [SeriesLabels], [CategoryLabels], [Replace]. Adds a Series to the collection. The Source parameter specifies either a range or an array of data points describing the new series (and all the points in it). The Rowcol parameter sets whether the row or the column of the Source contains a series of points. Set SeriesLabels or CategoryLabels to True to make the first row or column of the Source contain the labels for the series and category, respectively.
Count	Long	Read Only. Returns the number of Series objects in the collection.
Extend	Variant	Method. Parameters: Source, [Rowcol], [CategoryLabels]. Adds the points specified by the range or array of data points in the Source parameter to the SeriesCollection. See the Add method for details on the other parameters.

Name	Returns	Description
Paste	Variant	Method. Parameters: Rowcol As XlRowCol, [SeriesLabels], [CategoryLabels], [Replace], [NewSeries]. Pastes the data from the clipboard into the SeriesCollection as a new Series. See the Add method for details on the other parameters.
New Series	Series	Method. Creates a new series and returns the newly created series

Series Common Properties

The Application, Creator, and Parent properties are defined at the beginning of this Appendix.

Series Properties

Name	Returns	Description
ApplyPict ToEnd	Boolean	Set / Get whether pictures are added to the end of the points in the series.
ApplyPict ToFront	Boolean	Set / Get whether pictures are added to the front of the points in the series.
ApplyPict ToSides	Boolean	Set / Get whether pictures are added to the sides of the points in the series.
AxisGroup	XlAxis Group	Set / Get the type of axis type being used by the series (primary or secondary)
BarShape	XlBar Shape	Set / Get the type of shape to use in a 3D bar or column chart (e.g. xlBox)
Border	Border	Read Only. Returns the collection of borders (sides) around the series. Each border's attributes can be accessed individually.
Bubble Sizes	Variant	Set / Get the cells reference (A1 reference style) that have the data relating to how big the bubble should be for bubble charts.
ChartType	XlChart Type	Set / Get the type of chart to use for the series.
ErrorBars	Error Bars	Read Only. Returns the error bars in a series. Use with HasErrorBars.

Table Continued on Following Page

Name	Returns	Description
Explosion	Long	Set / Get how far out the slices (points) of a pie or doughnut chart will explode out. 0 for no explosion.
Fill	Chart Fill Format	Read Only. Returns an object containing fill formatting options for the series of points on a chart.
Formula	String	Set / Get the type of formula label to use for the series.
Formula Local	String	Set / Get the formula of the series in the language of the user using the A1 style references.
Formula R1C1	String	Set / Get the formula of the series in the language of the macro using the R1C1 style references.
Formula R1C1Local	String	Set / Get the formula of the series in the language of the user using the R1C1 style references.
Has3D Effect	Boolean	Set / Get if bubble charts have a 3D appearance.
HasData Labels	Boolean	Set / Get if the series contains data labels.
HasError Bars	Boolean	Set / Get if the series contains error bars. Use with the ErrorBars property.
HasLeader Lines	Boolean	Set / Get if the series contains leader lines. Use with the LeaderLines property.
Interior	Interior	Read Only. Returns an object containing options to format the inside area of the series (e.g. interior color).
InvertIf Negative	Boolean	Set / Get whether the color of the series' points should be the inverse if the value is negative.
Leader Lines	Leader Lines	Read Only. Returns the leader lines associated with the series.
Marker Background Color	Long	Set / Get the color of the series points marker background. Use the RGB function to create the color value.

Name	Returns	Description
Marker Background ColorIndex	XlColor Index	Set / Get the color of the series points marker background. Use the XlColorIndex constants or an index value in the current color palette.
Marker Foreground Color	Long	Set / Get the color of the series points marker foreground. Use the RGB function to create the color value.
Marker Foreground ColorIndex	XlColor Index	Set / Get the color of the series points marker foreground. Use the XlColorIndex constants or an index value in the current color palette.
MarkerSize	Long	Set / Get the size of the point key marker.
Marker Style	XlMarker Style	Set / Get the type of marker to use as the point key (e.g. square, diamond, triangle, picture, etc.)
Name	String	Set / Get the name of the series.
Picture Type	XlChart Picture Type	Set / Get how an associated picture is displayed on the series (e.g. stretched, tiled). Use the XlPictureType constants.
Picture Unit	Long	Set / Get how many units a picture represents if the PictureType property is set to xlScale.
PlotOrder	Long	Set / Get the plotting order for this particular series in the SeriesCollection.
Shadow	Boolean	Set / Get whether the points in the series will have a shadow effect.
Smooth	Boolean	Set / Get whether scatter or line charts will have curves smoothed.
Type	Long	Set / Get the type of series.
Values	Variant	Set / Get the range containing the series values or an array of fixed values containing the series values.
XValues	Variant	Set / Get the array of x values coming from a range or an array of fixed values.

Series Methods

Name	Returns	Parameters	Description
Apply CustomType		ChartType As XlChartType	Changes the chart type to the one specified in the ChartType parameter.
ApplyData Labels	Variant	Type As XlData LabelsType, [LegendKey], [AutoText], [HasLeader Lines]	Applies the data label properties specified by the parameters to the series. The Type parameter specifies whether no label, a value, a percentage of the whole, or a category label is shown. The legend key can appear by the point by setting the LegendKey parameter to True. Set the HasLeaderLines to True to add leader lines the series.
Clear Formats	Variant		Clears the formatting made on the series.
Copy	Variant		Copies the series into the clipboard.
DataLabels	Object	[Index]	Returns the collection of data labels in a series. If the Index parameter is specified then only a single data label is returned.
Delete	Variant		Deletes the series from the series collection

Name	Returns	Parameters	Description
ErrorBar	Variant	[Direction As XlErrorBarDirection], [Include As XlErrorBarInclude], [Type As XlErrorBarType], [Amount], [MinusValues]	Adds error bars to the series. The Direction parameter chooses whether the bar appears on the X or Y axis. The Include parameter specifies which error parts to include. The Type parameter decides the type of error bar to use. The Amount parameter is used to choose an error amount. The MinusValues parameter takes the negative error amount to use when the Type parameter is xlErrorBarTypeCustom.
Paste	Variant		Uses the picture in the clipboard as the marker on the points in the series.
Points	Variant	[Index]	Returns either the collection of points associated with the series or a single point if the Index parameter is specified.
Select	Variant		Selects the series' points on the chart.
Trendlines	Variant	[Index]	Returns either the collection of trendlines associated with the series or a single trendline if the Index parameter is specified.

Example: Series Object and the SeriesCollection Collection

See the DataLabel object for an example of using the Series object

SeriesLines Object

The `SeriesLines` object access the series lines connecting data values from each series. This object only applies to 2D stacked bar or column chart groups. The parent of the `SeriesLines` object is the `ChartGroup` object.

SeriesLines Common Properties

The `Application`, `Creator`, and `Parent` properties are defined at the beginning of this Appendix.

SeriesLines Properties

Name	Returns	Description
Border	Border	Read Only. Returns the border's properties around the series lines.
Name	String	Read Only. Returns the name of the `SeriesLines` object.

SeriesLines Methods

Name	Returns	Parameters	Description
Delete	Variant		Deletes the `SeriesLines` object.
Select	Variant		Selects the series lines in the chart.

Example: SeriesLines Object

```
Sub FormatSeriesLines()
    Dim oCG As ChartGroup
    Dim oSL As SeriesLines

    'Loop through the column groups on the chart
    For Each oCG In Charts(1).ColumnGroups

        'Make sure we have some series lines
        oCG.HasSeriesLines = True

        'Get the series lines
        Set oSL = oCG.SeriesLines

        'Format the lines
        With oSL
            .Border.Weight = xlThin
            .Border.ColorIndex = 5
        End With
    Next
End Sub
```

ShadowFormat Object

The `ShadowFormat` object allows manipulation of the shadow formatting properties of a parent `Shape` object. Use the `Shadow` property of the `Shape` object to access the `ShadowFormat` object.

ShadowFormat Common Properties

The Application, Creator, and Parent properties are defined at the beginning of this Appendix.

ShadowFormat Properties

Name	Returns	Description
ForeColor	Color Format	Read Only. Allows manipulation of the shadow fore color.
Obscured	MsoTri State	Set / Get whether the shape obscures the shadow or not.
OffsetX	Single	Set / Get what the horizontal shadow offset is.
OffsetY	Single	Set / Get what the vertical shadow offset is.
Transparency	Single	Set / Get how transparent the shadow is (0 to 1 where 1 is clear).
Type	MsoShadow Type	Set / Get the shadow type.
Visible	MsoTri State	Set / Get whether the shadow is visible.

ShadowFormat Methods

Name	Returns	Parameters	Description
Increment OffsetX		Increment As Single	Changes the horizontal shadow offset.
Increment OffsetY		Increment As Single	Changes the vertical shadow offset.

Example: ShadowFormat Object

```
Sub AddShadow()
    Dim oSF As ShadowFormat

    Set oSF = ActiveSheet.Shapes.Range(1).Shadow

    With oSF
        .Type = msoShadow6
        .OffsetX = 5
        .OffsetY = 5
        .ForeColor.SchemeColor = 2
        .Visible = True
    End With
End Sub
```

Shape Object and the Shapes Collection

The Shapes collection holds the list of shapes for a sheet. The Shape object represents a single shape such as an AutoShape, a freeform shape, an OLE object (like an image), an ActiveX control or a picture. Possible parent objects of the Shapes collection are the Worksheet and Chart object. The Shapes collection has a few methods and properties besides the typical collection attributes. They are listed in the following table.

Shapes Collection Properties and Methods

Name	Returns	Description
Count	Long	Read Only. Returns the number of shapes in the collection.
Range	Shape Range	Read Only. Parameters: Index. Returns a ShapeRange object containing only some of the shapes in the Shapes collection.
Add Callout	Shape	Method. Parameters: Type As MsoCalloutType, Left As Single, Top As Single, Width As Single, Height As Single. Adds a callout line shape to the collection.
Add Connector	Shape	Method. Parameters: Type As MsoConnectorType, BeginX As Single, BeginY As Single, EndX As Single, EndY As Single. Adds a connector shape to the collection.
AddCurve	Shape	Method. Parameters: SafeArrayOfPoints. Adds a Bezier curve to the collection.
AddForm Control	Shape	Method. Parameters: Type As XlFormControl, Left As Long, Top As Long, Width As Long, Height As Long. Adds an Excel control to the collection.
AddLabel	Shape	Method. Parameters: Orientation As MsoTextOrientation, Left As Single, Top As Single, Width As Single, Height As Single. Adds a label to the collection.
AddLine	Shape	Method. Parameters: BeginX As Single, BeginY As Single, EndX As Single, EndY As Single. Adds a line shape to the collection.

Name	Returns	Description
AddOLE Object	Shape	Method. Parameters: [ClassType], [Filename], [Link], [DisplayAsIcon], [IconFileName], [IconIndex], [IconLabel], [Left], [Top], [Width], [Height]. Adds an OLE control to the collection.
Add Picture	Shape	Method. Parameters: Filename As String, LinkToFile As MsoTriState, SaveWithDocument As MsoTriState, Left As Single, Top As Single, Width As Single, Height As Single. Adds a picture object to the collection
Add Polyline	Shape	Method. Parameters: SafeArrayOfPoints. Adds an open polyline or a closed polygon to the collection.
Add Shape	Shape	Method. Parameters: Type As MsoAutoShapeType, Left As Single, Top As Single, Width As Single, Height As Single. Adds a shape using the Type parameter to the collection.
Add Textbox	Shape	Method. Parameters: Orientation As MsoTextOrientation, Left As Single, Top As Single, Width As Single, Height As Single. Adds a textbox to the collection.
AddText Effect	Shape	Method. Parameters: PresetTextEffect As MsoPresetTextEffect, Text As String, FontName As String, FontSize As Single, FontBold As MsoTriState, FontItalic As MsoTriState, Left As Single, Top As Single. Adds a WordArt object to the collection.
Build Freeform	Freeform Builder	Method. Parameters: EditingType As MsoEditingType, X1 As Single, Y1 As Single. Accesses an object that allows creation of a new shape based on ShapeNode objects.
Select All		Method. Selects all the shapes in the collection.

Shape Common Properties

The `Application`, `Creator`, and `Parent` properties are defined at the beginning of this Appendix.

Shape Properties

Name	Returns	Description
Adjustments	Adjustments	Read Only. An object accessing the adjustments for a shape.
Alternative Text	String	Set / Get the alternate text to appear if the image is not loaded. Used with a web page.
AutoShape Type	MsoAuto ShapeType	Set / Get the type of AutoShape used.
BlackWhite Mode	MsoBlack WhiteMode	Property used for compatibility to other drawing packages only. Does not do anything.
BottomRight Cell	Range	Read Only. Returns the single cell range that describes the cell under the lower-right corner of the shape.
Callout	Callout Format	Read Only. An object accessing the callout properties of the shape.
Connection SiteCount	Long	Read Only. Returns the number of potential connection points (sites) on the shape for a connector.
Connector	MsoTriState	Read Only. Returns whether the shape is a connector.
Connector Format	Connector Format	Read Only. Returns an object containing formatting options for a connector shape. Shape must be a connector shape.
Control Format	Control Format	Read Only. Returns an object containing formatting options for an Excel control. Shape must be an Excel control.
Fill	FillFormat	Read Only. Returns an object containing fill formatting options for the Shape object.

Name	Returns	Description
FormControl Type	XlForm Control	Read Only. Returns the type of Excel control the current shape is (e.g. xlCheckBox). Shape must be an Excel control.
GroupItems	GroupShapes	Read Only. Returns the shapes that make up the current shape.
Height	Single	Set / Get the height of the shape.
Horizontal Flip	MsoTriState	Read Only. Returns whether the shape has been flipped.
Hyperlink	Hyperlink	Read Only. Returns the hyperlink of the shape, if any.
Left	Single	Set / Get the horizontal position of the shape.
Line	LineFormat	Read Only. An object accessing the line formatting of the shape.
LinkFormat	LinkFormat	Read Only. An object accessing the OLE linking properties.
LockAspect Ratio	MsoTriState	Set / Get whether the dimensional proportions of the shape is kept when the shape is resized.
Locked	Boolean	Set / Get whether the shape can be modified if the sheet is locked (True = cannot modify).
Name	String	Set / Get the name of the Shape object.
Nodes	ShapeNodes	Read Only. An object accessing the nodes of the freeform shape.
OLEFormat	OLEFormat	Read Only. An object accessing OLE object properties if applicable.
OnAction	String	Set / Get the macro to run when the shape is clicked.
Picture Format	Picture Format	Read Only. An object accessing the picture format options.
Placement	XlPlacement	Set / Get how the object will react with the cells around the shape.
Rotation	Single	Set / Get the degrees rotation of the shape.

Table Continued on Following Page

Name	Returns	Description
Script	Script	Read Only. Returns the VBScript associated with the shape.
Shadow	Shadow Format	Read Only. An object accessing the shadow properties.
TextEffect	TextEffect Format	Read Only. An object accessing the text effect properties.
TextFrame	TextFrame	Read Only. An object accessing the text frame properties.
ThreeD	ThreeD Format	Read Only. An object accessing the 3-D effect formatting properties.
Top	Single	Set / Get the vertical position of the shape.
TopLeftCell	Range	Read Only. Returns the single cell range that describes the cell over the upper-left corner of the shape.
Type	MsoShape Type	Read Only. Returns the type of shape.
VerticalFlip	MsoTriState	Read Only. Returns whether the shape has been vertically flipped.
Vertices	Variant	Read Only. Returns a series of coordinate pairs describing the Freeform's vertices.
Visible	MsoTriState	Set / Get whether the shape is visible.
Width	Single	Read Only. Returns the type of shape.
ZOrder Position	Long	Read Only. Returns where the shape is in the z-order of the collection (e.g. front, back)

Shape Methods

Name	Returns	Parameters	Description
Apply			Activates the shape.
Copy			Copies the shape to the clipboard.

Name	Returns	Parameters	Description
Copy Picture		[Appearance As XLPicture Appearance], [Format As XlCopyPictureFormat], [Size As XlPicture Appearance]	Copies the range into the clipboard as a picture. The Appearance parameter can be used to specify whether the picture is copied as it looks on the screen or when printed. The Format parameter can specify the type of picture that will be put into the clipboard.
Cut			Cuts the shape and places it in the clipboard.
Delete			Deletes the shape.
Duplicate	Shape		Duplicates the shape returning the new shape.
Flip		FlipCmd As MsoFlipCmd	Flips the shape using the FlipCmd parameter.
Increment Left		Increment As Single	Moves the shape horizontally.
Increment Rotation		Increment As Single	Rotates the shape using the Increment parameter as degrees.
IncrementTop		Increment As Single	Moves the shape vertically.
PickUp			Copies the format of the current shape so another shape can then apply the formats.

Table Continued on Following Page

Name	Returns	Parameters	Description
Reroute Connections			Optimizes the route of the current connector shape connected between two shapes. Also, this method may be used to optimize all the routes of connectors connected to the current shape.
ScaleHeight		Factor As Single, RelativeTo OriginalSize As MsoTriState, [Scale]	Scales the height of the shape by the Factor parameter.
ScaleWidth		Factor As Single, RelativeTo OriginalSize As MsoTriState, [Scale]	Scales the width of the shape by the Factor parameter.
Select		[Replace]	Selects the shape in the document.
SetShapes Default Properties			Sets the formatting of the current shape as a default shape in Word.
Ungroup	ShapeR ange		Breaks apart the shapes that make up the Shape object.
ZOrder		ZOrderCmd As MsoZOrderCmd	Changes the order of the shape object in the collection.

Example: Shape Object and the Shapes Collection

The Shape object is a generic container object for other object types. Examples of using the Shapes collection and Shape object are included under the specific objects.

ShapeNode Object and the ShapeNodes Collection

The ShapeNodes collection has the list of nodes and curved segments that make up a freeform shape. The ShapeNode object specifies a single node or curved segment that makes up a freeform shape. The Nodes property of the Shape object is used to access the ShapeNodes collection.

The ShapeNodes collection has a few methods besides the typical collection attributes listed in the following table.

ShapeNodes Collection Properties and Methods

Name	Returns	Description
Count	Integer	Read Only. Returns the number of ShapeNode objects in the collection.
Delete		Method. Parameters: Index As Integer. Deletes the node specified by the Index.
Insert		Method. Parameters: Index As Integer, SegmentType As MsoSegmentType, EditingType As MsoEditingType, X1 As Single, Y1 As Single, X2 As Single, Y2 As Single, X3 As Single, Y3 As Single. Inserts a node or curved segment in the Nodes collection.
Set Editing Type		Method. Parameters: Index As Integer, EditingType As MsoEditingType. Sets the editing type for a node.
Set Position		Method. Parameters: Index As Integer, X1 As Single, Y1 As Single. Moves the specified node.
Set Segment Type		Method. Parameters: Index As Integer, SegmentType As MsoSegmentType. Changes the segment type following the node.

ShapeNode Common Properties

The Application, Creator, and Parent properties are defined at the beginning of this Appendix.

ShapeNode Properties

Name	Returns	Description
Editing Type	MsoEditing Type	Read Only. Returns the editing type for the node.
Points	Variant	Read Only. Returns the positional coordinate pair.
Segment Type	MsoSegment Type	Read Only. Returns the type of segment following the node.

Example: ShapeNode Object and the ShapeNodes Collection

```
Sub ToggleArch()
   Dim oShp As Shape
   Dim oSN As ShapeNodes

   Set oShp = ActiveSheet.Shapes(1)

   'Is the Shape a freeform?
   If oShp.Type = msoFreeform Then

       'Yes, so get its nodes
       Set oSN = oShp.Nodes

       'Toggle segment 3 between a line and a curve
       If oSN.Item(3).SegmentType = msoSegmentCurve Then
           oSN.SetSegmentType 3, msoSegmentLine
       Else
           oSN.SetSegmentType 3, msoSegmentCurve
       End If
   End If
End Sub
```

ShapeRange Collection

The ShapeRange collection holds a collection of Shape objects for a certain range or selection in a document. Possible parent items are the Range and the Selection object. The ShapeRange collection has many properties and methods besides the typical collection attributes. These items are listed below.

However, some operations will cause an error if performed on a ShapeRange collection with multiple shapes.

ShapeRange Properties

Name	Returns	Description
Adjustments	Adjustments	Read Only. An object accessing the adjustments for a shape.
Alternative Text	String	Set / Get the alternate text to appear if the image is not loaded. Used with a web page.
AutoShape Type	MsoAuto ShapeType	Set / Get the type of AutoShape used.

Name	Returns	Description
BlackWhite Mode	MsoBlack WhiteMode	Property used for compatibility to other drawing packages only. Does not do anything.
Callout	Callout Format	Read Only. An object accessing the callout properties of the shape.
Connection SiteCount	Long	Read Only. Returns the number of potential connection points (sites) on the shape for a connector.
Connector	MsoTriState	Read Only. Returns whether the shape is a connector.
Connector Format	Connector Format	Read Only. Returns an object containing formatting options for a connector shape. Shape must be a connector shape.
Count	Long	Read Only. Returns the number of shapes in the collection.
Fill	FillFormat	Read Only. An object accessing the fill properties of the shape.
GroupItems	GroupShapes	Read Only. Returns the shapes that make up the current shape.
Height	Single	Set / Get the height of the shape.
Horizontal Flip	MsoTriState	Read Only. Returns whether the shape has been flipped.
Left	Single	Set / Get the horizontal position of the shape.
Line	LineFormat	Read Only. An object accessing the line formatting of the shape.
Lock Aspect Ratio	MsoTriState	Set / Get whether the dimensional proportions of the shape is kept when the shape is resized.
Name	String	Set / Get the name of the shape.
Nodes	ShapeNodes	Read Only. Returns the nodes associated with the shape.
Picture Format	Picture Format	Read Only. An object accessing the picture format options.

Table Continued on Following Page

Name	Returns	Description
Rotation	Single	Set / Get the degrees rotation of the shape.
Shadow	Shadow Format	Read Only. An object accessing the shadow properties.
Text Effect	TextEffect Format	Read Only. An object accessing the text effect properties.
Text Frame	TextFrame	Read Only. An object accessing the text frame properties.
ThreeD	ThreeDFormat	Read Only. An object accessing the 3-D effect formatting properties.
Top	Single	Set / Get the vertical position of the shape.
Type	MsoShapeType	Read Only. Returns the type of shape.
VerticalFlip	MsoTriState	Read Only. Returns whether the shape has been vertically flipped.
Vertices	Variant	Read Only. Returns a series of coordinate pairs describing the Freeform's vertices.
Visible	MsoTriState	Set / Get whether the shape is visible.
Width	Single	Set / Get the width of the shape.
ZOrder Position	Long	Read Only. Changes the order of the object in the collection

ShapeRange Methods

Name	Returns	Parameters	Description
Align		AlignCmd As MsoAlignCmd, RelativeTo As MsoTriState	Aligns the shapes in the collection to the alignment properties set by the parameters.
Apply			Applies the formatting that was set by the PickUp method.
Delete			Deletes the shape.

Name	Returns	Parameters	Description
Distribute		DistributeCmd As MsoDistribute Cmd, RelativeTo As MsoTriState	Distributes the shapes in the collection either evenly either horizontally or vertically.
Duplicate	Shape Range		Duplicates the shape and returns a new ShapeRange.
Flip		FlipCmd As MsoFlipCmd	Flips the shape using the FlipCmd parameter.
Group	Shape		Groups the shapes in the collection.
Increment Left		Increment As Single	Moves the shape horizontally.
Increment Rotation		Increment As Single	Rotates the shape using the Increment parameter as degrees.
Increment Top		Increment As Single	Moves the shape vertically.
PickUp			Copies the format of the current shape so another shape can then Apply the formats.
Regroup	Shape		Regroup any previously grouped shapes.
Reroute Connections			Optimizes the route of the current connector shape connected between two shapes. Also, this method may be used to optimize all the routes of connectors connected to the current shape.

Table Continued on Following Page

Name	Returns	Parameters	Description
ScaleHeight		Factor As Single, RelativeTo OriginalSize As MsoTriState, [Scale]	Scales the height of the shape by the Factor parameter.
ScaleWidth		Factor As Single, RelativeTo OriginalSize As MsoTriState, [Scale]	Scales the width of the shape by the Factor parameter.
Select		[Replace]	Selects the shape in the document.
SetShapes Default Properties			Sets the formatting of the current shape as a default shape in Word.
Ungroup	Shape Range		Breaks apart the shapes that make up the Shape object.
ZOrder		ZOrderCmd As MsoZOrderCmd	Changes the order of the shape object in the collection.

Example: ShapeRange Collection

```
Sub AlignShapeRanges()
    Dim oSR As ShapeRange

    'Get the first two shapes on the sheet
    Set oSR = ActiveSheet.Shapes.Range(Array(1, 2))

    'Align the left hand edges of the shapes
    oSR.Align msoAlignLefts, msoFalse
End Sub
```

Sheets Collection

The Sheets collection contains all of the sheets in the parent workbook. Sheets in a workbook consist of chart sheets and worksheets. Therefore, the Sheets collection holds both the Chart objects and Worksheet objects associated with the parent workbook. The parent of the Sheets collection is the Workbook object.

Sheets Common Properties

The Application, Creator, and Parent properties are defined at the beginning of this Appendix.

Sheets Properties

Name	Returns	Description
Count	Long	Read Only. Returns the number of sheets in the collection (and therefore workbook)
HPage Breaks	HPage Breaks	Read Only. Returns a collection holding all the horizontal page breaks associated with the Sheets collection.
VPage Breaks	VPage Breaks	Read Only. Returns a collection holding all the vertical page breaks associated with the worksheets of the Sheets collection.
Visible	Variant	Set / Get whether the sheets in the collection are visible. Also can set this to xlVeryHidden to not allow a user to make the sheets in the collection visible.

Sheets Methods

Name	Returns	Parameters	Description
Add		[Before], [After], [Count], [Type]	Adds a sheet to the collection. You can specify where the sheet goes by choosing which sheet object will be before the new sheet object (Before parameter) or after the new sheet (After parameter). The Count parameter decides how many sheet are created. The Type parameter can be used to specify the type of sheet using the xlSheetType constants.
Copy		[Before], [After]	Adds a new copy of the currently active sheet to the position specified at the Before or After parameters.
Delete			Deletes all the sheets in the collection. Remember a workbook must contain at least one sheet.
Fill Across Sheets		Range As Range, Type As XlFillWith	Copies the values in the Range parameter to all the other sheets at the same location. The Type parameter can be used to specify whether cell contents, formulas or everything is copied.

Table Continued on Following Page

Name	Returns	Parameters	Description
Move		[Before], [After]	Moves the current sheet to the position specified by the parameters. See the Add method.
Print Out		[From], [To], [Copies], [Preview], [Active Printer], [Print ToFile], [Collate], [PrToFile Name]	Prints out the sheets in the collection. The printer, number of copies, collation, and whether a print preview is desired can be specified with the parameters. Also, the sheets can be printed to a file using the PrintToFile and PrToFileName parameters. The From and To parameters can be used to specify the range of printed pages.
Print Preview		[Enable Changes]	Displays the current sheet in the collection in a print preview mode. Set the EnableChanges parameter to False to disable the Margins and Setup buttons, hence not allowing the viewer to modify the page setup.
Select		[Replace]	Selects the current sheet in the collection.

SoundNote Object

The SoundNote object is not used in the current version of Excel. It is kept here for compatibility purposes only. The list of its methods is shown below.

SoundNote Methods

Name	Returns	Parameters
Delete	Variant	
Import	Variant	Filename As String

Name	Returns	Parameters
Play	Variant	
Record	Variant	

Style Object and the Styles Collection

The `Styles` collection holds the list of user-defined and built-in formatting styles, such as `Currency` and `Normal`, in a workbook or range. Each `Style` object represents formatting attributes associated with the parent object. There are some Excel built-in `Style` objects, such as `Currency`. Also, new styles can be created. Possible parents of the `Styles` collection are the `Range` and `Workbook` objects.

> *Styles can be accessed by the end user using the* **Style** *dialog box from the* **Format | Style** *menu.*

The Styles collection has three extra attributes besides the typical collection ones. The `Count` property returns the number of `Style` objects in the collection. The `Add` method uses the `Name` parameter to add a new style to the collection. The `BasedOn` parameter of the `Add` method can be used to specify a range that the new style will be based on. The `Merge` method merges the styles in the workbook specified by the `Workbook` parameter into the current parent workbook.

Style Common Properties

The `Application`, `Creator`, and `Parent` properties are defined at the beginning of this Appendix.

Style Properties

Name	Returns	Description
AddIndent	Boolean	Set / Get whether text associated with the style is automatically indented if the text alignment in a cell is set to equally distribute.
Borders	Borders	Read Only. Returns the collection of borders associated with the style. Each border side can be accessed individually.
BuiltIn	Boolean	Read Only. Returns whether the style is built-in.
Font	Font	Read Only. Returns an object containing `Font` options for the associated style.

Table Continued on Following Page

Name	Returns	Description
Formula Hidden	Boolean	Set / Get whether formulas associated with the style will be hidden if the workbook / worksheet is protected.
Horizontal Alignment	XlHAlign	Set / Get how the cells associated with the style are horizontally aligned. Use the XlHAlign constants.
Include Alignment	Boolean	Set / Get whether the styles includes properties associated with alignment (i.e. AddIndent, HorizontalAlignment, VerticalAlignment, WrapText, and Orientation)
Include Border	Boolean	Set / Get whether border attributes are included with the style (i.e. Color, ColorIndex, LineStyle, and Weight)
IncludeFont	Boolean	Set / Get whether font attributes are included in the style (i.e. Background, Bold, Color, ColorIndex, FontStyle, Italic, Name, OutlineFont, Shadow, Size, Strikethrough, Subscript, Superscript, and Underline).
Include Number	Boolean	Set / Get whether the NumberFormat property is included in the style.
Include Patterns	Boolean	Set / Get whether interior pattern related properties are included in the style (i.e. Color, ColorIndex, InvertIfNegative, Pattern, PatternColor, and PatternColorIndex).
Include Protection	Boolean	Set / Get whether the locking related properties are included with the style (i.e. FormulaHidden and Locked).
IndentLevel	Long	Set / Get the indent level for the style.
Interior	Interior	Read Only. Returns an object containing options to format the inside area of the style (e.g. interior color).

Name	Returns	Description
Locked	Boolean	Set / Get whether the style properties can be changed if the workbook is locked.
MergeCells	Variant	Set / Get whether the current style contains merged cells.
Name	String	Read Only. Returns the name of the style.
NameLocal	String	Read Only. Returns the name of the style in the language of the user's computer.
Number Format	String	Set / Get the number format associated with the style.
Number FormatLocal	String	Set / Get the number format associated with the style in the language of the end user.
Orientation	Xl Orientation	Set / Get the text orientation for the cell text associated with the style. A value from –90 to 90 degrees can be specified or a XlOrientation constant.
ReadingOrder	Long	Set / Get whether the text associated with the style is from right-to-left (xlRTL), left-to-right (xlLTR), or context sensitive (xlContext).
ShrinkToFit	Boolean	Set / Get whether the cell text associated with the style will automatically shrink to fit the column width
Value	String	Read Only. Returns the name of the style.
Vertical Alignment	XlVAlign	Set / Get how the cells associated with the style are vertically aligned. Use the XlVAlign constants.
WrapText	Boolean	Set / Get whether cell text wraps in cells associated with the style.

Style Methods

Name	Returns	Parameters	Description
Delete	Variant		Deletes the style from the collection.

Example: Style Object and the Styles Collection

```
Sub UpdateStyles()
    Dim oStyle As Style

    Set oStyle = ActiveWorkbook.Styles("Editing")

    'Update the Editing style to be unlocked with a default background
    With oStyle
        .IncludePatterns = True
        .IncludeProtection = True
        .Locked = False
        .Interior.Pattern = xlNone
    End With
End Sub
```

TextEffectFormat Object

The TextEffectFormat object contains all the properties and methods associated with WordArt objects. The parent object of the TextEffectFormat is always the Shape object.

TextEffectFormat Common Properties

The Application, Creator, and Parent properties are defined at the beginning of this Appendix.

TextEffectFormat Properties

Name	Returns	Description
Alignment	MsoText Effect Alignment	Set / Get the alignment of the WordArt.
FontBold	MsoTri State	Set / Get whether the WordArt is bold.
Font Italic	MsoTri State	Set / Get whether the WordArt is italic.
FontName	String	Set / Get the font used in the WordArt.
FontSize	Single	Set / Get the font size in the WordArt.
KernedPairs	MsoTri State	Set / Get whether the characters are kerned in the WordArt.
Normalized Height	MsoTri State	Set / Get whether both the uppercase and lowercase characters are the same height.

Name	Returns	Description
Preset Shape	MsoPreset TextEffect Shape	Set / Get the shape of the WordArt.
PresetText Effect	MsoPreset TextEffect	Set / Get the effect associated with the WordArt.
Rotated Chars	MsoTri State	Set / Get whether the WordArt has been rotated by 90 degrees.
Text	String	Set / Get the text in the WordArt.
Tracking	Single	Set / Get the spacing ratio between characters.

TextEffectFormat Methods

Name	Returns	Parameters	Description
Toggle Vertical Text			Toggles the text from vertical to horizontal and back.

Example: TextEffectFormat Object

```
Sub FormatTextArt()
    Dim oTEF As TextEffectFormat
    Dim oShp As Shape

    Set oShp = ActiveSheet.Shapes(1)

    If oShp.Type = msoTextEffect Then

        Set oTEF = oShp.TextEffect

        With oTEF
            .FontName = "Times New Roman"
            .FontBold = True
            .PresetTextEffect = msoTextEffect14
            .Text = "Hello World!"
        End With
    End If
End Sub
```

TextFrame Object

The TextFrame object contains the properties and methods that can manipulate text frame shapes. Possible parent objects of the TextFrame object are the Shape and ShapeRange objects.

TextFrame Common Properties

The Application, Creator, and Parent properties are defined at the beginning of this Appendix.

TextFrame Properties

Name	Returns	Description
AutoMargins	Boolean	Set / Get whether Excel will calculate the margins of the text frame automatically. Set this property to False to use the MarginLeft, MarginRight, MarginTop, and MarginBottom properties.
AutoSize	Boolean	Set / Get whether the size of the text frame changes to match the text inside.
Horizontal Alignment	XlHAlign	Set / Get how the text frame is horizontally aligned. Use the xlHAlign constants.
MarginBottom	Single	Set / Get the bottom spacing in a text frame.
MarginLeft	Single	Set / Get the left spacing in a text frame.
MarginRight	Single	Set / Get the right spacing in a text frame.
MarginTop	Single	Set / Get the top spacing in a text frame.
Orientation	MsoText Orientation	Set / Get the orientation of the text in the text frame.
ReadingOrder	Long	Set / Get whether the text in the frame is read from right-to-left (xlRTL), left-to-right (xlLTR), or context sensitive (xlContext).
Vertical Alignment	XlVAlign	Set / Get how the text frame is vertically aligned. Use the XlVAlign constants.

TextFrame Methods

Name	Returns	Parameters	Description
Characters	Characters	[Start], [Length]	Returns an object containing all the characters in the text frame. Allows manipulation on a character-by-character basis and to retrieve only a subset of text in the frame.

Example: TextFrame Object

```
Sub SetShapeAutoSized()
    Dim oTF As TextFrame
    Dim oShp As Shape

    Set oShp = ActiveSheet.Shapes(1)
    Set oTF = oShp.TextFrame

    oTF.AutoSize = True
End Sub
```

ThreeDFormat Object

The ThreeDFormat object contains all of the three-dimensional formatting properties of the parent Shape object. The ThreeD property of the Shape object is used to access the ThreeDFormat object.

ThreeDFormat Common Properties

The Application, Creator, and Parent properties are defined at the beginning of this Appendix.

ThreeDFormat Properties

Name	Returns	Description
Depth	Single	Set / Get the 'depth' of a 3D shape.
Extrusion Color	ColorFormat	Read Only. An object manipulating the color of the extrusion.
Extrusion ColorType	MsoExtrusion ColorType	Set / Get how the color for the extrusion is set.
Perspective	MsoTriState	Set / Get whether the shape's extrusion has perspective.
Preset Extrusion Direction	MsoPreset Extrusion Direction	Read Only. Returns the direction of the extrusion.

Table Continued on Following Page

Name	Returns	Description
Preset Lighting Direction	MsoPreset Lighting Direction	Set / Get the directional source of the light source.
Preset Lighting Softness	MsoPresetLight ingSoftness	Set / Get the softness of the light source.
Preset Material	MsoPreset Material	Set / Get the surface material of the extrusion.
PresetThree DFormat	MsoPresetThree DFormat	Read Only. Returns the preset extrusion format.
RotationX	Single	Set / Get how many degrees the extrusion is rotated.
RotationY	Single	Set / Get how many degrees the extrusion is rotated.
Visible	MsoTriState	Set / Get whether the 3D shape is visible.

ThreeDFormat Methods

Name	Returns	Parameters	Description
Increment RotationX		Increment As Single	Changes the RotationX property.
Increment RotationY		Increment As Single	Changes the RotationY property.
Reset Rotation			Resets the RotationX and RotationY to 0.
Set Extrusion Direction		PresetExtrus ionDirection As MsoPreset Extrusion Direction	Changes the extrusion direction.
SetThreeD Format		PresetThreeD Format As MsoPreset ThreeDFormat	Sets the preset extrusion format.

Example: ThreeDFormat Object

```
Sub SetShape3D()
    Dim o3DF As ThreeDFormat
    Dim oShp As Shape
```

```
Set oShp = ActiveSheet.Shapes(1)
Set o3DF = oShp.ThreeD

With o3DF
    .Depth = 10
    .SetExtrusionDirection msoExtrusionBottomRight
End With
End Sub
```

TickLabels Object

The `TickLabels` object contains the formatting options associated with the tick-mark labels for tick marks on a chart axis. The parent of the `TickLabels` object is the `Axis` object.

TickLabels Common Properties

The `Application`, `Creator`, and `Parent` properties are defined at the beginning of this Appendix.

TickLabels Properties

Name	Returns	Description
Alignment	Long	Set / Get the alignment of the tick labels. Use the `XlHAlign` constants.
AutoScale Font	Variant	Set / Get whether the font size will change automatically if the parent chart changes sizes
Depth	Long	Read Only. Returns how many levels of category tick labels are on the axis.
Font	Font	Read Only. Returns an object containing `Font` options for the tick label text.
Name	String	Read Only. Returns the name of the `TickLabels` object.
Number Format	String	Set / Get the numeric formatting to use if the tick labels are numeric values or dates.
Number FormatLinked	Boolean	Set / Get whether the same numerical format used for the cells containing the chart data is used by the tick labels.
Number FormatLocal	Variant	Set / Get the name of the numeric format being used by the tick labels in the language being used by the user.

Table Continued on Following Page

Name	Returns	Description
Offset	Long	Set / Get the percentage distance between levels of labels as compared to the axis label's font size.
Orientation	XlTickLabel Orientation	Set / Get the angle of the text for the tick labels. The value can be in degrees (from –90 to 90) or one of the XlTickLabelOrientation constants.
ReadingOrder	Long	Set / Get how the text is read (from left to right or right to left). Only applicable in appropriate languages.

TickLabels Methods

Name	Returns	Parameters	Description
Delete	Variant		Deletes the tick labels from the axis labels.
Select	Variant		Selects the tick labels on the chart.

Example: TickLabels Object

```
Sub FormatTickLabels()
    Dim oTL As TickLabels

    Set oTL = Charts(1).Axes(xlValue).TickLabels

    With oTL
        .NumberFormat = "#,##0"
        .Font.Size = 12
    End With
End Sub
```

TreeviewControl Object

The TreeviewControl object allows manipulation of the hierarchical member-selection of a cube field. This object is usually used by macro recordings and not when building VBA code. The parent of the TreeviewControl object is the CubeField object.

TreeviewControl Common Properties

The Application, Creator, and Parent properties are defined at the beginning of this Appendix.

TreeviewControl Properties

Name	Returns	Description
Drilled	Variant	Set / Get a string array describing the drilled status of the members of the parent cube field.
Hidden	Variant	Set / Get the hidden status of the members in a cube field.

Trendline Object and the Trendlines Collection

The Trendlines collection holds the collection of trendlines in a chart. Each TrendLine object describes a trendline on a chart of a particular series. Trendlines are used to graphically show trends in the data and help predict future values. The parent of the Trendlines collection is the Series object.

The Trendlines collection has one property and one method besides the typical collection attributes. The Count property returns the number of TrendLine objects in the collection. The Add method adds a trendline to the current chart. The Add method has a Type, Order, Period, Forward, Backward, Intercept, DisplayEquation, DispayRSquared, and Name parameter. See the Trendline Properties section for more information.

Trendline Common Properties

The Application, Creator, and Parent properties are defined at the beginning of this Appendix.

Trendline Properties

Name	Returns	Description
Backward	Long	Set / Get how many periods the trendline extends back.
Border	Border	Read Only. Returns the border's properties around the trendline.
DataLabel	DataLabel	Read Only. Returns an object to manipulate the trendline's data label.
Display Equation	Boolean	Set / Get whether the equation used for the trendline is displayed on the chart.
DisplayR Squared	Boolean	Set / Get whether the R-squared value for the trendline is displayed on the chart.
Forward	Long	Set / Get how many periods the trendline extends forward.

Table Continued on Following Page

Name	Returns	Description
Index	Long	Read Only. Returns the spot in the collection that the current object is.
Intercept	Double	Set / Get at which point the trendline crosses the value (y) axis.
Intercept IsAuto	Boolean	Set / Get whether the point the trendline crosses the value axis is automatically calculated with regression.
Name	String	Set / Get the name of the Trendline object.
Name IsAuto	Boolean	Set / Get whether Excel automatically chooses the trendline name.
Order	Long	Set / Get the order of a polynomial trendline. The Type property must be xlPolynomial.
Period	Long	Set / Get what the period is for the moving-average trendline.
Type	XlTrendline Type	Set / Get the type of the trendline (e.g. xlExponential, xlLinear, etc).

Trendline Methods

Name	Returns	Parameters	Description
Clear Formats	Variant		Clears any formatting made on the trendlines.
Delete	Variant		Deletes the trendlines.
Select	Variant		Selects the trendlines on the chart.

Example: Trendline Object and the Trendlines Collection

```
Sub AddTrendLine()
    Dim oSer As Series
    Dim oTL As Trendline

    Set oSer = Charts(1).SeriesCollection(1)
    Set oTL = oSer.Trendlines.Add(xlLinear)

    With oTL
        .DisplayEquation = True
        .DisplayRSquared = True
    End With
End Sub
```

UpBars Object

The UpBars object contains formatting options for up bars on a chart. The parent of the UpBars object is the ChartGroup object. To see if this object exists use the HasUpDownBars property of the ChartGroup object.

UpBars Common Properties

The Application, Creator, and Parent properties are defined at the beginning of this Appendix.

UpBars Properties

Name	Returns	Description
Border	Border	Read Only. Returns the border's properties around the up bars.
Fill	ChartFill Format	Read Only. Returns an object containing fill formatting options for the up bars of a chart.
Interior	Interior	Read Only. Returns an object containing options to format the inside area of the up bars (e.g. interior color).
Name	String	Read Only. Returns the name of the up bars.

UpBars Methods

Name	Returns	Parameters	Description
Delete	Variant		Deletes the up bars
Select	Variant		Selects the up bars in the chart.

Example: UpBars Object

```
Sub AddAndFormatUpBars()
    Dim oUpBars As UpBars

    'Add Up/Down bars to the chart
    Charts(1).ChartGroups(1).HasUpDownBars = True

    'Get the collection of UpBars
    Set oUpBars = Charts(1).ChartGroups(1).UpBars

    'Format the up bars
    With oUpBars
        .Interior.ColorIndex = 3
        .Interior.Pattern = xlSolid
    End With
End Sub
```

Validation Object

The Validation object contains properties and methods to represent validation for a range in a worksheet. The Range object is the parent of the Validation object.

Validation Common Properties

The `Application`, `Creator`, and `Parent` properties are defined at the beginning of this Appendix.

Validation Properties

Name	Returns	Description
Alert Style	Long	Read Only. Returns the manner the user will be alerted if the range includes invalid data. Uses the `XlDVAlertStyle` constants.
Error Message	String	Set / Get the error message to show for data validation.
Error Title	String	Set / Get what the title is for the error data validation dialog box.
Formula1	String	Read Only. Returns the value, cell reference, or formula used for data validation.
Formula2	String	Read Only. Returns the second part of the value, cell reference, or formula used for data validation. The `Operator` property must be `xlBetween` or `xlNotBetween`.
Ignor eBlank	Boolean	Set / Get whether a blank cell is always considered valid.
IMEMode	Long	Set / Get how the Japanese input rules are described. Use the `XlIMEMode` constants.
InCell Dropdown	Boolean	Set / Get whether a drop-down list of valid values are displayed in the parent range. Used when the `Type` property is `xlValidateList`.
Input Message	String	Set / Get the validation input message to prompt the user for valid data.
Input Title	String	Set / Get what the title is for the input data validation dialog box.
Operator	Long	Read Only. Returns the operator describing how `Formula1` and `Formula2` are used for validation. Uses the `XlFormatConditionOperator` constants.
Show Error	Boolean	Set / Get whether the error message will be displayed when invalid data is entered in the parent range.
Show Input	Boolean	Set / Get whether the input message will be displayed when the user chooses one of the cells in the parent range.

Name	Returns	Description
Type	Long	Read Only. Returns the data validation type for the range. The XlDVType constants can be used (e.g. xlValidateDecimal, xlValidateTime)
Value	Boolean	Read Only. Returns whether if the validation is fulfilled for the range.

Validation Methods

Name	Returns	Parameters	Description
Add		Type As XlDVType, [AlertStyle], [Operator], [Formula1], [Formula2]	Adds data validation to the parent range. The validation type (Type parameter) must be specified. The type of validation alert (AlertStyle) can be specified with the XlDVAlertStyle constants. The Operator parameter uses the XlFormatConditionOperator to pick the type of operator to use. The Formula1 and Formula2 parameters pick the data validation formula.
Delete			Deletes the Validation method for the range.
Modify		[Type], [AlertStyle], [Operator], [Formula1], [Formula2]	Modifies the properties associated with the Validation. See the properties of the Validation object for a description of the parameters.

Example: Validation Object

```
Sub AddValidation()
    Dim oValid As Validation

    Set oValid = Selection.Validation

    With oValid
        .Delete
        .Add Type:=xlValidateWholeNumber, AlertStyle:=xlValidAlertStop, _
            Operator:=xlBetween, Formula1:="10", Formula2:="20"

        .ShowInput = False
        .ShowError = True
        .ErrorTitle = "Error"
        .ErrorMessage = "Number must be between 10 and 20"
    End With
End Sub
```

VPageBreak Object and the VPageBreaks Collection

The VPageBreaks collection contains all of the vertical page breaks in the printable area of the parent object. Each VPageBreak object represents a single vertical page break for the printable area of the parent object. Possible parents of the VPageBreaks collection are the WorkSheet and the Chart objects.

The VPageBreaks collection contains one property and one method besides the typical collection attributes. The Count property returns the number of VPageBreak objects in the collection. The Add method is used to add a VPageBreak object to the collection (and vertical page break to the sheet). The Add method has a Before parameter to specify the range to the right of where the vertical page break will be added.

VPageBreak Common Properties

The Application, Creator, and Parent properties are defined at the beginning of this Appendix.

VPageBreak Properties

Name	Returns	Description
Extent	XlPage Break Extent	Read Only. Returns whether the vertical page break is full screen or only for the print area.
Location	Range	Set / Get the cell that the vertical page break is located. The left edge of the cell is the location of the page break.
Type	XlPage Break	Set / Get whether the page break is automatic or manually set.

VPageBreak Methods

Name	Returns	Parameters	Description
Delete			Deletes the page break.
DragOff		Direction As XlDirection, RegionIndex As Long	Drags the page break out of the printable area. The Direction parameter specifies the direction the page break is dragged. The RegionIndex parameter specifies which print region the page break is being dragged out of.

Example: VPageBreak Object and the VPageBreaks Collection

```
Sub AddVPageBreaks()
    Dim oCell As Range

    'Loop through all the cells in the first column of the sheet
    For Each oCell In ActiveSheet.UsedRange.Rows(1).Cells

        'If the font size is 16, add a page break to the left of the cell
        If oCell.Font.Size = 16 Then
            ActiveSheet.VPageBreaks.Add oCell
        End If
    Next
End Sub
```

Walls Object

The `Walls` object contains formatting options for all the walls of a 3D chart. The walls of a 3D chart cannot be accessed individually. The parent of the `Walls` object is the `Chart` object.

Walls Common Properties

The `Application`, `Creator`, and `Parent` properties are defined at the beginning of this Appendix.

Walls Properties

Name	Returns	Description
Border	Border	Read Only. Returns the border's properties around the walls of the 3D chart.
Fill	ChartFill Format	Read Only. Returns an object containing fill formatting options for the walls of a 3D chart.
Interior	Interior	Read Only. Returns an object containing options to format the inside area of the walls (e.g. interior color).
Name	String	Read Only. Returns the name of the `Walls` object.
Picture Type	Variant	Set / Get how an associated picture is displayed on the walls of the 3D chart (e.g. stretched, tiled). Use the `XlPictureType` constants.
Picture Unit	Variant	Set / Get how many units a picture represents if the `PictureType` property is set to `xlScale`.

Walls Methods

Name	Returns	Parameters	Description
Clear Formats	Variant		Clears the formatting made on the Walls object.
Paste			Deletes the Walls object.
Select	Variant		Selects the walls on the parent chart.

Example: Walls Object

```
Sub FormatWalls()
    Dim oWall As Walls

    Set oWall = Charts(1).Walls

    With oWall
        .Fill.PresetTextured msoTextureCork
        .Fill.Visible = True
    End With
End Sub
```

WebOptions Object

The WebOptions object contains attributes associated with opening or saving Web pages. The parent of the WebOptions object is the Workbook object. The properties set in the WebOptions object override the settings of the DefaultWebOptions object.

WebOptions Common Properties

The Application, Creator, and Parent properties are defined at the beginning of this Appendix.

WebOptions Properties

Name	Returns	Description
AllowPNG	Boolean	Set / Get whether Portable Network Graphics Format (PNG) is allowed as an output format. PNG is a file format for the lossless, portable, well-compressed storage of images.
Download Components	Boolean	Set / Get whether Office components are downloaded to the end user's machine when viewing Excel files in a web browser.
Encoding	Mso Encoding	Set / Get the type of code page or character set to save with a document.

Name	Returns	Description
Folder Suffix	String	Read Only. Returns what the suffix name is for the support directory created when saving an Excel document as a web page. Language dependent.
LocationOf Components	String	Set / Get the URL or path that contains the Office Web components needed to view documents in a web browser.
OrganizeIn Folder	Boolean	Set / Get whether supporting files are organized in a separate folder from the document.
PixelsPer Inch	Long	Set / Get how dense graphics and table cells should be when viewed on a web page.
RelyOnCSS	Boolean	Set / Get whether Cascading Style Sheets (CSS) is used for font formatting.
RelyOnVML	Boolean	Set / Get whether image files are not created when saving a document with drawn objects. Vector Markup Language is used to create the images on the fly. VML is an XML-based format for high-quality vector graphics on the Web.
ScreenSize	MsoScreen Size	Set / Get the target monitor's screen size.
UseLong FileNames	Boolean	Set / Get whether links are updated every time the document is saved.

WebOptions Methods

Name	Returns	Parameters	Description
UseDefault FolderSuff ix			Tells Excel to use its default naming scheme for creating supporting folders.

Example: WebOptions Object

```
Sub SetWebOptions()
    Dim oWO As WebOptions

    Set oWO = ActiveWorkbook.WebOptions

    With oWO
        .ScreenSize = msoScreenSize800x600
        .RelyOnCSS = True
        .UseDefaultFolderSuffix
    End With
End Sub
```

Window Object and the Windows Collection

The Windows collection holds the list of windows used in Excel or in a workbook. Each Window object represents a single Excel window containing scrollbars and gridlines for the window. The parents of the Windows collection can be the Application object and the Workbook object. The Windows collection has a Count property and an Arrange Method besides the typical collection attributes. The Count property returns the number of Window objects in the collection. The Arrange method arranges the windows in the collection in the manner specified by the ArrangeStyle parameter. Use the xlArrangeStyle constants to set the ArrangeStyle parameter. Set the ActiveWorkbook parameter to True to arrange only the windows associated with the open workbook. Set the SyncHorizontal parameter or the SyncVertical parameter to True so the windows will scroll horizontally or vertically together, respectively.

Window Common Properties

The Application, Creator, and Parent properties are defined at the beginning of this Appendix.

Window Properties

Name	Returns	Description
Active Cell	Range	Read Only. Returns the cell in the window where the cursor is.
Active Chart	Chart	Read Only. Returns the currently selected chart in the window. If no chart is currently selected Nothing is returned.
ActivePane	Pane	Read Only. Returns the active pane in the window.
Active Sheet		Read Only. Returns the active sheet in the window.
Caption	Variant	Set / Get the caption that appears in the window.
Display Formulas	Boolean	Set / Get whether formulas are displayed in the window. Not valid in a Chart sheet.
Display Gridlines	Boolean	Set / Get whether worksheet gridlines are displayed.
Display Headings	Boolean	Set / Get whether row and column headings are displayed. Not valid in a Chart sheet.
Display Horizontal ScrollBar	Boolean	Set / Get whether the horizontal scrollbar is displayed in the window.

Name	Returns	Description
DisplayOut line	Boolean	Set / Get whether display...
Display RightTo Left	Boolean	Set / Get whether displayed fr... languages tha...
Display Vertical ScrollBar	Boolean	Set / Get wheth... displayed in the w...
Display Workbook Tabs	Boolean	Set / Get whether wor... displayed.
Display Zeros	Boolean	Set / Get whether zero valu... Not valid with Chart sheets.
Enable Resize	Boolean	Set / Get whether a user can res... window.
Freeze Panes	Boolean	Set / Get whether split panes are fro... valid with Chart sheets.
Gridline Color	Long	Set / Get the color of the gridlines. Use th... RGB function to create the color value.
Gridline ColorIndex	XlColor Index	Set / Get the color of the gridlines. Use the XlColorIndex constants or an index value in the current color palette.
Height	Double	Set / Get the height of the window.
Index	Long	Read Only. Returns the spot in the collection that the current object is located.
Left	Double	Set / Get the distance from the left edge of the client area to the window's left edge.
OnWindow	String	Set / Get the name of the procedure to run whenever a window is activated.
Panes	Panes	Read Only. Returns the panes that are contained in the window.
Range Selection	Range	Read Only. Returns the selected range of cells or object in the window.
Scroll Column	Long	Set / Get the column number of the left-most column in the window.
ScrollRow	Long	Set / Get the row number of the top-most row in the window.

Table Continued on Following Page

	Returns	Description
	Sheets	Read Only. Returns all the selected sheets in the window.
n	Object	Read Only. Returns the selected object in the window.
	Boolean	Set / Get whether the window is split into panes.
mn	Long	Set / Get which column number the window split is going to be located.
it izontal	Double	Set / Get where the horizontal split of window will be located, in points.
lit ow	Long	Set / Get which row number the window split is going to be located.
Split Vertical	Double	Set / Get where the vertical split of window will be located, in points.
TabRatio	Double	Set / Get how big a workbook's tab is as a ratio of a workbook's tab area width to the window's horizontal scrollbar width.
Top	Double	Set / Get the distance from the top edge of the client area to the window's top edge.
Type	XlWindow Type	Read Only. Returns the window type.
Usable Height	Double	Read Only. Returns the maximum height that the window can be.
Usable Width	Double	Read Only. Returns the maximum width that the window can be.
View	XlWindow View	Set / Get the view in the window (e.g. xlNormalView, xlPageBreakPreview)
Visible	Boolean	Set / Get whether the window is visible.
Visible Range	Range	Read Only. Returns the range of cells that are visible in the current window.
Width	Double	Set / Get the width of the window.
Window Number	Long	Read Only. Returns the number associated with a window. Typically used when the same workbook is opened twice (e.g. MyBook.xls:1 and MyBook.xls:2)

Name	Returns	Description
Window State	XlWindow State	Set / Get the state of window: minimized, maximized, or normal.
Zoom	Variant	Set / Get the percentage window zoom.

Window Methods

Name	Returns	Parameters	Description
Activate	Variant		Sets focus to the window.
Activate Next	Variant		Activates the next window in the z-order.
Activate Previous	Variant		Activates the previous window in the z-order.
Close	Boolean	[SaveChanges], [Filename], [Route Workbook]	Closes the window. Set SaveChanges to True to automatically save changes in the window's workbook. If SaveChanges is False then all changes are lost. The Filename parameter can be used to specify the filename to save to. RouteWorkbook is used to automatically route the workbook onto the next recipient, if applicable.
Large Scroll	Variant	[Down], [Up], [ToRight], [ToLeft]	Causes the document to scroll a certain direction a screen-full at a time as specified by the parameters.
NewWindow	Window		Creates and returns a new window.
PointsTo Screen PixelsX	Long	Points As Long	Converts the horizontal document coordinate Points parameter to screen coordinate pixels.

Table Continued on Following Page

Name	Returns	Parameters	Description
PointsTo Screen PixelsY	Long	Points As Long	Converts the vertical document coordinate Points parameter to screen coordinate pixels.
PrintOut	Variant	[From], [To], [Copies], [Preview], [Active Printer], [PrintToFile], [Collate], [PrToFileName]	Prints out the document in the window. The printer, number of copies, collation, and whether a print preview is desired can be specified with the parameters. Also, the sheets can be printed to a file with using the PrintToFile and PrToFileName parameters. The From and To parameters can be used to specify the range of printed pages.
Print Preview	Variant	[Enable Changes]	Displays the current workbook in the window in a print preview mode. Set the EnableChanges parameter to False to disable the **Margins** and **Setup** buttons, hence not allowing the viewer to modify the page setup.
RangeFrom Point	Object	x As Long, y As Long	Returns the shape or range located at the x and y coordinates. Returns Nothing if there is no object at the x, y coordinates.

Name	Returns	Parameters	Description
Scroll IntoView		Left As Long, Top As Long, Width As Long, Height As Long, [Start]	Scrolls the spot specified by the Left, Top, Width, and Height parameters to either the upper-left corner of the window (Start = True) or the lower-right corner of the window (Start = False). The Left, Top, Width, and Height parameters are specified in points.
Scroll Workbook Tabs	Variant	[Sheets], [Position]	Scrolls through the number of sheets specified by the Sheets parameter or goes to the sheet specified by the position parameter (xlFirst or xlLast).
Small Scroll	Variant	[Down], [Up], [ToRight], [ToLeft]	Causes the document to scroll a certain direction a document line at a time as specified by the parameters.

Example: Window Object and the Windows Collection

```
Sub MinimiseAllWindows()
   Dim oWin As Window

   For Each oWin In Windows
      oWin.WindowState = xlMinimized
   Next
End Sub
```

Workbook Object and the Workbooks Collection

The Workbooks collection contains the list of open workbooks. A Workbook object represents a single workbook. The parent of the Workbook is the Application object.

Workbooks Properties and Methods

Name	Returns	Description
Count	Long	Read Only. Returns the number of Workbook objects in the collection.
Add	Work book	Method. Parameters: [Template]. Adds a new workbook to the collection. Using a template name in the Template parameter can specify a template. As well the XlWBATemplate constants can be used to open up a type of workbook.
Close		Method. Closes the workbook.
Open	Work book	Method. Parameters: Filename As String, [UpdateLinks], [ReadOnly], [Format], [Password], [WriteResPassword], [IgnoreReadOnlyRecommended], [Origin], [Delimiter], [Editable], [Notify], [Converter], [AddToMru]. Opens a workbook specified by the Filename parameter and adds it to the collection. Use the UpdateLinks parameter to choose how links in the file are updated. Set ReadOnly to True to open up the workbook in read-only mode. If the file requires a password, use the Password or WriteResPassword parameters. Set AddToMru to True to add the opening workbook to the recently used files list.
		If the file to open is a delimited text file then there are some parameters that can be used. Use the Format parameter to choose the text delimiter character if opening a text file. Use the Origin parameter to choose the code page style of the incoming delimited text file. Use the Delimiter parameter to specify a delimiter if 6 (custom) was chosen for the Format parameter.

Name	Returns	Description
Open Text		Method. Parameters: `Filename As String`, `[Origin]`, `[StartRow]`, `[DataType]`, `[TextQualifier As XlTextQualifier]`, `[ConsecutiveDelimiter]`, `[Tab]`, `[Semicolon]`, `[Comma]`, `[Space]`, `[Other]`, `[OtherChar]`, `[FieldInfo]`, `[TextVisualLayout]`, `[DecimalSeparator]`, `[ThousandsSeparator]`. Opens the text file in `Filename` and parses it into a sheet on a new workbook. Origin is used to choose the code page style of the file (`XlPlatform` constant). `StartRow` decides the first row to parse. `DataType` decides if the file is `xlDelimited` or `xlFixedWidth`. Setting `ConsecutiveDelimiter` to `True` to treat consecutive delimiters as one. Set `Tab`, `Semicolon`, `Comma`, `Space`, or `Other` to `True` to pick the delimiter character. Use the `DecimalSeparator` and `ThousandsSeparator` to pick the numeric characters to use.

Workbook Common Properties

The `Application`, `Creator`, and `Parent` properties are defined at the beginning of this Appendix.

Workbook Properties

Name	Returns	Description
AcceptLabels InFormulas	Boolean	Set / Get whether labels can be used in worksheet formulas.
ActiveChart	Chart	Read Only. Returns the active chart in the workbook.
ActiveSheet		Read Only. Returns the active sheet (chart or workbook) in the workbook.
AutoUpdate Frequency	Long	Set / Get how often a shared workbook is updated automatically, in minutes.
AutoUpdate SaveChanges	Boolean	Set / Get whether changes made to a shared workbook are visible to other users whenever the workbook is automatically updated.

Table Continued on Following Page

Name	Returns	Description
Builtin Document Properties	Document Properties	Read Only. Returns a collection holding all the built-in properties of the workbook. Things like Title, Subject, Author, and Number of Words of the workbook can be accessed from this object.
Calculation Version	Long	Read Only. Returns the version number of Excel that was last used to recalculate the Excel spreadsheet.
Change History Duration	Long	Set / Get how far back, in days, a shared workbook's change history is visible.
Charts	Sheets	Read Only. Returns the charts in the workbook.
CodeName	String	Read Only. Returns the name of the workbook that was set at design time in the VBA editor.
Colors	Variant	Parameters: [Index]. Set / Get the color palette colors for the workbook. There are 56 possible colors in the palette.
CommandBars	Command Bars	Read Only. Returns an object to manipulate the command bars in Excel.
Conflict Resolution	XlSave Conflict Resolution	Set / Get how shared workbook conflicts are resolved when they are being updated (e.g. xlLocalSessionChanges means that the local user's changes are always accepted).
Container	Object	Read Only. Returns the object that contains the workbook, if applicable.
CreateBackup	Boolean	Read Only. Returns whether a backup file is created whenever the workbook is saved.
Custom Document Properties	Document Properties	Read Only. Returns a collection holding all the user-defined properties of the workbook.
CustomViews	Custom Views	Read Only. Returns the collection of custom views in a workbook.

Name	Returns	Description
Date1904	Boolean	Set / Get whether the 1904 date system is used in the workbook.
Display Drawing Objects	xlDisplay Drawing Objects	Set / Get if shapes are displayed, placeholders are displayed or shapes are hidden.
Envelope Visible	Boolean	Set / Get whether the envelope toolbar and email composition header are visible.
Excel4Intl MacroSheets	Sheets	Read Only. Returns the collection of Excel 4.0 international macro sheets in the workbook.
Excel4Macro Sheets	Sheets	Read Only. Returns the collection of Excel 4.0 macro sheets in the workbook.
FileFormat	XlFile Format	Read Only. Returns the file format of the workbook.
FullName	String	Read Only. Returns the path and file name of the workbook.
HasPassword	Boolean	Read Only. Returns whether the workbook has a protection password.
HasRouting Slip	Boolean	Set / Get whether the workbook has a routing slip. Use with the RoutingSlip object.
Highlight ChangesOn Screen	Boolean	Set / Get whether changes in a shared workbook are visible highlighted.
HTML Project	HTML Project	Read Only. Returns an object to access the project explorer of the script editor.
IsAddin	Boolean	Set / Get whether the current workbook is running as an Addin.
IsInplace	Boolean	Read Only. Returns whether the workbook is being edited as an object (True) or in Microsoft Excel (False).
KeepChange History	Boolean	Set / Get whether changes are tracked in a shared workbook.
ListChanges OnNewSheet	Boolean	Set / Get whether a separate worksheet is used to display changes of a shared workbook.

Table Continued on Following Page

Name	Returns	Description
Mailer	Mailer	Read Only.
MultiUser Editing	Boolean	Read Only. Returns whether a workbook is being shared.
Name	String	Read Only. Returns the file name of the workbook.
Names	Names	Read Only. Returns the collection of named ranges in the workbook.
Path	String	Read Only. Returns the file path of the workbook.
PersonalView ListSettings	Boolean	Set / Get whether a user's view of the workbook includes filters and sort settings for lists.
PersonalView Print Settings	Boolean	Set / Get whether a user's view of the workbook includes print settings.
PrecisionAs Displayed	Boolean	Set / Get whether the precision of numbers in the workbook are as displayed in the cells. Used for calculations.
Protect Structure	Boolean	Read Only. Returns whether the sheet order cannot be changed in the workbook.
Protect Windows	Boolean	Read Only. Returns whether the workbook windows are protected
Publish Objects	Publish Objects	Read Only. Returns access to an object used to publish objects in the workbook as web pages.
ReadOnly	Boolean	Read Only. Returns whether the workbook is in read-only mode.
ReadOnly Recommended	Boolean	Read Only. Returns whether the user is prompted with a message recommending that you open the workbook as read-only.
Revision Number	Long	Read Only. Returns how many times a shared workbook has been saved while open.
Routed	Boolean	Read Only. Returns whether a workbook has been routed to the next recipient.

Name	Returns	Description
RoutingSlip	Routing Slip	Read Only. Returns access to a RoutingSlip object that can be used to add a routing slip for the workbook. Use with the HasRoutingSlip property.
Saved	Boolean	Set / Get whether a workbook does not have changes that need saving.
SaveLink Values	Boolean	Set / Get whether values linked from external sources are saved with the workbook.
Sheets	Sheets	Read Only. Returns the collection of sheets in a workbook (Chart or Worksheet).
ShowConflict History	Boolean	Set / Get whether the sheet containing conflicts related to shared workbooks are displayed.
Styles	Styles	Read Only. Returns the collection of styles associated with the workbook.
Template Remove ExtData	Boolean	Set / Get whether all the external data references are removed after a workbook is saved as a template.
UpdateRemote References	Boolean	Set / Get whether remote references are updated for the workbook.
UserStatus	Variant	Read Only. Returns the name of the current user.
VBASigned	Boolean	Read Only. Returns whether the VBA Project for the workbook has been digitally signed.
VBProject	VBProject	Read Only. Returns access the VBE editor and associated project.
WebOptions	WebOptions	Read Only. Returns an object allowing manipulation of web related properties of the workbook.
Windows	Windows	Read Only. Returns the collection of windows that make up the workbook.
Worksheets	Sheets	Read Only. Returns the collection of worksheets that make up the workbook.

Table Continued on Following Page

Name	Returns	Description
Write Reserved	Boolean	Read Only. Returns whether the workbook can be modified.
Write ReservedBy	String	Read Only. Returns the name of the person with write permission to the workbook.

Workbook Methods

Name	Returns	Parameters	Description
Accept AllChanges		[When], [Who], [Where]	Accepts all the changes made by other people in a shared workbook.
Activate			Activates the workbook.
AddTo Favorites			Adds the workbook shortcut to the Favorites folder.
ChangeFile Access		Mode As XlFileAccess, [Write Password], [Notify]	Changes access permissions of the workbook to the one specified by the Mode parameter. If necessary, the WritePassword can be specified. Set Notify to True to have the user notified if the file cannot be accessed.
ChangeLink		Name As String, NewName As String, Type As XlLinkType	Changes the link from the workbook specified by the Name parameter to the NewName workbook. Type chooses the type of link (e.g. OLE, Excel)

Name	Returns	Parameters	Description
Close		[Save Changes], [Filename], [Route Workbook]	Closes the workbook. Set SaveChanges to True to automatically save changes in the workbook. If SaveChanges is False then all changes are lost. The Filename parameter can be used to specify the filename to save to. RouteWorkbook is used to automatically route the workbook onto the next recipient, if applicable.
Delete Number Format		NumberFormat As String	Deletes the number format in the NumberFormat parameter from the workbook.
Exclusive Access	Boolean		Gives the current user exclusive access to a shared workbook.
Follow Hyperlink		Address As String, [SubAddress], [NewWindow], [AddHistory], [ExtraInfo], [Method], [HeaderInfo]	Opens up the appropriate application with the URL specified by the Address parameter. Set NewWindow to True to open up a new window for the hyperlink. Use the ExtraInfo and Method parameters to send more information to the hyperlink (say for an ASP page). The Method parameter uses the MsoExtraInfo Method constants.

Table Continued on Following Page

Name	Returns	Parameters	Description
Highlight Changes Options		[When], [Who], [Where]	Set / Get when changes are viewed in a shared workbook (When), whose workbook changes can be viewed (Who), and the range that the changes should be put in (Where). Use the XlHighlight ChangesTime constants with the When parameter.
LinkInfo	Variant	Name As String, LinkInfo As XlLinkInfo, [Type], [EditionRef]	Returns the link details mentioned in the LinkInfo parameter for the link specified by the Name parameter. Use the Type parameter with the XlLinkInfoType constants to pick the type of link that will be returned.
Link Sources	Variant	[Type]	Returns the array of linked documents, editions, DDE and OLE servers in a workbook. Use the Type parameter with the XlLinkInfoType constants to pick the type of link that will be returned.
Merge Workbook		Filename	Merges the changes from the Filename workbook into the current workbook.
NewWindow	Window		Opens up a new window with the current workbook.

Name	Returns	Parameters	Description
OpenLinks		Name As String, [ReadOnly], [Type]	Opens the Name link and supporting documents. Set ReadOnly to True to open the documents as read-only. Use the Type parameter with the XlLinkInfoType constants to pick the type of link that will be returned.
Pivot Caches	Pivot Caches		Returns the collection of PivotTable caches in the workbook.
Post		[DestName]	Posts the workbook into a Microsoft Exchange public folder.
PrintOut		[From], [To], [Copies], [Preview], [Active Printer], [PrintTo File], [Collate], [PrToFile Name]	Prints out the workbook. The printer, number of copies, collation, and whether a print preview is desired can be specified with the parameters. Also, the sheets can be printed to a file with using the PrintToFile and PrToFileName parameters. The From and To parameters can be used to specify the range of printed pages.
Print Preview		[Enable Changes]	Displays the current workbook in a print preview mode. Set the EnableChanges parameter to False to disable the Margins and Setup buttons, hence not allowing the viewer to modify the page setup.

Table Continued on Following Page

Name	Returns	Parameters	Description
Protect		[Password], [Structure], [Windows]	Protects the workbook from user changes. A protect Password can be specified. Set the Structure parameter to True to protect the relative position of the sheets. Set the Windows to True to protect the workbook windows.
Protect Sharing		[Filename], [Password], [WriteRes Password], [ReadOnly Recommended], [Create Backup], [Sharing Password]	Protects and saves the workbook for sharing. The file is saved to the Filename parameter with the optional passwords in Password, WriteResPassword, and SharingPassword parameters. Set ReadOnlyRecommend ed to True to display a message to the user every time the workbook is opened. Set CreateBackup to True to create a backup of the saved file.
Purge Change HistoryNow		Days As Long, [Sharing Password]	Deletes the entries in the change log for the shared workbook. The Days parameter specifies how many days back to delete the entries. A SharingPassword may be required.
RefreshAll			Refreshes any external data source's data into the workbook.

Name	Returns	Parameters	Description
Reject AllChanges		[When], [Who], [Where]	Rejects all the changes in a shared workbook
ReloadAs		Encoding As MsoEncoding	Re-opens the workbook using the web page related Encoding parameter.
RemoveUser		Index As Long	Disconnects the user (specified by the user index in the Index parameter) from a shared workbook.
ReplyAll			Replies to all recipients of the sent workbook. Valid only in the Macintosh Edition of Excel.
Reset Colors			Resets the colors in the color palette to the default colors.
Route			Rout the workbook using the routing slip.
RunAuto Macros		Which As XlRunAuto Macro	Runs the auto macro specified by the Which parameter.
Save			Saves the workbook.

Table Continued on Following Page

Name	Returns	Parameters	Description
SaveAs		Filename, FileFormat, Password, WriteRes Password, ReadOnly Recommended, CreateBackup, AccessMode As XlSaveAs AccessMode, [Conflict Resolution], [AddToMru], [Text Codepage], [TextVisual Layout]	Saves the workbook as FileName. The type of file to be saved can be specified with the FileFormat parameter. The file can be saved with the optional passwords in the Password and WriteResPassword parameters. Set ReadOnlyRecommend ed to True to display a message to the user every time the workbook is opened. Set CreateBackup to True to create a backup of the saved file. Use the AccessMode to choose how the workbook is accessed (e.g. xlShared, xlExclusive). Use the ConflictResolutio n parameter to decide how shared workbooks resolve change conflicts. Set the AddToMru parameter to True to add the workbook to the recently opened files list.
SaveCopyAs		[Filename]	Saves a copy of the workbook as the FileName.

Name	Returns	Parameters	Description
SendMail		Recipients, [Subject], [Return Receipt]	Sends the workbook through the default mail system. The recipient or recipients and subject can be specified with the parameters. Set ReturnReceipt to True to request a return receipt.
SendMailer		FileFormat, Priority As XlPriority	
SetLink OnData		Name As String, [Procedure]	Runs the procedure in the Procedure parameter whenever the DDE or OLE link in the Name parameter is updated.
Unprotect		[Password]	Unprotects the workbook with the password if necessary.
Unprotect Sharing		[Sharing Password]	Unprotects the workbook from sharing and saves the workbook.
UpdateFrom File			Re-loads the current workbook from the file if the file is newer then the workbook.
UpdateLink		[Name], [Type]	Updates the link specified by the Name parameter. Use the Type parameter with the xlLinkInfoType constants to pick the type of link that will be returned.
WebPage Preview			Previews the workbook as a web page.

Workbook Events

Name	Parameters	Description
Activate		Triggered when the workbook is activated.
Addin Install		Triggered when the workbook is opened as an Addin.
Addin Uninstall		Triggered when the workbook opened as an Addin is uninstalled.
Before Close	Cancel As Boolean	Triggered just before the workbook closes. Set the Cancel parameter to True to cancel the closing.
Before Print	Cancel As Boolean	Triggered just before the workbook is printed. Set the Cancel parameter to True to cancel the printing.
BeforeSave	SaveAsUI As Boolean, Cancel As Boolean	Triggered just before the workbook is saved. Set the Cancel parameter to True to cancel the saving. Set the SaveAsUI to True for the user to be prompted with the **Save As** dialog box.
Deactivate		Triggered when the workbook loses focus.
NewSheet	Sh As Object	Triggered when a new sheet is created in the workbook. The Sh parameter passes in the new sheet.
Open		
Sheet Activate	Sh As Object	Triggered when a sheet is activated in the workbook. The Sh parameter passes in the activated sheet.
Sheet Before Double Click	Sh As Object, Target As Range, Cancel As Boolean	Triggered when a sheet is about to be double-clicked. The sheet and the potential double-click spot are passed into the event. The double-click action can be canceled by setting the Cancel parameter to True.
Sheet Before Right Click	Sh As Object, Target As Range, Cancel As Boolean	Triggered when a sheet is about to be right-clicked. The sheet and the potential right-click spot are passed into the event. The right-click action can be canceled by setting the Cancel parameter to True.
Sheet Calculate	Sh As Object	Triggered when a sheet is recalculated passing in the recalculated sheet.

Name	Parameters	Description
Sheet Change	Sh As Object, Target As Range	Triggered when the contents of a cell are changed in any worksheet in the workbook. E.g. triggered by entering new data, clearing the cell, deleting a row/column. **NOT** triggered when inserting rows/columns.
Sheet Deactivate	Sh As Object	Triggered when a sheet loses focus. Passes in the sheet.
Sheet Follow Hyperlink	Sh As Object, Target As Hyperlink	Triggered when the user clicks on a hyperlink on a sheet. Passes in the sheet and the clicked hyperlink.
Sheet Selection Change	Sh As Object, Target As Range	Triggered when the user selects a different cell on the sheet. Passes in the new range and the sheet where the change occurred.
Window Activate	Wn As Window	Triggered when a workbook window is activated (brought up to the front of other workbook windows). The workbook and the window are passed in.
Window Deactivate	Wn As Window	Triggered when a workbook window loses focus. The related workbook and the window are passes in.
Window Resize	Wn As Window	Triggered when a workbook window is resized. The resized workbook and window are passed into the event.

Example: Workbook Object and the Workbooks Collection

Please refer to Chapter 4 for Workbook object examples

Worksheet Object and the Worksheets Collection

The Worksheets collection holds the collection of worksheets in a workbook. The Workbook object is always the parent of the Worksheets collection. The Worksheets collection only holds the worksheets. The Worksheet objects in the Worksheets collection can be accessed using the Item property. Either the name of the worksheet can be specified as a parameter to the Item's parameter or an index number describing the position of the worksheet in the workbook (from left to right). The Worksheet object allows access to all of the attributes of a specific worksheet in Excel. This includes worksheet formatting and other worksheet properties. The Worksheet object also exposes events that can be used programmatically.

The Worksheets collection has a few properties and methods besides the typical collection attributes. These are listed in the following table.

Worksheets Collection Properties and Methods

Name	Returns	Description
Count	Long	Read Only. Returns the number of worksheets in the collection.
HPage Breaks	HPage Breaks	Read Only. Returns a collection holding all the horizontal page breaks associated with the Worksheets collection.
VPage Breaks	VPage Breaks	Read Only. Returns a collection holding all the vertical page breaks associated with the Worksheets collection.
Visible	Variant	Set / Get whether the worksheets in the collection are visible. Also can set this to xlVeryHidden to not allow a user to make the worksheets in the collection visible.
Add		Method. Parameters: [Before], [After], [Count], [Type]. Adds a worksheet to the collection. You can specify where the worksheet goes by choosing which sheet object will be before the new worksheet object (Before parameter) or after the new worksheet (After parameter). The Count parameter decides how many worksheets are created.
Copy		Method. Parameters: [Before], [After]. Adds a new copy of the currently active worksheet to the position specified at the Before or After parameters.
Delete		Method. Deletes all the worksheet in the collection.
Fill Across Sheets		Method. Parameters: Range As Range, Type As XlFillWith. Copies the range specified by the Range parameter across all the other worksheets in the collection. Use the Type parameter to pick what part of the range is copied (e.g. xlFillWithContents, xlFillWithFormulas)
Move		Method. Parameters: [Before], [After]. Moves the current worksheet to the position specified by the parameters.

Name	Returns	Description
Print Preview		Method. Parameters: [EnableChanges]. Displays the current worksheet in the collection in a print preview mode. Set the EnableChanges parameter to False to disable the **Margins** and **Setup** buttons, hence not allowing the viewer to modify the page setup.
PrintOut		Method. Parameters: [From], [To], [Copies], [Preview], [ActivePrinter], [PrintToFile], [Collate], [PrToFileName]. Prints out the worksheets in the collection. The printer, number of copies, collation, and whether a print preview is desired can be specified with the parameters. Also, the sheets can be printed to a file with using the PrintToFile and PrToFileName parameters. The From and To parameters can be used to specify the range of printed pages.
Select		Method. Parameters: [Replace]. Method. Parameters: [Replace]. Selects the current worksheet in the collection.

Worksheet Common Properties

The Application, Creator, and Parent properties are defined at the beginning of this Appendix.

Worksheet Properties

Name	Returns	Description
AutoFilter	AutoFilter	Read Only. Returns an AutoFilter object if filtering is turned on.
AutoFilter Mode	Boolean	Set / Get whether AutoFilter drop-down arrows are currently displayed on the worksheet.
Cells	Range	Read Only. Returns the cells in the current worksheet.
Circular Reference	Range	Read Only. Returns the cell range that contains the first circular reference on the worksheet.

Table Continued on Following Page

Name	Returns	Description
CodeName	String	Read Only. Returns the name of the worksheet set at design time in the VBA editor.
Columns	Range	Read Only. Returns a range of the columns in the current worksheet
Comments	Comments	Read Only. Returns the collection of comments in the worksheet.
Consolidation Function	Xl Consolidation Function	Read Only. Returns the type of consolidation being used in the worksheet (e.g. xlSum, xlMax, xlAverage).
Consolidation Options	Variant	Read Only. Returns a one-dimensional array containing three elements of Booleans. The first element describes whether the labels in the top row are used; the second element describes whether the labels in the left-most column; and the third element describes whether links are created to the source data.
Consolidation Sources	Variant	Read Only. Returns the array of strings that describe the source sheets for the current worksheet's consolidation.
DisplayPage Breaks	Boolean	Set / Get whether page breaks are displayed.
DisplayRight ToLeft	Boolean	Set / Get whether the worksheet contents are displayed from right to left. Valid only with languages that support right to left text.
EnableAuto Filter	Boolean	Set / Get whether the AutoFilter arrows are enabled when a worksheet is user interface-only protected.
Enable Calculation	Boolean	Set / Get whether Excel will automatically recalculate the worksheet as necessary.

Name	Returns	Description
Enable Outlining	Boolean	Set / Get whether outlining symbols are enabled when a worksheet is user interface-only protected.
Enable PivotTable	Boolean	Set / Get whether PivotTable controls and related actions are enabled when a worksheet is user interface-only protected.
Enable Selection	XlEnable Selection	Set / Get what objects can be selected when a worksheet is protected (e.g. xlNoSelection, xlNoRestrictions).
FilterMode	Boolean	Read Only. Returns whether a worksheet is in a filter mode
HPageBreaks	HPageBreaks	Read Only. Returns a collection holding all the horizontal page breaks associated with the worksheet.
Hyperlinks	Hyperlinks	Read Only. Returns the collection of hyperlinks in the worksheet.
Index	Long	Read Only. Returns the spot in the parent collection that the current worksheet is located.
Name	String	Set / Get the name of the worksheet.
Names	Names	Read Only. Returns the collection of named ranges in the worksheet.
Next		Read Only. Returns the next sheet in the workbook (from left to right) as an object.
Outline	Outline	Read Only. Returns an object to manipulate an outline in the worksheet.
PageSetup	PageSetup	Read Only. Returns an object to manipulate the page setup properties for the worksheet.
Previous		Read Only. Returns the previous sheet in the workbook (from right to left) as an object.

Table Continued on Following Page

Name	Returns	Description
Protect Contents	Boolean	Read Only. Returns whether the worksheet and everything in it is protected from changes.
Protect Drawing Objects	Boolean	Read Only. Returns whether the shapes in the worksheet can be modified (ProtectDrawingObjects = False).
Protection Mode	Boolean	Read Only. Returns whether protection has been applied to the user interface. Even if a worksheet has user interface protection on, any VBA code associated with the worksheet can still be accessed.
Protect Scenarios	Boolean	Read Only. Returns whether the worksheet scenarios are protected.
QueryTables	QueryTables	Read Only. Returns the collection of query tables associated with the worksheet.
Range	Range	Read Only. Parameters: Cell1, [Cell2]. Returns a Range object as defined by the Cell1 and optionally Cell2 parameters.
Rows	Range	Read Only. Returns a Range object containing the rows of the current worksheet.
Scripts	Scripts	Read Only. Returns the collection of VBScript code associated with a worksheet (typically to later use on Web pages).
ScrollArea	String	Sets the A1-style reference string describing the range in the worksheet that can be scrolled. Cells not in the range cannot be selected.
Shapes	Shapes	Read Only. Returns all the shapes contained by the worksheet.
Standard Height	Double	Read Only. Returns the default height of the rows in the worksheet, in points.

Name	Returns	Description
Standard Width	Double	Read Only. Returns the default width of the columns in the worksheet, in points.
Transition ExpEval	Boolean	Set / Get whether evaluates expressions using Lotus 1-2-3 rules in the worksheet.
Transition FormEntry	Boolean	Set / Get whether formula entries can be entered using Lotus 1-2-3 rules.
Type	XlSheetType	Read Only. Returns the worksheet type (e.g. xlWorksheet, xlExcel4MacroSheet, xlExcel4IntlMacroSheet)
UsedRange	Range	Read Only. Returns the range in the worksheet that is being used.
Visible	XlSheet Visibility	Set / Get whether the worksheet is visible. Also can set this to xlVeryHidden to not allow a user to make the worksheet visible.
VPageBreaks	VPageBreaks	Read Only. Returns a collection holding all the vertical page breaks associated with the worksheet.

Worksheet Methods

Name	Returns	Parameters	Description
Activate			Activates the worksheet.
Calculate			Calculates all the formulas in the worksheet.
Chart Objects		[Index]	Returns either a chart object (ChartObject) or a collection of chart objects (ChartObjects) in a worksheet.

Table Continued on Following Page

Name	Returns	Parameters	Description
Check Spelling		[Custom Dictionary], [Ignore Uppercase], [Always Suggest], [SpellLang]	Checks the spelling of the text in the worksheet. A custom dictionary can be specified (CustomDictionary), all UPPERCASE words can be ignored (IgnoreUppercase), and Excel can be set to display a list of suggestions (AlwaysSuggest).
Circle Invalid			Circles the invalid entries in the worksheet.
Clear Arrows			Clears out all the tracer arrows in the worksheet.
Clear Circles			Clears all the circles around invalid entries in a worksheet.
Copy		[Before], [After]	Adds a new copy of the worksheet to the position specified at the Before or After parameters.
Delete			Deletes the worksheet.
Evaluate	Variant	Name	Evaluates the Name string expression as if it were entered into a worksheet cell.
Move		[Before], [After]	Moves the worksheet to the position specified by the parameters.
OLE Objects		[Index]	Returns either a single OLE Object (OLEObject) or a collection of OLE objects (OLEObjects) for a worksheet.

Name	Returns	Parameters	Description
Paste		[Destination], [Link]	Pastes the contents of the clipboard into the worksheet. A specific destination range can be specified with the Destination parameter. Set Link to True to establish a link to the source of the pasted data. Either the Destination or the Link parameter can be used.
Paste Special		[Format], [Link], [DisplayAsIcon], [IconFileName], [IconIndex], [IconLabel]	Pastes the clipboard contents into the current worksheet. The format of the clipboard data can be specified with the string Format parameter. Set Link to True to establish a link to the source of the pasted data. Set DisplayAsIcon to True to display the pasted data as an icon and the IconFileName, IconIndex, and IconLabel to specify the icon and label. A destination range must be already selected in the worksheet.
Pivot Tables		[Index]	Returns either a single PivotTable report (PivotTable) or a collection of PivotTable reports (PivotTables) for a worksheet.

Table Continued on Following Page

Name	Returns	Parameters	Description
Pivot Table Wizard	Pivot Table	[SourceType], [SourceData], [Table Destination], [TableName], [RowGrand], [Column Grand], [SaveData], [HasAuto Format], [AutoPage], [Reserved], [Background Query], [Optimize Cache], [PageField Order], [PageField WrapCount], [ReadData], [Connection]	Creates a PivotTable report. The SourceType uses the XLPivotTableSourceTyp e constants to specify the type of SourceData being used for the PivotTable. TableDestination holds the range in the parent worksheet that report will be placed. TableName holds the name of the new report. Set RowGrand or ColumnGrand to True to show grand totals for rows and columns, respectively. Set HasAutoFormat to True for Excel to format the report automatically when it is refreshed or changed. Use the AutoPage parameter to set if a page field is created for consolidation automatically. Set BackgroundQuery to True for Excel to query the data source asynchronously. Set OptimizeCache to True for Excel to optimize the cache when it is built. Use the PageFieldOrder with the xlOrder constants to set how new page fields are added to the report. Use the PageFieldWrapCount to set the number of page fields in each column or row. Set ReadData to True to copy the data from the external database into a cache. Finally, use the Connection parameter to specify an ODBC connection string for the PivotTable's cache.

Name	Returns	Parameters	Description
PrintOut		[From], [To], [Copies], [Preview], [Active Printer], [PrintTo File], [Collate], [PrToFile Name]	Prints out the worksheet. The printer, number of copies, collation, and whether a print preview is desired can be specified with the parameters. Also, the sheets can be printed to a file with using the PrintToFile and PrToFileName parameters. The From and To parameters can be used to specify the range of printed pages.
Print Preview		[Enable Changes]	Displays the worksheet in a print preview mode. Set the EnableChanges parameter to False to disable the **Margins** and **Setup** buttons, hence not allowing the viewer to modify the page setup.
Protect		[Password], [Drawing Objects], [Contents], [Scenarios], [User Interface Only]	Protects the worksheet from changes. A case sensitive Password can be specified. Also, whether shapes are protected (DrawingObjects), the entire contents are protected (Contents), and whether the only the user interface is protected (User InterfaceOnly).
ResetAll Page Breaks			Resets all the page breaks in the worksheet.

Table Continued on Following Page

Name	Returns	Parameters	Description
SaveAs		Filename As String, [FileFormat], [Password], [WriteRes Password], [ReadOnly Recommended], [Create Backup], [AddToMru], [Text Codepage], [TextVisual Layout]	Saves the worksheet as FileName. The type of file to be saved can be specified with the FileFormat parameter. The file can be saved with the optional passwords in the Password and WriteResPassword parameters. Set ReadOnlyRecommended to True to display a message to the user every time the worksheet is opened. Set CreateBackup to True to create a backup of the saved file. Set the AddToMru parameter to True to add the worksheet to the recently opened files list.
Scenarios		[Index]	Returns either a single scenario (Scenario) or a collection of scenarios (Scenarios) for a worksheet.
Select		[Replace]	Selects the worksheet.
Set Background Picture		Filename As String	Sets the worksheet's background to the picture specified by the FileName parameter.
ShowAll Data			Displays all of the data that is currently filtered.
ShowData Form			Displays the data form that is part of the worksheet.

Name	Returns	Parameters	Description
Unprotect		[Password]	Deletes the protection set up for a worksheet. If the worksheet was protected with a password, the password must be specified now.

Worksheet Events

Name	Parameters	Description
Activate		Triggered when a worksheet is made to have focus.
Before Double Click	Target As Range, Cancel As Boolean	Triggered just before a user double-clicks on a worksheet. The cell closest to the point double-clicked in the worksheet is passed in to event procedure as Target. The double-click action can be canceled by setting the Cancel parameter to True.
Before Right Click	Cancel As Boolean	Triggered just before a user right-clicks on a worksheet. The cell closest to the point right-clicked in the worksheet is passed in to event procedure as Target. The right-click action can be canceled by setting the Cancel parameter to True.
Calculate		Triggered after the worksheet is recalculated.
Change	Target As Range	Triggered when the worksheet cell values are changed. The changed ranged is passed into the event procedure as Target.
Deactivate		Triggered when the worksheet loses focus.
Follow Hyperlink	Target As Hyperlink	Triggered when a hyperlink is clicked on the worksheet. The hyperlink that was clicked is passed into the event procedure as Target.
Selection Change	Target As Range	Triggered when the selection changes in a worksheet. The new selected range is passed into the event procedure as Target.

Example: Worksheet Object and the Worksheets Collection

Please refer to Chapter 4 for Worksheet object examples

WorksheetFunction Object

The WorksheetFunction object contains all of the Excel worksheet function. The WorksheetFunction object allows access to Excel worksheet function in Visual Basic code. The parent of the WorksheetFunction object is the Application object.

WorksheetFunction Common Properties

The Application, Creator, and Parent properties are defined at the beginning of this Appendix.

WorksheetFunction Methods

Name	Returns	Parameters	Description
Acos	Double	Arg1 As Double	Returns the arccosine of the Arg1 number. Arg1 must be between −1 to 1.
Acosh	Double	Arg1 As Double	Returns the inverse hyperbolic cosine of the Arg1 number. Arg1 must be >= 1.
And	Boolean	Arg1, [Arg2], ... [Arg30]	Returns True if all the arguments (from Arg1 up to Arg30) evaluate to True.
Asc	String	Arg1 As String	Returns the half-width character equivalent of the full width characters in the Arg1 string. Not the same as the VBA Asc() function which returns the ASCII code of the first character in the string.
Asin	Double	Arg1 As Double	Returns the arcsine of the Arg1 number. Arg1 must be between −1 and 1.
Asinh	Double	Arg1 As Double	Returns the inverse hyperbolic sine of the Arg1 number.

Name	Returns	Parameters	Description
Atan2	Double	Arg1 As Double, Arg2 As Double	Returns the arctangent of the x and y coordinates specified in the Arg1 and Arg2 parameters, respectively.
Atanh	Double	Arg1 As Double	Returns the inverse hyperbolic tangent of the Arg1 number. Arg1 must be between −1 and 1.
AveDev	Double	Arg1, [Arg2], ... [Arg30]	Returns the average of the absolute deviation from the mean of the Arg1 to Arg30 number parameters.
Average	Double	Arg1, [Arg2], ... [Arg30]	Returns the average of the numbers in Arg1 to Arg30.
BetaDist	Double	Arg1 As Double, Arg2 As Double, Arg3 As Double, [Arg4], [Arg5]	Returns the cumulative beta probability. Arg1 is the number to evaluate. Arg2 is the Alpha part of the distribution. Arg3 is the Beta part of the distribution. Arg4 and Arg5 can be the lower and upper bounds of the interval in Arg1.
BetaInv	Double	Arg1 As Double, Arg2 As Double, Arg3 As Double, [Arg4], [Arg5]	Returns the inverse of the cumulative beta probability density. Arg1 is the probability of the distribution. Arg2 is the Alpha part of the distribution. Arg3 is the Beta part of the distribution. Arg4 and Arg5 can be the lower and upper bounds of the evaluated number.

Table Continued on Following Page

Name	Returns	Parameters	Description
Binom Dist	Double	Arg1 As Double, Arg2 As Double, Arg3 As Double, Arg4 As Boolean	Returns the individual term binomial distribution probability. Arg1 is the number of successes in the trails. Arg2 holds the total number of trials. Arg3 is the probability of success on a single trial. Arg4 sets whether the method returns the cumulative distribution function (True) or the probability mass function (False).
Ceiling	Double	Arg1 As Double, Arg2 As Double	Returns the nearest number to Arg1 that is a multiple of Arg2, rounded positively.
ChiDist	Double	Arg1 As Double, Arg2 As Double	Returns the one-tail probability of the chi-squared distribution. Arg1 is the number to evaluate. Arg2 is the number of degrees of freedom.
ChiInv	Double	Arg1 As Double, Arg2 As Double	Returns the inverse of the one-tail probability of the chi-squared distribution. Arg1 is the probability. Arg2 is the number of degrees of freedom.
ChiTest	Double	Arg1, Arg2	Returns the chi-squared distribution test for independence. Arg1 holds the range of data that will be tested against the expected values. Arg2 holds the range of expected data.

Name	Returns	Parameters	Description
Choose	Variant	Arg1, Arg2, [Arg3], . . . [Arg30]	Returns one of the parameter values (Arg2 to Arg30) given the index value in Arg1. For example, if Arg1 is 2 then the value in Arg3 is returned.
Clean	String	Arg1 As String	Returns the string in Arg1 without any nonprintable characters.
Combin	Double	Arg1 As Double, Arg2 As Double	Returns the total possible number of combinations of a group of Arg2 items in a total number of Arg1 items.
Confidence	Double	Arg1 As Double, Arg2 As Double, Arg3 As Double	Returns a range on either side of a sample mean for a population mean. Arg1 is the Alpha value use to determine the confidence level. Arg2 is the standard deviation for the data range. Arg3 is the sample size.
Correl	Double	Arg1, Arg2	Returns the correlation coefficient of the arrays in Arg1 and Arg2. The parameters can also be cell ranges.
Cosh	Double	Arg1 As Double	Returns the hyperbolic cosine of the Arg1 number.
Count	Double	Arg1, [Arg2], . . . [Arg30]	Returns the number of numeric values in the arguments. Arg1 to Arg30 can be values or range references.

Table Continued on Following Page

Name	Returns	Parameters	Description
CountA	Double	Arg1, [Arg2], . . . [Arg30]	Returns the number of non-empty values in the arguments. Arg1 to Arg30 can be values or range references.
CountBlank	Double	Arg1 As Range	Returns the number of empty values in the range in Arg1.
CountIf	Double	Arg1 As Range, Arg2	Counts the number of cells in the Arg1 range that meet the criteria in Arg2
Covar	Double	Arg1, Arg2	Returns the covariance of the arrays or ranges in Arg1 and Arg2.
CritBinom	Double	Arg1 As Double, Arg2 As Double, Arg3 As Double	Returns the smallest value where the cumulative binomial distribution is greater then or equal to the criterion value. Arg1 is the number of Bernoulli trials. Arg2 is the probability of success for each trial. Arg3 is the criterion value.
DAverage	Double	Arg1 As Range, Arg2, Arg3	Returns the average of the column specified by Arg2 in the range of cells in Arg1. Arg3 contains the criteria used to choose rows of records to be averaged.

Name	Returns	Parameters	Description
Days360	Double	Arg1, Arg2, [Arg3]	Returns the difference of days between the Arg1 and Arg2 dates (Arg1 – Arg2). If the Arg3 method is set to True then the European method of calculation is used. If Arg3 is set to False or omitted then the US method of calculation is used.
Db	Double	Arg1 As Double, Arg2 As Double, Arg3 As Double, Arg4 As Double, [Arg5]	Returns depreciation for a specified period using the fixed-declining balance method. Arg1 is the initial cost to depreciate. Arg2 is final salvage cost (cost at end of depreciation). Arg3 is the number of periods to depreciate. Arg4 is the specific period from Arg3 to depreciation. Arg5 can be the number of months in the first year that depreciation will start.
Dbcs	String	Arg1 As String	Returns the Double-Byte-Character-Set string of the given ASCII string. Opposite of the Asc function.
DCount	Double	Arg1 As Range, Arg2, Arg3	Returns the number of cells that match the criteria in Arg3. Arg1 specifies the range of rows and columns to count and Arg2 is used to choose the field name or number to count.

Table Continued on Following Page

Name	Returns	Parameters	Description
DCountA	Double	Arg1 As Range, Arg2, Arg3	Returns the number of non-blank cells that match the criteria in Arg3. Arg1 specifies the range of rows and columns to count and Arg2 is used to choose the field name or number to count.
Ddb	Double	Arg1 As Double, Arg2 As Double, Arg3 As Double, Arg4 As Double, [Arg5]	Returns depreciation for a specified period using the double-declining balance method. Arg1 is the initial cost to depreciate. Arg2 is final salvage cost (cost at end of depreciation). Arg3 is the number of periods to depreciate. Arg4 is the specific period from Arg3 to depreciation. Arg5 can be the rate at which the balance declines.
Degrees	Double	Arg1 As Double	Converts the radians in Arg1 into degrees and returns the degrees.
DevSq	Double	Arg1, [Arg2], ... [Arg30]	Returns the sum of the squares of deviations of the Arg1 to Arg30 from their mean.
DGet	Variant	Arg1 As Range, Arg2, Arg3	Returns the cell value that matches the criteria in Arg3. Arg1 specifies the range of rows and columns to count and Arg2 is used to choose the field name or number to count. Criteria must match a single cell.

Name	Returns	Parameters	Description
DMax	Double	Arg1 As Range, Arg2, Arg3	Returns the largest value that matches the criteria in Arg3. Arg1 specifies the range of rows and columns to count and Arg2 is used to choose the field name or number to count.
DMin	Double	Arg1 As Range, Arg2, Arg3	Returns the smallest value that matches the criteria in Arg3. Arg1 specifies the range of rows and columns to count and Arg2 is used to choose the field name or number to count.
Dollar	String	Arg1 As Double, [Arg2]	Returns a currency-type string of the number in Arg1 with the decimal points specified in Arg2.
DProduct	Double	Arg1 As Range, Arg2, Arg3	Returns the multiplication product of the values that matches the criteria in Arg3. Arg1 specifies the range of rows and columns to count and Arg2 is used to choose the field name or number to count.
DStDev	Double	Arg1 As Range, Arg2, Arg3	Returns the estimated standard deviation of the values that matches the criteria in Arg3. Arg1 specifies the range of rows and columns to count and Arg2 is used to choose the field name or number to count.

Table Continued on Following Page

Name	Returns	Parameters	Description
DStDevP	Double	Arg1 As Range, Arg2, Arg3	Returns the standard deviation of the values that matches the criteria in Arg3 assuming the entire population is given. Arg1 specifies the range of rows and columns to count and Arg2 is used to choose the field name or number to count.
DSum	Double	Arg1 As Range, Arg2, Arg3	Returns the sum of the values that matches the criteria in Arg3. Arg1 specifies the range of rows and columns to count and Arg2 is used to choose the field name or number to count.
DVar	Double	Arg1 As Range, Arg2, Arg3	Returns the variance of the values that matches the criteria in Arg3. Arg1 specifies the range of rows and columns to count and Arg2 is used to choose the field name or number to count.
DVarP	Double	Arg1 As Range, Arg2, Arg3	Returns the variance of the values that matches the criteria in Arg3 assuming that the entire population is given. Arg1 specifies the range of rows and columns to count and Arg2 is used to choose the field name or number to count.

Name	Returns	Parameters	Description
Even	Double	Arg1 As Double	Converts the Arg1 number into the nearest even whole number, rounded up, and returns it.
ExponDist	Double	Arg1 As Double, Arg2 As Double, Arg3 As Boolean	Returns the exponential distribution of a value. Arg1 is the value of the function. Arg2 is the Lambda parameter value. Set Arg3 to True for the method to return the cumulative distribution. Set Arg3 to False to return the probability density.
Fact	Double	Arg1 As Double	Returns the factorial of Arg1.
FDist	Double	Arg1 As Double, Arg2 As Double, Arg3 As Double	Returns the F probability distribution of a value. Arg1 is the value to evaluate the function. Arg2 is the numerator degrees of freedom and Arg3 is the denominator degrees of freedom.
Find	Double	Arg1 As String, Arg2 As String, [Arg3]	Finds the text in Arg1 from the text in Arg2 and returns the starting position of the found text. Arg3 can specify the starting position to search in Arg2.
FindB	Double	Arg1 As String, Arg2 As String, [Arg3]	Finds the text in Arg1 from the text in Arg2 and returns the starting position of the found text. Arg3 can specify the starting byte position to search in Arg2.

Table Continued on Following Page

Name	Returns	Parameters	Description
FInv	Double	Arg1 As Double, Arg2 As Double, Arg3 As Double	Returns the inverse of the F probability distribution. Arg1 is the probability that is associated with the F cumulative distribution. Arg2 is the numerator degrees of freedom and Arg3 is the denominator degrees of freedom.
Fisher	Double	Arg1 As Double	Returns the Fisher transformation at the Arg1 value.
FisherInv	Double	Arg1 As Double	Returns the inverse of the Fisher transformation given the value Arg1.
Fixed	String	Arg1 As Double, [Arg2], [Arg3]	Rounds the number Arg1 to the decimal points Arg2 and returns the value as a string. Set Arg3 to True to put commas in the returned text. Set Arg3 to False to not put commas in the returned text.
Floor	Double	Arg1 As Double, Arg2 As Double	Returns the nearest number to Arg1 that is a multiple of Arg2, rounded down towards 0.
Forecast	Double	Arg1 As Double, Arg2, Arg3	Returns a predicted y value for a given x value (Arg1) by using the existing value pairs. Arg2 is an array or range corresponding to the y's known values. Arg3 is an array or range corresponding to the x's known values.

Name	Returns	Parameters	Description
Frequency	Variant	Arg1, Arg2	Returns an array of numbers describing the frequency of values in the array Arg1 that are in the intervals specified by the Arg2 array. Arg1 and Arg2 can also be references to a range.
FTest	Double	Arg1, Arg2	Returns the result of an F-test of the arrays in Arg1 and Arg2. Arg1 and Arg2 can also be references to a range.
Fv	Double	Arg1 As Double, Arg2 As Double, Arg3 As Double, [Arg4], [Arg5]	Returns the future value of an investment for a time period. Arg1 is the interest rate per period. Arg2 is the total number of payment period. Arg3 is the payment per period. Arg4 is the initial value. Arg5 determines if payments are due at the end of the period (0) or the beginning of the period (1).
GammaDist	Double	Arg1 As Double, Arg2 As Double, Arg3 As Double, Arg4 As Boolean	Returns the gamma distribution. Arg1 is the value to evaluate. Arg2 is the alpha parameter to the distribution. Arg3 is the beta parameter to the distribution. Set Arg4 to True for the method to return the cumulative distribution. Set Arg4 to False to return the probability density.

Table Continued on Following Page

Name	Returns	Parameters	Description
GammaInv	Double	Arg1 As Double, Arg2 As Double, Arg3 As Double	Returns the inverse of the gamma cumulative distribution. Arg1 is the gamma distribution probability. Arg2 is the alpha parameter to the distribution. Arg3 is the beta parameter to the distribution.
GammaLn	Double	Arg1 As Double	Returns the natural logarithm of the gamma function with the Arg1 number.
GeoMean	Double	Arg1, [Arg2], . . . [Arg30]	Returns the geometric mean of the numbers in Arg1 to Arg30. Arg1 to Arg30 can also be a reference to a range.
Growth	Variant	Arg1, [Arg2], [Arg3], [Arg4]	Returns the predicted exponential growth of y values (Arg1) for a series of new x values (Arg3). Arg2 can be used to set the series of existing x values. Arg4 can be set to False to make the 'b' part of the equation equal to one.
HarMean	Double	Arg1, [Arg2], . . . [Arg30]	Returns the harmonic mean of the numbers in Arg1 to Arg30. Arg1 to Arg30 can also be a reference to a range.

Name	Returns	Parameters	Description
HLookup	Variant	Arg1, Arg2, Arg3, [Arg4]	Looks up the value specified by Arg1 in the table array (or range reference) Arg2 first row. Arg3 specifies the row number in the table array that contains the matching value. Set the Arg4 to True to find approximate data or set Arg4 to False to only lookup exact values.
HypGeom Dist	Double	Arg1 As Double, Arg2 As Double, Arg3 As Double, Arg4 As Double	Returns the hypergeometric distribution probability. Arg1 is the number of successes in the trails. Arg2 holds the total number of trials. Arg3 is the number of successes in the trial. Arg4 is the size of the population.
Index	Variant	Arg1, Arg2 As Double, [Arg3], [Arg4]	May return the cell or array of cells from Arg1 that has a row number of Arg2 and a column number of Arg3. May also return the cell or range of cells that have a row number of Arg2 and a column number of Arg3. If Arg1 contains many areas then Arg4 can be used to specify the area.

Table Continued on Following Page

Name	Returns	Parameters	Description
Intercept	Double	Arg1, Arg2	Returns the point where the X-axis and Y-axis coordinates intersect. Arg1 represents the array of known y values and Arg2 represents the array of known x values.
Ipmt	Double	Arg1 As Double, Arg2 As Double, Arg3 As Double, Arg4 As Double, [Arg5], [Arg6]	Returns the interest amount paid for an investment for a time period. Arg1 is the interest rate per period. Arg2 is the period that you want to find the amount of interest. Arg3 is the total number of payment periods. Arg4 is the initial value. Arg5 is the future value that is wanted to be attained. Arg6 determines if payments are due at the end of the period (0) or the beginning of the period (1).
Irr	Double	Arg1, [Arg2]	Returns the rate of return for an array of values in Arg1. Arg2 can be used to specify a guess of the Irr result.
IsErr	Boolean	Arg1	Returns whether the cell Arg1 contains an error value (except #N/A).
IsError	Boolean	Arg1	Returns whether the cell Arg1 contains any error value.
IsLogical	Boolean	Arg1	Returns whether the cell or value Arg1 contains a logical value.

Name	Returns	Parameters	Description
IsNA	Boolean	Arg1	Returns whether the cell Arg1 contains the #N/A value.
IsNonText	Boolean	Arg1	Returns whether the cell Arg1 does not contain text.
IsNumber	Boolean	Arg1	Returns whether the cell Arg1 contains a numeric value.
Ispmt	Double	Arg1 As Double, Arg2 As Double, Arg3 As Double, Arg4 As Double	Returns the interest amount paid for an investment at a particular period. Used for compatibility purposes. Arg1 is the interest rate per period. Arg2 is the period that you want to find the amount of interest. Arg3 is the total number of payment periods. Arg4 is the initial value.
IsText	Boolean	Arg1	Returns whether the cell Arg1 contains a text value
Kurt	Double	Arg1, [Arg2], ... [Arg30]	Returns the kurtosis of the values in Arg1 to Arg30. Also, Arg1 can be a reference to a cell range.
Large	Double	Arg1, Arg2 As Double	Returns the Arg2 largest value in the array or cell reference specified by Arg1 (e.g. second largest, third largest).

Table Continued on Following Page

Name	Returns	Parameters	Description
LinEst	Variant	Arg1, [Arg2], [Arg3], [Arg4]	Returns an array describing a straight line that best fits the data of known y values (Arg1) and known x values (Arg2). Set Arg3 to False to make the 'b' part of the calculations equal to 0. Set Arg4 to True to return additional statistics.
Ln	Double	Arg1 As Double	Returns the natural logarithm of the Arg1 number.
Log	Double	Arg1 As Double, [Arg2]	Returns the logarithm of the Arg1 number to the base specified in Arg2. Arg2 is 10 by default.
Log10	Double	Arg1 As Double	Returns the base-10 logarithm of the Arg1 number.
LogEst	Variant	Arg1, [Arg2], [Arg3], [Arg4]	Returns an array describing the curved line that best fits the data of known y values (Arg1) and known x values (Arg2). Set Arg3 to False to make the 'b' part of the calculations equal to 0. Set Arg4 to True to return additional statistics.
LogInv	Double	Arg1 As Double, Arg2 As Double, Arg3 As Double	Returns the inverse of the lognormal cumulative distribution of a value. Arg1 is the probability that will have to be inversed. Arg2 is the mean of ln(value). Arg3 is the standard deviation of ln(value).

Name	Returns	Parameters	Description
LogNorm Dist	Double	Arg1 As Double, Arg2 As Double, Arg3 As Double	Returns the cumulative lognormal distribution of Arg1. Arg2 is the mean of ln(Arg1) and Arg3 is the standard deviation of ln(Arg1).
Lookup	Variant	Arg1, Arg2, [Arg3]	The value Arg1 is searched for in the single row or column in Arg2. A value from the matching spot in another array, Arg3, is returned.
Match	Double	Arg1, Arg2, [Arg3]	Returns the relative position of an item in an array, Arg2, which matches a specific value, Arg1. Use Arg3 to set the type of match.
Max	Double	Arg1, [Arg2], . . . [Arg30]	Returns the largest value in the numbers Arg1 to Arg30. Arg1 can also be a cell range.
MDeterm	Double	Arg1	Returns the matrix determinant of the matrix array specified by Arg1. Arg1 can also be a cell range. Cell elements cannot contain text or be empty. There must be an equal amount of rows to columns.
Median	Double	Arg1, [Arg2], . . . [Arg30]	Returns the median value in the numbers Arg1 to Arg30. Arg1 can also be a cell range
Min	Double	Arg1, [Arg2], . . . [Arg30]	Returns the smallest value in the numbers Arg1 to Arg30. Arg1 can also be a cell range

Table Continued on Following Page

Name	Returns	Parameters	Description
MInverse	Variant	Arg1	Returns the inverse matrix for the matrix array in Arg1. Arg1 can also be a cell range. Cell elements cannot contain text or be empty. There must be an equal amount of rows to columns.
MIrr	Double	Arg1, Arg2 As Double, Arg3 As Double	Returns the modified rate or return for a series of values in Arg1. Arg2 is the interest rate paid. Arg3 is the interest rate received as the cash flow values are re-invested.
MMult	Variant	Arg1, Arg2	Returns the matrix product of the two matrix arrays Arg1 and Arg2. The number of columns in Arg1 must be the same as the number of rows in Arg2. Arg1 and Arg2 can also be a cell range. Cell elements cannot contain text or be empty.
Mode	Double	Arg1, [Arg2], ... [Arg30]	Returns the most frequently occurring number in Arg1 to Arg30. Arg1 can also be a cell range.
NegBinom Dist	Double	Arg1 As Double, Arg2 As Double, Arg3 As Double	Returns the negative binomial distribution of the arguments. Arg1 is the number of failures in the trails. Arg2 holds the threshold number of successes. Arg3 is the probability of success on a single trial.

Name	Returns	Parameters	Description
NormDist	Double	Arg1 As Double, Arg2 As Double, Arg3 As Double, Arg4 As Boolean	Returns the normal cumulative distribution for the value to distribute (Arg1), the mean (Arg2), and the standard deviation (Arg3). Set Arg4 to True to return the cumulative distribution and False to return the probability mass.
NormInv	Double	Arg1 As Double, Arg2 As Double, Arg3 As Double	Returns the inverse of the normal cumulative distribution given a probability (Arg1), the mean (Arg2), and the standard deviation (Arg3).
NormSDist	Double	Arg1 As Double	Returns the standard normal cumulative distribution for the value to distribute (Arg1).
NormSInv	Double	Arg1 As Double	Returns the inverse of the standard normal cumulative distribution for a given probability (Arg1).

Table Continued on Following Page

Name	Returns	Parameters	Description
NPer	Double	Arg1 As Double, Arg2 As Double, Arg3 As Double, [Arg4], [Arg5]	Returns the number of periods for an investment. Arg1 is the interest rate per period. Arg2 is the payment amount made each period. Arg3 is the initial value. Arg4 is the future value that is wanted to be attained. Arg5 determines if payments are due at the end of the period (0) or the beginning of the period (1).
Npv	Double	Arg1 As Double, Arg2, [Arg3], . . . [Arg30]	Returns the net present value of an investment using a discount rate (Arg1) and many future payments and income (Arg2 to Arg30).
Odd	Double	Arg1 As Double	Converts the Arg1 number into the nearest odd whole number, rounded up, and returns it.
Or	Boolean	Arg1, [Arg2], . . . [Arg30]	Returns True if any of expressions in Arg1 to Arg30 returns True.
Pearson	Double	Arg1, Arg2	Returns the Pearson product moment correlation coefficient containing an array of values. Arg1 is the array of independent values and Arg2 is the array of dependent values. Arg1 and Arg2 can also be cell references.

Name	Returns	Parameters	Description
Percentile	Double	Arg1, Arg2 As Double	Returns the Arg2 percentile of values in the Arg1 range of cells or array.
Percent Rank	Double	Arg1, Arg2 As Double, [Arg3]	Returns how the value Arg2 ranks in the Arg1 range of cells or array. Arg3 can specify the number of significant digits for the returned percentage.
Permut	Double	Arg1 As Double, Arg2 As Double	Returns the total possible number of permutations of a group of Arg2 items in a total number of Arg1 items.
Phonetic	String	Arg1 As Range	Returns the phonetic characters from the Arg1 text string.
Pi	Double		Returns pi (3.14) to 15 decimal places.
Pmt	Double	Arg1 As Double, Arg2 As Double, Arg3 As Double, [Arg4], [Arg5]	Returns the payment for a loan. Arg1 is the interest rate per period. Arg2 is the number of payments for the loan. Arg3 is the initial value. Arg4 is the future value that is wanted to be attained. Arg5 determines if payments are due at the end of the period (0) or the beginning of the period (1).

Table Continued on Following Page

Name	Returns	Parameters	Description
Poisson	Double	Arg1 As Double, Arg2 As Double, Arg3 As Boolean	Returns the Poisson distribution given the number of events (Arg1) and the expected numeric value (Arg2). Set Arg3 to True to return the cumulative probability and False to return the probability mass.
Power	Double	Arg1 As Double, Arg2 As Double	Returns the base number Arg1 raised to the power of Arg2.
Ppmt	Double	Arg1 As Double, Arg2 As Double, Arg3 As Double, Arg4 As Double, [Arg5], [Arg6]	Returns the payment on the principal of an investment for a given period of time. Arg1 is the interest rate per period. Arg2 specifies the period to look at. Arg3 is the total number of payments. Arg4 is the initial value. Arg5 is the future value that is wanted to be attained. Arg6 determines if payments are due at the end of the period (0) or the beginning of the period (1).
Prob	Double	Arg1, Arg2, Arg3 As Double, [Arg4]	Returns the probability that the values in the Arg1 array and associated Arg2 array are within the lower limit (Arg3) and upper limit (Arg4).
Product	Double	Arg1, [Arg2], ... [Arg30]	Returns the multiplication product of all the values in Arg1 to Arg30.

Name	Returns	Parameters	Description
Proper	String	Arg1 As String	Capitalizes the start of every word in Arg1 and make everything else lower case.
Pv	Double	Arg1 As Double, Arg2 As Double, Arg3 As Double, [Arg4], [Arg5]	Returns the present value of an investment. Arg1 is the interest rate per period. Arg2 is the number of payments for the loan. Arg3 is the payment amount made per period. Arg4 is the future value that is wanted to be attained. Arg5 determines if payments are due at the end of the period (0) or the beginning of the period (1).
Quartile	Double	Arg1, Arg2 As Double	Returns the quartile specified by Arg2 of the array in Arg1. Arg2 can be 0 (Minimum value), 1 (first quartile), 2 (second quartile), 3 (third quartile), or 4 (maximum value).
Radians	Double	Arg1 As Double	Converts the Arg1 number from degrees to radians and returns the new value.
Rank	Double	Arg1 As Double, Arg2 As Range, [Arg3]	Returns the rank of Arg1 in the range Arg2. Arg3 can be used to set how to rank Arg1.

Table Continued on Following Page

Name	Returns	Parameters	Description
Rate	Double	Arg1 As Double, Arg2 As Double, Arg3 As Double, [Arg4], [Arg5], [Arg6]	Returns the interest rate per period for a value. Arg1 is the total number of payments. Arg2 is payment amount per period. Arg3 is the initial value. Arg4 is the future value that is wanted to be attained. Arg5 determines if payments are due at the end of the period (0) or the beginning of the period (1).
Replace	String	Arg1 As String, Arg2 As Double, Arg3 As Double, Arg4 As String	Replaces part of the text in Arg1 with the text in Arg4. The starting character of the replacement is at the number Arg2 and Arg3 specifies the number of replaced characters in Arg1.
ReplaceB	String	Arg1 As String, Arg2 As Double, Arg3 As Double, Arg4 As String	Replaces part of the text in Arg1 with the text in Arg4. The starting character of the replacement is at the number Arg2 and Arg3 specifies the number of replaced bytes in Arg1.
Rept	String	Arg1 As String, Arg2 As Double	Repeats the string in Arg1 by Arg2 number of times and returns that new string.

Name	Returns	Parameters	Description
Roman	String	Arg1 As Double, [Arg2]	Returns the number in Arg1 to a Roman numeral equivalent. Arg2 can specify the style of Roman numerals. 0 or True is the classic style. 4 or False is the simplified style. The other options are 1, 2, and 3 that set the style to varying degrees of simplification.
Round	Double	Arg1 As Double, Arg2 As Double	Returns the Arg1 number rounded to the number of digits specified in Arg2.
RoundDown	Double	Arg1 As Double, Arg2 As Double	Returns the Arg1 number rounded to the number of digits specified in Arg2. The number is rounded down towards 0.
RoundUp	Double	Arg1 As Double, Arg2 As Double	Returns the Arg1 number rounded to the number of digits specified in Arg2. The number is rounded up towards 0.
RSq	Double	Arg1, Arg2	Returns the square of the Pearson product moment correlation coefficient containing an array of values. Arg1 is the array of y values and Arg2 is the array of x values. Arg1 and Arg2 can also be cell references.

Table Continued on Following Page

Name	Returns	Parameters	Description
Search	Double	Arg1 As String, Arg2 As String, [Arg3]	Finds the text in Arg1 from the text in Arg2 and returns the starting position of the found text. Arg3 can specify the starting position to search in Arg2.
SearchB	Double	Arg1 As String, Arg2 As String, [Arg3]	Finds the text in Arg1 from the text in Arg2 and returns the starting position of the found text. Arg3 can specify the starting byte position to search in Arg2.
Sinh	Double	Arg1 As Double	Returns the hyperbolic sine of the Arg1 number.
Skew	Double	Arg1, [Arg2], . . . [Arg30]	Returns how skewed the numbers in Arg1 to Arg30 are. The arguments can also be a range reference.
Sln	Double	Arg1 As Double, Arg2 As Double, Arg3 As Double	Returns the simple straight-line depreciation of an asset costing Arg1 with a salvage value of Arg3 over Arg2 number of periods.
Slope	Double	Arg1, Arg2	Returns the slope of the linear regression line through the data points of the x values (Arg1) and y values (Arg2).
Small	Double	Arg1, Arg2 As Double	Returns the Arg2 smallest value in the array or cell reference specified by Arg1 (e.g. second smallest, third smallest).

Name	Returns	Parameters	Description
Standardize	Double	Arg1 As Double, Arg2 As Double, Arg3 As Double	Returns the normalized value from a distribution given a value (Arg1), a mean (Arg2), and a standard deviation (Arg3).
StDev	Double	Arg1, [Arg2], . . . [Arg30]	Returns the estimated standard deviation of the values in Arg1 to Arg30. The arguments can also be a range reference.
StDevP	Double	Arg1, [Arg2], . . . [Arg30]	Returns the standard deviation of the values in Arg1 to Arg30 based on the all the values. The arguments can also be a range reference.
StEyx	Double	Arg1, Arg2	Returns the standard error of the predicted y values for each of the x values in the regression given some know y values (Arg1) and x values (Arg2).
Substitute	String	Arg1 As String, Arg2 As String, Arg3 As String, [Arg4]	Substitutes all occurrences of the Arg2 text with the Arg3 text in the original Arg1 text string. Arg4 can be used to specify which occurrence to replace.

Table Continued on Following Page

Name	Returns	Parameters	Description
Subtotal	Double	Arg1 As Double, Arg2 As Range, [Arg3], . . . [Arg30]	Returns subtotals for the ranges or references specified in the Arg2 to Arg30 parameters. Arg1 is a number describing what type of function to use for calculating the subtotal. Valid function numbers are from 1 to 10 representing Average, Count, CountA, Max, Min, Product, StDev, StDevP, Sum, Var, and VarP in numerical order.
Sum	Double	Arg1, [Arg2], . . . [Arg30]	Returns the sum of all the numbers in Arg1 to Arg30.
SumIf	Double	Arg1 As Range, Arg2, [Arg3]	Returns the sum of the cells in the range Arg1 with the criteria matching Arg2. A different range to sum can be specified with Arg3. The columns or rows in Arg1 and Arg3 have to be the same.
SumProduct	Double	Arg1, [Arg2], . . . [Arg30]	Multiplies each corresponding element in the arrays Arg1 to Arg30 and returns the sum of the products. The arrays in Arg1 to Arg30 must have the same dimension.
SumSq	Double	Arg1, [Arg2], . . . [Arg30]	Returns the sum of the square roots of the number in Arg1 to Arg30.

Name	Returns	Parameters	Description
SumX2MY2	Double	Arg1, Arg2	Subtracts the squares of the corresponding elements in the arrays Arg1 and Arg2 and returns the sum of all the new elements.
SumX2PY2	Double	Arg1, Arg2	Adds the squares of the corresponding elements in the arrays Arg1 and Arg2 and returns the sum of all the new elements.
SumXMY2	Double	Arg1, Arg2	Subtracts the corresponding elements in the arrays Arg1 and Arg2, squares the difference and returns the sum of all the new elements.
Syd	Double	Arg1 As Double, Arg2 As Double, Arg3 As Double, Arg4 As Double	Returns the sum-of-years digits depreciation of an asset over a specified period. Arg1 is the initial cost. Arg2 is the salvage cost. Arg3 is the number of periods to depreciate the asset over. Arg4 is the specified period to return.
Tanh	Double	Arg1 As Double	Returns the hyperbolic tangent of the Arg1 number.

Table Continued on Following Page

Name	Returns	Parameters	Description
Tdist	Double	Arg1 As Double, Arg2 As Double, Arg3 As Double	Returns the probability for the Student's t-distribution for a value, Arg1, is a calculated value of 't'. Arg2 indicates the number of degrees of freedom. Set Arg3 to 1 to return a one-tailed distribution. Set Arg3 to 2 to return a two-tailed distribution.
Text	String	Arg1, Arg2 As String	Converts the value in Arg1 into text using the formatting in Arg2.
Tinv	Double	Arg1 As Double, Arg2 As Double	Returns the t-value of the Student's t-distribution given the probability (Arg1) and the degrees of freedom (Arg2).
Transpose	Variant	Arg1	Transposes the range specified by Arg1 from column to row or vice versa and returns the new range.
Trend	Variant	Arg1, [Arg2], [Arg3], [Arg4]	Returns the values associated with a linear trend given some y values (Arg1), some x values (Arg2), and some new x values (Arg3). Set Arg4 to False to make 'b' equal to 0 in the equation.
Trim	String	Arg1 As String	Returns the string in Arg1 without leading and trailing spaces.

Name	Returns	Parameters	Description
TrimMean	Double	Arg1, Arg2 As Double	Returns the mean of the interior of the data array in Arg1. Use Arg2 to specify the fractional part of the data array to exclude.
Ttest	Double	Arg1, Arg2, Arg3 As Double, Arg4 As Double	Returns the probability associated with a Student's t-test given the two sets of data in Arg1 and Arg12. Set Arg3 to 1 to return a one-tailed distribution. Set Arg3 to 2 to return a two-tailed distribution. Set Arg4 to 1, 2, or 3 to set the type of t-test to paired, two-sample equal variance, or two-sample unequal variance, respectively.
USDollar	String	Arg1 As Double, Arg2 As Double	Returns a currency-type string of the number in Arg1 with the decimal points specified in Arg2.
Var	Double	Arg1, [Arg2], . . . [Arg30]	Returns the estimated variance based on the numbers in Arg1 to Arg30. The arguments can also be range references.
VarP	Double	Arg1, [Arg2], . . . [Arg30]	Returns the variance based on the numbers in Arg1 to Arg30 as an entire population. The arguments can also be range references.

Table Continued on Following Page

Name	Returns	Parameters	Description
Vdb	Double	Arg1 As Double, Arg2 As Double, Arg3 As Double, Arg4 As Double, Arg5 As Double, [Arg6], [Arg7]	Returns the double-declining balance method depreciation (unless otherwise specified) of an asset for specified periods. Arg1 is the initial cost. Arg2 is the salvage cost. Arg3 is the number of periods to depreciate the asset over. Arg4 is the starting period to calculate depreciation. Arg5 is the ending period to calculate depreciation. Arg6 is the rate at which the balance declines. Set Arg7 to True to keep the calculation using the double-declining balance method. Set Arg7 to False to have Excel switch to straight-line depreciation when necessary.
Vlookup	Variant	Arg1, Arg2, Arg3, [Arg4]	Looks up the value specified by Arg1 in the table array (or range reference) Arg2 first column Arg3 specifies the column number in the table array that contains the matching value. Set the Arg4 to True to find approximate data or set Arg4 to False to only lookup exact values.
Weekday	Double	Arg1, [Arg2]	Returns the numerical day of the week for the date in Arg1. Arg2 specifies which day is the start of the week.

Name	Returns	Parameters	Description
Weibull	Double	Arg1 As Double, Arg2 As Double, Arg3 As Double, Arg4 As Boolean	Returns the Weibull distribution using the value (Arg1). Arg2 is the alpha parameter to the distribution. Arg3 is the beta parameter to the distribution. Set Arg4 to True to return the cumulative probability and False to return the probability mass.
Ztest	Double	Arg1, Arg2 As Double, [Arg3]	Returns the two-tailed P-value of a z-test. Arg1 is the array or range of data to test against Arg2. Arg2 is the value to test. Arg3 is the population standard deviation.

Example: WorksheetFunction Object

```
Sub GetBiggest()
    Dim oWSF As WorksheetFunction
    Dim vaArray As Variant

    Set oWSF = Application.WorksheetFunction

    vaArray = Array(10, 20, 13, 15, 56, 12, 8, 45)

    MsgBox "Biggest is " & oWSF.Max(vaArray)
End Sub
```

VBE Object Model

Officially known as *'Microsoft Visual Basic for Applications Extensibility 5.3'*, the VBE object library provides access to the code and forms within an application and to the various objects that comprise the **Visual Basic Integrated Development Environment** (VBIDE). By default, this object library is *not* included in the list of referenced libraries for new projects. In order to use the objects refered to in this chapter, a reference to the **Microsoft Visual Basic for Applications Extensibility 5.3** library must be created using the **Tools | References** menu in the VBE.

Many of the objects in the VBE object model have the same names as objects in the Excel object model. To distinguish the libraries and to ensure that you have the object from the VBE library you need to include the VBIDE library name in any Dim statements you may use:

```
Dim oWinVB As VBIDE.Window      'Always gives a VBE Window
Dim oWinXL As Excel.Window      'Always gives an XL Window
Dim oWin As Window              'Gives an XL Window
```

All of the applications in Office 2000 share the same development environment — the VBE. The code and forms that belong to each Excel workbook, Word document, Access database or PowerPoint presentation (i.e. the 'host document') are grouped into Visual Basic projects (the VBProject object). There is one project for each host document. FrontPage and Outlook have a single Project each, which 'belongs' to the application. Additionally, the Developer Edition of Office 2000 supports stand-alone projects, which are not linked to any of the Office applications and can be compiled into ActiveX DLLs.

Links Between the Excel and VBE Object Models

There are a number of properties of Excel objects that provide links to the VBE object model. Similarly, there are a number of properties in the VBE object model that provide a link back into Excel. Many of the code examples in this appendix and in Chapter 17 on Programming the VBE use these links:

Excel to VBE	
Excel Property	**Resulting VBE Item**
`Application.VBE`	VBE object
`Workbook.VBProject`	`VBProject` object
`Workbook.CodeName`	The name of the workbook-level `VBComponent` in the workbook's VBProject, usually 'ThisWorkbook' in English versions of Excel 2000.
`Worksheet.CodeName` `Chart.CodeName`	The name of the sheet-level `VBComponent` in the workbook's `VBProject`, usually 'Sheet1', 'Chart1' etc in English versions of Excel 2000.

VBE to Excel	
VBE Property	**Resulting Excel Item**
`VBProject.FileName`	The full name of the workbook, if the `VBProject` is an Excel workbook project and the workbook has been saved.
`VBComponent.Properties ("Name")`	The file name of the workbook, if the `VBComponent` is the workbook-level item (e.g. 'ThisWorkbook'), or the name of the sheet for sheet-level `VBComponents`.
`VBComponent.Properties ("<Other Properties>")`	The properties associated with the Excel object to which the `VBComponent` applies (if any).

Common Properties and Methods

Most of the objects in the VBE object library have the following common properties. To avoid redundancy, these properties will be listed for each object, but will not be explained.

Name	Returns	Description
`Collection`		Read Only. Returns the collection to which an object belongs. For example, a `Reference` object belongs to the `References` collection. The `Collection` property is used for objects that belong to collections.

Name	Returns	Description
Parent		Read Only. Return the object to which an object belongs. For example, a References collection belongs to a VBProject object. The Parent property is used for objects that do not belong to collections.
VBE	VBE	Read Only. Returns the Visual Basic Editor object, which is analagous to the Application object in the Excel Object Model.

Most of the objects in the VBE Object Model are contained in associated collections. The collection object is usually the plural form of the associated object. For example, the Windows collection holds a collection of Window objects. For simplicity, each object and associated collection will be grouped together under the same heading. The common properties and methods of the collection objects are the same as in the Excel Object Model, and are listed in Appendix A. Only unique properties, methods or events will be mentioned for each object.

AddIn Object and AddIns Collection

Not to be confused with Excel's Addin object, VBE Addins are DLLs that conform to Microsoft's Component Object Model architecture and are more commonly known as 'COM Addins'. These Addins are typically created using C++, Visual Basic, or the Developer Edition of Office 2000. If you have any installed, they can be found under the VBE's Add-Ins menu and can be loaded and unloaded using the Add-Ins | Add-In Manager... menu item.

AddIn Common Properties

The Collection and VBE properties are defined at the beginning of this section.

AddIn Properties

Name	Returns	Description
Connect	Boolean	Whether the COM Addin is currently connected (i.e. active). Can be set to True to load and run the Addin. Similar to the Installed property of an Excel Addin.
Description	String	The text that appears in the 'Description' box of the VBE Add-In Manager.

Table Continued on Following Page

Name	Returns	Description
Guid	String	Read Only. Returns the globally unique identifier for the Addin. The Guid is created by Excel/VB when the Addin is compiled.
Object		In the AddIn's OnConnection method, it can expose an object to the VBE (typically the root class of its object model, if it has one). You can then use the AddIn's Object property to access this object and through it, the rest of the AddIn's object model. Few Addins currently expose an Object.
ProgId	String	Read Only. Returns the program ID for the Addin, which is comprised of the name of the Addin project and the name of the connection class (usually a connection designer). For example, if you have an Addin project called MyAddin and an Addin Designer class called dsrMyConnection, the ProgId will be 'MyAddin.dsrMyConnection'.

AddIns Collection Methods

Name	Returns	Description
Item	Addin	Read Only. Parameters: Item As Variant. Returns an Addin associated with the item. The parameter can be either a number or the ProgId of the Addin (e.g. MyAddin.dsrMyConnection)
Update		Method. Updates the list of available COM Addins from the Registry. This should only need to be used if you are compiling an Addin through code (e.g. using VBProject.MakeCompiledFile).

AddIn Examples

The following example iterates through all the AddIns registered for use in the VBE and prints information about those that are active.

```
Sub ListRunningAddins()
    'Define as a VBE Addin, not an Excel one
    Dim oAddin As VBIDE.Addin

    'Loop through the VBE's addins
    For Each oAddin In Application.VBE.AddIns
```

```
        'Is it active (i.e. connected)?
        If oAddin.Connect Then

            'Yes, so show it's ID and description
            Debug.Print oAddin.ProgId, oAddin.Description
        End If
    Next
End Sub
```

Note that VBE Addins do not have a property to provide their name, as shown in the list in the **Add-In Manager** dialog.

CodeModule Object

The CodeModule object contains all of the code for a single VBComponent (i.e. Module, UserForm, Class Module or Excel sheet). There is only ever one CodeModule for a component — its methods and properties enable you to locate, identify, modify and add lines of code to a project's components. There can be more than one procedure of the same name in a module, if they are Property procedures:

```
Dim msSelection As String
Property Get TheSelection() As String
    TheSelection = msSelection
End Property

Property Let TheSelection(NewString As String)
    MsSelection = NewString
End Property
```

Hence, to uniquely identify a procedure, you need to supply both its name ('TheSelection' in this example) and the type of procedure you're looking for (i.e. vbext_pk_Get for Property Get, vbext_pk_Let for Property Let, vbext_pk_Set for Property Set or vbext_pk_proc for Subs and Functions). The ProcOfLine function provides this information for a given line number — the name of the procedure is the return value of the function and the type of procedure is returned in the variable you supply to its ProcKind argument. It is one of the few properties in the whole of Office 2000 that returns values by modifying the arguments passed to it.

CodeModule Common Properties

The Parent and VBE properties are defined at the beginning of this section (its Parent being the VBComponent.)

CodeModule Properties

Name	Returns	Description
CodePane	CodePane	Read Only. Returns the active CodePane for the module. If there is no visible CodePane, one is created and displayed. Note that a CodeModule can have up to two code panes, but there is no CodePanes collection for them!

Table Continued on Following Page

Name	Returns	Description
| CountOf Declaration Lines | Long | Read Only. Returns the number of lines at the top of the module used for Dim, Type and Option statements. If there are any such items at the top of the module, any comments following them are considered to be part of the following procedure, not the declarations. The following has two declaration lines:<br><br>```
Option Explicit
Dim msSelection As String

'My Comment
Sub ProcedureStart()
```<br>If no such statements exist, comments appearing at the top of the module are counted as declaration lines, if they are followed by a blank line. The following has one declaration line:<br><br>```
'My Comment

Sub ProcedureStart()
```<br>If the comment is immediately followed by the procedure, it is included in the procedure's lines, so the following has no declaration line:<br><br>```
'My Comment
Sub ProcedureStart()
``` |
CountOf Lines	Long	Read Only. Returns the total number of lines of code in the module, with line continuations counted as separate lines.
Lines	String	Read Only. Parameters: StartLine As Long, Count As Long. Returns a block of code, starting from Startline and continuing for Count lines.
Name	String	(Hidden) Read Only. Returns the name of the associated VBComponent.
ProcBody Line	Long	Read Only. Parameters: ProcName As String, ProcKind As vbext_ProcKind. Returns the line number of the start of the procedure, not including any preceding comments — i.e. it gives the line number of the Sub, Function or Property statement.
```

Name	Returns	Description
ProcCount Lines	Long	Read Only. Parameters: ProcName As String, ProcKind As vbext_ProcKind. Returns the number of lines used by the procedure, including preceding comments, up to the End Sub, End Function or End Property statement.
ProcOfLine	String	Read Only. Parameters: Line As Long [in], ProcKind As Long [out]. Returns the name of the procedure that a line is located within. The ProcKind argument is also modified to return the type of procedure (Sub/Function, Property Let, Get or Set). This is usually the first property to be called; the name and type returned from this are then used in calls to the other methods.
ProcStart Line	Long	Read Only. Parameters: ProcName As String, ProcKind As vbext_ProcKind. Returns the line number of the start of the procedure, including comments. Hence, ProcBodyLine — ProcStartLine gives you the number of preceding comment lines.

CodeModule Methods

Name	Returns	Parameters	Description
AddFromFile		FileName As String	Reads code from a text file and adds it to the end of the code module. It does not check if the names of procedures read from a file already exist in the module.
AddFrom String		String As String	Adds code from a string to the end of the code module.

Table Continued on Following Page

Name	Returns	Parameters	Description
CreateEvent Proc	Long	EventName As String, ObjectName As String	Creates an empty event procedure in a module, filling in the event parameters for you. Cannot be used on standard modules, as they do not support events. The ObjectName must be a valid object for the class module, and the EventName must be a valid event for that object.
DeleteLines		StartLine As Long, Count As Long	Deletes lines from a code module, starting at StartLine, for Count lines.
Find	Boolean	Target As String, StartLine As Long, Start Column As Long, EndLine As Long, EndColumn As Long, WholeWord As Boolean, MatchCase As Boolean, Pattern Search As Boolean	Locates a string within a code module, or section of a code module. It provides the same functionality as the VBE's Find dialog.
InsertLines		Line As Long, String As String	Adds code from a string into the middle of a code module, inserting the code before the Line given.
ReplaceLine		Line As Long, String As String	Adds code from a string into the middle of a code module, replacing the Line given.

CodeModule Examples

There are a number of `CodeModule` examples in the chapter on 'Programming the VBE'. The example below identifies the procedure for a given line and displays its type, name and line count:

```
Sub WhichProc()
    Dim lLine As Long, iProcKind As Long, lLineCount As Long
    Dim sProc As String, sMsg As String
    Dim oActiveCM As VBIDE.CodeModule

    lLine = CLng(InputBox("Which line?"))

    'Cancelled?
    If lLine = 0 Then Exit Sub

    'Get the currently active code module
    Set oActiveCM = Application.VBE.ActiveCodePane.CodeModule

    'Get the name and type of the procedure at that line
    'iProcKind is filled in
    sProc = oActiveCM.ProcOfLine(lLine, iProcKind)

    If sProc = "" Then
        'We didn't get a name, so you must be in the Declarations section
        sMsg = "You are in the Declarations section"
        lLineCount = oActiveCM.CountOfDeclarationLines
    Else
        sMsg = "You are in "

        'Display the type of the procedure...
        Select Case iProcKind
            Case vbext_pk_Proc
                sMsg = sMsg & "Sub or Function procedure"

            Case vbext_pk_Get
                sMsg = sMsg & "Property Get procedure"

            Case vbext_pk_Let
                sMsg = sMsg & "Property Let procedure"

            Case vbext_pk_Set
                sMsg = sMsg & "Property Set procedure"

        End Select

        '... its name ...
        sMsg = sMsg & " '" & sProc & "'"

        '... and how many lines it has.
        lLineCount = oActiveCM.ProcCountLines(sProc, iProcKind)
    End If

    'Display the message
    MsgBox sMsg & vbCrLf & "which has " & lLineCount & " lines."
End Sub
```

CodePane Object and CodePanes Collection

A `CodePane` is a view of a `CodeModule`, providing you with access to the interaction layer between the developer and the code being edited. Most VBE Addins use this layer to identify which line in which `CodePane` is currently being edited, and then modify the code at the line, using `CodeModule`'s methods and properties. Note that there can be more than one `CodePane` for a `CodeModule` (e.g. by splitting a code window into two panes with the horizontal splitter bar).

CodePane Common Properties

The Collection and VBE properties are defined at the beginning of this section.

CodePane Properties

Name	Returns	Description
CodeModule	CodeModule	Read Only. Returns the CodeModule which contains the code being viewed in the CodePane.
CodePaneView	vbext_Code PaneView	Read Only. Returns whether the CodePane is set to show one procedure at a time, or a full-module view with separator lines between procedures.
CountOf VisibleLines	Long	Read Only. Returns the number of lines visible in the CodePane. This and the TopLine property can be used to center a line in the CodePane window (see example below).
TopLine	Long	The CodeModule line number of the first line visible in the CodePane window.
Window	Window	Read Only. Returns the Window object containing the CodePane(s).

CodePane Methods

Name	Returns	Parameters	Description

GetSelection		StartLine As Long, StartColumn As Long, EndLine As Long, EndColumn As Long	Used to retrieve the currently selected text. All of the arguments are passed ByRef and are modified within the procedure to return the selection. All arguments are required, but it is only required to pass arguments for those items you want to retrieve. For example, to get only the start line, you can use:
			
			``vb
			Dim lStart As Long
			Application.VBE _
			   .ActiveCodePane _
			   .GetSelection lStart, _
			   0, 0, 0
			``

SetSelection		StartLine As Long, StartColumn As Long, EndLine As Long, EndColumn As Long	Used to set the position of the currently selected text. A program would typically read the selection using GetSelection, modify the code, then set the selection back again using SetSelection. See the 'PrintProcedure' routine in the Chapter 17 for an example of this.
Show			Opens and displays the CodePane, making it active.

CodePanes Collection Properties

The CodePanes collection contains all of the open CodePane objects in the VBE.

Name	Returns	Description
Current	CodePane	Read Only. Returns the currently active CodePane, and is the same as Application.VBE.ActiveCodePane.

CodePane Examples

There are a number of CodePane examples in the Chapter 17 of this book. The example below identifies the current selection and centers it in the CodePane window:

```
Sub CenterSelectionInWindow()
    Dim oCP As VBIDE.CodePane
    Dim lStartLine As Long, lEndLine As Long
    Dim lVisibleLines As Long, lNewTop As Long

    'Get the active CodePane
    Set oCP = Application.VBE.ActiveCodePane

    'Using the CodePane object...
    With oCP
        'Get the start and end lines of the selection
        .GetSelection lStartLine, 0, lEndLine, 0

        'How many lines fit in the window?
        lVisibleLines = .CountOfVisibleLines

        'So what should the new top line be?
        lNewTop = (lStartLine + lEndLine - lVisibleLines) \ 2

        'Set the window to display code from that line
        .TopLine = lNewTop
    End With
End Sub
```

CommandBarEvents Object

Within the VBE, the OnAction property of a command bar button has no effect — the routine named in this property is *not* run when the button is clicked. Instead, the VBE object model provides you with the CommandBarEvents object, which hooks into whichever command bar button you tell it to, either your own custom buttons or built-in items, and raises events for the button's actions. In Office 2000 it only raises the Click event, and hence provides exactly the same functionality as Excel's OnAction. The main difference is that the Click event has some arguments to enable you to modify its behaviour. The CommandBarEvents object also provides an extensible interface, allowing Microsoft to provide a richer event model in future versions of the VBE (such as BeforePopUp, BeforeRightClick and standard mouse events).

CommandBarEvents Events

Name	Parameters	Description
Click	CommandBarControl As Object, handled As Boolean, CancelDefault As Boolean	Triggered when a hooked command bar button is clicked. The CommandBarControl is passed to the event. A single control can be hooked by many CommandBarEvents objects. The events are fired in reverse order of setting up (i.e. most recently set up fires first). An event handler can set the handled flag to True to tell subsequent handlers that the event has already been processed. The CommandBarEvents object can also be used to hook into built-in menu items. If you want to handle the event through code, you can set the CancelDefault flag to True to stop the menu's normal action.

CommandBarEvents Examples

In a class module called CBarEvents, add the following code:

```
Public WithEvents oCBEvents As VBIDE.CommandBarEvents

'Hook into the Click event for the menu item
Private Sub oCBEvents_Click(ByVal CommandBarControl As Object, _
        handled As Boolean, CancelDefault As Boolean)

    Debug.Print "Clicked " & CommandBarControl.Caption
End Sub
```

In a normal module, add the following code:

```
'Declare a collection to hold all the instances of
'our events class
Dim ocolMenus As New Collection

Sub AddMenus()

    'Declare some CommandBar items
    Dim oBar As CommandBar
    Dim oBtn1 As CommandBarButton, oBtn2 As CommandBarButton

    'And an object to hold instances of your events class
    Dim oCBE As CBarEvents

    'Get the VBE's menu bar
    Set oBar = Application.VBE.CommandBars("Menu Bar")

    'Add a menu item to it
    Set oBtn1 = oBar.Controls.Add(Type:=msoControlButton, temporary:=True)
    oBtn1.Caption = "Menu1"
    oBtn1.Style = msoButtonCaption
```

```
    'Create a new instance of your CommandBarEvent handler
    Set oCBE = New CBarEvents

    'Link your CommandBarEvent handler to the menu item you just created
    Set oCBE.oCBEvents = Application.VBE.Events.CommandBarEvents(oBtn1)

    'And add the instance of your event handler to the collection
    ocolMenus.Add oCBE

    'Repeat for a second menu
    Set oBtn2 = oBar.Controls.Add(Type:=msoControlButton, temporary:=True)
    oBtn2.Caption = "Menu2"
    oBtn2.Style = msoButtonCaption

    Set oCBE = New CBarEvents
    Set oCBE.oCBEvents = Application.VBE.Events.CommandBarEvents(oBtn2)
    ocolMenus.Add oCBE
End Sub
```

When you run the AddMenus routine, two menus are added to the VBE standard menu bar which both use your CommandBarEvents handling class to hook into their Click event. When you click each of the menu items, the Immediate window displays the menu's caption.

Events Object

The Events object is a high-level container for the VBE's event model. In Office 2000, it contains event objects associated with clicking a command bar button and adding/removing references. The VBE extensibility model is based on the Visual Basic extensibility model, which contains a much richer set of events.

Events Properties

Name	Returns	Description
CommandBar Events	CommandBar Events	Read Only. Parameters: CommandBarControl. Performs the linking required to hook a CommandBarEvents object to a specific command bar button.
References Events	References Events	Read Only. Parameters: VBProject. Performs the linking required to hook a ReferencesEvents object to a specific project.

Events Examples

Examples of the Events object are included in the CommandBarEvents and ReferencesEvents sections.

LinkedWindows Collection

The LinkedWindows collection contains all the docked windows in the VBE workspace. COM Addins written in VB5/6 (but not in the Developer edition of Office 2000) can add their own windows to this collection. Within the Office environment, you are limited to docking or undocking the built-in windows. Note that if you undock, then dock a built-in window, it does *not* go back to its original position.

LinkedWindows Collection Methods

Name	Returns	Description
Add		Method. Parameters: Window As Window. Docks the specified window.
Remove		Method. Parameters: Window As Window. Undocks the specified window.

Property Object and Properties Collection

All of the VBComponents in a project have a Properties collection. The properties contained in the collection correspond to the items shown in the Properties Window of the VBE. For the VBComponents that correspond to the Excel objects, the Properties collection of the VBComponents also includes many of the properties of the Excel object.

Property Common Properties

The Collection, Parent and VBE properties are defined at the beginning of this section.

Property Properties

Name	Returns	Description
IndexedValue	Variant	Parameters: Index1, [Index2], [Index3], [Index4]. The Property's Value can be an array of up to 4 indices. The IndexedValue can be used to read a single item in the returned array.
Name	String	Read Only. Returns the name of the property, and is also used to refer to a specific property.

Table Continued on Following Page

Name	Returns	Description
NumIndices	Integer	Read Only. If the Property's value is an array, this returns the number of indices (dimensions) in the array. If not an array, it returns zero.
Object	Object	The Object propety is used to obtain a reference to the object returned by the Property, if any.
Value	Variant	The Property's value

It is easy to get confused with the Name property:

Item	Refers to
Worksheet.CodeName	The code name of the VBComponent (read only).
VBComponent.Name	The code name of the VBComponent (read/write).
VBComponent .Properties("CodeName")	The code name of the VBComponent (read only).
VBComponent .Properties("_CodeName")	The code name of the VBComponent (read/write).[1]
VBComponent .Properties("Name")	The name of the worksheet (read/write).
VBComponent .Properties("Name").Name	"Name".

[1] This was the only reliable way to change a worksheet's CodeName in Excel 97.

Property Examples

This simple example identifies the workbook containing a given VBComponent:

```
Dim oBk As Workbook

'Get the workbook containing a given VBComponent
Set oBk = Application.VBE.ActiveVBProject.VBComponents("Sheet1") _
          .Properties("Parent").Object
MsgBox oBk.Name
```

Reference Object and References Collection

A Reference is a link from your VBProject to an external file, which may be an object library (e.g. linking to the Word object library), a control (e.g. Windows Common Controls), an ActiveX DLL, or another VBProject. By creating a reference to the external object, you can implement early binding — meaning that the referenced objects run in the same memory area, all the links are evaluated at compile time and Excel provides tool-tip programming help when working with the referenced objects.

When you run your application on another machine, it may not have all the objects that your application requires. The Reference object and References collection provide access to these references, allowing you to check that they are all present and working before you try to use them.

Reference Common Properties

The Collection and VBE properties are defined at the beginning of this section.

Reference Properties

Name	Returns	Description
BuiltIn	Boolean	Read Only. Returns if the reference is built-in or added by the developer. The 'Visual Basic for Applications' and 'Microsoft Excel 9.0 Object Library' references are built-in and cannot be removed.
Description	String	Read Only. Returns the description of the reference, which is the text shown in the Object Browser.
FullPath	String	Read Only. Returns the path to the workbook, DLL, OCX, TLB or OLB file that is the source of the reference.
Guid	String	Read Only. Returns the globally unique identifier for the reference.
IsBroken	Boolean	Read Only. Returns True if the reference is broken (i.e. not available on the machine).
Major	Long	Read Only. Returns the major version number of the referenced file.
Minor	Long	Read Only. Returns the minor version number of the referenced file.

Table Continued on Following Page

Name	Returns	Description
Name	String	Read Only. Returns a short name for the reference (e.g. 'VBA' or 'Excel')
Type	vbext_RefKind	Read Only. Returns the reference type, vbext_rk_TypeLib for DLLs etc., or vbext_rk_Project for other VBProjects.

References Collection Methods

Name	Returns	Description
AddFromFile	Reference	Method. Parameters: FileName As String. Adds a reference between the VBProject and a specific file. This should only be used to create references between workbooks.
AddFromGuid	Reference	Method. Parameters: Guid As String, Major As Long, Minor As Long. Adds a reference between the VBProject and a specific DLL, Typelib etc. A library's file name, location and version may change over time, but its Guid is guaranteed to be constant. Hence, when adding a reference to a DLL, Typelib etc,. the Guid should be used. If you require a specific version of the DLL, you can request the major and minor version numbers.
Remove		Method. Parameters: Reference As Reference. Removes a reference from the VBProject.

References Collection Events

The References collection provides two events, which you can use to detect when items are added to or removed from the collection. You could use this, for example, to create a 'Top 10 References' dialog, by using the Application's events to detect when a workbook is opened or created and hooking into the workbook's VBProject's References collection events to detect when a particular Reference is added to a project. You could maintain a list of these and display them in a dialog box, similar to the existing Tools | References dialog in the VBE (but without all the clutter).

Name	Parameters	Description
ItemAdded	Reference As VBIDE.Reference	Triggered when a Reference is added to the VBProject being watched.
ItemRemoved	Reference As VBIDE.Reference	Triggered when a Reference is removed from the VBProject being watched.

Reference Examples

This example checks for broken references and alerts the user.

```
Function HasMissingRefs() As Boolean
   Dim oRef As VBIDE.Reference

   'Loop through all the references for the project
   For Each oRef In ThisWorkbook.VBProject.References

      'Is it missing?
      If oRef.IsBroken Then

         'Yes - show different messages for workbook and DLL references
         If oRef.Type = vbext_rk_Project Then
            MsgBox "Could not find the workbook " & oRef.FullPath & _
                  ", which is required by this application."
         Else
            MsgBox "This application requires the object library '" & _
                  oRef.Description & "', which has not been installed."
         End If

         'Return that there are some missing references
         HasMissingRefs = True
      End If
   Next
End Function
```

The following example shows the core code to watch when the user adds or removes references to any project (so that you could, for example, create a 'Top 10' references picker). There are four steps to take:

When started, hook into the References events of the VBProjects in all open workbooks. Hook into the Application's events to detect workbooks being created or opened. When a workbook is created or opened, hook its VBProject's References events. When a References event is triggered, do something (here, you just print it out).

In a class module, CRefEvents (for step 4):

```
'The WithEvents object to hook the References events
Public WithEvents oRefEvt As VBIDE.References

'We'll also store the workbook you're tracking
Public oWorkbook As Workbook

'We added a reference to a workbook
Private Sub oRefEvt_ItemAdded(ByVal Reference As VBIDE.Reference)
   Debug.Print "Added Reference '" & Reference.Description & "' to " & _
      oWorkbook.Name
End Sub
```

```vb
'We removed a reference from a workbook
Private Sub oRefEvt_ItemRemoved(ByVal Reference As VBIDE.Reference)
    Debug.Print "Removed Reference '" & Reference.Description & "' from " _
                              & oWorkbook.Name
End Sub
```

In a class module, CAppEvents (for step 3):

```vb
'WithEvents object to hook the Application's events
Public WithEvents oApp As Application

'Hook the References events for new workbooks
Private Sub oApp_NewWorkbook(ByVal Wb As Workbook)

    'A new References event handler instance
    Dim oRefEvents As New CRefEvents

    'Tell it which workbook you're hooking
    Set oRefEvents.oWorkbook = Wb

    'And give it the References object to hook into
    Set oRefEvents.oRefEvt = Wb.VBProject.References

    'Add the event handler to your collection of such handlers
    oRefHooks.Add oRefEvents
End Sub

'Hook the References events for opened workbooks
Private Sub oApp_WorkbookOpen(ByVal Wb As Workbook)
    Dim oRefEvents As New CRefEvents

    Set oRefEvents.oWorkbook = Wb
    Set oRefEvents.oRefEvt = Wb.VBProject.References
    oRefHooks.Add oRefEvents
End Sub
```

In a normal module (for steps 1 and 2):

```vb
'One instance of Application events hook
Public oAppHooks As New CAppEvents

'Lots of instances of References events hooks
Public oRefHooks As New Collection

Sub SetUpReferenceHooking()
    Dim oRefEvents As CRefEvents
    Dim oBk As Workbook

    Set oRefHooks = Nothing

    'Step 1: Loop through the existing projects, hooking their references
    'events
    For Each oBk In Workbooks
        If Not oBk Is ThisWorkbook Then
            Set oRefEvents = New CRefEvents
            Set oRefEvents.oWorkbook = oBk
            Set oRefEvents.oRefEvt = oBk.VBProject.References
            oRefHooks.Add oRefEvents
        End If
    Next

    'Step 2: Hook the Application events to watch for new projects to hook
    Set oAppHooks.oApp = Application
End Sub
```

ReferencesEvents Object

In a similar manner to the way in which the CommandBarEvents object provides the Click event for a command bar, the ReferencesEvents object provides two events related to a VBProject's References collection. The ReferencesEvents object appears to be redundant — all of the events it handles are also included in a VBProject's References object. The only difference (apart from the definition) is that the ReferencesEvents object works with a VBProject object instead of the VBProject's References collection. Note that a VBProject is compiled when a Reference is added or removed, resulting in the loss of any variables and instances of classes. Hence a VBProject cannot monitor its own References events.

ReferencesEvents Events

Name	Parameters	Description
ItemAdded	Reference As VBIDE.Reference	Triggered when a Reference is added to the VBProject being watched.
ItemRemoved	Reference As VBIDE.Reference	Triggered when a Reference is removed from the VBProject being watched.

ReferencesEvents Examples

The examples for the ReferencesEvents object are the same as the References Collection Events. The only difference is the way the events are handled (shown in bold in the code):

In the CRefEvents class:

```
'The WithEvents object to hook the References events
Public WithEvents oRefEvt As VBIDE.ReferencesEvents
```

In the CAppEvents class:

```
'Hook the References events for opened workbooks
Private Sub oApp_WorkbookOpen(ByVal Wb As Workbook)
    Dim oRefEvents As New CRefEvents

    Set oRefEvents.oWorkbook = Wb
    Set oRefEvents.oRefEvt = Application.VBE.Events _
                             .ReferencesEvents(Wb.VBProject)
    oRefHooks.Add oRefEvents
End Sub
```

In the normal module:

```
    Set oRefEvents.oWorkbook = oBk
    Set oRefEvents.oRefEvt = Application.VBE.Events _
                             .ReferencesEvents(oBk.VBProject)
```

VBComponent Object and VBComponents Collection

The VBComponents collection contains all the modules, class modules (including code behind worksheets) and UserForms in a VBProject; they are all different types of VBComponent. Every VBComponent has a CodeModule to stores its code and some VBComponents (such as a UserForm) have a graphical development interface, called its Designer. Through the Designer, you can modify the graphical elements of the VBComponent, such as adding controls to a UserForm.

VBComponent Common Properties

The Collection and VBE properties are defined at the beginning of this section.

VBComponent Properties

Name	Returns	Description
CodeModule	CodeModule	Read Only. Returns the CodeModule for the component, used to store its VBA code.
Designer		Read Only. Returns the Designer object for the component, which provides access to the design-time graphical elements of the component.
DesignerID	String	Read Only. Returns an identifier for the Designer, so you know what sort of designer it is. For example, a UserForm's designer ID is Forms.Form, while that of the Addin Connection designer in Office 2000 Developer is MSAddnDr.AddInDesigner.
Designer Window	Window	Read Only. Returns a Window object, representing the Window displaying the Designer. (Shown as a method in the Object Browser, as it opens the Window if not already open).
HasOpen Designer	Boolean	Read Only. Identifies if the component's Designer is open.
Name	String	The name of the VBComponent.

Name	Returns	Description
Properties	Properties	Read Only. Returns the component's Properties collection, providing access to the items shown in the Property Window and to many of the associated Excel object's properties if the VBComponent represents the code behind an Excel object. See the Property Object for more information
Saved	Boolean	Read Only. Returns whether the contents of the VBComponent has changed since the last save. It is analogous to an Excel workbook's Saved property, but applies to each component individually.
Type	vbext_ComponentType	Read Only. Returns the type of the component: vbext_ct_StdModule Normal module vbext_ct_ClassModule Class module vbext_ct_MSForm UserForm vbext_ct_Document Excel object vbext_ct_ActiveXDesigner All other types

VBComponent Methods

Name	Returns	Parameters	Description
Activate			Displays the VBComponent's main window (code module or designer) and sets the focus to it.
Export		FileName As String	Saves the component as a file, separate from the workbook.

VBComponents Collection Methods

Name	Returns	Description
Add	VBComponent	Parameters: ComponentType. Add a new, built-in, VBComponent to the project. The ComponentType can be one of vbext_ct_StdModule, vbext_ct_ClassModule or vbext_ct_MSForm.
AddCustom	VBComponent	Parameters: ProgId. Add a new, custom, VBComponent to the project. The result is always of type vbext_ct_ActiveXDesigner. It seems that custom VB components can only be added to ActiveX DLL projects and not to Excel workbook projects.
Import	VBComponent	Parameters: FileName. Add a new VBComponent to the project from a file (usually a previously-exported VBComponent).
Remove		Parameters: VBComponent. Removes a VBComponent from a project.

VBComponent Examples

Many of the examples in this section and in Chapter 17 use the VBComponent object and its properties and methods. The example below exports a UserForm from the workbook containing the code, imports it into a new workbook and renames it. It then adds a standard module, fills in some code to show the form, then calls the routine to show the form in the new workbook:

```
Sub CopyAndShowUserForm()
    Dim oNewBk As Workbook, oVBC As VBIDE.VBComponent

    'Create a new workbook
    Set oNewBk = Workbooks.Add

    'Export a UserForm from this workbook to disk
    ThisWorkbook.VBProject.VBComponents("UserForm1").Export "c:\temp.frm"

    'Import the UserForm into the new workbook
    Set oVBC = oNewBk.VBProject.VBComponents.Import("c:\temp.frm")

    'Rename the UserForm
    oVBC.Name = "MyForm"

    'Add a standard module to the new workbook
    Set oVBC = oNewBk.VBProject.VBComponents.Add(vbext_ct_StdModule)

    'Add some code to the standard module, to show the form
    oVBC.CodeModule.AddFromString _
            "Sub ShowMyForm()" & vbCrLf & _
            "    MyForm.Show" & vbCrLf & _
            "End Sub" & vbCrLf
```

```
'Close the code pane the Excel opened when you added code to the module
oVBC.CodeModule.CodePane.Window.Close

'Delete the exported file
Kill "c:\temp.frm"

'Run the new routine to show the imported UserForm
Application.Run oNewBk.Name & "!ShowMyForm"
End Sub
```

VBE Object

The VBE object is the top-level object in the VBIDE object library and hence is
analagous to the Application object in the Excel library. Its main jobs are to act as a
container for the VBIDE's command bars, addins, windows etc and to provide
information about the objects currently being modified by the user. Unfortunately, it
does not expose any of the VBIDE's options settings (e.g. code settings, edit formats,
error handling etc), nor does it provide any editing events (such as selecting a different
project, adding or deleting lines of code, etc).

VBE Properties

Name	Returns	Description
ActiveCode Pane	CodePane	Returns or sets the CodePane currently being edited by the user. Typically used to identify which object is being worked on, or to force the user to work with a specific code pane.
Active VBProject	VBProject	Returns or sets the VBProject selected in the Project Explorer window. If the Project Explorer is showing a VBComponent selected, this property returns the VBProject containing the component.
Active Window	Window	Read Only. Returns the active Window, which may be a code pane, designer or one of the VBIDE windows (i.e. Project Explorer, Immediate Window etc).
Addins	Addins	Read Only. Returns a collection of all the COM Addins registered for use in the VBIDE. See the Addin object for more information.
CodePanes	CodePanes	Read Only. Returns a collection of all the open CodePanes in the VBIDE. See the CodePane object for more information.

Table Continued on Following Page

Name	Returns	Description
CommandBars	CommandBars	Read Only. Returns a collection of all the command bars in the VBIDE.
Events	Events	Read Only. Returns an object containing all the events in the VBIDE. See the Events object for more information.
MainWindow	Window	Read Only. Returns a Window object representing the main window of the VBIDE.
Selected VBComponent	VBComponent	Read Only. Returns the VBComponent object that is shown as selected in the Project Explorer window. Note that this usually, but not always, corresponds to the ActiveCodePane.
VBProjects	VBProjects	Read Only. Returns a collection of all the VBProjects in the VBIDE, both Excel workbooks and ActiveX DLLs.
Version	String	Read Only. Returns the version number of the Extensibility library (shows 6.0 for Office 2000).
Windows	Windows	Read Only. Returns a collection of all the open windows in the VBIDE. See the Windows object for more information.

VBE Examples

Most of the examples in this section and in Chapter 17 include the VBE's properties. The following line displays the VBE:

```
Application.VBE.MainWindow.Visible = True
```

VBProject Object and VBProjects Collection

A VBProject represents all of the code for a workbook, including code behind sheets, modules, class modules and UserForms. In the Developer edition of Office 2000, a VBProject can also be a standalone project, compiled as an ActiveX DLL.

VBProject Common Properties

The Collection and VBE properties are defined at the beginning of this section.

VBProject Properties

Name	Returns	Description
BuildFile Name	String	For ActiveX DLLs only, get/set the name of the DLL file to compile the project into.
Description	String	For ActiveX DLLs only, the description of the DLL, as it will appear in the Tools | References list.
FileName	String	Read Only. For workbook projects, returns the full name of the workbook. For ActiveX DLL projects, returns the name of the source code version of the project *.vba. If the file has not been saved, a run-time-error occurs if you try to read this property.
HelpContext ID	Long	Identifies the default help file context ID for the project.
HelpFile	String	Get/Set the help file for a project. Each of the UserForms and controls within the project can be assigned a context ID to show a page from this help file.
Mode	vbext_ VBAMode	Read Only. Returns the VBProject's operation mode (Design, Run or Break). Note that VBProjects can have different execution modes (for example, an ActiveX COM Addin project can be running while you are in Design mode on a different project).
Name	String	The name of the project.
Protection	vbext_ Project Protection	Read Only. Returns whether the project is locked for viewing. Locked projects only expose their VBProject object. Any attempt to navigate below the VBProject level results in an error. Note that if a VBProject is set to Protected, but is unprotected by the user during a session, it's Protection property shows as vbext_pp_none for the remainder of that session.

Table Continued on Following Page

Name	Returns	Description
References	References	Read Only. Returns the collection of References for the VBProject. See the References object for more information.
Saved	Boolean	Read Only. Returns whether the VBProject has been changed since the last save. For Excel projects, this should agree with the workbook's Saved property.
Type	vbext_ ProjectType	Read Only. Returns the type of project — host project (i.e. an Excel workbook, Word document, Access database etc.) or an ActiveX DLL project.
VBComponents	VBComponents	Read Only. Returns the collection of VBComponents in the project. See the VBComponent object for more information.

VBProject Methods

Name	Returns	Parameters	Description
MakeCompiled File			For ActiveX DLL projects only. Compiles the project and makes the DLL file.
SaveAs		FileName As String	For ActiveX DLL projects only. Saves the project file.

VBProjects Collection Methods

Name	Returns	Description
Add	VBProject	Method. Parameters: Type. Adds a new project to the VBE. Can only successfully add stand-alone (i.e. ActiveX DLL) projects using this method.
Remove		Method. Parameters: lpc As VBProject. Removes a VBProject from the VBE. Can only be used for ActiveX DLL projects.

VBProject Examples

Most of the examples in this section use the VBProject object and its properties. This example lists the names of all the VBComponents in all the unlocked projects in the VBE:

```
Sub PrintComponents()
   Dim oVBP As VBIDE.VBProject
   Dim oVBC As VBIDE.VBComponent

   'Loop through all the projects in the VBE
   For Each oVBP In Application.VBE.VBProjects

      'If the project is not protected...
      If oVBP.Protection = vbext_pp_none Then

         '... loop through its components
         For Each oVBC In oVBP.VBComponents
            Debug.Print oVBP.Name & "." & oVBC.Name
         Next
      End If
   Next
End Sub
```

Window Object and Windows Collection

The Window object represents a single window in the VBE, including the VBE's main window, the built-in Project Explorer, Immediate, Debug and Watch Windows etc, as well as all open CodePanes and Designer Windows.

Window Common Properties

The Collection and VBE properties are defined at the beginning of this section.

Window Properties

Name	Returns	Description
Caption	String	Read Only. Returns the caption of the Window, as shown in its title bar.
Height	Long	The height of the Window, in twips (1 twip = 1/20 points). Does not affect docked windows.
HWnd	Long	Read Only. Returns a handle to the Window, for use in Windows API calls.
Left	Long	The left edge of the Window on the screen, in twips (1 twip = 1/20 points). Does not affect docked windows.
Linked Window Frame	Window	Read Only. Multiple windows can be linked together in the VBE (e.g. while docking them). This property returns another Window that represents the frame surrounding the docked windows. Returns Nothing if the window is not linked.

Table Continued on Following Page

Name	Returns	Description
Linked Windows	Linked Windows	Read Only. Returns a collection of windows linked to the Window (e.g. when docked).
Top	Long	The top of the Window on the screen, in twips (1 twip = 1/20 points). Does not affect docked windows.
Type	vbext_ WindowType	Read Only. Returns the window type, such as CodePane, Immediate Window, Main Window etc.
Visible	Boolean	Get/Set whether or not the window is visible
Width	Long	The width of the Window, in twips (1 twip = 1/20 points). Does not affect docked windows.
WindowState	vbext_ WindowState	The Window state — minimized, maximized or normal.

Window Methods

Name	Returns	Parameters	Description
Close			Closes the window.
SetFocus			Opens and activates the window, displays it and gives it the focus.

Windows Collection Methods

Name	Returns	Description
CreateTool Window	Window	Parameters: AddInInst, ProgId, Caption, GuidPosition, DocObj. This method is only used when creating COM Addins using Visual Basic 5 or 6, to create a dockable window in the VBE.

Window Examples

This example closes all code and designer windows in the VBE:

```
Sub CloseAllCodeWindows()
    Dim oWin As VBIDE.Window

    'Loop through all the open windows in the VBE
    For Each oWin In Application.VBE.Windows

        'Close the window, depending on its type
        Select Case oWin.Type
            Case vbext_wt_Browser, vbext_wt_CodeWindow, vbext_wt_Designer

                'Close the Object Browser, code windows and designer windows
                Debug.Print "Closed '" & oWin.Caption & "' window."
                oWin.Close

            Case Else
                'Don't close any other windows
                Debug.Print "Kept '" & oWin.Caption & "' window open."
        End Select
    Next
End Sub
```

Index

Index

Index

Index

Index

Index

Index

Index

Index